InDesign® CS4 Bible

InDesign® CS4 Bible

Galen Gruman

WILEY

Wiley Publishing, Inc.

InDesign® CS4 Bible

Published by
Wiley Publishing, Inc.
10475 Crosspoint Boulevard
Indianapolis, IN 46256
www.wiley.com

Copyright © 2009 by Wiley Publishing, Inc., Indianapolis, Indiana

Published simultaneously in Canada

ISBN: 978-0-470-40511-6

Manufactured in the United States of America

10 9 8 7 6 5 4 3 2 1

For general information on our other products and services or to obtain technical support, please contact our Customer Care Department within the U.S. at (800) 762-2974, outside the U.S. at (317) 572-3993 or fax (317) 572-4002.

Library of Congress Control Number: 2008941629

About the Author

Galen Gruman is the principal at The Zango Group, an editorial development and book production firm. As such, he has produced several books for Wiley Publishing and is a regular contributor to *Macworld* and *CIO*. He is author or coauthor of 22 other books on desktop publishing. Gruman led one of the first successful conversions of a national magazine to desktop publishing in 1986 and has covered publishing technology since then for several publications, including the trade weekly *InfoWorld,* for which he began writing in 1986 and of which he is now executive editor; *Macworld,* whose staff he was a member of from 1991 to 1998; and, most recently, *Layers Magazine*.

To my colleague and friend Carol Person, who has been a great partner in so many endeavors.

Credits

Associate Acquisitions Editor
Aaron Black

Project Editor
Susan Christophersen

Technical Editor
Jonathan Woolson

Copy Editor
Susan Christophersen

Editorial Manager
Robyn Siesky

Business Manager
Amy Knies

Senior Marketing Manager
Sandy Smith

Vice President and Executive Group Publisher
Richard Swadley

Vice President and Executive Publisher
Barry Pruett

Project Coordinator
Lynsey Stanford

Graphics and Production Specialists
Stacie Brooks
Sarah Philippart
Christin Swinford

Quality Control Technician
Laura Albert

Proofreading and Indexing
Broccoli Information Management
Nancy L. Reinhardt

Contents

Contents

Part II: Document Fundamentals   129

Chapter 4: Creating, Opening, and Saving Documents 131

Contents

Contents

Contents

Contents

Contents

Part VII: Output Fundamentals   655

Chapter 28: Preparing for Color Prepress. 657

Chapter 29: Preparing for Printing 679

Contents

Part VIII: Electronic Publishing Techniques 753

Contents

Foreword

In many ways, my career started in page layout. I was lucky enough to show up on the doorstep of my college newspaper the very year it switched from old-school paste-up to the new-fangled world of page-layout software. Being comfortable with both computers and journalism, I embraced the new technology, became a page-layout whiz, and now I write about computers and technology for a living.

The tool of choice back then was Aldus PageMaker, but in the intervening years the state-of-the-art tools have migrated from PageMaker to QuarkXPress to Adobe InDesign. In the years since the first version of InDesign was released, the product has gone from being a strange amalgam of PageMaker and XPress to a design juggernaut, and the publishing industry has embraced this new tool with a speed that I would not have thought possible.

But the more powerful a tool becomes, the more complicated it becomes. InDesign CS4 alone introduces a score of new features, including conditional text, Flash integration, smart guides and smart spacing, and several interface tweaks. That's why you need a tool like the *Adobe InDesign CS4 Bible*. This book, written by an expert who is also an expert communicator, will let you in on the secrets of InDesign, from the classic features you never knew about to the exciting new features in the CS4 update that will save you time and make you more productive.

Your guide along this journey of InDesign discovery is Galen Gruman, a guy who knows a thing or two about desktop publishing. I first met Galen more than a decade ago, when he was the editor of *Macworld*. Galen was *Macworld's* go-to author for desktop publishing back then, and in the intervening years he has continued his mastery of the subject, including the authoring of every edition of the *Adobe InDesign Bible*. You couldn't find a better person to show you the ins and outs of Adobe's powerful page-creation application.

Jason Snell

Editorial Director

Macworld

Preface

Every two years, give or take, Adobe comes out with yet another version of its Creative Suite applications, including InDesign. I always wonder, "What are they going to find to change this time?!" After all, they've been working on these programs for one to two decades, so there can't be a lot left to add or change. Well, Adobe always finds something — a collection of tiny to moderate enhancements and a handful (and sometimes more) of major additions or changes. Version 6 of InDesign — popularly known as InDesign CS4 — follows that tradition.

The big news is the ability to export files for use in Flash animation, a key part of Adobe's recent efforts to blur the boundaries between print and online, so documents can work in multiple media, taking advantage of any individual's special abilities but not limited to them.

Ironically, I doubt most users will do that much with the Flash capabilities, as the Flash Professional where the heavy lifting comes in is really designed to program automation, which uses a very different part of the brain than a mouse-oriented designer uses when working on layouts. No matter, we'll all learn a little Flash as a result and get just that more flexible in our work.

For the rest, though, there are other exciting additions, from cross-references and conditional text on one end to on-the-fly, user-definable preflighting and the Kuler color theme creation capability on the other. Oh, and the new smart guides are an amazingly effective yet simple way to help you be more precise when mousing around.

Although Adobe has also made some features such as the Links panel and the docks work a little more intuitively in this newest version of InDesign, the good news in this revision is that the basic user interface remains intact, so you can get productive more quickly. Still, at the end of the day, even with a less-dramatic interface change this round, the fact remains that InDesign does a lot of things for a wide range of users, so it remains daunting. And you'll continue to discover features that you never knew about that have been around at least a version or two — I still do.

The software is certainly more complex than ever, a whopping collection of capabilities that you may never glimpse more than a fraction of in your daily use. I'm very much reminded of a trip to the Louvre: You just can't take it all in during one or even a few visits.

Layout artists have an incredibly powerful tool in the form of InDesign to let them deliver on their creative aspirations and vision. I can only hope that this book helps you achieve and indeed increase those ambitions.

Acknowledgments

Thanks to the development and product marketing staff at Adobe for providing early versions of the InDesign CS4 software, providing insights into their thinking as they brought in new features, and listening to suggestions on making it even better. Thanks to the editors and production staff at Wiley Publishing for their efforts in making this book possible, especially to project editor Susan Christophersen and technical editor Jonathan Woolson for their improvements to the book's content and clarity.

The www.InDesignCentral.com Web site and its contents are copyrighted by The Zango Group.

Original photographs are copyrighted by Ingall W. Bull III, unless otherwise credited.

Introduction

Welcome to *Adobe InDesign CS4 Bible* — your personal guide to a powerful, full-featured publishing program that offers precise but flexible control over all aspects of page design. My goal is to guide you each step of the way through the publishing process, showing you how to make Adobe's InDesign CS4 work for you. You'll also learn tips and tricks about publishing design that you can use in any document, whether it was created in InDesign or not.

Taking the best from the two schools of thought on desktop publishing, when it appeared in 1999, InDesign was a ground-breaking merger of the highly structured approach of programs such as QuarkXPress and the bygone Ventura Publisher with the more naturalistic approach of Adobe PageMaker, which it essentially replaced. Nearly a decade later, InDesign continues this "have it both ways" approach while offering an incredibly wide range of desktop-publishing capabilities for sophisticated designers who develop magazines, books, ads, and product brochures. It also gives the power of the press to individuals and groups who use the program's impressive set of publishing tools to communicate their thoughts, dreams, and philosophies.

Version CS4 of InDesign takes this strong legacy and makes it even better, often in subtle ways meant to make the workflow process easier and more intuitive. While InDesign's abundance of features necessarily makes its interface complex, Adobe continues to find ways to simplify it while adding yet more capabilities. In the case of InDesign CS4, the new functions are fairly self-contained, so they haven't caused a major rippled effect in terms of the overall user interface as was the case in InDesign CS3. And Adobe has also added new features, from small enhancements in multilingual hyphenation and spell-checking and in links management to significant additions like smart guides, Flash export capability, and conditional text. Many existing features are extended with new capabilities, such as the ability to create nested styles for lines of text, to add page-transition effects for PDF and Flash files, and to rotate spreads for easier editing of rotated objects (sorry, they won't print rotated).

InDesign lets you take advantage of modern electronic publishing's full range of possibilities. Not only can you produce high-quality, lively flyers, newsletters, magazines, and similar publications in InDesign, you can also create rich, colorful documents that can be viewed on the Web, distributed by CD, or sent directly to a printing press for faithful print reproduction.

In a nutshell, InDesign is meant to help those who educate, inform, and document today's world. Join me in learning how to use this powerful program.

What This Book Offers

So, because InDesign comes with good documentation that is full of examples, why do you need this book? To see the bigger picture. Publishing design involves much more than understanding a particular program's tools; it involves knowing when, how, and, most importantly, *why* to use them. In this book, I help you realize the potential of InDesign by applying its tools to real-world publishing design needs. I also identify any weaknesses and explain how to overcome them — something that vendor manuals rarely do.

Some desktop publishers have years of high-end creative, design-intensive experience. Others are just getting started in publishing, perhaps by producing simple newsletters or flyers to advertise a community event. Not a few are exploring the brave new world of Web publishing.

Desktop publishers fall into several classes:

- Designers new to InDesign but familiar with other desktop publishing software
- Designers familiar with print publishing but new to electronic publishing
- Experienced designers new to desktop technologies
- Novice designers new to desktop technologies

No matter which class you're in, this book addresses your needs. You don't need a degree in design or ten years' experience producing national ad campaigns — you can use this book if you're responsible for developing and implementing the look of any document, whether it's a four-page company newsletter or a four-color billboard ad. The basic techniques and issues are the same for both ends of the spectrum. And of course, this book covers in detail the specialized needs — table creation, image control, color output, and electronic publishing for example — of specialty designers. (If you're just learning such advanced techniques, be sure to read the sidebars that explain the underlying issues.) Regardless of your level of experience with desktop publishing, this book can help you use InDesign efficiently, and guide you to discovering more of the program's potential.

What distinguishes this book from the rest of its type is that it does not attempt to be a substitute for the documentation that accompanies InDesign. Instead, it guides you through the *process* of publishing a document, regardless of whether that document is your first or your thousandth.

How to Read This Book

Adobe InDesign CS4 Bible is made up of 37 chapters and four appendixes divided into 11 parts, in addition to the QuickStart that appears just before Part I begins. If you're a novice InDesign user but familiar with desktop publishing, I suggest you read the book in order, because the process of page design is presented in the typical publishing workflow. You first learn how (and why) to create basic pages, containers, placeholders, and templates; then you learn how to work with specific elements (such as text and graphics); and finally, you learn how to use special effects and deal with prepress issues (such as output control, image manipulation, trapping, and printing).

If you're new to the new forms of electronic publishing, be sure to start with Part VIII, Electronic Publishing Techniques, which teaches novice publishers the basics of Web, PDF, and Flash document creation. Experienced publishers should at least skim this part as well — you're likely to find new ideas and perspectives on how you approach your work.

Whether you're reading the book sequentially or nonsequentially, you'll find the many cross-references helpful. Publication design is ultimately successful because the result is more than the sum of its parts, and the tools used to create and implement your designs cannot be used in isolation. Because this is true, having one "right" order or grouping of content is impossible. The cross-references let you know where to get additional information when what you're seeking to understand or learn doesn't fit the way I've organized this book.

Following is a brief description of the parts in *Adobe InDesign CS4 Bible*.

InDesign QuickStart

This guide walks you through the creation of a document to give you a quick tour of the program, from creation to printing. It's a convenient way to see the main InDesign features in action and quickly get a sense of how they work, whether you're new to publishing or new to InDesign.

Part I: Welcome to InDesign

This part walks you through the initial steps of using InDesign to create your publications. I give you a basic introduction to InDesign itself, explaining the concepts it uses in its layout approach. I also highlight what's special about InDesign in general and about InDesign CS4 in particular. But most of the part focuses on understanding all the tools and panels available to you and all the preferences you can set, so you can see the big picture all in one place.

Part II: Document Fundamentals

This part explains how to create the basic containers — documents, pages, and layers — of a publishing project and how to set the standards for your documents, from master pages, libraries, and templates to guides and colors. InDesign comes with a set of tools that lets you automate repetitive work, apply common elements to a range of pages, and customize page settings, among other capabilities. This part walks you though the ins and outs of all of them.

Part III: Object Fundamentals

This part explains how InDesign's frame and line tools work so you can create and manipulate layout objects. With these building blocks, you construct and alter almost all the components in a layout, from the frame containers that hold text and pictures to original artwork you create in InDesign. You'll also learn how to move, group, copy, and lock such objects and how to automate repetitive object actions to save time. You can learn about the many transformations and effects you can apply to objects, from skews to drop shadows, from text wrap to transparency. You can also learn how to manage the relationships between imported objects and their original files.

Part IV: Text Fundamentals

This part shows you how to import and work with text files, including the application of typographic features to really jazz up your layout and the tools to ensure that spelling and hyphenation are always correct. You can learn how to set up styles to automate the application of typography to document text, as well as how to use the insanely wide range of special symbols and characters available in InDesign.

Part V: Business Document Fundamentals

This part covers the features — old and new — that appeal most to business document creators, from annual reports to product manuals. But of course you don't have to create these kinds of documents to take advantage of features such as tables, text variables, footnotes, indexes, tables of contents, and multi-chapter projects, so don't let the part's title intimidate you.

Part VI: Graphics Fundamentals

This part explains how to use InDesign to manipulate and work with graphics in your layout, whether imported from another program or created within InDesign. Although text carries the message, a picture is what gets your attention and often can say more than any collection of words. This part helps you get the most out of your graphics in InDesign. It also shows you how you can use the tools in InDesign to create a variety of shapes that can be used as original artwork or as specialty containers for text and images.

Part VII: Output Fundamentals

This part walks you though the output steps of publishing. You'll learn what you need to be aware of as well as how to output your documents for printing, whether to a local printer or through a service bureau.

Part VIII: Electronic Publishing Techniques

InDesign lets you create all sorts of documents for electronic distribution, such as on the Web or on CDs. This part explains how to take advantage of hyperlinks, video, audio, and interactive buttons for use in PDF files and Flash animations, as well as how to create Web pages and eBooks files. Finally, you can learn the basics of working with XML, the structured content system widely used by Web-oriented content engines. InDesign can both create XML files and use XML files to turn templates into completed InDesign documents for automated publishing systems.

Part IX: Workgroup Publishing Techniques

Very few publishers work by themselves, and most have a whole raft of tools to work their miracles. The chapters in this part expose you to key insights in working beyond InDesign, covering workgroup issues and the InCopy add-on program for multi-user editing.

Part X: Extending InDesign

This part helps you expand your InDesign horizons through the use of plug-ins to add new capabilities, and the use of scripts to automate your work.

Part XI: Appendixes

The appendixes in this book take you through the ins and outs of how to install Adobe InDesign, what is new in version CS4, and how to use the Version Cue virtual server environment from Adobe for file management in a shared workgroup. Appendix D includes all the shortcuts for both Macs and PCs in one place.

The companion Web site

No application exists in a vacuum. A publishing program is especially dependent on other applications: those that create the source files, those that manage printing, and those that manage fonts, for example. And applications change — sometimes, a vendor like Adobe adds features to a shipping product or fixes ones that don't work as expected. The companion site, `www.InDesignCentral.com`, is where you can keep current on the InDesign ecosystem, with links to related software tools, the sample files used in this book's QuickStart chapter, links to helpful resources such as user groups, and if needed, updates to this book.

Conventions Used in This Book

Before I begin showing you the ins and outs of InDesign, I need to spend a few minutes reviewing the terms and conventions used in this book.

InDesign commands

The InDesign commands that you select by using the program menus appear in this book in normal typeface. When you choose some menu commands, a related pull-down menu or a pop-up menu appears. If this book describes a situation in which you need to select one menu and then choose a command from a secondary menu or list box, it uses an arrow symbol. For example, "Choose Layout⇨Margins and Columns" means that you should choose the Margins and Columns command from the Layout menu.

Dialog boxes, panels, and panes

As do most modern programs, InDesign uses dialog boxes to offer up a bunch of related features in one place. It also uses a similar mechanism called a panel, which is essentially a dialog box that you can always keep open for easy access. Both of these mechanisms use an interface feature that has proved to be quite popular called *tabbed panes*. This is a method of stuffing several dialog boxes into one dialog box or several panels into one panel. You see tabs, like those in file folders, and by clicking a tab, the pane of options for that tab comes to the front of the dialog box or panel. This book will tell you to go to the pane, which you do by clicking the tab where the name of the pane is to display the pane. For example, "Go to the General pane" means click the General tab in the current dialog box or panel.

Keyboard conventions

This book provides both the Macintosh and Windows shortcuts throughout, with the Mac shortcut first. In most cases, the Mac and Windows shortcuts are the same, except for the names of the keys, as follows.

 InDesign for Mac's user interface uses symbols to indicate special keys in shortcuts, such as ⌘, whereas the Windows version uses the actual key names, such as Ctrl.

- The Mac's Command key (⌘) is the most-used shortcut key. Its Windows equivalent is Ctrl. (This key is sometimes known as the Apple key, since the key has both the ⌘ symbol and an open Apple logo [] printed on it. But because there is also the Apple menu, indicated by a solid Apple logo [], in the Mac OS, it's best *not* to call this key the Apple key and then get confused with the Apple menu.)

- Shift is the same on the Mac and Windows. In many Mac program menus — including InDesign — Shift is displayed by the symbol ⇧.

- The Option key on the Mac is usually the same as the Alt key in Windows. In many Mac program menus — including InDesign — you see the symbol ⌥ used.

- The Control key on the Mac has no Windows equivalent (it is *not* the same as the Windows Ctrl key). Many Mac programs — including InDesign — indicate it with the symbol ^ in their menus.

- The Tab key is used both to move within fields in panes and dialog boxes and to insert the tab character in text. InDesign and many other Mac programs indicate it in menus with the symbol ⇥.

- The Return key (Mac) or Enter key (Windows) is used to apply a dialog box's settings and close the dialog box (equivalent to clicking OK or Done), as well as to insert a hard paragraph return in text. In InDesign and many other Mac programs, it is indicated in menus by the symbol ↵. Note that there is another key labeled Enter on most keyboards, in the numeric keypad. This sometimes works like the regular Return or Enter, but in InDesign text, it inserts a column break. I refer to it as *keypad Enter* in this book. In InDesign and many other Mac programs, it is indicated in menus by the symbol ⌤.

- The Delete key (Mac) and Backspace key (Windows) deletes text, one character at a time, to the *left* of the text-insertion point. In InDesign and many other Mac programs, the Delete key is indicated in menus by the symbol ⌫.

- Windows also has a separate Delete key that deletes text, one character at a time, to the *right* of the text-insertion point. Macs with an extended keyboard — one with a numeric keypad — have a second Delete key (below Help and next to End) that acts like the Windows Delete key in many programs, including InDesign. In InDesign and many other Mac programs, this other, "forward" Delete key is indicated in menus by the symbol ⌦.

If you're supposed to press several keys at the same time, I indicate that by placing plus signs (+) between them. Thus, Shift+⌘+A means press and hold the Shift and ⌘ keys and then press A. After you've pressed A, let go of all three keys. (You don't need to hold down the last character in the sequence.)

I also use the plus sign (+) to join keys to mouse movements. For example, Option+drag means to press and hold the Option key while dragging the mouse on the Mac, and Alt+drag means to press and hold the Alt key while dragging the mouse in Windows.

Also note that InDesign lets you change the shortcuts associated with menu and other commands (by choosing Edit⇨Keyboard Shortcuts). Throughout the book, I assume the shortcuts in use are the default ones and that you haven't altered them.

Icons

I've used special graphic symbols, or *icons,* throughout this book. These icons call your attention to points that are particularly important or worth noting:

 The New Feature icon indicates a technique or action that is new to or revised in InDesign CS4.

 The Tip icon indicates a technique or action in InDesign that will save you time or effort.

 The Note icon indicates information that you should remember for future use — something that may seem minor or inconsequential but will, in reality, resurface.

 The Caution icon is used to warn you of potential hang-ups or pitfalls you may encounter while using InDesign (and how to avoid them).

CROSS-REF The Cross-Reference icon points you to different parts of the book that contain related or expanded information on a particular topic.

 The Platform Differences icon alerts you to differences using InDesign on the Macintosh versus in Windows.

Dealing with Computer-Platform Appearance Issues

InDesign CS4 runs on Mac OS X 10.4 (Tiger), Mac OS X 10.5 (Leopard), Windows XP with Service Pack 2 or later installed, and Windows Vista. Most desktop publishers use Apple's Macintosh, and thus most readers of this book will likely be Mac-based. That's why I use Mac screenshots in the illustrations throughout this book. (Plus, Adobe uses Windows screen shots in its documentation.) Adobe has done a good job of ensuring that the interface for InDesign is almost identical — within the natural differences between Mac and Windows — on the two platforms.

Quick Start

Building a Document from Start to Finish

Although InDesign CS4 is a complex program that lets you do everything from designing a fashion magazine to indexing a book to generating separation plates for professional printing, you can get started building documents with just a few simple skills. If you're in a hurry to get started on a document — or you have a job interview tomorrow based on your "proficiency" in InDesign — work through the steps in this section. You can learn the basic building blocks of documents (frames and lines) and the two primary tools (Selection and Direct Selection).

By all means, do not assume that these steps provide all you need to know about InDesign CS4. From here, head to related sections of the book and explore the full functionality of the program. If you're not sure where to start, figure out what you'll be doing the most. For example, if you'll be flowing text into a newsletter template, head to Part IV.

To create the sample document shown in Figure QS.1 — from my book *QuarkXPress to InDesign: Face to Face* (Wiley, 2005) — you need InDesign, a text file from a program such as Microsoft Word, a graphic file such as a TIFF file, and a laser or inkjet printer. You can follow the steps exactly (substituting your own text, graphic, and fonts), or you can vary the design as much as you want.

> **TIP** You can download the text and graphics used in this QuickStart example at www.InDesignCentral.com/QS.html. You have to supply your own fonts, however.

FIGURE QS.1

Combining formatted text and several graphics with a few simple frames and lines produces a completely designed book.

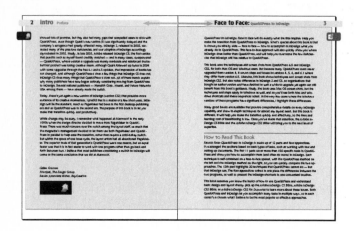

Creating a New Document

In this QuickStart, I assume that your copy of InDesign has been set with picas as the default measurement for vertical and horizontal measurement, one of two typical settings for publications. (The other is to set horizontal measurements at picas and vertical measurements at inches.) But for those who think in inches, I also provide values in inches. You set measurement defaults in the Ruler Units section of the Units & Increments pane of the Preferences dialog box, which you access by choosing InDesign ⇨ Preferences ⇨ Units & Increments or pressing ⌘+K on the Mac, or by choosing Edit ⇨ Preferences ⇨ Units & Increments or pressing Ctrl+K in Windows.

I also assume that your coordinates are set for the entire spread, not for individual pages. To make sure they are set for the spread, go to the Units & Increments pane of the Preferences dialog box and be sure that Spread is selected in the Origin pop-up menu.

When you create a new document in InDesign, you're actually specifying the final size and setup of the pages in the document.

1. **Start InDesign.**

2. **Choose File ⇨ New ⇨ Document or press ⌘+N or Ctrl+N.** The New Document dialog box appears (see Figure QS.2).

3. **In the Width field, enter 44p3 or 7.375 in (based on your preferences for picas or inches). In the Height field, enter** 55p6 or 9.25 in. Notice how the Page Size pop-up menu changes to Custom.

4. **Select the Facing Pages check box, because this is a book printed on two sides, thus it needs both left- and right-page versions.**

FIGURE QS.2

Set up the page size and other attributes for your document in the New Document dialog box.

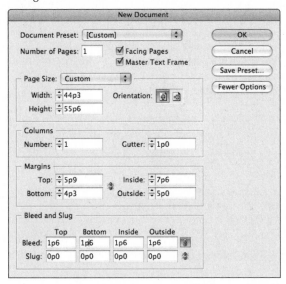

5. Select the Master Text Frame check box.

6. Set the number of columns to 1.

7. In the Margins area, click the Make All Settings the Same iconic button (the chain icon) so that the broken chain changes to an unbroken chain. (This lets you set the margins independently.) Set the Inside margin to **7p6** (or **1.25 in** if you prefer inches), Top to **5p9** (**0.95833 in**), Bottom to **4p3** (**0.70833 in**), and Outside to **5p** (**0.833 in**).

8. Click the More Options button to get the Bleed and Slug area. Make sure the closed-chain icon displays in the Bleed area (click it if not), and enter 1p6 (0.25 in) as the bleed margin in any of the four fields.

9. Click the Save Preset button, and give these specifications a name, such as *Book*. Assigning a name to these specifications lets you select these exact settings for future documents for this publication by choosing the preset name from the Document Preset pop-up menu.

10. Click OK to create the new document's new layout. InDesign creates one page.

11. Choose File ⇨ Save As or press Shift+⌘+S or Ctrl+Shift+S.

12. In the Save As field, type Book Intro.indd. Choose a location for the file and then click Save.

 For more information about creating a new document, see Chapter 4.

Working with Frames and Pages

By using the automatic text frame, you've already created the frame for the article text. But the article has colored frames at the top for the story title that you need to create via frames.

NOTE   **All measurements in this QuickStart are from the upper-left corner of the frames. In the Control panel, be sure that the upper-left square in the array of nine squares (the reference points) is black, which makes that point the *control point* from which all dimensions and transformations are applied. (All the other reference points will be white.) If it's not black, simply click it to make it the control point.**

Frames can exist on document pages or on master pages. A master page is essentially an internal page template that you can apply to document pages, adding all the master page's attributes to any document pages you prefer. This speeds formatting of repetitive elements such as footers, headers, and folios.

To create a master page:

1. **Go to the Pages panel.** (If it is not available at the right-hand side of your screen, open it by choosing Window ⇨ Pages or by pressing ⌘+F12 or Ctrl+F12.)

2. **From the panel's flyout menu (the icon below the panel's close box), choose New Master.**

3. **In the New Master dialog box, enter a name for the master page that will help you remember what it is used for (such as *Intro* in this case), and make sure Number of Pages is set to 2 so that InDesign creates a master spread. Click OK.** InDesign will then open the master spread for you.

You're now ready to add objects to the master spread. You start with the page background, add the folio at top, and finally place the logos on the outside margins.

Before you start, make sure InDesign is set to display transformation values so that it can give you feedback as to objects' location and size as you work on them. To display transformation values, ensure that Show Transformation Values is selected in the Interface pane of the Preferences dialog box (choose InDesign ⇨ Preferences ⇨ Interface or press ⌘+K on the Mac, or choose Edit ⇨ Preferences ⇨ Interface or press Ctrl+K in Windows).

1. **Select the Rectangular Frame tool.** To see the names of tools, point at them until a Tool Tip displays.

2. **On the left-hand page, click and drag to create a frame that is approximately 43p3 (7.20833 in) wide and 49p9 (8.291667 in) tall, as shown in Figure QS.3.** You fine-tune the size and placement in the next steps. The new frame is selected, as indicated by the white handles. If the frame becomes deselected in the following steps, click it to select it.

3. **Highlight the X field in the Control panel (if it's not visible, choose Window ⇨ Control or press Option+⌘+6 or Ctrl+Alt+6), which specifies the item's origin across (placement from the left edge of the page).** Be sure the Selection tool (the solid-arrow pointer) is active and that the new frame is selected. Type **1p** (or **0.1667 in** if you prefer inches) in this field.

FIGURE QS.3

Use any of the frame tools to create background shapes into which you can import a picture. Use the Control panel (at top) and the transformation-values display (near the mouse) to precisely control position and size.

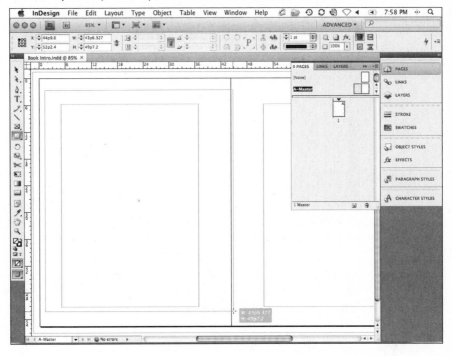

4. **Tab to the Y field, which specifies the item's origin down (placement from the top of the page).** Type **3p (0.5 in)** in this field.

5. **Tab to the W field, which specifies the item's width.** Type **41p3 (7.20833 in)** in this field.

6. **Tab to the H field, which specifies the item's height.** Type **49p9 (8.291667 in)** in this field.

7. **Press Return or Enter to reposition.** The frame now resizes itself according to the values entered.

8. **Choose Item ➪ Duplicate or press Option+Shift+⌘+D or Ctrl+Alt+Shift+D.** If necessary, first click the new frame with the Selection tool to select it.

9. **Highlight the X field in the Control panel.** Type **44p3 (7.375 in), as shown in Figure QS.4**

10. **Tab to the Y field.** Then type **3p (0.5 in)**. You add color to this frame later.

FIGURE QS.4

Resizing and repositioning the second frame with the Control panel

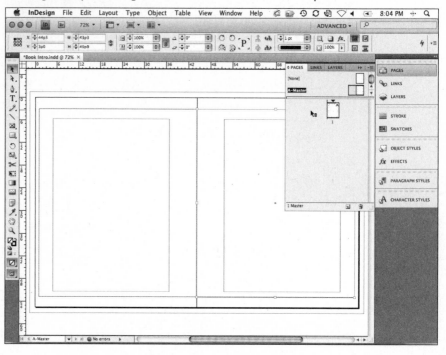

Now, create the frames for the icons that hang outside the margins:

- **Left-hand icon frame:** X: −1p6, Y: 4p6, W: 4p, and H: 2p3. (Or X: −0.25 in, Y: 0.75 in, W: 0.667 in, H: 0.375 in.)
- **Right-hand icon frame:** X: 86p3, Y: 4p6, W: 4p, and H: 2p3. (Or X: 14.375 in, Y: 0.75 in, W: 0.667 in, H: 0.375 in.)

In Figure QS.1, you may have noticed that the corners of these icon frames are slightly rounded. That's easy to do in InDesign:

1. **Select the two folio frames (click one, Shift+click the other).**
2. **Choose Object ⇨ Corner Options to open the Corner Options dialog box.**
3. **Choose Rounded from the Effect pop-up menu and enter** 0p6 (0.5 in) **in the Size field.** Click OK.

With the basic master spread created, it's time to add some pages to your document and apply the master spread to them:

1. **Add as many pages as you think you might need by choosing Insert Pages from the Pages panel's flyout menu. Enter the number of pages desired in the Insert Pages dialog box's Pages field — enter** 5 **in this example.**

   Be sure to select the name of the master page you just selected — such as A-Master — in the Master pop-up menu. Now click OK. The new pages are added to the Pages panel, with the letter of the master page applied in the upper corner of each page. (Note that you can always add more pages or delete extra ones later.)

   If you jumped the gun and added the pages without applying the master page, in the Pages panel's flyout menu, choose Apply Master to Pages. In the Apply Master dialog box, choose the master spread you just created from the Apply Master pop-menu and enter **1–6** in the To Pages field. Then click OK.

2. **Choose File ➪ Save or press ⌘+S or Ctrl+S to save your work.**

 **For more information about working with frames, see Part III. For more on master pages, see Chapter 6.**

Working with Text

In InDesign, text goes inside a text frame. You can type text into the frame or import a text file in various formats. After text is inside the frame, you can change the font, size, color, and many more options.

TIP **What's nice about InDesign is that you can put text in any frame, whether it started life as a text frame or not. The only catch: If the frame has a graphic in it, you can't make it into a text frame without first clearing out the graphic, as I describe in Chapter 9.**

Now you create the frames for the folios on the master page you created in the last section:

1. **Select the Type tool.** (You can also use the Rectangle tool or the Rectangular Frame tool.)

   Be sure you are on your master pages; double-click the master page in the Pages panel to be sure. Use the same process as in the previous section to create the two folio frames at top. The dimensions for each are in Step 2.

   Also set both frames to have rounded corners, using the same settings as for the icon frames, as I described in the previous section.

2. **Follow the frame creation steps from the previous section and create two frames with the following positions and dimensions:**

   ▪ **Left-hand folio frame:** X: –1p6, Y: 1p3, W: 40p9, and H: 1p9. (Or X: –0.25 in, Y: 0.208333 in, W: 6.45833 in, and H: 0.291667 in.)

   ▪ **Right-hand folio frame:** X: 51p9, Y: 1p3, W: 38p9, and H: 1p9. (Or X: 8.625 in, Y: 0.208333 in, W: 6.875 in, and H: 0.291667 in.)

3. Be sure to select the Type tool. Click in the left-hand folio frame to enter its folio. Type a tab character and then choose Type ⇨ Insert Special Character ⇨ Markers ⇨ Current Page Number or press Option+Shift+⌘+N or Ctrl+Alt+Shift+N. Type a tab character, the text Intro, an em space (press Shift+⌘+M or Ctrl+Shift+M), and the text Preface. Don't worry about text alignment for now.

4. Click in the right-hand folio frame and type Face to Face: QuarkXPress to InDesign; next, type a tab character; and finally, enter an automatic current page number by pressing Option+Shift+⌘+N or Ctrl+Alt+Shift+N. Note how the page number appears as a letter — the same letter as the master page number, in fact.

5. First in the left-hand frame and then in the right-hand frame, highlight the entire phrase and choose a font from the Control panel's Font menu (be sure the A iconic button is selected); the example uses Formata Regular). In the Font Size field, choose or enter 12 pt.

6. In the left-hand frame, highlight the automatic page number and choose a bolder font style from the Control panel's Font Style menu (the example uses Medium). Also choose or enter 19 pt in the Font Size field. In the right-hand frame, highlight *Face to Face:* and then apply a bolder style (the example uses Medium) as the Font Style and 19 pt as the Font Size. Highlight the automatic page number and set the Font Size to 19 pt. Figure QS.5 shows an example.

FIGURE QS.5

When text is highlighted, you can format it using controls on the left side of the Control panel.

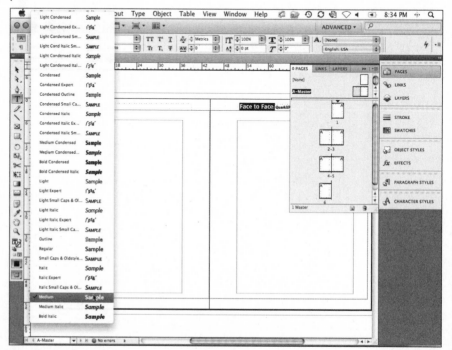

Now you put text in the text frame that was created through the automatic text frame feature earlier:

1. **Go to the document page by double-clicking the desired page in the Pages panel.** In this case, go to page 1.

2. **Choose File ⇨ Place or press ⌘+D or Ctrl+D.** The Place dialog box (shown in Figure QS.6) appears.

FIGURE QS.6

Choose File ⇨ Place or press ⌘+D or Ctrl+D to import text from a word processor.

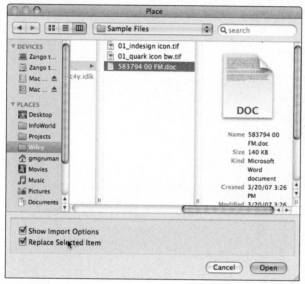

3. **Select Show Import Options.**

4. **Locate a text file in a format such as Microsoft Word.**

5. **Click to select the text file and then click Open.** The Microsoft Word Import Options dialog box appears.

6. **Be sure that Use Typographer's Quotes is selected.** In most cases, you want the Import Styles Automatically radio button selected, with both the Paragraph Style Conflicts and Character Style Conflicts pop-up menus set to Use InDesign Style Definition. You can save Word import settings for reuse later by clicking the Save Preset button.

7. **Click OK to import the file.** InDesign shows the loaded-text icon (it looks like a tiny paragraph and also shows the first few words of the text) that indicates a file ready to be placed into a frame, as shown in Figure QS.7.

FIGURE QS.7

The loaded-text icon has a preview of the file you are importing.

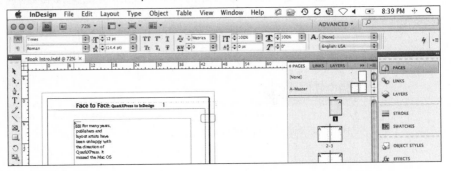

8. **Shift+click at the upper-left corner of the master text frame on page 1 to tell InDesign to pour the text into it and to all subsequent pages' master text frames.** (If you were placing the text in another frame, you would just click the frame.)

9. **Choose File ⇨ Save or press ⌘+S or Ctrl+S to save your work.**

NOTE   **If the text file you import does not fit in the frame, a red square in the lower-right corner indicates that text is overflowing. There is no need to worry about that for these purposes. If you do not have a text file, simply type another sentence in the frame.**

With the text placed, you now need to format it. Ideally, your Word file uses styles so that the imported text has Word's styles associated with it. You then can edit those styles in InDesign to change the formatting globally.

Assuming that your Word text uses styles, modify them in InDesign as follows:

1. **Go to the Paragraph Styles panel (choose Type ⇨ Paragraph Styles or press ⌘+F11 or Ctrl+F11).**

2. **Using the Type tool, click in any text that whose formatting you want to change.** The current style applied, if any, is highlighted in the panel's style list. (If there is no style, [Basic Paragraph] is highlighted instead.)

3. **Double-click the style name to edit it. Go through the various panes' options and click OK when done.** All text using that style is updated automatically.

4. **Repeat Steps 2 and 3 for all styles that you want to edit.**

5. **Create any needed styles by choosing New Paragraph Style from the Paragraph Styles panel's flyout menu. Go through the various panes to set the desired formatting, and click OK when you're done.**

6. **Apply styles to paragraphs with no styles, or to text with the wrong styles, by clicking the appropriate paragraphs (or by highlighting a range of paragraphs) using the Type tool. Then click the desired style from the Paragraph Styles panel, or choose it from the Control panel, as shown in Figure QS.8.** If you want to override all local formatting applied within the paragraphs, Option+click or Alt+click the style name instead.

7. **Choose File ⇨ Save or press ⌘+S or Ctrl+S to save your work.**

FIGURE QS.8

After you import text and apply styles, your pages should look something like this. Use the Paragraph Styles panel to modify and apply styles as needed.

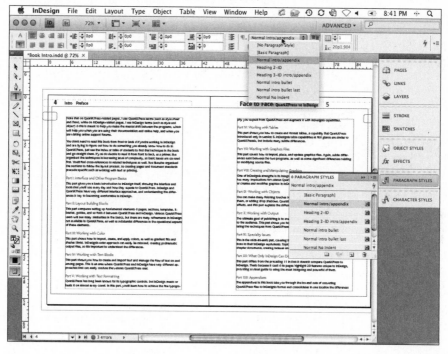

You can also create additional styles in InDesign and apply them to text by placing the text cursor anywhere in the desired paragraph and then clicking the desired style from the Paragraph Styles panel; to apply character styles, highlight the text with the Type tool and then click the desired style from the Character Styles panel.

This is a good time to clean up the positioning of text in the folios, which involves setting tab stops:

1. After switching back to the master page that contains the folios via the Pages panel, open the Tabs panel by choosing Type ⇨ Tabs or pressing Shift+⌘+T or Ctrl+Shift+T.

2. With the Type tool, click in the left-hand page's folio text.

3. Enter 3p3 (or 0.541667 in if you prefer inches) in the X field to set the first tab stop.

4. Click the tab ruler in the band above the numbers near the 6p (1 in) position. Enter 5p (0.833 in) in the X field to move the tab to that location if necessary. Figure QS.9 shows the result.

5. Now click in the right-hand page's folio using the Type tool.

6. Enter 34p3 (5.70833 in) the X field.

7. Click the right tab iconic button (the third from the left) at the top of the Tabs panel to right-align the page number.

8. To move the folio away from the arrowhead, enter 2p3 (0.375 in) in the Left Indent field in the Control panel (be sure the ¶ iconic button is selected).

9. Choose File ⇨ Save or press ⌘+S or Ctrl+S to save your work.

FIGURE QS.9

Setting tabs in the Tabs panel

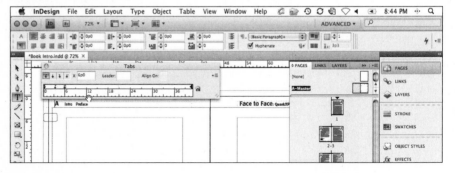

CROSS-REF   For more information about entering, importing, and formatting text, see Part IV. For more on tabs, see Chapter 21.

Working with Lines

You can create lines of any shape and size and then change the style, width, and color. Here, I'm adding two arrowheads to the document's master page so that it appears on all pages. To work on a master page, double-click a master page icon in the Pages panel (choose Window ⇨ Pages or press ⌘+F12 or Ctrl+F12).

Here's how to add the arrows:

1. **Select the Line tool.**

2. **Be sure the Stroke iconic button in the Tools panel or Swatches panel is set to [Black]** — click the icon, go to the Swatches panel (choose Window ➪ Swatches or press F6), and click the [Black] swatch.

3. **Position the mouse where you want to draw the line (here, starting at the gutter above the master text frame on the left-hand page) and then click and Shift+drag it to the left about 10p (1.667 in) to create a line, as shown in Figure QS.10.** (Pressing the Shift key while you drag constrains the Line tool to drawing a horizontal or vertical line.) When you release the mouse, the new line is selected, as indicated by the white handles. If the line becomes deselected in the following steps, click it to select it.

FIGURE QS.10

Use the Line tool to create lines at any angle.

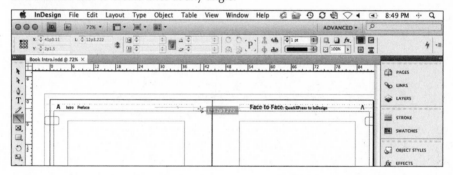

4. **Now set the line thickness and the arrowhead using the Stroke panel (choose Window ➪ Stroke or press ⌘+F10 or Ctrl+F10). Enter 6 in the Weight field and choose Triangle in the End pop-up menu.** The arrow should point to the left. If it is pointing the wrong way, choose Triangle in the Start pop-up menu and choose None in the End pop-up menu. (Note that you can also set the weight in the Control panel.)

5. **Now go to the right-hand page and draw another arrow, also from the gutter, but this time Shift+drag it to the right about 10p (1.667 in).** It's okay that the right-hand pages arrow overlaps the folio text on that page.

6. **Precisely place and size the lines using the Control panel, as follows:**

   ▪ **Left-hand line:** X: 34p3, Y: 1p6, and L: 10p. (Or X: 5.70833 in, Y: 0.25 in, and L: 1.667 in.)

   ▪ **Right-hand line:** X: 44p3, Y: 1p6, and L: 10p. (Or X: 7.375 in, Y: 0.25 in, and L: 1.667 in.)

   Figure QS.11 shows the result.

7. **Choose File ➪ Save or press ⌘+S or Ctrl+S to save your work.**

FIGURE QS.11

How the arrowhead lines should look

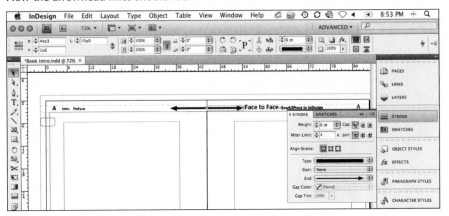

CROSS-REF For more information about working with lines, see Chapter 8.

Creating and Applying Colors

To apply the color you want to an item or text, first you need to create that color. By default, InDesign provides a few colors: cyan, magenta, yellow, [Black], red, blue, green, [Paper] (white), [None], and [Registration]. (The names that InDesign puts in brackets are colors that cannot be deleted or modified.) In most cases, you create additional colors to suit your documents.

1. **To open the Swatches panel, where you create, modify, and apply colors, choose Window⇨Swatches or press F5.**

2. **From the flyout menu, choose New Color Swatch to open the New Color Swatch dialog box shown in Figure QS.12.**

3. **From the Color Mode pop-up menu, choose Pantone Solid Uncoated and then type 1675 in the field after labeled Pantone. Now click OK.** This adds the premixed ink Pantone 1675U to the Swatches panel, to be printed as a spot color (separate ink). Note that if you want to create more colors, click Add instead. Click OK only when you want to close the dialog box.

FIGURE QS.12

Select the color mode that contains the ink you want and then choose the desired ink from the list or, if you know its number, enter it.

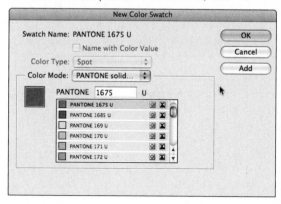

You can apply colors to frame backgrounds, lines, strokes, some imported images, and text. Here's how you apply colors to the frames you created in the master spread in the earlier section.

1. **Be sure the Swatches panel is open (choose Window ⇨ Swatches or press F5).**

2. **Using the Selection tool, select the left-hand page's large frame.**

3. **Make sure the Fill iconic button is selected in the Tools panel or Swatches panel, as it is in Figure QS.13.** This tells InDesign what you want to color the object, not any strokes it may have.

4. **Click the name of the color you created in the previous section.** In this example, select [Black]. The selected frames now fill with the color.

5. **Now lighten the solid black to a light shade of gray by entering 10 in the Swatch panel's Tint field.**

6. **Be sure there is no colored stroke (outline) around the frame.** To do so, select the Stroke iconic button in the Tools panel or Swatches panel and then select the [None] swatch. You can also go to the Stroke panel (choose Window ⇨ Stroke or press ⌘+F10 or Ctrl+F10) and enter **0** in the Weight field.

7. **Repeat Steps 3 through 6 for the right-hand page's large frame.** However, this time, apply the color Pantone 1675U to it, also with a 10 percent tint.

FIGURE QS.13

Click a color swatch to apply it to the background of a frame.

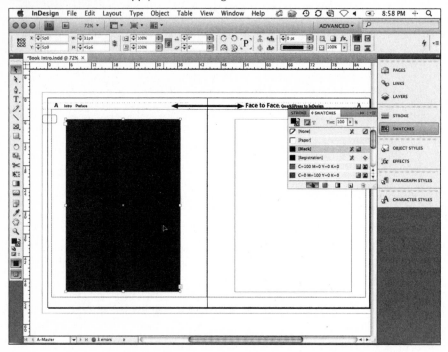

8. **Using the same process, apply a 10 percent tint of Pantone 1675U to the left-hand page's folio frame and a 10 percent tint of [Black] to the right-hand page's folio frame.**

9. **Click the Stroke iconic button in the Tools panel or Swatches panel and then apply a 40 percent tint of Pantone 1675U to the left-hand page's arrow and a 40 percent tint of [Black] to the right-hand page's arrow.** Yes, this means that the gray folio and arrow appear on the page with the light-orange background and vice versa.

10. **Choose File ➪ Save or press ⌘+S or Ctrl+S to save your work.**

CROSS-REF   **For more information about creating and applying colors, see Chapter 7 and the special color insert.**

The process is the same for text, except that you highlight the text with the Type tool before applying a color to its fill. For this exercise, set the folios' text color as follows:

■ On the left-hand page, set all the text except the automatic page number to Pantone 1675U. Apply a 70 percent tint to the word *Preface*.

■ On the left-hand page, apply a 70 percent tint of [Black] to the text *QuarkXPress to InDesign* and set the automatic page number to Pantone 1675U.

Working with Graphics

In InDesign, any image that you import into a layout — whether it's a digital photograph, chart, or line drawing — is referred to as a graphic. Graphics go inside graphics frames, either ones you create before you place graphics or ones that InDesign creates automatically when you import graphics but have no frames selected. After a graphic is inside a frame, you can change its size and placement.

> **TIP** Another thing that's nice about InDesign is that you can put a graphic in any frame, whether it started life as a graphics frame or not. The only catch: If the frame has text in it, the graphic gets inserted as an inline graphic, making InDesign treat it as if it were text, as described in Chapter 12.

Earlier, you created frames for the icons that appear on the outside margins of pages. Now you import the graphics into them:

1. **To import a graphic, be sure no frame or text is selected and choose File ⇨ Place or press ⌘+D or Ctrl+D.** The dialog box is essentially the same as the one you used to import the text file, though the import options differ significantly.

2. **Locate the graphics file (in formats such as a TIFF, JPEG, GIF, or EPS); select each one (Shift+click for a range; ⌘+click or Ctrl+click individual items) and click Open.** For the left-hand page, choose `quark icon bw.tif`. For the right-hand page, choose `indesign icon bw.tif`.

   The loaded-graphic icon appears, with a numeral 2 indicating that there are two graphics to be placed.

3. **Click first in the icon frame on the left-hand page to place the QuarkXPress icon.** (If the loaded-graphic icon shows the InDesign icon, press → or ← to have it switch to the QuarkXPress icon.) Click in the icon frame on the right-hand page to place the InDesign icon.

4. **Apply a Pantone 1675U color with 100 percent tint to the InDesign icon in the right-hand folio frame, using the techniques described in the previous section.**

5. **Now adjust the placement of the icons in the frame.** Using the Direct Selection tool (the hollow-arrow pointer), click in the left-hand page's icon frame and enter **15** in the Control panel's Scale X Percentage field and **–1p6** (or **–0.25 in** if you prefer inches) in the X+ field. Then click the right-hand page's icon frame and enter **15** in the Scale X Percentage field.

   Note how the Y Percentage field changes to match the X Percentage field. If it does not, click the Constrain Proportions for Scaling iconic button (the chain icon) so that it becomes a solid chain. Then reenter the desired scale. You can also resize the image to fit the frame by choosing Object ⇨ Fitting ⇨ Fit Content Proportionally or pressing Option+ Shift+⌘+E or Ctrl+Alt+Shift+E. Figure QS.14 shows the result.

6. **Choose File ⇨ Save or press ⌘+S or Ctrl+S to save your work.**

> **CROSS-REF** For more information about working with pictures, see Part V. For more on manipulating objects, see Part III.

FIGURE QS.14

The placed graphics, scaled to fit

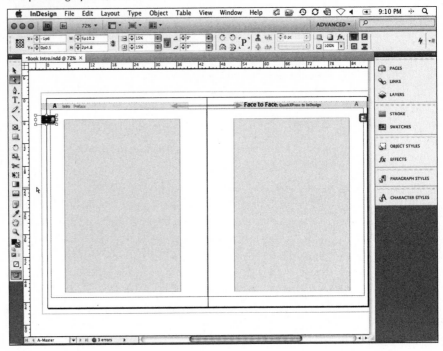

Adding Special Effects

InDesign CS4 has lots of special lighting effects such as transparency, drop shadows, and embossing. It's easy to add them using the Effects panel:

1. Select the object you want to add one or more effects to using the Selection tool.

2. Go to the Effects panel (choose Window ➪ Effects or press Shift+⌘+F10 or Ctrl+Shift+F10).

CROSS-REF For more information about special effects, see Chapter 11.

3. From the flyout menu, choose Effects and then the desired effect from the submenu. I chose Bevel and Emboss for the effect shown in Figure QS.15.

4. In the Settings For pop-menu, select what to apply the effect to: Object, Stroke, Fill, or Text. I chose Object for this exercise.

FIGURE QS.15

A bevel effect applied to the icon

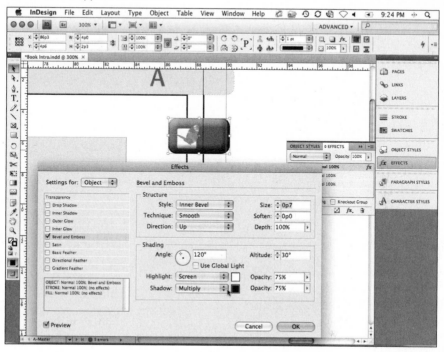

Note that you can apply different effects to different components of an object by using the Settings For pop-up menu and then selecting the effects from the list at left. You can also apply multiple effects simultaneously to the object and/or any of its components.

5. **Experiment with the effects and settings — be sure the Preview check box is selected so that you can see how they look.** Here, I chose the defaults: Inner Bevel as the Style, Smooth as the Technique, Up as the Direction (for the light), 0p7 for the Size, 120° for the Angle, 30° for the Altitude, Screen for the Highlight, Multiply for the Shadow, and 75% for the Opacity of both the highlight and shadow.

6. **Click OK when you are done.**

7. **Choose File ⇨ Save or press ⌘+S or Ctrl+S to save your work.**

Printing a Composite

Whether you're designing a document for black-and-white photocopying, color printing, professional printing, or even a PDF, you need to review drafts. By default, InDesign is set up to your system's default printer with just a few clicks.

1. Choose File ➪ Print or press ⌘+P or Ctrl+P.

TIP If you press Return or Enter as soon as the Print dialog box displays, chances are that InDesign will print a usable draft on your laser printer. However, if you've selected a different page size, orientation, or other option, you may want to confirm the other settings.

2. **At the top of the dialog box, the Printer pop-up menu is usually set to your system's default printer.** You can leave this setting or locate and select the printer you're actually using. It's best to select your actual printer.

3. **Go to the Output pane and make sure the Color pop-up menu is set to Composite Grayscale if you're printing to a black-and-white laser printer and to Composite CMYK if you're printing to a color inkjet or laser printer.**

4. **Look at the page preview at the lower-left of the dialog box and make sure the page (indicated by the light-gray rectangle) fits within the printer paper (indicated by the blue line), as shown in Figure QS.16.**

5. **Click Print.**

CROSS-REF For more information about printing, see Part VII: Output Fundamentals.

FIGURE QS.16

The Print dialog box lets you confirm that your document fits on the paper in the selected printer, as well as set the appropriate print settings for your document and target printer.

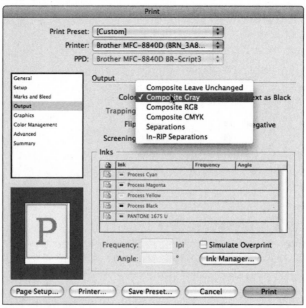

Part I

Welcome to InDesign

Chapter 1

What InDesign Can Do for You

InDesign CS4 is the sixth version of Adobe's flagship publishing tool, a product that came into its own with the third version (CS, which stands for Creative Suite). Widely regarded as the best layout tool today, InDesign CS4 continues to benefit from continued investment by its makers at Adobe Systems.

Every new version of InDesign has brought significant new capabilities to your fingertips, and CS4 is no different. This new version introduces several key additions that make it easier to produce flexible documents, such as the ability to export files for use in Flash multimedia projects, as well as enhanced capabilities for its conditional text feature that lets a document have different versions of, say, a chapter heading or copyright line. Catalog publishers, for example, will love these additions.

Adobe has also improved lots of features — some big, some small — to both simplify the product's use and to enhance its capabilities. For example, the new "smart guides" feature makes it much easier to align, resize, rotate, and place objects precisely when you're using the mouse. The Links panel has been redesigned to better match how Adobe Bridge works, as well as make it easier to substitute FPO (for position only) files quickly. And InDesign now alerts you as you're working if your document has any issues that may affect final output quality.

But if you're upgrading from InDesign CS3, what you'll notice most is a slightly cleaned-up user interface — using modern standards such as tabbed panes to hold documents, as well as simpler icons in the panels — rather than obvious new features. InDesign CS4 has many nice additions, but it's very much a continuance of what you know from CS3. Most of its enhancements are subtle, the kind you may not even notice right away.

IN THIS CHAPTER

Learning what InDesign can do

Understanding global and local control

Identifying InDesign terminology

> **CROSS-REF** If you want a quick overview of what's new in InDesign CS4, flip forward to Appendix B.

InDesign users fall into two camps: Recent converts from QuarkXPress or even the long-defunct PageMaker and people who've used at least one previous version of InDesign. If you're an experienced user of previous InDesign versions, you already know the InDesign approach. That's great — you're a step ahead! Feel free to skip this chapter or just skim it for a refresher. But if you're new to InDesign, please read on.

InDesign's Flexible Approach

So what can InDesign do for you? A lot. For years, layout designers had to choose between a free-form but manual approach to layout (PageMaker) and a structured but easily revised approach (QuarkXPress). For years, most chose the latter. But with InDesign, you can choose both, which is a key reason why it is now so widely acknowledged as the best publishing tool. InDesign's flexible approach is important for both novice and experienced users because there is rarely a one-size-fits-all answer for all your design challenges. Sometimes (for example, if your project is a onetime publication or an experimental effort), creating a layout from scratch — almost as if you were doing it by hand on paper — is the best approach. And sometimes using a highly formatted template that you can modify as needed is the best approach because you don't need to reinvent the wheel for common documents.

InDesign can handle sophisticated tasks such as magazine and newspaper page layout, but its simple approach to publishing also makes it a good choice for smaller projects such as flyers and newsletters. InDesign is also a good choice for corporate publishing tasks such as proposals and annual reports. Plug-in software from other vendors adds extra capabilities; for example, Virginia Systems offers several plug-ins that make InDesign a good tool for books and academic papers.

> **CROSS-REF** For more on plug-in software, see Chapter 36.

But that's not all. InDesign is not merely a merger of QuarkXPress and PageMaker — though it may seem that way to experienced users. It is designed from the ground up as an *electronic* publishing tool. That means you can easily send documents to service providers and printing presses for direct output, saving you lots of time and money. It also means you can create documents for electronic distribution, particularly using the Adobe Portable Document Format (PDF) or the Web's XHTML format, though the latter capability assumes that you'll redesign the content's appearance in a Web editing program such as Adobe Dreamweaver. These electronic files can include interactive features such as forms and sounds. And InDesign uses a whole bunch of automation techniques — from text variables through sharable styles and swatches — to ease the effort required to produce and maintain your documents.

> **CROSS-REF** For more in-depth coverage of output and electronic-document fundamentals, see Parts VII and VIII, respectively.

In this chapter, I detail the wide range of uses and features of InDesign, point out the ways in which InDesign can be useful to you, and describe the basic metaphor on which the program is based. I also provide a comprehensive list of the terms, clearly and concisely defined, that I use throughout the book. So whether you're an expert or novice, read on and prepare yourself for a great InDesign adventure.

Understanding Global and Local Control

The power of desktop publishing in general, and InDesign in particular, is that it lets you automate time-consuming layout and typesetting tasks while letting you customize each step of the process according to your needs. This duality of structure and flexibility — implemented via the dual use of the frame-based and free-form layout metaphors — carries over to all operations, from typography to color. You can use *global* controls to establish general settings for layout elements and then use *local* controls to modify those elements to meet specific publishing requirements. The key to using global and local tools effectively is to know when each is appropriate.

Global tools include:

- General preferences and application preferences (see Chapter 3)
- Master pages (see Chapter 6)
- Text styles (see Chapter 19)
- Table and cell styles (see Chapter 21)
- Object styles (see Chapter 12)
- Stroke styles (see Chapter 11)
- Text variables (see Chapter 22)
- Sections of page numbers (see Chapter 5)
- Color definitions (see Chapter 7)
- Hyphenation and justification (see Chapter 17)
- Libraries (see Chapter 6)

NOTE Styles and master pages are the two main global settings that you can expect to override locally throughout a document. This is the case because although the layout and typographic functions that styles and master pages automate are the fundamental components of any document's look, they don't always work for all of a publication's specific content.

Local tools include:

- Frame and shape tools (see Part III and Chapters 26 and 27)
- Character and paragraph tools (see Chapters 16 through 19)
- Graphics tools (see Part VI)

InDesign Vocabulary 101

InDesign comes with its own terminology, much of it adopted from other Adobe products. The general terms include the following:

- **Frame:** The container for an object, whether text, graphic, or color fill.

- **Link:** The connection that InDesign makes to an imported file. The link contains the file's location, last modification date, and last modification time. A link can reference any image or text file that you have imported into a layout. InDesign can notify you when a source text or graphics file has changed, so you can choose whether to update the version in your layout. (A *hyperlink,* often also abbreviated to *link* in casual conversation, connects elements in a Web page to other Web pages or other resources such as PDF files.)

- **Package:** The collection of all files needed to deliver a layout for commercial printing. InDesign has a package feature that collects all these files for you.

- **Pane:** A section of a dialog box or panel whose options change based on the set of controls you've selected in the dialog box or panel.

- **Panel:** A container for controls that stays on-screen even when you aren't using it (in contrast to a dialog box, which appears only while you are using it). Panels can be docked to the right edge of the screen or free floating. Panels can be combined into a single container called a *panel group*.

- **Path:** A shape in which the endpoint and start point are separate, keeping the shape "open." Lines are a straight type of path.

- **PDF:** The Adobe Portable Document Format is the standard for electronic documents. No matter what kind of computer it is viewed on (Windows, Macintosh, Palm, or Unix), a PDF document retains high fidelity to the original in typography, graphics representation, and layout. InDesign can both place PDF files as if they were graphics and export its own pages as PDF files.

- **Place:** To import a graphics file or text file.

- **Plug-in:** A piece of software that loads into InDesign and becomes part of it, adding more capabilities.

- **Stroke:** The outline of an object (whether a frame, a line, or an individual text character).

- **Thread:** The links between text frames that route stories among them.

In many cases, it's obvious which tool to use. If, for example, you maintain certain layout standards throughout a document, then using master pages is the obvious way to keep your work in order. Using styles is the best solution if you want to apply standard character and paragraph formatting throughout a document. When you work with special-case documents, such as single-page display ads, it doesn't make much sense to spend time designing master pages and styles — it's easier just to format one-of-a-kind elements on the fly.

In other cases, deciding which tool is appropriate is more difficult. For example, you can create a *drop cap* (a large initial letter set into a paragraph of type, like the one that starts each chapter in this book) as a character option in the Character panel, or you can create a *character style* (formatting that you can apply to any selected text, ensuring that the same formatting is applied each time) that contains the drop-cap settings and apply that style to the drop cap. The method you choose depends on the complexity of your document and how often you need to perform the action. The more often you find yourself doing something, the more often you should use a global tool (such as character styles).

Fortunately, you don't have to decide between global and local tools right away while designing a document. You can always create styles from existing formatting later or add elements to a master page if you find that you need them to appear on every page.

Another situation in which you can choose between local or global controls is specifying measurement values. Regardless of the default measurement unit you set (and that appears in all dialog boxes and panels), you can use any unit when entering measurements in an InDesign dialog box. If, for example, the default measurement is picas but you're accustomed to working with inches, go ahead and enter measurements in inches.

 Chapter 3 covers how to apply measurement values and set your preferred defaults.

Summary

InDesign offers a strong set of features for professional publishers working on brochures, magazines, advertisements, and similar publications. It combines the ability to create documents on the fly with the ability to create structured documents for use as templates, allowing for efficient while still creative design workflows.

Chapter 2

Inside the InDesign Interface

The first time you use a program, it can be overwhelming. You're not sure what you can actually do with the program, and each program has its own interface idiosyncrasies. InDesign is no different. If you're familiar with other Adobe applications, such as Dreamweaver or Photoshop, the InDesign software interface will be familiar to you. Even if you've been using QuarkXPress, you'll be able to translate much of what you see in InDesign to QuarkXPress terms.

But because every program is unique, each has its own style and approaches. So now that you're ready to start using InDesign, follow through this chapter to find out where InDesign puts its capabilities and how to access them. When you first launch InDesign, you see the Tools panel on the left, and you may see several other panels on the right. InDesign is ready and waiting for you to open a document and start working.

However, taking a few minutes to familiarize yourself with the interface is invaluable to learning new software. After all, without a basic understanding of what you're looking at on-screen, it's difficult to begin working in InDesign. And even if you've used InDesign before, Adobe has made some changes to its interface in this version, so it's worth your while to peruse this chapter to see what's changed.

NOTE InDesign lets you change both its menu options and the shortcuts associated with menu and other commands (see Chapter 3). Throughout the book, I assume that the menu arrangements and shortcuts you're using are the default ones.

IN THIS CHAPTER

Discovering what's inside the application folder

Exploring the document window

Working with multiple document windows

Using tools, panels, and docks

Reviewing menu commands

Undoing what you've just done if you change your mind

29

Exploring the InDesign Application Folder

Often, users simply launch an application from an alias or shortcut and never even look in the application folder. This approach is just fine until it comes time to install a new plug-in or to share important information with other users. Familiarizing yourself with the basic contents helps ensure that you're not throwing away anything important and that you're working with the correct files and folders.

If you locate the InDesign application folder on your hard drive and open it, you see that it's chock-full of stuff you may not even recognize. The three folders you need to know about in this folder are the `Presets` folder, the `Plug-ins` folder, and the `Required` folder.

The Presets folder

The `Presets` folder contains seven kinds of standards: Shortcut sets, color swatch libraries, scripts, workspaces, glyph sets, auto-correction tables, find-change tables, and stored document sizes. InDesign lets you create shortcut sets so that different users can have their own shortcut definitions. These preferences are stored in the InDesign shortcut sets folder in the `Presets` folder. Because these preferences are stored in files, they can be copied to other users' `Presets` folder to help ensure consistent options among all users in a workgroup.

 Chapters 3 ands 34 cover the `Presets` folder in more detail.

The Plug-ins folder

The `Plug-ins` folder in the `InDesign` folder contains small software modules, called *plug-ins*, that add both core features and additional, optional features to InDesign. The `Plug-ins` folder contains a variety of subfolders, such as `Dictionaries`, `Filters`, and `Graphics`, that make locating files easy.

To install additional plug-ins from Adobe or other companies, add them to the `Plug-ins` folder. Follow the instructions provided by each vendor — some have an installation program, whereas others have you copy the plug-in file to the `Plug-ins` folder.

To remove a plug-in, simply click and drag it out of the subfolder of the `Plug-ins` folder and store it someplace else or delete it.

TIP **To keep track of required files and plug-ins versus optional ones, you may want to create an `Optional Plug-ins` folder and install any optional plug-ins there. As long as the `Optional Plug-ins` folder is inside the `Plug-ins` folder, InDesign will load them when it starts up.**

You also use the `Plug-ins` folder to access any customizations you make to the spelling or hyphenation dictionaries in InDesign. These custom settings are saved in the files inside the `Dictionaries` folder. If you're in a workgroup, the only way to ensure that everyone is working with the same spelling and hyphenation standards — so that text flows the same way on everyone's computer — is to share the dictionary files.

CROSS-REF See Chapter 34 for more information on maintaining standards across workgroups. See Chapter 36 for details on managing plug-ins.

The Required folder

The Required folder is similar to the Plug-ins folder in that it contains components of InDesign. The difference is that the components in the Required folder are necessary for InDesign to function, so you should not modify this folder or its contents.

Exploring the Document Window

When you're running InDesign, the first thing to do is create a new, empty document by choosing File ➪ New ➪ Document, or pressing ⌘+N or Ctrl+N, and clicking OK immediately. Doing so gives you a document window so that you can start exploring the application. (Never mind the settings for now — you're just exploring.)

No matter what size document you're dealing with or how many pages it has, all documents are contained within a standard window. The window provides controls that help you create and place objects, change the view scale, and navigate between pages. Figure 2.1 shows all the standard elements of a new document window.

NEW FEATURE Gone in InDesign CS4's default view are the Structure panel and the Show/Hide Structure button for that panel at the lower left of the document window. (You use the Structure panel when working on XML documents, as Chapter 33 explains.) You can still display or hide this panel by choosing View ➪ Structure ➪ Show/Hide Structure or by pressing Option+⌘+1 or Ctrl+Alt+1.

Title tab

When you open or create a document, by default InDesign opens a new tabbed window within the application frame. Each window is accessed via a tab; click the tab and the desired window appears. Each tab has the name of the document, as well as other information about the document:

- The current view percentage is shown at the end of the filename, such as "@ 74%" to indicate that the document is displayed at 74 percent of actual size.

- An asterisk (*) displays in front of the filename if the document has unsaved changes.

- If multiple windows are open for the same document, InDesign indicates the various windows by adding ":1," ":2," and so on to each window, with ":1" indicating the first window, ":2" the second, and so on. (Note that a colon precedes the number.)

NEW FEATURE InDesign CS4 puts documents in tabbed windows by default, instead of in free-floating windows as in previous editions.

FIGURE 2.1

The standard document window provides controls for managing documents on-screen, changing the view scale, displaying different pages, and placing objects on pages.

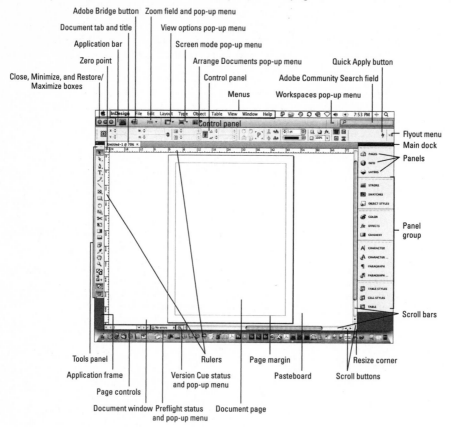

You can close a document quickly by clicking the Close box (the "X" icon) on the document's tab.

Later in this chapter, I explain how to work with multiple documents, as well as how to use the old-style document windows instead of the new tabbed ones.

Rulers

Document windows always display a horizontal ruler across the top and a vertical ruler down the left side. The horizontal ruler measures from the top-left corner of the page across the entire spread; the vertical ruler measures from the top to the bottom of the current page.

You can use these rulers to judge the size and placement of frames and lines on your page. Although InDesign provides more precise methods for placing objects — such as the Control panel, in which you can enter exact values — designers often use the rulers for rough placement while they experiment with a design, as shown in Figure 2.2.

NEW FEATURE When you create new objects, move them, resize them, or rotate them, InDesign now provides an indicator near the mouse to show you the object's current status — called the transformation value — such as size or rotation angle, as you can see in Figure 2.2.

FIGURE 2.2

This frame's top is aligned with the 9-pica mark on the vertical ruler.

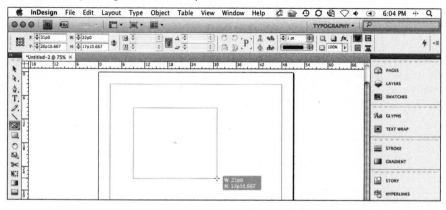

By default, both rulers display increments in picas, but you can change the measurement system for each ruler in the Units & Increments pane of the Preferences dialog box (choose InDesign ⇨ Preferences ⇨ Units & Increments or press ⌘+K on the Mac, or choose Edit ⇨ Preferences ⇨ Units & Increments or press Ctrl+K in Windows). If you do make such a change while no documents are open, the rulers in all new documents appear in your preferred measurement systems. If a document is open, the rulers are changed only in that open document.

CROSS-REF Chapter 3 explains ruler increments in more detail.

If you need more space on-screen or want to preview a design without all the layout tools, you can hide the rulers by choosing View ⇨ Hide Rulers or pressing ⌘+R or Ctrl+R. Most users show the rulers all the time out of habit, but the rulers aren't really necessary in template-driven documents such as magazines in which all the placement decisions are indicated by guides and master pages. If you're editing text on a smaller monitor, you might appreciate the space gain of not having rulers, minimal though it might be.

Zero point

The intersection of the rulers in the upper-left corner of the page is called the *zero point*. Known as the *ruler origin* in other applications, this is the starting place for all horizontal and vertical measurements. If you need to place items in relation to another spot on the page (for example, from the center of a spread rather than from the left-hand page), you can move the zero point by clicking and dragging it to a new location. The X and Y values in the Control panel and Transform panel update as you click and drag the zero point so that you can place it precisely. The zero point is document-wide, so it changes for all pages or spreads in the document. To restore the zero point to the upper-left corner of the left-most page, double-click the intersection of the rulers in the upper-left corner.

After the zero point is moved, all the objects on the page display new X and Y values even though they haven't moved. Objects above or to the left of the zero point have negative X and Y values, and the X and Y values of other objects do not relate to their actual position on the page or spread.

The effects of changing the zero point can be confusing, especially if you're in a workgroup with other users who may change the zero point and forget to restore it to the upper-left corner. To prevent this problem, you can lock the zero point, making it more difficult for users to change it. To lock the zero point, Control+click or right-click the zero point and choose Lock Zero Point from the contextual menu.

Of course, a user determined to change the zero point can simply choose Unlock Zero Point from the contextual menu. But doing so is a conscious act on someone's part, and the fact that you locked the zero point usually sends the message that you want to keep it that way.

Keep Your Bearings Straight

A powerful but confusing capability in InDesign is something called a *reference point*. InDesign lets you work with objects from nine reference points — any of the four corners, the middle of any of the four sides, or the center — such as when you're positioning the object precisely or rotating the object. You choose these reference points in the Control panel or Transform panel, using the grid of nine points arranged in a square.

By default, InDesign works with the central reference point, which is great for rotating an object but can lead to confusion when you enter in the X and Y coordinates to place it precisely. That's because most people use the upper-left corner of an object when specifying its coordinates, not the center of the object. So be sure to change the reference point to the upper left whenever entering X and Y coordinates in the Control or Transform panels. (I use the upper-left reference point in this book unless otherwise indicated.)

How do you change which reference point is active? That's easy: Just click the point in that preview grid. The active reference point — called the control point — is black, whereas the others are white.

Scroll bars

Standard scroll bars run down the right side and across the bottom of the document window. As in most applications, you can either click and drag the scroll bars or click the scroll buttons to move around on a page or move to other pages in the document.

Pasteboard, pages, and guides

Inside the rulers, you see a white area surrounding the black, drop-shadowed outlines of your pages (refer to Figure 2.1). The work area surrounding the page is called the *pasteboard,* and it's designed as a workspace for creating, experimenting with, and temporarily storing objects. You can also use the pasteboard to bleed objects off a page so that they print to the edge of a trimmed page. In contrast to PageMaker (and like QuarkXPress), each page or spread in InDesign has its own pasteboard. By default, there's 1 inch of pasteboard above and below each page, and a space equal to the page width to the left and right of each page or spread. (As Chapter 3 explains, you can change the pasteboard height.) For example, a spread consisting of two 4-inch pages has 4 inches of pasteboard to the left and 4 inches of pasteboard to the right.

Pages, drawn with black outlines, reflect the page size you set up in the New Document dialog box (choose File ➪ New ➪ Document or press ⌘+N or Ctrl+N). If it looks like two pages are touching, you're looking at a multipage spread. By default, you see magenta lines across the top and bottom of each page showing the top and bottom margins you specified when you created the document. Violet-colored lines indicate the left and right margins (for single-page documents) or inside and outside margins (for facing-page documents). These lines are nonprinting guides that can help you position objects.

You can change the placement of these guides by choosing Layout ➪ Margins and Columns, and you can create additional guides by clicking and dragging them off the horizontal and vertical rulers.

CROSS-REF I cover guides in detail in Chapter 6.

If you can't see the guide colors well, you can change them for all new documents. When no documents are open, choose new colors in the Guides & Pasteboard pane of the Preferences dialog box (choose InDesign ➪ Preferences ➪ Guides & Pasteboard or press ⌘+K on the Mac, or choose Edit ➪ Preferences ➪ Guides & Pasteboard or press Ctrl+K in Windows). The Margins color changes the horizontal guides and the Columns color affects the vertical guides.

Page controls

InDesign has several controls for maneuvering through pages: page-turning buttons, and the Page field and pop-up menu. In the document window, next to the Zoom pop-up menu, you have the Page field and pop-up menu available to navigate pages. Figure 2.3 shows the page controls.

Iconic buttons in the application bar (at left) let you flip from page to page. You can also use the Page pop-up menu to select a specific page.

Next to the application bar's Zoom pop-up menu, you can find a combined page-number field and pop-up menu encased by two sets of arrows, shown in Figure 2.3. These arrows are page-turning buttons, which let you turn pages sequentially or jump to the first or last page in the document. From left to right, clicking these arrows takes you to the first page, the previous page, the next page, and the last page.

The document window also provides a control for jumping to a specific page or master page in a document. To jump to a specific page number, highlight the current number in the Page field, type a new page number, and press Return or Enter.

NEW FEATURE The Zoom pop-up menu and pop-up menu have moved to the new application bar from their former position at the bottom of the document window. Also, the shortcut ⌘+J or Ctrl+J that used to highlight the current number in the Page field now opens the Go to Page dialog box instead, which performs the same action.

To jump to a master page, type the first few characters of the master page's name in the field. Jumping to document pages can be a little more complicated. Because the page number that displays and prints on the document page does not have to match the position of the page in the document — for example, the third page might be labeled *iii* instead of *3* — there are two methods for entering the page number you want to jump to: section page numbers and absolute page numbers. (Chapter 5 covers these methods in detail.)

You can also use the pop-up menu to the right of the Page field to get a list of available pages, including master pages (see Figure 2.3).

CROSS-REF Chapter 5 details the other methods for navigating pages.

Version Cue pop-up menu

As Figure 2.4 shows, InDesign uses the Version Cue pop-up menu to show you the status of your document in the Version Cue version-management system that comes with InDesign CS4 and other Creative Suite 4 programs. For example, Version Cue lets you see other versions of a document, revert to the project's version of the file, and show the source file in the Adobe Bridge browser window or in the Finder (Mac) or Explorer (Windows) interface. At the left of the pop-up menu is an information display that indicates the document's current Version Cue status.

FIGURE 2.4

An unlabeled pop-up menu at the bottom of the document window lets you open other versions of your document, find the file in the Adobe Bridge browser (or in the Mac Finder or Windows Explorer), or revert to the project's master version. To the left of this pop-up menu, InDesign displays the document's current Version Cue status.

NOTE If Version Cue is not enabled, or if the current document has not been saved to a Version Cue folder, the Version Cue pop-up menu — as well as the related Check In command in the File menu and in the Links panel's flyout menu — is grayed out or don't even display.

CROSS-REF Appendix C covers Version Cue in detail.

Application frame

InDesign CS4 introduces the application frame. At least if you are a Mac user, it does. Previously, on a Mac, all the InDesign elements such as document windows and panels just floated on-screen, and pieces of other open applications could peek through any open spaces between the InDesign elements. Some people found that display confusing, so the new version lets you put all the InDesign elements in their own container, preventing them from floating freely and keeping other applications from peeking through.

The Windows version of InDesign has always had an application frame that contained all the interface elements. In InDesign CS4 for Windows, you can now turn that off so that the display has the same free-floating appearance as the Mac version has always had.

You can hide the application frame (or bring it back) by choosing Window ➪ Application Frame.

PLATFORM DIFFERENCES On the Mac, the application frame is turned off by default. In Windows, it is turned on by default.

Application bar

Above the Control panel is the new application bar, which offers easy access to other Adobe applications, such as Bridge, and to controls pertaining to various view options (see Chapter 3). The application bar appears by default if the application frame is enabled, as shown in Figure 2.1. But when the application frame is hidden, you can show or hide the application bar by choosing Window ➪ Application Bar.

 The application bar is new to InDesign CS4.

The application bar has several handy elements. From left to right:

- The first element is the set of quick-access buttons to Bridge and other Adobe software.

- The second element is the Zoom Level field and pop-up menu, which replaces the Zoom pop-up menu that used to be at the bottom of the document window (see later in this chapter).

- The third element is the View Options pop-up menu, which lets you hide and show frames edges, rulers, various guides and grids, and hidden characters from one handy location. These options previously existed, but only in a variety of scattered View menu options and by choosing Type ➪ Show/Hide Hidden Characters (where they also remain).

- The fourth element, the Screen Mode pop-up menu, duplicates the screen-mode buttons' settings at the bottom of the Tools panel (covered later in this chapter).

- The fifth element, the new Arrange Documents pop-up menu, gives you fast access to InDesign CS4's new controls over how document windows are arranged (covered later in this chapter).

- The sixth element, the Workspaces pop-up menu, gives you quick access to the work-spaces you've defined (covered in Chapter 3).

- At far right is the Adobe Community Search field, a new feature that lets you find help on the Adobe Community Web site (covered at the end of this chapter).

Zoom field and pop-up menu

In the application bar, you use the Zoom field and pop-up menu, which let you change the document's view scale. The view scale can be as small as 5 percent and as large as 4,000 percent, and you can modify it in 0.01 percent increments. (Chapter 3 covers zoom controls in more detail.)

NEW FEATURE   The Zoom field and pop-up menu have moved from the bottom of the document window into the application bar in InDesign CS4. But how they work has not changed.

You have two options for using the Zoom field and pop-up menu:

- To change the view to a preset value, click the arrow on the field and choose an option from the pop-up menu, as shown in Figure 2.5.

- To change the view to a specific value, highlight the value in the field, type a new value, and press Return or Enter.

NEW FEATURE   Gone in InDesign CS4 is the ability to jump into the View field quickly by pressing press Option+⌘+5 or Ctrl+Alt+5, typing a specific value, and then pressing Return or Enter.

FIGURE 2.5

You can choose from a list of preset view percentages using the list in the Zoom pop-up menu.

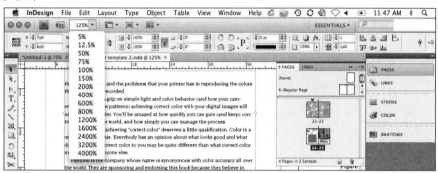

Adobe Community Search field

This new field — the one at the upper-right of the document window, preceded by a magnifying glass icon — lets you enter phrases you want to search for help on in the new Adobe Community service hosted by Adobe. Here, Adobe, other vendors, and other users can post information and answer questions. The service is based on the wiki concept, which lets multiple people directly support each other from a common set of editable files. This free service does not replace the Help menu's InDesign Help and Search options but just supplements it.

 **The Adobe Community Search capability is new to InDesign CS4.**

Working with Multiple Document Windows

If you like to work on more than one project at one time, you've come to the right program. InDesign lets you have several documents open simultaneously. It also lets you have multiple windows for an individual document open simultaneously. A large monitor (or having multiple monitors connected) makes this multiwindow feature even more useful. By opening multiple windows, you can

- **Display two (or more) different pages or spreads at one time.** You still have to work on the documents one at a time, but no navigation is required — you need only to click within the appropriate window.

- **Display multiple magnifications of the same page.** For example, you can work on a detail at high magnification in one window and display the entire page — and see the results of your detail work — at actual size in another window.

- **Display a master page in one window and a document page based on that master page in another window.** When you change the master page, the change is reflected in the window in which the associated document page is displayed.

NEW FEATURE As explained earlier in this chapter, document windows are now, by default, accessed through a set of tabs below the Control panel, rather than as a series of cascaded windows as in previous versions of InDesign.

When multiple windows are open, you activate a window by clicking a window's title tab or anywhere within its window. That window then displays in place of whatever other window had been previously active. Also, the names of all open documents are displayed at the bottom of the Window menu. Choosing a document name from the Window menu brings that document to the front. If multiple windows are open for a particular document, each window is displayed (they're displayed in the order in which you created them) in the Window menu.

To show multiple windows on-screen at one time, choose Window ⇨ Arrange ⇨ Tile. When you choose the Tile command, all open windows are resized and displayed side by side or in a grid, depending on how many windows are open. Or use one of the new window-layout options in the new Arrange Documents pop-up menu's options (in the application bar). How they display depends on the option you choose. Either way, note that when you resize any individual document window, the others will be resized accordingly so that they don't overlap.

To put all these tiled windows back into their regular tabs so that only one document window is visible on screen at a time, choose Window ⇨ Arrange ⇨ Consolidate All Documents, or choose the Consolidate All Documents option (single-window icon) in the Arrange Documents pop-up menu in the application bar.

If you don't like the tabbed approach to windows and instead want to use the old-style approach of stacked windows, you can. First, enable cascading windows by going to the Interface pane of the Preferences dialog box and then deselecting the Open New Documents as Tabs option. (Choose In Design ⇨ Preferences ⇨ Interface or press ⌘+K on the Mac, or choose Edit ⇨ Preferences ⇨ Interface or press Ctrl+K in Windows, to open the Preferences dialog box.) Now, all windows are floating — displayed stacked and staggered on top of each other as they are opened. The front-most document window is visible; the title bars of the other windows are visible above the front-most document. (You can still, of course, use the tiling features described earlier and then revert to cascaded windows by choosing Window ⇨ Arrange ⇨ Cascade.)

TIP To quickly take a specific tabbed window and make it into a free-floating window, just click and drag its title tab away from the other tabs.

TIP To close all windows for the currently displayed document, press Shift+⌘+W or Ctrl+Shift+W. To close all windows for all open documents, press Option+Shift+ ⌘+W or Ctrl+Alt+Shift+W.

Not only do you get separate document windows for each open document, you can also create multiple windows for an individual document so that you can see different parts of it at the same time. To open a new window for the active document, choose Window ⇨ Arrange ⇨ New Window (or use the New Window option in the new Arrange Documents iconic pop-up menu in the application bar). The new window is displayed in its own tab.

NOTE You can tell that a document window shows a different view of an existing document by looking at the name of the document in the window's title. At the end of the document name is a colon (:) followed by a number. For example, Newsletter.indd:1 would be a document's first window, Newsletter.indd:2 would be its second window, and so on.

Using Tools

InDesign by default displays a docked panel on the left side of the screen called the *Tools panel* (longtime users also know it as the *Toolbox*, the name used in early InDesign documentation), which contains 32 tools plus 13 other functions. It appears by default at the upper-left of the screen (see Figure 2.6).

FIGURE 2.6

InDesign's Tools panel has 32 tools available (at left), many via pop-out menus (shown at center). You can see a tool's name by hovering the mouse over it to get a Tool Tip (at right).

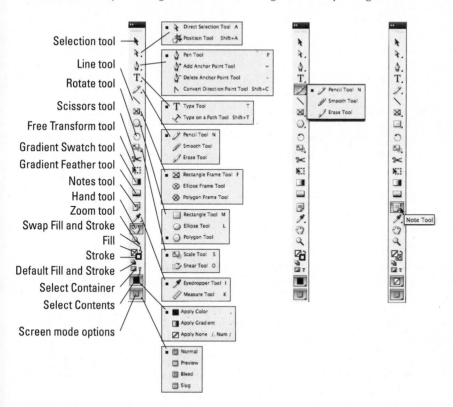

The tools let you create and manipulate the objects that make up your pages. The tools work similarly to those in other Adobe products (such as Photoshop, Illustrator, and Dreamweaver) and they work somewhat like the tools in QuarkXPress. But the tools do not work like the toolbars in your word processor, which are more like macros that make something happen. With InDesign's tools, for the most part, you select the tool and do something with it — draw a new frame, rotate a line, crop an image, and so on.

NOTE   **The one tool not directly accessible from the Tools panel is the Marker tool. But you can switch to it from the Eyedropper tool by holding Option or Alt. (Chapter 7 and the special color insert explain its use.)**

With so many tools, all of which perform limited functions, understanding what each tool does is imperative. When it comes to tools, InDesign has little intuition — it requires you to select the precise tool for the action you want to complete. The software is unable to predict that you might want to make a box slightly larger while you're editing text, or that you might want to reshape a frame at the same time you're resizing it. You need to learn which tool to use and get used to switching tools — a lot.

Selecting tools

To select a tool and start using it, click it in the Tools panel. As long as you're not using the Type tool, you can also press a keyboard shortcut displayed in parentheses in the Tool Tips (covered later in this chapter).

In addition to the tools you can see, the Tools panel contains a few hidden tools that are consolidated into little pop-out menus. Any tool with a small arrow in its lower-right corner is hiding one or more similar tools, as shown in Figure 2.6. To access these "hidden" tools, Control+click or right-click a tool that has a pop-out indicator. When the pop-out displays, click one of the new tools to replace the standard tool with the pop-out tool. Note that many of the pop-out tools also have keyboard shortcuts, as Figure 2.6 shows.

NEW FEATURE   **The ability to select pop-out tool menus by Control+clicking or right-clicking is new to InDesign CS4. You can still use the old method: Click and hold the mouse over a tool that has a pop-out menu.**

NEW FEATURE   **InDesign CS4's Tools panel doesn't have a Button tool as the previous versions did; that function is now handled through the Buttons panel, as described in Chapter 32. The Gradient Feather tool has taken its place on the Tools panel and is no longer available as a pop-out tool from the Gradient Swatch tool.**

Understanding what the tools do

In real life, you can often get by using the wrong tool for a job — using a flat screwdriver instead of a Phillips, or a shoe instead of a fly swatter. This doesn't work in InDesign. Whether you're typing text, reshaping an object, or applying a color, there's one — and only one — tool for each job.

Loosely organized with the most commonly used tools at the top, the Tools panel includes tools for creating and manipulating frames and lines — the objects that make up your designs (see Figure 2.6).

> **NOTE** Frames are shapes and containers that you can size, position, and reshape with precision. InDesign has three types of frames: Empty (unassigned) frames for blocks of color, text frames for type, and graphics frames for imported images. By default, most frames are empty but you can easily convert them to text or graphics frames. Other frames are created specifically as text or graphics frames.

Selection tool

The Selection tool (shortcut V) lets you select objects on the page and move or resize them. You might want to rename this tool in your mind as the Mover tool because it's the only tool that lets you drag objects around on-screen.

> **TIP** If you're working with text and have the Type tool selected, you can switch to the Selection tool by holding down ⌘ or Ctrl instead of using the Tools panel.

Here's how the Selection tool works:

- **To select any object on a document page, click it.** If you can't seem to click it, it might be an object placed by a *master page* (a preformatted page used to format pages automatically) or it might be behind another object.

- To select an object placed by a master page, press Shift+⌘ or Ctrl+Shift while you click.

- **To select an object that is completely behind another object,** ⌘+click it or Ctrl+click it.

- **To select multiple objects, click and drag around the objects or Shift+click them individually.** Because you need to press the Shift key anyway while selecting objects placed by master pages, you can always multiple-select those objects.

- **To move selected objects, click somewhere within the objects and drag the mouse.**

- **To resize a selected object, click and drag any handle.** Press Shift+⌘ or Ctrl+Shift while you drag to maintain the proportions of the object.

- **To resize both a selected frame and its graphic, press ⌘ or Ctrl while you drag.** Press Shift+⌘ or Ctrl+Shift to keep things proportional.

> **TIP** To resize multiple objects simultaneously via the mouse, you must first group them (choose Object ⇨ Group or press ⌘+G or Ctrl+G). Otherwise, only the object whose handle is being dragged will resize. Ungroup by choosing Object ⇨ Ungroup or pressing Shift+⌘+G or Ctrl+Shift+G. You can resize multiple selected — but ungrouped — objects by using the Control panel or Transform panel.

Direct Selection tool

The Direct Selection tool (shortcut A) lets you select individual handles on objects to reshape them, and it lets you move graphics independently of their frames.

Here's how the Direct Selection tool works:

- **To select an object to reshape it, click it to display anchor points on the edges.** (The anchor points are hollow handles that you can select individually, as shown in Figure 2.7.) You can drag the anchor points to reshape the object.

- **To select objects placed by a master page, Shift+⌘+click or Ctrl+Shift+click, as with the Selection tool.** The Direct Selection tool lets you easily select objects behind other objects and select items within groups.

- **To select multiple objects, click and drag around the objects or Shift+click them.** Because you need to press the Shift key anyway while selecting objects placed by master pages, you can always multiple-select those objects.

- **To move a graphic within its frame, click inside the frame and drag the graphic.**

- **To move a frame leaving the graphic in place, click an edge of the frame and drag it.**

NOTE   In addition to using the Selection tool for *threading* (linking) text frames (see Chapter 14), you can use the Direct Selection tool. This is one of the few cases when you have more than one tool to handle a task.

FIGURE 2.7

Clicking and dragging a hollow anchor point with the Direct Selection tool lets you reshape items.

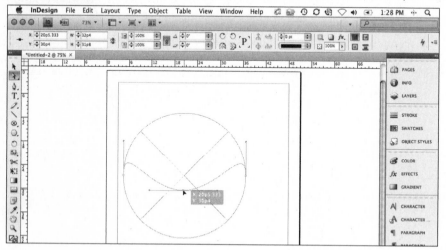

Position tool

The Position tool (no shortcut) is a renamed version of PageMaker's Crop tool. You access it from the pop-out menu in the Direct Selection tool. The Position tool combines some aspects of the Selection tool with some aspects of the Direct Selection tool:

- As with the Selection tool, you can resize an object's frame by dragging its handles.

- As with the Direct Selection tool, you can click a graphic and reposition it (crop it) within the frame by dragging.

Pen tool

The Pen tool (shortcut P) lets you create paths consisting of straight and curved segments. Modeled after the Pen tools in Illustrator and Photoshop, this is the tool for creating simple illustrations within InDesign. (See Chapter 27.)

If a path you create with the Pen tool is left open, the object is essentially a line that you can color or adjust stroke settings for. If the path is closed, the object is basically an empty frame. You can import text or graphics into the paths using the Place command (choose File ⇨ Place or press ⌘+D or Ctrl+D) or you can type into the path using the Type tool. If you decide to place text or graphics in an open path, the path closes automatically and becomes a frame. (To place text on a path, first select the Type on a Path tool [shortcut Shift+T] and then click the path.)

Here's how the Pen tool works:

- **To create straight segments of a path, click to establish an anchor point, move the mouse to the next location, click again, and so on.** To move an anchor point after clicking, press the spacebar and drag the segment.

- **To create curved segments of a path, click and drag; then, release the mouse button to end the segment.**

- **To close a path and create a frame, click over the first anchor point created (the hollow one).**

- **To leave a path open and create a line, ⌘+click or Ctrl+click away from the path or select another tool.**

Anchor and direction point tools

The Pen tool includes a pop-out menu containing three additional tools for reshaping lines and frames: Add Anchor Point (shortcut =), Delete Anchor Point (shortcut – [hyphen]), and Convert Direction Point (shortcut Shift+C).

 **For more information about using the Pen and anchor point tools, see Chapter 27.**

Type tool

The Type tool (shortcut T) lets you type, edit, and format text. The Type tool also lets you create rectangular text frames as you need them. (See Chapters 9, 14, and 15.)

Here's how the tool works:

- To create a rectangular text frame, click and drag; hold the Shift key to create a perfect square.
- To begin typing or editing text, click in a text frame or in any empty frame.
- To highlight text so that you can format it, cut and paste it, drag-move it, and so on.
- To select a word, double-click anywhere in the word.
- To select a paragraph, triple-click anywhere in the paragraph.
- To select all the text in a *story* (a series of threaded text frames), choose Edit ➪ Select All or press ⌘+A or Ctrl+A.

You can place or drag and drop text files, and you can *thread* (link) text frames with either of the selection tools, but those tools won't let you touch the text.

Type on a Path tool

The Type tool has a pop-out menu to select the Type on a Path tool (shortcut Shift+T), which lets you select a path or frame and type text onto it so that it follows the path or frame's outline. (See Chapter 18.)

Pencil tool

The Pencil tool (shortcut N) lets you draw free-form shapes by having InDesign trace your mouse movements, creating a curve based on that automatically. (See Chapter 27.)

Smooth tool

The Pencil tool has a pop-out menu to select the Smooth tool, which lets you smooth lines, curves, and shapes. It has no shortcut. (See Chapter 27.)

Erase tool

The Pencil tool also has a pop-out menu to select the Erase tool, which lets you erase portions of an object. It has no shortcut. (See Chapter 27.)

Line tool

The Line tool (shortcut E) lets you draw freestanding lines (rules) on your page. To use this tool, simply click it and drag the mouse. You can use the rulers, the Control panel, or the Transform panel to size and position the line precisely. Pressing the Shift key while you click and drag constrains the line angle to 45-degree increments, which is useful for creating straight horizontal and vertical lines. (See Chapter 8.)

Frame tools

InDesign has three frame tools: Rectangle Frame (shortcut F), Ellipse Frame, and Polygon Frame. Their icons are distinguished by a large X inside. The latter two tools, which have no shortcuts, are available from the Rectangle Frame tool's pop-up menu. The frames created by these tools are meant to hold either graphics or text. To create frames with these tools, click and drag using the rulers or information in the Control panel or Transform panel to judge the size and placement. To create a perfect circle with the Ellipse Frame tool or a perfect square with the Rectangle Frame tool, press the Shift key while you click and drag. (See Chapter 8.)

You can fill and stroke the empty frames for use as design elements or you can import text and graphics into them using the Place command (choose File ➪ Place or press ⌘+D or Ctrl+D). You can also click in an empty frame with the Type tool to begin typing in it. (See Chapters 13 and 25.)

Shape tools

If you'd rather create actual graphics frames, use the Rectangle (shortcut M), Ellipse (shortcut L), or Polygon tools. (The Ellipse and Polygon tools are pop-out tools available from the Rectangle tool.) The tools are meant to create shapes that you use as artwork rather than as containers. But you can place text or graphics into one of these shapes the same way as you would a frame. (See Chapter 8.) Essentially, the shape tools are superfluous and you can ignore them.

Scissors tool

The Scissors tool (shortcut C) lets you cut paths into separate paths. When you cut an open path (a line or curve), you get two separate lines. When you cut a closed path in one place, you get an open path. When you cut a closed path (a frame) in two places, you get two closed paths containing the same contents. Note that you cannot cut paths containing text. (See Chapter 27.)

Rotate tool

The Rotate tool (shortcut R) lets you change the angle of selected items visually. To use the Rotate tool, first select an item with the Selection tool or the Direct Selection tool and then select the Rotate tool. Or ⌘+click or Ctrl+click an object with the Rotate tool. Click and drag in any direction. The object rotates from the location of the active reference point, as shown in Figure 2.8.

FIGURE 2.8

Objects rotate based on the active reference point: At left, the active reference point is the centerpoint; at right it is the upper-left corner.

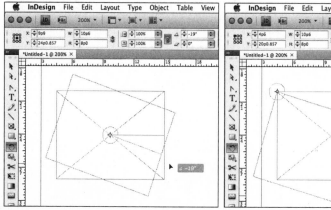
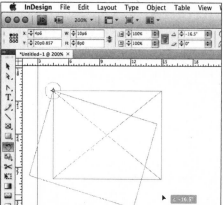

The active reference point is indicated through the nine boxes in the upper left of the Control panel or Transform panel — the black square is the active reference point (also called *control point*) from which the rotation will pivot and from which all coordinates originate. Just click whatever square you want to be the active reference point. You can also click and drag the active reference point to a new location for a custom rotation.

 **To rotate an object in 45-degree increments, press the Shift key while you click and drag.**

Scale tool

The Scale tool (shortcut S) lets you grab any object and resize it horizontally, vertically, or proportionally. When you scale text or graphics frames, the text or image within them is resized as well. As with the Rotate tool, the Scale tool doesn't let you select items to scale. You either need to select an object first with a selection tool or ⌘+click or Ctrl+click it with the Scale tool. (See Chapter 10.)

Shear tool

Available through the Scale tool's pop-out menu, the Shear tool (shortcut O) works much the same as the Scale tool. Rather than resize the object and contents, the Shear tool slants selected objects in the direction you drag. But it also rotates the object, creating a more three-dimensional perspective effect. (See Chapter 10.)

Gradient Swatch tool

The Gradient Swatch tool (shortcut G) lets you change the direction of existing gradient fills or strokes applied to objects. To apply gradients to objects, you use the Gradient panel. (See Chapter 7.)

Gradient Feather tool

The Gradient Feather tool (shortcut Shift+G) acts just like the Gradient Swatch tool except that it fades the gradient to transparent instead of to a solid color, providing a quick way to apply a feathering effect. (See Chapter 11.)

Free Transform tool

The Free Transform tool (shortcut E) is handy because it lets you move, rotate, and reshape objects all with one tool. If you click and hold the mouse within the object, you can drag it. If you click any of the handles on the object frame, you can resize it. If you click and hold on any edge (except where there is a handle) or anywhere outside the object, you can rotate the object. (See Chapter 10.)

Note tool

The Note tool lets you insert a nonprinting note (such as a reminder to yourself or another designer) in text. After selecting the tool, click in any text to insert the note. The Notes panel will display, in which you can type the note and navigate to other notes. (See Chapter 15.)

Eyedropper tool

The Eyedropper tool (shortcut I) samples the color settings for the object at the location you click with it. This is handy way to find out the color makeup of imported graphics so that you can then create a color swatch that matches it exactly or apply that sampled color to other objects. If the Eyedropper tool is selected, pressing Alt or Option switches you to the Marker tool, which lets you apply the color you just sampled to any object. (See Chapter 7.)

Measure tool

Available through the Eyedropper tool's pop-out menu, the Measure tool (shortcut K) opens the Info panel and lets you draw a line whose dimensions appear in that panel so that you can measure an arbitrary distance. You can see objects' dimensions in the Control, Transform, and Info panels, but the value of the Measure tool is that it determines the distance between objects rather than the dimensions of objects. It can also come in handy when you're measuring the distance across multiple objects. (See Chapter 9.)

Hand tool

The Hand tool (shortcut H) lets you scoot pages around to view a different portion of a page or another page entirely. The Hand tool is an entirely visual method of scrolling, allowing you to see the page contents at all times. To use the Hand tool, click and drag in any direction. You can access the Hand tool temporarily without actually switching tools by pressing Option+spacebar or Alt+spacebar. (See Chapter 3.)

Zoom tool

The Zoom tool (shortcut Z) lets you increase and decrease the document view scale. You can highlight a specific area on a page to change its view or you can click on-screen to change the view scale within InDesign's preset increments (shown in the Zoom field and pop-up menu in the application bar). (See Chapter 3.)

Color buttons

The bottom portion of the Tools panel contains buttons for applying colors to the edges of objects (*strokes*) and the insides of objects (*fills*). You use these buttons with the Stroke, Color, Gradient, and Swatches panels to apply and experiment with the colors applied to objects. (Refer to Chapter 7.) Figure 2.6 identifies these buttons.

View buttons

At the very bottom of the Tools panel are the two view-oriented iconic buttons: Normal View Mode and Preview Mode. The first shows the pasteboard, margins, and guidelines, and the second hides those to give an unadorned preview of the final document.

Two preview options are available via a pop-up menu in the Preview Mode iconic button: Bleed Mode and Slug Mode. Bleed Mode shows any objects that bleed beyond the page boundaries, and Slug Mode shows the space reserved for information such as crop marks and color separation names used in final output, as covered in Chapters 4 and 30. You set these up when you create new documents or by choosing File ➪ Document Setup or pressing Option+⌘+P or Ctrl+Alt+P.

NOTE **These four view modes are also accessible by choosing View ➪ Screen Mode and then the desired option from the submenu, as well as from the Screen Mode iconic pop-up menu in the new application bar (covered earlier in this chapter).**

Using Tool Tips and keyboard shortcuts

To start getting familiar with the tools, first make sure that the Tool Tips pop-up menu is set to Normal or Fast in the Interface pane of the Preferences dialog box (choose InDesign ➪ Preferences ➪ Interface or press ⌘+K on the Mac, or choose Edit ➪ Preferences ➪ Interface or press Ctrl+K in Windows). Point at each tool to learn its official name, as shown earlier in Figure 2.6; let the pointer rest on the tool for a few seconds (if Tool Tips is set to Normal) and a Tool Tip appears, telling you the name and shortcut key of that tool. Knowing the actual name is the key to learning about any tool — after all, neither the InDesign documentation's index nor this book's index lists tools by the way they look (for example, *little black pointer* or *empty square*); instead, if you want to look up a tool, you need to know the tool's name (Selection tool or Rectangle tool, for example).

While you're learning the tool names, you may notice a single letter in parentheses next to each tool name. This is the shortcut key to selecting that tool. For example, the (T) next to the Type tool indicates that pressing T selects the Type tool. The Tools panel's shortcuts don't use modifier keys such as ⌘ and Ctrl. If you're editing text or otherwise have the Type tool selected — or if you're in a text-entry field in a panel or dialog box — typing these shortcuts simply inserts the text where your cursor is.

CAUTION **If you're not careful, you can type nonsense text in your articles because of the way the Tools panel's shortcuts work (without having to press ⌘ or Ctrl).**

 **To avoid typing these extra letters into your text, always use ⌘+click or Ctrl+click to click anywhere on the page or pasteboard. Doing so "releases" the live text that you were working on before typing a single-letter keyboard shortcut.**

After you learn all the keyboard commands, you can create and refine a layout without ever reaching for the Tools panel. In no time, you'll be switching from the Scale tool to the Rotate tool with a quick punch of the R key, and then you'll be pressing T to add a text frame. Now, obviously, you can't use the keyboard commands for selecting tools while typing or editing text, but they are worth remembering for switching tools while designing a layout. In many production environments, copy editors handle text changes, whereas layout artists handle design issues. In such environments, the layout artists learn these shortcuts and the copy editors avoid them.

Opening and closing the Tools panel

Opening and closing the Tools panel is easy. One method of opening (or closing) the Tools panel is to choose Window ➪ Tools. The other method of opening (or closing) the Tools panel is more obscure: Pressing the Tab key (with any tool but the Type tool selected) closes all open panels, including the Tools panel. To reopen those panels, press Tab again. To reopen just the Tools panel, choose Window ➪ Tools. You can also close a floating Tools panel by clicking its Close box.

By default, the Tools panel is docked under the Control panel, but you can drag it out (drag the dark area at the very top) and make it a free-floating panel. Drag it back to the left of the monitor screen, right under the Control panel, to re-dock it.

You can change the Tools panel's appearance, as Figure 2.9 shows, by clicking the double-arrow iconic button in the dock that contains the Tools panel. If the Tools panel is docked, you can make the panel toggle between single-column and double-column. If the Tools panel is undocked, you get a third state: single-column horizontal. (Note how the double-arrow icons change direction as you toggle through the various states.) You can also set the display to any of these three settings — whether the panel is docked or not — in the Interface pane of the Preferences dialog box, using the Floating Tools Panel pop-up menu.

FIGURE 2.9

The five forms of the Tools panel: docked and single-column, docked and double-column, undocked and single-column, undocked and double-column, and undocked and horizontal.

Close box

Tools panel
display toggle

Docked panels

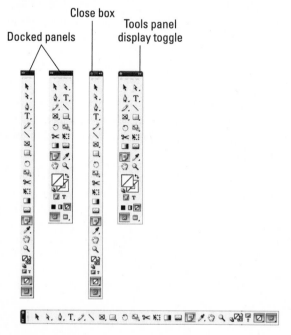

Working with Panels and Docks

Initially, software developers used floating palettes to provide convenient access to commonly used options such as swatches, fonts, and styles. Palettes provide a more interactive method of working with features because the screen is not obscured by a large dialog box and you can access the controls quickly. Eventually, palettes started to move away from serving as a convenient alternative to commands and became the primary method — often the *only* method — for performing many tasks. InDesign calls these floating palettes *panels*. Panels can have multiple sets of functions, with each set in its own tabbed pane. Figure 2.10 shows the interface elements in panels.

FIGURE 2.10

Anatomy of a panel. Panels contain a flyout menu that provides additional options. Floating panel groups also have a Close box to remove them from the display. Some panels have a hide/show options button to display and hide additional fields.

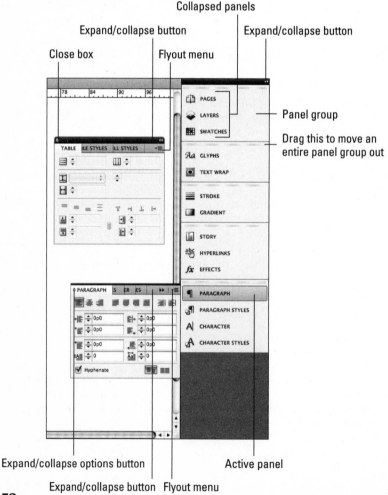

NEW FEATURE InDesign CS4 has changed the appearance of its panels slightly. The biggest functional appearance-related change is that the flyout menus are now clearly separated from the collapse/expand buttons so that you don't accidentally collapse a panel when trying to open the flyout menu, as could happen in InDesign CS3.

There are so many panels in InDesign CS4 — even more than in previous versions — that you might want to consider hooking up a second monitor for displaying them. And break out the computer glasses and your decoder ring, because the panels are small and laden with mysterious icons.

As with the tools, if you make sure Tool Tips is selected in the Interface pane of the Preferences dialog box (choose InDesign ⇨ Preferences ⇨ Interface or press ⌘+K on the Mac, or choose Edit ⇨ Preferences ⇨ Interface or press Ctrl+K in Windows), you can get some pretty good hints as to what the panel icons and fields do.

You can also manage what panels display, and switch among these view settings, using the workspaces feature described in Chapter 3.

Arranging panels

InDesign places a set of panels in a dock at the right edge of your screen. The goal of this dock is to keep panels in a self-contained area, minimizing interface clutter. Because the Tools panel resides in its own dock, I call the one at the right side of the screen the *main dock*.

NOTE The only panel that cannot be docked is the Quick Apply panel.

You access a panel by clicking its tab (if it is on-screen) and/or by choosing the desired panel from the Window menu. If you choose a panel from the Window menu that is not already in the dock, that selected panel displays on-screen as a free-floating panel.

NEW FEATURE InDesign CS4 displays just a limited set of panels in the main dock when you install it — those in the Essentials workspace. I suggest that you switch to the Advanced workspace to get a useful set of panels in the dock as your default; to do so, choose Advanced from the Workspaces menu at the right side of the application bar, or choose Window ⇨ Workspace ⇨ [Advanced]. (Chapter 3 explains how to work with, and create your own, workspaces.)

You can move panels in and out of panel groups, dragging them by their tabs. You can drag panels within the main dock or outside the dock (dragging them outside the dock makes them free-floating). (If the dock is collapsed, just drag the panels by their names to pull them out or move them.) You can also drag free-floating panels into the dock.

TIP To drag an entire panel group — all the panels whose tabs are in the same row in the dock — hold Option or Alt when you drag the tab of one of its panels. If a panel group is collapsed into the dock, just drag the dashed line that appears over its name to drag the entire panel group out of the dock.

Some panels have additional fields that you can display by clicking the up/down arrow iconic button in its tab. Clicking the icon again returns the panel to the normal display.

NEW FEATURE In InDesign CS4, you can no longer close an individual panel, whether it's inside the main dock or free floating; there is no longer a Close box on its tab. Instead, you must drag it out into its own free-floating panel and then close that panel using its Close box. (To bring back a closed panel, select it from the Window menu.) The exception: The free-floating Control panel has no Close box, so it must be closed from the Window menu. Note that you *can* close an entire panel group by clicking its Close box.

Changing the dock display

As with the Tools panel, you can now drag the main dock from the right side of the screen and make it float, as well as drag it back and dock it there. (You can also drag the Control panel to make it free floating.)

In addition to being able to move the main dock, you can adjust how it displays. You can widen or narrow the dock by its left edge when docked, and any edge when undocked.

NEW FEATURE The ability make the main dock free floating is new to InDesign CS4. The method to resize it is also new, although you could resize it in InDesign CS3 using a different approach.

You can also add panels to it by dragging them at the boundary of any existing panel or panel group on the dock, as well as remove panels and panel groups from the dock, as explained in the previous section.

The Interface pane of the Preferences dialog box gives you additional control over the dock's display: If you select Auto-Collapse Icon Panels, an open panel will close as soon as you click somewhere else in the program. This way is handier than manually collapsing the panel when done.

NEW FEATURE You can now collapse floating panel groups in InDesign CS4. They will display as a set of names, just like collapsed panels in the main dock. Previously, you could reduce the panel group's size to just its tabs, an option no longer available.

Sometimes, panels get in the way of working on your layout. To quickly hide all panels, press Tab. (Make sure no text is selected if the Type tool is active; otherwise, you'll enter a tab in your text. And make sure no dialog box or panel field is enabled; otherwise, you'll move to another field.) To get them all back, press Tab again.

NEW FEATURE If you enable the Auto-Show Hidden Panels option in the Interface pane of the Preference dialog box, you can quickly open certain panels. (To set this preference, choose InDesign ⇨ Preferences ⇨ Interface or press ⌘+K on the Mac, or choose Edit ⇨ Preferences ⇨ Interface or press Ctrl+K in Windows.) When you hide all panels by pressing Tab, you'll see a dark gray border on the left and right sides of InDesign's document window. Hover your mouse over the left border to display the Tools panel. Hover over the right border to display the main dock and any floating panels. (Note you cannot show the Control panel this way; you must press Tab again.)

Using panels

To use a panel, first you need to activate it. You can do this by clicking its tab (if the panel containing it is open) or by choosing its menu command in the Window menu (if the panel is not open or if another pane in that panel is active). You'll need to be on the lookout here — if a menu command brings a panel forward in the main dock or in a free-floating panel group, you might not even notice.

When a panel is active, you use its controls in the following ways:

- Click a pop-up menu to display and select an option, or click an icon to select an option; the changes take effect immediately.

- Highlight a value in a field to enter a new value. To implement the value, press Shift+ Return or Shift+Enter. Or you can press Tab to move to the next field or Shift+Tab to the previous field. Or just click in a different field or elsewhere in the document. To get out of a field you've modified, leaving the object unscathed, press Esc.

- Some fields include up and down arrows that you can click to increase or decrease the value in the field.

- Fields accept values in all different measurement systems. (I cover field values in detail in Chapter 3.)

- In addition to typing values in fields, you can enter calculations. You can add to, subtract from, multiply, and divide values in fields using the following operators: +, −, * (multiply), and / (divide). For example, to reduce the width of a frame by half, you might type **/2** next to the current value in the Width field (such as 4.5"/2). Or, to increase the length of a line by 6 points, you can type **+6** next to the current value in the Length field (such at 23pt+6).

TIP You can also use percentages in fields, such as 50%, which adjusts the current value by that percentage.

- Most panels provide a pop-up menu, called a *flyout menu*, that you can display by clicking the iconic button in the upper-right corner. The flyout menu provides commands related to the current panel's contents, as shown earlier in Figure 2.10.

Checking out the panels

As does each tool in InDesign, each panel has a distinct function. I cover the use of each panel in detail in the appropriate chapters throughout this book. (For example, the Layers panel is covered in Chapter 5.) But with the help of Tool Tips and a quick introduction to their primary purpose, you can start using many of the panels to begin performing basic functions.

TIP All but one of the text-oriented panels are available from the Type menu: Character, Character Styles, Glyphs, Index, Paragraph, Paragraph Styles, Tabs, and Table. (The Table panel and its related Table Styles and Cell Styles panels are not available here, but that's because they have their own Table menu for accessing their controls.) Having this menu provides faster access than choosing Window ➪ Type & Tables ➪ *submenu* does.

Customizing the Control Panel

InDesign lets you customize the Control panel, which you do using the Customize flyout menu option. This is especially useful if you are working with a monitor whose screen resolution is set at less than 1152 × 872 pixels, because InDesign automatically removes options from the Control panel at smaller screen sizes. By customizing the Control panel, you can keep the options you want and remove the ones you don't, rather than accept what InDesign thinks you should have.

In the Customize Control Panel dialog box that appears when you select Customize from the flyout menu, you can select and deselect sets of iconic buttons to control which ones display. These objects are grouped into five categories — Object, Character, Paragraph, Tables, and Other. You can control individual buttons within these categories by clicking the right-facing arrow icon to the left of each group's name; you'll get a list of options within that group that you can individually control.

The Control panel also adds several functions to its options if you have a wide-screen monitor. For example, with a monitor set at a width of 1280 pixels, you see both the character and paragraph options simultaneously, rather than have to toggle between them. When you've selected an object with the Selection tool at that resolution, you see extra controls such as frame alignment and frame fitting.

Here is a quick summary of the InDesign panels. Note that in the figures of the various panels, the full panel is shown for any that have the option of showing just some options; these panels have an up-down arrow iconic button to the left of the panel name.

NEW FEATURE   **Panels new to InDesign CS4 are the Conditional Text, Connections, Kuler, Page Transitions, and Preflight panels. Gone is the Navigator panel, replaced with the new quick zoom option described in Chapter 3. Also gone is the Command Bar panel. The Buttons panel replaces the previous versions' States panel.**

There is also a new menu item, Window ➪ Type & Tables ➪ Cross-References, which actually opens the Hyperlinks panel. That panel contains a new Cross-References section. InDesign does not have a separate Cross-References panel, as you might expect.

- **Tools panel (choose Window ➪ Tools):** As I covered earlier in this chapter, the Tools panel is the mechanism by which you select the appropriate tool to accomplish various layout tasks.

- **Control panel (choose Window ➪ Control or press Option+⌘+6 or Ctrl+Alt+6):** The Control panel is one of the most useful features in InDesign. It combines many attributes for the currently selected object so that you can minimize the use of other panels and menu items. The panel changes based on what you select, as shown in Figure 2.11.

  The Control panel adjusts its display based on what the current object is, so you get just the relevant options. For example, when you select a text frame, the Control panel provides the most functions of the Transform, Character Style, Character, Paragraph, Paragraph Styles, and Stroke panels. And the wider your screen, the more options display in it.

FIGURE 2.11

From top to bottom: The Control panel for frames, text paths, and Bézier shapes selected with the Selection tool; the Control panel for frames with frames and Bézier shapes with graphics in them selected with the Direct Selection tool; and the two Control panel versions for text frames and text paths with text selected with the Type tool. More options display if your monitor resolution is 1152 pixels or wider.

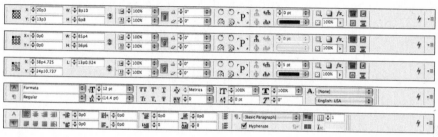

- **Links panel (choose Window ⇨ Links or press Shift+⌘+D or Ctrl+Shift+D):** The Links panel shows the original location of imported graphics and text files (see Figure 2.12).

- **Info panel (choose Window ⇨ Info or press F8):** The Info panel (shown in Figure 2.12) shows some of the characteristics — such as size, position, and cropping — of selected objects. It also displays the results of using the Measure tool.

FIGURE 2.12

The Links panel (left), the Info panel (upper right), the Attributes panel (middle right), and the Story panel (lower right)

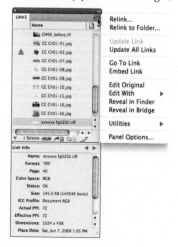
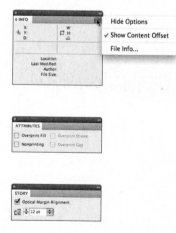

■ **Attributes panel (choose Window ⇨ Attributes):** The Attributes panel (shown in Figure 2.12) lets you specify that the stroke or fill in selected objects overprints the background. (Note that the Attributes panel has no flyout menu.)

■ **Story panel (choose Type ⇨ Story or Window ⇨ Type & Tables ⇨ Story):** Small but important, the Story panel (shown in Figure 2.12) lets you specify hanging punctuation for all the frames in a story by checking Optical Margin Alignment. You can also change the type size at which alignment begins if the need arises. (Note that the Story panel has no flyout menu.)

■ **Character panel (choose Type ⇨ Character or Window ⇨ Type & Tables ⇨ Character or press ⌘+T or Ctrl+T):** Use the Character panel (shown in Figure 2.13) to change common attributes of highlighted text such as the font, size, leading, kerning, tracking, and scaling).

■ **Paragraph panel (choose Type ⇨ Paragraph or Window ⇨ Type & Tables ⇨ Paragraph or press Option+⌘+T or Ctrl+Option+T):** Use the Paragraph panel (shown in Figure 2.13) to change common attributes of selected paragraphs such as alignment, indents, space before and after, and hyphenation.

FIGURE 2.13

The Character panel (left) and the Paragraph panel (right)

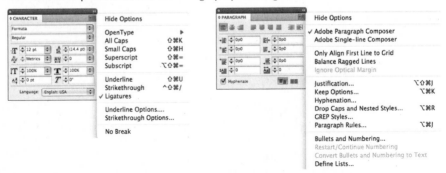

■ **Character Styles panel (choose Type ⇨ Character Styles or Window ⇨ Type & Tables ⇨ Character Styles or press Shift+⌘+F11 or Ctrl+Shift+F11):** Use the Character Styles panel (shown in Figure 2.14) to create and apply styles consisting of character-level formats.

■ **Paragraph Styles panel (choose Type ⇨ Paragraph Styles or Window ⇨ Type & Tables ⇨ Paragraph Styles or press ⌘+F11 or Ctrl+F11):** Use the Paragraph Styles panel (shown in Figure 2.14) to create and apply styles consisting of paragraph-level formats.

FIGURE 2.14

The Character Styles panel (left) and Paragraph Styles panel (right)

- **Table panel (choose Window ⇨ Type & Tables ⇨ Table or press Shift+F9):** The Table panel (shown in Figure 2.15) lets you adjust table settings.
- **Tabs panel (choose Type ⇨ Tabs or press Shift+⌘+T or Ctrl+Shift+T):** The Tabs panel (shown in Figure 2.15) lets you create tab stops for selected paragraphs; you can also specify alignment, position, and leader characters for the tabs. Note that Adobe calls this panel a dialog box, but it does not work like any other dialog box: It has no OK or Cancel buttons, and — unlike when a regular dialog box is open — you can select items in your layout while it is open. It really is a panel, except that it uses a nonstandard Close box and has no Minimize box. So I'm still calling it a panel.

FIGURE 2.15

The Table panel (left) and the Tabs panel (right)

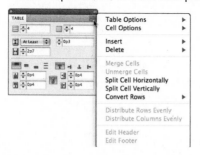
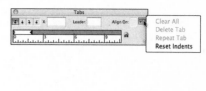

- **Table Styles panel (choose Window ⇨ Type & Tables ⇨ Table Styles):** The Table Styles panel (shown in Figure 2.16) lets you specify and apply styles for tables.

The Table Styles panel (left) and Cell Styles panel (right)

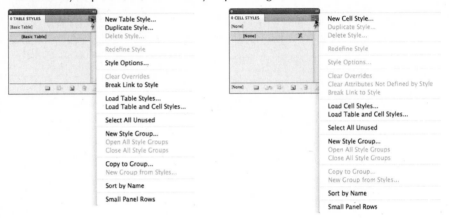

- **Cell Styles panel (choose Window ⇨ Type & Tables ⇨ Cell Styles):** The Cell Styles panel (shown in Figure 2.16) lets you specify and apply styles for table cells.

- **Glyphs panel (choose Type ⇨ Glyphs or Window ⇨ Type & Tables ⇨ Glyphs or press Option+Shift+F11 or Alt+Shift+F11):** The Glyphs panel lets you access special characters within a font. Figure 2.17 shows the Glyphs panel.

- **Conditional Text panel (choose Windows ⇨ Type & Tables ⇨ Conditional Text):** The new Conditional Text panel is where you apply or remove conditions applied to text, as Chapter 22 explains. Figure 2.17 shows the panel.

The Glyphs panel (left) and Conditional Text panel (right)

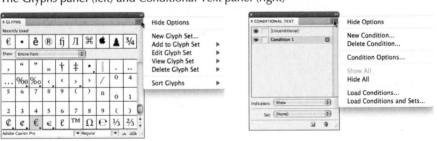

- **Index panel (choose Window ⇨ Type & Tables ⇨ Index or press Shift+F8):** The Index panel (shown in Figure 2.18) lets you add and manage index entries.

FIGURE 2.18

The Index panel (left) and Data Merge panel (right)

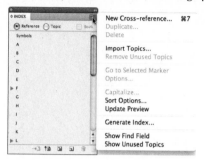

- **Data Merge panel (choose Window ⇨ Automation ⇨ Data Merge):** The Data Merge panel (shown in Figure 2.18) lets you import data for use in form letters, labels, and other "mail-merge" documents.

- **Text Wrap panel (choose Window ⇨ Text Wrap or press Option+⌘+W or Ctrl+ Alt+W):** The Text Wrap panel (shown in Figure 2.19) provides iconic buttons for controlling how text runs around selected objects.

- **Object Styles panel (choose Window ⇨ Object Styles or press ⌘+F7 or Ctrl+F7):** Use the Object Styles panel (shown in Figure 2.19) to create and apply styles for frames, lines, and other objects.

FIGURE 2.19

The Text Wrap panel (left) and Object Styles panel (right)

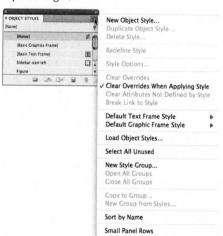

- **Transform panel (choose Window ⇨ Object & Layout ⇨ Transform):** The Transform panel (shown in Figure 2.20) lets you specify size, placement, scale, rotation, and shear of selected objects. It duplicates much of the Control panel, so it's seldom used.

FIGURE 2.20

The Transform panel (left) and Align panel (right)

- **Align panel (choose Window ⇨ Object & Layout ⇨ Align or press Shift+F7):** The Align panel (shown in Figure 2.20) provides buttons that let you evenly distribute or realign multiple selected objects with one click.
- **Pages panel (choose Window ⇨ Pages or press ⌘+F12 or Ctrl+F12):** Use the Pages panel (shown in Figure 2.21) to create master pages and to add, rearrange, and delete document pages. You can also create sections of page numbers using the Pages panel's flyout menu.

FIGURE 2.21

The Pages panel (left) and the Layers panel (right)

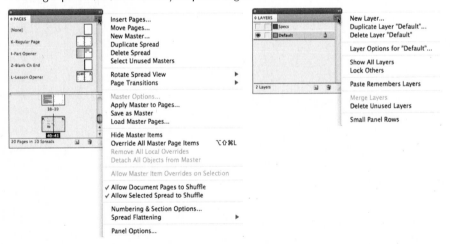

- **Layers panel (choose Window ⇨ Layers or press F7):** The Layers panel (shown in Figure 2.21) provides access to vertical slices of a document that you can use to control the stacking order of objects, to isolate specific portions of a design, or to store revisions of the same document.

- **Swatches panel (choose Window ⇨ Swatches or press F5):** The Swatches panel (shown in Figure 2.22) lets you create named colors such as those using Pantone, Focoltone, and Toyo inks, and apply the colors to text, strokes, and fills.

FIGURE 2.22

The Swatches panel (left), the Color panel (upper right), and the Gradient panel (lower right)

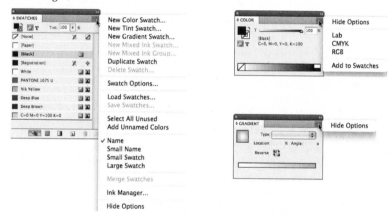

- **Color panel (choose Window ⇨ Color or press F6):** The Color panel (shown in Figure 2.22) lets you create Lab, CMYK, and RGB colors, and apply the colors to text, strokes, and fills. (Lab, CMYK, and RGB are all composite color models, in which all colors are made by mixing a small number of primary colors.) Chapter 7 describes these models in detail.

- **Gradient panel (choose Window ⇨ Gradient):** Use the Gradient panel (shown in Figure 2.22) to create a stroke or fill consisting of a graduated blend between two colors.

- **Kuler panel (choose Windows ⇨ Extensions ⇨ Kuler):** Use the new Kuler panel (with its three panes shown in Figure 2.23) to load color palettes created by others, modify them, and create your own, as well as transfer them to the Swatches panel and share them with other Kuler.com users.

FIGURE 2.23

The Kuler panel's three panes

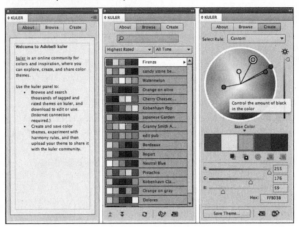

- **Stroke panel (choose Window ⇨ Stroke or press ⌘+F10 or Ctrl+F10):** Use the Stroke panel (shown in Figure 2.24) to outline the edges of frames and lines; you have control over the thickness and the pattern of the outlines.

- **Pathfinder panel (choose Window ⇨ Object & Layout ⇨ Pathfinder):** The Pathfinder panel (shown in Figure 2.24) lets you manipulate paths, enabling you to combine, separate, and otherwise work with open and closed paths. It also now lets you convert shapes. (Note that the Pathfinder panel has no flyout menu.)

FIGURE 2.24

The Stroke panel (left) and the Pathfinder panel (right)

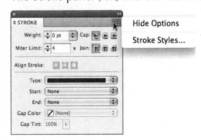 

- **Effects panel (choose Window ⇨ Effects or press Shift+⌘+F10 or Ctrl+Shift+F10):** The Effects panel (shown in Figure 2.25) lets you adjust the solidity of images to create transparency and lighting effects.

- **Preflight panel (choose Window ⇨ Output ⇨ Preflight or press Option+Shift+⌘+F or Ctrl+Alt+Shift+F):** The new Preflight panel (shown in Figure 2.25) lets you determine what settings InDesign should check for output violations as you work on your file, as well as see what current object have such violations.

FIGURE 2.25

The Effects panel (left) and the Preflight panel (right)

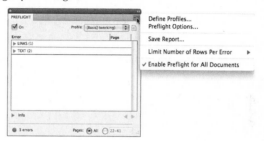

- **Flattener Preview panel (choose Window ⇨ Output ⇨ Flattener):** The Flattener Preview panel (shown in Figure 2.26) lets you see what page items (typically those with transparency) are *flattened* (made solid) during printing or exporting to Encapsulated PostScript (EPS), Scalable Vector Graphics (SVG, a vector format for the Web), or Portable Document Format (PDF) formats. Flattening occurs for printing devices and graphics export formats that don't support transparency.

FIGURE 2.26

The Separations Preview panel (upper left), the Trap Presets panel (right), and the Flattener Preview panel (lower left)

The Quick Apply Panel

A fast way to apply various attributes to layout elements is by using the Quick Apply panel. Quick Apply is a consolidated list of styles, scripts, text variables, and other attributes that you access by choosing Edit ⇨ Quick Apply, by clicking the Quick Apply button (the lightning-bolt icon) in many panels, or by pressing ⌘+Return or Ctrl+Enter. The Quick Apply panel presents all available options in an alphabetical list. You can scroll down to the one you want or type the first few letters of the attribute in the text field at the top to jump to attributes beginning with those letters, and then navigate to the one you want and press Return or Enter, which brings you back to where you were working and closes the Quick Apply panel.

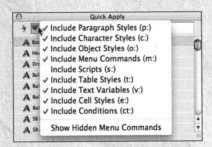

This feature can be handy if you're working on layouts from your keyboard — perhaps you're a layout artist working on a notebook while commuting. For example, you can switch to the Quick Apply panel, apply a style, and return to your object or text, all without touching the mouse.

But there are so many options in the Quick Apply panel's default state that you can quickly get overwhelmed. To remove attributes you likely will never use in this panel — such as scripts and menu customizations — choose the unnamed pop-up menu at the top of the panel, and deselect unwanted attributes (the check marks indicate attributes that will display).

- **Separations Preview panel (choose Window ⇨ Output ⇨ Separations or press Shift+F6):** The Separations Preview panel (shown in Figure 2.26) lets you see page items with various color plates enabled, as well as preview the effects of different ink densities.

- **Trap Presets panel (choose Window ⇨ Output ⇨ Trap Presets):** The Trap Presets panel (shown in Figure 2.26) lets you set and apply different trapping settings to objects, which controls how abutting and overlapping objects print to avoid gaps caused by paper-feed variations during printing.

- **Assignments panel (choose Window ⇨ Assignments):** The Assignments panel (shown in Figure 2.27) lets you make individual stories in your layout available to a user of the InCopy add-on program. For example, with InCopy, a copy editor can check out a story from your layout to proofread it while you're still working on the layout.

- **Notes panel (choose Window ⇨ Notes):** The Notes panel (shown in Figure 2.27) lets you insert and manage nonprinting notes used as reminders for yourself or other people working on the layout.

FIGURE 2.27

The Assignments panel (left) and the Notes panel (right)

- **Hyperlinks panel (choose Window ⇨ Interactive ⇨ Hyperlinks or Window ⇨ Type & Tables ⇨ Cross-References):** The Hyperlinks panel (shown in Figure 2.28) lets you set up hyperlinks from and to document objects and pages, as well as to World Wide Web locations. It also now lets you create cross-references for use in automatic text.

- **Bookmarks panel (choose Window ⇨ Interactive ⇨ Bookmarks):** The Bookmarks panel (shown in Figure 2.28) creates the bookmarks used in PDF files to create clickable indexes and tables of contents.

FIGURE 2.28

The Hyperlinks panel (left) and the Bookmarks panel (right)

■ **Buttons panel (choose Window ⇨ Interactive ⇨ Buttons):** The Buttons panel (formerly called the States panel and shown in Figure 2.29) sets button actions for PDF and Flash files.

■ **Page Transitions panel (choose Window ⇨ Interactive ⇨ Page Transitions):** The Page Transitions panel (shown in Figure 2.29) sets page-transition effects for PDF and Flash files.

FIGURE 2.29

The Buttons panel (left) and the Page Transitions panel (right)

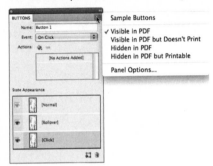 

■ **Scripts panel (choose Window ⇨ Automation ⇨ Scripts or press Option+⌘+F11 or Ctrl+Alt+F11):** The Scripts panel (shown in Figure 2.30) shows available AppleScripts, VBA scripts, and Java scripts in the `Scripts` folder in the `InDesign` folder.

■ **Script Label panel (choose Window ⇨ Automation ⇨ Script Labels):** The Script Label panel (shown in Figure 2.30) lets you change the label of an object for use by scripts. (Note that the Script Label panel has no flyout menu.)

FIGURE 2.30

The Scripts panel (left) and the Script Label panel (right)

■ **Tags panel (choose Window ⇨ Tags):** The Tags panel (shown in Figure 2.31) lets you add XML tags and map them to paragraph and character styles. XML tags determine the formatting for XML data sources used in XML documents.

■ **Connections panel (choose Window ⇨ Extensions ⇨ Connections):** The new Connections panel (shown in Figure 2.31) lets you set up access to Adobe Connections, a members-only set of online services such as discussion groups.

FIGURE 2.31

The Tags panel (left) and the Connections panel (right)

Reviewing Menu Commands

With so many panels, menu commands take on a more secondary function in InDesign. Many menu commands do nothing but display a panel or bring it forward — this is especially true in the Type and Table menus. But to get comfortable in InDesign, you need to know the basic function of each menu.

InDesign menu

Available only on Mac OS X, the InDesign menu, shown in Figure 2.32, contains preference and plug-in settings, as well as the command to exit the program and to hide it. The Services menu option contains Mac OS X functions, not any InDesign-specific options. Note that none of these menu items' functions are available in panels.

PLATFORM DIFFERENCES The InDesign menu is available only on the Mac. In Windows, the About InDesign and Configure Plug-ins menu options reside in the Help menu, the Preferences menu option resides in the Edit menu, and the Quit InDesign menu option resides in the File menu. The other InDesign menu options are specific to Mac OS X.

File menu

The File menu (shown in Figure 2.32) lets you perform actions on entire documents, libraries, and books, including creating, opening, saving, closing, exporting, and printing. The Place command lets you import graphics and text files, and the Export command lets you save documents in different formats such as EPS, RTF, XML, and PDF. The Windows version also includes the Quit menu option. Note that none of these menu items' functions are available in panels.

FIGURE 2.32

From left to right: the InDesign menu (in Mac OS X only), File menu, Edit menu, and Layout menu

NEW FEATURE The File menu now includes the **Share My Screen** option, which lets Adobe Connection subscribers share their live screens with other users, such as to help each other out or look at layouts together. There's no cost for up to three simultaneous users; Adobe sells a service for larger groups.

The File menu's Cross-Media Export option is now gone, and its Dreamweaver and Digital Editions submenus are now on the File menu itself.

Edit menu

InDesign's Edit menu (shown in Figure 2.32) provides access to its invaluable multiple undo and redo features, as well as the standard Cut, Copy, Paste, and Clear commands. You'll find Duplicate, and Step and Repeat here, even though you might be searching the Object menu for them. The Edit menu also provides commands for searching and replacing text and formats, checking spelling, and editing spelling and hyphenation dictionaries, as well as for opening the Story Editor text-editing feature and setting up stories for the InCopy add-on program. It also provides access to color settings and keyboard shortcut preferences. The Windows version also contains the Preferences menu option (which is in the InDesign menu on the Mac). Note that these menu items' functions, except for Quick Apply, are not available in panels.

NEW FEATURE The Edit menu now includes an **Edit With** option, which lets you choose which program to open a file with, such as an image.

Layout menu

With the Layout menu (shown in Figure 2.32), you can change the position of the column and margin guides you established in the New Document dialog box, create guides at specific locations, and resize an entire document proportionally. You can also turn pages in a document and insert automatic page numbers using Layout menu commands. Finally, this menu contains the commands for setting up tables of contents. Note that these menu options' functions — except for the Pages, page-navigation, and Numbering & Section Options menus — are not available in panels.

Type menu

The Type menu (shown in Figure 2.33) provides all your controls for formatting text — character formats, paragraph formats, tabs, and styles. The Story command lets you specify hanging punctuation for all the frames in a story (the same function as in the Story panel). You can also convert text to a frame and insert special characters using a dialog box rather than keyboard shortcuts. Note that the Find Font, Change Case, Type on a Path, Document Footnote Options, Text Variables, Insert Character, Fill with Placeholder text, and Show Hidden Characters menu items' functions are not available though panels.

NEW FEATURE The Type menu adds a new menu option: Hyperlinks and Cross-References, providing menu access to some of the Hyperlinks panel's functions.

The Notes menu is gone from InDesign CS4 and is now a submenu of the Type menu.

FIGURE 2.33

From left to right: the Type menu, Object menu, Table menu, and View menu

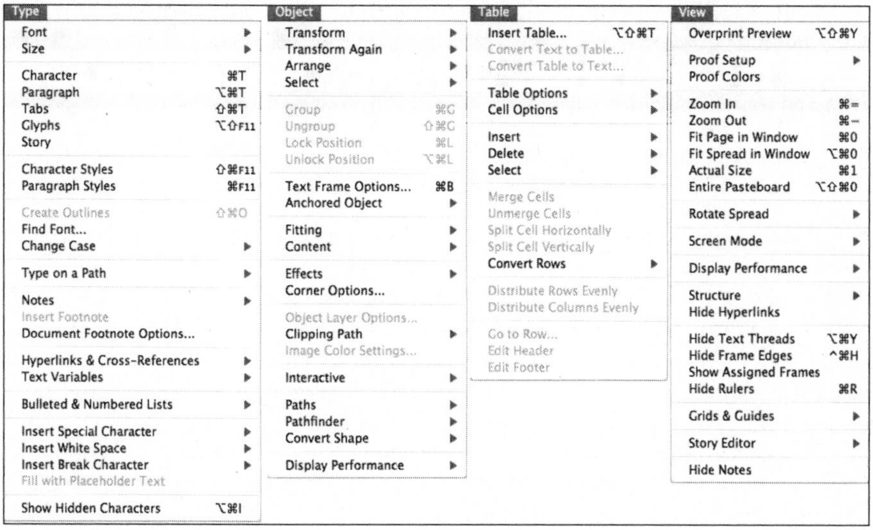

Object menu

Use the Object menu (shown in Figure 2.33) for layout functions such as controlling the stacking order of lines and frames, grouping objects together, locking objects to the page, and wrapping text around objects.

You can manipulate objects, such as changing the number of columns and text inset in the Text Frame Options dialog box or fine-tuning the corners of a frame using the Corner Options dialog box. For working with graphics, the Object menu lets you fit graphics to frames and frames to graphics, create clipping paths, merge and separate paths, convert shapes, apply colors to some types of images, and create drop shadows and apply other lighting effects. It also lets you insert movies and audio files for interactive PDF documents.

Note that the Text Frame Options, Anchored Object, Corner Options, Clipping Path, and Convert Shape menu items' functions are not available through panels.

Table menu

The Table menu (shown in Figure 2.33) contains the controls to create and edit tables. Using commands from this menu, you create tables, modify them, convert text into tables and vice versa, manage table cells, and control row and column spacing. Note that this menu's functions are available through panels.

View menu

With the View menu (shown in Figure 2.33), you can change the view scale of the document, choose whether objects placed by master pages appear, and specify which layout tools are visible: *Threads* (links between text frames), the edges of frames, rulers, guides, the baseline grid, and the document grid. You can also specify whether guides are locked and whether items snap to guides and the document grid. Note that none of these menu items' functions, except for Screen Mode and the zoom controls, are available in panels.

 If you're expecting to use the View menu to show and hide invisible characters such as spaces and tabs, look in the Type menu instead.

 The View menu adds the Rotate Spread option to make it easier to work on pages that have rotated elements.

Window menu

For the most part, the Window menu (shown in Figure 2.34) opens panels or brings panels forward within their panel group. Other commands let you manage document windows, opening additional windows for the same document and redistributing document windows on-screen. Currently open documents are listed at the bottom of the menu. The window display and workspace functions are not available via panels.

FIGURE 2.34

The Window menu (left) and the Help menu (right)

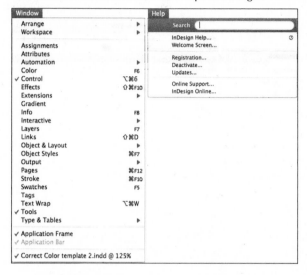

 NEW FEATURE The Window menu lets you show and hide the new application bar and application frame, described in the "Exploring the Document Window" section, earlier in this chapter.

Help menu

The Help menu (shown in Figure 2.34) contains links to Adobe's HTML help files, as well as to Adobe's program update, registration, and activation functions. The Windows version also contains the About InDesign and Configure Plug-ins menu options that are in the InDesign menu on the Mac. Note that none of these menu items' functions are available in panels.

Contextual menus

An interface element you'll find quite useful in InDesign is the contextual menu. By Control+ clicking or right-clicking the document, an object, the rulers, items listed in a panel, and so on, you can display a menu of options for modifying whatever it is you're clicking. Figures 2.35 through 2.37 show 11 contextual menus: two variants of one contextual menu for frames, two variants when you're using the Type tool, two affecting the rulers, one for the document tab, one for a panel group, and three examples of contextual menus for panels.

NEW FEATURE When you Control+click or right-click a Tools panel icon that has a triangle in its lower-right corner, you get a pop-out menu of alternative tools. Essentially, these menus are now treated like contextual menus. You can, however, still access these pop-out menus the previous way: by clicking and holding the mouse button on them until the pop-out menu appears.

FIGURE 2.35

From left to right: The contextual menus for a graphics frame, for a text frame, for a text-insertion point, and for selected text

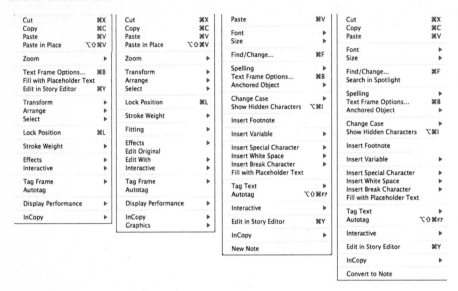

FIGURE 2.36

From left to right: The contextual menus for the zero point, rulers, a document tab, and a panel group

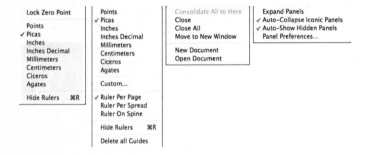

FIGURE 2.37

Many panels offer contextual menus for listed items, such as (from left to right) the Paragraph panel, Pages panel, and Swatches panel.

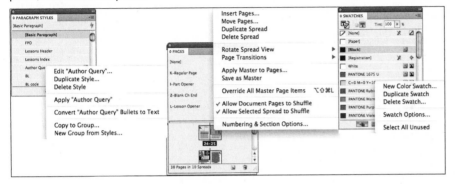

Undoing What You've Just Done

Sometimes, you do something you didn't mean to — or you did mean to do it but don't like the results. InDesign gives you several ways to deal with changing your mind:

- Choosing Edit ⇨ Undo or pressing ⌘+Z or Ctrl+Z for most actions. (Some actions, particularly actions such as scrolling that do not affect any items or the underlying document structure, are not undoable.) You can undo multiple actions in the order they were done by choosing Edit ⇨ Undo or pressing ⌘+Z or Ctrl+Z — each time you undo, and the previous action is undone.

- If you change your mind while InDesign is still completing the action, pressing Esc usually cancels the operation.

- When working in most dialog boxes, you can revert all settings to what they were when you opened the dialog box: Just press Option or Alt, which changes the Cancel button into a Reset button, and then click Reset.

If you've undone something that you decide you didn't want to undo, InDesign has a way to help here as well: Choose Edit ⇨ Redo or press Shift+⌘+Z or Ctrl+Shift+Z. This will redo whatever you undid by choosing Edit ⇨ Undo or pressing ⌘+Z or Ctrl+Z. It does not reinstate a canceled operation or a reverted dialog box.

Alternatively, choosing Undo and Redo is a handy way of seeing a before/after view of a particular change. As with Undo, you can redo multiple undone actions in the order in which they were undone. If you've made lots of changes to your document and you want to jettison them all, you can choose File ⇨ Revert to reopen the file as it was when you last saved it.

Summary

InDesign stores its preferences in a file that you can copy and send to other users to ensure that you use a standard interface in workgroups. It offers its functionality through a variety of interface methods: tools, panels, menu options, and contextual menus, as well as through some navigation controls in the document window. Panels are the primary vehicle for accessing InDesign features, whereas tools — accessed via the Tools panel — are the primary vehicle for determining what actions are possible.

You can move panels into the main dock to keep them self-contained at the right side of your screen. You can also move, separate, and combine panels into panel groups of your choice, either within the main dock or as free-floating panel groups. New panels are Assignments, Notes, Cell Styles, and Table Styles.

The Control panel is a great timesaver, grouping many functions into one panel, showing only the relevant options for different kinds of objects as they are selected.

InDesign displays documents in separate tabs, whose display you can control. The new application bar also gives you quick access to many InDesign display-oriented functions such as zooming and managing document display.

You can undo and redo most actions, giving you greater ability to experiment.

Chapter 3

Getting InDesign Ready to Go

Although you may not realize it, Adobe has made a variety of educated guesses about the way you work. For example, it assumes you work in picas, that you prefer low-resolution previews of images, and that you use typographers' quotes. Adobe has also made decisions about the default properties of text, the default color swatches included with documents, and the default attributes of some objects. In all cases, Adobe tried to make the defaults appropriate for most publishers.

But no matter how much thought Adobe put into making these educated guesses, they don't work for everybody. In fact, it's unlikely that every single setting is appropriate for you. So no matter how tempted you are to jump in and start working, take a minute to prepare InDesign for the way you actually work. Otherwise, you end up conforming the way you work to InDesign's decisions, making it more difficult to learn the program and get your work done; or you end up making the same changes to document after document, wasting time in the process.

Working with Preferences Files

InDesign stores preferences in several places. Some are stored in the documents themselves, so they work as expected as they are moved from user to user. Others are stored in files on your computer and affect only you.

InDesign Defaults file

The preferences you set in InDesign, from measurement units to color-calibration settings, are all stored in the InDesign Defaults file:

- On the Mac, this file is in the `Users: current user:Library:Preferences: Adobe InDesign:Version 6.0` folder on the drive that contains the Mac OS X System folder.

- In Windows XP, it is in the `\Document and Settings\current user\ Application Data\Adobe\InDesign\Version 6.0` folder on the drive that contains Windows.

- In Windows Vista, it is in the `\Users\current user\AppData\Local\Adobe\ InDesign\Version 6.0` folder on the drive that contains Windows.

CROSS-REF In Windows, these folders may be hidden. Chapter 34 explains how to make them accessible.

To specify these defaults, you modify settings in the Preferences dialog box when no documents are open. All new documents you create are based on these settings.

Because some of the information affects how text flows and how documents look, you may want to standardize it for a workgroup by setting preferences once and sharing the InDesign Defaults file. (Sharing the file is a simple matter of giving copies of the file to other InDesign users to place in the appropriate system folder.)

TIP To return to a blank slate, you can delete the InDesign Defaults preference files when opening InDesign; press Control+Option+Shift+⌘ or Ctrl+Alt+Shift when launching InDesign.

NOTE If you make changes to preferences while a document is open, the changes save with that document and not in the InDesign Defaults file. The document remembers its own preference settings so that it looks the same when it's opened on other computers running InDesign.

Presets folder

The Presets folder — which is inside the folder containing the InDesign application — contains 10 kinds of stored preferences: shortcut sets, color swatch libraries, workspaces, auto-correction tables, find/change tables, the button library, page transitions, page sizes, icon images, and start-page settings. (The latter two relate to InDesign's interface, not preferences related to your work.) Because these preferences are stored in files, they can be copied to other users' Presets folders to help ensure consistent options among all users in a workgroup. Here are the eight folders that contain users' stored preferences:

- **Autocorrect:** This folder includes XML documents that store the automatic text-correction rules that display in the Autocorrect pane of the Preferences dialog box — both those that come with InDesign and those you add yourself (see Chapter 16). If you are knowledgeable in XML, you can edit this file to add more correction rules outside of InDesign (which may be helpful for a production programmer, for example).

- **Button Library:** This folder contains a standard InDesign library file named `ButtonLibrary.indl` that contains the buttons defined in the Buttons panel.

■ **Find-Change Queries:** This folder includes XML documents that store common find/ change queries, such as replacing two paragraph returns with one, as shown in the Query pop-up menu of the Find/Change dialog box. (See Chapter 15.) If you are knowledgeable in XML, you can edit this file to add more correction rules outside of InDesign.

■ **InDesign Shortcut Sets:** InDesign lets you create custom shortcut sets, so if you don't like the shortcuts that Adobe assigned to various commands — or if you want to add shortcuts to features when Adobe doesn't provide them — you can make InDesign work your way. This also lets different users have their own shortcut definitions on the same computer.

■ **InDesign Workspaces:** This folder contains workspace definitions. A *workspace* is a set of panels and panel positions that you can save for easy switching among different inter-faces optimized for different layout tasks. For example, you can have all text-editing pan-els appear when you're working on text, and graphics and object-handling panels appear while you're laying out elements.

■ **Page Sizes:** This folder contains presets of custom page sizes, all stored in a single file: the New Doc Sizes.txt file. It contains any custom page sizes you have created; you edit this text file in any text editor to create your own. These custom page sizes display in the New Document and Document Setup dialog boxes' Page Size pop-up menus. An example is building a custom page size for every standard ad size for a magazine or news-paper to ensure correct dimensions on new ad documents. Just add a new line in the New Doc Sizes.txt file for each document style as follows: name→width→height. For example: Business card→3.5"→2". (The → character here indicates a tab; you should press the Tab key.)

■ **Page Transitions:** This folder contains the Adobe Flash movie (.swf) files used in page transitions in the new Page Transitions panel.

■ **Swatch Libraries:** This folder contains color-swatch libraries — both those that come with InDesign and any you might add yourself.

NEW FEATURE The Page Transitions and Button Library preset folders are new to InDesign CS4, storing presets for new features. The Page Sizes folder is also new, but it's just a new location for the New Doc Sizes.txt file that used to be in the main Presets folder. Gone is the Glyph Sets folder; it has moved to your operating system's preferences folder, as described in Chapter 34.

CROSS-REF I cover workspaces in Chapter 2; shortcut sets later in this chapter; document creation in Chapter 4; swatch libraries in Chapter 7; search and replace and auto-correction in Chapter 15; glyph sets in Chapter 20; buttons and page transitions in Chapter 32; and scripts in Chapter 37.

Using the Preferences Dialog Box

Preferences are settings that affect an entire document — such as what measurement system you're using on rulers, what color the guides are, and whether substituted fonts are highlighted. In InDesign, you access these settings through the Preferences dialog box (choose InDesign ⇨ Preferences ⇨ *desired pane* or press ⌘+K on the Mac, or choose Edit ⇨ Preferences ⇨ *desired pane* or press Ctrl+K in Windows). They are stored in the InDesign Defaults file in your InDesign application folder.

NOTE You must select a specific pane from the Preferences submenu. For example, you might choose InDesign ⇨ Preferences ⇨ Composition on the Mac or Edit ⇨ Preferences ⇨ Composition in Windows. If you use the keyboard shortcut ⌘+K or Ctrl+K, you will get the General pane, from which you can then select the desired pane from the list on the left.

InDesign has two methods for changing preferences: You can change preferences when no documents are open to create new settings for all future documents, or you can change preferences for the active document, which affects only that document. Your strategy for changing preferences depends on the way you work and the needs of specific documents. For example, if you generally prefer to work in points, you might change the default measurement system to points with no documents open. However, you might have a design such as an envelope that makes more sense in inches, so you can change the measurement system for that specific document.

The Preferences dialog box provides 17 types of settings divided into panes: General, Interface, Type, Advanced Type, Composition, Units & Increments, Grids, Guides & Pasteboard, Dictionary, Spelling, Autocorrect, Notes, Story Editor Display, Display Performance, Appearance of Black, File Handling, and Clipboard Handling. The steps for setting preferences stay the same, regardless of the changes you need to make.

When using the Preferences dialog box:

1. **Determine whether the change is for a specific document or for all future documents and then open or close documents accordingly.** If no documents are open, the changes are stored in your preferences file and will be remembered for all new documents. If a document is open, the changes are in effect for that document only.

2. **Choose InDesign ⇨ Preferences ⇨ General or press ⌘+K on the Mac, or choose Edit ⇨ Preferences ⇨ General or press Ctrl+K in Windows, to open the General pane.**

3. **To switch to a specific pane, click an option from the list at the left of the dialog box, as shown in Figure 3.1.**

4. **Change any settings in any of the panes and then click OK.** The changes are saved with the active document or in the InDesign Defaults file.

NOTE In this section, I take a comprehensive look at all the preferences in InDesign. I explain references that affect specific features again in the relevant chapters. For example, I cover Dictionary preferences in Chapter 15.

CAUTION In contrast to most actions you perform in InDesign, you cannot reverse changes to preferences using the Undo command (choose Edit ⇨ Undo, or press ⌘+Z or Ctrl+Z). If you change your mind about a preference setting, open the Preferences dialog box and change the setting again.

General preferences

Options in the General pane (see Figure 3.1) affect the operation of several InDesign features.

FIGURE 3.1

The General pane of the Preferences dialog box

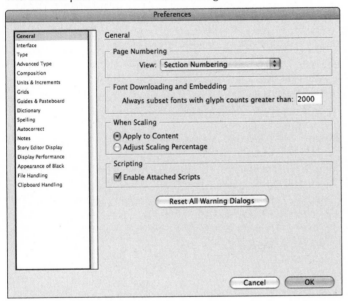

Page Numbering area

In the Page Numbering area of the Preferences dialog box, the View pop-up menu controls how page numbers appear in the fields such as the page number field on the document window. Here are the controls:

- **Section Numbering:** This is the default setting, which means that InDesign shows the page numbers according to the information in the Section Options dialog box accessed through the Pages panel's flyout menu. When Section Numbering is selected, by default you need to type section page numbers, such as Sec2:3, in fields.

- **Absolute Numbering:** This option, which I prefer, shows page numbers according to each page's position in the document. For example, the first page is 1, the second page is 2, and the third page is 3, even if the pages display the Roman numerals i, ii, and iii. When this option is selected, you can always jump to the first page in a document by typing 1 in the Page Number box.

Font Downloading and Embedding area

The Always Subset Fonts with Glyph Counts Greater Than field is used for OpenType fonts that have many special characters, such as accented letters, symbols, and diacritical marks. To prevent output files from getting clogged with very large font files, this option lets you set the maximum number of characters (glyphs) that can be downloaded from a font file into an output file. Any characters actually used are always downloaded; the reason you might want to download an entire font is so that someone could edit the file as a PDF or EPS file and have access to all characters in the proper fonts for such editing.

When Scaling area

When the Apply to Content radio button is selected and you resize an object with no stroke, InDesign will display the new scale whether you select the *object* using the Selection tool or Position tool or you select its *content* using the Direct Selection tool or Position tool. This option makes it easy to see which objects have had their content scaled when selected with the Selection tool.

When the Adjust Scaling Percentage option is selected instead, InDesign shows the resized object as 100 percent when you select it with the Selection tool or Position tool, but shows the actual new scale only when you select its content using the Direct Selection tool or Position tool. This has always been InDesign's standard behavior. (If the object has a stroke, InDesign shows the new scale no matter what tool you select it with — also InDesign's longstanding normal behavior.)

 Chapter 10 explains how to scale objects and their contents.

Scripting area

If selected (the default), the Enable Attached Scripts option lets scripts run automatically whenever you open a specific menu. This feature lets script developers write scripts that don't require you to explicitly run them from the Scripts panel; instead, the scripts run themselves as you select certain menu items.

Reset All Warning Dialogs button

Use this button to turn on warning dialogs you may have turned off. Most warning dialog boxes have an option to turn off future warnings, and this option resets them so that they all appear again.

Interface preferences

InDesign has seven options in this pane, shown in Figure 3.2:

- The Floating Tools Panel pop-up menu lets you set the Tools panel as double-column width, single row, or the default single-column width. This is a matter of personal preference.
- The Tool Tips pop-up menu has three options: Normal, Fast, and None. None turns off *Tool Tips,* the labels that pop up when the mouse hovers over a panel's icons. Fast makes the labels appear faster, which is best for new users learning the interface. Normal is the default setting and is the best for experienced users because it waits a bit before displaying the label so that it doesn't pop up if you're just moving the mouse slowly.

- The Show Thumbnails on Place option, if selected, shows you a small preview icon of an imported text or graphics file when you use the Place command to bring them into InDesign.

- The Show Transformation Values, if selected, displays near the mouse the new settings as you move the mouse for sizing, scaling, and rotating objects. It is selected by default.

- If the Auto-Collapse Icon Panels option is selected, InDesign automatically closes an open panel when the mouse is no longer within that panel. But this feature works only if the main dock has been collapsed and you are accessing the panels from it in that collapsed view. (Free-floating panels are not affected.)

- The Auto-Show Hidden Panels option, if selected, adds dark gray borders to the sides of the InDesign window when you hide panels by pressing Tab. Hover the mouse over the left border to redisplay the Tools panel; hover over the right border to redisplay the main dock. (Press Tab again to get all panels back.)

- The Open New Documents as Tabs option, if selected, puts new documents into tabs rather than in free-floating windows. It is selected by default.

NEW FEATURE The Show Transformation Values setting is new to InDesign CS4. Chapter 10 shows what this new feature does. Auto-Show Hidden Panels is also new, as is Open New Documents as Tabs. (Chapter 2 covers tabbed documents.)

FIGURE 3.2

The Interface pane of the Preferences dialog box

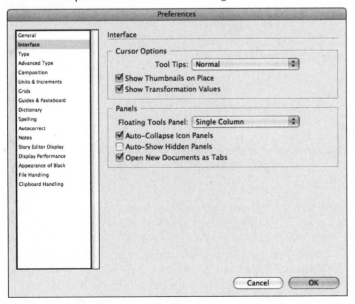

Type preferences

Options in the Type pane of the Preferences dialog box, shown in Figure 3.3, affect how several character formats work, whether you use typographer's quotes, and how text appears on-screen.

FIGURE 3.3

The Type pane of the Preferences dialog box

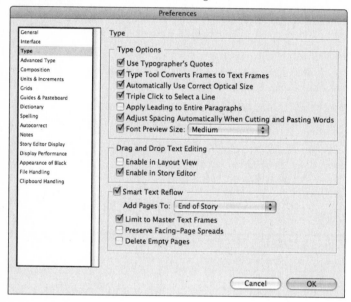

NEW FEATURE The Links area has moved to the File Handling pane.

Type Options area

These options control how InDesign handles character formatting behind the scenes as you work. Note that the first four of the seven Type Options that control different aspects of InDesign's character handling are selected by default.

- **Use Typographer's Quotes:** When you press the quotation mark key on the keyboard with Use Typographer's Quotes selected, InDesign inserts the correct typographer's quotation marks (often called *curly quotes*) for the current language in use. For example, for U.S. English, InDesign inserts typographic single quotation marks (' ') or double quotation marks (" ") rather than straight quotation marks. For French and some other languages, InDesign inserts double angle brackets (« »). InDesign knows what language's characters to use based on the Language pop-up menu in the Character panel (choose

Type ⇨ Character or press ⌘+T or Ctrl+T), or in the Paragraph Style and Character Style panels' Advanced Character Formats pane (choose Type ⇨ Paragraph Styles or press ⌘+F11 or Ctrl+F11, and choose Type ⇨ Character Styles or press Shift+⌘+F11 or Ctrl+Shift+F11).

- **Type Tool Converts Frame to Text Frames.** Selected by default, this option has InDesign automatically convert an empty frame to a text frame if you click it with the Type tool. If this option is not selected, you have to choose Object ⇨ Content ⇨ Text to convert a selected graphics or unassigned frame to a text frame.

- **Automatically Use Correct Optical Size:** When selected, this option automatically accesses OpenType and PostScript fonts that include an optimal size axis, which ensures optimal readability at any size.

- **Triple Click to Select a Line:** When this option is selected, InDesign lets you triple-click anywhere in a line to select the whole line. This used to be a standard shortcut in Mac applications but has fallen into disuse recently.

- **Apply Leading to Entire Paragraphs:** If this option is selected, InDesign applies leading changes to the entire paragraph as opposed to the current line. In most cases, you want the leading (the spacing between lines) to be applied to all paragraphs, so I recommend that you click this option. (It is not selected by default in InDesign.)

- **Adjust Spacing Automatically When Cutting and Pasting Words:** This option is selected by default and adds or deletes spaces around words when you cut and paste so that words don't abut or have too many spaces next to them.

- Font Preview Size: If selected, this option displays a preview in all menus in which lists of fonts appear. The preview shows the actual font so that you can see what you'll get before selecting the font. The pop-up menu at right lets you select the size of the preview. Figure 3.4 shows an example. Note that if you have lots of fonts, the preview menu size quickly becomes unwieldy.

FIGURE 3.4

Example of a font menu that appears when Font Preview Size is selected and set to medium size

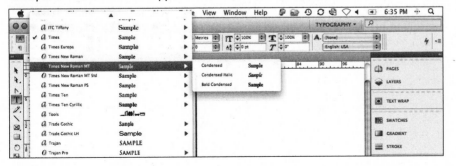

Drag and Drop Text Editing area

The options here control whether you can drag and drop text selections within a document. By default, Enable in Story Editor is selected, whereas Enable in Layout View is deselected. These default settings mean you can drag and drop text in the Story Editor but not when working on a layout, the rationale being that a layout artist could inadvertently move text if it were selected for the layout view.

Smart Text Reflow area

The options here control how text is auto-flowed into blank and new pages:

- **Add Pages To:** This pop-up menu determines how pages are added to accommodate new text. The menu options are End of Story, End of Section, and End of Document.

- **Limit to Master Text Frames:** If selected, this option adds text only using the master page text frame defined for your document (as described in Chapter 5). It is selected by default.

- **Preserve Facing-Page Spreads:** If selected, this option won't let pages be added in such a way that breaks apart facing-page spreads that have objects already on them.

- **Delete Blank Pages:** If selected, this option will delete any blank ages in the document after the new pages are inserted, including blank pages that you may have created but not yet added objects to (in other words, not just those at the end of the document).

 The smart text reflow options are new to InDesign CS4; Chapter 14 explains how this new feature works.

Advanced Type preferences

The Advanced Type pane includes additional typographic settings, as shown in Figure 3.5.

The flyout menu on the Character panel (choose Type ⇨ Character or press ⌘+T or Ctrl+T) lets you format highlighted characters as Superscript (reduced and raised above the baseline), Subscript (reduced and dropped below the baseline), or Small Caps (reduced versions of capital letters). Note that Superscript, Subscript, and Small Caps characters do not need to be reduced — they can actually be enlarged instead. The controls in the Advanced Type pane govern precisely how these characters are placed and resized, as well as control the handling on non-Latin text entry.

Character Settings area

This area controls the size of subscripts, superscripts, and small caps:

- The Size fields let you specify how much to scale these characters. The default is 58.3 percent, but you can type a value between 1 and 200 percent. I prefer 60 or 65 percent, depending on the type size and font.

- The Position fields let you specify how much to shift Superscript characters up and Subscript characters down. The default is 33.3 percent, but you can type a value between −500 and 500 percent. I prefer 30 percent for subscripts and 35 percent for superscripts.

- The Small Cap field lets you specify the scale of Small Caps characters in relation to the actual capital letters in the font. The default is 70 percent, but you can type a value between 1 and 200 percent.

FIGURE 3.5

The Advanced Type pane of the Preferences dialog box

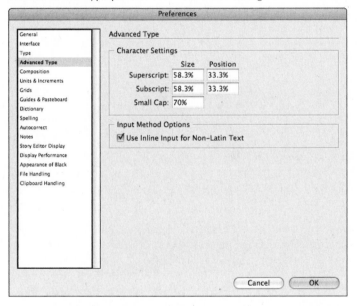

Input Method Options area

The Use Inline Input for Non-Latin Text option enables input method editors (IMEs) from Microsoft, Apple, or other companies, if installed on your computer, for typing Chinese-, Japanese-, and Korean-language (CJK) characters on non-CJK operating systems. It's meant for the occasional use of CJK characters. If you publish regularly in these languages, you should use the appropriate CJK version of InDesign.

Composition preferences

In general, preferences in the Composition pane, shown in Figure 3.6, affect entire paragraphs rather than individual characters.

FIGURE 3.6

The Composition pane of the Preferences dialog box

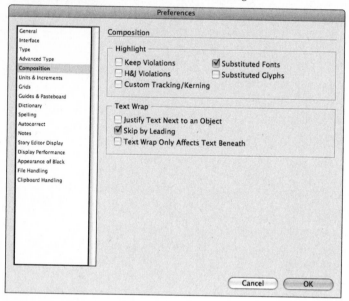

Highlight area

The options in the Highlight area control whether InDesign calls attention to possible typesetting problems by drawing a highlighter-pen effect behind the text.

- **Keep Violations:** This option is deselected by default and highlights the last line in a text frame when it cannot follow the rules specified in the Keep Options dialog box in the Paragraph panel's flyout menu (choose Type➪Paragraph or press Option+⌘+T or Ctrl+Alt+T). For example, if the Keep Options settings require more lines to stay together than fit in the text frame, thereby bumping all the text in a frame to the next text frame in the chain, the Keep Options rules are violated and the last line of text is highlighted so that you know to change the frame size or the Keep Options rules for that text.

- **H&J Violations:** When selected, H&J Violations uses three shades of yellow to mark lines that might be too loose or too tight because of the combination of spacing and hyphenation settings. The darker the shade, the worse InDesign considers the problem to be. H&J Violations is deselected by default; you might want to select it while fine-tuning type and then deselect it when you're finished.

- **Custom Tracking/Kerning:** If this option is selected, it highlights custom tracking and kerning (essentially, anywhere you override the defaults) in a bluish green. It's handy for copy editors, helping them quickly find such overrides to make sure they're not too tight or loose for readability reasons.

- **Substituted Fonts:** This option is selected by default and uses pink highlight to indicate characters in fonts that are not available to InDesign. InDesign actually uses Adobe Sans MM or Adobe Serif MM to create a replacement for missing fonts so that the text looks as close as possible to the actual font. For editing purposes, the substituted fonts work fine, although the pink highlight can be distracting. But for output purposes, it's important that you have the correct fonts, so you may want to live with the irritation and have InDesign highlight substituted fonts for you.

- **Substituted Glyphs:** This option highlights in yellow any glyphs (special characters) that are substituted. This usually occurs when you have multiple versions of the same font, with different special characters in each version. For example, a file using the euro (€) currency symbol might have been created in the newest version of, say, Syntax. But a copy editor working on the same file may have an older version of Syntax that doesn't have the euro symbol in it. Selecting Substituted Glyphs ensures that such a problem is highlighted. Substituted Glyphs also highlights characters of an OpenType font that have been changed on the fly by turning on some OpenType features from the Control panel's or Character panel's flyout menu, such as Discretionary Ligatures, Swashes, Small Caps, Slash Zero, and so on. I recommend you select this option.

NOTE InDesign is hypersensitive to fonts (see Chapter 16), so you'll get such highlighting even when you have the correct font installed but the wrong face applied to it (such as Normal rather than Regular); in these cases, the font style will have brackets ([ ]) around it in the Character or Control panel.

Text Wrap area

As the label makes clear, the three options here affect how text wraps:

- **Justify Text Next to an Object:** If this option is selected, it overrides any local justification settings that justify text that wraps around an object. That means the text smoothly follows the object's shape, rather than keeps any ragged margins that can make the wrap look strange. This option comes into play when you wrap ragged (left-aligned or right-aligned) text around objects; I recommend that you avoid wrapping text on its ragged side; doing so looks awkward. Although this option eliminates the awkwardness of ragged text that wraps around an object, it presents a different awkwardness: having some text ragged (that which is not wrapping) and some text justified (that which is wrapping).

- **Skip by Leading:** When selected, this option uses the text's leading to determine how much space follows an object that it is wrapping. This option has an effect only if you choose the Jump Object text-wrap option in the Text Wrap panel. (See Chapter 12 for more on text wrap.)

- **Text Wrap Only Affects Text Beneath:** If selected, this option has only text that's below an object wrap around that object. This lets some text overlap an image and some text overwrap it, depending on the text's location in the stacking order.

Units & Increments preferences

The measurement systems you use for positioning items and the way the arrows on the keyboard increase or decrease settings are controlled by settings in the Units & Increments pane, shown in Figure 3.7.

FIGURE 3.7

The Units & Increments pane of the Preferences dialog box

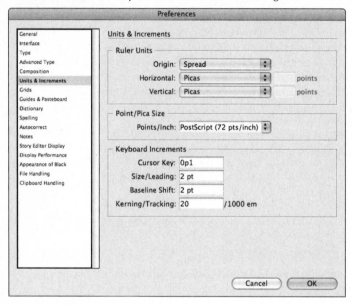

Ruler Units area

The Ruler Units area affects three things: the origin point (by page, by spread, or by the spine), the measurement system displayed on the horizontal and vertical ruler on the document window, and the default values in fields used for positioning objects.

The Origin pop-up menu determines the zero point (typically, the upper-left corner of the page) for object positions. If you choose Page, objects' positions are relative to each page's upper-left corner. If you choose Spread, objects' positions are relative to the current spread's upper-left corner. If you choose Spine, objects' positions are relative to the binding spine of each spread — the very top and center of where the two pages meet.

NEW FEATURE   **Previous versions of InDesign often miscalculated object positions when you chose the Spine option. That's now been fixed.**

With the Horizontal and Vertical pop-up menus, you can specify one measurement system for the horizontal ruler and measurements and specify another measurement system for the vertical ruler and measurements. For example, you might use points for horizontal measurements so that you can use the rulers to gauge tab and indent settings while using inches for vertical measurements. If you use inches for both the Horizontal and Vertical Ruler Units, not only do the rulers display inches, but the X, Y, W, and H fields on the Control panel (choose Window ➪ Control or press Option+⌘+6 or Ctrl+Alt+6) or Transform panel (choose Window ➪ Object & Layout ➪ Transform) display values in inches as well.

NOTE   To display the document ruler, choose View ➪ Show Ruler or press ⌘+R or Ctrl+R.

TIP   The default horizontal and vertical measurement system is picas. If you aren't accustomed to working in picas, be sure to change the default Horizontal and Vertical Ruler Units when no documents are open. Changing the default this way ensures that all future documents use your preferred measurement system. (If you make the change with a document open, the change applies only to the open document.)

To specify the measurement systems you want to use, click an option from the Horizontal pop-up menu and from the Vertical pop-up menu. The following options are available:

■ **Points:** A typesetting measurement equal to $\frac{1}{72}$ of an inch. To enter values in points, type a **p** before the value or **pt** after the value (**p6** or **6 pt**, for example).

TIP   InDesign doesn't care if you put spaces between numbers and the abbreviations in your measurements — `3 p` is read the same as `3p`, and `0.4inch` is read the same as `0.4 inch`, for example.

■ **Picas:** A typesetting measurement equal to $\frac{1}{6}$ of an inch. To enter values in picas, type a **p** after the value (for example, **6p**).

■ **Inches:** An English measurement system that is divided into sixteenths. To enter values in inches, type **i**, **in**, **inch**, or **"** after the value. For example, `3i`, `3in`, `3 inch`, and `3"` are all read by InDesign as `3 inches`.

■ **Inches decimal:** Inches divided into tenths on the ruler rather than sixteenths. To enter values in inches decimal, include a decimal point as appropriate and type **i**, **in**, **inch**, or **"** after the value.

■ **Agates:** Typically used in newspapers, an agate is $\frac{1}{14}$ of an inch, usually the depth of a line in the small type of classified ads, stock tables, and sports statistics boxes. To enter values in agates, type **ag** after the value (for example, **10ag**).

■ **Millimeters:** A metric measurement that is $\frac{1}{10}$ of a centimeter. To enter values in millimeters, type **mm** after the value (for example, **14mm**).

■ **Centimeters:** A metric measurement that is about $\frac{1}{3}$ of an inch. To enter values in centimeters, type **cm** after the value (for example, **2.3cm**).

■ **Ciceros:** A European typesetting measurement that is slightly larger than a pica. To enter values in ciceros, type **c** after the value (for example, **2c**).

■ **Custom:** This option lets you set a custom number of points as your measurement unit, placing a labeled tick mark at every point increment you specify. You get to customize the number of tick marks between the labeled marks by typing a value in the Points field. For example, if you type **12** in the field, you get a tick mark at each pica, because there are 12 points in a pica. A good opportunity to use this is if you need to have the rulers show tick marks at whole-line increments; in that case, if your leading is 8 points, you'd set the Custom field to **8**.

> **TIP** Despite the Ruler Units you specify, you can type values in any fields using any supported measurement system. For example, if you're working in picas, you can type an inch value in the Width field by typing 1 in. InDesign automatically converts the value to picas for you. You can type values in picas and points by placing a p between the two values. For example, typing 1p2 indicates 1 pica and 2 points.

Point/Pica Size area

The Points/Inch pop-up menu lets you specify how a point (pt) is calculated. The default is PostScript (72 pts/in). You can also select Traditional (72.27 pts/in), which had been the standard before electronic publishing took hold in the 1980s, as well as 72.23 and 72.3. You can also enter a value of between 60 and 80. Leave this at PostScript (72 pts/in) unless you or your service bureau has a reason to select a different option.

Keyboard Increments area

The arrow keys on the keyboard let you move selected objects right, left, up, or down. You can also use the arrow keys and other keyboard shortcuts to change some text formatting. You can customize the way these shortcuts work. For example, you can specify how far each click of an arrow key moves an item.

The options for setting keyboard shortcut increments are as follows:

■ **Cursor Key field:** When you select an object with the Selection tool or the Direct Selection tool, you can move it up, down, left, or right using the arrow keys on the keyboard. By default, the item moves 1 point. You can change the increment to a value between 0.001 and 100 points (equal to 8p4 or 1.3888 inches). For example, if you're using a document grid, you might change the increment to match the grid lines.

■ **Size/Leading field:** The value you type in this field, which is 2 points by default, specifies how much point size or leading is increased or decreased when implemented with keyboard commands. You can type a value between 1 and 100.

■ **Baseline Shift field:** You can shift the baseline of highlighted text up or down by clicking in the Baseline Shift field on the Character panel and then pressing the up or down arrow on the keyboard. You can change the default value of 2 points to any value between 1 and 100. If you press Shift while clicking, the increment is multiplied by five.

■ **Kerning field:** To kern text with keyboard commands, you position the cursor between two letters and then Option+click or Alt+click the right arrow key to increase kerning or the left arrow to decrease kerning. By default, each click changes kerning by $^{20}/_{1000}$ of an em dash — shown on-screen as 20/1000 em. You can change this value to anything between 1 and 100, in increments of $^1/_{1000}$ of an em dash. Hold the ⌘ or Ctrl key to multiply the increment by five.

Note that InDesign does not use these preferences consistently to modify the arrow keys or keyboard shortcuts. Here are the various ways they are applied so that you know what to expect:

- The Cursor Key field works with all four arrow keys.

- The Size/Leading value works with the up and down arrow keys for leading, as well as with the keyboard shortcuts to change size and leading.

- The Kerning field works with the left and right arrows.

- The Baseline Shift field works only while you're pressing the arrow keys when the Baseline Shift field is highlighted on the Character panel.

Keyboard Options for Cursor Movements

Whatever you enter as the values for the Cursor Key fields, when you are working in InDesign, you can use several keys to change how much the values actually change and/or make a copy of the moved object:

- If you press the Shift key while you press an arrow key, the object moves ten times the amount specified in the Cursor Key field.

- Holding the Option or Alt key while you press an arrow key creates a copy of the selected object at the distance specified in the Cursor Key field.

- Holding the Shift key with the Option or Alt key while you press an arrow key creates a copy of the selected object at ten times the amount specified in the Cursor Key field. This last combination is a very simple and quick way to create a grid of text or image boxes with equal spacing between them.

Similarly, you can use keys to modify how the Size/Leading field values are applied:

- To increase the point size of selected text, press Shift+⌘+. (period) or Ctrl+Shift+. (period).

- To decrease the point size, press Shift+⌘+, (comma) or Ctrl+Shift+, (comma).

- Add Option or Alt to the combination to multiply the increment by five.

- To modify leading for selected text, Option+click or Alt+click the up or down arrow on the keyboard.

There are two other ways to use keys to change how cursors are applied:

- In the Character panel's Baseline Shift field, press Shift while clicking to multiply the increment by five.

- In the Character panel's kerning field, hold the ⌘ or Ctrl key to multiply the increment by five.

Grids preferences

Grids preferences let you set up a baseline grid, which you commonly use to space text evenly across columns, and a document-wide grid, which you can use for positioning or drawing objects. If you're planning a structured design that uses a grid, you want to set it up before you start working in the document. It's likely that each design you create will have different grid settings based on its individual content, so you probably won't change Grids preferences unless you have a document open. The Grids pane is shown in Figure 3.8.

FIGURE 3.8

The Grids pane of the Preferences dialog box

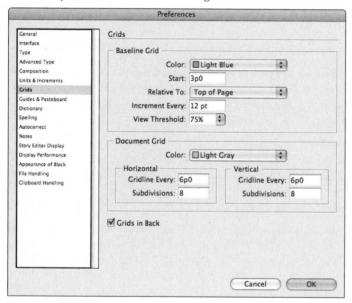

> **NOTE** By default, both the baseline grid and the document grid appear on every spread behind all objects; the document grid appears on the pasteboard as well. Both grids cover the entire document and cannot be associated with a specific master page or layer. You can have grids appear in front by deselecting the Grids in Back option.

Baseline Grid area

You can specify the color of the baseline grid, where it starts, how far apart each grid line is, and when it appears. To display the baseline grid for a document, choose View ➪ Grids & Guides ➪ Show Baseline Grid or press Option+⌘+' (apostrophe) or Ctrl+Alt+' (apostrophe). You have the following options:

- **Color pop-up menu:** The default color of the baseline grid is Light Blue. If this color is difficult for you to see, or if you're accustomed to the pink lines in QuarkXPress and prefer something similar, you can select a different color from the Color pop-up menu. Choose Other to access the system color picker and create your own color.

- **Start field:** This value specifies how far down from the top of the page the grid starts. The Start value, which defaults to 3p0, usually matches your top margin.

- **Relative To pop-up menu:** InDesign lets you set where the grid starts, which is at Top of Page or Top Margin.

- **Increment Every field:** The amount of space between grid lines is specified in the Increment Every field. The default value of 1p0 usually changes to match the leading of your body text so that text aligns with the grid.

- **View Threshold pop-up menu.** You can prevent the baseline grid from appearing when you decrease the view percentage. If you use the default setting, the baseline grid does not appear at views below 75 percent. You can type a value between 5 and 4,000 percent.

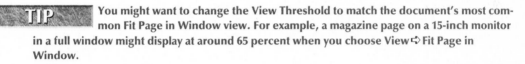 **You might want to change the View Threshold to match the document's most common Fit Page in Window view. For example, a magazine page on a 15-inch monitor in a full window might display at around 65 percent when you choose View ⇨ Fit Page in Window.**

Document Grid area

The document grid consists of intersecting horizontal and vertical gridlines, forming a pattern of small squares that you can use for object placement and for drawing symmetrical objects. You can customize the color and spacing of the grid lines. To display the document grid, choose View ⇨ Grids & Guides ⇨ Show Document Grid or press ⌘+' (apostrophe) or Ctrl+' (apostrophe). You have the following options:

- **Color pop-up menu:** The default color of the document grid is Light Gray. Although this light shade is unobtrusive, you might want to change it to something brighter or darker so that you can see it better. You can choose a different color from the Color pop-up menu or choose Other to create your own.

- **Gridline Every field:** The major grid lines, which are slightly darker, are positioned according to this value. The default value is 6p0; in general, you want to specify a value within the measurement system you're using. For example, if you're working in inches, you might type **1 inch** in the Gridline Every field. That way, the gridlines match the major tick marks on the ruler. You set the horizontal and vertical settings separately.

- **Subdivisions field:** Although this is a number and not a measurement, it ends up specifying the amount of space between grid lines. The major grid lines established in the Gridline Every field are divided according to the value you type here. For example, if you type **1 inch** in the Gridline Every field, and you type **4** in the Subdivisions field, you get a gridline at each quarter inch. The default number of subdivisions is 8. You set the horizontal and vertical settings separately.

Guides & Pasteboard preferences

When you create a new document, you set up margins in the New Document dialog box (choose File ⇨ New ⇨ Document or press ⌘+N or Ctrl+N). For more alignment options within a document, you can create guidelines by clicking and dragging them off the rulers or clicking Layout ⇨ Create Guides. Settings in the Guides & Pasteboard pane of the Preferences dialog box, shown in Figure 3.9, control the color and other attributes of the margins and guides.

The Guides & Pasteboard pane of the Preferences dialog box

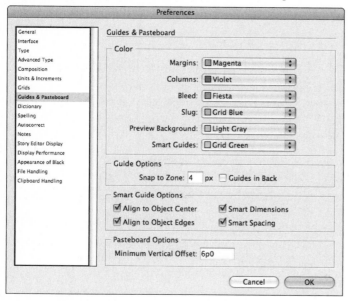

Color area

In the Color area, the Color pop-up menus for Margins, Columns, Bleed, Slug, Preview Background, and Smart Guides let you select colors other than the defaults. If you want to make your own color, choose Custom to access the system color picker. The Margins color (Magenta by default) displays on all horizontal guides; the Columns color (Violet by default) displays on all vertical guides. To display guides in a document, choose View ⇨ Grids & Guides ⇨ Show Guides or press ⌘+; (semicolon) or Ctrl+; (semicolon).

 Smart guides are a new method in InDesign CS4 to align objects on the fly (see Chapter 9), so the various smart guide options in this pane are new as well.

Guide Options area

This area controls guide snap-to and placement:

- **Snap to Zone:** This field's value specifies how close you need to drag an object to a grid line or guideline to make it *snap to* the line (think of it as the line's magnetic field). The default Snap to Zone value is 4 pixels, but you can type a value between 1 and 36. You enable snapping to the grid through the Snap to Document Grid and Snap to Guides commands in the View menu.

- **Guides in Back:** By default, margins and guides appear in front of all objects. If you prefer to have objects obscure margins and guides, select the Guides in Back option in the Guide Options area. Note that baseline grids and document grids always appear behind all objects, regardless of this setting.

Smart Guides area

The new smart guides feature has four options for when objects you are creating, resizing, moving, or rotating snap to nearby items:

- **Align to Object Center:** If this option is selected, InDesign will create guidelines as you get near the center point of nearby objects so that you can align the center of the object you are working with to that of a nearby object.

- **Align to Object Edge:** If this option is selected, InDesign will create guides on the fly based on the edges of nearby objects, against which you can align the object you are working with.

- **Smart Dimensions:** If this option is selected, InDesign will highlight when any size of an object you are creating or resizing matches that of a nearby object. For example, it will highlight the width of the two objects when they match, or the depth. Similarly, it will highlight when the rotation angles match. (See Chapter 9 for examples of how InDesign this feature works and how it highlights matches.)

- **Smart Spaces:** If this option is selected, InDesign will highlight when nearby objects are spaced equidistantly along the horizontal or vertical axes so that you can precisely space them if desired. (See Chapter 6 for examples of how this feature works.)

Pasteboard Options area

The Pasteboard Options area has the Minimum Vertical Offset field, in which you specify the amount of pasteboard to appear above and below your pages. The default is 6p0 (1 inch).

Dictionary preferences

The Dictionary pane, shown in Figure 3.10, sets options related to hyphenation and spelling dictionaries, as well as to quotation marks.

FIGURE 3.10

The Dictionary pane of the Preferences dialog box

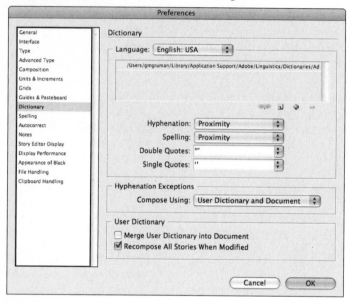

Language area

The Language area begins with a pop-up menu that lets you choose a language. You choose a language when you want to replace the existing one, or add new, hyphenation and spelling dictionaries for that language. You can therefore control the dictionaries used by each language separately. For example, if you want to replace the French dictionaries, choose French in the pop-up menu and then select the new French dictionaries elsewhere in this pane. The current dictionaries for the selected language appear in the window beneath it, and there are four buttons (from left to right) to link, add, delete, or save dictionary files.

NEW FEATURE InDesign CS4 adds the All Languages option to the pop-up menu, which allows for multilingual hyphenation in the document.

CROSS-REF InDesign lets you associate multiple user dictionaries with each language. Chapter 15 explains how to create, edit, remove, and otherwise manage dictionaries.

In addition, the Language area offers these controls over dictionaries:

- **Hyphenation:** This pop-up menu lets you choose from any hyphenation dictionaries installed for the selected language. Typically, there is only the default dictionary, Proximity, in this pop-up menu.

- **Spelling:** This pop-up menu lets you choose from any spelling dictionaries installed for the selected language. Typically, there is only the default dictionary, Proximity, in this pop-up menu.

How to Install Dictionaries

To install different dictionaries, place them in the Dictionaries folder inside the Plug-ins folder (inside your InDesign application folder). Press Option+⌘+/ or Ctrl+Alt+/ to update the pop-up menus in the Dictionary pane without restarting InDesign. (In a workgroup, it's important that everyone uses the same dictionaries.)

Eventually, you may be able to purchase third-party spelling or hyphenation dictionaries for InDesign — although no third-party commercial dictionaries have been released since InDesign was created in 1999. For example, you might be able to purchase a different Traditional German dictionary with more words than the one InDesign has. In that case, when you check the spelling of a word with Traditional German as its language format, InDesign would consult the third-party dictionary rather than the default. More likely, you will use this feature to create your own project-specific dictionaries, such as a dictionary of technical terms.

The Language area also lets you set the quotation marks you want to use. Different languages use different symbols for quotation marks, and InDesign adjusts the quotation marks automatically when you switch the language. However, in some cases you might want to override the language's default quotation-mark settings, which you can do in the Double Quotes and Single Quotes pop-up menus.

Note that changing the quotation-mark options for one language does not affect the settings for others. Each language can have independent settings for the quotation marks used.

CAUTION After you change a language's quotation-mark settings, you can't reset them to the language defaults except by choosing the proper options from the pop-up menus. You therefore need to remember or record what the original, correct setting was.

Hyphenation Exceptions area

The Compose Using pop-up menu has three options that specify what to use for hyphenation exceptions, which override the language dictionary's hyphenation rules. For example, you may choose not to hyphenate a short word like "preset" that has a legitimate hyphenation as "pre-set." And you may correct the hyphenation of specialized terms not in the language's dictionary.

The options here dictate how you manage those exceptions. By default, InDesign stores hyphenation exceptions in an outside file, so multiple users can standardize on the same exceptions list. But you can also store exceptions in a document, perhaps for unique needs. The Compose Using pop-up menu lets you select from Document, User Dictionary, and User Dictionary and Document options. Choose User Dictionary if you want to override any exceptions stored in the document; perhaps they're wrong or the copy editors want to rely only on a standard exception list. Choose Document if you want to ignore exceptions stored in an outside file. Choose User Dictionary and Document if you want to use both.

User Dictionary area

This area has two options that are selected by default and should stay that way:

- **Merge User Dictionary into Document:** If selected, this option copies the user dictionary file into the document, so if the file is sent to someone else who doesn't have access to that dictionary, the hyphenation in the document is preserved. The main reason to deselect this option is if you need to keep your files to a minimum size; otherwise, selecting this option prevents reflow when you pass a document to a service bureau or another designer, especially if you have any custom hyphenations.

- **Recompose All Stories When Modified:** If selected, this option redoes the document's hyphenation to reflect the changed user dictionary.

Spelling preferences

The Spelling pane, shown in Figure 3.11, lets you control what the InDesign spell checker examines when it checks spelling in a document.

FIGURE 3.11

The Spelling pane of the Preferences dialog box

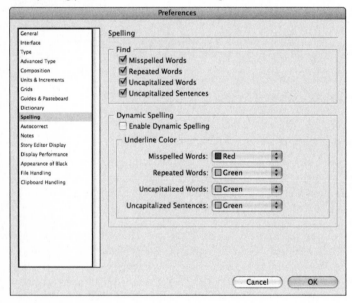

Spelling area

There's little reason not to select all four options in this area — Misspelled Words, Repeated Words, Uncapitalized Words, and Uncapitalized Sentences. Note that Uncapitalized Words checks for known proper nouns that aren't capitalized.

Dynamic Spelling area

This area lets you enable whether InDesign checks spelling in your documents as you type and import text. If enabled (by selecting the Enable Dynamic Spelling option), InDesign highlights on-screen any errors using the colors selected for the four types of errors it checks for: Misspelled Words, Repeated Words, Uncapitalized Words, and Uncapitalized Sentences. Select the desired color from the appropriate pop-up menu.

Autocorrect preferences

This pane, shown in Figure 3.12, lets you turn on automatic text correction, select which dictionary to use to detect misspellings, and specify which words are to be replaced in the list below.

FIGURE 3.12

The Autocorrect pane of the Preferences dialog box

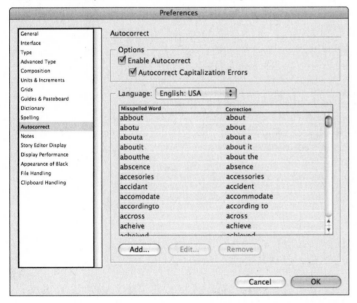

Turn on auto-correction by selecting the Enable Autocorrect option. If you want the auto-correction feature to also fix capitalization errors, be sure to select Autocorrect Capitalization Errors. Select the dictionary against which to check spelling from the Language pop-up menu.

You can modify the list of words to be automatically corrected using the list below the Language pop-up menu. Click Add to add a misspelled word and its correction. To delete an auto-correction rule, select it in the Misspelled Word list and click Remove.

NOTE You might think you can use the auto-correction feature to have InDesign substitute special characters for codes you enter, to save the hassle of memorizing the keyboard shortcuts or using the Glyphs panel. But you can't: InDesign won't let you enter special characters in the Correction field after you click the Add button. That means, for example, you *cannot* have InDesign change -- to an em dash (—), or change (r) to ® using this feature.

CROSS-REF Chapter 15 explains how to work with InDesign's spell-checking capabilities.

Notes preferences

The Notes pane sets up how notes are handled in InDesign. Notes are nonprinting blocks of text that you can insert within the document's text as reminders for yourself or others (see Chapter 15). Figure 3.13 shows the pane.

FIGURE 3.13

The Notes pane of the Preferences dialog box

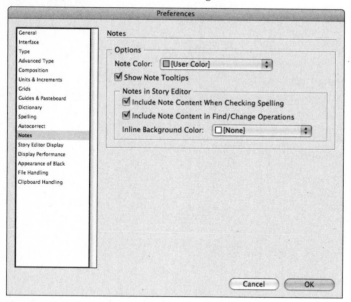

The Note Color pop-up menu lets you control the color of notes, to help make them stand out from other layout elements. If selected (the default), the Show Note Tool Tips option controls whether a pop-up box displaying the note appears when your mouse hovers over a note character in text.

The Notes in Story Editor area has three options. The first two, selected by default, are self-explanatory: Include Note Content When Checking Spelling and Include Note Content in Find/Change Operations. The third option, the Inline Background Color pop-up menu, controls whether there is no color (the default) or the note color displayed behind the special, nonprinting character in your text that "anchors" the note. Selecting the note color option makes the notes easier to find, but it can also be distracting.

Story Editor Display preferences

The Story Editor Display pane controls how the Story Editor displays text and the text cursor. Figure 3.14 shows the pane.

CROSS-REF Chapter 15 covers the Story Editor in detail.

FIGURE 3.14

The Story Editor Display pane of the Preferences dialog box

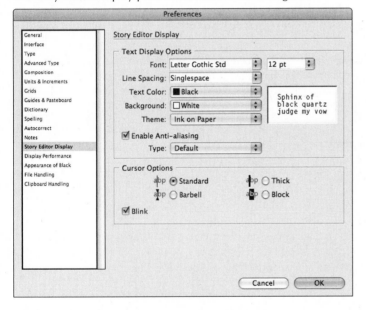

Text Display Options area

The Text Display Options area determines how text displays in the Story Editor. All options are meant to make it easy to edit text on-screen.

The first set of options lets you customize the text itself in the Story Editor. The Font pop-up menu lets you choose a font that is easy to read — you can use any active font available on your computer — as well as a point size (the default of 12 points is usually quite readable, but you may want to enlarge or reduce that in specific cases). The Line Spacing pop-up menu lets you change the default Singlespace setting to 150%, Doublespace, and Triplespace. You may prefer 150% or Doublespace if you have a wide Story Editor window to help make reading the text easier.

Two pop-up menus control the basic display: Text Color and Background. You rarely want to change either of these from the default of black for the text color and white for the background. (However, if you do change the background color, you might want to choose a light yellow or green that's a bit easier on the eye.)

The Theme pop-up menu has four predefined text color/background combinations that override any changes you make to the Text Color and Background pop-up menus. Of those four themes, you want to keep Ink on Paper, which is simply black text on a white background. The other three options provide hard-to-read displays modeled after the very first computer displays in the 1970s and early 1980s.

The Enable Anti-aliasing option, if selected, smoothes text display for better readability in the Story Editor. You choose the smoothing type — Default, Best for LCD Display, or Soft — you prefer in the Type pop-up menu. Note that both Windows and the Mac OS offer similar capabilities system-wide, so you may not want to set antialiasing in InDesign if you have already set it for your whole computer.

Cursor Options area

InDesign gives you a choice of the text cursor that appears in the Story Editor. In the Cursor Options area, choose whichever looks best on-screen and is easy to find without obscuring the text under it. That varies based on the font and point size you choose. If you want the text cursor to blink — that might help you find it more easily — be sure to select the Blink option.

Display Performance preferences

The Display Performance pane, shown in Figure 3.15, controls how images and text appear on-screen.

Options area

In the Default View pop-up menu in the Options area, you can choose from three view settings: Typical, Fast, and High Quality. These affect only what appears on-screen, not what is printed. The three options correspond to how you set the options in the Adjust View Settings area of this pane.

If selected, the Preserve Object-Level Display Settings option overrides any global view settings here with those you have set for specific images. Images that have no individual view settings set will still take on the settings in this pane.

You can override these view settings by choosing Object ⇨ Display Performance and then picking Fast Display (press Option+Shift+⌘+Z or Ctrl+Alt+Shift+Z), Typical Display (press Option+⌘+Z or Ctrl+Alt+Z), or High Quality Display (press Command+Option+⌘+H or Ctrl+Alt+H) from the submenu. The new setting remains in effect until you change it or until the next time you launch InDesign. Furthermore, you can set display settings for individual objects by ensuring that Allow Object-Level Display Settings is checked in that submenu (choose it if not) and then selecting the desired objects and applying the desired display settings to them. These settings remain in effect until you change them or clear them all by choosing View ⇨ Clear Object-Level Display Settings.

FIGURE 3.15

The Display Performance pane of the Preferences dialog box

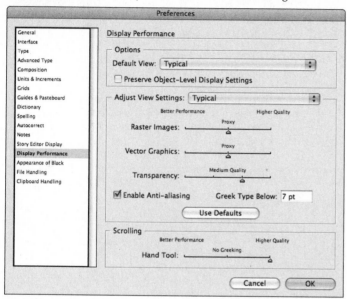

Adjust View Settings area

Use the Adjust View Settings area to determine what Typical, Optimized, and High Quality should mean in your copy of InDesign. Click the tick mark for the quality level you want to set in each of the three graphical view aspects (Raster Images, Vector Images, and Transparency). You can also click and drag the sliders to the desired tick mark. Note that you must move the slider all the way to a tick mark; you cannot choose a setting in-between tick marks.

For *raster* (bitmap) images and *vector* images, you have three options: Gray Out, Proxy, and High Resolution. Proxy means a low-resolution version (72 dpi). For transparency, there are three quality levels available — Low, Medium, and High — as well as Off, which doesn't display objects behind transparent portions of an image.

The Adjust View Settings area also has two controls for text:

- **Enable Anti-aliasing:** When this option is selected, it smoothes text display. Note that you may already have set antialiasing in your Windows or Mac OS X systemwide display preferences, in which case you probably don't need to also set them in InDesign.

- **Greek Type Below:** This field is where you set the size text appears as gray lines rather than as actual characters.

Click Use Defaults to return to InDesign's default setting for this pane.

Scrolling area

You can adjust screen refresh while scrolling by setting your preferred options in the Hand Tool slider. Either click the desired tick mark or move the slider to the desired tick mark. Selecting the leftmost tick mark means you see less detail appear as you scroll. This can speed up scrolling in complex documents. It has no effect on image preview when you stop scrolling, or on printing quality.

Appearance of Black preferences

InDesign lets you control how black appears on-screen and when printing, as seen in Figure 3.16.

FIGURE 3.16

The Appearance of Black pane of the Preferences dialog box

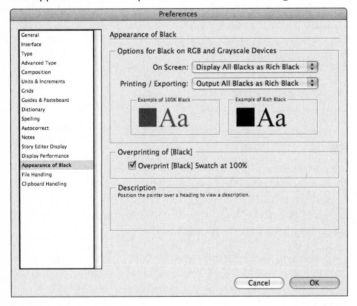

Options for Black on RGB and Grayscale Devices area

This area lets you control the display of blacks, as well as the output when printing and exporting to PDF. Using the On Screen and Printing/Exporting pop-up menus, you can choose Display All Blacks Accurately or Display All Blacks as Rich Black. *Rich black* (also called *superblack*) is created by combining black and magenta to create a darker appearance. Chapter 7 covers this concept in more detail.

Overprinting of [Black] area

By default, the Overprint [Black] Swatch at 100% option is selected so that any black text, strokes, or fills overprint. This usually results in clearer text and lines. (This option applies to the [Black] color in the Swatches panel, rather than, say, a black swatch that you create.) If you deselect Overprint [Black], all black text, strokes, and fills knock out of their backgrounds, which results in a lighter black and could cause some misregistration when printing.

CROSS-REF See Chapters 7 and 28 for more details on creating colors and trapping colors, respectively.

File Handling preferences

The File Handling pane, shown in Figure 3.17, controls how recovery files and document previews are handled. It also controls how snippets are handled and how various links are handled.

NEW FEATURE The Version Cue control is now gone from this pane. Instead, you now turn on Version Cue globally in the Adobe Bridge CS4 program, as Appendix C describes.

FIGURE 3.17

The File Handling pane of the Preferences dialog box

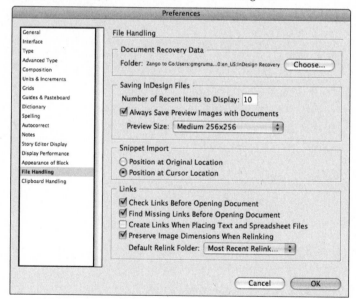

Document Recovery Data area

In this area, InDesign lets you specify the folder that contains auto-recovery files, which are files that let you recover most or all of your work in case of a program or system crash. You can click Choose to select an alternate directory, but there's really no reason to change the default, which places the recovery folder safely inside the appropriate location based on your operating system:

- On the Mac, this location is the `Users:current user:Library:Preferences:Adobe InDesign:Version 6.0:Caches` folder on the drive that contains the Mac OS X System folder.

- In Windows XP, it is the `\Document and Settings\current user\Application Data\Adobe\InDesign\Version 6.0\Caches` folder on the drive that contains Windows.

- In Windows Vista, it is the `\Users\current user\AppData\Local\Adobe\InDesign\Version 6.0\Caches` folder on the drive that contains Windows.

Saving InDesign Files area

The Always Save Preview Images with Documents option, if selected, lets InDesign save a thumbnail view of the document's first page. Select a preview size from the Preview Size pop-up menu. That preview appears in the Open a File dialog box instead of the InDesign logo when you select a file. It's handy when you've got a ton of files in a folder and can't remember which is which. But using this preview can eat up a lot of disk space and slow down file transfers because it adds a lot of image data to the InDesign document file.

NEW FEATURE New to InDesign CS4 is the ability to change how many recently saved files are displayed in the Open Recent submenu that appears under the Open option in the File menu after you have opened a file. You can change this number using the Number of Recent Items to Display option in the Saving InDesign Files area of the File Handling pane.

Snippet Import area

Snippets are files that contain pieces of an InDesign layout exported for use by others. The radio buttons here give you the choice of having any snippet that you drag into the layout placed at its original coordinates (that is, at the same coordinates it had in its original document) or at the cursor (mouse pointer) location when you drag it to in the new document. The default is Position at Cursor Location, which is typically where you'd expect it.

Links area

There are several link-related controls in this area:

- **Check Links Before Opening Document:** This option has InDesign look to see whether any linked files, such as graphics, are missing or updated as it opens the document so that it can alert you to any in the Links panel (see Chapter 12).

- **Find Missing Links Before Opening Document:** This option has InDesign look for any missing files — such as those that may have been moved — while opening the document and relinking to them if it can.

- **Default Relink Folder:** This pop-up menu lets you tell InDesign to start looking for missing files in the most recent folder in which it found missing files or in the original folder in which it found them. The first option is the default, and usually makes relinking files a bit easier because missing files tend to have been moved to new folders or disks, so it's a good bet that if one file was moved to that new location, others were, too.

NEW FEATURE The preceding three options are new to InDesign CS4. Previous versions would automatically look for missing files when you opened a document. Now you can choose when not to, such as when you know you are working with a copy that doesn't have the images (for example, when you send a document for copy editing or proofreading).

■ **Create Links When Placing Text and Spreadsheet Files:** This option creates links to your source text files. InDesign can alert you when those files change so that you can reimport them if desired. (InDesign always does this for graphics files.) Select this option if you want InDesign to track such links in the Links panel (choose Window⇨Links or press Shift+⌘+D or Ctrl+Shift+D).

NEW FEATURE The option above had resided in the Type pane of the Preferences dialog box in previous versions of InDesign.

■ **Relink Preserves Dimensions:** This option, which is selected by default, ensures that if you update a link to a graphics file using the Relink command that any dimensions such as position and scale that you applied to the original file are retained after the relink.

Clipboard Handling pane

The Clipboard Handling pane, shown in Figure 3.18, controls how image and text formatting are handled when you copy elements to or from the Clipboard.

FIGURE 3.18

The Clipboard Handling pane of the Preferences dialog box

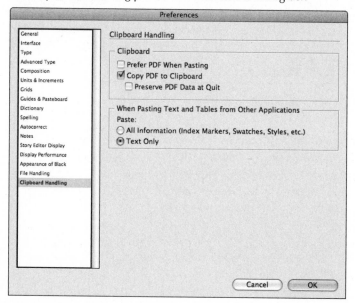

When you choose Edit ➪ Copy or press ⌘+C or Ctrl+C, and choose Edit ➪ Cut or press ⌘+X or Ctrl+X, in any application, you place a copy on the Mac or Windows Clipboard. Placing an item on the Clipboard lets items be shared among applications. Items in the Clipboard are pasted into your current document using the standard Paste commands: Edit ➪ Paste or ⌘+V or Ctrl+V.

Clipboard area

The Clipboard area has three options that control how PDF data is handled between the Clipboard and InDesign.

- **Prefer PDF When Pasting:** Selecting this option converts items copied from Adobe Illustrator into PDF files so that transparency objects, blends, and patterns are preserved during the paste operation into InDesign.

- **Copy PDF to Clipboard:** Selecting this option creates a temporary PDF file when you copy items from InDesign for pasting into applications such as Illustrator.

- **Preserve PDF Data at Quit:** Selecting this option keeps any pasted PDF information in the Clipboard's memory when you quit InDesign. You usually don't need to select this option.

When Pasting Text and Tables from Other Applications area

This area gives you a choice as to how formatting is handled when you paste textual objects from other applications: Using the two Paste radio buttons, you click either All Information or Text Only. The default is Text Only. This can be helpful or a pain, depending on whether you want copied text to preserve its formatting or you prefer copied text to take on the formatting of the destination location's text. The right answer depends on your specific layouts.

Setting Other Global Preferences

There are several global preferences handled outside the Preferences dialog box.

Setting up automatic program updates

The Adobe Updater Preferences dialog box, shown in Figure 3.19, lets you decide whether to let InDesign connect automatically to Adobe's servers over your Internet connection to download and install product updates.

FIGURE 3.19

The Adobe Updater status dialog box (right) and the Adobe Updater Preferences dialog box (left)

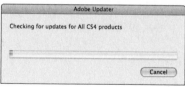
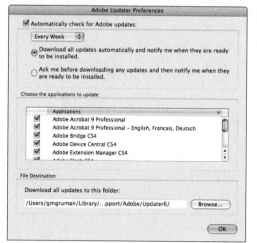

To open this dialog box, choose Help ➪ Updates. InDesign will then display the Adobe Updater dialog box that displays the status of the update process. After it has completed its search for any current updates, the Preferences button appears in the Adobe Updater dialog box, along with the Quit button. Click preferences to make the Adobe Updater Preferences dialog box appear.

In this dialog box, select the Automatically Check for Adobe Updates option to enable the auto-update feature and then choose the frequency (Every Week or Every Month) in the companion pop-up menu. You can also determine whether to have InDesign install the updates after they are downloaded or to ask you for permission first. You can also change the download folder for updater files and select which Adobe applications are updated. (Doing so lets you conveniently set automatic updating for all your Adobe applications without having to go to this dialog box in each application.)

Customizing keyboard shortcuts

InDesign provides keyboard shortcuts for accessing most tools and menu commands, and for many pane options. For the most part, the keyboard shortcuts selected by Adobe either match platform standards — such as ⌘+X or Ctrl+X for Edit ➪ Cut — or they're based on keyboard shortcuts in PageMaker, Photoshop, and Illustrator. Fortunately, you're not stuck with the keyboard shortcuts Adobe decided on — I say fortunately because a few decisions and omissions are a little odd.

To Customize or Not to Customize

The ability to customize keyboard shortcuts, letting you work the way you want, is great — or is it? Maybe it is only if you work alone and never talk to others about your work or their work. Modified keyboard shortcuts can lead to confusion when discussing techniques, reading documentation, or sharing computers. While modifying keyboard shortcuts — or even while considering it — keep the following in mind:

- You can specify keyboard shortcuts for specific fonts and faces that you use frequently, such as a shortcut for, say, Gill Sans Bold Italic. For the font to be listed in the Commands area, you need to make sure it's available to InDesign when you open the Keyboard Shortcuts dialog box.

- Don't change systemwide conventions such as the shortcuts for New, Open a File, Save, and Print.

- Don't change common keyboard commands to harmful shortcuts — for example, don't use ⌘+F or Ctrl+F for changing leading rather than invoking Find/Change.

- If you share computers in any way — even just another user reaching over your shoulder to provide assistance — adding keyboard shortcuts is safer than changing them. Your shortcuts are slightly customized, but other users are able to use your copy of InDesign without unexpected results.

- If you're at a 24-hour production shop in which two or three people share computers, each person can have his or her own set of named keyboard shortcuts. But this requires each user to remember to activate his or her own set.

- You can't export keyboard shortcuts to share with other users. If consistency is important, make sure everyone creates the same set.

- Don't modify keyboard shortcuts for computers in public places such as training centers or photocopy centers.

- QuarkXPress users coming to InDesign have to learn new software anyway, so they will benefit in the long run from learning new keyboard shortcuts rather than use InDesign's QuarkXPress shortcuts option. Even though using your old shortcuts would ease the initial transition, the frustration caused by missing or different shortcuts is worse than learning new ones. So don't prolong the switch by using this option.

- When you're specifying keyboard shortcuts, remember to use a modifier key or keys: ⌘, Option, Shift, or Control on the Mac and Ctrl, Alt, or Shift on Windows. You obviously can't use single-letter or single-numeral commands (which Adobe uses for selecting tools) while you're editing text.

If my words of caution make me seem negative about customizing keyboard shortcuts, I'm really not. Just consider all the ramifications before you do any customizing.

The Keyboard Shortcuts dialog box (choose Edit ➪ Keyboard Shortcuts), shown in Figure 3.20, provides all the tools you need for modifying keyboard shortcuts.

FIGURE 3.20

The Keyboard Shortcuts dialog box lets you create new sets of keyboard shortcuts.

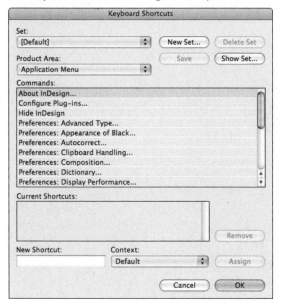

Using and modifying default shortcuts

When you first launch InDesign, you're using the default set of shortcuts, which you can view in menus, in some Tool Tips, and in your documentation. (This book lists default shortcuts as well.) You cannot modify the default set, but you can create a new set based on it and then modify the shortcuts in that set.

The Keyboard Shortcuts dialog box (choose Edit ➪ Keyboard Shortcuts), shown in Figure 3.20, provides all the tools you need for modifying keyboard shortcuts. To use the standard keyboard shortcuts after switching to another set, choose Default from the Set pop-up menu at the top of the dialog box and then click OK.

Here's how to create a new set:

1. **Choose Edit ➪ Keyboard Shortcuts.**
2. **Click New Set.**
3. **In the New Set dialog box, choose Default from the Based On Set pop-up menu.**

4. Type a different name for the set in the Name field and then click OK to create the set.

5. **To start modifying the commands, select a menu or type of shortcut to change from the Product Area pop-up menu.** For example, you can choose File Menu, Object Editing, or Typography.

6. **Scroll through the Commands area, and click to select a command so that you can change its shortcut.** The Current Shortcuts area shows you the command's existing shortcut (if there is one).

7. **Click in the New Shortcut field. You have three options at this point:**

   ▪ If a keyboard shortcut exists for this command, you can click Remove to delete it and free it for another command.

   ▪ If no keyboard shortcut exists for this command, you can press the actual modifier keys and command and then click Assign.

   ▪ If a keyboard shortcut exists for this command but you want to override it, you can press the actual modifier keys and command and then click Assign. (The shortcut you are overriding appears below the Assign button.)

8. **Typically, you leave the Context pop-up menu at Default, but if you want the shortcut to be active for a specific context, choose Alerts Dialogs, Tables, XML Selection, or Text.** This context determines when InDesign treats the keyboard shortcut as a shortcut rather than as simple text.

9. **Click Save after modifying a shortcut set.**

10. **When you're finished editing (and saving) keyboard shortcuts, click OK to exit the dialog box.** For the shortcuts that don't appear in menus, you can print a list to use as a reference. See the section "Viewing and printing shortcuts," later in this chapter.

 **You might consider adding a keyboard shortcut for Layout ⇨ Create Guides, such as the unused Option+Shift+G or Alt+Shift+G.**

Viewing and printing shortcuts

After you modify keyboard shortcuts, you may need a list for reference. (In addition, reviewing the entire QuarkXPress set before you start editing it is helpful.)

Click Show Set in the Keyboard Shortcuts dialog box (choose Edit ⇨ Keyboard Shortcuts) to view a list of shortcuts for the currently selected set. The shortcuts appear in TextEdit (on the Macintosh) or in WordPad (in Windows). You can then print the list from that application.

Customizing menus

Sometimes, the sheer number of menu options in InDesign — in the standard menus at the top of the screen, in contextual menus, and in panel menus — can be overwhelming. So InDesign lets you customize your menu options, such as to remove options you don't use. You can even save these custom menus as part of workspaces, which are collections of interface preferences, such as which panels display. (Workspaces are covered in the next section.)

Using and Modifying QuarkXPress Shortcuts

If you're switching to InDesign from QuarkXPress and are not accustomed to using Photoshop or Illustrator, the keyboard shortcuts in InDesign may seem odd. To ease the transition to InDesign, Adobe has provided a set of keyboard shortcuts based on those in QuarkXPress 4.0. I say "based on" because some QuarkXPress commands don't have equivalents and some work very differently, while other QuarkXPress shortcuts conflict with long-established Adobe shortcuts. And commands unique to InDesign still have their own keyboard shortcuts; for example, you can still select tools with the single letters shown in the Tool Tips.

Among the shortcuts you might miss or be confused by are the following:

- Option or Alt for the Page Grabber Hand is missing (use the quick zoom function instead, as described later in this chapter).

- ⌘+K or Ctrl+K for deleting selected objects is missing. (You can always use the Delete key unless the Type tool is selected.) That's because even though InDesign's QuarkXPress 4.0 shortcut set maps the Preferences dialog box to QuarkXPress 4's ⌘+Y or Ctrl+Y short-cut, it also retains the standard Adobe shortcut of ⌘+K or Ctrl+K to open the Preferences dialog box.

If you want to use the QuarkXPress set of keyboard shortcuts, choose Set for QuarkXPress 4.0 from the Set pop-up menu at the top of the Keyboard Shortcuts dialog box (choose Edit ⇨ Keyboard Shortcuts). You might want to print the list of keyboard shortcuts and review them so that you know what's available and what's different. (See the section "Viewing and printing shortcuts," later in this chapter.)

If you decide to use the QuarkXPress set of keyboard shortcuts, you might want to create a copy and modify some of them. For example, you can assign ⌘+K or Ctrl+K to Clear (rather than leave it set to open the Preferences dialog box) because you're accustomed to using it for deleting items. You can also repair the incorrect commands, although in many cases they're assigned to other commands and must be replaced.

However, hiding menu options can be confusing because you may forget that you hide an option and come to believe that the feature does not exist. If you do hide menu options and then want to get them all back, choose Window ⇨ Workspace ⇨ Show Full Menus. Do note that this option affects only the current workspace; if you switch workspaces, you won't see full menus in the new workspace unless you choose Window ⇨ Workspace ⇨ Show Full Menus again there.

InDesign CS4 also lets you turn on all options individually for each menu that has been hidden; the Show All Menu Items option will appear at the bottom of a menu if any menu options are hidden.

CAUTION   Changing menus can be a bad idea. You might forget about a feature that you later want to use, for example. People sharing a computer may get confused when the interface looks different than they are used to and they can't find the commands they're used to.

If you do decide to customize your menus, the process is simple:

1. **Choose Edit ⇨ Menus to open the Menu Customization dialog box shown in Figure 3.21.**

2. **Using the Category pop-up menu, select the category of menu you want to modify: Application Menus or Context & Panel Menus.**

3. **In the list of application menu commands that displays, choose the menu option you want to show or hide, or color.** Click the eye icon in the Visibility column to remove a menu option (the icon goes blank); to restore a menu option, click a blank icon in the Visibility column (the icon becomes an eye). You can also give the menu item a color background by choosing a color in the Color column's pop-up menus. Note that to access submenus, you click the right-pointing triangle to the left of a menu's name to expand the list of submenu options.

4. **When you're done, click Save As.** Then enter a name in the Save Menu Set dialog box and click OK.

5. **When you're done changing menus, click OK to return to InDesign.**

FIGURE 3.21

The Menu Customization dialog box

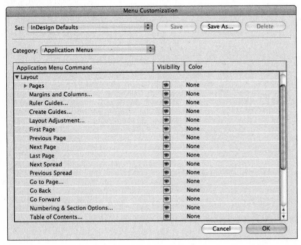

To modify an existing customized menu set, choose it from the Set pop-up menu, make your changes as described previously, and click Save when done. Similarly, to delete a set, choose it from the Set pop-up menu and then click Delete.

To reset InDesign to use the standard menus, choose Window ⇨ Arrange ⇨ Reset Menus.

Workspaces

To try to gain some control over InDesign's panel profligacy, you can create *workspaces,* which are essentially memorized panel collections. First, display the panels you want, where you want them. Then customize menus as desired (see the previous section of this chapter). Now you create a new workspace by choosing Window ➪ Workspace ➪ New Workspace. The New Workspace dialog box will let you name the workspace, as well as give you options to save the panel locations and menu commands:

- If you don't choose the Panel Locations option, the new workspace will remember which panels you added, rearranged, and removed, but not their location on the screen. If you don't choose the Menu Commands option, the new workspace will not save with it any menu changes.

- When you name the workspace, be sure to give it a name that makes sense, such as Text Panels. That new workspace is now available by clicking Window ➪ Workspace ➪ *workspace name.*

By having several such workspaces, you can quickly switch among collections of panels based on the tasks you're focused on.

InDesign comes with several predefined workspaces, whose names are in brackets so that you know they are the predefined ones. When you first launch InDesign, the limited [Essentials] workspace is used.

Note that you cannot edit the predefined workspaces, but if you make changes — such as turning on full menus, adding or moving panels, or editing menus — they will stick until you choose Window ➪ Workspace ➪ Reset *workspace name.* For workspaces you create, your changes also stick until you reset them. The difference is that you can save changes to any workspaces you create by choosing Window ➪ Workspace ➪ New, giving the modified workspace the same name as the original version, and clicking OK; if you confirm that you want to replace the original workspace with the new one, InDesign will update that workspace.

NEW FEATURE   **You can select workspaces not only from the Window menu's Workspace submenu but also via the Workspaces iconic pop-up menu on the application bar. InDesign has more predefined workspaces than before.**

Workspaces now save not only the locations of open and docked panels but also any custom menus in effect when you created the workspace.

NOTE   **The new [Essentials] default workspace hides too many features to be used in a professional setting. I recommend you use the [Advanced] workspace instead, or create your own custom workspace.**

To delete a custom workspace, choose Window ➪ Workspace ➪ Delete Workspace. You'll get a dialog box that asks which workspace to delete.

Color management settings

You can customize the way color management works in InDesign and across Adobe Creative Suite applications. The Color Settings dialog box (choose Edit ➪ Color Settings) lets you customize the default color transformations used for viewing and outputting colors.

CROSS-REF   See Chapter 28 for details on color management and how to set the defaults.

Modifying Defaults for Documents, Text, and Objects

When you create a new document, start typing, or create a new object, it is based on default settings that you can change. For example, by default, a new document is always letter-sized, but if you design only CD covers, you can change the default.

You may need to work with InDesign for a while to determine which of these settings to change and which settings you prefer. When you identify a problem — for example, you realize that you always end up changing the inset for text frames — jot down a note about it or close all documents right then. When no documents are open, change the setting for all future documents.

Document defaults

You can modify the default size, margins, and columns in new documents; the default attributes of guides; and the way layouts are adjusted. To modify document defaults, choose the following with no documents open:

- **File ➪ Document Setup (Option+⌘+P or Ctrl+Alt+P):** The Document Setup dialog box, shown in Figure 3.22, lets you modify the default settings in the New Document dialog box for the Number of Pages, Page Size, Facing Pages, and Master Text Frame, as well as for bleeds and slugs if you click the More Options button. (When you click More Options, the Bleeds and Slugs area appears, and the button changes to Fewer Options, as shown in the figure.)

- **Layout ➪ Margins and Columns:** The Margins and Columns dialog box, shown in Figure 3.22, lets you modify the default settings in the New Document dialog box for the Margins and Columns areas.

- **Layout ➪ Ruler Guides:** This adjusts the View Threshold and Color for all new guides. It opens the Ruler Guides dialog box, which is shown in Figure 3.22.

- **Layout ➪ Layout Adjustment:** The Layout Adjustment dialog box, shown in Figure 3.23, lets you resize entire layouts and customize how they are resized.

When no documents are open, the Document Setup dialog box (left) lets you customize default settings in the New Document dialog box. Use the Margins and Columns dialog box (upper right) when no documents are open to establish default margins and columns. And when no documents are open, the Ruler Guides dialog box (lower right) lets you customize default settings for ruler display.

Use the Layout Adjustment dialog box when no documents are open to establish default layout-adjustment settings.

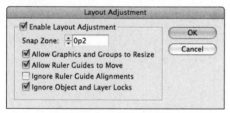

Text defaults

When you start typing in a new text frame, the text is formatted with default character formats, paragraph formats, and s tory attributes. You can also choose to show invisible characters such as spaces and tabs by default; otherwise you need to activate their display in each text-heavy document. To modify text defaults, choose:

- **Type ⇨ Character (⌘+T or Ctrl+T):** Select default options for character formats such as font, size, and leading from the Character panel. (You can also choose Window ⇨ Type & Tables ⇨ Character.)

- **Type ⇨ Paragraph (Option+⌘+T or Ctrl+Alt+T):** Select defaults for paragraph formats such as alignment, indents, spacing, and so on from the Paragraph panel. (You can also choose Window ⇨ Type & Tables ⇨ Paragraph.)

- **Type ⇨ Paragraph Styles (⌘+F11 or Ctrl+F11):** Select defaults for the [Basic Paragraph] style, which is what all unstyled imported text, as well as text typed in a new text frame in InDesign, will use. (You can also choose Window ⇨ Type & Tables ⇨ Paragraph Styles.)

- **Type ⇨ Story:** This lets you activate Optical Margin Alignment. Because Optical Margin Alignment works best for display type rather than body type, it's unlikely that you'll make Optical Margin Alignment your default setting. (You can also choose Window ⇨ Type & Tables ⇨ Story.)

- **Type ⇨ Show Hidden Characters (⌘+Option+I or Ctrl+Alt+I):** Select this option if you often edit in InDesign and always end up turning on Show Hidden Characters.

You can also edit the spelling and hyphenation dictionaries while no documents are open by choosing Edit ⇨ Spelling ⇨ Dictionary. However, because all the edits are saved in the same file, it doesn't matter whether documents are open.

Object defaults

When you create new objects, they're based on some default settings. For example, you can specify how text wraps around objects. To modify object defaults, use the following commands:

- **Object ⇨ Text Frame Options (⌘+B or Ctrl+B):** The Text Frame Options dialog box lets you specify the default Columns, Inset Spacing, First Baseline, and Ignore Text Wrap settings for new text frames.

- **Window ⇨ Object Styles (⌘+F7 or Ctrl+F7):** Select defaults for the [Normal Graphics Frame] and [Normal Text Frame] object styles, which are what all new frames created in InDesign use.

- **Window ⇨ Text Wrap (⌘+Option+W or Ctrl+Alt+W):** The Text Wrap panel lets you specify how text wraps around all new objects.

- **Object ⇨ Corner Options (⌘+Option+R or Ctrl+Alt+R):** The Corner Options dialog box lets you choose a style for the corners of all new frames except those created with the Type tool.

- **Object ⇨ Clipping Path (Option+Shift+⌘+K or Ctrl+Alt+Shift+K):** The Clipping Path dialog box lets you specify the default attributes of clipping paths imported into graphics frames.

- **Window ⇨ Stroke (⌘+F10 or Ctrl+F10), Window ⇨ Swatches (F5), Window ⇨ Gradient (F6), and Window ⇨ Attributes:** These panels let you specify other default properties of objects. For example, if all objects you create are stroked (framed), specify a weight in the Stroke panel.

- **Double-click the Polygon tool or Polygon Frame to open the Polygon Settings dialog box (there is no menu command or keyboard shortcut):** This lets you specify the default number of sides and the inset for the first new polygon in a new document. Note that you can set the two tools differently, letting you have two types of polygons remembered for you.

Modifying Defaults for Views

Another way to customize your copy of InDesign is to specify which layout tools appear by default. The lower two-thirds of the View menu, shown in Figure 3.24, let you do this. If you'd prefer not to view the edges of frames, you can hide them by default. Or if you always want to start with a document-wide grid, you can show it by default. To modify viewing defaults, choose the appropriate menu options. Note that the menu names toggle between Show and Hide each time you select them. (Therefore, if the menu option begins with Hide, it means that attribute is currently being displayed; if it starts with Show, it means the attribute is currently not being displayed.)

FIGURE 3.24

The View menu commands that are available when no documents are open

- **View ⇨ Show/Hide Text Threads (Option+⌘+Y or Ctrl+Alt+Y):** This shows or hides the links between text frames.

- **View ⇨ Show/Hide Frame Edges (Control+⌘+H or Ctrl+H):** This shows or hides the edges of frames.

- **View ▷ Show/Hide Rulers (⌘+R or Ctrl+R):** This shows or hides the horizontal and vertical ruler.

- **View ▷ Grids & Guides ▷ Show/Hide Guides (⌘+; [semicolon] or Ctrl+; [semicolon]):** This shows or hides margin, column, and layout guides.

- **View ▷ Grids & Guides ▷ Show/Hide Baseline Grid (Option+⌘+' [apostrophe] or Ctrl+Alt+' [apostrophe]):** This shows or hides the baseline grid established in the Grids pane of the Preferences dialog box. You can access this pane on a Mac by choosing InDesign ▷ Preferences ▷ Grids or pressing ⌘+K; choose Edit ▷ Preferences ▷ Grids or press Ctrl+K in Windows.

- **View ▷ Grids & Guides ▷ Show/Hide Document Grid (⌘+' [apostrophe] or Ctrl+' [apostrophe]):** This shows or hides the document-wide grid established in the Grids pane of the Preferences dialog box.

In addition to changing which layout tools appear by default, you can control some of their default behavior. Choose the appropriate menu options to select or deselect them. Note that if the menu option is currently selected, a check mark appears next to its name, in which case choosing it again deselects the option and the check mark disappears.

- **View ▷ Grids & Guides ▷ Lock Guides (Option+⌘+; [semicolon] or Ctrl+Alt+; [semicolon]):** Disabled by default; when you choose this option to enable it, all ruler guides are locked in place.

- **View ▷ Grids & Guides ▷ Lock Column Guides:** Enabled by default; when you choose this option to disable it, all column guides are no longer locked in place.

- **View ▷ Grids & Guides ▷ Snap to Guides (Shift+⌘+; [semicolon] or Ctrl+Shift+; [semicolon]):** Enabled by default; when you choose this option to disable it, aligning objects with guides is more difficult, but positioning objects near guides is easier.

- **View ▷ Grids & Guides ▷ Snap to Document Grid:** Disabled by default; when you choose this option to enable it, objects are easy to align with document grid lines whether or not they're showing.

- **View ▷ Grids & Guides ▷ Smart Guides (⌘+U or Ctrl+U):** Enabled by default, this new option provides visual feedback to help you size, align, and rotate objects via the mouse, as Chapter 6 explains.

CROSS-REF Chapter 6 covers how to use guides and grids in your layout. Chapter 9 covers the new smart guides feature,

Setting Color and Style Defaults

If you find yourself creating the same colors, paragraph styles, character styles, table styles, cell styles, and/or object styles over and over again, create them with no documents open. They will be available to all future documents. To create these elements, use the New command in the flyout menus for the following panels: Swatches (F5), Character Styles (Shift+⌘+F11 or Ctrl+Shift+F11), Paragraph Styles (⌘+F11 or Ctrl+F11), Table Styles, Cell Styles, and Object Styles (⌘+F7 or

Ctrl+F7). You can also use the flyout menus' Load commands to import colors and styles from existing documents instead of creating them from scratch.

Reverting Preferences and Defaults

If you inherit a copy of InDesign from another user, or if you've been changing preferences and defaults at random and are unhappy with the results, you can revert InDesign to all its default settings. You particularly want to do this if you're learning InDesign using tutorial files or in a class setting.

> **TIP** To revert all preferences and defaults, deleting the InDesign Defaults preference files when opening InDesign, press Control+Option+Shift+⌘ or Ctrl+Alt+Shift when launching InDesign.

> **NOTE** Keep in mind that you need to re-enable any custom keyboard shortcut set you were using by choosing it from the Set pop-up menu in the Keyboard Shortcuts dialog box (choose Edit ⇨ Keyboard Shortcuts).

Changing Views

Customizing also involves the way you look at your work. InDesign provides a variety of options for magnifying and displaying your work. Understanding these ahead of time and memorizing the ones that work best for your type of work, your eyesight, and your monitor can help you get started with InDesign.

Desktop-publishing pioneers in the late 1980s often worked on publications using 9-inch black-and-white monitors, and they spent as much time zooming in, zooming out, and pushing oversized pages around on undersized screens as they did formatting text and modifying graphics. The best present you could give yourself — or your employer could give you — is a large monitor (two large monitors aren't bad, either). In this era of proliferating panels, there's no such thing as too much screen space. But even if you have a huge monitor, you're going to find yourself zooming in and out and using InDesign's other display-related features to control what you see on-screen and help you work more efficiently.

Zooming and scrolling

When you begin building a page, it's often easiest to display the entire page (choose View ⇨ Fit Page in Window or press ⌘+0 or Ctrl+0) or spread (choose View ⇨ Fit Spread in Window or press Option+⌘+0 or Ctrl+Alt+0) — note the use of the numeral 0, not the letter O, in the shortcuts — and work somewhat roughly — creating the required objects and positioning them more or less where you want them. After you add text and graphics to your frames, you probably want to begin polishing the page by modifying individual objects. At this point, seeing a reduced view of an entire page or spread isn't the best way to work. If you need to work on details, it's best to pull out a magnifying glass. With InDesign, this means tapping into the program's view-magnification capabilities.

Using Gestures on a Multi-Touch Trackpad

If you use a MacBook Air or a 2008-or-newer-model MacBook Pro, you can use gestures on its Multi-Touch trackpad (first introduced in the iPhone) to navigate your document in InDesign CS4. (If Apple adds the Multi-Touch to other Macs in the future, they also would support these gestures in InDesign.) There are three navigation actions you can do via gestures on these computers:

- **Zoom in or out:** Use the pinch gesture (two fingertips moving closer) to zoom in and the expand gesture (two fingers moving apart) to zoom out.

- **Rotate:** Use the rotate gesture (twisting two fingertips clockwise or counterclockwise) to rotate selected objects. If no objects are selected, your pasteboard is rotated in 90-degree increments.

- **Scroll:** To scroll from one page to the next, use the swipe gesture (drag three fingertips from right to left); to scroll to the previous page, swipe from left to right. (This gesture acts as if you were pressing PageUp and PageDown keys.)

Remember: To use gestures, you place the number of fingertips indicated on the touchpad and then move them as described.

You can zoom in to magnifications up to 4,000 percent and zoom out to magnifications as small as 10 percent. Like many other features, you have several options for changing view magnification. You can zoom in and out using:

- The Zoom tool
- The zoom commands in the View menu
- The Zoom pop-up menu or the accompanying box in the left side of the application bar (see Chapter 2)

The Zoom tool

If you're the type of designer who prefers the click-and-drag solution when it's available, you probably want to use the Zoom tool to enlarge a portion of a page. Here's how it works:

1. **Select the Zoom tool or press Z if the Type tool is not selected.**

2. At this point you have two options:

   - **You can move the Zoom pointer over the area you want to see and click the mouse.** Each click enlarges the view to the next preset magnification percentage. (To display these percentages, click the pop-up menu next to the Zoom field at the bottom-left corner of the document window.)

   - **You can click and drag a rectangle that encloses the area you want to see.** When you release the mouse, the area is centered in the document window. (When you hold Option or Alt, the plus sign in the Zoom pointer changes to a minus sign. Clicking or clicking and dragging in this situation zooms out instead of in.)

TIP   You never have to actually select the Zoom tool. Instead, use its keyboard shortcuts: ⌘+spacebar or Ctrl+spacebar (for zooming in) and ⌘+Option+spacebar or
Ctrl+Alt+spacebar (for zooming out).

Zoom options in the View menu

The third group of commands in the View menu, shown earlier in Figure 3.24, lets you change the view magnification. Here's a brief description of each command:

- **Zoom In (⌘+= or Ctrl+=):** This enlarges the display magnification to the next higher percentage. (When no objects are active, the Zoom In command is also available in the contextual menu.)

- **Zoom Out (⌘+− [hyphen] or Ctrl+− [hyphen]):** This reduces the display magnification to the next lower percentage. (When no objects are active, the Zoom Out command is also available in the contextual menu.)

TIP   If an object is active when you choose Zoom In or Zoom Out or use the Zoom field
or pop-up menu, the object is centered in the document window after the view
changes.

- **Fit Page in Window (⌘+0 [zero] or Ctrl+0 [zero]):** This reduces or enlarges the display magnification of the currently displayed page (the current page number is displayed in the page number field at the lower left of a document window) so that the entire page is visible (and centered) in the document window.

- **Fit Spread in Window (Option+⌘+0 [zero] or Ctrl+Alt+0 [zero]):** This is similar to Fit Page in Window, except you use it if you're working on a facing-page document and want the entire spread to be on-screen.

- **Actual Size (⌘+1 or Ctrl+1):** This displays the document at 100 percent magnification. When you choose Actual Size, a pica is a pica and an inch is an inch — if your monitor is appropriately configured.

TIP   Double-clicking the Zoom tool is the same as choosing View ⇨ Actual Size; it displays a document at 100 percent magnification.

- **Entire Pasteboard (Option+Shift+⌘+0 [zero] or Ctrl+Alt+Shift+0 [zero]):** This reduces the display magnification so that the current page or spread and its surrounding pasteboard are visible within the document window.

TIP   To switch back and forth between the last two magnification percentages, press
Option+⌘+2 or Ctrl+Alt+2.

The Zoom field and pop-up menu

The Zoom field in the application bar and its accompanying Zoom pop-up menu, shown in Figure 3.25, offer two additional methods for changing display magnification. To use the field, simply type a value between 5 percent and 4,000 percent and then press Return or Enter. To use the pop-up menu, click the arrow and then choose one of the preset magnification values.

FIGURE 3.25

The Zoom field and the Zoom pop-up menu

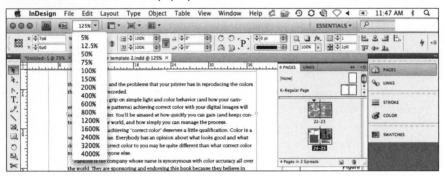

The Hand tool

Sometimes after you've zoomed in to work on a particular object, you want to work on a portion of the page that's not currently displayed. You can always zoom out and then use the Zoom tool or the Zoom commands to zoom back in, or you can "push" the page around within the window until you can see the portion of the page you want to work on. To scroll, you can use the scroll bars and boxes on the right and bottom of the document window, or you can use the Hand tool (press H if the Type tool is not selected). Simply select it and then click and drag to move the currently displayed page or spread around within the document window. When you can see what you want, release the mouse.

TIP   To temporarily access the Hand tool when the Type tool is not selected, press the spacebar. The hand pointer appears. Click and drag to move the page within the document window. (This is one of InDesign's most useful keyboard shortcuts!)

The quick zoom function

For a quick way to pan through your document, you can use the new quick zoom feature. First, make sure the Hand tool is active. Then click and hold the mouse. InDesign will zoom out and display a red rectangle, as Figure 3.26 shows. If you move the mouse, InDesign CS4 stops zooming and instead lets you move the rectangle to a new area of focus. Let go to have InDesign display that part of the document back at the original zoom setting. If the autozoom is too fast, you can use the up and down arrow keys instead to manually move through various zoom levels. And if you decide you've navigated some place you didn't mean to, just press Esc — as long as the mouse is still pressed — to start over.

NEW FEATURE   This new quick zoom function replaces previous versions' Navigator panel and its features.

FIGURE 3.26

The quick zoom function

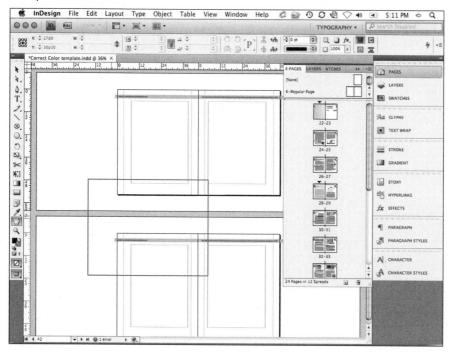

Object display options

Generally, you're going to want to display the objects you've placed on your pages. After all, what's displayed on-screen is what gets printed, right? Not exactly. For example, text and graphic frames are displayed on-screen with blue borders, even if they're empty, but the borders don't print. In addition to the six zoom commands (covered earlier in this chapter), there are two other commands that affect how objects appear:

■ **View ⇨ Show/Hide Frame Edges (Control+⌘+H or Ctrl+H):** When you click Hide Frame Edges, text and graphics frames are not displayed with a blue border. Additionally, an *X* does not appear in empty graphics frames when frame edges are hidden. You might want to hide frame edges to see how a page will look when printed.

TIP When you move an object by clicking and dragging, you have the choice of displaying the entire object (including the contents of a frame) or displaying only the bounding box. If you begin dragging immediately after clicking to select an object, only the bounding box appears as you drag. If you pause after clicking an object until the stem of the arrow pointer disappears and then begin dragging, the entire object appears.

- **In the Pages panel's flyout menu, choose View ➪ Show/Hide Master Items.** When you choose Show Master Items, any objects on the currently displayed document page's master page appear. When you choose Hide Master Items, master objects on the currently displayed page are hidden. This command is page-specific, so you can show or hide master objects on a page-by-page basis.

Summary

InDesign provides extensive controls for setting preferences for everything from how objects appear on-screen and how text spelling and hyphenation are managed to how keyboard shortcuts work and how color is handled. You can also reset all preference changes to their defaults with just one command.

Part II

Document Fundamentals

Chapter 4

Creating, Opening, and Saving Documents

You're pumped up. You've purchased a copy of InDesign, installed it, checked out the interface, and now you're ready to put the program to work. So, what's next? Launch the application and start clicking? Hardly. Creating a publication with InDesign is much like going on a trip. You don't reach your destination unless you've prepared a plan for getting there. And you reach your destination more quickly and more easily if your plan is a sound one.

Remember, too, that most trips don't go exactly according to plan. InDesign is both versatile and forgiving. As you create a publication, you should feel free to change your mind, experiment, and let your creativity roam. As long as you reach your destination (on time!), taking a few detours is acceptable, and encountering a few roadblocks (small ones, you hope) is inevitable.

IN THIS CHAPTER

Planning a publication

Creating a new document

Opening native and foreign documents and templates

Saving documents and templates

Exporting documents and document elements

Taking Stock before You Begin

Before you launch InDesign, open a new document, and begin working, you must answer several fundamental questions about the publication you are producing:

- What is the basic nature of the piece? Will it be printed, or will it be distributed over the Internet or an intranet? Is it going to be published as a print, PDF, Flash, or Web piece, or perhaps in several formats?

- What are its dimensions?

- How many pages will it have? If it will be a multipage publication, will it have facing pages like a book or a catalog, or will it be single-sided like a flip chart?

- How many columns will each page have? How wide will the margins be?

- Does the budget allow for the use of color? If so, how many colors? What kind of paper will it be printed on? What kind of printer or printing press will be used?

- How will the publication be distributed? Under what circumstances will it be read? What's the life expectancy of the publication?

- If the publication is bound for the Internet, will you create an HTML file (which can be viewed by anybody with a Web browser), as a Flash presentation (which will require further work in Adobe Flash Professional and require users to have the free Adobe Flash viewer application or browser plug-in), or a PDF file (which requires viewers to have the free Adobe Reader application or browser plug-in)?

- And what about the content of your publication? What programs were used to create the text files and graphic files your publication will contain? Did you create the content yourself, or did others? What file formats were used for text and graphic files? What is the most effective way to present the content given the production requirements and budget?

As you answer these questions, a rough image of your publication begins to take shape in your mind. When you're ready to begin turning your ideas into an actual publication, you have a couple of choices. Many designers whose skills date back to the days of traditional paste-up still prefer to use traditional tools — a drawing pad and colored markers or pencils in this case — to create rough sketches before they fire up their page-layout or illustration program. Other designers who were never exposed to such archaic tools are comfortable doing their brainstorming and sketching on the fly, using their favorite software. Whatever method suits you is fine. Keep in mind that, at this early stage, you shouldn't be spending much time fine-tuning details. You can do that later with InDesign.

An overly careful person can plan forever, in which case, nothing actually gets done. At some point, when the image you have of the publication you're creating is clear enough in your mind to begin work, it's time to create a new InDesign document.

Setting Up a New Publication

After you launch InDesign, you have two options: You can choose the Open command (choose File ➪ Open or press ⌘+O or Ctrl+O) to open a previously created document or template (more on opening documents and templates later in this chapter), or you can choose File ➪ New ➪ Document or press ⌘+N or Ctrl+N to create a new document.

When you create a new document, the New Document dialog box, shown in Figure 4.1, appears. It is here that you implement many of the decisions, including page size, number of pages, number of columns, and margin width you arrived at during the planning stage. Although you're free to change your mind later, you save yourself time and potential headaches by sticking with the basic page parameters you establish in the New Document dialog box.

FIGURE 4.1

The settings you make in the New Document dialog box establish the basic framework for the pages in your publication. This example shows the settings used to create a 48p9-x-65p3 (8⅛-x10⅞-inch) magazine page.

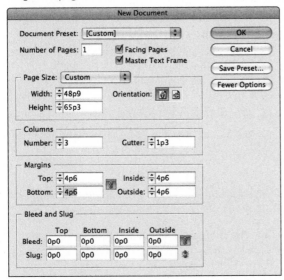

> **TIP**   To change the measurement units displayed in the New Document dialog box, choose InDesign ⇨ Preferences ⇨ Units & Increments or press ⌘+K on the Mac, or choose Edit ⇨ Preferences ⇨ Units & Increments or press Ctrl+K in Windows. Next, choose the measurement system you want from the Horizontal and Vertical pop-up menus in the Ruler Units area. If you change preferences when no documents are open, your changes are applied to all subsequently created documents.

Creating new documents

Here's how to create a new document:

1. **Choose File ⇨ New ⇨ Document or press ⌘+N or Ctrl+N.**

2. **If you know exactly how many pages your publication will have, type the number in the Number of Pages field.** If you don't know for sure, you can always add or delete pages later as needed.

3. **Select the Facing Pages option if you're creating a multipage publication that will have a spine, such as a book, catalog, or magazine.** You do not need to select this option if you're creating a one-page document, such as a business card, an ad, or a poster. Some publications, such as flip charts, presentations, and three-ring bound documents, have multiple pages but use only one side of the page. For such documents, don't select the Facing Pages option, either.

4. **If you want to flow text from page to page in a multipage document, such as a book or a catalog, select the Master Text Frame option.** (See Chapter 14 for more information on using master text frames.) When you select this option, InDesign automatically adds a text frame to the document's master page and to all document pages based on this master page. This saves you the work of creating a text box on each page and manually threading text through each frame.

5. **In the Page Size area, you can choose one of the predefined sizes from the pop-up menu.** Your options are Letter (8.5" × 11"), Legal (8.5" × 14"), Tabloid (11" × 17"), Letter Half (5.5" × 8.5"), Legal Half (7" × 8.5"), A4 (210mm × 297mm), A3 (297mm × 420mm), A5 (148mm × 210mm), B5 (176mm × 250mm), Compact Disc (4.7222" × 4.5"), eight variations of Web page sizes, or Custom. Other options may appear in this menu if you've defined your own page sizes as described in Chapter 3.

NEW FEATURE   The eight Web-page sizes — 600×300, 640×480, 760×420, 800×600, 984×588, 1024×768, 1240×620, and 1280×800 points — are new to InDesign CS4. Pity, no iPhone page size (240×416 points).

TIP   For the purposes of InDesign page dimensions, you can think of a pixel as equivalent to a point, so specify Web-oriented page sizes in points in InDesign.

If you choose Custom as the page size, you can type values in the Width and Height fields. But you don't have to actually choose Custom: No matter what page size is selected, if you type values in those fields, the Page Size automatically changes to Custom. The minimum height and width is 1 pica (0.1667"); the maximum is 216". Clicking the Portrait iconic button next to Orientation produces a vertical page (the larger of the Height and Width values is used in the Height field); clicking the Landscape iconic button produces a horizontal page (the larger of the Height and Width values is used in the Width field). You can also specify Height and Width values by clicking the up and down arrows associated with these fields.

TIP   When you specify page size, make sure the values you type in the Height and Width fields are the size of the final printed piece — and not the size of the paper in your printer. For example, if you're creating a standard-sized business card, type 3.5i in the Width field and 2i in the Height field.

TIP   If you want to print *n*-up — meaning several "pages" on one sheet, such as several business cards on an 8½-×-11-inch sheet of paper — you can create a letter-sized document (8.5" × 11"), but you have to arrange the business cards within the page boundary and add your own crop marks for each card.

6. **Specify margin values in the Margins area.** The *margin* is the white area around the outside of the page within which page elements — text and graphics — are placed. A document doesn't have to have margins (you can type **0** into these fields), and if you want, you can place text and graphics in the margin area. If the Facing Pages option is selected, Inside and Outside fields are available in the Margins area. Designers often specify larger inside margins for multipage publications to accommodate the fold at the spine. If Facing Pages is not selected, Left and Right fields replace the Inside and Outside fields. You can also specify margin values by clicking the up or down arrows associated with the fields.

7. **Type a value in the Columns field to specify how many columns your pages have.** You can also specify the number of columns by clicking the up or down arrow associated with the Column field.

8. **Specify a gutter distance (the gutter is the space between columns) in the Gutter field.** You can also specify a gutter width value by clicking the up and down arrows associated with the Gutter field.

9. **If you click More Options, the Bleed and Slug area of the New Document dialog box appears (refer to Figure 4.1), and the More Options button changes to Fewer Options.** The More Options button expands the dialog box to provide options to set bleed and slug areas. (The button then changes to Fewer Options, which if clicked hides the Bleed and Slug area.) A *bleed area* is a margin on the outside of the page for objects you want to extend past the edge of the page — you want them to extend at least $1/8$ inch so if there is any shifting of the paper during printing, there's no white space where the image should be (touching the edge of the page). The *slug area* is an area reserved for printing crop marks, color plate names, and other printing information — some output devices cut these off during printing unless a slug area is defined. For both bleed and slug areas, you can set the top, bottom, left, and right margins independently.

10. **Click OK to close the New Document dialog box.** When you do, your new, blank document appears in a new document window. Figure 4.2 shows the window of a newly created document that uses the settings shown in Figure 4.1. Note how the zoom level displays both in the Zoom field in the application bar and after the name of the document in the document tab.

TIP   **You can bypass the New Document dialog box by pressing Shift+⌘+N or Ctrl+Shift+N. When you use this method, the most recent settings in the New Document dialog box are used for the new document.**

FIGURE 4.2

The magazine page settings in the New Document dialog box shown in Figure 4.1
resulted in the document you see here.

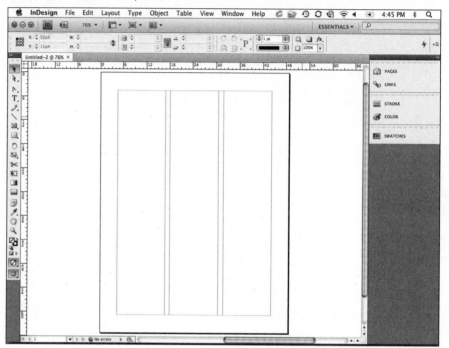

Creating your own document types

InDesign lets you create predefined document types, called *document presets*, to supplement the
standard ones such as Letter. Note that a preset is much more than a saved page size; it also
includes margins, columns, and the other setting specified in the New Document dialog box.

There are two ways to create document presets:

- You can save these new-document settings by clicking Save Preset in the New Document
  dialog box. These saved settings appear in the Document Style pop-up menu in the future.
- You can choose File ⇨ Document Presets ⇨ Define to create (by clicking New) a new document style or import (by clicking Load) one from another document. It opens the dialog
  box shown in Figure 4.3. When you create a new preset, or edit an existing one, you get
  a dialog box that essentially matches the New Document Setup dialog box, shown earlier
  in Figure 4.1. Modify the settings as desired and click OK to return to the Document
  Presets dialog box.

FIGURE 4.3

The Document Presets dialog box lets you create, import, edit, and delete document styles.

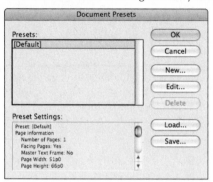

Opening Documents and Templates

Opening documents with InDesign is pretty much the same as opening documents with any program. Simply choose File ⇨ Open or press ⌘+O or Ctrl+O, locate and click the document on which you want to work, and then click Open. But InDesign offers a few options for opening documents you don't find in every program. For example, you can:

- Open more than one document at a time.

- Open a copy of a document instead of the original. This keeps you from overwriting the original file accidentally — very helpful if you're making several variations of one document.

- Open a template under its own name. This makes editing templates easier than it is with other programs, specifically QuarkXPress.

- Open documents created with some versions of PageMaker and QuarkXPress: QuarkXPress and QuarkXPress Passport versions 3.3 through 4.1 and PageMaker versions 6.0 through 7.0.

NEW FEATURE InDesign's File menu displays the names of the 10 most recently saved documents in the Open Recent submenu that appears under the Open option in the File menu after you have opened a file. New to InDesign CS4 is the ability to change how many recently saved files are displayed. You can change this number using the Number of Recent Items to Display option in the File Handling pane of the Preferences dialog box (choose InDesign ⇨ Preferences ⇨ File Handling or press ⌘+K on the Mac, or choose Edit ⇨ Preferences ⇨ File Handling or press Ctrl+K in Windows).

To open a file:

1. **Choose File ➪ Open or press ⌘+O or Ctrl+O.** The Open a File dialog box shown in Figure 4.4 appears.

FIGURE 4.4

The Open a File dialog box. When you open a file, you have the option to open it normally (Open Normal/Normal), open the original copy of a template (Open Original/Original), or open a copy of the file (Open Copy/Copy).

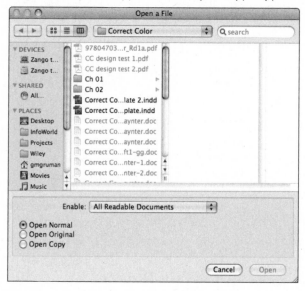

2. **Locate and open the folder that contains the documents you want to open.** Click a filename or press and hold ⌘ or Ctrl and click multiple filenames.

   In Windows, the Files of Type pop-up menu offers several options: PageMaker 6.0–7.0 files, QuarkXPress 3.3–4.1 files, InDesign files, InDesign Interchange, Adobe PDF Creation Settings Files, and All Formats. Choose any of these options to display a specific file format in the file list. (Choose All Files in the Files of Type pop-up menu to display files with no extensions.) Note that InDesign CS4 can open files created by any previous version of InDesign, in addition to CS4-created files. The InDesign Interchange format is a variation of the standard InDesign CS4 format that lets InDesign CS3 read your CS4 files, minus any CS4-specific formatting.

   On a Mac, the Open a File dialog box displays any supported file formats that have filename extension, and the dialog box includes a Preview pane that displays a thumbnail version of the selected file or, more commonly, its icon. (Choose All Documents in the Enable pop-up menu to display files without the filename extensions.)

The name of the pop-up menu for selecting file types differs between the Mac and Windows versions of InDesign, as does the menu option for displaying all files (including those with no filename extensions).

3. **Click Open Normal (Mac) or Normal (Windows) at the bottom of the Open a File dialog box if you want to open the original document (rather than a copy of the document); click Open Copy (Mac) or Copy (Windows) to open a copy of a document.** When you open a copy of a document, it's assigned a default name (Untitled-1, Untitled-2, and so on). If you want to use a template to create a new version of a publication, select Normal; InDesign creates a document based on the template. To open a template under its own name so that you can edit it, click Open Original (Mac) or Original (Windows). Templates are explained in the following section, "Opening documents versus opening templates." (For documents, selecting Open Normal/Normal or Open Original/Original does the same thing: It opens the document for editing.)

4. **Click OK to close the dialog box.** Each document you open appears in a separate document window. The page and view magnification displayed when a document was last saved is used when you open the document.

TIP You can also open an InDesign document or template by double-clicking its file icon. If InDesign is not running, double-clicking a document or template file — as long as it has the proper filename extension (`.indd` for documents and `.indt` for templates) — launches the application and opens the document/template. If InDesign is already running, the document appears in a new window.

Opening documents versus opening templates

Whenever you save a document, you have the option of saving a standard document file or a template (more on saving templates later in this chapter). A *template* is an InDesign file that's used to create multiple iterations of the same publication. For example, if you produce a monthly newsletter, you can save gobs of time and ensure consistency from issue to issue by using a template as the starting point for each edition of the newsletter. A template is essentially the shell of a publication that contains the basic framework — page layout, master pages, styles, and so on — but doesn't contain any actual content.

CROSS-REF For more information about creating templates, see Chapter 6.

When you open a template, you have two choices: You can open a copy of the file and use it to create a new publication, or you can open the original file, make changes, and then save an updated version of the template.

If you want to use a template as the starting point for a new publication, choose File ➪ Open or press ⌘+O or Ctrl+O, locate and select the template, and make sure Open Normal (Mac) or Normal (Windows) is selected in the Open a File dialog box (refer to Figure 4.4) before you click Open.

Displaying Filename Extensions

Both Windows and the Mac OS use icons to show you (and tell programs) what format a file is in. Windows and Mac OS X (but not earlier versions of the Mac OS) use filename extensions to identify the file type. But by default these are hidden from view when you open folders.

InDesign uses the filename extension .indd to denote InDesign documents. Without this filename extension, you won't be able to double-click a file icon to open it, although you can still open the file from InDesign's Open a File dialog box (choose File ⇨ Open or press ⌘+O or Ctrl+O), as long as you select All Documents from the Enable pop-up menu (on the Mac) or All Files from the Files of Type pop-up menu (in Windows). Note that the Place dialog box for importing text and graphics — covered in Chapters 13 and 25 — does not have the Enable pop-up menu on the Mac; InDesign will show all files, even unsupported ones, in this dialog box.

If filename extensions are hidden in Windows XP, open any folder, choose Tools ⇨ Folder Options, and then select the View tab. (You have to have a disk or folder open to have the View menu.) Select the Show Hidden Files and Folders option and then click OK.

In Windows Vista, choose Start ⇨ Computer and then choose Organize ⇨ Folder and Search Options in the dialog box that appears. Go to the View pane and select the Show Hidden Files and Folders option; then click OK.

If filename extensions are hidden in Mac OS X 10.4.8 (Tiger) or Mac OS X 10.5 (Leopard), click Finder ⇨ Preferences, go to the Advanced pane, select the Show All File Extensions option, and close the dialog box. (You have to be using the Finder, not be in an application, to get this menu.)

If you want to modify a template, click Open Original (Mac) or Open (Windows) at the bottom of the dialog box. If Open Normal (Mac) or Normal (Windows) is selected, clicking Open opens a new document window and assigns the document a default name, Untitled-1, Untitled-2, and so on. If Open Original (Mac) or Original (Windows) is selected, the original file opens and the original name appears in the title bar.

Working with files in the Bridge file system

There's another way to open documents and templates in InDesign CS4: Choose File ⇨ Browse in Bridge or press Option+⌘+O or Ctrl+Alt+O to open documents or templates, or choose File ⇨ New ⇨ Document from Template to open just templates. Choosing either option opens the Adobe Bridge program, shown in Figure 4.5, where you can browse for a file to open.

Bridge is designed to be a central repository for Creative Suite programs and support files, mainly for use in workgroup situations but also as an Adobe-centric alterative to the standard Mac and Windows file systems. Bridge's biggest attraction is that it lets you see previews of and file information for almost all the files types you'd be working with in your layouts. (And Bridge does come with several canned templates created by Adobe that you might want to consider using.)

FIGURE 4.5

You can access files through the Adobe Bridge program, a common file environment for Creative Suite applications.

There's no difference in the documents or templates available via Bridge than those available via the regular Open a File dialog box — it's just a different organizational structure for your files.

If you want to access the template files stored in Bridge's InDesign folder without using Bridge itself, navigate to `Library:Application Support:Adobe:Templates:InDesign` on the Mac, to `Program Files/Common Files/Adobe/Templates/InDesign` in Windows. Of course, if you do prefer to use Bridge to store template files, you use InDesign's regular Save As dialog box, select InDesign CS4 Template as the file format, and navigate to the Bridge application's `InDesign` folder.

You can access Bridge files directly from the Bridge application, using its folder-based interface to find files of interest.

CROSS-REF Most of Bridge's features are oriented to Photoshop users, so chances are you can just ignore Bridge. But it does have some utility in workgroup environments, as I explain in Chapter 34.

Converting documents created with other programs

One of InDesign's hallmarks is its capability to open documents from some versions of QuarkXPress and PageMaker and convert them to InDesign documents. If InDesign comes across any formatting it can't retain from foreign files, it displays an alert (Figure 4.6). It cannot open documents created by Microsoft Publisher or Apple Pages, but Markzware does offer a utility to convert Publisher files to InDesign format. (At press time, no third-party conversion tools were available for Pages files.)

Also, InDesign cannot import PDF files, but it can bring in PDF files as graphics for placement in your document. Chapter 25 covers this process in detail. It can also import PDF job-option files, so you can reuse the same settings already developed for Adobe Acrobat Distiller when you export to PDF, as Chapter 31 covers.

CROSS-REF For links to Markzware and other providers of InDesign tools, visit this book's companion Web site at www.InDesignCentral.com.

CAUTION Because other programs' formats are so different from InDesign's, and their capabilities differ as well, the chances of being able to import a foreign document and have it flawlessly convert to InDesign are small. Use this feature to do the first step in the conversion process, but expect to spend time cleaning up the converted files by hand.

FIGURE 4.6

InDesign shows the Warnings dialog box if there are any conversion issues when importing foreign file formats.

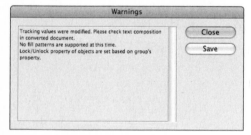

QuarkXPress

InDesign can read QuarkXPress and QuarkXPress Passport files from versions 3.3, 4.0, and 4.1. (Adobe has no plans to support files in the version 5, 6, 7, or 8 formats of QuarkXPress, though Markzware offers a conversion utility for these formats.)

Because there are so many differences between QuarkXPress and InDesign, it's impossible to predict all the conversion issues that may arise. The good news is that a great many things work well, but some don't. Here are some common conversion issues to which you should pay attention:

■ If your QuarkXPress document relies on XTensions (a type of plug-in) to add capabilities (such as table creation), it does not convert correctly into InDesign and may not even import at all. Examples include any documents built with QuarkXPress's indexing and book features.

■ QuarkXPress's leading model is different than InDesign's, so expect leading to sometimes vary significantly, especially if you use additive leading as the automatic leading method in QuarkXPress.

■ InDesign doesn't retain kerning-table adjustments in QuarkXPress files. (It does retain any kerning applied manually.)

■ The customizable dashes in QuarkXPress are converted to solid and dashed lines. (Note that stripes *do* convert properly.)

■ Special gradient blends, such as the diamond pattern, are converted to linear blends or circular blends.

■ Text on a curved path is converted to regular text in a rectangular frame, even though InDesign supports text on paths.

■ H&J sets don't have an equivalent in InDesign, so they do not convert, although any H&J settings are carried over into the converted paragraph styles.

■ Libraries don't convert.

■ Printer styles don't convert.

PageMaker

InDesign can read PageMaker 6.0, 6.5, and 7.0 files. Because PageMaker and InDesign offer many of the same features, there are fewer translation issues between them. Some to take note of include:

■ Fill patterns aren't supported.

■ Libraries won't convert.

■ Printer styles won't convert.

Recovering a document after a crash or power failure

InDesign includes an automatic recovery feature that protects your documents in the event of a power failure or a system crash. As you work on a document, any changes you make after saving it are stored in a separate, temporary file. Under normal circumstances, each time you choose Save, the information in the temporary file is applied to the document. The data in the temporary file is important only if you aren't able to save a document before crashing. A word of warning: Although InDesign's automatic recovery feature is a nice safety net, you should still be careful to save your work often. Here's how it works:

1. **Relaunch InDesign or, if necessary, restart your computer and then launch InDesign.**

2. **If automatic-recovery data is available, InDesign automatically opens the recovered document and displays the word "Recovered" in the document's title bar.** This lets you know that the document contains changes that were not included in the last saved version.

3. If you want to save the recovered data, choose File ➪ Save or press ⌘+S or Ctrl+S; "Recovered" is removed as part of the filename, and InDesign asks whether you want to overwrite the old file. Overwriting the old file is easier than choosing File ➪ Save As or pressing Shift+⌘+S or Ctrl+Shift+S and then typing a name, unless you do want to save a copy of the file in case you want to go back to the old version later. If you want to use the last saved version of the document (and disregard the recovered data), close the file (choose File ➪ Close or press ⌘+W or Ctrl+W) without saving and then open the file (choose File ➪ Open press or ⌘+O or Ctrl+O).

NOTE   Sometimes, InDesign can't automatically recover the documents for you. Instead, it gives you the choice of recovering any files open during a crash or power outage, saving the recovery data for later, or deleting the recovery data. You typically want to recover the files immediately.

Saving Documents and Templates

When you open a new document, it's assigned a default name (Untitled-1, Untitled-2, and so on) and the first page appears in the document window. At this point, you're like a painter standing in front of a blank canvas. But painters don't have to worry about system crashes and power failures; you do. Make sure that when you work on InDesign documents, you follow the first rule of safe computing: Save early and often.

The second group of commands — Close, Save, Save As, Save a Copy, Check In, and Revert — in InDesign's File menu provides options for saving the active/frontmost document. Here's a rundown of what each command does:

- **Close (choose File ➪ Close or press ⌘+W, Ctrl+W, or Ctrl+F4):** This closes the active document. If the document has never been saved or if it's been changed since it was last saved, a dialog box appears that lets you save, close without saving, or cancel and return to the document.

- **Save (choose File ➪ Save or press ⌘+S or Ctrl+S):** This saves changes you've made to the active document since you last saved. If you choose Save for a document that hasn't yet been saved, the Save As dialog box appears. This dialog box lets you name and choose a storage folder for the document.

TIP   If you have more than one document open, you can save the documents all at one time by pressing Option+Shift+⌘+S or Ctrl+Alt+Shift+S.

- **Save As (choose File ➪ Saves As or press Shift+⌘+S or Ctrl+Shift+S):** This lets you save a copy of the active document in a different (or in the same) folder using a different (or the same) name. When you choose Save As and when you choose Save for an unsaved document, the Save As dialog box (see Figure 4.7) appears.

- **Save a Copy (choose File ➪ Close or press Option+⌘+S or Ctrl+Alt+S):** This lets you create a copy of the active document in a different (or in the same) folder using a differ- ent (or the same) name. When you use the Save a Copy command, the original document remains open and retains its original name. It differs from Save As only in that it keeps the original document open.

- **Check In (choose File ⇨ Check In):** This saves the current document as a version within a Version Cue project. This latest save is considered a version of the previously saved file. (See Appendix C for details.)

- **Revert (choose File ⇨ Revert):** This undoes all changes you've made to a document since you last saved it. There is no way to undo this and reinstate all your changes after you revert, so be careful.

FIGURE 4.7

The Save As dialog box.

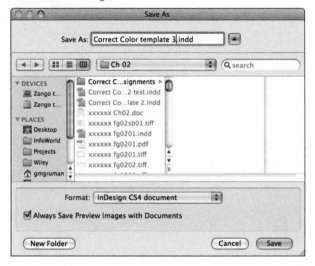

Saving documents versus saving templates

Whenever you save a document for the first time or you use the Save As or Save a Copy command, the Save As dialog box lets you save a standard InDesign document file or a template.

In an ideal world, you would create a finished template, save it, and then open a copy of the template and use it to create an actual publication. In the real world, however, templates are often created by yanking the content out of a finished publication and then saving the gutted file as a template. Regardless of how you create your templates, make sure you remember to select the InDesign CS4 Template option in the Save As dialog box.

 **Where you choose the desired format varies based on the operating system. On the Mac, use the Enable pop-up menu. In Windows, use the Save as Type pop-up menu.**

If you forget to save a document as a template, it opens under its actual name. If you then make any changes and choose File ➪ Save or press ⌘+S or Ctrl+S, the changes are saved with the original document. If this happens, simply save the document again and choose the InDesign CS4 Template option.

> **TIP** Choosing File ➪ Package or pressing Option+Shift+⌘+P or Ctrl+Alt+Shift+P lets you save a copy of a document along with all files — linked graphics, fonts, and ICC color profiles — required to print the document. This feature is particularly handy if you intend to send an InDesign document to an output provider. (See Chapter 29 for more information about the Package command.)

Knowing how to not save changes

As I mentioned earlier in this chapter, InDesign is a very forgiving program. If you make a mistake, change your mind, or work yourself into a complete mess, you don't have to remain in your predicament or save your work. InDesign offers an escape route.

You can revert to your last saved version. To do this, choose File ➪ Revert. This undoes all changes you made since last saving a document. There is no way to undo this and reinstate all your changes after you revert, so be careful.

Saving Files in Other Formats

InDesign's Save, Save As, Save a Copy, and Check In commands let you save documents and templates using InDesign's native file format. The Export command (choose File ➪ Export or press ⌘+E or Ctrl+E) opens the Export dialog box, from which you can save documents and some individual document elements such as stories and graphics in several other formats. And InDesign has separate menu commands for exporting Web and eBook documents, as Chapter 32 explains.

Export formats for whole documents

To export entire documents, InDesign provides the following options (accessed from the Export dialog box unless otherwise indicated):

- **InDesign Interchange format:** This format lets InDesign CS4 save files readable by InDesign both CS3 and CS4, so users of the previous and next versions of InDesign can exchange files. (Therefore, InDesign Interchange CS4 files will be readable by InDesign CS5 as well, and CS5 Interchange files will be readable by InDesign CS4, when InDesign CS5 becomes available.) The trick is to export, not save as, files to the InDesign Interchange format. Interchange files have the filename extension .inx.

- **Production formats.** You can save the document as an EPS or a PDF file for use by prepress tools and service bureaus or for import into other applications as a graphic. You get the choice of exporting individual pages and page ranges, not just the whole document. Choose the Adobe PDF or EPS options in the Format pop-up menu (called Save as Type when you use click Use Adobe Dialog in Windows) in the Export dialog box.

■ **Online formats.** You can save the document in XML format for use in online database-oriented content-management systems by choosing the XML option in the Format pop-up menu (called Save as Type when you use click Use Adobe Dialog in Windows) in the Export dialog box. InDesign CS4 also adds new options in the Export dialog box for exporting to Flash presentation files (SWF) and Flash project files (XFL). You can also export your document to the Web's structured HTML format (XHTML) by choosing File ➪ Export for Dreamweaver. (Despite the menu option's name, any Web browser and most creation tools can work with these exported files). Finally, you can export to the eBook format meant for Web-based distribution of rich-media documents — by choosing File ➪ Export for Digital Editions.

NEW FEATURE The menu options for exporting to HTML and eBook formats have moved into the File menu in InDesign CS4 and have slightly different names than in prior versions. Previously, they had been accessed as submenus when choosing File ➪ Cross-Media Export. Also, the ability to export SWF and XFL files is new to InDesign CS4.

CROSS-REF Chapter 31 covers how to export PDF files. Part VIII covers the creation of interactive PDF and eBook files, how to export to XHTML, eBook, and Flash formats, and how to import, export, and use XML files.

Export formats for document elements

You can also export pieces of your document, such as text files and graphics. Be sure to select the objects (use the Type tool for text and the Direct Selection tool for graphics) and then choose the appropriate options from the Export dialog box (choose File ➪ Export or press ⌘+E or Ctrl+E):

■ **Word processing formats.** If you place the text cursor into a story, you can export its text (select a range of text if you want to export only that selection) into one of three formats: RTF (Rich Text Format) for import into word processors with only basic formatting retained and Text Only for import into word processors that don't support RTF (no formatting is retained). You can also export selected stories to the InCopy or InCopy CS format, for use in that add-on program (see Chapter 35); exported stories appear in the Assignments panel.

NOTE If you need to export several stories from the same document, it's better to use the Assignments panel to create an assignment file that contains multiple stories, as described in Chapter 35. If you export multiple stories to one of the InCopy formats in the Export dialog box, each story is exported to its own file — and that can create a confusing number of files.

■ **InDesign Tagged Text format.** Whether you select text using the Type tool, you can save the story in the InDesign Tagged Text format (for editing in a word processor and later reimporting into InDesign with all InDesign formatting retained).

■ **InDesign Markup Language format.** This new format is meant to allow document exchange with future versions of InDesign and with InCopy CS4; developers can also use it to open InDesign files in applications they create.

- **Graphics formats.** You can export individual or multiple graphics as well as entire pages and layouts to the JPG format by choosing the JPEG option in the Export dialog box. You can also export text frames, which convert the exported text to an uneditable image.

- **Animation formats.** You can export InDesign pages and documents as Flash presentations (SWF files) or Flash Pro projects (XFL files) for further work in Adobe Flash Professional.

- **Document snippets.** You can also export selected elements to a snippet file; choose InDesign Snippets from the Export dialog box. A snippet contains all the formatting information and contents for whatever you select, so it can be brought into other layouts completely intact. It's a very handy way to share pieces of your layout with other users and other layouts. You can also simply drag objects from your page to the Mac or Windows desktop to create a snippet; you import snippets by dragging the snippet file (which has the filename extension .inds) into your document from the desktop. (Chapter 9 covers snippets in more detail.)

NEW FEATURE   **The IDML format is new to InDesign CS4. Gone is InDesign CS4 is the ability to export SVG graphics files.**

Working with exported tagged text files

No matter which layout program they use, most people don't use the Tagged Text option because the coding can be tortuous. Because you can't use tagged-text codes with your word processor's formatting, you must code everything with tagged text and save the document as an ASCII file. So why have Tagged Text at all? A good reason is because this format is the one format sure to support all the formatting you do in InDesign as well as make it easy for you to automate the layout of database-derived documents such as catalogs. (See Chapter 22 for details on database publishing.)

The usefulness of Tagged Text is not in creating text for import but in transferring files created in InDesign to another InDesign user (including someone working on another platform) or to a word processor for further work. You can export an InDesign story or piece of selected text in the Tagged Text format and then transfer the exported file to another InDesign user or to a word processor for further editing.

Exporting a Tagged Text file into a word processor makes sense if you want to add or delete text without losing special formatting, such as fonts, kerning, or style tags, that your word processor doesn't support. After you edit the text, you can save the altered file (make sure that it is saved as ASCII text) and reimport it into your InDesign layout.

The best way to understand the Tagged Text format is to export some of your own documents to it, and open the resulting file in a word processor to see how InDesign coded the file. A warning: The Tagged Text format can be complex, especially because most codes have two forms: a short (abbreviated) form and a long (verbose) form; you choose which InDesign form exports from the Export dialog box in InDesign (choose File ➪ Export or press ⌘+E or Ctrl+E, and then choose InDesign Tagged Text as the file format). Note that a Tagged Text file is simply an ASCII text file, so it has the filename extension .txt and uses the standard text-only file icon in Windows and on the Mac.

Here's an example of verbose coding (because the code is so long, I had to add line breaks; slightly indented lines are actually part of the same code segment):

```
<ASCII-WIN>
<DefineParaStyle:Normal=<Nextstyle:Normal><cTypeface:Regular>
    <cSize:10.000000><pHyphenationLadderLimit:0><pHyphenation:0>
    <pHyphenationZone:18.000000><cFont:Times New Roman>
    <cColorTint:100.000000>>
<DefineCharStyle:Default Paragraph Font=<Nextstyle:Default Paragraph
    Font>>
<DefineCharStyle:Hyperlink=<BasedOn:Default Paragraph Font>
    <Nextstyle:Hyperlink><cColor:Blue><cTypeface:Regular>
    <cSize:10.000000><cHorizontalScale:1.000000>
    <cBaselineShift:0.000000><cCase:Normal><cStrokeColor:>
    <cUnderline:1><cFont:Times New Roman><cPosition:Normal>
    <cStrikethru:0><cColorTint:100.000000>>
<ColorTable:=<Black:COLOR:CMYK:Process:0.000000,0.000000,0.000000,1.0
    00000><Blue:COLOR:RGB:Process:0.000000,0.000000,1.000000>>
<ParaStyle:Normal><pHyphenation:1><CharStyle:Default Paragraph Font>
    <CharStyle:><CharStyle:Hyperlink>www.adobe.com<CharStyle:>
    <CharStyle:Default Paragraph Font>. <CharStyle:><pHyphenation:>
```

Here is the same text with abbreviated tags:

```
<ASCII-WIN>
<dps:Normal=<Nextstyle:Normal><ct:Regular><cs:10.000000><phll:0>
    <ph:0><phz:18.000000><cf:Times New Roman><cct:100.000000>>
<dcs:Default Paragraph Font=<Nextstyle:Default Paragraph Font>>
<dcs:Hyperlink=<BasedOn:Default Paragraph Font><Nextstyle:Hyperlink>
    <cc:Blue><ct:Regular><cs:10.000000><chs:1.000000><cbs:0.000000>
    <ccase:Normal><csc:><cu:1><cf:Times New Roman><cp:Normal>
    <cstrike:0><cct:100.000000>>
<ctable:=<Black:COLOR:CMYK:Process:0.000000,0.000000,0.000000,1.00000
    0><Blue:COLOR:RGB:Process:0.000000,0.000000,1.000000>>
<pstyle:Normal><ph:1><cstyle:Default Paragraph Font>
    <cstyle:><cstyle:Hyperlink>www.adobe.com<cstyle:>
    <cstyle:Default Paragraph Font>. <cstyle:><ph:>
```

What does all that coding mean? It's for a one-page document with one frame that has simply one line of text: This is a hyperlink to www.adobe.com. The text is black, except for the Web address, which is in blue underline.

As you can see, there's a lot to Tagged Text codes. InDesign comes with a complete list of codes in a PDF file called Tagged Text.pdf that you can find in the Tagged Text folder within the Adobe Technical Info folder on the InDesign CD-ROM.

In practical terms, you may not mind editing Tagged Text slightly or leaving the tags in a file when you alter the files text. But you're not likely to forgo the friendly formatting available in your word processor and in InDesign to apply Tagged Text coding to everything in your text files.

149

Exporting files as JPEG graphics

The process for exporting to JPEG is simple: Select the objects to export, choose File ⇨ Export, choose the desired format in the Export dialog box, and click Save to get the Export JPEG dialog box (shown in Figure 4.8).

FIGURE 4.8

The Export JPEG dialog box

In the Export section of the Export JPEG dialog box, you choose whether to export the selected graphics, entire pages and page ranges, or the entire document using the controls in the Export area Pages area.

 If you select multiple objects and choose Selection, they will be combined into one graphic in the exported file.

You also can control quality, format, and resolution settings.

Your options (all in the Image area) are the following:

- The Quality pop-up menu lets you control the image quality, with choices of Low, Medium, High, and Maximum. Note that the higher the quality, the less the JPEG image can be compressed.

- The Format Method pop-up menu controls how the JPEG image displays in a browser. The default Baseline option displays the entire image at one time, whereas the Progressive option has it build up line by line — a good option for very large files so that viewers can tell something is happening as the image loads.

- The Resolution field lets you specify the output resolution in dots per inch (dpi); 72 dpi is appropriate for the Web, assuming that the image will be used at the same size, but you should pick a value of 300 for images to be published at the same size in print.

Click Export when done setting these options.

Summary

When you're ready to begin working on a new document, choose File ➪ New ➪ Document or press ⌘+N or Ctrl+N, and then use the controls in the New Document dialog box to specify the page size, margins, column format, and any bleed and slug areas for the document. You can also save these settings for easy future use as document styles from the New Document dialog box.

After opening a new document, choose File ➪ Save or press ⌘+S or Ctrl+S to save a standard InDesign document file or a template file. (A *template* is a preconstructed document that you use to create multiple versions of a publication.) You can choose File ➪ Save As or press Shift+⌘+S or Ctrl+Shift+S to save a copy of the current document, or you can choose File ➪ Revert to discard your most recent round of changes. If you want to work on a document you've previously saved, choose File ➪ Open or press ⌘+O or Ctrl+O.

In addition to opening InDesign documents and templates, you can open QuarkXPress and QuarkXPress Passport 3.3, 4.0, and 4.1 documents, as well as PageMaker 6.0, 6.5, and 7.0 documents. Choosing File ➪ Export or pressing ⌘+E or Ctrl+E lets you save InDesign documents as InDesign Interchange, IDML, EPS, PDF, JPEG, SWF, XFL, and XML formats.

With the InDesign Interchange format, InDesign can export in a format readable by the previous version of InDesign. IDML likewise lets you exchange InDesign documents with future versions of InDesign and with custom programs. You can save entire pages or selected objects as PDF, EPS, SWF, XFL, and XML files for use on the Web (PDF, SWF, XML), or within other graphics (PDF, EPS), layout (PDF, EPS, XML) and Flash files (XFL, SWF. You can export individual objects, groups or objects, individual pages, ranges of pages, or entire documents to the JPEG graphics format.

You can also save individual stories or text selections in RTF, text-only, InCopy, and InDesign Tagged Text formats. You can also export selected objects as snippet files that preserve all content and formatting, making it easy to share elements across documents.

Last, you can create structured HTML files for use in Web creation programs by choosing File ➪ Export for Dreamweaver and rich-media eBook files for the Web by choosing File ➪ Export for Digital Editions.

Chapter 5

Working with Pages and Layers

I't's a rare InDesign user who creates only one-page documents. Even if business cards, ads, and posters are your bread and butter, you'll probably produce at least a few multipage documents. If you plan to create newsletters, newspapers, books, catalogs, or any other such multipage publications, you need to know how to add pages to your document, move pages around if you change your mind, and delete pages if necessary.

In addition to letting you create multipage documents — something that most illustration and image-editing programs don't — InDesign lets you divide multipage documents into independently numbered sections. As documents grow in size, your ability to navigate quickly to the page you want to work on becomes an important consideration. The longer you spend getting to the page you want, the less time you have to work on it. Fortunately, InDesign provides several navigation aids that make it easy to move around on a page or in a document.

Working with Multipage Documents

If you intend to create a multipage document, you should select the Facing Pages option in the New Document dialog box (choose File ➪ New ➪ Document or press ⌘+N or Ctrl+N) when you create the document. You also want to display the Pages panel (choose Window ➪ Pages or press ⌘+F12 or Ctrl+F12), shown in Figure 5.1, because it provides the controls that let you add pages (document and master), delete and move pages, apply master pages to document pages, and navigate through a document.

ROSS-REF For more information about using the Pages panel to work on master pages, see Chapter 6.

IN THIS CHAPTER

Adding, removing, and rearranging document pages

Adjusting page numbers

Working with sections

Navigating through a document and scrolling in a page

Working with transparency, page rotation, and page transitions

Adjusting page layouts and objects

Understanding layers

Creating and managing layers

Working with object on layers

NOTE The overwhelming majority of multipage documents are facing-page publications such as books, catalogs, and magazines. Some exceptions are flip charts, Web pages, and three-hole-punched publications printed on only one side. In this chapter, the figures show examples of a facing-page document. If you're creating a single-sided multipage document, the techniques are the same as for facing-page documents, but the icons in the Pages panel show only single-sided page icons (the icons aren't dog-eared).

FIGURE 5.1

The Pages panel and its flyout menu. This is how the panel looks when you open a new, facing-page document. (Here, it happens to have one page.)

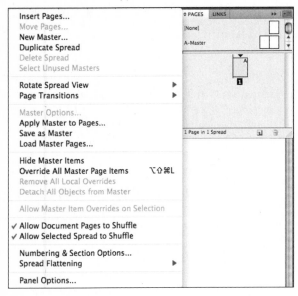

Adding pages

A document can contain as many as 9,999 pages, although you'd never want to create a document nearly that long. In general, try to break up long publications into logical pieces. For example, if you're creating a book, it's a good idea to create separate documents for the front matter, each chapter, the index, and any other parts (appendixes and so on). Also, if you're producing a long document, you want to take advantages of master pages (covered in Chapter 6), which save you the work of building each page from scratch.

When you create a multipage document, you're free to add however many pages you want. But be careful. Even though InDesign lets you create a seven-page newsletter, in real life, facing-page publications always have an even number of pages — usually a multiple of 4 and often a multiple of 16 because of the way printers arrange multiple pages on a single sheet of paper.

Here's how to add pages to a document:

1. **If it's not displayed, open the Pages panel by choosing Window⇨Pages or pressing ⌘+F12 or Ctrl+F12.**

2. **From the Pages panel's flyout menu, choose Insert Pages.** The Insert Pages dialog box, shown in Figure 5.2, appears.

FIGURE 5.2

The Insert Pages dialog box

---

3. **In the Pages field, type the number of pages you want to add.**

4. **Select an option from the Insert pop-up menu: After Page, Before Page, At Start of Document, or At End of Document.** Be careful: If you've already started working on page 1, for example, make sure you add new pages after page 1. Otherwise, it isn't page 1 anymore and you have to move the objects you already created.

5. **Type a page number in the field next to Insert or use the arrows to increase or decrease the value in one-page increments.**

6. **From the Master pop-up menu, select the master page you want to apply to the new pages.**

7. **When you're finished, click OK to close the dialog box.**

You can also add new pages or spreads — spreads are added if a spread is selected in the Pages panel — one at a time at the end of a document by clicking the Create New Page iconic button at the bottom of the Pages panel. When you use this method, the master page applied to the last document page is applied to each new page. Pages are added after the currently selected page in the panel.

Speedy Page Actions

There is a faster way to add and manipulate pages if you don't happen to have the Pages panel already open: Choose Layout⇨Pages and then select the appropriate option, such as Add Pages, from the submenu. The resulting dialog boxes match those accessed from the Pages panel.

If you want to quickly add just one page after the current page, click Layout⇨Pages⇨Add Page or press Shift+⌘+P or Ctrl+Shift+P. Note that this menu shortcut is not available through the Pages panel's flyout menu, although, of course, you can use the keyboard shortcut at any time.

You can also click and drag a master page icon (or both pages in a facing-pages spread to add a spread) from the top of the Pages panel to add a page using a master page's settings (use the [None] page for a plain page) between any pair of document page spreads or to the right of the last document spread. If a vertical bar appears when you release the mouse button, the spread is placed between the spreads on either side of the bar. If a vertical bar does not appear between document page spreads when you release the mouse button, the new spread is placed at the end of the document.

Deleting pages

InDesign offers several choices for deleting pages from a document. You can:

- Select one or more page icons in the Pages panel and either click and drag them to the pane's Delete Selected Pages iconic button (the trash can icon) or simply click the Delete Selected Pages iconic button. Click a spread's page numbers to select both pages. You can click a page icon or spread number and then Shift+click another page icon or spread number to select a range of pages. Hold down the ⌘ or Ctrl key and click page icons or spread numbers to select multiple, noncontiguous pages.

- Select one or more page icons in the Pages panel and then click Delete Pages or Delete Spreads from the panel's flyout menu.

- Choose Layout ➪ Pages ➪ Delete Pages. Any pages or spreads selected in the Pages panel are deleted. (If one or more spreads are selected, the menu option is Delete Spreads.) This is not a terribly useful option because you have to have the Pages panel open and thus may as well just use its flyout menu to delete pages.

Copying and moving pages

InDesign lets you copy and move pages from one document to another, as well as copy and move pages within a document.

Working within a document

To *duplicate* the current spread within the current document, click Duplicate Spread from the Pages panel's flyout menu or by choosing Layout ➪ Pages ➪ Duplicate Spread. (If you're not working with spreads because Facing Pages is deselected in the Document Setup dialog box, the menu option is still named Duplicate Spread.)

To *move* a page within a document, click its icon in the Pages panel and then drag the hand pointer between two spreads or between the pages of a spread inside the Pages panel. A vertical bar indicates where the selected page is placed. Release the mouse button when the vertical bar is where you want to move the page. To move a spread, click the page numbers beneath the icons (rather than on the page icons) before dragging them to the new location.

NEW FEATURE   In Design CS4 now carries along any objects in the page's bleed and slug area when you move the page. Previous versions left such objects behind.

Or you can choose Move Pages from the Pages panel's flyout menu or choose Layout ⇨ Pages ⇨ Move Pages. Either way, the Move Pages dialog box appears (refer to Figure 5.3). In that dialog box, you can specify where to move the pages: After a specific page, before a specific page, at the beginning of the document, or at the end of the document.

Working across documents

You can also copy and move pages to other documents. Note that the other documents must be open for the following techniques to work.

The easiest way is to select the page in the Pages panel and then drag its icon to the document you want to copy it to. (You'll need to have both documents visible, either by tiling or cascading the document windows, as explained in Chapter 3.) The Insert Pages dialog box then appears, giving you a choice of where to insert the page in the new document.

Slightly harder is the Move Pages dialog box I described earlier: Just be sure to select the target document in the Move To pop-up menu. Your page is then copied to the target document at the location you specified.

To *move* a page rather than copy it, be sure to select the Delete Pages After Inserting option in the Insert Pages dialog box, or select the Delete Pages After Moving option in the Move Pages dialog box.

Figure 5.3 shows both the Insert Pages and Move Pages dialog boxes.

FIGURE 5.3

The Insert Pages dialog box (top) displays when you drag pages between documents, whereas the Move Pages dialog box (bottom) displays through a menu option.

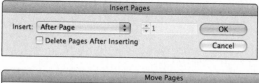

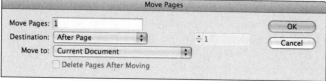

The Dangers of Shuffling

Although you can move pages around in a document, do so only with great care, if at all. Generally, if you want to move the *objects* on one page to another page, it's safer to cut (choose Edit ⇨ Cut or press ⌘+X or Ctrl+X) or copy (choose Edit ⇨ Copy or press ⌘+C or Ctrl+C) the objects than to move the page, which might cause subsequent pages to shuffle.

What's the big deal about shuffling? Shuffling moves pages around to make space for the moved page, and that can move what had been left-hand pages to the right-hand side of the spread and vice versa. If you have different alignments on left and right pages — such as having page numbers on the outside of pages — this shuffling can wreak havoc with that alignment.

If you absolutely must move a single page, it's safer to move its spread. (Of course, if you're working on a single-sided facing-page document, shuffling is not an issue.)

Starting documents on a left page

By default, InDesign starts all documents with a right-hand page. As a default, that makes sense, because the first sheet in a document always is a right-hand page. But sometimes, you want documents to start on a left-hand page, particularly if they are a chapter or section in a larger document. For example, magazine articles often start on a left page, giving the introduction a full spread. To start a document on a left page:

1. Select the first page in the Pages panel and then choose Numbering & Section Options from the panel's flyout menu, or choose Layout ⇨ Numbering & Section Options.

2. Select the Start Section option.

3. Select the Start Page Numbering At option and enter an even number such as 2 in the field to its right.

4. Click OK.

5. The Pages panel updates, showing the start page on the left of the spine.

6. You may not want to assign a starting page number (for example, if the starting page number is unknown because the number of pages that precede this document is unknown, and you are letting the book feature determine the page numbers later). In this case, repeat Step 1 but deselect Start Section. This leaves the page as a left-hand page but lets the book feature figure out the page number.

CROSS-REF For more on the book feature, see Chapter 24. Sections are covered in more detail later in this chapter.

Controlling page shuffling

When you insert new pages, existing pages after the inserted pages are automatically changed from left-hand (*verso*) pages to right-hand (*recto*) pages, and vice versa, as needed when individual pages are added and removed in a facing-pages document. You can prevent that for selected spreads, such as a two-page table, that you don't want to have broken apart when other pages are added or deleted. Of course, for proper printing, you may need to move that spread so that it follows a complete spread when you're done adding or deleting pages.

To disable shuffling for selected spreads, first select them in the Pages panel and then choose Allow Selected Spread to Shuffle in the flyout menu. By default, this menu option will have a check mark to its left, indicating that the spreads can shuffle; selecting it turns off the option, meaning that the selected spreads will *not* shuffle. (If the menu option has no check mark next to it, selecting it turns shuffling back on and the check mark reappears.)

 When you designate pages not to shuffle — that is, to be kept together — the page numbers below the spread in the Pages panel are displayed in brackets.

You can also disable shuffling for all spreads by choosing Allow Document Pages to Shuffle in the flyout menu: If the check mark is not there, the pages will *not* shuffle.

Creating gatefold spreads

Have you ever seen a publication, a magazine perhaps, that had a foldout page? Often such pages are ads (publishers love advertisers who buy multipage ads) or special sections. Or maybe you've seen a two-sided, multifold brochure with several panels, each the same size. A multipage spread of this type is often called a *gatefold spread*. Some people call it an *accordion page* or (as it was known in early versions of InDesign) an *island spread*.

When you designate a spread a gatefold spread, the spread's pages don't move if you add or delete any document pages in front of it. (Normally, when you add or delete pages, all subsequent pages bump backward or shuffle.)

When you create a gatefold spread of three pages in a facing-page publication, you should always create them in pairs because, in an actual printed publication, if you add a third page to a two-page spread, the backside of the page becomes the third page in another three-page spread. Along the same lines, if you create a four-panel, trifold brochure, both the front and the back have four panels. If this is difficult to visualize, take a look at Figure 5.4.

One last word about gatefold spreads: They require special care throughout the production process, and they cost you extra at the printer and bindery. If you're creating a modest, black-and-white newsletter for a local nonprofit organization, throwing in a three-panel gatefold probably isn't an option. On the other hand, if you can find an advertiser with deep pockets, InDesign lets you create gatefold spreads with up to ten pages.

FIGURE 5.4

In this example, pages 1, 2, and 3 are a gatefold, as are pages 4, 5, and 6.

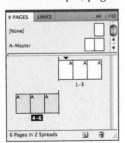

To create a gatefold spread, first select the pages that you want to make into a gatefold and then deselect the Allow Selected Pages to Shuffle option from the panel's flyout menu. Now, drag any of the pages you just unmarked as Allow Selected Pages to Shuffle to create the gatefold spread; that is, drag pages to the spread that will contain the multiple pages. A vertical bar indicates where the page will be placed. When the bar is where you want to place the page, release the mouse button.

To clear a gatefold, select it in the Pages panel and then reselect the Allow Selected Pages to Shuffle option in the panel's flyout menu.

Figure 5.4 shows a pair of three-page gatefold spreads in a facing-pages publication.

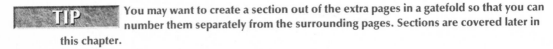

TIP You may want to create a section out of the extra pages in a gatefold so that you can number them separately from the surrounding pages. Sections are covered later in this chapter.

Working with page numbers

Pages are numbered automatically starting at 1 based on the order in which they appear in the Pages panel. But you can change the page numbering from Arabic numerals to Roman numerals or letters, as well as change the start page to be something other than 1. To do so, select the first page in the document in the Pages panel and choose Layout ⇨ Page Numbering & Sections or choose Numbering & Section Options from the Pages panel's flyout menu. Either way, you get the dialog box shown in Figure 5.5. (Its name will be New Section if the page has no section already applied to it. Otherwise, the name will be Numbering & Section Options.)

TIP A quick way to edit an existing section is to double-click its icon — the triangle that appears over the section's starting page in the Pages panel. You'll then get the Numbering & Section Options dialog box.

To change the initial page number, select the Start Page Numbering At option and type a new starting page number in its field. To change the page numbering style from the default of Arabic numerals (1, 2, 3, 4, . . .), use the Style pop-up menu and choose from I, II, III, IV, . . .; i, ii, iii, iv, . . .; A, B, C, D, . . .; and a, b, c, d, ...

FIGURE 5.5

The New Section dialog box lets you change the starting page number and the types of numerals used. (This dialog box is named Numbering & Section Options if you are working with a page that was previously made a section start.)

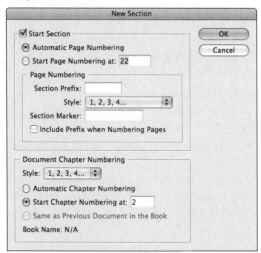

TIP To have a facing-pages document start on a left-hand page, you must have the starting page number be even.

CROSS-REF InDesign lets you create automatic page numbers, which lets you add the current page number to a folio or to automatically update the page number in a cross-reference such as a continued line. Chapter 22 covers this feature in detail.

It also lets you specify a chapter number for each document for use in book projects so that InDesign can use the text variables feature to automatically enter the chapter number in text such as folios for you. Chapter 22 covers text variables and Chapter 24 covers books.

Dividing a document into sections

Some long documents are divided into parts that are numbered separately from the other parts. For example, the page numbers for the front matter of books are often Roman numerals, whereas those for the body of the book are standard Arabic numerals. If a book has appendixes, a separate numbering scheme can be applied to these pages. In InDesign, such independently numbered parts are referred to as *sections*.

A multipage document can contain as many sections as you want (a section has to contain at least one page). If each section of a document uses a different page layout, you probably want to create a different master page for each section. Here's how to create a section:

1. **If it's not displayed, open the Pages panel by choosing Window ⇨ Pages or pressing ⌘+F12 or Ctrl+F12.**

2. **Click the icon of the page where you want to start a section.**

3. **Choose Numbering & Section Options from the panel's flyout menu.** If the page is not already a section start, the New Section dialog box, shown in Figure 5.5, appears. Otherwise, the identical Numbering & Section Options dialog box appears. (You can also create a section starting at the current page in your document by choosing Layout ⇨ Numbering & Section Options.) By default, the Start Section option is selected. Leave it selected.

4. **In the Section Prefix field, type up to eight characters that identify the section in the page-number box at the lower-left corner of the document window.** For example, if you type Sec2, the first page of the section is displayed as Sec2:1 in the page-number box.

5. **From the Style pop-up menu, choose the Roman numeral, Arabic numeral, or alphabetic style you want to use for page numbers.**

6. **For Page Numbering, select the Automatic Page Numbering option if you want the first page of the section to be one number higher than the last page of the previous section.** The new section uses the specified style; the previous section may use this style or another style.

7. **Select the Start Page Numbering at option and type a number in the accompanying field to specify a different starting number for the section.** For example, if a book begins with a section of front matter, you could begin the body section of a book on page 1 by choosing Start At and typing 1 in the field. If you select Continue from Previous Section, the first page of the body section would begin one number higher than the Roman numeral on the last page of the front matter.

8. **In the Section Marker field, type a text string that you can later automatically apply to pages in the section.** You might want to enter something straightforward, such as **Section 2**, or, if the section is a chapter, the name of the chapter.

> **TIP** You can insert the section marker name so that it prints in folios, chapter headings, and story text by choosing Type ⇨ Insert Special Character ⇨ Markers ⇨ Section Marker. This is a great way to get a chapter name (if you use it as the section marker) in your folio or to have cross-references in text to a section whose name might later change. You can also specify a chapter for automatic insertion into folios or other text. Chapter 22 explains both in detail.

9. **Click OK to close the dialog box.**

When you create a section, it's indicated in the Pages panel by a small, black, inverted triangle over the icon of the first page in the section, as shown at the top of the Pages panel in Figure 5.6. (If you move the mouse pointer over the black triangle, the name of the section appears.) The page-numbering scheme you've specified is reflected in the page numbers below the page icons. When you begin a section, it continues until the end of the document or until you begin a new section.

TIP By default, the Pages panel displays section numbers beneath the icons of document pages. To display absolute page numbers — the first page is page 1 and all other pages are numbered sequentially — choose InDesign ⇨ Preferences ⇨ General or press ⌘+K on the Mac, or choose Edit ⇨ Preferences ⇨ General or press Ctrl+K in Windows, and select Absolute Numbering from the View pop-up menu.

If you decide that you want to remove a section, navigate to the page that begins the section, choose Numbering & Section Options from the Pages panel's flyout menu, or choose Layout ⇨ Numbering & Section Options, and deselect the Section Start option.

Targeting Versus Selecting Spreads

Depending on the task you're working on, you may want to use the Pages panel to *target* a spread or to *select* a spread. The choice you make determines the actions you can perform.

A targeted spread is the spread to which copied objects will be placed when you choose Edit ⇨ Paste or press ⌘+V or Ctrl+V, or to which library objects will be placed when you choose Place Items from a library panel's flyout menu. The target spread is the one that's in the center of the document window and is indicated by the page number displayed in the page-number field at the lower-left corner of the document window. Only one spread can be the target spread at any one time. At reduced magnifications, it's possible to display several spreads in the document window. In this case, the number in the page-number field indicates the target spread.

When you select one or more spreads, you can then perform several page-level modifications, such as adjusting margin and column guides, applying a master page, or deleting the pages, in a single operation.

There are several ways to target a spread. You can:

- Modify an object on the spread or its pasteboard.
- Click a spread or its pasteboard.
- In the Pages panel, double-click the page numbers below the spread's page icons. (This also moves you to the document pages in the spread.)

You also have several options for selecting a page or spread:

- Click a page icon once to select one page of a spread; click the page numbers to select both pages. If you click twice, the page or spread is selected and targeted.
- Click a page icon or spread number and then Shift+click another page icon or spread number to select a range of pages.
- Hold down ⌘ or Ctrl and click page icons or spread numbers to select multiple, noncontiguous pages.

In the Pages panel, the page numbers of the target spread are displayed reversed, white numbers in a black rectangle, whereas the page icons are highlighted in a light-blue color.

Navigating pages

Moving from page to page in a long document and scrolling around a large or magnified page are among the most common tasks you'll perform in InDesign. The more time you spend displaying the page or page area you want to work on, the less time you have to do the work you need to do. As with most trips, the less time you spend between destinations, the better.

You can always just go to the page you want, but for navigating through the pages of a document when you don't know which page has the content you are seeking, the Pages panel (choose Window ⇨ Pages or press ⌘+F12 or Ctrl+F12) offers the fastest ride. For navigating around in a page, you may want to switch to the navigator function, described in Chapter 3.

Navigating by page number

InDesign lets you easily move through pages by just selecting the desired page — if you know its number, of course. To do so, enter the desired page number in the Page field and then press Enter or Return, or select the page from the Page pop-up menu, both of which are at the left side of the application bar, as shown in Chapter 3.

 Use the shortcut ⌘+J or Ctrl+J to open the Go to Page dialog box, where you can enter the desired page number.

Navigating with the menus and shortcuts

InDesign also offers several menu commands and keyboard shortcuts to quickly navigate your layout, as Table 5.1 details.

TABLE 5.1

Page Navigation Menus and Shortcuts

Navigation	Menu Sequence	Macintosh Shortcut	Windows Shortcut
Go to a specific page	Layout ⇨ Go to Page	⌘+J	Ctrl+J
Go to first page	Layout ⇨ First Page	Shift+⌘+PgUp	Ctrl+Shift+Page Up
Go back one page	Layout ⇨ Previous Page	Shift+PgUp	Shift+Page Up
Go forward one page	Layout ⇨ Next Page or Layout ⇨ Go Forward	Shift+PgDn or ⌘+PgDn	Shift+Page Down or Ctrl+keypad PgDn
Go to last page	Layout ⇨ Last Page	Shift+⌘+PgDn	Ctrl+Shift+Page Down
Go to last page viewed	Layout ⇨ Go Back	⌘+PgUp	Shift+Page Up or Ctrl+keypad PgUp
Go forward one spread	Layout ⇨ Next Spread	Option+PgUp	Alt+Page Up
Go back one spread	Layout ⇨ Previous Spread	Option+PgDn	Alt+Page Down

Understanding Special Page Numbers

When entering in page numbers for page navigation, printing, or other functions, you usually can use regular numbers, such as 5 for the fifth page. But there are some occasions where that won't get what you want; these occasions involve the use of sections.

A *section page number,* specified through the Numbering & Section Options dialog box (choose Layout ⇨ Numbering & Section Options or choose Numbering & Section Options in the Pages panel's flyout menu) is a customized page number. You use section numbers if your document needs to start on a page other than 1 — for example, if you're working on a magazine and each article is saved in a different document, or if you have a preface using Roman numerals (such as *iv*). A single document can have multiple sections of page numbers and can use section page numbers to change the format of numbers to Roman numerals, letters, and so on.

If your sections use different numbering styles such as letters, Roman numerals, and Arabic numerals, you can go to the desired page as long as the page number you enter is unique: iii, c, and 3 would represent different pages, and InDesign would know which is which because their numbering is different.

But if your document uses the same page numbers more than once, such as page 51 in two different sections, you can't just enter 51 to get to page 51, since InDesign won't know which page 51 to go to. That's where section page numbers come in. To jump to or print a page with a section page number, you need to indicate which section it is and what page number appears on the page. InDesign provides a default name for sections, starting at Sec1. When you enter a section page number, you must separate the section name and the page number with a colon. For example, if you start the page numbering on page 51, you need to type **Sec1:51** in the page number field to jump to that page. Having to include this undisplayed section information makes this option fairly unappealing, so you may prefer to use absolute page numbers.

An *absolute page number* indicates a page's position in the document, such as 1 for the first page, 2 for the second page, and so on. To specify an absolute page number in the page number field or other dialog box (such as Print) that involves selecting pages, you type a plus sign before the number that represents the page's position. For example, the first page in the document is always +1, the second page is always +2, and so on. If you don't type a plus sign, the first page with the number 1 is what InDesign will assume you mean — although this may not be the first page in the document. For example, perhaps you have a 5-page section with Roman numerals followed by a 30-page section with Arabic numerals. Type just **1**; this goes to the first page in the Arabic-numbered section, whereas entering **+1** goes to the first page in the document (*i*, in this case).

Navigating with the Pages panel

When the Pages panel appears, you can use it to quickly move from page to page in a multipage document and to switch between displaying master pages and document pages. To display a particular document page, double-click its icon. The selected page is centered in the document window. To display a master spread, double-click its icon in the lower half of the panel.

> **TIP**   You can reverse the order of master pages and regular pages in the Pages panel by choosing the Panel Options option in the flyout menu. Then select Pages on Top instead of the Default Masters on Top. You can also control whether pages and master pages appear as preview thumbnails, whether they display vertically or horizontally, whether they appear in fixed sizes or in proportion to their actual dimensions, and what size their icons should be.

> **TIP**   The Fit Page in Window command (choose View⇨ Fit Page in Window or press ⌘+0 or Ctrl+0) and Fit Spread in Window command (choose View⇨ Fit Page in Window or press Option+⌘+0 or Ctrl+Alt+0) let you enlarge or reduce the display magnification to fit the selected page or spread in the document window. When you have lots of objects parked on the pasteboard, also useful is choosing View⇨ Entire Pasteboard or pressing Option+Shift+⌘+0 or Ctrl+Alt+Shift+0. (Note that all the shortcuts use the numeral *0*, not the letter *O*.)

Working with specialty page controls

InDesign offers three specialty controls over pages: transparency, rotation, and transitions. And the Panel Options dialog box is where you tell InDesign to highlight whether those controls are in use. Figure 5.6 shows the Pages panel with indicators for all three, as well as the Panel Options dialog box. (You also set whether page thumbnails display and the relative position of document and master pages in the Pages panel via this dialog box.) Choose Panel Options from the Pages panel's flyout menu to get this dialog box.

FIGURE 5.6
_____

The Pages panel (at left) has several iconic indicators. The small inverted triangle above a page icon (page 4, here) represents a section start. There are also indicators for pages that have transparent objects, whose views are rotated, and that have page transitions applied. You control the display of these last three indicators in the Panel Options dialog box (at right).

Section start Transparency

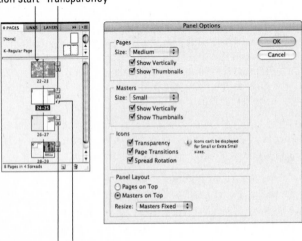

Page transition Rotated view

NEW FEATURE The ability to control whether the transparency icon displays is new to InDesign CS4. The ability to rotate page views and apply page transitions is also new, as are the controls to display the icons indicating their usage.

Transparency alert

InDesign is a pioneer in the use of transparency for layouts, but that feature can trip up some printers. To help you identify pages that use transparency, InDesign can automatically add an icon to the right of the page number in the Pages panel if that page uses transparency — and if the Panel Options dialog box is set to display the transparency icon (it is turned off by default). Chapters 11 and 30 cover transparency in detail.

Rotated page views

Sometimes, rotated objects — especially those containing text — can be hard to edit in the regular view of a page. InDesign CS4 thus lets you rotate a spread so that you can view it at 90-, 180-, and 270-degree views — in addition to the standard 0-degree view, of course. Note that the actual spread isn't rotated, just its appearance in InDesign; it will print correctly. Figure 5.7 shows an example; note the rotation icon that appears in the pages panel to the right of the rotated spread.

There are two ways to rotate a spread's view: Choose View ⇨ Rotate Spread and then choose the desired rotation amount from the submenu, or select the desired spread for which to rotate its view in the Pages panel and then choose Rotate Spread View and the desired rotation amount from the submenu. To set the view back to normal, choose the Clear Rotation option in the submenu.

Page transitions

Another new feature in InDesign CS4 is the ability to apply page transitions, such as you would see in a PowerPoint presentation or video. These transitions have no effect on printed documents, but will appear in PDF and Flash files exported from InDesign.

To apply page transitions, select the pages you want to apply them to and then either choose Layout ⇨ Pages ⇨ Page Transitions ⇨ Choose or, in the Pages panel's flyout menu, choose Page Transitions ⇨ Choose. The Page Transitions dialog box, shown in Figure 5.8, will appear, and you can choose the desired transition effect. To apply the effect to all spreads, be sure to select the Apply to All Spreads option at the bottom of the dialog box.

You can edit page transitions on selected pages by choosing Edit instead of Choose in the above two menu sequences, which opens the Page Transitions panel shown in Figure 5.8. You can also open the Page Transitions panel by choosing Window ⇨ Interactive ⇨ Page Transitions. Here, you can change not only the transition effect but also control its direction and speed, using the three pop-up menus. In its flyout menu, you can choose Apply to All Spreads if you hadn't done so previously.

Note that the only way to turn off the Apply to All Spreads setting is in the Page Transitions dialog box — you cannot do so in the Page Transitions panel. To get rid of all page transitions applied, choose Layout ⇨ Pages ⇨ Page Transitions ⇨ Clear All, or in the Pages panel's flyout menu choose Page Transitions ⇨ Clear All.

FIGURE 5.7

Rotating a spread's view helps you work on rotated text and other rotated objects.

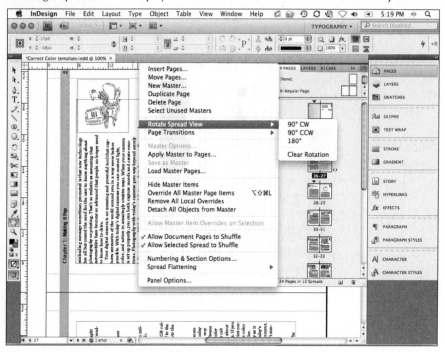

FIGURE 5.8

The Page Transitions dialog box (left) and the Page Transitions panel (right)

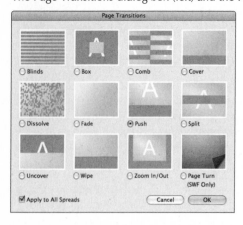

 Chapter 32 covers the creation of PDF, Flash, and other electronic documents.

Adjusting page layouts

If you've ever created and worked with a document all the way to the finishing touches and then discovered that the page size was wrong from the beginning, you know the meaning of frustration. Manually adjusting the size and placement of all the objects in a document is an ugly chore and one you want to avoid at all costs. However, should the unthinkable happen — you have to modify the size, orientation, or margins of a document that is partially or completely finished — InDesign automatically resizes and repositions objects when you change its basic layout.

For example, maybe you've created a magazine for an American audience that subsequently needs to be converted for publication in Europe. Most newsletters in the United States use letter-sized pages (8½ × 11 inches), whereas in Europe the standard page size for such publications is A4 (210 × 297 mm), which is slightly narrower and slightly taller than U.S. letter size. Of course, you have to change *color* to *colour*, *apartment* to *flat*, and so on. But you also have to both squeeze (horizontally) and stretch (vertically) every item on every page to accommodate the A4 page's dimensions.

The Layout Adjustment command (choose Layout ⇨ Layout Adjustment) gives you the option of turning this chore over to InDesign, which automatically adjusts object shape and position according to the new page size, column guides, and margins.

The Layout Adjustment dialog box lets you turn layout adjustment on or off and specify the rules used to adjust objects when you change page size or orientation (via the Document Setup dialog box; choose File ⇨ Document Setup or press Option+⌘+P or Ctrl+Alt+P) or margins or columns (via the Margin and Columns dialog box, accessed by choosing Layout ⇨ Margins and Columns). To adjust a layout:

1. **Choose Layout ⇨ Layout Adjustment to display the Layout Adjustment dialog box, shown in Figure 5.9.**

FIGURE 5.9

The Layout Adjustment dialog box

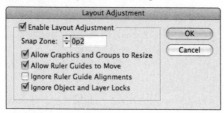

2. **Select the Enable Layout Adjustment option to turn on the feature; deselect it to turn it off.**

3. **In the Snap Zone field, type the distance within which an object edge automatically snaps to a guideline when layout adjustment is performed.**

4. **Select the Allow Graphics and Groups to Resize option if you want InDesign to resize objects when layout adjustment is performed.** If you don't select this option, InDesign moves objects but does not resize them (the preferred option).

5. **Select the Allow Ruler Guides to Move option if you want InDesign to adjust the position of ruler guides proportionally according to a new page size.** Generally, ruler guides are placed relative to the margins and page edges, so you probably want to select this option.

6. **Select the Ignore Ruler Guide Alignments option if you want InDesign to ignore ruler guides when adjusting the position of objects during layout adjustment.** If you think that objects may snap to ruler guides that you don't want them to snap to during layout adjustment, select this option. If selected, InDesign still snaps object edges to other margin and column guides.

7. **Select the Ignore Object and Layer Locks option to let InDesign move locked objects (either objects locked directly by choosing Object ⇨ Lock Position or by pressing ⌘+L or Ctrl+L, or objects that reside on a locked layer).** Otherwise, locked objects are not adjusted.

8. **When you're done, click OK to close the dialog box.**

The Layout Adjustment feature works best when the layout is not complex and does not contain more than one or two text frames. But if you radically change a document that you've already done considerable work on, the Layout Adjustment feature usually creates more work than it saves. For example, the switch from a U.S. letter-sized page to an A4-sized page is a relatively minor change and the layout adjustments will probably be barely noticeable. But if you decide to change a tabloid-sized poster into a business card in midstream, well, you're better off starting over.

Here are a few things to keep in mind if you decide to use InDesign's Layout Adjustment feature:

- If you change page size, the margin widths (the distance between the left and right margins and the page edges) remain the same.

- If you change page size, column guides and ruler guides are repositioned proportionally to the new size.

- If you change the number of columns, column guides are added or removed accordingly.

- If an object edge is aligned with a guideline before layout adjustment, it remains aligned with the guideline after adjustment. If two or more edges of an object are aligned with guidelines, the object is resized so that the edges remain aligned with the guidelines after layout adjustment.

- If you change the page size, objects are moved so that they're in the same relative position on the new page.

- If you've used margin, column, and ruler guides to place objects on pages, layout adjustment are more effective than if you've placed objects or ruler guides randomly on pages.

- Check for text reflow when you modify a document's page size, margins, or column guides. Decreasing a document's page size can cause text to overflow a text frame whose dimensions have been reduced.

- Check everything in your document after the adjustment is complete. Take the time to look over every page of your document. You never know what InDesign has actually done until you see it with your own eyes.

TIP If you decide to enable layout adjustment for a particular publication, you may want to begin by using the Save As command (choose File ➪ Save As or press Shift+⌘+S or Ctrl+Shift+S) to create a copy. That way, if you ever need to revert back to the original version, you can simply open the original document.

Working with Layers

Publishers seem to spend a lot of time doing the same things: creating several different versions of the same ad for different markets or flowing text in another language into a design. The goal of software is to automate the predictable so that you have more time for creativity. Toward this goal, InDesign provides a method for preserving the time you put into creating and editing a layout that is used for more than one purpose: *layers*.

If you've ever seen a series of clear plastic overlays in presentations, understanding layers is easy. In one of those old overhead presentations, the teacher might have started with one overlay containing a graphic and then added another overlay with descriptive text, and then added a third overlay containing a chart. Each overlay contained distinct content, but you could see through each one to the others to get the entire message. InDesign's layers are somewhat like this, letting you isolate content on slices of a document. You can then show and hide layers, lock objects on layers, rearrange layers, and more.

Each document contains a default layer, Layer 1, which contains all your objects until you select and create a new layer. Objects on the default layer — and any other layer for that matter — follow the standard *stacking order* of InDesign. (The first object you create is the backmost object, the last one you create is the frontmost, and all the other objects fall somewhere in between. See Chapter 12 for detailed information about stacking orders.)

As with the clear plastic overlays, the order of the layers also affects the stacking order of the objects. Objects on the bottom layer are behind other objects, and objects on the top layer are in front of other objects. In Figure 5.10, the Default layer at the top of the list contains the business card's standard graphics and the main text. Two additional layers contain different sets of contact information, in separate text frames, for different people.

FIGURE 5.10

A business card with different layers for each person's card. The graphics common to all cards are on their own layer (Default).

Object icon (indicates layer the selected object is on)

Pen icon (indicates active layer)

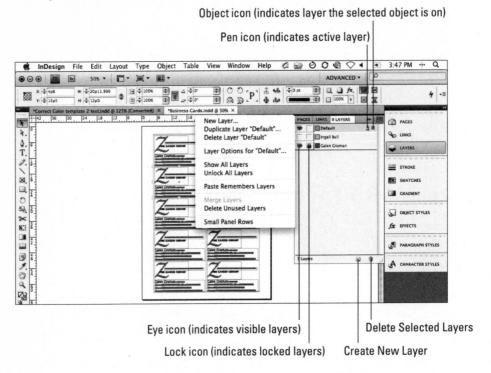

Eye icon (indicates visible layers)   Delete Selected Layers

Lock icon (indicates locked layers)   Create New Layer

Although layers are often compared to plastic overlays, there's one big difference: Layers are not specific to individual pages. Each layer encompasses the entire document, which doesn't make much difference when you're working on a one-page ad but makes a significant difference when it comes to a 16-page newsletter. Layers help you enforce the stacking order of your page elements, making it easier to manage them. Layers are essential to grouping chunks of similar elements that can be altered quickly.

The Layers panel (choose Window ➪ Layers or press F7) is your gateway to creating and manipulating layers. Its controls are mostly iconic, but, as with other panels, when Tool Tips are turned on via the Tool Tips pop-up menu in the Interface panel of the Preferences dialog box, you can learn what controls do by pointing at them. (Choose InDesign ➪ Preferences ➪ Interface or press ⌘+K on the Mac, or choose Edit ➪ Preferences ➪ Interface or press Ctrl+K in Windows.) If you know what the controls do, you can intuit a great deal of how to work with layers.

When, Where, and Why to Use Layers

The layers feature is one that many users ignore. It's true that if you never looked at the Layers panel, you could continue to do your work in InDesign. But that would be a mistake. So take a look at the possibilities and see whether they fit into your workflow. In the long run, using layers can save you time and help you prevent mistakes that can result when you need to track changes across multiple documents.

Say you've created an ad with the same copy in it but a different headline and image for each city where the ad runs. You can place the boilerplate information on one layer and the information that changes on other layers. If any of the boilerplate information changes, you only need to change it once. To print different versions of the ad, you control which layers print.

You might use layers in the following situations:

- **A project with a high-resolution background image:** For example, a background such as a texture might take a long time to redraw. You can hide that layer while designing other elements and then show it occasionally to see how it works with the rest of the design.

- **A document that you produce in several versions:** For example, a produce ad may have different prices for different cities, or a clothing catalog may feature different coats depending on the climate in each area. You can place the content that changes on separate layers and then print the layers you need.

- **A project that includes objects you don't want to print:** If you want to suppress printout of objects for any reason, the only way you can do this is to place them on a layer and hide the layer. You might have a layer that's used for nothing but adding editorial and design comments, which you can delete when the document is final. (Even though InDesign supports nonprinting notes, you can insert them only into text; therefore, having a design-comments layer is still useful to be able to make annotations for frames, images, and other nontextual elements.)

- **A publication that is translated into several languages:** Depending on the layout, you can place all the common objects on one layer and then create a different layer for each language's text. Changes to the common objects need to happen only once — in contrast to if you created copies of the original document and flowed the translated text into the copies.

- **To experiment with different layouts of the same document:** You can show and hide layers to present different options to your supervisor or client. This strategy lets you use common elements, such as the logo and legal information, in several versions of the same design.

- **A complex design with overlapping objects, text wraps, and grouped objects:** Say the background of a page consists of a checkerboard pattern made up of filled, rectangular frames. You don't want to accidentally select the blocks while you're working with other objects. If you isolate complex objects on their own layer, you can show only that layer to work on it, hide that layer to concentrate on other layers, lock the layer so that you can't select objects, and otherwise manipulate the layer.

continued

continued

- **To create bulletproof templates:** Locked layers are a great way to decrease the possibility of items in a template being moved or deleted. Move all the objects you don't want moved or deleted on a layer and lock the layer. Although you can unlock layer, a locked layer keeps the people who use the template from accidentally moving or removing anything too quickly.

- **To ensure that folios and the like are never overprinted.** Placing folios (the document's page numbers, running headings, and so forth) on their own layer, uppermost in the layer stack, ensures that they are never accidentally obscured by other objects.

- **To help text print properly over transparent elements.** Layers are useful to isolate text above other objects with transparency effects. This avoids the rasterizing of text during output to plate or film — something that can make the text quality look poor.

When determining whether objects should go on a layer, remember that layers are document wide and not page specific.

Creating layers

Each document contains a default layer, Layer 1, which contains all the objects you place on master pages and document pages — until you create and activate new layers. You can create as many layers as you need. After you create a new layer, it's activated automatically so that you can begin working on it.

The Layers panel (choose Window ⇨ Layers or press F7) provides several methods for creating new layers. It doesn't matter which document page is displayed when you create a layer because the layer encompasses all the pages in the document. To create a layer, do one of the following:

- To create a new layer *on top of all existing layers*, click the Create New Layer iconic button on the Layers panel to get the New Layer dialog box. The layer gets the default name of Layer *x*.

- To create a layer *above the selected layer*, ⌘+click or Ctrl+click the Create New Layer iconic button. The layer will get the default name of Layer *x*.

- To create a new layer *on top of all existing layers but customize its name and identifying color*, Option+click or Alt+click the Create New Layer iconic button, or choose New Layer from the flyout menu. Use the New Layer dialog box to specify options for the layer, as described shortly. (The New Layer dialog box — set with a custom name and color — is shown in Figure 5.11.)

FIGURE 5.11

The New Layer dialog box

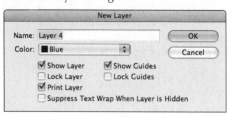

> **NOTE**   You can create a layer while a master page is displayed. Objects you create on a layer while a master page is displayed are placed on all pages based on that master page. However, the layer is not specific to that master page. It is available for all document pages — even those based on other master pages — and you can place objects on it.

> **TIP**   To change a layer's settings, double-click it or choose Layer Options for *name of layer* from the flyout menu to display the Layer Options dialog box.

Whether you're using the New Layer dialog box shown in Figure 5.11 or the nearly identical Layer Options dialog box, the customization options work the same:

- **Name field:** Type a descriptive name for the layer. For example, if you're using layers for multilingual publishing, you might have a U.S. English layer, a French layer, and a German layer. If you're using layers so that you can hide background objects while you're working, you might have a Background Objects layer.

- **Color pop-up menu and button:** A layer's color helps you identify which layer an object is on. The color appears to the left of the layer name in the Layers panel and appears on each object on that layer. The color is applied to frame edges, selection handles, bounding boxes, text ports, and text wraps. Note that the display of frame edges is controlled by choosing View ➪ Show/Hide Frame Edges or pressing Control+⌘+H or Ctrl+H. By default, InDesign applies a different color to each new layer, but you can customize it to something meaningful for your document and workflow. Choose a color from the list or double-click the color swatch to use from the operating system's color picker.

> **CROSS-REF**   I cover the other layer manipulation features in these dialog boxes later in this chapter.

Working with objects on layers

Whether you're designing a magazine template from the ground up or modifying an existing ad, you can isolate specific types of objects on layers. You can create objects on a layer, move objects to a layer, or copy objects to a layer.

The active layer

The *active layer* is the one on which you're creating objects — whether you're using tools, importing text or graphics, clicking and dragging objects in from a library, or pasting objects from other layers or other documents. A pen icon to the right of a layer's name means it's the active one (refer to Figure 5.10). Although you can select more than one layer at a time, only one layer can be active. To switch the active layer to another layer, click to the right of the layer name that you want to be active; the pen icon moves, making that the new active layer. Keep in mind that for a layer to be activated, it must be visible.

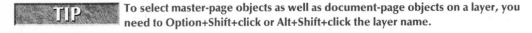

NOTE Regardless of which layer is the active layer, you can select, move, and modify objects on any visible, unlocked layer. You can even select objects on different layers and manipulate them.

Selecting objects on layers

The Layers panel helps you work with selected objects in the following ways:

- To determine to which layer an object belongs, match the color on its bounding box, handles, and so on, to a color to the left of a layer name.

- To determine which layers contain active objects, look to the right of the layer names. A small box — the object icon — next to a layer name (refer to Figure 6.2) indicates that it contains an active object.

- To select all the objects on a layer, Option+click or Alt+click the layer's name in the Layers panel. The layer must be active, unlocked, and visible.

TIP To select master-page objects as well as document-page objects on a layer, you need to Option+Shift+click or Alt+Shift+click the layer name.

Placing objects on layers

To place objects on a layer, the layer must be active as indicated by the pen icon. To place objects on the layer, use any of these options:

- Use any tools to create paths and frames.

- Use the Place command (choose File ⇨ Place or press ⌘+D or Ctrl+D) to import graphics or text.

- Use the Paste command (choose Edit ⇨ Paste or press ⌘+V or Ctrl+V) to paste objects from the Clipboard onto the layer.

- Click and drag objects to the layer from a library or another document.

NOTE When you create objects on master pages, they are placed on the default layer and are therefore behind other objects on document pages. To create objects on master pages that are in front of other objects, place the objects on a different layer while the master page is displayed.

You can cut and paste objects from one page to another but have the objects remain on their original layer — without concern about the active layer. To do this, use the Paste Remembers Layers command in the Layers panel's flyout menu rather than Edit ⇨ Paste, or press ⌘+V or Ctrl+V. You might do this if you're moving the continuation of an article from one page to another but you want the text to remain on the same layer. (For example, if you're working on a multilingual document with separate layers for English, French, and Spanish text, using Paste Remembers Layer ensures that text frames cut or copied from the French layer are pasted onto the French layer on the new location.)

Moving objects to different layers

After an object is on a layer, it isn't stuck there. You can copy and paste objects to selected layers, or you can move them using the Layers panel. When you move an object to a layer, it's placed in front of all other objects on a layer. To select multiple objects, remember to Shift+click them and then move them in one of the following ways:

- **Paste objects on a different layer.** First cut or copy objects to the Clipboard. Activate the layer on which you want to put the objects and then use the Paste command (choose Edit ⇨ Paste or press ⌘+V or Ctrl+V). This method works well for moving objects that are currently on a variety of layers.

- **Move objects to a different layer.** Click and drag the active objects' object icon (to the right of a layer's name) to another layer. When you use this method, it doesn't matter which layer is active. However, you can't move objects from multiple layers to a single layer using this method. (If you select multiple objects that reside on different layers, dragging the icon moves only objects that reside on the first layer on which you selected an object.)

- **Move objects to a hidden or locked layer.** Press ⌘ or Ctrl while you click and drag the active objects' object icon.

- **Copy rather than move objects to a different layer.** Press Option or Alt while you click and drag the active objects' object icon.

- **Copy objects to a hidden or locked layer.** Press Option+⌘ or Ctrl+Alt while you drag the active objects' object icon.

TIP After designing a new template, you might realize that it would be easier to work with if you had isolated certain objects on layers. You can create new layers and then move objects to them at this point. Just make sure the layers are in the same stacking order as the original objects.

Manipulating layers

Using the Layers panel, you can select and manipulate entire layers. These changes affect all the objects on the layer — for example, if you hide a layer, all its objects are hidden; if you move a layer up, all its objects appear in front of objects on lower layers. Functions that affect an entire layer include hiding, locking, rearranging, merging, and deleting.

Selecting layers

The active layer containing the pen icon is always selected. You can extend the selection to include other layers the same way you multiple-select objects: Shift+click for a continuous selection and ⌘+click or Ctrl+click for a noncontiguous selection. When layers are selected, you can move them within the stacking order of layers, modify attributes in the Layer Options dialog box, merge them, or delete them.

Hiding layers

When you hide a layer, none of the objects on that layer displays or prints. You might hide layers for a variety of reasons, including to speed screen redraw by hiding layers containing high-resolution graphics, to control which version of a publication prints, and to simply focus on one area of a design without the distraction of other areas. To show or hide layers using the Layers panel, do one of the following:

- Click the eye icon in the first column to the left of a layer's name. When the eye icon is blank, you just see an empty square in the column, and the layer is hidden. Click the empty square to show the layer; the eye icon will appear in that square. You can also double-click a layer and select or deselect the Show Layer option in the Layer Options dialog box.

- If no layers are hidden, you can show only the active layer by choosing Hide Others from the flyout menu.

- Regardless of the state of other layers, you can show only one layer by Option+clicking or Alt+clicking in the first column next to its name. All other layers will be hidden.

- If any layers are hidden, you can show all layers by choosing Show All Layers from the flyout menu. You can also Option+click or Alt+click twice in the first column to show all layers.

The Suppress Text Wrap When Layer Is Hidden option in the flyout menu prevents text wrapping around the layer's objects when the layer is hidden. Be sure to select this option when you use multiple layers for variations of the same content — such as multilingual text or different contacts for business cards. Otherwise, your layer's text cannot display because it is wrapping around a hidden layer with an object of the same size in the same place.

Locking layers

When you lock a layer, you cannot select or modify objects on it — even if the locked layer is active. You might lock a layer containing boilerplate text or a layer containing a complex drawing that you don't want altered. Locking and unlocking layers is easy, so you might lock one layer while focusing on another, and then unlock it. To lock or unlock layers using the Layers panel, do one of the following:

- Click the blank square in the second column to the left of a layer's name. When the lock icon appears in the square, the layer is locked. Click the lock icon to unlock the layer; the square becomes blank. You can also double-click a layer and select or deselect the Lock Layer option in the Layer Options dialog box.

- If no layers are locked, you can lock all but the active layer by choosing Lock Others from the flyout menu.

- If any layers are locked, you can unlock all layers by choosing Unlock All Layers from the flyout menu.

- You can toggle between Lock Others Unlock All Layers by Option+clicking or Alt+clicking the blank box or the lock icon.

NOTE When you lock an object to a page (choose Object ⇨ Lock Position or press ⌘+L or Ctrl+L), as described in Chapter 9, the object's position stays locked regardless of its layer's lock status.

Preventing layers from printing or exporting

InDesign lets you designate layers as nonprinting, separately from being hidden. Select the layers you don't want to print or export and then choose Layer options from the Layers panel's flyout menu and deselect Print Layer. Layers that won't print show their names in italic in the Layers panel. (In addition, hidden layers also do not print.)

CROSS-REF When you do print or export, you can override layers' nonprinting status, as explained in Chapters 30 and 31.

Rearranging layers

Each layer has its own front-to-back stacking order, with the first object you create on the layer being its backmost object. You can modify the stacking order of objects on a single layer using the Arrange commands in the Object menu, as explained in Chapter 9. Objects are further stacked according to the order in which the layers are listed in the Layers panel. The layer at the top of the list contains the frontmost objects, and the layer at the bottom of the list contains the backmost objects.

If you find that all the objects on one layer need to be in front of all the objects on another layer, you can move that layer up or down in the list. In fact, you can move multiple-selected layers up or down, even if the selection is noncontiguous. To move layers, click the selection and drag it up or down in the Layers panel. When you move layers, remember that layers are document wide, so you're actually changing the stacking order of objects on all the pages.

TIP You might be accustomed to moving objects to the front of the stacking order to make them easily editable. Working this way, you might be tempted to bring a layer up to the top of the layer stacking order so that you can edit it easily and then move it back to its original location. Try to get out of that habit, though, and into the habit of simply showing the layer you need to work on and hiding the others.

Combining layers

If you decide that all the objects on one layer belong on a different layer — throughout the document — you can merge the layers. When you're learning about the power of layers, it's easy to create a document that is unnecessarily complex (for example, you might have put each object on a different layer and then realized that the document has become difficult to work with). The good news is that you can also merge all the layers in a document to *flatten* it to a single layer. To flatten all layers:

1. **Select the *target layer* (where you want all the objects to end up) by clicking it.**

2. **Select the *source layers* (which contain the objects you want to move) in addition to the target layer.** Shift+click, or ⌘+click or Ctrl+click, to add the source layers to the selection.

3. **Make sure the target layer displays the pen icon and that the target and source layers are all selected.**

4. **Choose Merge Layers from the Layers panel's flyout menu.** All objects on the source layers are moved to the target layer, and the source layers are deleted.

NOTE   When you merge layers, the stacking order of objects does not change, so the design looks the same — with one notable exception: If you created objects on a layer while a master page was displayed, those objects go to the back of the stacking order with the regular master-page objects.

Deleting layers

If you've carefully isolated portions of a document on different layers and then find that you don't need that portion of the document, you can delete the layer. For example, if you have a U.S. English and an International English layer, and you decide that you can't afford to print the different versions and one dialect's readers will simply have to suffer, you can delete the unneeded layer. You might also delete layers that you don't end up using to simplify a document.

When you delete layers, all the objects on the layer throughout the document are deleted. To ensure that you don't need any of the objects before deleting a layer, you can hide all other layers and then look at the remaining objects on each page. If you think you might need them later for this or another document, you can click and drag them to the pasteboard or place them in a library.

Using the Layers panel, you can delete selected layers in the following ways:

- Click and drag the selection to the Delete Selected Layers iconic button (the trash can icon).
- Click the Delete Selected Layers iconic button. (The current layer, the one with the pen icon, is deleted.)
- Choose Delete Layer from the Layers panel's flyout menu.

If any of the layers contain objects, a warning reminds you that they will be deleted. And, of course, the ubiquitous Undo command (choose Edit ➪ Undo or press ⌘+Z or Ctrl+Z) lets you recover from accidental deletions.

   To remove all layers that do not contain objects, choose Delete Unused Layers from the Layers panel's flyout menu.

Controlling guides

The New Layer and Layer Options dialog boxes give you control over how guides work for specific layers:

- **Show Guides option:** This lets you control the display of guides that were created while the selected layer was active. When selected, as it is by default, you can create guides while any layer is active and view those guides on any layer. When deselected, you cannot create guides. Any guides you create while that layer is active are not displayed, but you can still see guides that were created while other layers were active. Note that when guides are hidden entirely (choose View ⇨ Grids & Guides ⇨ Hide Guides or press ⌘+; [semicolon] or Ctrl+; [semicolon]), this command has no apparent effect.

- **Lock Guides option:** This works similarly to Show Guides in that it affects only guides that are created while the layer is active. When deselected, as it is by default, you can move guides on any layer for which Lock Guides is deselected. When selected, you cannot move guides created while that layer was active. You can, however, move guides on other layers for which Lock Guides is deselected. Note that when all guides are locked (choose View ⇨ Grids & Guides ⇨ Lock Guides or press Option+⌘+; [semicolon] or Ctrl+Alt+; [semicolon]), this command has no apparent effect.

Summary

If you're working on a multipage document, you want to display the Pages panel. It lets you add, move, and delete document pages as well as create multipage spreads called *gatefold spreads*.

If you're working on a long document with multiple parts and want to number each part separately, you can create sections to manage these multiple page-numbering schemes within the document. You can also have InDesign automatically add the correct page numbers for folios and continued lines, as well as section names in folios and other text.

As you work on a long document, you can use the Pages panel to target a specific page or spread in the document window; to select multiple pages or spreads so that you can move, modify, or delete them collectively; and to navigate from page to page in a multipage document.

InDesign provides visual indicators that let you know whether pages contain transparent objects, have their views rotated, or have page transition effects applied. You can also rotate page views and apply transition effects with the Pages panel and related Layout ⇨ Page submenus.

If you decide to change the layout of a publication after you've started work, you can use the Layout Adjustment feature to automatically adjust the size and position of objects and guidelines when you change the document's page size, margins, or columns.

If you take the time to integrate layers into your workflow, you can save time and effort in creating multilingual publications, produce multiple versions of a document, and benefit from greater flexibility with objects. Until you create new layers, all the objects are placed on the default layer. Although each layer has its own stacking order, the order of layers also affects stacking order.

You can create objects on the active layer, and you can move objects to different layers. Even though objects are on layers, you can continue to select and modify them as you normally would — provided that the layers are visible and unlocked. Hiding layers suppresses the printout of objects as well as prevents their display. There's also a separate control to prevent unhidden layers from printing. To streamline a document, you can merge and delete layers.

Chapter 6

Creating Layout Standards

Think for a moment about the publications you produce. Chances are that most of your work involves creating multiple iterations of a basic set of publications, and each publication looks more or less the same from issue to issue. For example, periodicals such as newsletters, magazines, and newspapers don't change much from one issue to the next (disregarding the occasional redesigns that all publications undergo). The ongoing uniformity of such things as page size, margins, page layouts, text formats, even the tone of the writing, gives each publication a unique look and feel.

If you had to start from scratch every time you created a publication, you'd spend the bulk of your time setting up your documents and have little time left to attend to the appearance of the content (you'd probably get terribly bored, too). Few things are less rewarding than doing the same job over and over. Fortunately, InDesign includes several extremely useful features that let you automate repetitive tasks. This chapter focuses on three of them: master pages, templates, and libraries.

IN THIS CHAPTER

Automating repetitive tasks

Working with master pages

Creating templates

Using libraries

Ensuring consistency with rulers, grids, and guides

- A *master page* is a preconstructed page layout that you can use when adding pages to a multipage document. With master pages, you can design a single background page and then use it as the basis for as many document pages as you want. Without master pages, you would have to create every page from scratch.

- A *template* is a preconstructed document that's used to create multiple iterations of the same design or publication. A template is a shell of a document that contains everything in a publication except content. Each time you need to create a new version of a repeatedly produced publication, you open its template, save the version as a new document file, add the content (text and graphics), tweak as desired, and then print. Next issue, same thing.

■ As its name suggests, a *library* is a place where you store things. Specifically, InDesign libraries are files for storing objects that you create in InDesign and that you intend to use repeatedly in multiple documents.

This chapter covers a fourth set of options — rulers, guides, and grids —that don't automate your work but do make it easier to be consistent across pages. Ensuring consistency is a key part of implementing layout standards, and it's easy to overlook these aids when using InDesign.

TIP Although this chapter begins with master pages, this doesn't mean that you should begin work on a publication by creating master pages. You may prefer to work on text-formatting tasks first and build styles before turning your attention to page-layout and document-construction tasks.

Adapting Layout Standards to Your Work

When you combine libraries, master pages, and templates with the capability to create character, paragraph, table, and cell styles (see Chapters 19 and 21) and object styles (see Chapter 12), you have a powerful set of automation tools. Styles automate text and object formatting; libraries automate object creation; master pages automate page construction; and templates automate document construction.

How and to what extent you use these features depends on your personal preferences and the publications you produce. You might think that something as small as a business card wouldn't benefit from any of these features, but if it's a business card for a corporate employee, the chances are that, other than the personal information, it's exactly the same as business cards of every other employee. By creating and saving a business-card template, you can quickly build cards for several or several hundred new employees. All you have to do is open the template; add the name, title, and phone number of the new employee; and then send to the printer.

For other publications, you might use several — perhaps all — of the aforementioned timesaving features. A good newsletter template, for example, contains a set of styles for formatting text, probably a master spread or two (depending on whether all pages share exactly the same design), and perhaps an associated library of frequently used objects — house ads, corporate logos, boilerplate text, and so on.

Creating and Applying Master Pages

Before the arrival of personal computers, publications were created by graphics designers who leaned over light tables and, armed with matte knives and waxing machines, stuck galleys of type, halftones, and plastic overlays onto paste-up boards. The paste-up boards were usually oversized sheets of white card paper on which was printed a grid of light-blue lines. The blue guidelines indicated such things as the edge of the final, trimmed page; the margins in which text and graphics were placed; column boundaries; and so on. These guidelines helped the designer position elements on a page and also helped ensure consistent placement of repeating page elements, such as page numbers.

Although there are no paste-up boards in the electronic publishing world, the concept has survived in the form of *master pages*. A master page is a building-block page that you can use as the background (that is, as the starting point) for document pages. The master pages themselves don't print, but any pages that use them print the items from their master page, in addition to any unique elements you add to those individual pages. Typically, master pages contain text and graphic elements, such as page numbers, headers, footers, folios, and so on, that appear on all pages of a publication. And as did their paste-up board ancestors, master pages also include guidelines that indicate page edges, column boundaries, and margins, as well as other manually created guidelines to aid page designers in placing objects. By placing items on master pages, you save yourself the repetitive work of placing the same items one by one on each and every document page.

NOTE Note that InDesign's menu options and other interfaces sometimes switch between *master page* and *master spread* based on which is selected, but the steps are the same even if I say *page* and InDesign shows *spread*.

By default, every InDesign document you create contains a master page. Whether you use the master page or create and use additional master pages depends on the kind of publication you're creating. If it's a single-page document, such as a business card or an advertisement, you don't need to worry about master pages at all. (Generally, master pages are of little use for one-page documents.) However, if you're creating a multipage document like a newsletter, a book, or a catalog, using master pages save you time and help ensure design consistency. It's impossible to overstate the importance of master pages. They're one of InDesign's most powerful features.

The Pages panel

When you work on multipage documents, you may want to display the Pages panel (choose Window➪Pages or press ⌘+F12 or Ctrl+F12), which is shown in Figure 6.1. The Pages panel displays a thumbnail preview of your document pages (bottom) and master pages (top) in the current document. The controls in the Pages panel and its accompanying flyout menu let you perform several master page-related tasks, including creating and deleting master pages, applying master pages to document pages, and creating master pages out of document pages. The Pages panel also lets you add and remove document pages.

FIGURE 6.1

The Pages panel. The document page icons at the bottom of the panel show that the publication has 34 pages. The master page icons at the top show the default master pages: [None], A-Master, B-Master, and so on.

CROSS-REF   See Chapter 5 for more information about adding and removing document pages.

Here's a quick rundown of the controls available in the Pages panel and the commands in its flyout menu:

- The page icons (by default at the top of the panel) represent master pages. Every document includes a master page called [None], which includes only margin guidelines, and A-Master, which reflects the margin and column settings you specify in the New Document dialog box when you create the document. If a letter appears on a master page icon, it indicates that the master spread is based on another (parent) master page; for example, if you have a master page named C-Master and the icons for C-Master have the letter *A,* then C-Master is based on A-Master. A master page's name appears below its icon. If a master page and its name are highlighted, it means that the master page appears in the document window. If a master page name appears in reverse type, it's currently displayed in the document window.

- The page icons (by default at the bottom of the panel) represent document pages. Dog-eared icons represent left and right pages in a facing-pages document. The letter displayed on a page icon indicates the master page it's based on. (If no letter appears, the page is based on the blank master page.) The numbers below the page icons indicate the page numbers, including section numbering, if any (sections are covered in Chapter 5; automatic page numbers are covered in Chapter 22). If a page and its number are highlighted, it means that page currently appears in the document window. If a page number appears in reverse type (that is, white characters on a black background), it means that it's currently displayed in the document window.

■ The Create New Page iconic button (notepad icon) at the bottom of the panel lets you add a new page with a mouse click. (When a master page is displayed, the button becomes the Create New Master button.)

■ The Delete Selected Pages iconic button (trashcan icon) lets you delete document and master pages. (When a master page is displayed, the button becomes the Delete Selected Masters button.)

■ The Insert Pages flyout menu option lets you add pages to a document and specify the master page on which they're based.

■ The Move Pages flyout menu option lets you move document pages using a dialog box in which you specify which pages to move and where to move them. You can also simply click the pages to select them and drag them to their new location within the Pages panel. When a master page is displayed, the menu option becomes Move Masters.

■ The New Master flyout menu option lets you add a new master page.

■ The Duplicate Spread and Duplicate Page flyout menu options do exactly what the names say. They let you duplicate a page or a facing-pages spread. The name of the command depends on whether a page or spread is highlighted in the panel. (When a master page is displayed, the menu options become Duplicate Master Spread and Duplicate Master Page.)

■ The Delete Page and Delete Spread flyout menu options let you delete single pages and facing-pages spreads. Again, the menu name changes based on what is selected in the panel. When a master page is displayed, the menu options become Delete Master Spread and Delete Master Page.

■ The Select Unused Masters flyout menu option selects all unused master pages and spreads, so you can easily identify and perhaps delete them.

■ The Master Options flyout menu option changes master page attributes, including name and parent master page (if you want to base a master page on another master page).

■ The Apply Master to Pages flyout menu command is used for applying a master page layout to one or more document pages.

■ The Save as Master flyout menu option lets you convert a document page into a master page.

■ The Hide Master Options flyout menu option hides any master page items in your document. The menu option then becomes Show Master Options so that you can redisplay them.

■ The Override All Master Page Items flyout menu option lets you have any local changes to the selected pages override the master page settings. This command moves all master items to the document page on the selected pages. You can also use the shortcut Option+Shift+⌘+L or Ctrl+Alt+Shift+L.

- The Remove All Local Overrides and the Remove Selected Local Overrides flyout menu options return master objects that you've modified on specific document pages to their original condition. If no object is selected and you are displaying a document page, the menu command is Remove All Local Overrides; if one or more objects are selected, the menu command is Remove Selected Local Overrides.

- The Detach All Objects from Master and Detach Selection from Master flyout menu options remove any master page items that had been modified on the selected pages from the master page *for those selected document pages* only. Essentially, this command prevents you from using the Remove All Local Overrides or Remove Selected Local Overrides commands for these document pages, permanently changing the master pages for them. If no object is selected and you are displaying a document page, the menu command is Detach All Objects from Master; if one or more objects are selected, the menu command is Detach Selection from Master.

- The Allow Master Item Overrides on Selection flyout menu option lets you change the object on document pages, by Shift+⌘+clicking or Ctrl+Shift+clicking it and changing attributes such as size, location, or color. If you deselect this option on the master page for any selected objects, then you cannot change the object on any document pages, which is a great way to prevent unauthorized changes for standard elements. Of course, all someone has to do is change the settings on the master page, but that kind of effort is usually enough to hinder unintentional changes this feature is really aimed at stopping.

- If selected, the Allow Document Pages to Shuffle flyout menu option ensures that pages within spreads are not split apart as you add pages. Normally, adding a single page shuffles all subsequent pages so that they form new spreads. With this command, existing spreads are maintained, so adding an odd number of pages does not cause them to be reshuffled.

- If selected, the Allow Selected Spread to Shuffle flyout menu option ensures that pages within this spread do split apart as you add pages.

- The Panel Options flyout menu option controls icon size, position, and other Pages panel display settings, as explained in Chapter 5.

- The Numbering & Section Options flyout menu option lets you establish independently numbered sections in a single document. For example, you can create a section if you want to use a different numbering scheme (Roman numerals, perhaps) for the front matter of a book than for the body.

- The Spread Flattening flyout menu option lets you control image flattening for specific spreads. *Flattening* is InDesign's term for reducing the resolution of graphics to save disk space and speed output time. Typically, you'd flatten images for Web-oriented documents because the Web displays images at the relatively low resolution of 72 dpi. You might also flatten high-resolution graphics when printing a draft version to speed up printing.

CROSS-REF See Chapter 5 for details on how the shuffling controls work, as well as for more information about sections and the Panel Options dialog box. Chapter 31 covers flattening in more detail.

Creating a new master page

If all the pages in the publication you're creating share essentially the same page design, you don't need to create a new master page. Instead, you can simply use the default master page called A-Master that every document has. But if you intend to use more than one page layout in your document — maybe you're building a magazine and you want some pages to use a three-column format and others to use a two-column format — you need to create additional master pages.

Before you create a new master page, you should have a general idea of how you want it to look. In particular, you should know where you want to place margins, column boundaries, and repeating elements, such as page numbers. (Laying out master pages is covered later in this section.) When you're ready to create a new master page, follow these steps:

1. **If the Pages panel is not displayed, choose Windows ⇨ Pages or press ⌘+F12 or Ctrl+F12.**

2. **From the Pages panel's flyout menu, choose New Master.** You can also press Option+⌘ or Ctrl+Alt and click the Create New Page iconic button at the bottom of the panel. The New Master dialog box, shown in Figure 6.2, appears.

FIGURE 6.2

The New Master dialog box

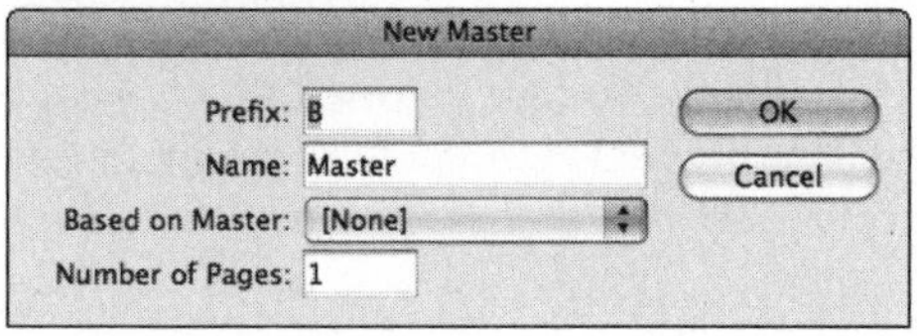

3. **In the Prefix field, specify a one-character prefix that's attached to the front of the master page name and appears on associated document page icons in the Pages panel.** The default is a letter such as B, C, or D.

4. **In the Name field, type a name for the master page.** Use something descriptive, such as 3-*Column Layout*, *Front Matter Layout*, or *Chapter Title Pages*.

5. **If you want to base the master page on another master page you've already created, select the parent master page from the Based on Master pop-up menu.** Basing a master page on another master page is covered in more detail later in this section.

6. **In the Number of Pages field, type the number of pages you want to include in the master spread.** Typically, you type **2** for a facing-pages document and **1** for a single-page document.

7. **When you finish specifying the attributes of the new master page, click OK to close the dialog box.**

After you create a new master page, it appears in the document window. (When a master page is displayed, its name appears in the Page field in the bottom-left corner of the document window.) You can modify any of a master page's attributes at any time by clicking its icon at the top of the Pages panel, choosing Master Options from the panel's flyout menu, and then changing any of the settings in the Master Options dialog box, which is identical to the New Master dialog box.

Basing a master page on another master page

If you find that a particular publication requires more than one master page, you may want to first lay out a base master page (you can use the default A-Master) and then create additional master pages that share the same basic layout but are slightly different. For example, if the magazine you're working on uses two-, three-, and four-column page layouts, you can create the two-column master spread first and include all repeating page elements. You can then create two additional master page spreads, base them on the two-column master, and specify different column formats. The two *children* masters are identical to the parent except for the number of columns. If you subsequently decide to modify, move, or delete a repeating page element, such as the issue date in the folio, you can make the change on the parent master and it is automatically applied to the children masters.

When you create a new master page, the New Master dialog box provides the option to base it on an existing master page. You can also choose or change a master spread's parent by:

- Choosing Master Options in the Pages panel's flyout menu and then choosing a master page from the Based on Master pop-up menu.

- Dragging and dropping the icon of a master spread (the parent) onto the icon of another master spread (the child). Be careful if you use this method. It's possible to base only one page of a master spread on another, but in most cases you want to base both pages of the child master on both pages of the parent master. To do so, make sure that when you release the mouse button both pages of the child are highlighted.

- Clicking the master spread you want to be the child and then pressing Option or Alt and clicking the master spread you want to be the parent.

When you base a master page on another master page, the prefix of the parent appears in the upper outside corner of the page icon of the child.

> **TIP** If you base a master page on another master page, you can still modify the master objects (that is, the objects inherited from the parent master) on the child master page. As with regular document pages, you have to Shift+⌘+click or Ctrl+Shift+click the object inherited from a parent master to release it before you can edit it on a child master.

Creating master pages from document pages

Generally, if you need a new master page, you begin by choosing New Master from the Pages panel's flyout menu. But you can also create a master page from a document page (or a master spread from a document spread). To do so, highlight the document page or spread by clicking the page number(s) below the page icon(s) in the Pages panel and then choose Save as Master from the Pages panel's flyout menu. The new page or master is assigned a default name and prefix. If you want to modify any of its attributes, click its name in the Pages panel and then choose Master Options from the pop-up menu.

Importing a master page

Sometimes another document has a master page that you'd like to use in your current layout. InDesign lets you import those master pages: Just choose Load Master Pages from the Pages panel's flyout menu and then select the source document in the dialog box that appears. InDesign will import all master pages from that document into your current one. There's no way to select specific master pages.

If any of the imported master pages have the same name as your current document's master pages (such as the default name A-Master), a dialog box appears giving you the choice of replacing the current master pages with the imported ones that use the same name or of renaming the imported master pages, so you keep what you have and add the imported ones. InDesign does the renaming for you, using the next available default name. For example, if your current document has master pages A-Master and B-Master already defined, it renames the imported A-Master to C-Master.

Note that InDesign also alerts you if the imported master pages use different dimensions than the current document's pages. But it won't adjust the imported pages to fit the current document's size, so some items may appear off the page if the imported master page has larger dimensions than the current document.

Duplicating a master

You can create a copy of a master page or spread by clicking its icon and then choosing Duplicate Master Spread from the Pages panel's flyout menu, or by clicking and dragging the master page's icon onto the Create New Master iconic button and releasing the mouse. If you duplicate a master page or spread, there is not a parent/child relationship between the original master and the copy (as there is when you base a master on another master).

Deleting a master

To delete a master page, click its name and then choose Delete Master Page from the Pages panel's flyout menu. You can also click the master page icon and then click the Delete Selected Masters iconic button (trashcan icon) in the Pages panel, or click and drag the master page icon directly to the Delete Selected Masters iconic button.

Laying out a master page

Because a master page is similar to a document page, you can use the same approach for building both master and document pages. Some designers prefer to do a preliminary sketch on paper and then re-create the design in InDesign. You may like to do your creative brainstorming at your computer, in which case you can use InDesign as your sketchpad. The main difference between document pages and master pages is that master pages don't contain any content (other than elements that appear on every page). So, when you're building a master page, you should be thinking more about the page's overall infrastructure than about details.

Here are a few things to keep in mind when designing master pages:

- If you're working on a facing-pages document (most multipage publications have facing pages), you can create facing-pages master spreads. The left-hand page (used for even-numbered document pages) and right-hand page (used for odd-numbered document pages) of the master spreads you create are more or less mirror opposites of each other. For example, page numbers are generally placed near the outside edge of facing pages so that they're visible when a reader thumbs through the pages. Or you may decide to place the publication name on one side of a spread and balance it by placing the date of publication in the same position on the other side.

- If you want to automatically place page numbers on document pages, you should add a page number character on each page of your master spreads. To add a page number character, draw a text frame with the Type tool and then choose Type ⇨ Insert Special Character ⇨ Markers ⇨ Auto Page Number or press Option+Shift+⌘+N or Ctrl+Alt+Shift+N. The prefix of the master page (A, B, C, and so on) is displayed on the master page, but on document pages, the actual page number is used. When you add a page number to a master page, make sure to format the numbers as you want them to look on document pages.

- Perhaps the most important elements of a master page are the margins and column guides. To specify margins and columns for a master page, make sure the page appears in the document window and then choose Layout ⇨ Margins and Columns. The Margins and Columns dialog box, shown in Figure 6.3, appears. The controls in this dialog box let you specify the position of the margins, the number of columns, and the gutter width (space between columns).

FIGURE 6.3

The Margins and Columns dialog box

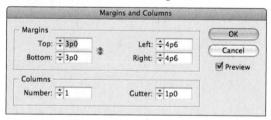

When placing text elements on master pages, you may want to use placeholder text instead of actual text. InDesign makes it easy to do so: Just choose Type ⇨ Fill with Placeholder Text. InDesign adds fake Latin text to the text frame until it is filled. In some cases, you want to add your own placeholder text. For example, if you produce a monthly magazine and you want to include the name of the month on each spread (perhaps opposite the name of the newsletter on the facing page), you can use placeholder text such as [Name of month] or [Add month here] or use the variable-text feature. If you use placeholder text, format it as you want the actual text to appear on document pages. Of course, be sure to replace the placeholder text with the actual text in your final document.

CROSS-REF Note that you can use the Section Marker feature in some cases to have InDesign automatically enter text, such as the issue month. See Chapter 5 for more details. Or you can use the more flexible variable-text feature, explained in Chapter 22.

- If you want to place additional guidelines on a master page, you can add as many custom guidelines as you want. Guidelines are covered later in this chapter.

- As with objects on document pages, the objects you place on master pages have a stacking order. On document pages, all master objects remain beneath any objects you add to the page.

Figure 6.4 shows a typical master page spread for a newsletter. Whenever you want to make a change to a master page, double-click its icon in the Pages panel to display it in the document window.

TIP To copy a master page from one document to another, display the source document, click the master's name in the Pages panel, drag it to the window of the target document, and release the mouse button.

FIGURE 6.4

A typical three-column master layout for a newsletter. The footer at the bottom of the left- and right-hand pages includes a page-number character on the outside. On a master page, the page number appears as the master page's prefix (A, in this case).

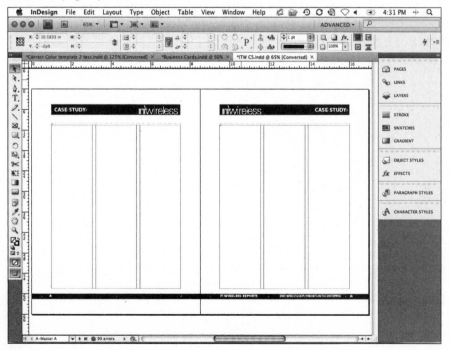

Applying a master page to document pages

After you've built a master page, you can apply it to new document pages as you add them or to existing pages (see Chapter 5 for information about adding and removing document pages). For facing-pages documents, you can apply both pages of a master spread to both pages of a document spread, or you can apply one page of a master spread to one page of a document spread. For example, you can apply a master page with a two-column format to the left-hand page of a document spread and apply a master page with a three-column format to the right-hand page.

To apply only one page of a master spread to a document page, click the icon of the master spread and then drag it onto the icon of the document page you want to format. When the target document page is highlighted (framed in a black rectangle as shown in the upper left side of Figure 6.5), release the mouse button. If both document pages are highlighted, both sides of the master spread are applied to the document spread.

To apply both pages of a master spread to both pages of a document spread, drag the master spread's icon below the right-hand page in the document spread (under its page icon). When both pages of the target document spread are highlighted, as shown in the right side of Figure 6.5, release the mouse button. Getting InDesign to select the entire spread can be tricky: You need to move the icon to just outside (vertically) and just inside (horizontally) a corner of a spread for the spread rather than an individual page to be highlighted.

FIGURE 6.5

Upper left: Applying a single page of a master spread to a document page using the mouse. Upper right: Applying both pages of a master spread to a document spread using the mouse. Bottom: The Apply Master dialog box lets you apply a master page to selected pages.

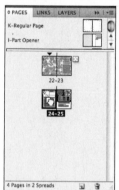
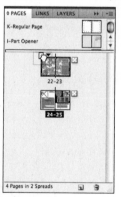
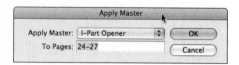

InDesign also lets you apply a master page to multiple document pages in a single operation. You can:

- **Select the document pages to which you want to apply a master.** Click a page and then Shift+click another page to select a range of pages, or press ⌘ or Ctrl and click pages to select nonconsecutive pages. After you select the document pages, press Option or Alt and click the master page you want to apply.

- **Choose Apply Master to Pages from the Pages panel's flyout menu.** The Apply Master dialog box, shown in Figure 6.5, appears. Choose the master page you want to apply from the Apply Master pop-up menu, and specify the pages to which you want to apply it in the To Pages field. Use commas to separate page numbers; use a hyphen to specify a range of pages. For example, type **2, 4–6, 8** to apply the selected master to pages 2, 4 through 6, and 8.

- **Choose Layout ⇨ Pages ⇨ Apply Master to Pages.** This works the same way as the Apply Master to Pages flyout menu option in the Pages panel.

You can also use these techniques to apply a different master page to a document page. If you want to disassociate a document page from its applied master page, you can apply the default [None] master page the same way you apply any other master page.

Modifying master items on document pages

As you work on a document page that's based on a master, you may find that you need to modify, move, or delete a master object. For example, you might apply a master to the first page of a newsletter and then decide that the page number you've placed on the master page isn't necessary for page 1. In this case, you'd select the master object on the document page and delete it. Any change you make to a master object on a local page is referred to as a *local override*.

If you remove a master object from a document page, you sever the object's relationship to the master page object for that document page only. If you subsequently move or modify the object on the master page, it doesn't affect the deleted object on the document page; it remains deleted on that particular document page.

However, you can modify a master object on a document page without completely breaking its relationship to the corresponding object on the master page. For example, if you change the size, position, or content of a master object on a document page, any subsequent size, position, or content change you make to the object on the master page does not affect the object you modified. But any changes you make to the stroke or fill of the object on the master page are applied to the overridden master object on the document page. Similarly, if you use any of the transformation tools or the corresponding controls in the Control panel or Transform panel to modify a master object on a document page, any similar transformation applied to the corresponding object on the master page is not applied to the overridden object.

In other words, any type of attribute applied to the item on a particular document page prevents any changes to the same attribute on the master page from affecting that document page.

> **TIP** The Show Master Items command (choose Show Master Items in the Pages panel's flyout menu) lets you show or hide master objects on document pages. (The name of the menu option is Show Master Items when items are hidden, Hide Master Items when they are not hidden.)

To modify a master object on a document page, you must select it. However, master objects behave slightly differently than other objects on document pages. Specifically, to select a master object on a document page, you press Shift+⌘ or Ctrl+Shift when you click the object with one of the selection tools. After you select a master object on a document page, you can modify it in the same manner as you modify nonmaster objects.

If you modify one or more master objects on a document page and then decide you want to revert back to using the original master objects, you can remove the local overrides. To do so, display the document page that contains the master objects you've modified, select the objects, and choose Remove Selected Local Overrides from the Pages panel's flyout menu. If no objects are selected, the command name changes to Remove All Local Overrides (if the selected spread doesn't have any modified master objects, the command is not available).

You can prevent master page objects from being modified at all. To do this, select them on the master page and then choose Allow Master Item Overrides on Selection so that the check mark disappears to its left. Now, you cannot change or even select these objects on the document page unless you come back to the master page and turn back on this option.

But note that if you use this technique in an existing document, any document pages where the selected master page objects have already been modified will retain those modifications and allow additional modifications. Only untouched objects will be made untouchable.

If you want to reset all overridden master page objects, before locking them down with the Allow Master Item Overrides menu option, you must first choose Remove All Overrides from the flyout menu.

Using Templates

A template is a preconstructed InDesign document that you can use as the starting point for creating multiple versions of the same design or publication. For example, if you are assigned the task of creating a dozen testimonial ads that share the same layout but use different graphics and text, you begin by creating a template that contains all the elements that are the same in every ad — placeholder frames for the graphics and text, guidelines, and so on. Along the same lines, if you produce periodicals such as a newsletter or a magazine, you should create a template for each one.

Creating templates

The process of creating a template is much the same as creating a document. You create the required character and paragraph styles, master pages, repeating elements (for example, the nameplate on the first page and mailing information on the back page), and so on. The only thing you don't add to a template is actual content.

It would be nice if designers had the luxury of creating a template up front for each new publication they produced. But in the real world, templates are often created by gutting an existing document. The first time you create a publication such as a newsletter, the main goal during production is getting a finished document to the printer —on time, you hope. After you finish the first issue of a publication (or a prototype), you can open the file, remove all objects and content that aren't repeated in every issue, and then save the gutted file as a template. This is probably how you'll build many of your templates.

Here are the steps in creating a template:

1. **Choose File ➪ Save As or press Shift+⌘+S or Ctrl+Shift+S to display the Save As dialog box.**

2. **Choose a storage folder and specify a name for the file.** Even though the template has the filename extension `.indt` as opposed to the `.indd` extension of a document, it's not a bad idea to add the word Template to the filename, if possible. It lets whoever uses the file quickly know its purpose.

3. **On a Mac, choose InDesign CS4 Template in the Format pop-up menu. On a PC, choose InDesign CS4 Template from the Save As Type pop-up menu.**

4. **Click Save to close the Save As dialog box and save the template.**

TIP If you're designing a template that others will use, you might want to add a layer of instructions. When it's time to print a document based on the template, simply hide the annotation layer, or mark it as nonprinting. (See Chapter 5 for more information about layers.)

Modifying templates

A template is almost exactly the same as a standard InDesign document with one major exception: A template is slightly protected from being overridden. When you open a template, it's assigned a default name (Untitled-1, Untitled-2, and so on). The first time you choose File ➪ Save or press ⌘+S or Ctrl+S, the Save As dialog box appears.

NOTE As you use a template over time, you're likely to discover that you forgot to include something — perhaps a style, a repeating element on a particular master page, or an entire master page. To modify a template, you must open it, make your changes, and then use the Save or Save As command to save the file in the same place and with the same name as the original.

To modify a template, you have two options:

- **Open it as a normal file, make your changes and then choose File ➪ Save As or press Shift+⌘+S or Ctrl+Shift+S to save it again as a template.** To open a file as a normal file, be sure that Open Normal (Mac) or Normal (Windows) is selected at the bottom of the Open a File dialog box; this is the default option.

■ **Open it as an original file (see Chapter 4), make your changes and then choose File ⇨ Save or press ⌘+S or Ctrl+S to save it again as a template.** To open a file as an original file, be sure that Open Original (Mac) or Original (Windows) is selected at the bottom of the Open a File dialog box. It's easy to forget to select this option, so most people end up using the previous technique to resave the template.

Creating documents from templates

It's very easy to create a document from a template: Just open a template file and then save it with a new name, making sure that InDesign CS4 Document is selected in the Format pop-up menu (Mac) or Save as Type pop-up menu (Windows) — this the default setting. Work on your document and continue to save changes normally.

A more complicated way to create a document from a template is to choose File ⇨ New ⇨ Document from Template. This opens the Adobe Bridge CS4 program, which can contain InDesign templates that you open and then save as documents. Chapter 34 covers Bridge in more detail.

Storing Objects in Libraries

If you're a savvy InDesign user, you should never need to build the same document twice. After all, that's what templates are for. Along the same lines, you never have to create the same object twice; that's what libraries are for. An InDesign *library* is a file — similar in some ways to a document file — in which you can store individual objects, groups and nested objects, ruler guides, and grids (ruler guides and grids are covered in the next section). For example, if you create a logo in InDesign and you want to use it in other documents, you can place it in a library. After you save an object in a library, it's as though you have an endless supply of copies. Every time you need a copy, all you have to do is click and drag one out of the library.

CROSS-REF You can also create files that contain pieces of your layout, called *snippets*, for use in other documents. Chapter 9 covers snippets in more detail.

Creating a library is easy: Choose File ⇨ New ⇨ Library, choose a location to save the library in, give the library a name, and click Save. InDesign automatically adds the filename extension `.indl`.

You can create as many libraries as you want and store them wherever is most convenient, including on a networked server so that other InDesign users can share them. When it comes to naming and organizing libraries, the choice is yours. If you work for an advertising agency, for example, you may decide to create a separate library for each client; each library can contain logos, images, boilerplate text (such as disclaimers, copyright information, and legal blurbs), and so on. If you work for an in-house art department, you can create separate libraries for corporate logos (black-and-white, gray-scale, and two-color/four-color variations), house ads, frequently used graphics, and standing art.

 **InDesign libraries are cross-platform. That is, you can open libraries created on a Mac using a PC and vice versa.**

After you create a new library, an empty library panel is displayed. (Each library you open is in its own panel.) The name you assigned is displayed in its title bar. You add items by dragging them to the panel. Figure 6.6 shows an example. You can group the panel with other panels (by dragging its tab onto another panel) or close it by clicking its Close box or choosing Close Library from its flyout menu.

FIGURE 6.6

A library and its accompanying flyout menu

Library Item Information   Delete Library Item

Show Library Subset New Library Item

At this point, you're ready to begin placing objects into the library, after which you can begin copying the objects into other documents. Before I cover moving items into and out of libraries, here's a brief description of the controls in a library panel and the commands in the accompanying flyout menu (refer to Figure 6.6):

- **Numbers in the lower-left corner of the panel:** These indicate the number of objects currently displayed in the pane (although not necessarily visible, depending on the size of the panel) and the number of objects in the library. Search capabilities let you display a subset of the entire library.

- **Close Library:** This flyout menu command does the same thing as clicking a library panel's Close box.

- **Library Item Information iconic button and Item Information menu option:** You can use the button or the menu item with a library item selected — as well as simply double-click the library item itself — to open the Item Information dialog box, shown in Figure 6.7. Here you can assign a name, type, and description to a library object. You can search for library objects based on these attributes.

FIGURE 6.7

The Item Information dialog box

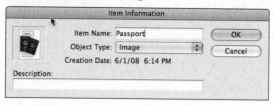

- **Show Library Subset iconic button and Show Subset menu option:** However you access this feature, it displays a dialog box that lets you locate and display objects that meet certain search criteria.

- **New Library Item iconic button and Add Item menu option:** However you access this feature, it lets you add selected objects on a document page to a library as separate items.

- **Add Items on Page:** This flyout menu option let you add all items on a document page to a library *as one library item.* You can also simply click and drag items together into the panel so that they're added as a single library item.

- **Add Items on Page as Separate Objects:** This flyout menu option lets you add all items on a document page to a library *as individual library items.*

- **Place Item(s):** This command lets you place copies of selected library objects into a document.

- **Delete Library Item iconic button and Delete Item(s) menu option:** However you access this feature, it lets you delete highlighted objects in the library.

- **Update Library Item:** Although you might think this menu option only updates the library item to reflect any changes made to the original item, that's not true. What this command really does is let you replace a library object, either a modified version of the original item or a completely different object. After you select the library object you want to replace, click whatever object you want to replace it with in your layout and then choose Update Library Item.

- **Show All:** This command displays all library objects (rather than a subset identified by a previous search).

- **List View:** When this option is selected, library objects appear in a list rather than as thumbnails.

- **Thumbnails View:** When this option is selected, each library object appears in its own thumbnail window.

- **Sort Items:** This command lets you sort library items by Name, Oldest, Newest, and Type. If you sort by Oldest or Newest, items are arranged based on the order in which they were placed into the library.

To open an existing library, choose File ➪ Open or press ⌘+O or Ctrl+O.

InDesign CS4 Color Techniques

Adobe InDesign offers a strong set of tools for color creation and control, as Chapters 7, 11, and 29 show in detail. This special eight-page color section shows some of these tools in action, using InDesign's actual capabilities.

Inside Color Models

Color is made up of light, but the printer and computer-monitor color models act very differently. Color printing is based on how light reflects off paper through inks. The standard inks in printing are cyan, magenta, yellow, and black (CMYK), although there are specialty inks such as Pantone, Toyo, and Trumatch. Each ink absorbs all colors but the one you see; for example, your eyes can see cyan because the cyan ink has absorbed all the other colors that light would normally pick up. That's why mixing several inks produces a dark brown or gray; most of the light is absorbed by the multiple inks. By contrast, computer monitors use a model based on how the three colors of light — red, green, and blue (RGB) — combine. All three combine to make white, whereas having none of the three colors gives you black. Because the physics of the two models is different, what you see on-screen — or what your scanner or digital camera sees when capturing an image — may not match what is printed.

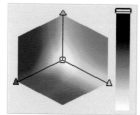

The CMYK model   *The RGB model*

The CMYK color and RGB color models (at left). For CMYK, the cube shows how cyan, magenta, and yellow combine in various percentages; the slider at the cube's right adds black, which has the effect of darkening the combination shown. In RGB, there's no slider because the three colors combine to produce all color shades (white is the absence of all colors). At bottom left are eight example ink swatches from specialty color libraries.

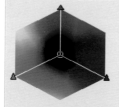

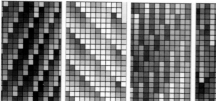

Pantone Solid ANPA   *Trumatch*   *Focoltone*

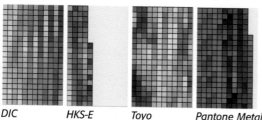

DIC   *HKS-E*   *Toyo*   *Pantone Metallic*

The Kuler panel lets you choose themed collections of RGB-based colors (left panel), as well as create your own using a variety of constraints (right panel).

Mixed Inks: Duotones and Beyond

A mixed-ink color combines spot colors and/or process colors to create a blended color. Such mixed-ink colors are mostly used for duotones and tritones, which combine one or two spot colors with black. A duotone (a spot color plus some black) is often used to simulate that dark brown of a very old photograph, for example. A tritone (two spot colors plus some black) creates richer or unusual colors that standard CMYK mixes can't create. But InDesign doesn't limit you to just duotones and tritones containing black; you can use yellow, cyan, and/or magenta as well — or create them solely from spot colors, with no process colors at all.

To create a mixed-ink color, you first must have created the spot colors you want to mix with the process colors. Then choose New Mixed Ink Swatch from the Swatches panel's flyout menu to get the New Mixed Ink Swatch dialog box. (Access the Swatches panel by choosing Window➪Swatches or pressing F5.) You can create solid colors, color tints, and gradients, as well as sets of color swatches using the mixed-ink capability. Here, you select the colors you want to mix and set the percentage of ink for each. Keep in mind that the more spot colors you use, the more it will cost to print the result (unless you convert them at print time to process colors).

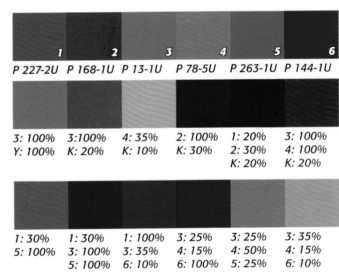

C	M	Y	K		
Cyan	Magenta	Yellow	Black		

1	2	3	4	5	6
P 227-2U	P 168-1U	P 13-1U	P 78-5U	P 263-1U	P 144-1U

3: 100%	3:100%	4: 35%	2: 100%	1: 20%	3: 100%
Y: 100%	K: 20%	K: 10%	K: 30%	2: 30%	4: 100%
				K: 20%	K: 20%

1: 30%	1: 30%	1: 100%	3: 25%	3: 25%	3: 35%
5: 100%	3: 100%	3: 35%	4: 15%	4: 50%	4: 15%
	5: 100%	6: 10%	6: 100%	5: 25%	6: 10%

You create mixed-ink swatches by combining colors at various percentages. The top row shows the four process colors (cyan, magenta, yellow, and black) and six Pantone uncoated colors. The middle row shows traditional duotones and tritones created with them. The bottom row shows mixed-ink colors composed of multiple spot colors. The captions show the mixes, using the codes in the upper row to identify the colors used. Below is the New Mixed Ink Swatch dialog box in which you actually mix the colors.

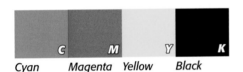

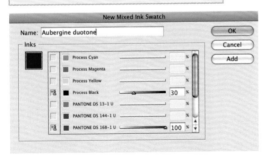

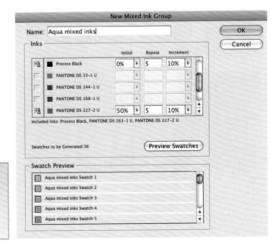

In addition to creating mixed-color swatches, InDesign can create a whole palette of related colors for you in one fell swoop, using the New Mixed Ink Group dialog box, shown at right. You get a swatch for each combination generated.

Copying Colors from an Image

Even if you have an excellent sense of color, matching colors by eye can be difficult. Because you may want to use a color from an image in your document — as a text color or for lines or strokes — an accurate color matching tool is a necessity. Fortunately, InDesign has the Eyedropper tool so you can sample a color and then apply it to an object or to text. You can also create a color swatch from the sample for use later.

After you click a color with the Eyedropper tool, the Eyedropper tool changes to the Marker tool, which applies the current fill and stroke to any text you highlight. For other objects, just click them with the Marker tool to apply the current fill to other objects. (Hold Shift to apply the stroke color to the current object's fill instead.) You can toggle back to the Eyedropper tool to sample another color by holding the Option or Alt key.

The color-selection process is simple: First, click the Fill iconic button or Stroke iconic button, in the Tools panel or the Swatches panel, to determine what will get the sampled color. Now select the Eyedropper tool in the Tools panel and click any colored object in your document with the tool (circled in yellow above). The Fill or Stroke button displays the sampled color.

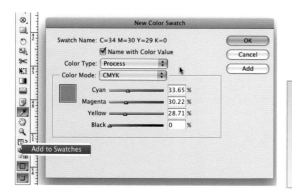

To add the color to your Swatches panel, just Control+click or right-click the color in the Tools panel; the color will be added as an RGB-based process color. Or select New Color Swatch from the Swatches panel's flyout menu to be able to name the color and set options such as the color model and color type.

Sharing Colors with Others

Although you can't use the Eyedropper tool to sample colors in Photoshop or Illustrator documents, you can share colors with users of those programs, as well as with other InDesign users. In InDesign, select any swatches you want to export — only mixed-ink swatches cannot be shared this way — and choose Save Swatches from the flyout menu. Now save the swatches as an Adobe Swatch Exchange (.ase) file, which other Creative Suite applications can open. (These are also called ColorBook files.) In Photoshop and Illustrator, choose Save Swatches for Exchange from their Swatches panels' flyout menus. In all three programs, import colors using the Load Swatches flyout menu commands. To import mixed-color swatches across InDesign documents, you must open the document containing those swatches and then apply each of them, even if just temporarily, to an object in the new target document. Doing so copies them to the target.

Working with Gradients

Gradients (also called blends) add a sense of motion or depth to a background or image. An image editor or illustration program such as Photoshop, Paint Shop Pro, Illustrator, or CorelDraw gives you very fine control over gradients, letting you control their shape and pattern. InDesign approaches the ability of such programs, and in some cases surpasses them. When combined with transparency and InDesign's light effects, you can really create some interesting effects, as shown in these two pages.

Two-color linear gradient   **Two-color radial gradient**

Example gradients (at left), using various settings for the stop and start colors, as well as for the gradient midpoint and, for linear gradients, the angle. At bottom left is the New Gradient Swatch dialog box in which you set the gradient's colors, stop points, angle, and other settings.

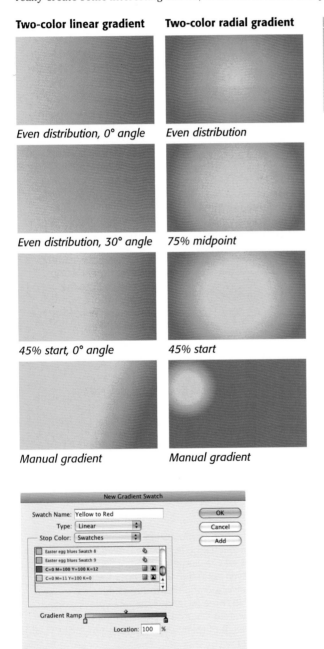

Even distribution, 0° angle   *Even distribution*

Even distribution, 30° angle   *75% midpoint*

45% start, 0° angle   *45% start*

Manual gradient   *Manual gradient*

Use the Gradient Swatch tool to manually set the gradient angle and stop points (top image below). The length of the line determines how tight the gradient ramp is, and the angle of the line sets the gradient angle. (The line does not print.) The bottom image below shows the new Gradient Feather tool, which does essentially the same thing but blends to transparent.

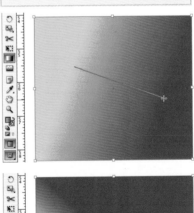

Applying Color Tints and Transparency

Adding color to a grayscale image, whether at full strength or as a lighter tint, can greatly change its character. And applying transparency (by reducing its opacity from solid, or 100%) to text, images, and other objects can greatly change their look and feel.

Original grayscale image

Content: swatch applied

Content: duotone applied

Content: tritone applied

Content: 20% [Black]

Content: [Paper] (white)
Fill: [Black]

Content: 20% Plum
Fill: 10% Plum

Content: 100% Plum
Fill: 20% Yellow

> From the Swatches panel, you can apply swatches to the contents of grayscale images to colorize them. (Be sure to select the images first with the Direct Selection tool.) By also coloring the fill (be sure to select the images with the Selection tool), you can achieve interesting effects — especially when combined with tints. For more-complex colorizing, use an image editor such as Adobe Photoshop or Corel Paint Shop Pro.

Applied via the Effects panel, transparency can give new dimension to text and graphics. At left, I applied 60% opacity to the banners to give a vellum effect. I then applied colored, partially transparent drop shadows to them.

Working with Lighting Effects

InDesign CS4 adopts a host of lighting effects that Photoshop has offered for a while (in its layer blending options), letting you create dimensional effects such as beveled edges and inner glows. Using the Effects panel, you can apply any of these effects (including several at one time) to your choice of an object's fill, stroke, and/or contents. Below are several examples of the effects, as well as the panel's Effects dialog box where you can find all the controls. Note that these effects rely on both transparency and color to carry out their design goals.

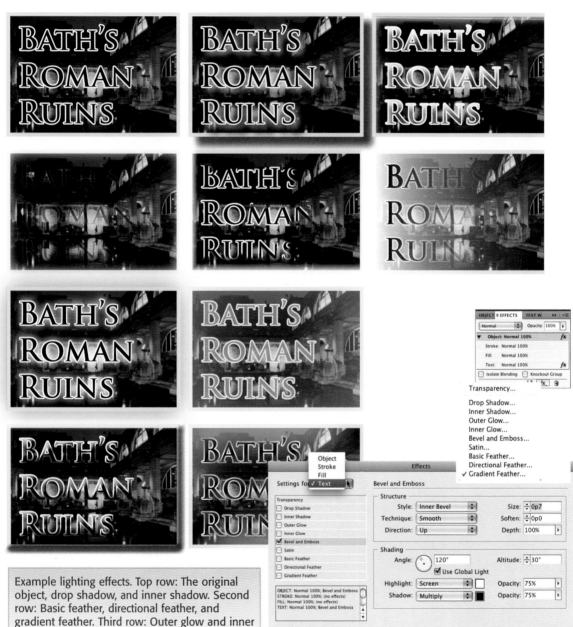

Example lighting effects. Top row: The original object, drop shadow, and inner shadow. Second row: Basic feather, directional feather, and gradient feather. Third row: Outer glow and inner glow. Bottom row: Bevel and emboss, and satin.

Normal	Lighten	Normal	Lighten
Multiply	Difference	Multiply	Difference
Overlay	Exclusion	Overlay	Exclusion
Soft Light	Hue	Soft Light	Hue
Hard Light	Saturation	Hard Light	Saturation
Color Dodge	Color	Color Dodge	Color
Color Burn	Luminosity	Color Burn	Luminosity
Darken		Darken	

The 15 blend modes affect how various lighting effects appear. At left, they are applied to the drop shadows of the text placed over a solid background. At right, the blend modes are applied to both the 80% opaque text and to its drop shadows over a 30% opaque image.

The Web's Limited Palette

Although the HTML supports thousands of colors, you can count on only 216 colors to display properly on popular Macintosh and Windows Web browsers. That's because most browsers play it safe and assume that people have just the basic video support on their computers: 8-bit color depth, which permits 256 colors. Of those 256, Windows reserves 40 for its interface, leaving 216 for the browser to use. Understanding this, InDesign comes with a Web-Safe swatch library that has only the colors that all browsers can display. Keep these limits in mind when you convert your print images to the Web's JPEG or GIF formats; whether you convert them using InDesign's Export to Dreamweaver feature or in a program such as Photoshop, expect the Web images' colors to shift and be less subtle.

The examples at left show how print-oriented colors (top row) are typically shifted when viewed in a Web browser (bottom row).

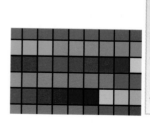

The InDesign swatch library at left shows all 216 Web-safe colors; by contrast, the number of colors that can be printed is in the millions.

Working with Traps

If you don't have your InDesign documents output to negatives or directly to plate and have them printed on a standard web offset press (SWOP, or Specifications for Web Offset Publications), you don't need to worry about trapping. But if you do such professional output, *trapping* is an issue you should be aware of. InDesign lets you control trapping in some situations, based on what kind of output device you are using. These controls are global — affecting everything in the document — so if you want to set specific trapping settings for graphics, for example, you need to do so as part of creating the illustration in a program such as Illustrator or CorelDraw. The one local control InDesign does offer is whether strokes and fills overprint or trap.

Knockout (no overlap of abutting colors)

Overprint

Centering (light color and dark color move into each other)

Choke (dark color moves into light color)

Spread (light color moves into dark color)

Above: The various trapping methods you can use in InDesign. Except for overprinting, each method is applied to every object in your document.

Adjusting Color for Output

As do most professional design tools, InDesign uses color profiles (choose Edit ➪ Color Settings) to help ensure that your output matches as closely as possible the original image's colors. (The capabilities and limits of your output device ultimately determine how close you can get.) By applying color profiles and using InDesign's Rendering Intent color settings, you can change the output character of your images.

You should set your document to use the appropriate RGB color profile for your monitor or scanner, as well as the appropriate CMYK profile for your printer or printing press to get the most accurate color. A mismatch between the profile and the input and output devices can shift the color of your images. The images at left have the following settings, clockwise from upper left: default settings; Tektronix Phaser III Pxi with relative colorimetric rendering; Euroscale v2 with absolute colorimetric rendering; and Kodak SWOP Proofer CMYK Coated with saturation rendering.

NOTE Multiple users can share a library, but only if it's locked (meaning people can use items in the library but not add new ones). To lock a library on the Mac, locate the library file in the Finder, select it, choose File ⇨ Get Info or press ⌘+I, and select the Locked option. In Windows, locate the library file in its current folder, right-click the filename or icon, and then select Read-Only from the Properties contextual menu's General pane.

To delete a library, you must delete the file. Either click and drag the file icon to the Trash (Mac) or move the file icon to the Recycle Bin (Windows).

Adding and deleting library objects

In addition to placing individual objects, such as text and graphics frames, into a library, you can also place multiple-selected objects, groups, nested frames, ruler guides, guidelines, and all objects on a page.

There are several ways to add objects to a library. You can:

- Select one or more objects and then drag and drop them into an open library panel.
- Select one or more objects and then click the New Library Item button at the bottom of an open library panel.
- Select one or more objects and then choose Add Item from the flyout menu of an open library panel.
- Go to the desired page and then choose Add Items on Page from the flyout menu of an open library panel to add all selected objects on the current page or spread *as one library item.*
- Go to the desired page and then choose Add Items on Page as Separate Objects from the flyout menu of an open library panel to add all selected objects on the current page or spread *as individual library items.*

TIP If you press and hold Option or Alt when adding an object to a library using any of the preceding methods, the Item Information dialog box appears. This dialog box lets you add searchable attributes to the object.

To delete a library object, click and drag its icon to the Delete Library Item iconic button (trashcan icon) at the bottom of the panel. You can also click the object once and then choose Delete Item(s) from the library panel's flyout menu or just click the Delete Library Item iconic button. You can select a range of objects by clicking on the first one and then Shift+clicking the last one. You can select multiple, noncontiguous objects by pressing and holding ⌘ or Ctrl and clicking each icon that you want to delete.

When you place an object into a library, all its attributes are saved. For example, if you import a graphic into a document and then place a copy of the graphic into a library, the path to the original graphics file is saved, as are any transformations you've applied to the graphic or its frame (scale, rotation, shear, and so on). If you save text in a library, all formats, including styles, are retained.

Library Caveats

Because the attributes of the original object are retained when you place a copy in a library, there are some pitfalls you have to watch out for:

- If you move, modify, or delete the original graphic files associated with a graphic you've placed in a library and then copy the library object into a document, the Links panel will report that the graphics file is modified or missing (just as it would if you imported the graphic and then moved, modified, or deleted the original). It's a good idea to store graphics files used in libraries in a common location, such as in a `Standards` folder on the network, so that the graphics files aren't accidentally moved or deleted when you delete or archive a set of project files that happen to contain objects placed in libraries.

- If you copy a text frame from a library onto a document page, any styles or swatches in the library object that have the same name as styles or swatches in the target document are replaced by those in the target document. If the target document does not contain styles or swatches in the placed text, they're added to the document.

- If you copy a text frame from a library onto a document page, make sure that the fonts are available. If they're not available, you have to select alternate fonts.

Cataloging library objects

If your libraries contain only a few objects, finding the one you're looking for isn't very hard. But a library can hold as many objects as you want, and as a library becomes bigger, locating a particular object gets increasingly difficult. To make library objects easier to find, InDesign lets you tag them with several searchable attributes.

To tag a library element, select it and then choose Item Information from the library panel's flyout menu. You can also display the Item Information dialog box by double-clicking on a library object or by clicking once on a library object and then clicking the Library Item Information iconic button at the bottom of the library panel. (Figure 6.7, earlier in the chapter, shows the Item Information dialog box.) Now specify an Item Name, an Object Type, and/or a Description. In the Description field, it's a good idea to type one or more keywords that describe the object so that you can easily find it later. Click OK to close the dialog box and return to the document.

InDesign lets you search for library objects based on the information specified in the Item Information dialog box. For example, if you've placed several different corporate logos into a library that includes many other objects, you could search for the term *logo* in the Name or Description field. If you used the word *logo* in either of these fields for your logos, a search of these fields for the word *logo* will identify and display your logos. The ability to search for library objects based on name and description is a good reason to name your library objects carefully and consistently and to specify keywords in the Description field of the Item Information dialog box. Follow these steps:

1. **Choose Show Subset from a library panel's flyout menu or click the Show Library Subset iconic button (glasses icon) at the bottom of the panel.** The Show Subset dialog box, shown in Figure 6.8, appears.

FIGURE 6.8

The Show Subset dialog box with two search options specified

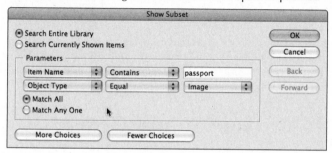

2. **To search the entire library, click Search Entire Library; to search only the objects currently displayed in the page, click Search Currently Shown Items.**

3. **From the leftmost pop-up menu in the Parameters area, choose the Item Information category you want to search from the first pop-up menu: Item Name, Creation Date, Object Type, or Description.**

4. **From the next pop-up menu, choose Contains if you intend to search for text contained in the chosen category; choose Doesn't Contain if you want to exclude objects that contain the text you specify.**

5. **In the rightmost field, type the word or phrase you want to search for (if Contains is selected) or exclude (if Doesn't Contain is selected).**

6. **To add more search criteria, click More Choices; to reduce the number of search criteria, click Fewer Choices.** You can add up to five levels of search criteria.

7. **To display objects that match all search criteria, select Match All; to display objects that match any of the search criteria, select Match Any One.** These options are available only if two or more levels of search criteria are displayed.

8. **Click OK to conduct the search and close the dialog box.**

All the objects that match the search criteria appear in the panel. The panel is empty if no objects match the search criteria. If you want to display all objects after conducting a search, choose Show All from the library panel's flyout menu.

Copying library objects onto document pages

Once you place an object into a library and, optionally, specify item information for the object, you can place copies of the library object into any document or into another library. To place a copy of a library object onto the currently displayed document page, click the object's icon in the library panel and drag it onto the page. As you drag, the outline of the library object appears. Release the mouse button when the outline is positioned where you want to place the object. You can also place a library object onto a document by clicking its icon and then choosing Place Item(s).

> **TIP**   You can copy an object from one library to another by clicking and dragging its icon from the source library panel and dropping it onto the target library panel. Press and hold Option or Alt when dragging and dropping an object between libraries to remove the original object from the source library (in effect moving it from one library to the other).

Using Ruler Guides and Grids

If you've ever seen a carpenter use a chalked string to snap a temporary line to use as an aid for aligning objects, you understand the concept behind guidelines. They're not structurally necessary and they don't show in the final product, yet they can still make your work easier. InDesign lets you create and display several types of nonprinting guidelines:

- **Ruler guide:** These are moveable guidelines that you can create by hand or automatically. They're helpful for placing items precisely and aligning multiple items.

- **Margin and column guides:** These guidelines are part of your page setup when you create or modify a document (see Chapter 4), providing the default margin around the sides of the page and the space between the default text frame's columns.

- **Baseline grid:** This is a series of horizontal lines that help you align lines of text and objects across a multicolumn page. When displayed, a baseline grid makes a page look like a sheet of lined paper.

- **Document grid:** This is a crisscross of horizontal and vertical lines that aid in object alignment and placement.

- **Frame-based grid:** This is like a page's baseline grid except that it is just for a specific text frame.

InDesign's grids and guides capabilities verge on overkill. Chances are you'll end up using a combination of ruler guides and the baseline or ruler guides and the document grid, but using all four is more complicated than necessary.

> **CROSS-REF**   InDesign also creates "smart guides" on the fly as you work with objects. They use the centerpoints and frame edges of nearby objects and display when your objects approach those coordinates so that you can line up your current object to match a nearby object's position or size. Chapter 9 explains how to take advantage of these as you're working with objects.

Ruler guides

InDesign lets you create individual ruler guides manually or a set of ruler guides automatically with the Create Guides command (choose Layout ➪ Create Guides).

Creating ruler guides manually

To create manual ruler guides, go to the page or spread onto which you want to place ruler guides. (If the rulers do not appear at the top and left of the document window, choose View ➪ Show Rulers or press ⌘+R or Ctrl+R.) Now click the horizontal ruler or vertical ruler, and drag the pointer onto a page or the pasteboard. Release the mouse button when the guideline is positioned where you want it. If you release the mouse when the pointer is over a page, the ruler guide extends from one edge of the page to the other (but not across a spread). If you release the mouse button when the pointer is over the pasteboard, the ruler guide extends across both pages of a spread and the pasteboard. If you want a guide to extend across a spread and the pasteboard, you can also press and hold down ⌘ or Ctrl as you drag and release the mouse when the pointer is over a page.

TIP You can place both a horizontal and vertical guide at the same time by pressing ⌘ or Ctrl and dragging the ruler intersection point onto a page. You can also place a guide that extends across the page or spread and pasteboard by double-clicking the vertical or horizontal ruler.

Ruler guides are cyan in color (unless you change the color by choosing Layout ➪ Ruler Guides and selecting a new color on the Color pop-up menu in the Ruler Guides dialog box that appears) and are associated with the layer onto which they're placed. You can show and hide ruler guides by showing and hiding the layers that contain them. You can even create layers that contain nothing but ruler guides and then show and hide them as you wish.

TIP If you want to create ruler guides for several document pages, create a master page, add the guides to the master page, and then apply the master to the appropriate document pages.

Creating a set of guides automatically

Follow these steps to create a set of ruler guides:

1. **If the document contains multiple layers, display the Layers panel (choose Window ➪ Layers or press F7) and click the name of the layer to which you want to add guides.**

CROSS-REF See Chapter 5 for more information about layers.

2. **Choose Layout ➪ Create Guides.** The Create Guides dialog box, shown in Figure 6.9, appears. Select the Preview option if you want to see the guides on the current document page as you create them.

FIGURE 6.9

The Create Guides dialog box, along with the guides it created

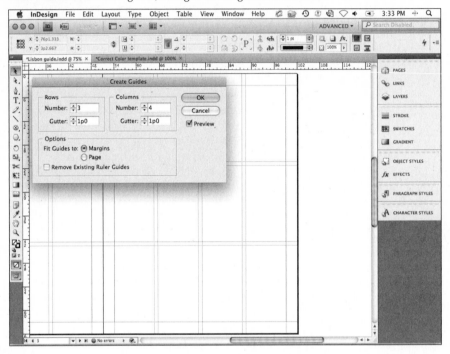

3. **In the Rows and Columns areas specify the number of guides you want to add in the Number fields and, optionally, specify a Gutter width between horizontal (Rows) and vertical (Columns) guides.** Type **0** in the Gutter fields if you don't want gutters between guides.

4. **In the Options area, click the Margins option to fit the guides in the margin boundaries; click the Page option to fit the guides within the page boundary.**

5. **Click the Remove Existing Ruler Guides option to remove any previously placed ruler guides.**

6. **When you're done specifying the attributes of the ruler guides, click OK to close the dialog box.**

Working with ruler guides

After you've created ruler guides, you can show or hide them, lock or unlock them, and select and move, copy and paste, or delete one or more guides at a time. Here are a few pointers for working with ruler guides:

■ To display or hide ruler guides, choose View ⇨ Grids & Guides ⇨ Show/Hide Guides or press ⌘+; (semicolon) or Ctrl+; (semicolon).

■ To lock or unlock all ruler guides, choose View ⇨ Grids & Guides ⇨ Lock Guides or press Option+⌘+; (semicolon) or Ctrl+Alt+; (semicolon). (If the menu option has a check mark to its left, the ruler guides are locked.) By default, InDesign unlocks ruler guides.

■ To select a ruler guide, click it with a selection tool. To select multiple guides, press and hold down Shift and click them. The color of a selected ruler guide changes from blue to the color of its layer.

■ To select all ruler guides on a page or spread, press Option+⌘+G or Ctrl+Alt+G.

■ To move a ruler guide, click and drag it as you would any object. (You can also change its coordinates in the Control panel or Transform panel.) To move multiple ruler guides, click and drag them. To move ruler guides to another page, select them, choose Edit ⇨ Cut or press ⌘+X or Ctrl+X, or choose Edit ⇨ Copy or press ⌘+C or Ctrl+C, display the target page, and then choose Edit ⇨ Paste or press ⌘+V or Ctrl+V. If the target page is the same shape as the source page, the ruler guides are placed in their original position.

■ To delete ruler guides, select them and then press Delete or Backspace.

■ To change the color of the ruler guides and the view percentage above which they're displayed (the default view threshold is 5 percent), choose Layout ⇨ Ruler Guides. The Ruler Guides dialog box appears. Modify the View Threshold value, choose a different color from the Color pop-up menu, and click OK. If you change the settings in the Ruler Guides dialog box when no documents are open, the new settings become defaults and are applied to all subsequently created documents.

■ To display ruler guides behind objects instead of in front, choose InDesign ⇨ Preferences ⇨ Guides & Pasteboard or press ⌘+K on the Mac, or choose Edit ⇨ Preferences ⇨ Guides & Pasteboard or press Ctrl+K in Windows, and select Guides in Back in the Guide Options section of the dialog box's Guides & Pasteboard pane.

Working with column guides

You can also adjust column guides if your document has them, though you don't get the same flexibility in adjusting column guides as you do ruler guides. Column guides are created when you create a new document and set it up with multiple columns (see Chapter 3).

By default, column guides are locked. To unlock them (or relock them) choose View ⇨ Grids & Guides ⇨ Lock Column Guides. (If the menu option has a check mark to its left, the column guides are locked.)

To move a column guide, click and drag it. Note that the color of a selected column guide does not change as the color of a selected ruler guide does. Also note that you cannot select multiple column guides or move them to other pages.

The only way to add or delete column guides is to change the number of guides in the Margins and Columns dialog box (choose Layout ⇨ Margins and Columns); adjusting the number of columns undoes any custom moves applied to column guides.

Working with the baseline grid

Every new document you create includes a baseline grid. If the document you're working on uses a multicolumn page layout, a baseline grid can be helpful for aligning text baselines across columns and for ensuring that object edges align with text baselines. Baseline grids aren't much use for small documents, such as business cards and ads, and one-column designs. Here's how to create them:

1. **Choose InDesign ⇨ Preferences ⇨ Grids or press ⌘+K on the Mac, or choose Edit ⇨ Preferences ⇨ Grids or press Ctrl+K in Windows, and choose the Grids pane.** The Grids pane, shown in Figure 6.10, appears.

FIGURE 6.10

The Grids pane of the Preferences dialog box

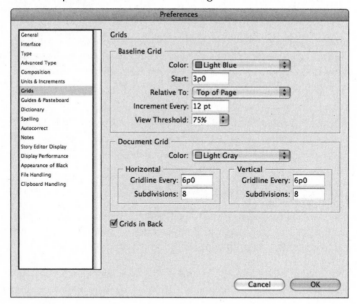

2. **Choose a color from the Color pop-up menu in the Baseline Grid area.**

3. **In the Start field, type the distance between the top of the page and the first grid line.** If you type **0**, the Increment Every value determines the distance between the top of the page and the first grid line.

4. **Type the distance between grid lines in the Increment Every field.** Generally, the value you type in this field will be the same as the leading value you use for the publication's body text.

5. **Choose a View Threshold percentage from the pop-up menu or type a value in the field.** Generally, you don't want to display the baseline grid at reduced view percentages because grid lines become tightly spaced.

6. **Click OK to close the dialog box and return to the document.**

A baseline grid is document-wide (that is, you can't change it from page to page), and grid lines are displayed behind all objects, layers, and ruler guides. The default baseline grid begins tyled inch from the top of a document page; the grid lines are light blue and placed 1 pica apart; and they are displayed at view percentages above 75 percent. If you change any of these settings when no documents are open, the changes are applied to all subsequently created documents; if a document is open, changes apply only to that document.

TIP The Show/Hide Baseline Grid command (choose View ⇨ Grids & Guides ⇨ Show/Hide Baseline Grid or press Option+⌘+′ [apostrophe] or Ctrl+Alt+′ [apostrophe]) lets you display and hide a document's baseline grid.

You set the baseline grid for a text frame in a very similar way. After selecting the text frame, choose Object ⇨ Text Frame Options (⌘+B or Ctrl+B) and then go to the Baseline Options pane, shown in Figure 6.11. Select the Use Custom Baseline Grid option to turn on the grid for this text frame and then choose the rest of the settings as appropriate to it. The Offset, Start, Relative To, Increment Every, and Color options work the same way as in the Grids pane of the Preferences dialog box.

FIGURE 6.11

The Baseline Options pane of the Text Frame Options dialog box

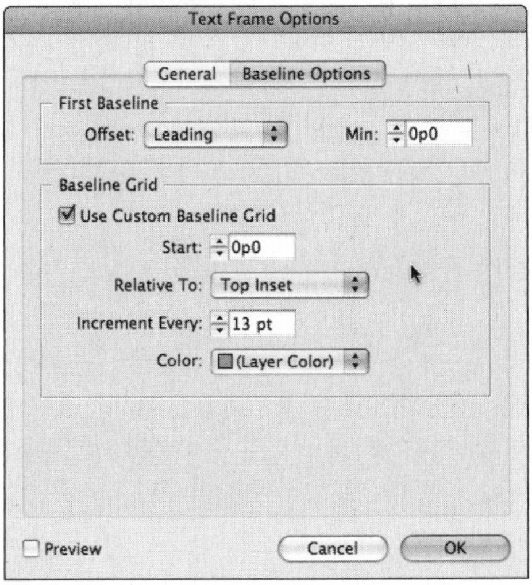

Working with the document grid

Just as every document includes a baseline grid, it also includes a default *document grid,* which is a set of horizontal and vertical lines. And like baseline grids, you may or may not find the document grid to be a useful aid for laying out pages. If you like working on graph paper in the real world, the document guide may be just your cup of tea. On the other hand, you may find document grids to be too constricting and opt not to use them. If you want to use document grids, follow these steps:

1. **Choose InDesign ⇨ Preferences ⇨ Grids or press ⌘+K on the Mac, or choose Edit ⇨ Preferences ⇨ Grids or press Ctrl+K in Windows.** The Grids pane appears (refer to Figure 6.10).

2. **Choose a color from the Color pop-up menu in the Document Grid area.**

3. **Type the distance between grid lines in the Gridline Every field.** If your basic measurement unit is an inch, you probably want to use the default value of 1 inch.

4. **Type the number of divisions between grid lines in the Subdivisions field.** If your basic measurement unit is an inch, you can specify a value of 6 to subdivide the grid into 1-pica squares. Or, if you prefer, you can type a value of 4, 8, 16, and so on to subdivide the grid into standard divisions of an inch.

5. **Click OK to close the dialog box and return to the document.**

> **TIP**   The Show/Hide Document Grid command (choose View ⇨ Grids & Guides ⇨ Show/Hide Document Grid or ⌘+' [apostrophe] or Ctrl+' [apostrophe]) lets you display and hide the document grid.

Snapping to guides

If the Snap to Guides command (choose View ⇨ Grids & Guides ⇨ Snap to Guides or press Shift+⌘+; [semicolon] or Ctrl+Shift+; [semicolon]) is selected, object edges snap to guidelines and grids when you drag them in the snap zone. To specify the *snap zone* (the distance — in pixels — at which an object snaps to a guide), choose InDesign ⇨ Preferences ⇨ Guides & Pasteboard or press ⌘+K on the Mac, or choose Edit ⇨ Preferences ⇨ Guides & Pasteboard or press Ctrl+K in Windows, and type a value in the Snap to Zone field in the Guide Options section of the dialog box.

Setting the snap zone is just the first step. You must turn on the snap-to feature in InDesign as well for whichever elements you want to snap to:

- For guidelines and baseline grids, be sure Snap to Guides is turned on. Choose View ⇨ Guides & Grids ⇨ Snap to Guides or press Shift+⌘+; [semicolon] or Ctrl+Shift+; [semicolon]). Note that the guidelines must be visible for objects to snap to them; to make them visible, choose View ⇨ Guides & Grids ⇨ Show Guides or press ⌘+; [semicolon] or Ctrl+; [semicolon]. But the baseline grid need not be visible.

- For document grids, be sure that Snap to Document Grid is turned on. Choose View ⇨ Guides & Grids ⇨ Snap to Document Grid or press Shift+⌘+' (apostrophe) or Ctrl+Shift+' (apostrophe).

In both cases, if the menu option has a check mark to its left, it is turned on. Choosing it toggles between turning on and off the snap-to feature.

Summary

If you want to be a true InDesign expert, you must take advantage of three of its most powerful features: master pages, templates, and libraries. All these features save time and ensure design consistency across documents. A master page is a preformatted page design that you can apply to document pages in a multipage publication; a template is a preconstructed document that serves as the starting point when you need to create multiple versions of the same publication; and a library is a storage file in which you can save any object you've created with InDesign for use in other publications.

To help you place and align objects, InDesign lets you create three types of guidelines: ruler guides, the baseline grid, and the document grid. You can also move the column guides that InDesign creates automatically for you. You can show or hide guidelines, and you have the option to snap object edges to guidelines when you click and drag them in the specified snap zone.

Chapter 7

Defining Colors, Tints, and Gradients

Although color is most widely used by high-end publishers — people producing magazines and catalogs — color is becoming more accessible to all publishers thanks to the recent emergence of inexpensive color printers, color copiers, and leading-edge desktop-publishing programs. Whether you want to produce limited-run documents on a color printer, create newsletters using spot colors, or publish magazines and catalogs using process colors and special inks, InDesign offers the tools that you need to do the job well.

But color is a complex issue in printing, which involves both physics and chemistry. The inks that produce color are designed chemically to retain those colors and to produce them evenly so that your images don't look mottled or faded. How light reflects off of ink and paper to your eye determines the color you see, and many factors (particularly different textures of paper) can affect the physics of how the light carries the color.

You also have implementation issues to consider: How many colors can your printing press produce, and how much will it cost? When do you decide to go for the exact pure color, and when do you decide to go with a close-enough version that costs less to print?

After you have figured out what your color capabilities are, you can get into the nitty-gritty of actually using color in your graphics or applying colors to text and layout elements (such as bars along the edge of a page). Or you can use color both ways. To a great extent, where you define and apply color determines what you can do with it.

CROSS-REF Chapter 28 covers color matching and other high-end color-output issues in depth. This chapter concentrates on how to create and apply colors within InDesign.

Defining Color Terms

Color is an expansive (and sometimes confusing and esoteric) concept in the world of publishing. The following definitions, however, should start you on your way to a clear understanding of the subject:

- **Build:** Attempts to simulate a color-model color by overlapping the appropriate percentages of the four process colors.

- **CIE Lab:** A standard that specifies colors by one lightness coordinate and two color coordinates, green-red and blue-yellow. The first part of the name means Commission Internationale de l'Éclairage (International Committee on Illumination), an international standards group, and the second part refers to the mathematical approach used to describe the colors in a cubic arrangement: luminance, *a*-axis, and *b*-axis (thus the term "Lab").

- **CMYK:** A standard that specifies colors as combinations of cyan, magenta, yellow, and black. These four colors are known as *process colors*.

- **Color gamut:** The range of colors that a device, such as a monitor or a color printer, can produce. Each color model has a different color gamut.

- **Color model:** An industry standard for specifying a color, such as CMYK or Pantone.

- **Color separation:** A set of four photographic negatives, one filtered for each process color, shot from a color photograph or image. When overlapped, the four negatives reproduce that original image.

- **Color space:** A method of representing color in terms of measurable values, such as the amount of red, yellow, and blue in a color image. The color space RGB represents the red, green, and blue colors on video screens.

- **Four-color printing:** The use of the four process colors in combination to produce most other colors.

- **Process color:** Any of the four primary colors in publishing — cyan, magenta, yellow, and black (known collectively as CMYK). A six-color, high-fidelity variant produced by Pantone is called Hexachrome.

- **RGB:** The standard used by monitors, and the abbreviation from the three colors in it: red, green, and blue. One of the biggest hurdles to producing color documents that look as you'd expect is that computers use RGB whereas printers use CMYK, and the two don't always produce colors at the same hue.

- **Spot color:** A single color applied at one or more places on a page, such as for a screen or as part of an illustration. You can use more than one spot color per page. Spot colors can also be process colors.

- **Swatchbook:** A table of colors collected together as a series of color samples. The printer uses premixed ink based on the color model identifier you specify; you look up the numbers for various colors in the table of colors in a swatchbook.

Understanding Process and Spot Color

In this section, I briefly explore the differences between spot and process colors, the two primary ways of indicating color in print documents.

Identifying methods of color printing

Several forms of color are used in printing, but the two most prevalent ones are process color and spot color.

Process color is the use of four basic colors — cyan, magenta, yellow, and black (known collectively as CMYK) — that are mixed to reproduce most color tones the human eye can see. A separate negative is produced for each of the four process colors. This method, often called *four-color printing*, is used for most color publishing.

> **NOTE** As is CMYK, RGB and Lab are created by mixing colors; however, InDesign refers to RGB and Lab colors as *mixed colors*, leaving the term *process color* for CMYK because that's an industry-standard term for CMYK.

Spot color is any color ink — whether one of the process colors or some other hue — used for specific elements in a document. For example, if you print a document in black ink but print the company logo in red, the red is a spot color. A spot color is often called a *second color* even though you can use several spot colors in a document. Each spot color is output to its own negative (and not color-separated into CMYK). Using spot color gives you access to special inks that are truer to the desired color than any mix of process colors can be. These inks come in several standards, and include metallics, neons, and milky pastels. You even can use varnishes as spot colors to give layout elements a different gleam from the rest of the page. Although experienced designers sometimes mix spot colors to produce special shades not otherwise available, you probably won't need to do so.

There are several advantages to spot colors. You can use colors like metallic inks that are impossible to create with CMYK. Also, your printed results will be more consistent than with CMYK separations, which can suffer from *color shift* (variation in the hue produced) over the length of a long printed piece. But spot colors work only in objects that have distinct, continuous hue, such as a solid brick red, that can be printed with just one ink. To produce any image with multiple colors, such as a photograph, you need to use multiple inks, and because printing presses can traditionally print only four to eight colors on a page, you have to mix colors to create the range of hues in such multicolor objects.

> **TIP** If you create spot colors, I suggest that you include the word *Spot* as part of the name so that you can quickly tell in a panel or menu whether a selected color will print on its own plate or be color-separated. InDesign does use an icon to tell you whether a color is process or spot, as well as what color model (CMYK, RGB, or Lab) in which it was defined (see Figure 7.1 later), but often it's easier to see the word than a tiny icon.

> **NOTE** Adobe programs, including InDesign, show that spot colors such as Pantone, Toyo, and DIC (Dainippon Ink & Chemical) are based on the CMYK color model, even though they're not. It doesn't really matter, because if you print them as a spot color, they get their own plate and your printer will use the actual Pantone, Toyo, or DIC ink. And if you color-separate them into process colors, you'll get the CMYK values shown in the Swatch Options dialog box; or you can hold the mouse over the color name in the Swatches panel (if the Tool Tips option is selected in the Preferences dialog box, as described in Chapter 3).

Mixing spot and process colors

Some designers use both process and spot colors in a document in a procedure known as using a *fifth color*. Typically, the normal color images are color-separated and printed using the four process colors, whereas a special element (such as a logo in metallic ink) is printed in a spot color. The process colors are output on the usual four negatives; the spot color is output on a separate, fifth negative and printed using a fifth plate, a fifth ink roller, and a fifth inkwell. You can use more than five colors, however; you're limited only by your budget and the capabilities of your printing plant. (Most commercial printers can handle six colors for each run through the press, and larger ones often can handle as many as eight colors.)

Converting spot color to process color

InDesign can convert spot colors to process colors. This handy capability lets designers specify the colors they want through a system with which they're familiar, such as Pantone, without the added expense of special spot-color inks and extra negatives. Conversions are never an exact match, but guidebooks are available that can show you in advance the color that will be created. And with several Pantone and HKS variations, designers can pick a Pantone or HKS color that color-separates predictably.

You can set InDesign to convert some spot colors in a document to process colors while leaving others alone: Just use the Color Mode pop-up menu in the Swatch Options dialog box, covered later in this chapter. (For example, you can keep a metallic silver as a spot color so it prints with a metallic ink, rather than be converted to a grayish color that is the closest the CMYK colors can produce to simulate a silver. But you would convert common colors such as deep blue, purple, and green to process colors, because the CMYK inks can combine fairly accurately to reproduce them.) You can also leave all spot colors as spot colors or convert all spot colors to process colors.

> **CAUTION** Colors defined in one model and converted to another may not reproduce exactly the same because the physics underlying each color model differ slightly. Each model was designed for use in a different medium, such as with paper or on a video monitor.

Working with Color Models

Once you understand color terminology and the difference between process and spot colors, you can start thinking about the type of colors you create in InDesign. (You define colors in the Swatches panel, as I describe later in this chapter.) The color models fall into two broad classes:

Using Color Swatchbooks

Anyone who uses a lot of color should have a color swatchbook handy. You probably can get one at your local art supply store or from your commercial printer (prices typically range from $50 to $100, depending on the color model and the type of swatchbook). But if you can't find a swatchbook, here's where to order the most popular ones:

- **Pantone:** Several Pantone swatchbooks are available, including ones for coated and uncoated paper, and for spot-color output and process-color output. If you are converting (called *building* in publishing parlance) Pantone colors to CMYK for four-color printing, I particularly recommend the *Pantone Process Color Imaging Guide: CMYK Edition* or the *Pantone Process Color System Guide* swatchbooks. www.pantone.com.

- **Hexachrome:** Pantone also created the Hexachrome standard that uses six colors rather than four to build truer-to-life colors. Pantone sells Hexachrome swatchbooks, but it no longer sells the HexWare software that added the Hexachrome output capability to Adobe Photoshop and Illustrator (InDesign does not natively support Hexachrome). Because InDesign can import Illustrator color swatch files, you can add Hexachrome swatches to InDesign by importing any Hexachrome swatch libraries created in earlier versions of Photoshop and Illustrator through the now-discontinued HexWare software.

- **Trumatch:** Based on a CMYK color space, Trumatch suffers almost no matching problems when converted to CMYK. Variants of the swatchbooks for coated and uncoated paper are available. www.trumatch.com.

- **ANPA:** Designed for reproduction on newsprint, these colors also are designed in the LAB color space. www.naa.org.

- **Focoltone:** As is Trumatch, this color model is based on the CMYK color space. www.apmedia.com.

- **HKS:** This color model is used mainly in Germany and other European countries, with variants for industrial printing such as on plastics. It uses various combinations of cyan, magenta, and yellow with black overlays to achieve different shades. www.hks-colour.de.

- **Dainippon Ink & Chemical (DIC):** As is Pantone, the DIC color set is a spot-color–based system. http://dicwww01.dic.co.jp/eng/index.html.

- **Toyo:** Similar to Pantone in that it is based on spot-color inks, this model is popular in Japan. www.toyoink.com.

- Those that let you define a color by selecting a color from a *color wheel* (which represents a spectrum of available colors) or by entering specific values for the color's *constituent colors* (the colors that make up the color), which include CMYK, RGB, Lab, and Multi-Ink.

- Those that have a predefined set of colors, which you select from a palette of swatches. These swatches include ANPA (American Newspaper Publishers Association), DIC (Dainippon Ink & Chemical), Focoltone, Trumatch, 13 variants of Pantone, eight variants of HKS, and two variants of Toyo. There are also two sets of colors meant for use on computer displays and a third for use on the Web. Plus, you can add additional palette sets.

> **NOTE** Most North American publishers use Pantone color models, also known as the Pantone Matching System (PMS). Focoltone, HKS, and Trumatch tend to be used in Europe. DIC, Focoltone, and Toyo tend to be used in Asia. ANPA is used by North American newspapers. And everyone uses CMYK.

> **NOTE** Several of the swatch library names are in all uppercase in InDesign's menus and dialog boxes. That's because they're trademarked names, which some people (such as those at Adobe) like to indicate by using all caps. That's just a convention and means nothing per se. (Legally, the word need only be treated as a proper adjective, although the owner needs to use the ® or ™ symbols in its own materials to assert ownership.)

Keep in mind that the colors displayed are only on-screen representations; the actual colors may be different. The differences are particularly noticeable if your monitor is running in 8-bit (256 hues) color mode. Check the actual color in a color swatchbook for the model you are using. (Art and printing supply stores usually carry these swatchbooks. See the sidebar "Using Color Swatchbooks" for lists of other sources.) You can also calibrate your monitor display with tools from X-Rite (www.xrite.com) and X-Rite's Pantone subsidiary (www.pantone.com); this keeps the colors as close as possible to actual output.

> **TIP** InDesign uses the same swatch format as Illustrator, so you can import color models into InDesign created in or for Illustrator. InDesign also supports the Adobe Swatch Exchange format that all Adobe CS2, CS3, and CS4 applications support for color exchange.

Understanding Paper Variation Models

Both the Pantone and HKS color models recognize that the type of paper on which you print affects how a color appears, so they have variations based on popular paper types. Here's how they work:

- **Pantone Process Coated:** Use this variant when you color-separate Pantone colors and your printer uses the standard Pantone-brand process-color inks on coated paper. Colors in this variant have the code DS added *before* the numerals in their names and the code C *after* the numerals.

- **Pantone Process Uncoated:** Use this variant when you color-separate Pantone colors and your printer uses the standard Pantone-brand process-color inks on coated paper. Colors in this variant have the code DS added *before* the numerals in their names and the code U *after* the numerals.

> **NOTE** The *DS* code stands for digital SWOP, or Specifications for Web Offset Publications, a prepress standard for the web-offset printing process used by magazines, catalog, and most high-run printing presses.

- **Pantone Solid Coated:** Use this variant when your printer uses actual Pantone-brand inks (as spot colors) when printing to coated paper stock. Colors in this variant have the code C appended to their names.

- **Pantone Solid Matte:** This is the same as Pantone Coated but for paper with a matte finish. Colors in this variant have the code M appended to their names.

- **Pantone Solid Uncoated:** This is the same as Pantone Solid Coated but for uncoated paper. Colors in this variant have the code U appended to their names.

- **Pantone Metallic Coated:** This contains metallic colors designed for coated papers (which helps make them shine like metal). Colors in this variant have the code C appended to their names.

- **Pantone Pastel Coated:** This contains pastel colors designed for coated papers (which helps make them more lustrous). Colors in this variant have the code C appended to their names.

- **Pantone Pastel Uncoated:** This contains pastel colors designed for uncoated papers (which helps make them have the visual texture of eggshells). Colors in this variant have the code U appended to their names.

- **Pantone Color Bridge:** This contains Pantone solid colors that reproduce well with process colors, for use on coated paper. Colors in this variant have the code PC appended to their names.

- **Pantone Color Bridge Uncoated:** This contains Pantone solid colors that reproduce well with process colors, for use on uncoated paper. Colors in this variant have the code U appended to their names.

- **Pantone Color Bridge Euro:** This contains Pantone solid colors that reproduce well with process colors on European printing presses, for use on any paper. Colors in this variant have the code EC appended to their names.

- **Pantone Solid to Process:** This contains Pantone solid colors that reproduce well with process colors, for use on any paper. Colors in this variant have the code PC appended to their names.

- **Pantone Solid to Process Euro:** This contains Pantone solid colors that reproduce well with process colors on European printing presses, for use on any paper. Colors in this variant have the code EC appended to their names.

- **HKS E:** Use this HKS variant for continuous-form stationery. Colors in this variant have the code E appended to their names.

- **HKS E Process:** Use this HKS variant for continuous-form stationery printed with process colors. Colors in this variant have the code E appended to their names.

- **HKS K:** Use this HKS variant for glossy art paper (highly coated). Colors in this variant have the code K appended to their names.

- **HKS K Process:** Use this HKS variant for glossy art paper (highly coated) printed with process colors. Colors in this variant have the code K appended to their names.

- **HKS N:** Use this HKS variant for natural paper (uncoated). Colors in this variant have the code N appended to their names.

- **HKS N Process:** Use this HKS variant for natural paper (uncoated) printed with process colors. Colors in this variant have the code N appended to their names.

- **HKS Z:** Use this HKS variant for newsprint. Colors in this variant have the code Z appended to their names.

- **HKS Z Process:** Use this HKS variant for newsprint printed with process colors. Colors in this variant have the code Z appended to their names.

 When printing on uncoated stock with any colors designed for use on coated stock, you will usually get weaker, less-saturated color reproduction.

Defining Colors and Tints

InDesign comes with a few predefined colors: [Black], [Registration] (black on each negative for the printing press), [Paper] (white), [None] (transparent), Cyan, Magenta, Yellow, Red, Green, and Blue. So you most likely want to add a few of your own.

Before you can apply any colors — whether to bitmap images or to layout elements such as strokes, text, frames, and shapes — you must first define the colors. InDesign offers four ways to create colors: via the Swatches panel, via the Kuler panel, via the Colors panel, and by double-clicking the Fill or Stroke iconic button on the Tools panel. You can also import colors from other Adobe programs and from some color images.

No matter how you define colors, you have a couple of decisions to make first:

■ Do you want to create your own color by mixing basic colors such as red, green, and blue (called RGB and typically used for screen display), or cyan, yellow, magenta, and black (called CMYK or *process colors*, and typically used for printing presses)?

■ Do you want to use a color from an ink maker such as Pantone or Toyo? These colors — called *spot colors* — are typically used as an extra ink on your document but can also be converted to the standard four-process colors; therefore, they're handy when you know the color you want when you see it.

All of InDesign's color-creation tools support both process and spot colors. And all have access to the predefined colors such as Pantone and Toyo as well as to the free-form color pickers for mixing CMYK or RGB colors. If you plan to print the color on its own plate, you need to use a predefined color so that you know the printer can reproduce it. If you plan to color-separate a color into the four CMYK plates, then it doesn't matter whether you use a predefined color or make one of your own. One advantage to using a predefined color is that it's easy to tell other designers what the color is; another is that you get very close matches if you start with a predefined color and then end up having it color-separated in some documents and kept as a spot color in others.

 If no document is open when you create, edit, or delete colors, the new color palette becomes the default for all future documents.

Creating colors the ideal way: the Swatches panel

The best way to create colors in InDesign is to use the Swatches panel. All colors in this panel get a unique name and are tracked by InDesign. That means each such color is available to be used on any object in your document, with no risk of having slightly different variants. Plus, you can modify a swatch and ensure that all objects using that swatch are updated, and you can delete a swatch and tell InDesign which color to use in its place. Furthermore, when you print, you have control over how each color is handled (whether it is printed to its own plate, whether it is printed at all, and whether there should be any adjustments to its ink density or screening angle.) Figure 7.1 shows the Swatches panel.

 You can drag the color from the Stroke or Fill iconic buttons onto the Swatches panel to create a swatch of that color.

TIP Because regular black can appear weak when it's overprinted by other colors, many designers create what printers call *superblack* or *rich black* by combining 100 percent black and 100 percent magenta. (Some use cyan instead of magenta.) You can define superblack as a separate color or redefine the registration color as 100 percent of all four-process colors, and use that as a superblack. Note that superblack should be used only in large areas — using it on type or small objects increases the chances of registration problems for those items.

FIGURE 7.1

The Swatches panel and its flyout menu

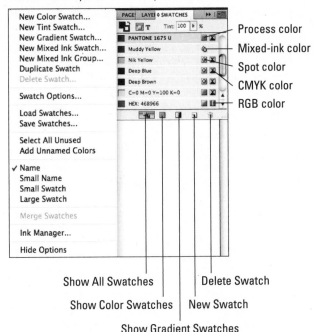

Personalizing the Swatches Panel

You can change the appearance of the entries in the Swatches panel by using the three options in the Swatches panel's flyout menu: Name (the default), Small Name (a tighter list view), Small Swatch (no names, just small icons), and Large Swatch (no names, just larger icons).

Also, use the Hide Options menu to suppress the display of the Stroke, Fill, Formatting Affects Container, and Formatting Affects Text iconic buttons and the Tint field and pop-up menu; Show Options brings them back.

Finally, you can use the Show All Swatches, Show Color Swatches, and Show Gradient Swatches iconic buttons at the bottom of the panel to control which swatches appear.

To create your own color, go to the Swatches panel (choose Window ➪ Swatches or press F5) and select New Color Swatch from the flyout menu. You get the New Color Swatch dialog box shown in Figure 7.2. Now follow these steps:

FIGURE 7.2

The New Color Swatch dialog box lets you define colors. (At left is the dialog box for CMYK color mixing; at right is the dialog box for the swatch-based spot colors such as Pantone colors.) An identical dialog box named Swatch Options lets you edit them.

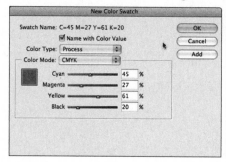 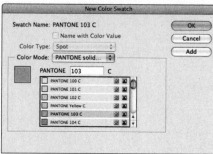

1. **In the Swatch Name field, give your color a name that describes it, such as Lime Green or Bright Purple.** You can also select the Name with Color Value option, which uses the color values to make up the color name as was done for the color under the Deep Brown swatch in Figure 7.1. This option is available only for CMYK, RGB, and Lab colors, not for swatch-based colors such as Pantone.

2. **In the Color Type pop-up menu, choose from Process or Spot.** These are covered earlier in this chapter; leave the color type at Process if you're not sure.

3. **In the Color Mode pop-up menu, choose the mixing system or swatch library (both are considered to be** *color models***) you want to use: CMYK, RGB, Lab, or a swatch-based model.** (These are covered earlier in this chapter.)

4. **For the CMYK, RGB, and Lab models, use the sliders to create your new color.** A preview appears in the box at left. For the swatch-based models, scroll through the lists of colors and select one.

5. **If you want to create multiple colors, click Add after each color definition and then click Done when done.** To create just one color, click OK instead of Add. You can also click Cancel to abort the current color definition.

Using Kuler to add to your color swatches

There's a Web site out there that lets users share palettes of colors they've created. The idea is to give people with little fashion sense sets of colors that work well together. InDesign CS4 lets you tap into these colors and add them to your Swatches panel, using the Kuler panel (choose Window ➪ Extensions ➪ Kuler). Note that you must have an active Internet connection to be able to use the Kuler panel.

NEW FEATURE Support for Kuler is new to InDesign CS4 and other applications, although an experimental (beta) version of Kuler had been available in Adobe Illustrator CS3.

You go to the Browse pane in the Kuler panel and choose from the color swatch palettes — called themes — already there. You can use the unlabeled pop-up menus at top and the search field to narrow down your choices. Click one you want and then click the Add Selected Theme to Swatches iconic button at the bottom right of the panel. Repeat for each theme you want to copy.

You can create your own themes in the Create pane (as well as edit an existing theme; click the Create Theme in Create Pane iconic button in the Browse pane to do so). First, be sure a document is open — you cannot add Kuler colors to the Swatches panel if no document is open, even though you can create swatches in the Swatches panel when no document is open so that they become default colors for all new documents.

You start the Kuler theme creation with the Base Color, the one that determines the starting point for the theme and any constraints applied to it. Use the color wheel and sliders to select a new value, or drag its current color (the circles) to a new location on the wheel. There are also two iconic buttons that let you take the color of a selected object and make that the base color: Add Current Fill Color as Base Color and Add Current Stroke Color as Base Color.

To add colors, click the Add a New Color to the Theme iconic button. Kuler has a maximum of five colors per theme. You can delete a color by selecting it and then clicking the Remove This Color from the Theme iconic button.

You can have Kuler constrain your color choices using the Select Rule pop-up menu, which has seven options: Analogous, Monochromatic, Triad, Complementary, Compound, Shades, and Custom. As you choose each one, you'll see its effect on your color choices. (Custom lets you choose any colors.) You can also constrain color options using the Affect the Other Colors in the Theme with a Harmony iconic button; this has Kuler change the colors to what it considers "harmonious."

How to Decide on a Color-Naming System

Vou can name a CMYK, RGB, or Lab color anything you want. (Colors defined in other models will use their official names, such as Pantone 147U or ANPA 1732-4 AdPro.) To make it easier to remember what a defined color looks like, you should use either descriptive names (such as Grass Green or Official Logo Blue) or use names based on the color settings. Choose one naming convention to keep things consistent.

The benefit of using descriptive names is that they have intrinsic meaning, which helps designers choose the right one. For example, there's no confusion that Official Logo Blue is the color to be used for the company logo, but the proper usage of the same color using a name based on its color values won't be so obvious.

The benefit of using color-value names is that designers who do a lot of color work know what that color is. Grass Green could be any of several colors, but C=30 M=0 Y=50 K=5 can be only one color.

A good strategy is to use the color-value names for all colors — with a twist: For colors that have specific usage, add that to the color name. For example, you might use a grassy green for a particular feature article, so you would just name it based on its color values (for example, C=30 M=0 Y=50 K=5). But your magazine logo color would be named something like Logo C=100 M=100 Y=20 K=25 so that you have a reminder of this swatch's designated usage.

InDesign names colors based on their values automatically if you select the Name with Color Value option and choose Process as the Color Type when you define the color. For example, if you create a color in the CMYK model, you might give it a name based on its mix, such as *55C 0M 91Y 0K* for that grass-green color — composed of 55 percent cyan, 0 percent magenta, 91 percent yellow, and 0 percent black. (Believe it or not, this naming convention is how professionals specify colors on paste-up boards.) InDesign's Name with Color Value option would name this color *C=55 M=0 Y=91 K=0*. The same system applies to the RGB, HSB, and Lab models.

You can apply a color at any time to a selected object in your layout by double-clicking the desired swatch in the Kuler panel. Note that this does not add the color to the Swatches panel automatically, creating the risk of an unnamed color in your document (more about this later in this chapter). To add the five colors in the Kuler panel, click the Add Selected Theme to Swatches iconic button at the bottom right of the panel. (Note that all Kuler colors are added as RGB process colors; you can change these using the Swatch Options dialog box described earlier, as for any color swatch.)

You can save the themes and upload them to the Kuler site for other users to enjoy using the Upload Theme to Kuler iconic button, if you have a Kuler account. You can also save a theme for later access by clicking the Save Theme button. This does not add the colors to the Swatches panel or upload them to Kuler; it does make the theme available in the Browse pane's filter pop-up menu.

Figure 7.3 shows both the Browse and Create panes of the Kuler panel. Not shown is the About pane, which just provides information about the Kuler site, nothing to actually use in InDesign.

FIGURE 7.3

The Kuler panel lets you copy predefined themes (left) — sets of colors — as well as create and even share your own (right).

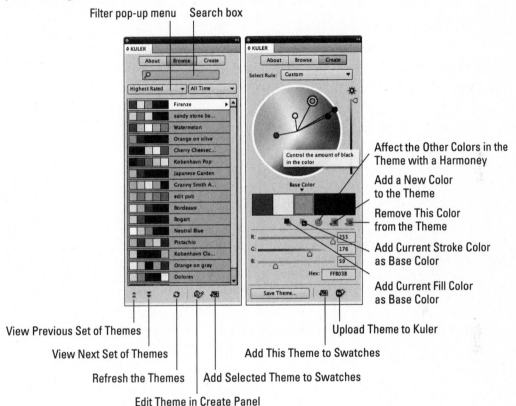

Creating tints

A *tint* is a shade of a color. InDesign lets you create such tints as separate color swatches, so they're easy to use for multiple items. The process is easy:

1. **In the Swatches panel, just select a color from which you want to create a tint.**

2. **Using the flyout menu, select New Tint Swatch.** You get the New Tint Swatch dialog box shown in Figure 7.4.

3. **Click and drag the slider to adjust the tint or type a value in the field at right.**

4. **Click Add to create another tint from the same base color and then click OK when you're finished.** (If you're adding a single tint, there's no need to click Add; just click OK when done.) Click Cancel to abort the current tint. Any new tint has the same name as the original color and the percentage of shading, such as Leaf Green 66%.

FIGURE 7.4

The New Tint Swatch dialog box lets you define colors; a nearly identical dialog box named Swatch Options lets you edit them. The difference is that, when editing, you can change all the other color values, not just the degree of tint.

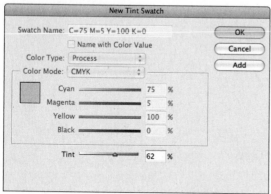

> **NOTE** You can create a tint from a tint, which can be confusing. Fortunately, InDesign goes back to the original color when letting you create the new tint. Thus, if you select Leaf Green 66% and move the slider to 33%, you get a 33 percent tint of the original Leaf Green, not a 33 percent tint of the Leaf Green 66% (which would be equivalent to a 22 percent tint of the original Leaf Green).

> **TIP** You can also apply tints to objects without creating a separate swatch for each tint. After applying the color (described later in this chapter), select the object and change the value in the Tint field of the Swatches panel, or use its pop-up menu's predefined tint values.

Mixing color swatches to create more colors

InDesign offers another type of color: mixed-ink color. Essentially, a mixed-ink color combines a spot color with the default process colors (cyan, magenta, yellow, and black) to create new color swatches. For example, you can combine 38 percent black with 100 percent Pantone 130C to get a darker version of Pantone 130C (called a *duotone,* though InDesign doesn't limit you to mixing spot colors with just black, as traditional duotones do).

To create a mixed-ink swatch, select the spot color you want to begin with and then choose New Mixed Ink Swatch from the Swatches panel's flyout menu. You get the dialog box shown in Figure 7.5, in which you select the percentages of the spot color and any or all of the default process colors you want to mix. You also give the new color a name. Click Add to add another mixed-ink swatch based on the current spot color and then click OK when you're finished. If you're creating just one color, click OK instead of Add. You can click Cancel to abort the current mixed-ink color definition.

> **TIP** Be sure to test such mixes by creating a color proof first. They may not look as you expect when actually printed because of how printing presses handle a color overlapping other colors.

The New Mixed Ink Swatch dialog box lets you mix one or more spot colors with any or all of the default process colors to create new shades and variations.

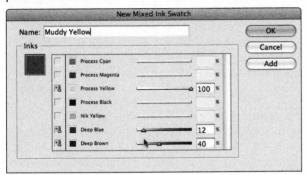

There's more to mixed-ink colors than creating them one by one. InDesign lets you create mixed-ink groups, which are a series of colors based on a spot color and one or more default process colors. Figure 7.6 shows the New Mixed Ink Group dialog box, in which you select the colors to mix as you do in the New Mixed Ink Swatch dialog box. This feature is handy to create a palette of colors within a color range, as well as to create color combinations known as *duotones* (a spot color mixed with black) and *tritones* (two spot colors mixed with black).

The New Mixed Ink Group dialog box lets you mix a selected spot color with any or all of the default process colors in user-defined increments to create a range of new shades and variations.

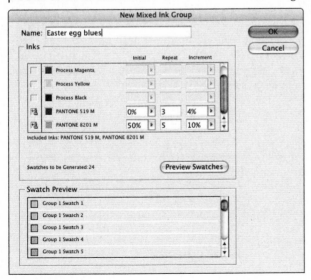

But you do more than simply mix the colors. In this dialog box, you specify an initial tint for each color you want to mix, then how many times you want to create a color using it, as well as the increment of color for each creation. This can be confusing, so I walk you through the options in Figure 7.6.

The spot color Pantone 519 M is chosen with an Initial value of 0%, a Repeat setting of 3, and an Increment of 4%. Also chosen is the spot color Pantone 8201 M, with an Initial value of 50%, a Repeat setting of 5, and an Increment of 10%. This combination creates 24 mixed-ink swatches, as shown in the Swatch Preview section (click Preview Swatches to display the preview colors in the Swatch Preview section of the dialog box).

InDesign uses the settings and first mixes 0 percent of Pantone 519 M with 50 percent of Pantone 8201 M. That's one swatch. Then it mixes 0 percent of Pantone 519 M with 60 percent of Pantone 8201 M (adding the increment of 10%). It does so four more times, for 70, 80, 90, and 100 percent of Pantone 8201 M mixed with the 0 percent of Pantone 519 M because there was a Repeat setting of 5. Note that InDesign stops at 100 percent saturation even if the Increment results in a higher number.

So that's six mixed-ink swatches based on 0 percent of Pantone 519 M. InDesign now repeats this six sets of Pantone 80201 M mixed with the next increment of Pantone 519 M (4 percent, based on the Increment value of 4% for that color). That's six more. The process is repeated two more times, one for 8 percent and one for 12 percent, to meet the Repeat setting of 3. So that's a total of 24 swatches.

> **TIP** To figure out how many swatches you can create using this feature, add 1 to the number in each of the Repeat fields and then multiply the values. In the preceding example, you get 24 — (3+1) × (5+1), or 4 × 6, or 24. That's because the Repeat setting indicates how many more variations to create *in addition to* those with the base (Initial) value.

Creating colors the risky way: Using the Colors panel

Many people may try to use the Color panel (choose Window ➪ Color or press F6) to define colors, but that can be a mistake. At first, you may not realize you can create colors from the Color panel. It shows a gradation of the last color used and lets you change the tint for that color on the current object. But if you go to the flyout menu and choose a color model (RGB, CMYK, or Lab), you get a set of mixing controls (see Figure 7.7).

FIGURE 7.7

The Color panel

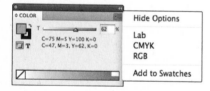

Managing Unnamed Colors

No matter how disciplined you are, chances are that you will get unnamed colors in your document. Fortunately, InDesign provides several ways to identify and convert those unnamed colors to swatches you can then edit, apply, and manage consistently:

- If you go to the Color panel and modify a color without thinking about it, choose Add to Swatches from the flyout menu to add the modified color to the Swatches panel.

- Choose Add Unnamed Colors from the Swatches panel's flyout menu, which adds all unnamed colors in one fell swoop.

- Drag an unnamed color from the Fill iconic button or Stroke iconic button on the Tools panel onto the Swatches panel to create a swatch.

- Use the Find/Change dialog box's Object pane to find unnamed colors in the Fill and/or Stroke panes in the Find Object Format Options dialog box and replace them with actual swatches. (See Chapter 10.) Note that this does not convert an unnamed color into a swatch but lets you eliminate the use of such colors.

So what's the problem? Colors created through the Color panel don't appear in your Swatches panel and so can't be used for other objects. Called *unnamed colors* because they don't appear anywhere, these can be dangerous for publishers to use. (Adobe added them to InDesign to be consistent with how Illustrator defines colors — a foolish consistency.)

First, you can't modify them later in the Swatches panel if you want to adjust the color for all objects using them.

TIP **You can double-click the Stroke and Fill iconic buttons on the Tools panel to create colors, using a Photoshop-style color picker. You can add any colors created this way to the Swatches panel using the Add Swatch button. Otherwise, you run the same risk as creating colors through the Color panel.**

Second, you can't specify the color to print as a spot color, which you might later decide is how you want to print a particular color. They print only as process colors and do not show up in the list of colors in the Color pane of the Print dialog box (see Chapter 30 for more details on this).

That's why it's best to think *Swatches panel* when you think about adding or editing colors instead of the more obvious *Color panel*. And even better is to remove the Colors panel from your user interface by clicking its Close box so that you don't get tempted to use it.

Importing and sampling colors

InDesign lets you add colors to your document from other sources, such as importing swatch files, adding colors from imported graphics automatically, and letting you sample a color from an imported image.

Importing swatches

You can import colors from other InDesign, Illustrator, and Illustrator EPS files by choosing Load Swatches from the Swatches panel's flyout menu. Plus, you can also import colors from Adobe Swatch Exchange library files this way. From the resulting dialog box, navigate to the file that contains the colors you want to import, select that file, and click Open.

TIP A quick way to import specific color swatches from another InDesign document or template is to click and drag the colors from that other file's Swatches panel into your current document or template.

So you can share those swatches with other Creative Suite 2, 3, and 4 users, InDesign lets you save swatches into color library files. Just select the colors you want to save and then choose Save Swatches from the Swatches panel's flyout menu. You'll be asked to give the Adobe Swatch Exchange file a name before you save it.

You can also import an Illustrator color library, adding its set of swatches to InDesign. To do so, create a new swatch as described earlier in this chapter. In the New Color Swatch dialog box, choose Other Library from the Color Mode pop-up menu. You'll get a dialog box from which you select the any color, tint, or gradient swatch library file in the old Adobe Illustrator 8 format. (You can't use Illustrator's patterned swatches, but don't worry if the swatch file contains them: InDesign simply ignores them.)

Importing colors from graphics

When you import a graphic file in EPS format or in PDF, any named colors (swatches) in that file are automatically added to the Swatches panel. But sometimes the colors won't print accurately from InDesign:

- Even though InDesign does not offer Hexachrome swatch libraries, it does retain any Hexachrome colors in an imported PDF file. These Hexachrome colors will print as CMYK if you print from InDesign; note that many Hexachrome colors do not print properly when converted to CMYK. But if you export your InDesign file to a PDF file, those Hexachrome colors are retained and will print as Hexachrone colors, assuming your printer can print PDF files directly.

- Colors in imported EPS files may not print as expected (you can minimize this chance by using popular programs such as the latest versions of Adobe Illustrator and CorelDraw. One of three things can happen:

  - Each color prints on its own plate (as if it were a spot color), even if you defined it as a process color.

  - A spot color is color-separated into CMYK even when you define it as a spot color in both the source program and in InDesign.

  - A color prints as black.

Color Considerations for Imported Graphics

When you work with imported graphics, whether they are illustrations or scanned photographs, color is part of the graphic file. So the responsibility for color controls lies primarily with the creator of the graphic. It is best to use color files in CMYK EPS or DCS format (for illustrations and vector art) or CMYK TIFF format (for scans and bitmaps). These standards are de facto for color publishing, so InDesign is particularly adept at working with them. (See Chapter 25 for details on preparing graphics files for import.)

Although printing uses CMYK, computers use RGB as the color model, since monitors use red, green, and blue electron guns to display images. The dilemma most designers face is that an RGB image displays properly on-screen but may appear with slightly adjusted hues in print, whereas a CMYK image may print correctly but appear incorrectly on-screen. Most designers get good at mentally shifting the colors from one model to another as they see the results of their work in print over time. Until that happens, rely on color proofs from your printer to see what your images actually look like when printed.

Do note that color files pasted via the Clipboard should print properly after they're pasted into an InDesign graphics frame. But problems, such as dropped colors or altered colors, sometimes occur depending on the applications involved and the amount of memory available. If you click and drag files from Photoshop or Illustrator directly into InDesign rather than using copy and paste, you should have no such problems.

Sampling colors

Many types of graphics, such as bitmap images, don't use named colors or swatches. But InDesign lets you *sample* colors in such graphics, determining the RGB values and then letting you create a swatch from them. Here's how:

1. **In the Tools panel or Swatches panel, choose the Fill iconic button or Stroke iconic button.** It doesn't really matter which unless you will immediately create a shape or enter text after capturing the desired color; in that case choose whichever aspect you'll want the new object or text to have the color applied to.

2. **Select the Eyedropper tool and then click the graphic where the desired color is used.** The Fill or Stroke iconic button will now have that color. (If the Eyedropper tool is not visible in the Tools panel, look for the Measure tool, then click and hold down its icon to get the pop-up menu that lets you select the Eyedropper tool.)

3. **The Eyedropper tool changes to the Marker tool.** Any object you select with the Marker tool will have the color applied to its fill or stroke, depending on whether the Fill or Stroke iconic button is active. Note you can switch between the Eyedropper and Marker tool to select different colors and apply them by holding the Option or Alt key to get the Eyedropper tool back and then releasing it to switch to the Marker tool.

CAUTION If you apply a sampled color via the Marker tool, it will be an unnamed color. It's best to first create a swatch from your sampled color so you can ensure consistent color usage.

4. **To add the new, unnamed color to the Swatches panel, Control+click or right-click the Fill iconic button or Stroke iconic button (whichever has the captured color) and choose Add to Swatches from the contextual menu that appears.** (Or just drag the color to the Swatches panel.) Now you can edit and apply the captured color as you can any other color swatch.

Figure 7.8 shows a composite image that highlights the Eyedropper tool at center left and the Marker tool at right.

FIGURE 7.8

At left: Sampling a color with the Eyedropper tool. At right: Applying that sampled color to an object using the Marker tool.

Working with Gradients

A technique that has been popular for a long time among designers is the gradient, which blends two or more colors in a sequence, going from, say, green to blue to yellow to orange. InDesign has a powerful gradient creation feature that lets you define and apply gradients to pretty much any object you create in InDesign: Text, lines, frames, shapes, and their outlines (strokes).

NOTE Gradients go by several names among artists. Included among them are *blends* and *graduated fills.*

Creating gradients

In the Swatches panel, where you define colors and tints you can also define gradients: Just use the New Gradient Swatch option in the flyout menu. You get the dialog box shown in Figure 7.9. The first two options are straightforward:

FIGURE 7.9

The New Gradient Swatch dialog box (left) and the Gradient panel (right)

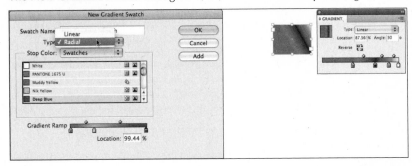

- **Type a name for the gradient in the Swatch Name field.** Picking a name is a bit more difficult than it is for a color, but use something like "Blue to Red" or "Bright Multihue" or "Logo Gradient" that has a meaning specific to the colors used or to its role in your document.

- **In the Type pop-up menu, choose Linear or Radial.** A linear blend goes in one direction, whereas a radial blend radiates out in a circle from a central point. (Later in this section, Figure 7.10 shows some example gradients.)

FIGURE 7.10

Examples of gradients. First column: A two-color linear gradient (top) with variations that have different transition controls. Second column: A four-color gradient (top) with variations that have different transition controls. Third column: The second column's gradients with various angles applied. Fourth column: A two-color radial gradient (top), the same gradient reversed (middle), and with a different transition control (bottom). Fifth column: The fourth column's gradients modified using the Gradient Swatch tool (see Figure 7.11).

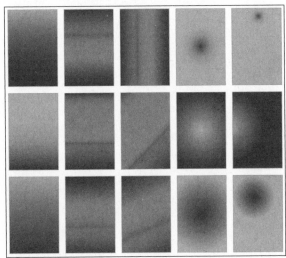

Now it gets a little tricky. Follow these steps:

1. **Select a stop point — one of the squares at the bottom of the dialog box, on either side of the gradient ramp that shows the gradient as you define it.** The stop points are essentially the from-and-to colors, with the from being the stop point at left and the to being the stop point at right. With a stop point selected, you can now define its color.

2. **Choose what color model you want to define the color in — select from CMYK, RGB, Lab, and Swatches in the Stop Color pop-up menu.** The area directly beneath the pop-up menu changes accordingly, displaying sliders for CMYK, RGB, and Lab, as well as a list of all colors from the Swatches panel for the Swatches option.

3. **Create or select the color you want for that stop point.**

 You can also click and drag swatches from the Swatches panel to the gradient ramp. (Use the [Paper] swatch for white.)

4. **Repeat Steps 1 and 2 for the other stop point.** Note that the color model for the two stop points don't have to be the same — you can blend from a Pantone spot color to a CMYK color, for example.

You now have a simple gradient. But you don't have to stop there. Here are your options:

■ You can change the rate at which the colors transition by sliding the diamond icon at the top of the gradient ramp.

■ You can create additional stop points by clicking right below the gradient ramp. By having several stop points, you can have multiple color transitions in a gradient. (Think of them like tab stops in text — you can define as many as you need.) You delete unwanted stop points by clicking and dragging them to the bottom of the dialog box.

Notice that there's a diamond icon between each pair of stop points — that means each can have its own transition rate. (Figure 7.9 shows a complex gradient being defined.)

 When you create a new gradient, InDesign uses the settings from the last one you created. To create a gradient similar to an existing one, click that existing gradient before selecting New Gradient Swatch from the flyout menu. InDesign copies the selected gradient's settings to the new one, which you can then edit. One reason to use this is to create, say, a radial version of an existing linear gradient.

The Swatches panel shows a preview of the actual gradient next to its name. You can also see the pattern in the Fill iconic button or Stroke iconic button in the Tools panel if that gradient is currently selected as a fill or stroke, as well as in the Gradient iconic button in that panel, whether or not it's currently applied as a fill or stroke.

NOTE If a gradient mixes spot colors and process colors, InDesign converts the spot colors to process colors.

Creating unnamed gradients

Just as it does with colors, InDesign lets you create *unnamed gradients* — gradients that have no swatches. My caution on using this feature for colors applies less for gradients because all colors in a gradient are converted to process colors and/or use defined spot-color swatches — so there are no unnamed colors in their output. Here's how it works:

1. **Select the object to which you want to apply the gradient.** Make sure the stroke or fill, as appropriate, is active in the Tools panel.

2. **Go to the Gradient panel (choose Window ⇨ Gradient), shown previously in Figure 7.9.**

3. **Select a stop point.**

4. **Now go to the Color panel or Swatches panel.** The Color panel is usually in the same panel group as the Gradient panel, but choose Window ⇨ Color or press F6 to display it if not. Open the Swatches panel by choosing Window ⇨ Swatches or pressing F5.

5. **In the Colors panel, create a color using the CMYK, RGB, or Lab models.** (Use the flyout menu to choose the model.) Or click and drag a swatch from the Swatches panel onto the stop point.

6. **Repeat Steps 2 through 5 for the other stop point.**

7. **Create any additional stop points by clicking below the gradient ramp, and adjust the transition controls as desired.**

Adjusting gradient angle and location

After you apply a linear gradient — whether via a gradient swatch or as an unnamed gradient — you can change the angle of the gradient, as was done with the gradient on the right side of Figure 7.9, shown previously.

To rotate a gradient, you use the Gradient panel — you cannot set rotation in a gradient swatch itself. In the Gradient panel, type a value in the Angle field to rotate the gradient's direction. That's it! You can't rotate a radial gradient because it's circular and, thus, any rotation has no effect. That's why InDesign grays out the Angle field for radial gradients.)

You can adjust the location of a linear or radial gradient by entering a value in the Location field in the Gradient panel or using the Gradient Swatch tool in the Tools panel. The Location field lets you specify a precise location for where the gradient starts, but it's not visually intuitive for most designers to work this way.

The Gradient Swatch tool provides a more visual approach. To use it, select the Gradient Swatch tool and draw a line in the object, as shown in Figure 7.11. The origination point, angle, and length of the line drawn with the Gradient Swatch tool determine the result. Shorter lines confine the color transition to a small area, whereas longer ones broaden it. Keep these points in mind when you use the tool:

- For a linear gradient, the start point corresponds to where you want the first stop point of the gradient to be, and the end point corresponds to the last point. This lets you stretch or compress the gradient, as well as offset the gradient within the object. Also, the angle at which you draw the line becomes the angle for the gradient.

- For a radial gradient, the line becomes the start and endpoint for the gradient, in effect offsetting it, as was done in the bottom-right gradient in Figure 7.10 (compare it to the standard radial-gradient setting for the object to its immediate left).

The Gradient Feather tool — accessed from the Gradient Swatch tool's pop-out menu or via the shortcut Shift+G — works just the same as the Gradient Swatch tool except that it makes a gradient that goes from transparent to the chosen color, as Figure 7.11 shows. To remove a gradient feather effect, deselect the Gradient Feather option in the Effects panel, as explained in Chapter 11.

FIGURE 7.11

The Gradient Swatch tool (left) lets you set the offset, adjust the gradient length, and (for gradient blends) adjust the gradient angle. The origination point, angle, and length of the line drawn with the Gradient Swatch tool determine the result. The Gradient Feather tool (right) acts the same as the Gradient Swatch tool except that it starts with transparent as the initial "color."

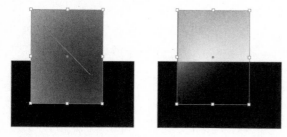

Managing Swatches

When you create colors, tints, and gradients (described later in this chapter), you may find it easy to go overboard and make too many. You'll also find that different documents have different colors, each created by different people, and you'll likely want to move colors from one document to another. InDesign provides basic tools for managing swatches in and across documents.

> **TIP** To help simplify working with swatches, you can have InDesign show just color and tint swatches, just gradient swatches, or all swatches by using the iconic buttons at the bottom of the Swatches panel. Figure 7.1 illustrates which iconic button does what.

Editing swatches

Editing swatches is pretty easy in InDesign: For any swatch in the Swatches panel, just double-click the swatch's preview or the swatch's name, or choose Swatch Options from the flyout menu.

The Swatch Options dialog box (called Gradient Options for gradient swatches) will then appear. The dialog box will differ based on what type of swatch you are editing, but in all cases it is identical except for the dialog box name to the dialog box you used to create the swatch with in the first place, such as the New Color Swatch or New Tint Swatch dialog boxes shown earlier in this chapter.

Make any adjustments and click OK when you're done. Voilà! Your swatch is now changed.

CAUTION When editing a tint, the Swatch Options dialog box also lets you change the other attributes of the color. If you change those settings in the tint, all other tints based on the original color, as well as the original color, are changed accordingly. If you want to change a setting of just the tint — such as making it a spot color while leaving the original color a process color — you need to duplicate the original color and make a tint from that duplicate.

Merging swatches

InDesign also lets you merge swatches — select multiple swatches and then choose Merge Swatches from the Swatches panel's flyout menu — but I suggest you avoid this. When InDesign merges swatches, it tries to calculate a new value based on the swatches' values, essentially weighting the CMYK values (RGB and other values are converted to CMYK first). But it's a crapshoot: You are not likely to get the color you expect. If you want a shade between two colors, I recommend you create it as a new swatch, manually entering the desired CMYK (or RGB or Lab) values.

Deleting swatches

InDesign makes deleting swatches easy: Just select the color, tint, or gradient in the Swatches panel. Then choose Delete Swatch from the flyout menu, or click the Delete Swatch iconic button at the bottom of the Swatches panel.

Well, that's not quite it. You then get the Delete Swatch dialog box, which lets you assign anything using the deleted swatch to a new color (the Defined Swatch option) or leave the color on any object that happens to be using it, but delete the swatch from the Swatches panel (the Unnamed Swatch option).

As I explain earlier in this chapter, unnamed colors should be avoided, so if your document is using a color, keep its swatch. But if you do delete a swatch and replace it with an unnamed swatch, you can recapture that deleted swatch later by choosing the Add Unnamed Colors menu item in the Swatches panel's flyout menu.

CAUTION If you delete a tint and replace it with another color, any object using that tint gets the full-strength version of the new color, not a tint of it.

Likewise, if you delete a color swatch that you've based one or more tints on, those tints are also deleted if you replace the deleted swatch with an unnamed swatch. However, if you delete a color swatch and replace it with another swatch, those tint swatches based on the original color swatch will remain but use the new color instead.

TIP InDesign offers a nice option to quickly find all unused colors in the Swatches panel — the flyout menu's Select All Unused option. Then you can just delete them in one fell swoop.

NOTE Remember that when you select swatches for deletion or duplication, you can ⌘+click or Ctrl+click multiple swatches to work on all of them at one time. Note that Shift+clicking selects all swatches between the first swatch clicked and the swatch that you Shift+click, whereas ⌘+click or Ctrl+click lets you select specific swatches in any order and in any location in the panel.

Duplicating swatches

To duplicate a swatch so you can create a new one based on it, use the Duplicate Swatch option in the Swatches panel. The word *copy* is added to its name, and you edit it — including its name — as you would any swatch.

Applying Colors, Tints, and Gradients

Applying colors, tints, and gradients to objects in InDesign is easy. Select the object and then click the Formatting Affects Text iconic button or Formatting Affects Container iconic button in the Swatches panel or Tools panel, as appropriate for what you want to apply the color to, and then click the appropriate swatch. In either case, you can also choose whether to apply the attribute to the object's fill or stroke by clicking the Fill or Stroke iconic button in the Swatches panel or Tools panel.

NOTE You can apply colors and tints to grayscale and black-and-white bitmapped images, such as those in the TIFF and Photoshop formats. But you cannot color vector-based graphics (such as those in the Illustrator and EPS formats) or color bitmapped images.

CROSS-REF Although you cannot apply a tint to a color bitmapped image, you can achieve a similar effect by making it (or any bitmapped image) partially or fully transparent, as explained in Chapter 11.

Once you've determined what you want to apply the color, tint, or gradient to, you can use the Swatches panel to select a swatch, or pick the last-used color and gradient from the Apply Color and Apply Gradient iconic buttons on the Tools panel. Figure 7.12 shows the panel. (You can't apply tints this way.)

For tints, you can also enter a tint value in the Swatches panel's Tint field. (You would use a swatch for tints you want to use repeatedly in your layout, such as for the background tint in sidebar boxes, to ensure consistency. You would use the Tint field for tints you are applying on the fly, typically for one-time use.)

You can also apply colors and tints (but not gradients) to *gaps* in strokes through the Stroke panel's flyout options menu: Select Show Options and select a swatch from the Gap Color pop-up menu. You can apply a tint by entering a value in the Gap Tint field, or by choosing a value from its pop-up menu.

FIGURE 7.12

The Tools panel lets you choose what part of an object you want to color, as well as apply the last-used color or gradient.

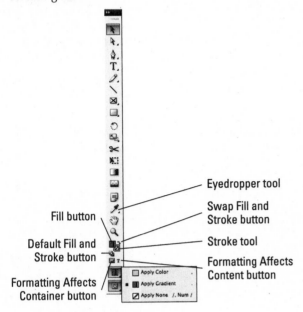

Eyedropper tool

Swap Fill and
Stroke button

Fill button

Stroke tool

Default Fill and
Stroke button

Formatting Affects
Content button

Formatting Affects
Container button

Apply Color
Apply Gradient
Apply None /, Num /

Summary

Using color in publishing involves complex decisions. There are many ways to define colors, but they don't all result in the same colors when you finally print your documents. That's why choosing the color models for your documents up front is important.

Color can also be expensive to print, so you may need to weigh when you use color and how you apply it. A spot color — a single ink — is cheaper to print than full color (produced by combining four process colors) but, of course, it gives you less visual flexibility. You can also mix spot colors with process colors to add special colors such as pastels and metallics that process colors cannot produce.

Key to defining colors is choosing the appropriate color model: spot or process. A spot color prints on its own plate, whereas a process color is separated into the four basic colors used in traditional color publishing. If you define too many colors as spot colors, you're likely to create an impossible-to-print or a very expensive-to-print document. InDesign lets you convert colors from spot to process and vice versa, so you can choose the right output options for each document. Similarly, it's best to create color images in the color model you intend to use for output: CMYK for traditional printing and RGB for on-screen display.

InDesign uses swatches to contain defined colors (including colors made up of other colors), tints, and gradient blends; the use of swatches lets you apply colors repeatedly with the assurance it's the same color each time, much as character and paragraph styles ensure consistent text formatting. Although you can also apply colors without using these swatches, doing so can cause output problems, especially when you're using color separations.

To maintain consistency of colors, InDesign can import colors from other InDesign documents, as well as from Adobe swatch files known as Adobe Swatch Exchange files. InDesign also imports colors used in EPS and PDF files, as well as colors defined by others using the Kuler.com Web site, which you can modify and even add your own color palettes to.

A powerful feature in InDesign is its capability to create gradient blends that can contain blends among multiple colors. No other layout program offers this level of control or flexibility on gradients, although image editors such as Photoshop go even further than InDesign does.

Part III

Object Fundamentals

Chapter 8

Adding Frames, Shapes, and Lines

W hen you create a new InDesign document, you make several important decisions, including the page size, number of columns, and gutter width, that determine the basic structure of your publication. After you click OK in the New Document dialog box (choose File ➪ New ➪ Document or press ⌘+N or Ctrl+N), you're greeted with a blank first page. Much like an artist confronting an empty canvas, it's now time for you to add the text, graphics, and graphic elements (shapes and lines) that make up the final piece.

InDesign uses *objects* as the building blocks you manipulate to create finished pages. An object is a container that can (but doesn't have to) hold text or graphics, as well as attributes such as color, strokes, and gradients; when an object contains an imported graphic or text, or if an object is created as a placeholder for a graphic or text, it's referred to as a *frame*. A frame looks and behaves much the same as an object but has some additional properties:

- If you change the size or shape of a frame that contains text, you affect the flow of text in the frame and in any subsequent frames of a multiframe story.

- If you change the size or shape of a frame that contains an imported graphic, you also change the portion of the graphic that's visible.

Designing pages in InDesign is largely a matter of creating and modifying frames and modifying the text and graphics the frames contain. If, for example, you're creating a simple, one-page publication such as a business card, an advertisement, or a poster, you likely add several text frames to the page; each text frame holds a different piece of textual information. In the case of a business card, text frames would contain the company name, the name and title of the cardholder, the company address and phone numbers, and so on.

IN THIS CHAPTER

Knowing how and when to create frames for text and graphics

Creating text frames

Creating graphics frames

Converting frames for specific content

Drawing straight lines

If you want to include photos or computer-generated illustrations in your piece — maybe you want to add an EPS version of a corporate logo to your business card or a scanned image to an ad — you must also add graphics frames. A graphics frame serves as the cropping shape for the graphic within.

In this chapter, I show you how to create and modify basic text frames, graphics frames, shapes, and straight lines. After you create a text frame, you can type text directly into it or you can place a text file from a word-processing program. (For information about importing, formatting, and flowing text through a document, see Part IV.) After you create a graphics frame, you can import a graphic into it and then crop, scale, or apply other effects to the graphic. (For more information about importing and modifying graphics, see Part VI.)

InDesign offers tools to create both frames and shapes, which work the same way as each other. Visually, a graphics frame has an X placed through it, as a reminder that you can place contents into it (an ancient layout convention), whereas a shape — what InDesign calls an *unassigned frame* — does not, presumably because you are using it not as a container but as a printing object. (A text frame looks just like a shape.) But the difference between frames and shapes is artificial, because a shape can easily become a frame simply by placing text or graphics into it. So for all practical purposes, shapes and frames are the same thing. In this book, I use the word *frame* to mean either frames or shapes.

This chapter focuses on creating simple frames and straight lines. But InDesign also lets you create complex shapes and convert them to frames for holding text and graphics. And you can modify frames and other shapes. For more information about using InDesign's Pen tool to create free-form shapes and curved lines and to modify existing frames and shapes, see Chapter 27.

Creating frames and lines is also typically just an early step in the layout process. You want to modify and use those objects for various layout objectives. The Control panel provides the basic controls for objects all in one place, and Chapter 9 covers this versatile panel in more depth. Chapter 10 covers ways to modify objects, and Chapter 11 covers special effects you can apply to objects. InDesign also lets you save object styles so that you can apply the same settings to multiple frames or lines and keep them in synch; Chapter 12 covers this feature in more detail.

TIP   **When you create a frame or line, you can align the frame edge with a guideline by clicking within the number of pixels specified in the Snap to Zone in the Guides & Pasteboard pane of the Preferences dialog box, as Chapter 3 explains. You can also have frames and lines align to other objects with the new smart guides feature explained in Chapter 9.**

Creating a Text Frame

All the text blocks, called *stories*, in an InDesign document are contained in text frames. Unlike a word-processing program, which lets you just start typing text on a blank page, InDesign requires you to create a text frame before you can add text to a page using the keyboard. (If you want to import the text from a word-processing file onto a page, you don't have to create a text frame before you import.) After you create a new text frame, you can type and format text, move or resize the frame, and add graphic effects to the frame edge and the frame background.

CROSS-REF For information about importing text, see Chapter 13. Chapter 12 shows you how to anchor frames to text so that frames follow the text as it reflows, a useful feature for figures, tables, and sidebars.

The Tools panel contains several tools for creating both shapes and graphics frames, and because any shape or graphics frame can be converted into a text frame, you can use any of these tools to create a container that you intend to fill with text. However, in most cases, your text is contained within simple, rectangular text frames, and the quickest and easiest way to create such a frame is with the Type tool; it's the tool with a big T on it.

TIP If you want to place a particular piece of text on every page in a multipage publication (for example, the title of a book), you should place the text frame on a master page, as explained in Chapter 6.

Here's how to create a text frame:

1. **Select the Type tool by clicking it or by pressing T.**

2. **Move the I-beam mouse pointer (also called the *text cursor*) anywhere within the currently displayed page or on the pasteboard.**

3. **Click and hold the mouse button, and while holding down the mouse button, drag in any direction.** As you drag, a cross-hair pointer appears in the corner opposite your starting point; a colored rectangle indicates the boundary of the frame, as shown in Figure 8.1. (The color is blue for objects on the default layer; objects on other layers have that layer's color. See Chapter 5 for more on layers.) You can look at the width and height values displayed in the Control panel or the Transform panel as you drag to help you get the size you want. Or, if it's turned on in the Preference dialog box's Interface pane, the transformation-values indicator near the mouse pointer will show you the current size and dimensions as you move the mouse (see Chapter 6). Holding down the Shift key as you drag creates a square.

FIGURE 8.1

Creating a text frame with the Type tool is a simple matter of clicking and dragging until the rectangle that appears as you drag is approximately the size and shape of the intended text block.

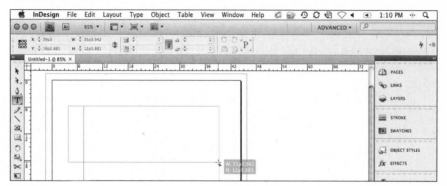

4. **When the frame is the size and shape you want, release the mouse button.** The flashing cursor appears in the finished frame, indicating that you can use the keyboard to type new text. Don't worry too much about being precise when you create a text frame: You can always go back later and fine-tune its size and position.

At this point, you can begin typing, or you can click and drag elsewhere on the page or pasteboard to create another text frame. You can create as many new text frames as you want. Just make sure not to click in an existing text frame when your intention is to create a new one. If you click within an existing frame when the Type tool is selected, the flashing cursor appears and InDesign thinks you want to type text.

CROSS-REF Chapter 13 covers the methods to add text to frames.

You can type or import text into *any* empty frame, not just those created with the Type tool. When creating nonrectangular frames, you cannot use the Type tool but must use the Pen, Pencil, or one of the frame or shape tools.

Creating a Graphics Frame

Although you can use InDesign's illustration features to create the kind of vector graphics that can be created with dedicated illustration programs such as Illustrator, FreeHand, Canvas, and CorelDraw, you may find yourself needing to import an illustration that you or somebody else created using another program. You may also want to add other kinds of digital images to a publication, such as a scanned photograph, a piece of clip art stored on a CD-ROM, or a stock photograph that you've downloaded from the Internet.

In InDesign, all imported graphics are contained within graphics frames or shapes. The Tools panel contains three tools for drawing graphics frames:

- **Ellipse Frame:** This tool lets you create oval and round frames.
- **Rectangle Frame:** This tool lets you create rectangular and square frames.
- **Polygon Frame:** This tool lets you create equilateral polygons and starburst-shaped frames.

There are three equivalent shape tools: Ellipse, Rectangle, and Polygon.

 You can also import graphics into so-called open shapes, such as curved lines, covered in Chapter 27.

The first time you use InDesign, the Rectangle Frame and Rectangle tools are displayed in the Tools panel. (The frame tools have an *X* through their icons.) To access the other frame tools, Control+click or right-click the Rectangle Frame tool to display a pop-out menu with the Ellipse Frame and Polygon Frame tools. (You can also click and hold on the tool to get the pop-out menu.) Drag and release to select a different frame tool. When you do, it replaces the Rectangle Frame tool in the Tools panel until the next time you change the tool. (You have the same options for the shape tools and for any tool that has a small triangle in its lower-right corner.)

Here's how to add a new graphics frame:

1. **Select the Ellipse Frame tool, the Rectangle Frame tool (or press F), or the Polygon Frame tool.**

2. **Move the cross-hair mouse pointer anywhere within the currently displayed page or on the pasteboard.**

3. **Click and hold the mouse button, and while holding down the mouse button, drag in any direction.** As you drag, the cross-hair pointer appears in the corner opposite your starting point and a blue shape indicates the boundary of the frame. As you drag, you can look at the transformation-values indicator near the mouse, or look at the width and height values displayed in the Control panel or Transform panel, to help you get the size you want. Holding down the Shift key as you drag creates a circle if the Ellipse Frame tool is selected, a square if the Rectangle Frame tool is selected, and an equilateral polygon or starburst if the Polygon Frame tool is selected.

4. **When the frame is the size and shape you want, release the mouse button.** Don't worry too much about being precise when you create a graphics frame. You can always go back later and fine-tune it. Figure 8.2 shows an oval graphics frame.

FIGURE 8.2

Creating a graphics frame with any of the frame-creation tools is the same as creating a text frame with the Type tool. Choose the appropriate frame tool and then click, drag, and release. In this example, an elliptical graphics frame has just been created; its bounding box appears with resizing handles.

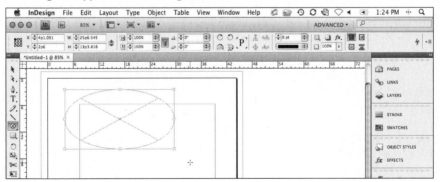

When any of the frame-creation tools is selected, you can create as many new frames as you want. Simply keep clicking, dragging, and releasing.

Creating Custom Polygons

You can configure the Polygon tool and the Polygon Frame tool to create either regular polygons or starburst shapes. Double-click either of the Polygon tools to display the Polygon Settings dialog box, shown below. The value in the Number of Sides field determines how many sides your polygons have. If you want to create a starburst shape, specify a value in the Star Inset field. As you increase the percentage value, the spikes become longer and pointier. When you change the values in the Polygon Settings dialog box, the new values are used for both versions of the polygon tool.

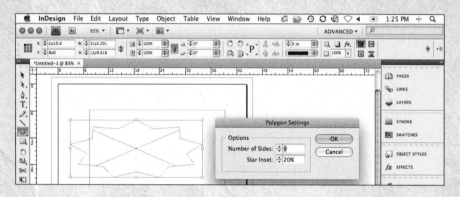

You cannot modify an existing polygon's attributes by selecting the polygon and then opening the Polygon Settings dialog box. You must either edit its shape with the Direct Selection tool, as covered in Chapter 27, or change attributes in the Polygon Settings dialog box and create a new polygon.

Note that you can set separate defaults for the Polygon Frame and Polygon tools, letting you have two default settings available at any time.

CAUTION   Don't try to click a frame handle when a frame-creation tool is selected. Instead of moving the handle you are clicking, you end up creating a new frame. You have to switch to one of the selection tools to move or resize a graphics frame.

CROSS-REF   See Part VI for details on importing graphics and modifying imported graphics.

Converting Frames for Specific Content

It makes no difference whether you use a frame tool or a shape tool — or even the Type tool — to create a frame that you want to hold a graphic. Similarly, you don't have to use the Type tool to create a frame that will hold text. Just select an empty frame and import text or a graphic into it. InDesign automatically converts the frame into the appropriate type.

Note that if you import a graphic into a text frame that already has text in it, the graphic is added as an inline graphic within the text, as Chapter 12 explains. (You cannot add text to a graphics frame that already has a graphic in it.)

You can also choose Object ⇨ Content ⇨ Graphic to convert a shape or text frame to a graphic frame. Or choose Object ⇨ Content ⇨ Unassigned to convert a text frame or graphics frame to a shape. There's really little reason to do so, given that InDesign converts the frame automatically when you place content into it. But you might use these commands to convert empty frames into the desired type so that it's clear later on what they're supposed to be used for.

Drawing Straight Lines

Although they're not as flashy or versatile as graphics shapes and frames, lines can serve many useful purposes in well-designed pages. For example, plain ol' vertical rules can be used to separate columns of text in a multicolumn page or the rows and columns of data in a table. Dashed lines are useful for indicating folds and cut lines on brochures and coupons. And lines with arrowheads are handy if you have to create a map or a technical illustration.

InDesign lets you create straight lines with the Line tool and zigzag lines, curved lines, and free-form shapes with the Pen and Pencil tools. In this chapter, I keep things simple and limit the coverage to the Line tool.

CROSS-REF For information about using the Pen and Pencil tools, see Chapter 27.

To draw a straight line:

1. **Select the Line tool (or press \).**

2. **Move the cross-hair mouse pointer (it will appear as a small cross) anywhere within the currently displayed page or on the pasteboard.**

3. **Click and hold the mouse button, and while holding down the mouse button, drag in any direction.** As you drag, a thin, blue line appears from the point where you first clicked to the current position of the cross-hair pointer. Holding down the Shift key as you drag constrains the line to horizontal, vertical, or a 45-degree diagonal.

4. **When the line is the length and angle you want, release the mouse button.** Don't worry too much about being precise when you create a line. You can always go back later and fine-tune it. Figure 8.3 shows a new line.

TIP When you create a line, it takes on the settings in the Stroke panel (choose Window ⇨ Stroke or press ⌘+F10 or Ctrl+F10). The default line width is 1 point. To change the width of a selected line, double-click the Line tool and adjust the Weight in the Stroke panel that appears. If you make this adjustment when no document is open, all new documents use the new settings.

When the Line tool is selected, you can create as many new lines as you want. Simply keep clicking, dragging, and releasing.

FIGURE 8.3

After you create a line with the Line tool, the active line appears either within a rectangular bounding box that has eight resizing handles (if the Selection tool was previously selected; left) or with anchor points at both ends (if the Direct Selection tool was previously selected; right).

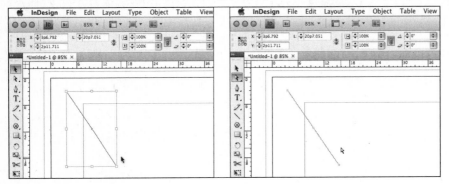

Summary

Empty objects, frames that hold text and graphics, and lines are the fundamental building blocks of pages. InDesign's Tools panel contains several tools for creating these objects. The easiest way to create a text frame is by clicking and dragging a rectangle with the Type tool.

Frames created for text or graphics, or to hold nothing, can actually hold text or graphics; InDesign converts them to the appropriate frame type based on what you put in them.

The Line tool lets you draw straight lines.

Chapter 9

Manipulating Objects

The primary purpose of the text frames and graphics frames that you add to the pages of your InDesign documents is to hold text and graphics, and much of the time you spend using InDesign involves modifying the appearance of the text and graphics you put in your frames. However, as with real-world containers — bags, boxes, cartons, and cans — text frames and graphics frames exist independently of their contents (they don't even have to have any contents), and you can modify the position, shape, and appearance of frames without affecting the text and graphics within.

In this chapter, you learn how to do perform basic manipulations on the objects that you add to your pages: select, move, copy, delete, and position. If you've ever worked with a page-layout or illustration program, many of the basic techniques for manipulating objects should seem very familiar.

CROSS-REF For information on resizing, rotating, and applying other transformations to objects, see Chapter 10. For information on applying strokes and other effects to objects, see Chapter 11. For information on working with the text within a frame, see Part IV; for information on working with imported graphics, see Part VI.

IN THIS CHAPTER

Selecting objects and understanding tool differences

Moving, copying, and deleting objects

Working with snippets

Preventing objects from printing

Aligning and distributing multiple objects

Using gridlines and guidelines when positioning objects

Aligning and spacing objects via smart guides

Selecting Objects

If you want to manipulate or transform an object, you must first select it. To select an object, you must first choose a selection tool. InDesign offers three tools for selecting objects: the Selection tool (the solid arrow icon; shortcut V), the Direct Selection tool (the hollow arrow icon; shortcut A), and the Pointer tool (the crop-tool-and-hand icon; no shortcut).

When an object is selected, various commands and controls for changing its position and appearance become available depending on how you select it, what panels are open, and what the object is.

Understanding the selection tools

All InDesign objects — unassigned shapes, text and graphics frames, and straight and curved lines — have at least two levels of selection. You can select the object itself, or you can select the rectangular bounding box that encloses the object. (For rectangular objects, the bounding box and the shape are the same.) The tool that you choose — typically, either the Selection tool or the Direct Selection tool — determines what you can do to the object you select:

- **Selection tool:** This tool lets you select an entire object by clicking anywhere in it. This is the best tool to use if you want to move or resize an object's container. For a text object, resizing the frame does not affect the text size, but for a graphics object, both the frame and graphic are resized. (You can also resize objects with the Direct Selection tool.) When you click an object with the Selection tool, the object's bounding box is selected.

- **Direct Selection tool:** This tool lets you select any of the individual anchor points (and direction handles of free-form shapes and curved lines) on an object. If you click with the Direct Selection tool on an object that has a bounding box, the shape within is selected; the bounding box is not selected. You use this tool to work on the object independently of its container frame. You can also move a graphic within its frame by clicking within the object with the Direct Selection tool and then dragging the graphic.

CROSS-REF   Chapter 15 covers how to select and work with text. Chapter 27 covers using the Direct Selection tool to select and change the shape of objects.

There's a third way to work with objects: the Position tool. (To access it, Control+click or right-click, or click and hold on, the Direct Selection tool until the pop-out menu appears, and then choose the Position tool.) Essentially a renamed version of PageMaker's Crop tool, the Position tool combines some aspects of the Selection tool with some aspects of the Direct Selection tool:

- As with the Selection tool, you can resize an object's frame by clicking and dragging its handles.

- As with the Direct Selection tool, you can click a graphic and reposition it (crop it) within the frame by dragging.

Unless you're a former PageMaker user who's totally mystified with the InDesign Selection and Direct Selection tools, you'll likely never use this tool. But if you do, note that you can change how quickly InDesign displays any masked portion of a selected graphic by double-clicking the tool and selecting the desired option from the dialog box that appears: After Short Delay, After Standard Delay, After Long Delay, Never, and No Delay.

Selecting objects

Here's how to select a frame, shape, line, or path — in other words, an object — with any of the selection tools:

1. **Select the desired selection tool by clicking it or, if the Type tool is not selected, by pressing V for the Selection tool or A for the Direct Selection tool.**

2. **Move the pointer anywhere within an object and then click and release.** To select an object with no background color, you must click its edge. If you click within it, the object is not selected. (The exception: Text frames are selected if you click within them.)

Choose View ⇨ Show Frame Edges or press Control+⌘+H or Ctrl+H to see object edges if they aren't already visible.

If you're using the Selection tool or the Position tool, when you release the mouse button, the object you clicked — or the object's bounding box if it has one — appears with a colored outline (the color is based on which layer it resides; blue is the default), eight resizing handles (four on the corners and four on the midpoints of the sides), and the solid centerpoint (which you can click and drag to move the object), as shown in Figure 9.1.

FIGURE 9.1

Left: When you select a frame with the Selection or Position tool (in this case an oval graphics frame), the bounding box appears with eight resizing handles, one of which I'm dragging to resize it. Right: When you select a frame with the Direct Selection tool (in this case an oval graphics frame), the frame's reference points appear. Here, I am moving one of those points. Note how it reshapes — not resizes — the frame.

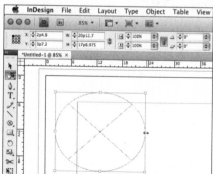
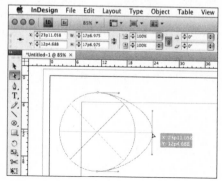

If you're using the Direct Selection tool, when you release the mouse button, the object you clicked appears, with a colored outline (the color is based on which layer it resides; blue is the default), reshaping handles (called *nodes* and located at corners and any other transition points), and the hollow centerpoint (which you can click and drag to move the object). Note that you can also select any of the frame segments to reshape the object. Figure 9.1 also shows the same graphics frame selected using the Direct Selection tool, with one of the points being dragged to reshape the frame.

There are several tricks to know when selecting objects:

■ You can also select an object with the Selection tool by clicking and dragging a rectangle around it; this is called a *marquee*. Simply click in an empty portion of the page or paste-board near the object you want to select and drag out a rectangle that intersects the object. (You don't have to enclose the entire object.) Clicking and dragging is a handy way to select multiple objects.

■ If an object is on a master page and you're working on a document page, you must Shift+⌘+click or Ctrl+Shift+click the object to select it. (If you try to select an object by clicking and it doesn't become selected, the object must be on a master page.) For more information about using master pages, see Chapter 6.

■ When you double-click an object other than a text frame, the selection tool switches between the Selection tool and the Direct Selection tool. If the Position tool is active, double-clicking the object switches to the Direct Selection tool, and double-clicking switches to the Selection tool. The only way to switch back to the Position tool is to select it from the Direct Selection tool's pop-out menu.

■ If you double-click a text frame, InDesign switches to the Type tool. Double-clicking again selects the text, as described in Chapter 14. If the Type tool is active, you can select the text frame by pressing Esc — a faster alternative to picking a selection tool and then selecting the frame with it.

■ If you want to select an object within a group, InDesign now lets you double-click the object to select just it. (Single-clicking selects the entire group.) Groups are covered in Chapter 12.

Selecting overlapping objects

You often have multiple objects overlapping in your layout, with some objects completely obscured by others. So how do you select them? InDesign gives you several options.

The Select submenu

One way to select overlapping objects is by choosing Object ➪ Select and then choosing the appropriate command. Figure 9.2 shows the Select submenu and its options, as well as the equivalent buttons in the Control panel.

The first four options let you select another object relative to the currently selected object:

■ **First Object Above** selects the topmost object.

■ **Next Object Above** selects the object immediately on top of the current object.

■ **Next Object Below** selects the object immediately under the current object.

■ **Last Object Below** selects the bottommost object.

If no objects are selected, InDesign bases its selection on the creation order.

FIGURE 9.2

The Select submenu in the Object menu (top) and the equivalent controls available in the Control panel (bottom).

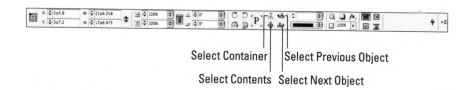

Select Container | Select Previous Object

Select Contents | Select Next Object

TIP You can also access these four selection options by Control+clicking or right-clicking an object and choosing Select from the contextual menu.

The Select submenu has four other options:

■ If an object has content (text or graphic) and you've selected its content, choose Object ⇨ Select ⇨ Container to choose the frame. This is the same as selecting it with the Selection tool.

■ If an object has content (text or graphic) and you've selected its frame, choose Object ⇨ Select ⇨ Content to choose the content within the object. This is basically the same as selecting it with the Direct Selection tool.

■ If you have selected an object in a group of objects, using the Direct Selection tool, choose Object ⇨ Select ⇨ Previous Object in Group to navigate to the previous object in the group.

■ Similarly, if you have selected an object in a group of objects, using the Direct Selection tool, choose Object ⇨ Select ⇨ Next Object in Group to navigate to the previous object in the group.

NOTE Object creation order determines what is "previous" or "next" in a group.

Keyboard shortcuts

You can use the keyboard shortcuts listed in this section. Although this approach takes memorizing the commands, it's the fastest way to change your selection because you don't have to mouse around to the menus.

- Option+Shift+⌘+] or Ctrl+Alt+Shift+] selects the topmost object.
- Option+⌘+] or Ctrl+Alt+] selects the object immediately on top of the current object.
- Option+⌘+[or Ctrl+Alt+[selects the object immediately under the current object.
- Option+Shift+⌘+[or Ctrl+Alt+Shift+[selects the bottommost object.

Control panel selection buttons

The Control panel also provides iconic buttons — Select Previous Object and Select Next Object — to select the next or previous object, as well as the Select Contents and Select Container iconic buttons to select the content or container (frame). Figure 9.2 shows the buttons.

If you Shift+click either selection button, InDesign jumps past four objects and selects the fifth one. If you ⌘+click or Ctrl+click either button, InDesign selects the bottommost or topmost object, respectively.

> **NOTE** If you use the Select Previous Object or Select Next Object buttons and reach the top or bottom of the object stack, InDesign loops back from the top to the bottom object or from the bottom to the top object.

Selecting multiple objects

When an object is selected, you can move or modify it. When several objects are selected, you can move or modify all the objects at one time, saving you the time and drudgery of selecting and performing the same modification to several objects one at a time. You have several options for selecting multiple objects. You can:

- Choose the Selection tool and hold down the Shift key while clicking in succession on the objects you want to select.
- Choose any of the selection tools and then click in an empty portion of the page and drag a rectangle (called a *marquee*) around any portion of each object you want to select. Make sure you don't click an item or you'll move it when you drag.
    - If you use the Selection or Position tool, the bounding box of each item is selected. You can resize any of the bounding boxes, but the anchor points and direction lines of the shapes within are not selected and cannot be moved.
    - If you use the Direct Selection tool, the anchor points and direction handles of the shapes in the bounding boxes are selected. You can change the shape of any of the objects by dragging an anchor point or a direction handle.

- If you want to select all items on a page or spread, choose Edit ⇨ Select All or press ⌘+A or Ctrl+A. (If the Type tool is selected and a text frame is active when you choose Select All, you highlight all the text, if any, in the frame.) If the Direct Selection tool is selected when you choose Select All, the anchor points and direction handles of the shapes in the selected objects' bounding boxes are selected. If any other tool is selected when you choose Select All, the bounding boxes of the objects are selected.

Deselecting objects

A selected object remains selected until you cause it to become deselected, and there are many reasons you might want to deselect an item. For example, you might want to deselect a text frame if you want to see how it looks when displayed without the frame's in and out ports visible. Or you might want to simply "let go" of an object you just finished working on. There are several ways to deselect a selected object. You can:

- Click in an empty portion of the page with any of the selection tools selected.

- Press and hold the Shift key with any of the selection tools selected and click the object you want to deselect.

- Choose any of the object-creation tools (the Pen, Pencil, Line, or any shape- and frame-creation tools) and then click and drag to create a new object.

- If you want to deselect all items on a page or spread, choose Edit ⇨ Deselect All or press Shift+⌘+A or Ctrl+Shift+A. (If the Type tool is selected and a text frame is active when you choose Deselect All, you'll deselect any text that's highlighted in the frame.)

Moving Objects

Before you can move an object, you must first select it. When an object is selected, InDesign provides several methods for moving or copying it.

You can move a selected object by:

- **Clicking and dragging it to a different location:** When you drag an object, you can move it anywhere within the current page or spread, into an open library (see Chapter 6 for more information about libraries), or into another document (if another document is open and its window is visible). If you drag an object from one document to another, a copy of the object is placed in the target document and the original object remains unchanged in the source document.

 **Press and hold down the Shift key as you drag to restrict the angle of movement to the nearest 45-degree angle based on the direction in which you're moving your mouse.**

- **Pressing any of the arrow keys:** Each time you press an arrow key, the object is nudged by the distance specified in the Cursor Key field in the Units & Increments pane of the Preferences dialog box (choose File ⇨ Preferences ⇨ Units & Increments or press ⌘+K on the Mac, or choose Edit ⇨ Preferences ⇨ Units & Increments or press Ctrl+K in Windows). The default nudge value is 1 point. If you press and hold the Shift key when using arrow keys, the nudge increment is 10 points.

- **Selecting it with the Selection or Direct Selection tool and then double-clicking the tool to open the Move dialog box:** You enter the desired horizontal (X) and vertical (Y) coordinates, or the distance from the current location and the angle of the new location from the existing one. (This does not work with the Position tool.)

- **Selecting it with any of the selection tools, then choosing Object ⇨ Transform ⇨ Move:** You enter the desired horizontal (X) and vertical (Y) coordinates, or the distance from the current location and the angle of the new location from the existing one.

- **Changing the X and Y values in the Control panel or in the Transform panel:** These values determine the distance between an object's control point and the ruler's zero point, where the horizontal and vertical rulers intersect (usually the upper-left corner of a page or spread). (If the Control panel is not displayed, activate it by choosing Window ⇨ Control or pressing Option+⌘+6 or Ctrl+Alt+6. If you want to use the Transform panel, activate it by choosing Window ⇨ Object & Layout ⇨ Transform.) Figure 9.3 shows the Control panel and Transform panel and their controls. If you want, change the object's control point — where the X and Y coordinates refer to.

FIGURE 9.3

The Control and Transform panels

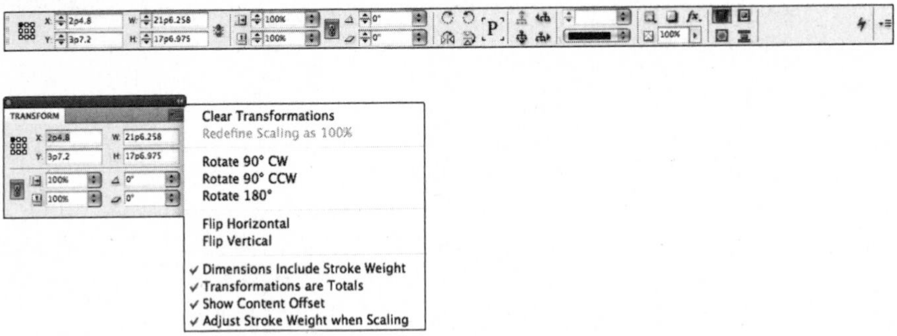

Each of the preceding methods for moving objects has its merits. The method you choose depends on how you prefer to work.

CROSS-REF Chapter 2 explains how to set the control point.

 InDesign lets you move and copy entire pages between documents, as described in Chapter 5.

Creating Copies of Objects

After you create something — a simple, rectangular frame or a complicated graphic made up of several dozen objects — InDesign makes it easy to reuse the original. InDesign provides many options for copying objects within documents as well as across them.

Copying objects within documents

Here are your options for copying objects within a document:

- **Copy and Paste commands (choose Edit ⇨ Copy or press ⌘+C or Ctrl+C; choose Edit ⇨ Paste or press ⌘+V or Ctrl+V):** Using these commands is a good choice if you have to copy something from one page to another. A great option is Paste in Place (choose Edit ⇨ Paste in Place or press Option+Shift+⌘+V or Ctrl+Alt+Shift+V), which pastes an object in the same place as the original object. It's very handy when copying an element from one page to another because it places the copy in the same location on the new page, saving you the effort of having to move it. (When copying among documents, Paste in Place uses the same X and Y coordinates as the original.)

- **Duplicate command (choose Edit ⇨ Duplicate or press Option+Shift+⌘+D or Ctrl+Alt+Shift+D):** The Duplicate command is quicker than using copy and paste. When you duplicate an object, the copy is placed one pica below and to the right of the original.

NOTE InDesign offsets a duplicate by whatever settings are in the Step and Repeat dialog box or by the distance and direction of the last Option+drag or Alt+drag copying of an object — whichever was done last.

- **Manual cloning:** When you drag and drop an object while pressing and holding Option or Alt, a copy of the selected object is created. If you're a drag-and-dropper, you may prefer this manual method to the Duplicate command.

- **Cloning with the transform tools:** If you press and hold Option or Alt while using any of the transform tools (Rotate, Shear, Scale, and Free Transform), a copy of the selected object is transformed. The selected item remains unchanged.

- **Control panel and Transform panel cloning:** If you press and hold Option or Alt when you exit the Control or Transform panels (by pressing Return or Enter or releasing the mouse after choosing an option from a menu), the transformation is applied to a copy of the selected item.

- **Step and Repeat command (choose Edit ⇨ Step and Repeat or press Shift+⌘+U or Ctrl+Shift+U):** Think of the Step and Repeat dialog box (shown in Figure 9.4) as the Duplicate command on steroids. It lets you create multiple duplicates of selected objects and specify the horizontal and vertical offset of the duplicates. This command is handy if you have to create, for example, a vertical and/or horizontal grid of lines on a page. Simply draw a horizontal line at the top of the page or a vertical line along the left edge of the page. With the line selected, use the Step and Repeat command to place and evenly space as many additional lines as you need.

Figure 9.4 shows a typical task that's easily handled with the Step and Repeat command. First, the top row was built by creating two copies of the original; the rest of the rows were created by step-and-repeating the four grouped objects in the top row.

> **TIP** If you need to use an object or a group of objects repeatedly, storing them in a library is a good idea. After you place something in a library, you can drag-copy as many clones as you want into any document. (Chapter 6 covers libraries.)

FIGURE 9.4

These business cards were created with two trips to the Step and Repeat dialog box. First, I copied the upper-left original to the right. Then I selected both cards and had them copied four times to fill out the page vertically.

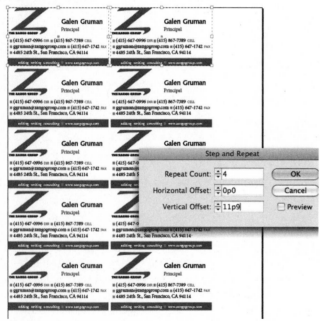

Copying objects between documents

Occasionally, you'll want to use something you've created in one InDesign document in another document. For example, maybe you need an ad that ran in last month's newsletter again for this month's edition. Or perhaps you created a small illustration for an ad that you want to use in a companion brochure. InDesign offers several options for moving objects between documents. You can:

- Open the document that contains the objects you want to copy, select the objects and then copy them to the clipboard by choosing Edit ➪ Copy or pressing ⌘+C or Ctrl+C. Open the target document and choose Edit ➪ Paste or press ⌘+V or Ctrl+V, to place the copied objects. You can also choose Edit ➪ Paste in Place or press Option+Shift+⌘+V or Ctrl+Alt+Shift+V to paste the object at the same X and Y coordinates as the original.

- If you need to use the objects in more than one document, you can copy them into a library, which lets you place as many copies as you want in any document. (Libraries are covered in Chapter 6.)

- You can open the source document (the one that contains the objects) and the target document and drag-copy the objects from the source document to the target document. (Choose Window ➪ Arrange ➪ Tile to display both document windows side by side; Chapter 3 covers working with multiple document windows in detail.)

- A very easy way to share parts of your document is to select the desired objects and drag them out of your document window into the Mac or Windows desktop or into a folder. You can also choose File ➪ Export or press ⌘+E or Crl+E and then choose InDesign from the Format pop-up menu in the Export dialog box to create snippets from selected objects. InDesign creates a file called a snippet file (with the filename extension .idms) that contains all the objects, formatting, and position information. You or another person can drag the file onto an InDesign document to place the objects, with all formatting intact.

NEW FEATURE The filename extension for snippets in InDesign CS4 has changed to .idms from .inds in previous versions.

Working with snippets is easy: Just drag objects from InDesign to the desktop or a folder to create the snippet file. And drag the snippet file on to a layout to place the objects on it. (You can also place the snippets the same as you can any other file by choosing File ➪ Place or pressing ⌘+D or Ctrl+D.) But don't let that simplicity blind you to a couple of cool attributes of snippets:

- You can send snippets to other users on storage drives, via e-mail, or over the network — as with any other file.

- You can control where a snippet's object are placed in your document. Select Position at Original Location or Position at Cursor Location in the Snippet Import section of the Preference dialog box's File Handling pane (choose InDesign ➪ Preferences ➪ File Handling or press ⌘+K on the Mac, or choose Edit ➪ Preferences ➪ File Handling or press Ctrl+K in Windows). The Position at Cursor Location option means the objects will be placed wherever you release the mouse when dragging the snippet.

NEW FEATURE You can now place — but not drag — snippets into text frames as inline graphics.

Deleting Objects

There are several ways to delete objects in InDesign. Most people either have a favorite method or use one that's easiest to adopt in their current state (such as using a mouse action to delete a frame when they're using the mouse already to size frames). No matter your preferred approach, be sure you select an object with the Selection tool. The methods are:

- Choose Edit ⇨ Cut or press ⌘+X or Ctrl+X to cut objects. Or choose the Cut command in the contextual menu you get when Control+clicking or right-clicking an object.

- Choose Edit ⇨ Clear or press ⌘+Delete or Backspace to delete (clear) the object.

- Drag the object to the Mac's Trash canor the Windows Recycle Bin; this clears the object.

 Cut objects can then be pasted elsewhere, at least until the time an object is cut or copied. Cleared objects cannot be pasted back.

Preventing Objects from Printing

InDesign lets you prevent an object from printing. To do so, select the object, open the Attributes panel (choose Window ⇨ Attributes), and then select the Nonprinting option. (The other settings in this panel control stroke settings, which Chapter 11 covers.)

You would use this feature for comments and other elements that should not print but that you need to have visible on-screen. Another approach to nonprinting objects is to place them all on a layer and make the entire layer nonprinting.

 Chapter 5 covers layers. Chapter 30 covers printing.

Aligning and Distributing Objects

A key task in any layout is to make sure that objects are correctly aligned and spaced. But that can be difficult to do precisely, given that designers tend to use the mouse to create and position objects; your hand-eye coordination is rarely exact for each and every object.

InDesign provides four ways to make sure that objects are precisely aligned and spaced:

- You can use the X, Y, W, and H coordinates in the Control panel or the Transform panel to specify the exact coordinates for every object. Just select an object and specify its coordinates in the panel. However, this often requires figuring out the math for the proper coordinates, which can be difficult, especially for visually oriented designers.

■ To take the math out of your hands, InDesign has the Align panel, which lets you align and distribute objects. The Align panel saves you the hassle of manually moving and placing each element, or it figures out the correct coordinates for elements' locations in the Control panel or Transform panel so that you can do so. The Align panel is where InDesign offers these timesaving capabilities.

■ You can use InDesign's guides and the "snap to" capability to help ensure that manually placed items at least align to your desired X or Y coordinates, as Chapter 6 explains.

■ The new smart-guides feature is particularly suited to visually oriented designers: It shows you on-screen — as you size, move, and rotate objects with the mouse — when the object you're working with aligns to nearby objects and when it is spaced equidistantly to other nearby objects. This feature provides the precision you want while you are doing actual work, saving you from having to fix alignment and spacing after the fact, which is what you have to do when you use the Control, Transform, or Align panels.

Working with the Align panel

The Align panel (choose Window➪Object & Layout➪Align or press Shift+F7), shown in Figure 9.5, has several iconic buttons that let you manipulate the relative position of multiple objects in two ways. (The buttons show the alignments they provide.)

FIGURE 9.5

The rectangles on the left were aligned along the left edge of the leftmost object by clicking the Align Left Edges iconic button in the Align panel, and then evenly distributed using the Distribute Top Edges iconic button. The result of the alignment operation is shown in the stack of rectangles on the right.

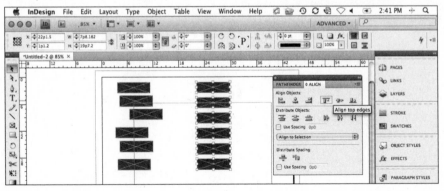

TIP   The Align panel's iconic buttons may also be available in the Control panel if you've selected multiple objects with the Selection tool, depending on how wide your screen is and how many buttons you've set the Control panel to display. (See Chapter 2 for how to customize the buttons it displays.)

With the Align panel, you can:

- **Line up objects along a horizontal or vertical axis.** For example, if you've randomly placed several small graphic frames onto a page, you can use the iconic alignment buttons in the Align panel to align them neatly — either horizontally or vertically. Figure 9.5 shows objects aligned with the Align panel.

- **Distribute space evenly among objects along a horizontal or vertical axis.** Here's a typical problem that's easily solved by using this feature: You've carefully placed five small graphics on a page so that the top edges are aligned across the page and there is equal space between each picture. Then you find out one of the graphics needs to be cut. After deleting the unneeded graphic, you could use the Align panel to redistribute the space among the remaining graphics so that they're again equally spaced. Figure 9.5 shows objects spaced evenly using the Align panel's Distribute Spacing capability.

NOTE The Align iconic buttons don't work with objects that have been locked with the Lock Position command. If the objects are on a locked layer, you need to unlock the layer. (Chapter 12 covers locking. Chapter 6 covers layers.)

When you click a button in the Align panel, selected objects are repositioned in the most logical manner. For example, if you click the Align Left Edges iconic button, the selected objects are typically moved horizontally (to the left, in this case) so that the left edge of each object is aligned with the left edge of the leftmost object. Along the same lines, if you click the Distribute Vertical Centers iconic button, the selected objects are moved vertically so that there's an equal amount of space between the vertical center of each object.

Spacing can appear uneven if you click the Distribute Horizontal Space or Distribute Vertical Space iconic buttons when objects of various sizes are selected. For objects of different sizes, you usually want to use the Distribute Spacing buttons (which make the space between objects even) rather than space objects based on their centers or sides (which is how the Distribute Object buttons work).

Note that the unnamed pop-up menu in the Align panel lets you choose where selected objects align to: Align to Selection (the default behavior), Align to Margins, Align to Page, and Align to Spread.

TIP Although InDesign has no default shortcuts for them, you can create keyboard shortcuts for the alignment and distribution buttons, as explained in Chapter 3.

NOTE If the two Distribute Spacing iconic buttons do not appear at the bottom of the panel and you want to distribute objects, choose Show Options from the flyout menu or click the double-arrow icon to the left of the panel name.

Using the Measure Tool and Info Panel

InDesign has two little-known methods to get dimension information about objects: the Measure tool and the Info panel. Because so much information about object size and position resides in the Control panel, these methods are little used. They're more vestiges of InDesign's pre-Control panel era. But they can be useful on occasion.

Available through the Eyedropper tool's pop-out menu or via the shortcut K, the Measure tool opens the Info panel and lets you draw a line whose dimensions appear in that panel (look for D1 in the upper left) so you can measure an arbitrary distance. You can measure the distance of two segments if you hold the Option or Alt key when dragging the tool for the second segment. Note that the second measurement must start where the first measurement left off — the two measurement lines must share a "corner." That second measurement displays in the D2 area, as shown in the figure.

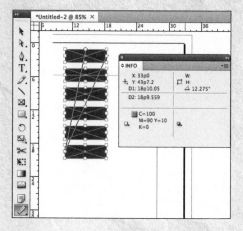

Although you can see objects' dimensions in the Control, Transform, and Info panels, the value of the Measure tool is that it enables you to determine the distance between objects rather than the dimensions of objects. It can also come in handy when you're measuring the distance across multiple objects. The figure shows the tool and Info panel.

When you select an object, the Info panel also shows its width and height, as well as any rotation angle, gradient, or stroke applied. While these are all bits of information you can get from the Control panel or Transform panel, the Info panel does show one bit of unique information: In its upper-left quadrant, the panel shows the current position of the mouse, providing a handy way to ensure that your starting and ending points when drawing something are exactly where you want them, especially when used with the new transformation-values indicator that appears next to the mouse pointer (see Chapter 6).

Working with smart guides

Using the new smart guides feature is easy. First, make sure that smart guides are enabled. You do so in the Smart Guide Options section of the Guides & Pasteboard pane of the Preferences dialog box by selecting the Align to Object Center and/or the Align to Object Edges options. (Choose InDesign ⇨ Preferences ⇨ Guides & Pasteboard or press ⌘+K on the Mac, or choose Edit ⇨ Preferences ⇨ Guides & Pasteboard or press Ctrl+K in Windows.)

NEW FEATURE Smart guides are new to InDesign CS4.

Aligning to an object's center tells InDesign to look for the centerpoint of other objects as you move or resize objects and use those as alignment targets. Aligning to object frame edges has it look for other objects' edges and use those as alignment targets. Turning on both produces more smart guides as you work on objects.

Figure 9.6 shows the smart guide feature in action in three sequences (in each sequence, at left is an existing object):

- The top sequence shows me adding a second frame. The mouse pointer is near neither the nearby object's centerpoint nor its edge, so no smart guide appears.

- The middle sequence shows what happens as the mouse pointer moves near the edge of the nearby object: InDesign displays a smart guide to let me know that if I want the bottom edge of the new frame to align with the bottom of the nearby object, all I have to do is let go.

- The third sequence shows me moving a circular frame from the bottom to the upper right of the page. You can see the smart guide that indicates the mouse is aligned to the centerpoint of the second object, and if I let go here, the circular frame's centerpoint will align to that other object's centerpoint.

Working with smart spacing and measurements

You probably noticed additional visual indicators in the third sequence of Figure 9.6: the spacing indicators between each set of objects. This visual indication is called *smart spacing,* which you also turn on in the Smart Guide Options section of the Guides & Pasteboard pane of the Preferences dialog box, following the two alignment options). When smart spacing is on, InDesign looks at the relative spacing of nearby objects as you work with one and highlights when the spacing is the same, or close to being the same (in which case it moves them for you).

A fourth "smart" feature option in the Smart Guides Options section of the Guides & Pasteboard pane: smart measurements. In this case, as you resize or rotate objects, InDesign shows a smart guide when the object being transformed matches the specs — such as dimensions or rotation angle — of other nearby angles, under the assumption that maybe you want them to be the same. As with the other smart-guide functions, let go of the mouse when the guides appear so that you can get those matching settings.

FIGURE 9.6

Smart guides in action. At top is a new frame being added (at right). The middle sequence shows a smart guide that automatically appears indicating an edge alignment, while the third sequence shows a smart guide indicating a centerpoint alignment, as well as two smart spacing indicators that show the spacing between the three objects is now equidistant.

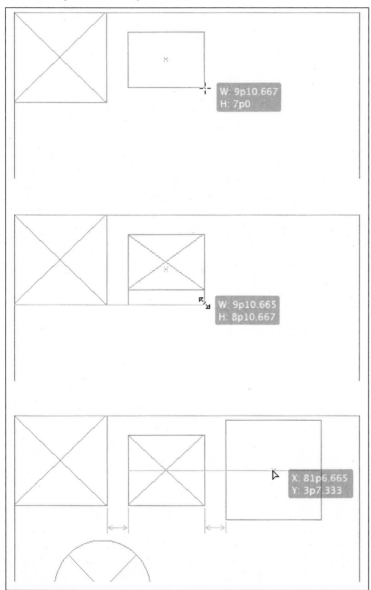

Summary

After you create an object, you can move, modify, or delete it. If the object is a frame, you also have the option of modifying the text or graphic within it. Before you can modify an object, you must select it. When an object is selected, commands and controls for changing its position and appearance become available. To select an object, you must first choose one of the three selection tools.

You can create a single copy of any object by using the Copy and Paste commands, by using the Duplicate command, or by Option+dragging or Alt+dragging a clone of the original. The Step and Repeat command lets you create multiple copies of objects and position the copies relative to the originals. The Paste in Place command pastes an object on a new page at the same X and Y coordinates as the original object.

You can prevent selected objects from printing using the Attributes panel.

The Align panel lets you align multiple objects and control the amount of space between them, while vertical and horizontal ruler guides and snap-to-grid features help you accurately position and align items. You can also distribute objects precisely using this panel. The smart guides capability lets you more easily align and size objects accurately; InDesign displays guides when your mouse location would make the object you're now working with have the same alignment, size, or spacing as nearby objects do, so if your intent is to create a similarly positioned, sized, or spaced object, you know when you have done so and thus can release the mouse button at the correct location.

Chapter 10

Transforming Objects

O ne of the wonders of desktop publishing is how you can make fundamental changes to objects. You can make them smaller, bigger, and wider. You can rotate them, flip them, and skew them. Try that with a printed photograph or strip of type.

The most common transformations include resizing frames and resizing (scaling) their contents. The other basic transformations — rotating, shearing, and flipping — are used less often, with rotation being the most widely useful and the other two usually limited to special effects.

For all of these controls, InDesign offers multiple ways to achieve the desired transformation: menu options, tools, panels, and dialog boxes. When you have a choice, pick whichever is most convenient at the moment.

CROSS-REF Chapter 9 covers how to select objects, as well as how to move, copy, delete, and align them. Chapter 11 covers special effects such as adding strokes and lighting effects.

The Control panel contains all sorts of transformation controls. Figure 10.1 identifies them.

IN THIS CHAPTER

Resizing and scaling objects

Rotating, shearing, and flipping objects

Controlling how InDesign displays transformation values

Repeating transformations

Undoing transformations

Replacing object attributes

FIGURE 10.1

The Control panel's transformation controls.

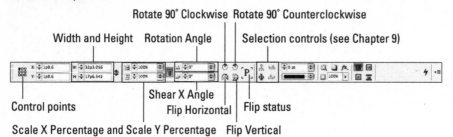

- Rotate 90° Clockwise Rotate 90° Counterclockwise
- Width and Height   Rotation Angle   Selection controls (see Chapter 9)
- Control points
- Shear X Angle
- Flip Horizontal   Flip status
- Scale X Percentage and Scale Y Percentage   Flip Vertical

Resizing and Scaling Objects

Two closely related transformation features are resizing and scaling. The difference is that resizing affects just the container — the frame or path — whereas scaling affects both the container and its contents. (For straight lines and for curved lines with no graphics or text, there is no difference between resizing and scaling, because there are no contents.)

Resizing methods

After you create a shape, frame, path, or line, you may find that it's too big or too small for your design. No problem. Resizing objects is as easy as moving them. And as is the case with repositioning objects, you have two basic options for resizing: the mouse or your choice of the Control or Transform panel.

Using the mouse

Click and drag the control handles on an object's bounding box using the Selection or Position tool. To change the width and height, drag a corner handle. To change only the width or height, drag a midpoint handle. If you press and hold Shift as you drag, the object's original proportions are retained.

> **TIP**   If you drag immediately after clicking a handle, only an object's bounding box is displayed as you drag. If you click and then pause until the pointer changes, the contents within are displayed as you drag.

Here's how the various selection tools act on objects — frames, paths, and lines — when you resize them via the mouse:

- **If you resize a graphics or text frame with the Selection tool, InDesign resizes just the frame.** Hold ⌘ or Ctrl to also scale the contents. For lines and paths, resizing the bounding box (the invisible "frame" that enclosed them) resizes the object but does not affect the thickness (weight) of any strokes unless you also hold the ⌘ or Ctrl key while dragging.

- **If you resize a graphics or text frame with the Position tool, InDesign resizes just the frame, as long as you selected the frame and not its contents.** If you selected the contents, InDesign resizes just the contents. The same is true when selecting paths. For lines, the Position tool acts like the Selection tool.

- **If you resize a graphic within a frame or path with the Direct Selection tool, only the graphic's size changes.** Just be sure that you select the graphic, not its frame. Hold ⌘ or Ctrl to also scale the frame (or the bounding box for a path).

- **If you resize a frame (rather than its contents) with the Direct Selection tool, the frame is reshaped.** If you select a path with the Direct Selection tool, its nodes appear so that you can reshape the path (see Chapter 27). If you select a line, dragging on its nodes will simply move the line, not resize it.

Using the Control or Transform panel

As with using the mouse, how you select an object determines what is resized (see the previous section). After selecting an object in the desired way, modify the horizontal and/or vertical dimensions by changing the W (width) and/or H (height) values in the Control panel or Transform panel. For a frame or path containing graphics, if the contents are selected rather than the bounding box or path outline, the new size values apply to the contents rather than to the container. Otherwise, the container is resized.

If you want to have the X and Y values change by the same amounts when you enter a new value for either, be sure that the Constrain Proportions for Width & Height iconic button shows a solid chain in the Control panel. If the button shows a broken chain, each dimension is changed independently. Toggle between the solid chain and broken chain by clicking the button. Note that the Transform panel does not have this button.

Resizing lines works a little differently: When a line is selected with any selection tool, the W and H fields are replaced by the L field, in which you can enter the line's new length. Doing so ensures that the line's angle is not changed by the resize.

Scaling methods

There are similar ways to change the scale of an object's contents:

- **Select the Scale tool.** If it's not already selected, click the object you want to scale and then drag the mouse in the direction you want to scale the object, as shown in Figure 10.2. (You don't need to drag on any handles.) If you want, you can click and drag the reference point from its default location in the upper-left corner of the bounding box to a different location. When the object grows or shrinks, the reference point doesn't move, but it does affect how InDesign interprets the direction and degree of scale desired as you move the mouse. Press and hold Shift and drag horizontally to apply only horizontal scale, vertically to apply only vertical scale, and diagonally to apply both horizontal and vertical scale and keep the object's original proportions. Release the mouse button when the object is the size you want. (If you select the object with the Direct Selection tool, only its contents will scale, not its frame.)

- **Choose the Free Transform tool, select an object handle, and drag in the direction you want to scale the object.** Selecting a corner handle scales in both dimensions, whereas selecting a side handle scales the contents only in that side's dimension.

- **Using the Selection or Position tool, click and drag a handle to resize a graphics or text frame.** To change the content's scale as well as the frame size while doing this, hold down ⌘ or Ctrl.

- **Select the object and then change the values in the Scale X Percentage and Scale Y Percentage fields in the Control panel or Transform panel.**

NOTE   If you want to have the X and Y percentage values change by the same amounts when you enter a new value for either, be sure the Constrain Proportions for Scaling iconic button shows a solid chain in the Control or Transform panel. If the button shows a broken chain, each dimension is changed independently.

FIGURE 10.2

Clicking and dragging with the Scale tool enlarges or reduces a frame. In this example, the Scale tool is being used to enlarge a frame.

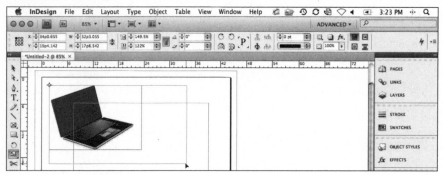

Here's how the Scale tool acts on objects based on what selection tool you used to select them:

- If you selected a graphics or text frame with the Selection or Position tool, InDesign scales the frame and the contents.

- If you selected a graphic within a frame with the Direct Selection or Position tool, only the content is scaled.

NOTE   When you select a scaled object with the Selection or Position tool, the Control or Transform panel may still show scale values of 100 percent. InDesign has a control in the Preference dialog box's General pane to change that odd behavior, as Chapter 3 explains.

Performing Other Transformations

In addition to the essential mundane capabilities to move, copy, delete, resize, and scale objects, InDesign provides tools and several controls in the Control panel and Transform panel that let you perform more dramatic effects on objects, such as rotation, mirroring, *shearing* (which distorts a shape by applying a combination of rotation and slant), and flipping.

For all these tools, keep these tips in mind:

■ If you press Option or Alt as you drag, you work on a copy of the object.

■ To get finer control as you drag, click farther from the active object's reference point.

■ If you drag immediately after clicking an object, the object appears in its original location and the object's bounding box moves as you drag. If you click and then pause until the cross hair changes to an arrowhead, the object is displayed as you drag.

■ A key consideration is what you use to select an object before applying a transformation. If you use the Selection or Pointer tool, the transformation will apply to the entire object. If you use the Direct Selection tool, the transformation will apply to the selected node or side (or segment). For example, to flip or rotate just a side of an object, select it with the Direct Selection tool. To rotate the entire object, use one of the other tools.

■ The Rotate and Shear tools rely on the object's control point — the black square in the matrix of nine reference points shown at the left of the Control and Transform panels — to determine where rotation and shearing are done from. You can also simply click anywhere in the document window with these tools to choose your own control point for the current operation. (This control point choice method also applies to the Scale tool.)

■ You can access all these functions by choosing Object ➪ Transform and then choosing the desired option from the submenu. These functions are also available from the contextual menu you get when Control+clicking or right-clicking an object. You can also double-click the tools themselves to get the same dialog boxes that these menus provide.

How you use these transformations is up to you and is limited only by your imagination. As always, discretion is advised. Just because InDesign has some pretty cool features doesn't mean that you should use them in every publication you create.

Rotating objects

If you need to rotate an object, you can do it via the mouse or via your choice of the Control panel or Transform panel.

Using the Rotate tool

The Rotate tool is best used when you want to experiment with different angles quickly, or if you want to preview the rotation to see what looks right. Here's how:

1. **Select the Rotate tool.** If the Type tool isn't selected, you can also press R to select the Rotate tool.

2. **If it's not already selected, click the object you want to rotate.** When using the Selection or Position tool, you can click and drag the bounding box's control point (which matches the control point set in the Control or Transform panel) to a different location. The object rotates around the control point. When using the Direct Selection tool, select the side (or segment) or node you want to rotate.

TIP   You can reposition the control point by simply dragging it on-screen to the desired location — you're not limited to using one of the previous control points in the Control panel or Transform panel. Figure 10.3 shows a graphics frame being rotated around a repositioned control point (coming in from the upper-left corner).

3. **Move the pointer away from the control point and then click and drag with a circular motion, clockwise or counterclockwise.** Press and hold Shift as you drag to constrain rotation increments to the nearest 45-degree angle. If the transformation-values indicator is turned on, as explained in Chapter 6, InDesign shows you the current rotation value near the mouse as you drag.

4. **Release the mouse button when the object is at the angle you want.**

FIGURE 10.3

Left: When you rotate an object with the Rotate tool, a moving bounding box appears along with the original object as you. You can move the control point, as done here. Right: the rotated object, with the moved control point highlighted.

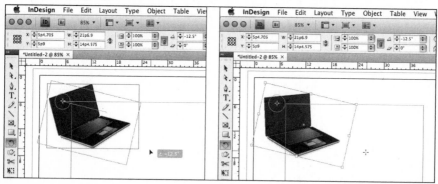

Using the panels

The Control panel and Transform panel give you more exact control and the ability to rotate an object's contents. The two panels have the Rotation Angle fields, in which you can enter precise rotation amounts. If the object is selected via the Selection or Position tool — or if an edge is selected with the Direct Selection tool — the value entered here rotates the entire object around the current control point. If you select the object's contents with the Direct Selection tool, the content rotates within the frame. Either way, note how the preview *P* icon in the Control panel shows the current rotation. (Figure 10.1 shows these controls.)

The Transform panel also lets you apply three predefined rotations to select an object through its flyout menu: Rotate 180°, Rotate 90° CW, and Rotate 90° CCW.

 **Negative numbers rotate counterclockwise, positive numbers clockwise.**

Using the Shear tool

When you shear an object with the Shear tool, you actually perform two transformations at one time: rotation and slant. Because the contents within text frames and graphics frames are distorted along with the frames when you shear an object, you'll probably use this tool only for special effects.

 **If you want to just slant an object, use the Shear X Angle field in the Control panel or Transform panel, or choose Object ↻ Transform ↻ Shear.**

To shear an object with the Shear tool:

1. **Select the Shear tool.** If the Type tool isn't selected, you can also press O (the letter) to select the Shear tool.

2. **If it's not already selected, click the object you want to shear.** If you want, you can drag the control point from its default location in the upper-left corner of the bounding box to a different location. When you shear an object, the control point doesn't move.

3. **Move the pointer away from the control point and then click and drag.** Hold the Shift key and drag to constrain rotation increments to multiples of 45 degrees. Figure 10.4 shows a frame being sheared.

FIGURE 10.4

Left: In this example, a frame is being sheared using the Shear tool. Right: The sheared object.

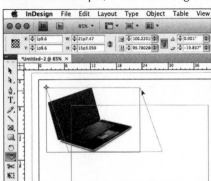 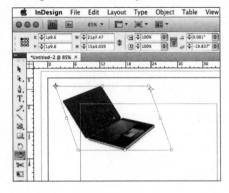

Controlling InDesign's Value Display

When you measure an object, do you include its stroke in that size? When you rotate an object's content, do you measure it relative to its frame or to the page? There are legitimate differences in how to calculate measurements, so InDesign provides controls that let you choose the methods you prefer. These options are available in the flyout menus of the Control and Transform panels.

Note that all these flyout menu options toggle between being selected (a check mark appears to an option's left) and deselected (nothing appears to an option's left) when you choose them.

Here are the available options:

- **Redefine Scaling as 100%:** Select this option to make the current scale appear as 100 percent in all panels. For example, if you scale an object to 75 percent and choose this option, all panels display its scale as 100 percent but leave the object at its current scale. Note this menu option is available only in the Transform panel.

- **Dimensions Include Stroke Weight:** If you select this menu option, the width of any stroke is added to the frame dimensions, and the dimensions shown in the Control panel and Transform panel reflect the strokes' widths (see Chapter 11). This option helps you with precise placement because frames extend beyond the frame, so adding a 6-point frame to a rectangle in effect increases its width and height by 12 points (6 points on each side).

- **Transformations Are Totals:** If you select this menu option, InDesign adds up all rotation angles, scale values, and so on that they are applied to an object as well as to any objects that contain the object. For example, if you rotate a frame 30 degrees but rotate its contents –30 degrees, InDesign shows the content's rotation as 0 degrees (30–30=0), its absolute rotation relative to the page. But if Transformation Are Totals is not selected, InDesign reports the content's rotation as –30 degrees — in other words, its relative rotation to the frame it is in. InDesign does the same with scales. For example, if you scale an object by 50 percent whose nested object was previously scaled by 50 percent, the nested object's scale still displays at its relative scale of 50 percent if Transformations Are Totals is not selected, but at its absolute scale of 25 percent if Transformations Are Totals is selected (0.5×0.5=0.25).

- **Show Content Offset:** If selected, this menu option shows the graphics content's position of the origin relative to the frame containing it in the X and Y fields in the Control panel and Transform panel. If you move a graphic within the frame, the offset will be positive as you move it to the right and/or down, and negative as you move it to the left and/or up. If this option is disabled, the Control panel and Transform panel instead show the graphics content's absolute position on the page relative to the current control point.

- **Adjust Stroke Weight While Scaling:** If selected, this menu option makes InDesign scale the frame's stroke as the frame is resized. For example, a frame with a 1-point stroke has its stroke scaled to 0.5 points if the frame is scaled to 50 percent. If this option is deselected, the stroke width is not affected when you scale the frame.

Flipping objects

InDesign also lets you flip objects horizontally, vertically, or in both directions. As you would expect, there are several ways to do this:

- Click the Flip Horizontal or Flip Vertical iconic buttons in the Control panel. (Notice how the *P* preview icon shows you the currently applied flip setting.)

- Choose Flip Horizontal or Flip Vertical from the Transform panel's flyout menu, choose Object ⇨ Transform ⇨ Flip Horizontal or Object ⇨ Transform ⇨ Flip Vertical, or choose Flip Horizontal or Flip Vertical from the contextual menu that appears when you Control+click or right-click an object.

- Drag an object's bounding box handle across and beyond the opposite corner or edge, as though you were resizing the object's frame. This also moves the object, as Figure 10.5 shows. (If you use the Direct Selection tool, the frame doesn't move, but the flipped contents move, usually outside the frame, so you'd need to reposition to contents in that case to make them visible again.)

FIGURE 10.5

Left: In this example, dragging a corner using the Selection tool causes a frame to be flipped in a user-determined direction and angle. Right: The flipped object.

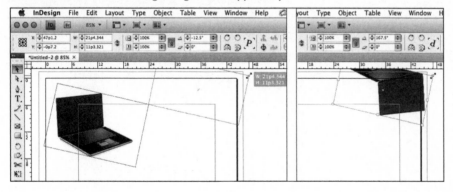

Using the Free Transform tool

InDesign has the Free Transform tool for you to use to move, resize, and rotate objects without having to switch among several tools. What it does matches the transformations already described. *How* it does it is a little different.

When you select the Free Transform tool and then move the mouse to an object, the mouse's location relative to that object determines what the Free Transform tool actually does, as Figure 10.6 shows:

- If the tool is inside the object's frame, it will move the object.
- If the tool is on an edge or on an edge or corner control point, it will resize the object.
- If the tool is slightly outside the edge, it will rotate the object.

As Figure 10.6 shows, the pointer changes according to the action the Free Transform tool can perform, which is based on its current position.

FIGURE 10.6

The Free Transform tool's actions (and pointer) depend on where the mouse is relative to an object: Left: Moving an object. Center: Resizing an object. Right: Rotating an object.

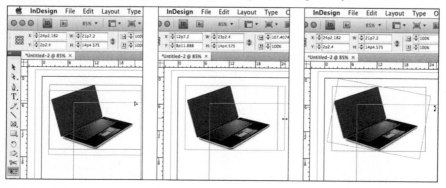

Repeating Transformations

Whatever transformations you use, you can apply them repeatedly. InDesign remembers the effects you apply to frames with the Control panel, Transform panel, and transform tools.

Choose Object ➪ Transform ➪ Transform Again or press Option+⌘+3 or Ctrl+Alt+3 to repeat the last transformation on the selected object (it can be a different object than you last applied a transformation to).

Or choose Object ➪ Transform ➪ Transform Sequence Again or press Option+⌘+4 or Ctrl+Alt+4 to apply all recent transformations to a select object. That sequence of transactions stays in memory until you perform a new transformation, which then starts a new sequence, so you can apply the same set of transformations to multiple objects.

CROSS-REF Not only can you apply transformations repeatedly, you can also save transformations, strokes, and other object attributes as object styles so that you can apply them at any time. Chapter 11 covers this feature in detail.

Undoing Transformations

Sometimes, you apply a series of transformations and realize you really hate the result and just want to start over. Sure, you can step back through each transformation by choosing Edit ⇨ Undo or pressing ⌘+Z or Ctrl+Z repeatedly, thereby undoing each transformation (and any other work) one step at a time until you get back to the point at which you want to start again. That process can be a long and tedious one, however.

Instead, for quick do-over, use the Clear Transformations option. This menu option undoes all transformations applied to an object in one fell swoop. Well, sort of. If you use this option when you're using the Direct Selection tool, only transformations applied through that tool (that is, those that affect the contents) are cleared. Likewise, if you use this option when you're using the Selection tool, only transformations applied through it (that is, those that affect the container) are cleared.

So, how do you get to the Clear Transformations menu option? Several methods are available, as follows:

- Choose Clear Transformations in the flyout menus of the Control and Transform panels.
- Choose Object ⇨ Transform ⇨ Clear Transformations.
- Control+click or right-click the *P* rotation preview in the Control panel and choose Clear Transformations from the contextual menu.

 The Object ⇨ Transform ⇨ Clear Transformations menu sequence is new to InDesign CS4.

Replacing Object Attributes

A really painstaking task in any layout is going through it to fix formatting to frames, lines, or other objects after the design standards have changed. InDesign has a very handy way to apply object formatting consistently to objects — the object styles feature described in Chapter 12 — but even if you use these styles, local formatting still applies to at least some objects. That's where the Object pane of the Find/Replace dialog box comes in, letting you replace attributes throughout your document, no matter what they are applied to. Figure 10.7 shows that pane.

Here's how it works:

1. **Open the Find/Change dialog box by choosing Edit ⇨ Find/Change and then going to the Object pane.**

2. **Select the desired object attributes by clicking the Specify Attributes to Find iconic button to the right of the Find Object Format list.** In the dialog box that displays (see Figure 10.8), select the attributes to search (choose one category at a time from the list at the left and then set the desired parameters in the pane that appears) and click OK when done. (This dialog box is nearly identical to the New Object Style dialog box covered in

Chapter 12.) The attributes appear in that Find Object Format attributes list in the Find/Change dialog box's Object pane. (Highlight an attribute in the list and click the Clear Specified Attributes iconic button — the trashcan icon — next to the Find Object Format attributes list if you want to remove an attribute from your search.)

3. **If you're replacing attributes, click the Specify Attributes to Change iconic button to the right of the Change Object Format attributes list.** These controls work like the Find Object Format controls.

4. **Limit or expand the search range by choosing an option from the Search pop-up menu: Selection, Document, and All Documents.** Also choose the type of frames to search in the Type pop-up menu: All Frames, Text Frames, Graphic Frames, and Unassigned Frames. Finally, to determine the scope of your search, select or deselect any of the six iconic buttons at the bottom of the pane (from left to right: Include Locked Layers, Include Locked Stories, Include Hidden Layers, Include Master Pages, and Include Footnotes). Note that the first two buttons apply only to finds; you cannot change the formatting of locked objects. (If an icon's background darkens, it is selected.)

5. **Click Find, Change, Change All, or Change/Find as desired to perform your search and/or replace operation.**

6. **Click Done when done.**

FIGURE 10.7

The Object pane of the Find/Change dialog box, with a Fill attribute selected in the Find Object Format attributes list

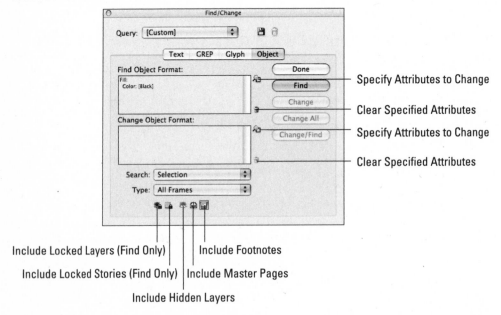

FIGURE 10.8

The Find Object Format Options dialog box, here showing the Fill pane. (The Change Object Format Options dialog box is identical.)

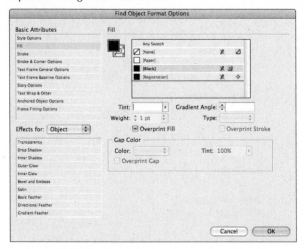

Find Object Format Options

Basic Attributes

Style Options
Fill
Stroke
Stroke & Corner Options
Text Frame General Options
Text Frame Baseline Options
Story Options
Text Wrap & Other
Anchored Object Options
Frame Fitting Options

Effects for: Object

Transparency
Drop Shadow
Inner Shadow
Outer Glow
Inner Glow
Bevel and Emboss
Satin
Basic Feather
Directional Feather
Gradient Feather

Fill

Any Swatch
[None]
[Paper]
[Black]
[Registration]

Tint: | Gradient Angle: |
Weight: 1 pt | Type: |
Overprint Fill | Overprint Stroke

Gap Color
Color: | - Tint: 100% |
Overprint Gap

Cancel | OK

Summary

InDesign's resizing controls let you change the size of a frame without affecting its contents, whereas scaling affects its contents as well as its size.

You can change an object's shape using the Rotate, Scale, or Shear tools or the corresponding fields in the Control panel or Transform panel. You can also resize objects' frames.

InDesign provides control over the display of transformed objects' values, such as the relative versus absolute scaling or rotation and whether an object's stroke is considered in calculating its dimensions.

A handy feature in InDesign lets you apply a sequence of transformations repeatedly to one or more objects. Another handy feature is the ability to search and replace object attributes.

Chapter 11

Applying Effects to Objects

InDesign has always been the leader when it comes to providing special effects, such as drop shadows and transparency, to layout elements, and accurately reproducing them in print. InDesign, in fact, has greatly blurred the role of a desktop publishing program, bringing in high-end graphics capabilities that had long been the province of image-manipulation programs such as Photoshop and illustration software such as Illustrator. The result is you have the ability to create more visually rich documents than you can with any other program.

InDesign's effects fall into two broad categories: strokes and lighting. The two types of effects are related in that they both interact with the edges of objects.

Strokes are the edges of all objects — frames, lines, and text — and InDesign lets you adjust their thickness, style, and color.

Lighting effects create a simulated three-dimensional appearance for objects, providing visual depth through drop shadows and embossing, for example. A related effect is transparency, which lets you control whether objects let elements below them show through, as well as create interesting fade effects.

CROSS-REF Chapter 7 covers how to create and apply colors, gradients, and tints as fills within objects and to text. You apply these same colors, gradients, and tints the same way to strokes as you do to fills.

NOTE Choose View ⇨ Show Frame Edges or press Control+⌘+H or Ctrl+H to see frame edges if they aren't already visible.

Working with Strokes

When you create a new frame or shape, there's not much to it. It has no content, no color (it's transparent or *none-colored* in InDesign's vocabulary), and no border. Text has color but no border. But both have strokes; they just happen to have a thickness of 0 points, so they are invisible at first. Lines (and paths) have an automatic stroke width of 1 point.

Adding strokes

In the old days of traditional paste-up, adding a simple, black border around a sidebar or a thin keyline around a graphic was a tedious and time-consuming process of laying out adhesive tape and then hoping that your meticulously placed rules remained straight and your perfectly square corners remained tight long enough to make it to the printer. If you were unlucky, your rules wound up on the floor or stuck to somebody's elbows. Nowadays, computers make adding borders to shapes an easy task. InDesign lets you quickly apply strokes to the shapes and text you create and modify the thickness, color, and style of strokes.

To add a stroke:

1. **Select any of the selection tools and click the frame, shape, line, or path to which you want to add a stroke.** For text, highlight the desired text with the Type tool.

2. **Click the Stroke iconic button in the Tools panel (see Figure 11.1) or in the Swatches panel.**

3. **You now can click a color, tint, or gradient from the Swatches panel, or click one of the three iconic buttons from the pop-out menu at the bottom of the Tools panel.** These buttons let you apply the last-selected color, last-selected gradient, or [None]. (Applying [None] removes the stroke's color, tint, and/or gradient.)

Note that if you don't see the stroke applied to the object, you may need to specify a stroke width, as I describe a little later in this section.

The controls in the Color panel (choose Window ➪ Color or press F6) let you change the tint of the color applied to a stroke, but I recommend you use the tint control on the Swatches panel (choose Window ➪ Swatches or press F5) instead so that you don't accidentally use unnamed colors (see Chapter 7 for more information on this issue). The Gradient panel (choose Windows ➪ Gradient) gives you the option to apply either a linear or radial gradient to strokes. For linear gradients, you can specify the angle using the Angle field.

CROSS-REF For information about adding colors, tints, and gradients to the Swatches panel, see Chapter 7.

TIP You can type percentages in panel fields for size- and scale-oriented items such as stroke widths. For example, to change a 1-point stroke to a hairline (0.25 points), you can type 0.25 pt or 25%.

FIGURE 11.1

The iconic buttons at the bottom of the Tools panel offer the quickest and easiest method of applying the last-used color or gradient to objects, or removing a color, tint, or gradient.

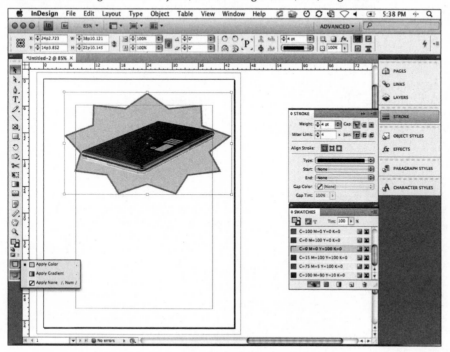

When you add a stroke, it's assigned by default a width of 1 point. You can change the width and several other characteristics of a stroke using the controls in the Stroke panel. Except when working with text, you can also change the stroke width and type in the Control panel.

When using the Stroke panel to modify a stroke:

1. **Select any of the selection tools and click the object whose stroke you want to modify.**

2. **If the Stroke panel is not displayed, show it by choosing Window ⇨ Stroke or pressing ⌘+F10 or Ctrl+F10.**

3. **To change the width of stroke, enter a new value in the Weight field.** You can also change the Weight value by choosing a new value from the field's pop-up menu or by clicking the up and down arrows. (Each click increases or decreases the stroke by 1 point.)

4. **Set the Miter Limit.** The default of 4 is fine for almost all frames.

NOTE The value in the Stroke panel's Miter Limit field determines when a corner point switches from *mitered* (squared off) to beveled. You'll rarely use this feature; it's useful when you have thick lines joining at sharp angles. In such cases, the lines may extend farther than needed, and the miter value (1 to 500, with 1 being the most conservative setting and 500 the most forgiving) tells InDesign when to change the squared-off corner to a beveled one, which prevents the problem.

NEW FEATURE InDesign CS4 lets you adjust stroke cap, end join, miter limit (if miter join is enabled), and stroke alignment (center or outside) for text; previous versions of InDesign could not apply these stroke settings to text.

5. **Click any of the three Cap iconic buttons to specify how dashes will look if you create a dashed stroke (covered in Step 9).** Figure 11.2 shows how each of the cap styles affect a line.

FIGURE 11.2

The line in this illustration was selected with the Direct Selection tool. Each of the three available endcap styles — butt (left), round (center), and projecting (right) — is shown.

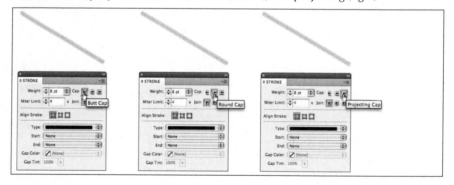

6. **Click any of the three Join iconic buttons to specify how corners are handled.** Figure 11.3 shows how each of the join styles affects a corner.

7. **Choose an Align Stroke option.** The default is the first iconic button, Align Stroke to Center, which has the stroke straddle the frame. You can also choose Align Stroke to Inside, which places the entire thickness inside the frame boundary, or Align Stroke to Outside, which places the entire thickness outside the frame boundary. Figure 11.4 shows the options.

FIGURE 11.3

The Stroke panel lets you apply mitered (left), rounded (center), and beveled (right) corners to shapes.

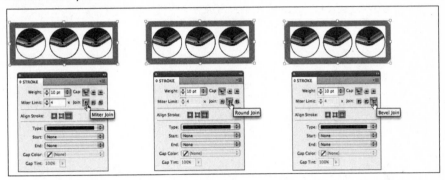

FIGURE 11.4

The Stroke panel lets you apply outside (left), centered (center), and inside (right) alignment to strokes.

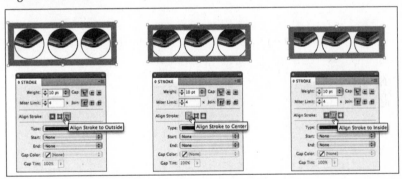

8. **You can also choose endpoints for your strokes (this affects lines only, not rectangles, ellipses, and other closed-loop shapes) using the Start and End pop-up menus.** Figure 11.5 shows the options.

9. **To create a dashed line instead of a solid line, choose an option from the Type pop-up menu.** (These are also available from the Control panel.) You see 18 types of predefined dashes and stripes, as shown in Figure 11.5. The Gap Color and Gap Tint fields at the bottom of the Stroke panel become active as well and let you choose a specific color and tint for the gaps in dashes and stripes.

FIGURE 11.5

Left: The Start options in the Stroke panel. (The End options are identical.) Right: The predefined dash and stripe options in the Stroke panel's Type pop-up menu

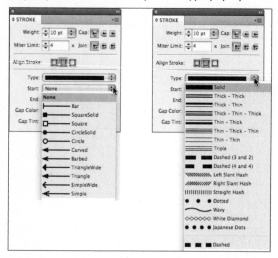

> **TIP**   To see the full Stroke panel, click the dual-arrow icon to the left of the Stroke panel's label. By default, the panel shows only the Weight, Cap, Miter Limit, and Join options.

> **TIP**   If you really want to turn heads, you can create reversed text within the frame by adding a fill color and lightening the text. But remember: Reversed text is harder to read, so keep the text size on the large side, and use this effect sparingly. You may want to make the reversed-out text boldface to aid in its readability.

Creating stroke styles

InDesign lets you create custom strokes, known as *stroke styles*, in any of three types: dashed, dotted, and striped lines. To create custom dashes or stripes, choose the Stroke Styles option in the Stroke panel's flyout menu. Figure 11.6 shows the Stroke Styles dialog box, from which you can create new strokes, edit or delete existing ones, and import (load) strokes from a stroke styles file that you create by saving a document's strokes as a separate file for import into other documents by clicking the Save button; stroke style files have the filename extension `.inst`.

Note that you cannot edit or delete the seven default stripe patterns shown in the figure, nor can you edit or delete the default dash patterns; they're not even available in the dialog box. When you edit or create a stroke pattern, you get the New Stroke Style dialog box, also shown in Figure 11.6. In the Name field, you type a name for your stroke. In the Type pop-up menu, you can choose to create (or convert a stripe you are editing to) a dashed, dotted, or striped stroke.

FIGURE 11.6

Upper left: The Stroke Styles dialog box. When you create a stroke, you get one of three New Stroke Style dialog boxes: the dashes version (upper right), the dots version (lower left) or the stripes version (lower right), based on the selection in the New Stroke Style dialog box's Type pop-up menu.

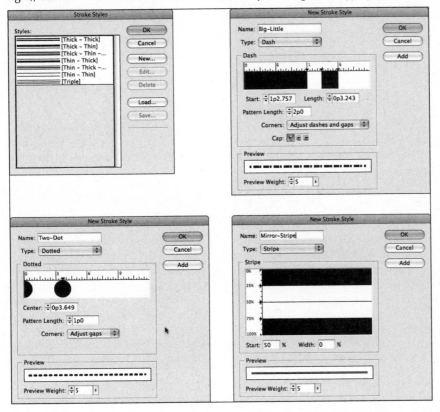

For dashes, you can resize the dash component by clicking and dragging the down-pointing triangle at the end of the dash in the ruler section. You can add dash segments by simply clicking on the ruler and dragging a segment to the desired width. Or you can use the Start and Length fields to manually specify them. The Pattern Length field is where you indicate the length of the segment you're defining; this is then repeated to fill the frame or line the stroke is applied to. In the Corners pop-up menu, you tell InDesign whether to adjust how the dashes and gaps are handled at corners; the default is Adjust Dashes and Gaps, a setting you should keep — it makes certain that your corners have dash segments that extend along both sides of the corner, which look neater. (Your other options are Adjust Dashes, Adjust Gaps, and None.) You can also choose a cap style and the stroke weight. The preview section of the pane lets you see your dash as you create or edit it.

Adding Fills

The option to add a stroke to any shape becomes even more powerful when combined with the option to fill any shape with a color or tint. For example, adding a stroke around a text frame is an effective way to draw attention to a sidebar.

Adding a fill to a shape is much like adding a stroke, and the options available for specifying color and tint are identical. The only difference is that you click the Fill iconic button in the Tools panel or Swatches panel rather than the Stroke iconic button.

For dots, you get a dialog box similar to dashes, as Figure 11.6 shows. The Start and Length fields disappear and are replaced with the Center field that determines where any added dots are placed on the ruler. (The initial dot, shown as a half-circle, starts at 0 and cannot be moved or deleted.) The Caps field is also gone.

 To delete a dash or dot segment, just click and drag it off the ruler to the left.

For stripes, you get the dialog box shown in Figure 11.6. The principle is the same as for dashes: You create segments (in this case vertical, not horizontal) for the stripes by dragging on the ruler. However, the stripes version of the dialog box expresses its values in percentages because the actual thickness of each stripe is determined by the stroke weight — the thicker the stroke, the thicker each stripe is in the overall stroke.

TIP **In all three versions of the New Stroke Style dialog box, you click Add to add the stroke to your document and then you can create a new one. When you're done creating strokes, click OK. (When editing a stroke, the Add button is not available.)**

TIP **Note the use of the Preview Weight pop-up menu and field in Figure 11.6. This lets you increase or decrease the preview size so you can better see thin or small elements in your stroke.**

Adding Corner Options

Anytime you're working on an object that has any sharp corners, you have the option to add a little pizzazz to the corners with InDesign's Corner Options feature (choose Object ➪ Corner Options). Five built-in corner options, shown in Figure 11.7, are available. Note that if the shape contains only smooth points, any corner option you apply won't be noticeable.

FIGURE 11.7

The Corner Options dialog box lets you apply any of these six options to frame corners. From left to right: None, Fancy, Bevel, Inset, Inverse Rounded, and Rounded.

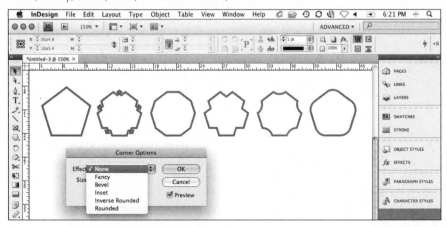

A word of caution about adding fancy corners: These effects are handy for such things as certificates and coupons, but don't get carried away and use them for everyday tasks such as frames for graphics and text unless you have a good reason. Few things kill a design like too much graphic embellishment.

NEW FEATURE The Corner Options dialog box's Size field now has nudge buttons to help you easily step through various sizes.

To add a corner option:

1. **Use any of the selection tools to select the object to which you want to add a corner option.** Then choose Object ➪ Corner Options to display the Corner Options dialog box.

2. **Choose an option from the Effect pop-up menu.**

3. **Type a distance in the Size field.** The Size value determines the length that the option extends from the corner. You can also use the new nudge buttons to step through sizes.

4. **Click OK to close the dialog box and apply your changes.**

TIP Select the Preview check box to view changes as you make them.

TIP If you can't see a corner effect after applying one, make sure that a color is applied to the stroke or try making the object's stroke thicker. Increasing the Size value in the Corner Options dialog box can also make a corner option more visible.

Using the Attributes Panel

One of InDesign's easily overlooked panels is the Attributes panel. It has two sets of controls: one set for controlling overprinting and one set (with just one control) for controlling whether an object prints. (The Nonprinting option is covered in Chapter 9.)

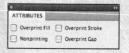

The three overprinting check boxes — Overprint Fill, Overprint Stroke, and Overprint Gap — control how any fills, strokes, and gaps in an object or its stroke are printed. By default, these are all dese-lected, and InDesign knocks out any colors beneath (such as for an object the current object overlaps or for an imported graphic in the frame) so you get the pure color specified for your fill, stroke, and/or gap. If these options are selected, InDesign will print the specific color on top of whatever colors might be underneath, essentially blending the colors. (Chapter 30 explains overprinting and knock-outs in detail.)

You typically enable overprinting as a special effect, where that blending is intentional, such as for a ghosting effect.

Applying Lighting Effects

InDesign offers sophisticated built-in drop shadow, feathering, and other options that let you cre-ate dimensional effects based on simulated lighting. It also lets you apply transparency to objects, so you can make them fade away or overlap so that the underlying object is somewhat visible. Figure 11.8 shows examples of the available lighting effects.

Using the Effects panel and related controls

You access InDesign's lighting effects from the Effects panel (choose Window ⟷ Effects or press Shift+⌘+F10 or Ctrl+Shift+F10). The panel itself offers controls for InDesign's transparency func-tions, but you can access the other lighting effects from it as well, either by choosing the desired option from the flyout menu's Effects menu option or by clicking the Add an Object Effect pop-up menu (the *fx* icon) at the bottom of the panel.

NOTE   The Add an Effect iconic pop-up menu is also available in the Control panel. And you can select the same options from the submenu when choosing Object ⟷ Effects. All these open the Effects dialog box.

FIGURE 11.8

Various effects applied to a set of objects, as well as the Effects panel and its flyout menu (bottom right). Top row: The original object, drop shadow, and inner shadow. Second row: Basic feather, directional feather, and gradient feather. Third row: Outer glow and inner glow. Bottom row: Bevel and emboss, and satin.

A cool capability in the Effects panel is the ability to apply effects separately to different parts of an object. In the panel, you see a list with four items: Object, Stroke, Fill, and Text. (If not, click the triangle to the left of Object to reveal the others.) Select the desired component in that list before applying the transparency settings (otherwise they apply to the entire object). You can also use the Apply Effect To iconic pop-up menu in the Control panel, or use the Settings For pop-up menu in each of the Effects dialog box's panes. (Note that the Apply Effect To icon will change based on what you choose from its pop-up menu. Also, the Tool Tip for the icon will reflect that choice, such as saying Apply Effects to Object if you selected Object in the pop-up menu, or Apply Effects to Text if you selected Text.)

NOTE Whatever you select in the Effects panel's list or via the Apply Effect To iconic pop-up menu becomes the default setting for the Settings For pop-up menu when you got to a pane in the Effects dialog box. You can always change that setting in the Settings For pop-up menu. Likewise, if you use the Drop Shadow iconic button in the Control panel, the drop shadow will be applied to whatever was last selected in the Effects panel's List or via the Apply Effects To iconic pop-up menu.

If the selected object has any lighting effects applied to it, in the Effects panel's list you see *fx* to the left of whichever object components (Object, Stroke, Fill, and Text) have these effects. If you hover the mouse over the *fx* symbol, InDesign lists what effects are applied.

Here's another cool feature: Click and drag the desired *fx* symbol to an object you want to apply the same effects to, releasing the mouse when it is over the desired object. (You of course can also use object styles, as described in Chapter 12, to apply multiple settings including lighting effects to objects, but this Effect panel drag-and-drop formatting provides a quick way for applying consistent formatting that you don't want to include in an object style.)

> **NOTE**   This ability to drag and drop lighting effects is not available if the only effect applied is transparency (including any blending mode settings).

The Effects panel's flyout menu also has two controls to undo your lighting effects: Clear Effects undoes lighting effects such as drop shadows for the selected object, whereas Clear All Transparency also removes the opacity settings for objects. These menu options have equivalent iconic buttons called Remove Effects and Clear All Effects, respectively, as Figure 11.9 shows.

> **NOTE**   You can apply multiple lighting effects, separately to each component of an object: Object, Fill, Stroke, and/or Text, to choose where each effect is applied. You can also select the part of the object you want to apply an effect to before you open these panes by using Apply or selecting from the four options in the Effects panel's list. (If the triangle under the Blending Modes menu is pointing to the right, click it to display these four options.)

FIGURE 11.9

The Effects panel and its Blending Modes menu, the effects-related iconic buttons in the Control panel, and an example of a transparency applied to both text and a photo

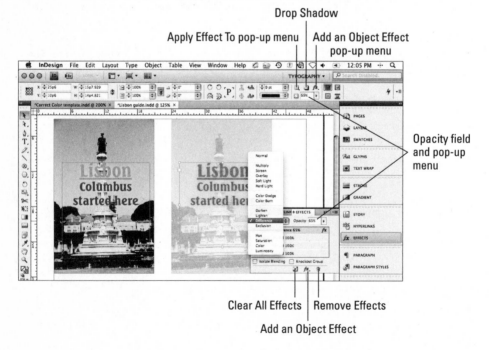

Applying transparency

One of InDesign's most sophisticated tools is its set of transparency options that lets you make items partially transparent. You apply transparency with the Effects panel (choose Window ⇨ Effects or press Shift+⌘+F10 or Ctrl+Shift+F10). Figure 11.9 shows example transparency settings for an image and text (the original objects are at left).

In the Opacity field of the Effects panel, the Control panel, or Effects dialog box's Transparency pane, enter a value or choose one from the unlabeled Opacity pop-up menu. A value of 0 is completely invisible; a value of 100 is completely solid.

NEW FEATURE The Effects dialog box's Opacity field now has nudge buttons to help you easily step through various percentages.

NOTE If you remove an object from a group that had transparency applied (via Cut and Paste or Copy and Paste), that pasted object does not have the group's transparency settings applied to it.

There are 16 transparency types, called *blending modes,* available in the unlabeled Blending Mode pop-up menu at the upper left of the Effects panel. The differences among them can be subtle or extreme, depending on a variety of issues. (Photoshop and Illustrator users will recognize these options from those programs.) You should experiment with them to see what effect works best in each case. The 16 modes are:

- **Normal:** Colors the selection with the blend color, without interaction with the base color. This is the default mode.

- **Multiply:** Multiplies the base color by the blend color. The resulting color is always a darker color. Multiplying any color with black produces black. Multiplying any color with white leaves the color unchanged. The effect is similar to drawing on a page with multiple magic markers.

- **Screen:** Multiplies the inverse of the blend and base colors. The resulting color is always a lighter color. Screening with black leaves the color unchanged. Screening with white produces white. The effect is similar to projecting multiple slide images on top of each other.

- **Overlay:** Multiplies or screens the colors, depending on the base color. Patterns or colors overlay the existing artwork, preserving the highlights and shadows of the base color while mixing in the blend color to reflect the lightness or darkness of the original color.

- **Soft Light:** Darkens or lightens the colors, depending on the blend color. The effect is similar to shining a diffused spotlight on the artwork. If the blend color (light source) is lighter than 50 percent gray, the artwork is lightened, as if it were dodged. If the blend color is darker than 50 percent gray, the artwork is darkened, as if it were burned in. Painting with pure black or white produces a distinctly darker or lighter area but does not result in pure black or white.

- **Hard Light:** Multiplies or screens the colors, depending on the blend color. The effect is similar to shining a harsh spotlight on the artwork. If the blend color (light source) is lighter than 50 percent gray, the artwork is lightened, as if it were screened. This is useful for adding highlights to artwork. If the blend color is darker than 50 percent gray, the artwork is darkened, as if it were multiplied. This is useful for adding shadows to artwork. Painting with pure black or white results in pure black or white.

- **Color Dodge:** Brightens the base color to reflect the blend color. Blending with black produces no change.

- **Color Burn:** Darkens the base color to reflect the blend color. Blending with white produces no change.

- **Darken:** Selects the base or blend color — whichever is darker — as the resulting color. Areas lighter than the blend color are replaced, and areas darker than the blend color do not change.

- **Lighten:** Selects the base or blend color — whichever is lighter — as the resulting color. Areas darker than the blend color are replaced, and areas lighter than the blend color do not change.

- **Difference:** Subtracts either the blend color from the base color or the base color from the blend color, depending on which has the greater brightness value. Blending with white inverts the base color values; blending with black produces no change.

- **Exclusion:** Creates an effect similar to, but lower in contrast than, the Difference mode. Blending with white inverts the base color components. Blending with black produces no change.

- **Hue:** Creates a color with the luminance and saturation of the base color and the hue of the blend color.

- **Saturation:** Creates a color with the luminance and hue of the base color and the saturation of the blend color. Using this mode in an area with no saturation (a gray) produces no change.

- **Color:** Creates a color with the luminance of the base color and the hue and saturation of the blend color. This preserves the gray levels in the artwork and is useful for coloring monochrome artwork and for tinting color artwork.

- **Luminosity:** Creates a color with the hue and saturation of the base color and the luminance of the blend color. This mode produces the inverse of the Color mode.

NOTE The Difference, Exclusion, Hue, Saturation, Color, and Luminosity modes do not blend spot colors, just process colors.

NOTE InDesign's blending calculations differ based on whether the document is to be printed (usually in CMYK) or seen on-screen (as RGB). Be sure to choose the right blending space based on the intended output. To do so, choose Edit ⇨ Transparency Blend Space ⇨ Document CMYK or Edit ⇨ Transparency Blend Space ⇨ Document RGB, as appropriate.

You have two other transparency-related options in the Effects panel:

- **Isolate Blending:** This option restricts the blending modes to the objects in a group, instead of also applying them to objects beneath the group. This can prevent unintended changes to those underlying objects.

- **Knockout Group:** This option obscures any objects below the selected group. But those objects beneath the knocked-out group are still affected by any blend mode settings applied to the group, unless the Isolate Blending option is also selected.

CROSS-REF Chapter 30 explains printing issues when using transparency.

Applying drop shadows and inner shadows

A drop shadow casts its shadow away from the object, as if it were blocking the light. An inner shadow casts its shadow inside, as if the frame were a wall blocking light that falls inside the object.

The Drop Shadow pane of the Effects dialog box, shown in Figure 11.10, is accessed by choosing Object ➪ Effects ➪ Drop Shadow or pressing Option+⌘+M or Ctrl+Alt+M. (You can also open this pane by choosing Effects ➪ Drop Shadow from the Effects panel's flyout menu, as well as from the Add an Object Effect pop-up menu [the *fx* iconic menu] in the Effects panel or Control panel. Even simpler: Click the Drop Shadow iconic button in the Control panel.)

FIGURE 11.10

The Drop Shadow pane of the Effects dialog box

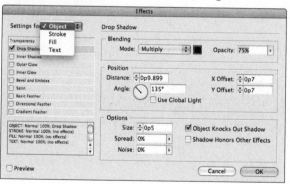

To apply a drop shadow to an object, you select it with a selection tool — you cannot apply the shadow to just highlighted characters. In the dialog box, you set the following options:

- Choose what component of the object to apply the drop shadow to by using the Settings For pop-up menu or by using the Apply Effect To iconic pop-up menu in the Control panel.

- Check the Drop Shadow option to turn on the drop shadow function for the selected component.

- Select a lighting type (technically, a blend mode) by choosing one of the 16 options in the Mode pop-up menu. These are the same blending modes used in transparencies and are covered earlier in this section.

- Choose a color source — Swatches, RGB, CMYK, and Lab — from the Color pop-up menu (the square swatch to the right of the Mode pop-up menu) and then select a color from the sliders or swatches below. You'll get sliders for RGB, CMYK, and Lab with which to mix a color if you selected RGB, CMYK, or Lab in the Color pop-up menu, and a set of previously defined color swatches if you selected Swatches in the Color pop-up menu.

- Specify the opacity by typing a value in the Opacity field; 0% is invisible, while 100% is completely solid.

- Specify the shadow's position relative to the object using the X Offset and Y Offset fields. A positive X Offset moves the shadow to the right, while a positive Y Offset moves the shadow down. Negative values go in the other direction.

- Specify the shadow's size by typing a value in the Distance field.

- Set the light source angle by entering a value in the Angle field or by clicking a location in the circle. You can also check Use Global Light to use those settings, as described in the sidebar "What Is Global Light?"

- To control the shadow's appearance, use the controls in the Options area of the pane. The Size field lets you specify the width of the shadow's fuzzy edge. (A value of 0 gives it a hard edge, a value as great as Distance fades the shadow over the whole shadow.) The Spread field and slider let you control where the shadow begins to get fuzzy. (A value of 0 starts immediately at the object edge, while a larger value pushes the fuzzy part away from the object.) The Noise field and slider let you add visual noise to the shadow, making it less smooth as the value increases. The other two controls — the Object Knocks Out Shadow and Shadow Honors Other Effects check boxes — are self-explanatory.

- To see the effects to your selected object as you experiment with various settings, select the Preview option.

 **Although traditionally associated with text, you can apply drop shadows to any objects, such as frames and shapes.**

The controls for the new inner shadow feature work almost exactly the same as the controls for drop shadows, with these exceptions:

- The Spread field in the Options area is called Choke. It does the same as Spread but applies inside the frame rather than outside of it.

- The Object Knocks Out Shadow and Shadow Honors Other Effects check boxes aren't available for inner shadows.

What Is Global Light?

The Global Light option — specified via the Effects panel's flyout menu and applied in various panes in the Effects dialog box — is a handy new feature to let you specify a standard lighting basis for all lighting effects. In the Global Light dialog box, you choose the origin of the light source that casts shadows in your lighting effects by entering a value in the Angle field (for the horizontal direction) and entering a value in the Altitude field (for the vertical direction). (New to InDesign CS4 are the nudge buttons to make it easier to step through various settings.) You can also just use the mouse to select a point in the wheel.

Once you've selected your light origin, just select the Use Global Light check box in the various panes of the Effects dialog box to ensure a consistent light source for those effects. You can, of course, not use Global Light at all, or use it sometimes and not others, based on the desired visual result.

Applying feathering

A similar option to drop shadows is feathering, which essentially softens the edges of objects. Figures 11.11 through 11.13 show all three types of feathering.

Applying basic feathering

To apply basic feathering, where the edges are blurred around all sides of an object, select the Basic Feather option. The controls are simple:

- In the Feather Width field, enter a value for the degree of feathering — smaller numbers have the least effect; larger numbers have the most effect. The featuring area starts at the outside edge of the object, so a larger number "eats into" the object, making it a wispier version of itself.

- The Choke field and pop-up menu let you set where the frame edge begins to get fuzzy (a value of 0 starts immediately at the object edge, while a larger value pushes the fuzzy part into the object).

- The Noise field and pop-up menu let you add visual noise to the shadow, making it less smooth as the value increases.

- The Corners pop-up menu gives you three options: Sharp, Rounded, and Diffused. The Sharp option retains the original corner shape as much as possible. The Rounded option rounds the corners of the object; it can distort the shape dramatically at larger Feather Width settings. The Diffused option creates a soft, almost smoky effect by making the object borders and corners more translucent.

FIGURE 11.11

The Basic Feather pane of the Effects dialog box

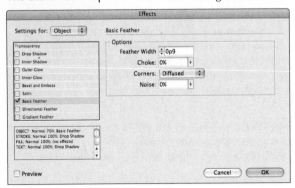

Applying directional feathering

The Directional Feather controls act like a drop shadow in that there is an external light source that determines how the feathering's blur appears along an object's edges. The effect is more like a shadowy smear. The controls are similar to that of Basic Feather, with these exceptions:

- Rather than have one Width setting, there are separate settings for the Top, Bottom, Left, and Right. If the chain icon is a solid chain, then all edges have the same width; click it to get the broken-chain icon, which lets you control each edge independently.

- The Shape pop-up menu lets you choose which edges are feathered: First Edge Only (the ones specified in the Width fields), Leading Edges (any in the path of the light source), and All Edges.

- Set the light source angle by entering a value in the Angle field or by clicking a location in the circle.

FIGURE 11.12

The Directional Feather pane of the Effects dialog box

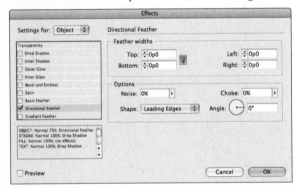

Applying gradient feathering

The Gradient Feather controls create the effect of having a strong light source near the object, washing out part of the object. Here's how the controls work:

- You set the gradient itself in the Gradient Stops area. You add stop points, choose opacity for each, and set the location for both gradient stops and transition points just as you do for any gradient (see Chapter 7). You can reverse the gradient's direction by clicking the iconic button to the right of the gradient ramp.

- In the Options area, you set the gradient type — Linear or Radial — and the lighting angle.

 You can also apply gradient feathering using the Gradient Feather tool, as described in Chapter 7.

FIGURE 11.13

The Gradient Feather pane of the Effects dialog box

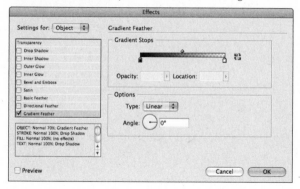

Applying outer and inner glows

Glows are what they sound like: A lighting effect that makes it seem as if there is light behind an object that causes it to glow (an outer glow) or a light source within the object's frame that causes a glow inside (an inner glow). Figure 11.14 and Figure 11.15 show the panes.

Applying an outer glow

Here's how the controls for outer glow work (note that the first three options are the same as for transparency effects):

- Choose the blending mode in the Mode pop-up menu, the glow color in the Color pop-up menu (the square swatch to the right of the Mode pop-up menu), and the transparency level in the Opacity field or pop-up menu.

- Choose the glows intensity by choosing Software or Precise in the Technique pop-up menu. The Precise option creates a more saturated, harsher glow.

- Choose how far away from the frame that the glow begins to dissipate by entering a value in the Spread field. A value of 0 starts the fade immediately.

- Choose the width of the glow in the Size field.

- Add visual noise to the shadow, making it less smooth as the value increases, by entering a value in the Noise field or choosing a value from the pop-up menu.

FIGURE 11.14

The Outer Glow pane of the Effects dialog box

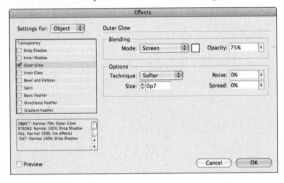

Applying an inner glow

The controls for inner glows are nearly identical to those for outer glows, with these two exceptions:

- The Spread field in the Options area is called Choke. It does the same as Spread but applies inside the frame rather than outside of it.

- The Source options — Center and Edge — let you choose the light source's location relative to the object.

FIGURE 11.15

The Inner Glow pane of the Effects dialog box

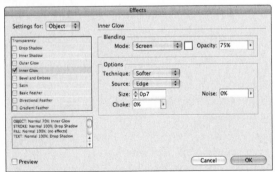

Applying beveling and embossing

Beveling means to make an object appear to be above the plane of other objects, thus casting a shadow at the edges. *Embossing* is a variation of beveling where only the edges are raised; the contents are lowered back to the normal plane. Figure 11.16 shows the Bevel and Emboss pane.

The controls for beveling and embossing combine controls from several other lighting effects:

- In the Structure area, choose the bevel or emboss style from the Style pop-up menu: Outer Bevel (the bevel extends outside the frame), Inner Bevel (the bevel extends inside the frame), Emboss, and Pillow Emboss (a shallower embossing).

- In the Technique pop-up menu, choose the type of shadow effects: Smooth, Chisel Hard, and Chisel Soft.

- Choose the apparent height of the effect by entering a value in the Depth field or using the Depth slider. Similarly, choose the shadow's thickness by entering a value in the Size field.

- Choose the direction of the effect by selecting either Up (raised) or Down (etched out) in the Direction pop-up menu.

- Adjust the shadow's intensity by entering a value in the Soften field.

- In the Shading area, choose the light source's direction by entering a value in the Angle field, clicking a point in the circle, or checking the Use Global Light option. Similarly, adjust the light source's height in the Altitude field.

- Adjust the blending mode applied to areas of the bevel or emboss that are "hit" by the light using the Highlight Mode pop-up menu and the blending mode applied to the shadowed areas using the Shadow Mode pop-up menu. In both cases, there is also a combination field and pop-up menu labeled Opacity where you can adjust the effect's transparency.

FIGURE 11.16

The Bevel and Emboss pane of the Effects dialog box

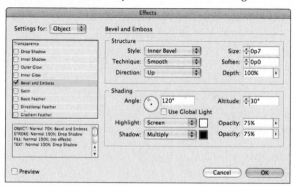

Applying satin effects

The satin effect is similar to a glow, except that it applies a shadow to the frame's edges, as if the object were made of satin cloth and bowed slightly out from its edges. Figure 11.17 shows the Satin pane.

To apply a satin effect:

- Choose the blending mode in the Mode pop-up menu, the glow color in the Color pop-up menu (the square swatch to the right of the Mode pop-up menu), and the transparency level in the Opacity field or pop-up menu.

- Choose the light source's direction by entering a value in the Angle field, clicking a point in the circle.

- Choose the width of the satin effect in the Size field.

- Specify the shadow's size by typing a value in the Distance field.

- To have the satin effect appear as if the object were sinking slightly from the edges (making it darker), check Invert.

FIGURE 11.17

The Satin pane of the Effects dialog box

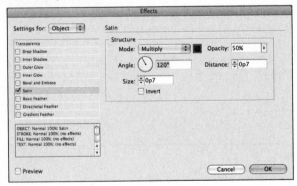

Summary

If you have a frame or shape selected, you can add a stroke around its border or add a color to its background, as well as apply transparency to an object or its contents. You can further enhance these attributes with the corner-options capabilities. You can apply strokes (and colors) to lines and text as well.

InDesign has a broad palette of lighting-effects capabilities, including inner shadow, glow, feather, bevel, emboss, and satin effects, as well as more traditional transparency and drop shadow effects. You can apply these effects to entire objects, to just their frames, just their fills, or just their text.

Chapter 12

Orchestrating Objects

Frames, shapes, lines, and paths are the building blocks with which you construct InDesign pages. Becoming familiar with creating and modifying individual objects, which is the focus of Chapters 8 through 11, is a key step in learning how to create publications with InDesign. The next step is to learn how to use several features that let you manipulate multiple objects simultaneously and quickly adjust the relationships among the various objects that make up a page. A good InDesign user can handle individual objects one at a time with ease; a virtuoso user can simultaneously juggle several objects with equal ease.

Think of it this way: As an InDesign user, you're much like an architect. You begin with a blueprint — perhaps a rough, felt-tip pen sketch or maybe just a graphic in your mind's eye — open a new document, and start construction. The settings you establish in the New Document dialog box (choose File ➪ New ➪ Document or press ⌘+N or Ctrl+N) — the page size, margin placement, column arrangement, and number of pages — serve as the foundation as you begin adding objects to your pages. You must then construct your building, or rather, your publication, using four basic components: text frames, graphics frames, shapes, and lines. You can tweak and twist each of those components in a nearly endless variety of ways while retaining basic properties. After all, a sheared (skewed) and mirrored text frame with a purple dashed stroke, a gradient background, and magenta text outlined in cyan is still just a text frame.

As a publication evolves, plans invariably change: An advertiser pulls out and a magazine article needs to be stretched an extra half-page by enlarging an InDesign-created illustration. A client loves his company's newsletter but wants the front-page graphic cropped differently. A new product is added to a catalog and half the pages reflow. If you build your documents soundly

IN THIS CHAPTER

Changing the stacking order of objects

Working with groups

Locking objects

Nesting objects

Inserting objects within a text thread

Anchoring objects to text

Setting text wrap

Working with object styles

Managing source links

from the ground up and use the features covered in this chapter, you should be prepared to handle even the most challenging page building — and rebuilding — tasks.

Stacking Objects

Each time you begin work on a new page, you start with a clean slate (unless the page is based on a master page, in which case the master objects act as the page's background; see Chapter 6 for more on master pages). Every time you add an object to a page — either by using any of InDesign's object-creation tools or with the Place command (choose File ➪ Place or press ⌘+D or Ctrl+D) — the new object occupies a unique place in the page's object hierarchy, or *stacking order*.

The first object you place on a page is automatically positioned at the bottom of the stacking order; the next object is positioned one level higher than the first object (that is, on top of and in front of the backmost object); the next object is stacked one level higher; and so on for every object you add to the page. It's not uncommon for a page to have several dozen or even several hundred objects.

TIP When building pages, always try to keep the number of objects to a minimum. For example, instead of putting a headline in one text frame and a subhead in a separate text frame directly below the one that contains the headline, use a single text frame. Lean documents save and print more quickly and are less problematic to modify than bloated documents.

Although each object occupies its own level, if the objects on a page don't overlap, then the stacking order is not an issue. But some of the most interesting graphic effects you can achieve with InDesign involve arranging several overlapping objects, so it's important to be aware of the three-dimensional nature of a page's stacking order.

Because objects are added in back-to-front order, it makes sense to build your pages from back to front. For example, if you want to use a lightly tinted version of a scanned image as the background for a page, you first place the image on the page and then add other objects on top of or in front of the graphics frame.

In an ideal world, the first object you place on a page would remain forever the backmost, the last object would be the frontmost, and every object in between — created in perfect order from back to front — would relate correctly with every other object. In this perfect world, you would never have to worry about moving objects backward or forward.

But the world is not perfect, and you may change your mind about what you want to achieve in your layout after you've already placed objects in it. To change an object's position in a page's stacking order, use the Arrange menu option (choose Object ➪ Arrange), which offers four submenus:

- Bring to Front (Shift+⌘+] or Ctrl+Shift+])
- Bring Forward (⌘+] or Ctrl+])
- Send to Back (Shift+⌘+[or Ctrl+Shift+[)
- Send Backward (⌘+[or Ctrl+[)

For example, you might want to see how a piece of text looks in front of an illustration. But if you create the text frame before you create or place the illustration, you have to move the text frame forward (or the illustration backward) in the stacking order.

CROSS-REF In addition to letting you change the stacking order of objects on a page, InDesign also lets you create document-wide layers. Each layer contains a separate collection of stacked objects. For more information about using layers, see Chapter 5.

To change the stacking order of objects:

1. **Use any of the object-creation tools to create four overlapping shapes, as shown in Figure 12.1.** The numbers in parentheses indicate the order in which you should create the shapes.

FIGURE 12.1
_____

Left: The first shape you create is the backmost, the second is one level above, and so on. In this example, the three smaller boxes partially overlap each other and they are all in front of the largest box. Right: Applying tints to the shapes lets you see the stacking order of the four rectangles. Every InDesign object occupies one level in the stacking order.

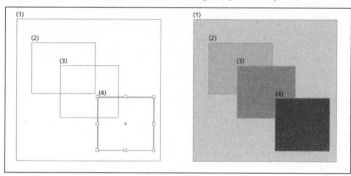

---

2. **If it's not already displayed, open the Swatches panel by choosing Window ⇨ Swatches or pressing F6.** You use this panel to change the shade of each object so you can easily tell them apart.

3. **Click the Selection tool, click the last object you created and then use the color tools in the Tools panel or the Swatches panel to fill the object with a color.**

CROSS-REF See Chapters 7 and 11 for more information about applying fills and strokes to objects.

4. **Use the Swatches panel to fill each of the remaining boxes with a successively lighter tint of the color, as shown in Figure 12.1.** In the example, the remaining shapes are tinted at 25 percent, 50 percent, and 75 percent, respectively.

5. **Click the frontmost shape (the last one you created) and then choose Object ⇨ Arrange ⇨ Send Backward or press ⌘+[or Ctrl+[.** Notice that the Bring to Front and Bring Forward menu options are not available. That's because you can't move the frontmost object any farther forward in the stacking order.

6. **Click the backmost shape (the first one you created) and then choose Object ⇨ Arrange ⇨ Bring Forward or press ⌘+] or Ctrl+].** When you bring the object forward, one of the objects becomes obscured.

7. **Choose Object ⇨ Arrange ⇨ Bring to Front or press Shift+⌘+] or Ctrl+Shift+].** The smaller shapes are now obscured by the largest one.

8. **Choose Object ⇨ Arrange ⇨ Send to Back or press Shift+⌘+[or Ctrl+Shift+[.** The hidden objects are once again visible.

To select an object that's hidden behind one or more other objects, press and hold ⌘ or Ctrl and then click anywhere within the area of the hidden object. The first click selects the topmost object; each successive click selects the next lowest object in the stacking order. When the bottom object is selected, the next click selects the top object. If you don't know where a hidden object is, you can simply click the object or objects in front of it and then send the objects to the back.

Another way to select objects that are in a stack or group is to use the Select Previous Object or Select Next Object iconic buttons in the Control panel. If you Shift+click either button, InDesign jumps past four objects and selects the fifth one. If you ⌘+click or Contrl+click either button, InDesign selects to the bottommost or topmost object, respectively.

 **See Chapter 9 for more details on selecting objects.**

Combining Objects into a Group

InDesign lets you combine several objects into a group. A group of objects behaves like a single object, which means that you can cut, copy, move, or modify all the objects in a group in a single operation. Groups have many uses. For example, you might create a group to:

■ Combine several objects that make up an illustration so that you can move, modify, copy, or scale all objects in a single operation.

■ Keep a graphics frame and its accompanying caption (text) frame together so that if you change your mind about their placement, you can reposition both objects at one time.

■ Combine several vertical lines that are used to separate the columns of a table so that you can quickly change the stroke, color, length, and position of all lines.

TIP **If you want to manipulate a group, select any object in the group with the Selection tool. The group's bounding box appears. Any transformation you perform is applied to all objects in the group. If you want to manipulate a specific object in a group, choose the Direct Selection tool.**

To create a group:

1. **Switch to a selection tool.**

2. **Select all the objects you want to include in your group.**

3. **Choose Object ⇨ Group or press ⌘+G or Ctrl+G.**

That's all there is to it. When you create a group from objects that do not occupy successive levels in the stacking order, the objects are shuffled as necessary so that the grouped objects are stacked on adjacent layers directly below the topmost object. If you create a group from objects on different layers, all objects are moved to the top layer and stacked in succession beneath the topmost object.

CROSS-REF See Chapter 5 for more about layers.

NOTE You cannot create a group if some of the selected objects are locked and some are not locked. All selected objects must be locked or unlocked before you can group them. (Locking and unlocking objects is covered later in this chapter.)

Using groups within groups

One nifty thing about groups is that you can include a group within a group. For example, all the objects in Figure 12.2 — five stars and two circles (a gray circle and a white circle form the moon) — have been grouped, making it easy to manipulate the whole illustration. But that's not all. The stars within the group are also a group. So are the two circles that make up the crescent moon. That is, first the stars were grouped together, then the two circles were grouped together, and finally then the group of stars was grouped with the circles that form the moon to create a larger group. Grouping the stars makes it easy to change all of them at one time, as shown in Figure 12.2. And grouping the two circles that make up the crescent moon makes it easy to move the moon.

FIGURE 12.2

The bounding box indicates that all the objects within it have been grouped (at left). What you can't tell from this illustration is that the five stars are a group within the larger group, which lets you move or modify all of them in a single operation, as shown at right.

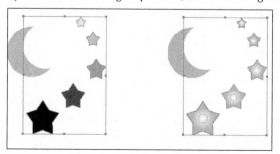

> **NOTE** A group can contain as many levels of subgroups, or *nested* groups, as you want, but it's best to keep things as simple as you can. The more levels of nested groups you have within a group, the more work it is to ungroup the objects.

Selecting objects within groups

The main reason you create groups in the first place is so that you can delete, copy, move, or modify all the objects at one time. But sometimes, you may want to modify an object within a group. No problem. You don't have to ungroup objects to modify an individual object. InDesign offers several options for selecting objects — and nested groups — within groups. You can:

- Select an individual object by clicking it with the Direct Selection tool or Position tool.

- Double-click an object in a group with the Selection tool to select just that object.

- Select the bounding box of an individual object by clicking it with the Direct Selection tool or Position tool and then switching to the Selection tool.

- If you have selected an object in a group of objects, choose Object ➪ Select ➪ Previous Object in Group to navigate to the previous object in the group, or choose Object ➪ Select ➪ Next Object in Group to navigate to the previous object in the group. Or use the Select Previous Object or Select Next Object iconic buttons in the Control panel, as shown in Figure 12.3.

- Select multiple objects within a group by Shift+clicking each object with the Direct Selection or Position tool.

- Select the bounding box of multiple objects within a group by Shift+clicking each object with the Direct Selection or Position tool and then switching to the Selection tool.

- Select a nested group by clicking any object within the nested group with the Direct Selection or Position tool and then pressing and holding Option or Alt and clicking the object again. Pressing and holding Option or Alt in this situation temporarily accesses the Group Selection tool, indicated by a small plus sign (+) below and to the right of the arrow pointer.

FIGURE 12.3

The selection buttons on the Control panel.

Select Previous Object

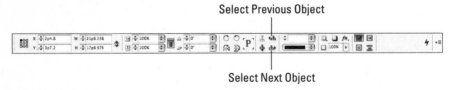

Select Next Object

Ungrouping

After creating a group, you may eventually decide that you want to return the objects to their original, ungrouped state. To do so, simply click any object in the group with the Selection tool to select the entire group and then choose Object ➪ Ungroup or press Shift+⌘+G or Ctrl+Shift+G. If you ungroup a group that contains a group, the contained group is not affected. To ungroup this subgroup, you must select it and then choose Ungroup again.

Locking Objects

If you're certain that you want a particular object to remain where it is, you can choose Object ➪ Lock Position or press ⌘+L or Ctrl+L, to prevent the object from being moved. Generally, you'll want to lock repeating elements such as headers, footers, folios, and page numbers so that they're not accidentally moved. (Such repeating elements are usually placed on a master page; you can lock objects on master pages, too.)

So what does locking do, exactly? A locked object can't be moved whether you click and drag it with the mouse or change the values in the X and Y fields in the Control panel or Transform panel. Not only can you not move a locked object, but you can't delete one, either. However, you can change other attributes of a locked object, including its stroke and fill.

To unlock an object, choose Object ➪ Unlock Position or press Option+⌘+L or Ctrl+Alt+L.

CROSS-REF You can also lock entire layers, as described in Chapter 5.

InDesign lets you not only combine several objects into a group but also place an object within the boundaries of a frame. Just as a group that's embedded within a larger group is said to be a *nested* group, an object that's been placed within another frame is said to be a *nested* object. When you place an object within a frame, the containing frame acts as the cropping shape for the object within.

One of the more common uses of nested frames is for cropping imported graphics. When you place a graphic onto a page, the graphic is automatically placed within a frame. (You can also place a graphic within an existing frame.) You can reveal and hide different areas of the graphic by resizing or reshaping the container frame. Figure 12.4 shows an imported graphic that's been placed within a circular frame.

Clicking the graphic with the Direct Selection tool selects the nested object rather than the container frame. To work on that nested object's frame, you can then switch to the Selection tool after the nested object is selected with the Direct Selection tool. To select the container frame's bounding box instead of the nested object, click the object with the Selection tool.

CROSS-REF For more information about importing and modifying graphics, see Part VI.

FIGURE 12.4

Left: In this example, the rectangle displayed with handles indicates the border of a graphic that's been placed into a triangular frame. Right: I created the squiggly line (left) with the Pen tool. I then copied and pasted it into (Edit ⇨ Paste Into) a circular frame (right). Selecting the line with the Direct Selection tool (not shown) would display the visible portion of the line within the oval cropping frame, as well as the parts of the line that are cropped.

As you can with groups, you can place a frame within a frame within a frame and so on, to create as many nested levels as you want. The same caveat applies: Keep things as simple as possible to achieve the desired effect. To nest a frame within a frame:

1. **Use any selection tool to select the frame you want to nest within another frame.**

2. **Choose Edit ⇨ Copy or press ⌘+C or Ctrl+C.**

3. Select the frame into which you want to place the copied object and then choose Edit ⇨ Paste Into or press Option+⌘+V or Ctrl+Alt+V. Figure 12.4 shows a before/after example of a squiggly line that's been pasted into a circular frame that serves as the masking shape for the line.

> **TIP**   Selecting nested objects can be tricky. In general, the same selection techniques that work with groups also work with nested frames. If you need to modify text within a nested or grouped text frame, simply click within the frame with the Type tool.

Creating Inline Frames

In most cases, you want the objects you place on your pages to remain precisely where you put them. But sometimes, you want to place objects relative to related text in such a way that the objects move when the text is edited. For example, if you're creating a product catalog that's essentially a continuous list of product descriptions and you want to include a graphic with each description, you can paste graphics within the text to create inline graphics frames.

An inline frame is treated like a single character. If you insert or delete text that precedes an inline frame, the frame moves forward or backward along with the rest of the text that follows the inserted or deleted text. Although inline frames usually contain graphics, they can just as easily contain text or nothing at all.

There are two ways to create an inline frame: using the Paste command and using the Place command.

CAUTION Inline frames may interfere with line spacing in paragraphs with automatic leading. If the inline frame is larger than the point size in use, the automatic leading value for that line is calculated from the inline frame. This leads to inconsistent line spacing in the paragraph. To work around this, you can either apply a fixed amount of leading to all characters in the paragraph, adjust the size of inline frames, place inline frames at the beginning of a paragraph, or place inline frames in their own paragraphs.

There are three ways to create inline frames. The first two are the simplest, but the third, using the Anchored Object command, gives you more control over the inline frame when you create it.

NOTE You can set text wraps on inline frames using the standard Text Wrap panel (Window ⇨ Text Wrap, or Option+⌘+W or Ctrl+Alt+W), as described later in this chapter. But note that such wraps affect only text that appears on the same line or below the inline frame, not text above the inline frame or text in other frames.

Creating an inline frame with the Paste command

If you want to create an inline frame from an object you've already created, all you have to do is copy or cut the object and then paste it into text as you would a piece of highlighted text. Here's how:

1. **Use the Selection or Position tool to select the object you want to paste within text.** You can use any type of object: a line, an empty shape, a text or graphics frame, even a group of objects.

2. **Choose Edit ⇨ Copy or press ⌘+C or Ctrl+C.** If you don't need the original item, you can use the Cut command (Edit ⇨ Cut, or ⌘+X or Ctrl+X) instead of the Copy command. An object that you cut or copy remains on the Clipboard until you cut or copy something else or you turn off your computer. If you intend to use the original object elsewhere, it's better to use the Copy command when creating an inline frame.

3. **Select the Type tool (or press T) and then click within the text where you want to place the copied object.** Make sure the cursor is flashing where you intend to place the inline frame.

4. Choose Edit ⇨ Paste or press ⌘+V or Ctrl+V. Figure 12.5 shows an example of an inline frame.

TIP Inline frames often work best when placed at the beginning of a paragraph. If you place an inline frame within text to which automatic leading has been applied, the resulting line spacing can be inconsistent. To fix this problem, you can resize the inline frame.

The icon identifying a tip (next to "Go Further") is placed in the text as an inline frame so that it moves up and down with the surrounding text.

To change the position of an inline frame, choose Object ➪ Anchored Object ➪ Options. The Anchored Object Options dialog box that appears is the same as the Insert Anchored Object dialog box covered later in this section and shown in Figure 12.6.

Creating an inline frame with the Place command

In addition to using the Paste command to create an inline frame from an existing object, you can use the Place command to create an inline graphics frame from an external graphics file. (You can't use this technique for inline text frames.) Here's how:

1. **Select the Type tool (or press T) and then click within a text frame to establish the insertion point.**

2. **Choose File ➪ Place or press ⌘+D or Ctrl+D.**

3. **Locate and select the graphics file (including InDesign files and snippets) you want to place within the text and then click Choose or Open.**

 **You can use the transform tools (Rotate, Scale, Shear, and Free Transform) and the Control panel or Transform panel to modify an inline frame as you modify any other frame.**

To delete an inline frame, you can select it and then choose Edit ➪ Clear or Edit ➪ Cut, or you can position the cursor next to it and then press Delete or Backspace.

FIGURE 12.6

The Insert Anchored Object dialog box for inline frames (left) and anchored objects (right)

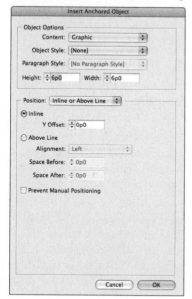
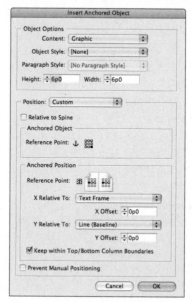

Creating an inline frame using the Anchored Object command

You can also choose Object ⇨ Anchored Object ⇨ Insert to insert an inline frame. This option opens a dialog box, shown in Figure 12.6, that lets you control the positioning of the inline frame as you insert it.

NOTE This method inserts a new frame in your text, in which you paste or place a graphic or text. To create an inline frame using an existing frame, use the cut-and-paste method described earlier in this section.

To create an inline frame with the Anchored Object command, follow these steps:

1. **Select the Type tool (or press T) and then click within a text frame to establish the insertion point.**

2. **Choose Object ⇨ Anchored Object ⇨ Insert.**

3. **Choose Inline or Line Above from the Position pop-up menu.** The Insert Anchored Object dialog box shown in Figure 12.6 appears.

4. **In the Object Options section, specify inline frame's settings.** You choose the type of frame (text, graphics, or unassigned) using the Content pop-up menu, apply an object style if desired using the Object Style pop-up menu, apply a paragraph style if desired using the Paragraph Style pop-up menu, and set the inline frame's dimensions using the Height and Width fields.

   Note that the Paragraph Style you choose, if any, applies to the inline frame, not to the paragraph in which the inline frame is embedded. Oddly, InDesign lets you apply a paragraph style to the inline frame even if it contains no text.

5. **In the lower part of the dialog box, set the desired position settings.** You have two basic choices for position:

   ▪ The Inline option, if selected, places the frame at the text-insertion point, setting it in the same line as that insertion point. You can adjust the inline frame's vertical position on that line by typing a value in the Y Offset field, which works like shifting the baseline of any text.

   ▪ The Above Line option, if selected, places the inline frame above the current line. Typically, you would use this when you want to place a frame above the first line of a paragraph. An example would be using graphics as the equivalent of headlines above specific paragraphs. You can adjust the alignment of the inline frame relative to the paragraph using the Alignment pop-up menu, as well as control how much space is above and below the inline frame using the Space Before and Space After fields.

   No matter which position you choose, selecting the Prevent Manual Positioning option ensures that the positions of individual frames can't be adjusted using InDesign's other text and frame controls (such as Baseline Shift). This forces users to use this dialog box to change the inline frame's position.

6. **Click OK to insert the inline frame.**

7. **Add any desired content to the inline frame as you would with any other frame.**

Anchored objects added by choosing Object ⇨ Anchored Object ⇨ Insert do not have text automatically wrapped around them. Use the Text Wrap panel (Window ⇨ Text Wrap, or Option+⌘+W or Ctrl+Alt+W) to open this panel and set text wrap. Figure 12.7 shows an inline frame before and after text wrap has been applied.

But anchored objects created by pasting a graphic into text do automatically have text wrap around them.

CAUTION   InDesign may not wrap text around inline graphics properly, no matter how you adjust the Text Wrap options. That typically occurs when you have cropped or resized the anchored graphic within its frame. InDesign still sees the old scale and size and tries to wrap around those, not the ones actually in effect. You have to crop and resize the graphic in a program such as Photoshop and then place it again in the anchored frame for InDesign to wrap text correctly around it.

FIGURE 12.7

Choosing Object ⇨ Anchored Object ⇨ Insert does not make InDesign wrap text around the resulting frame (top). Use the Text Wrap panel to set text wrap for such objects (bottom).

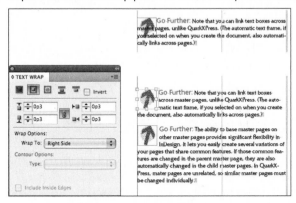

Adjusting inline frames

After you create an inline frame, you can adjust its position vertically or horizontally. Again, there are several methods.

A quick-and-easy trick to move an inline frame vertically is as follows:

1. **Use the Type tool to highlight the inline frame as you would highlight an individual text character.** In the Character panel or Control panel, type a positive value in the Baseline Shift field to move the inline frame up; type a negative value to move the frame down.

2. **Use a selection tool to select the inline frame and then drag the frame up or down.**

A quick way to move an inline frame horizontally is as follows:

1. **With the Type tool selected, click between the inline frame and the character that precedes it.**

2. **Use the kerning controls in the Character panel or Control panel to enlarge or reduce the space between the inline frame and the preceding character.**

Note that these preceding methods work only if the Prevent Manual Positioning option remains unselected in the Insert Anchored Object dialog box or Anchored Object Options dialog box. (This option is not selected by default.) You can also adjust the vertical (Y) position of an inline frame by choosing Object ⇨ Anchored Object ⇨ Options. The resulting Anchored Object Options dialog box is the same as the Insert Anchored Object dialog box covered previously in this section and shown in Figure 12.6, except the Anchored Object Options dialog box does not have the Object Options section.

Of course, you can also adjust its other attributes, such as strokes, fills, dimensions, rotation, and skew, as needed using the Tools panel, Control panel, and other panels.

Deleting inline frames

It's easy to delete an inline frame: Select the frame with the Selection or Direct Selection tool and then choose Edit ⇨ Clear or press Delete or Backspace. If you want to remove the object but keep it in the Clipboard for pasting elsewhere, choose Edit ⇨ Cut or press ⌘+X or Ctrl+X.

Setting Up "Follow Me" Anchored Frames

InDesign offers another way to associate frames to text, and this one can make it easier to have sidebars, pull-quotes, info boxes, and other elements that relate to a specific piece of text remain near that text even as it reflows. The difference between an inline frame and an anchored frame is that an anchored frame is not embedded in the text frame — it is simply leashed to it.

 InDesign retains anchored frames set up in Microsoft Word documents. It also preserves anchored frames when exporting text as RTF files.

When to use anchored frames

Before I explain how to create anchored frames, it's important for you know when to use them. There are several caveats to consider:

- Because an anchored frame follows its text as it flows throughout a document, you need to ensure your layout retains clear paths for those anchored objects to follow. Otherwise, you could have anchored frames overlap other frames as those anchored frames move.

- Anchored frames should generally be small items and/or used sparingly. The more items you have anchored to text, the greater the chance that they will interfere with each other's placement. Likewise, you can move large items only so far within a page, so the benefit of keeping them close to their related text goes away.

- Items such as pull-quotes are obvious candidates for use as anchored frames. But in many layouts you want the pull-quotes to stay in specific locations on the page for good visual appearance. The InDesign anchored-frame function can accommodate that need for specific positioning on a page, but you need to be careful as you add or delete text so that you do not end up with some pages that have no pull-quotes at all because there is so much text between the pull-quotes' anchor points. Conversely, you need to make sure you don't have too many pull-quotes anchored close to each other, which could result in overlapping objects.

Typically, you would use anchored frames for small graphics or icons that you want to stay next to a specific paragraph. Another good use would be for cross-reference ("For More Information") text frames.

Earlier, Figure 12.6 shows the Insert Anchored Object dialog box for an anchored object, while Figure 12.8 shows an example of an anchored frame in use.

FIGURE 12.8

Example of an anchored frame

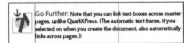

Adding anchored frames

The process for adding an anchored frame is similar to that for inline frames (described in the previous section). But the controls over positioning are quite different.

Here are the steps:

1. **Select the Type tool (or press T) and then click within a text frame to establish the insertion point.**

2. **Choose Object ⇨ Anchored Object ⇨ Insert.**

3. **Choose Custom from the Position pop-up menu.** The Insert Anchored Object dialog box, shown previously in Figure 12.6, appears.

4. **In the Object Options section, specify the inline frame's settings.** Choose the type of frame (text, graphics, or unassigned) using the Content pop-up menu; apply an object style, if desired, using the Object Style pop-up menu; apply a paragraph style, if desired, using the Paragraph Style pop-up menu; and set the inline frame's dimensions using the Height and Width fields.

   Note that the Paragraph Style you choose, if any, applies to the inline frame, not to the paragraph in which the inline frame is embedded. Oddly, InDesign lets you apply a paragraph style to the inline frame even if it contains no text.

5. **Decide whether to select the Relative to Spine option.** If this option is not selected, the anchored frame is placed on the same side of the text frame on all pages, whether left-facing or right-facing. If this option is selected, InDesign places the text frame on the outside of both pages or inside of both pages, depending on how the anchored position is set. In other words, if the anchored frame is set to be on the left of the reference text for a left-hand page, selecting this option puts the anchored frame to the right of the reference text on a right-hand page. If this option is not selected, InDesign places the anchored frame to the left of the text frame on both left-hand and right-hand pages.

6. **In the Anchored Object section of the dialog box, click one of the positioning points (the squares) to set up the text frame's relative position.** Note that you need to think about both the horizontal and vertical position you desire. For example, if you want the

anchored frame to appear to the right of the text reference, click one of the right-hand points. (Remember that selecting the Relative to Spine option overrides this, making the right-hand pages' positions mirror that of the left-hand pages, rather than be identical to them.) If you choose the topmost right-hand point, the anchored frame is placed to the right of the text reference and vertically appears at or below that text reference. But if you choose the bottommost right-hand point, you're telling InDesign you want the anchored frame to appear vertically above the text reference.

You need to experiment with your layout to see what works best in each case.

7. **In the Anchored Position section of the dialog box, click one of the positioning points to set up the text reference's relative position.** (Position points are similar to the reference points in the Control and Transform panels, covered in Chapter 2.) Although there are nine points shown, the only three that matter are those in the middle row. Typically, you'd have the text reference be on the opposite side of the anchored frame; if you want the anchored frame to be to the left, you thus would indicate that the text reference is to the right. (If you set the text reference to be on the same side as the anchored frame, InDesign places the anchored frame over the text.) The reason there are three points (left, middle, and right) is to accommodate layouts where you want some anchored frames to appear to the left of the text and some to the right; in that case, choose the middle position here and select the right- or left-hand position in the Anchored Object section as appropriate to that object.

I mentioned that you can ignore the top and bottom row of position points in the Anchored Section. If you click any left-hand position point, InDesign sets the position as if you clicked the middle row's left-hand position point. If you click any right-hand position point, InDesign treats it as if you clicked the middle right-hand position point. The only reason the nine points are there is for consistency with the Anchored Object section's position points.

8. There are three options in the Anchored Position section that you may need to set that give InDesign more precise instructions on how to place the anchored frames:

   - The X Relative To pop-up menu tells InDesign from where the horizontal location is calculated, using the following options: Anchor Marker, Column Edge, Text Frame, Page Margin, and Page Edge. The right option depends both on where you want the anchored frames placed and whether you have multicolumn text frames (in which case Text Frame and Column Edge result in different placement, while in a single-column text frame they do not).

     You can also specify a specific amount of space to place between the chosen X Relative To point and the anchored frame by typing a value in the X Offset field.

   - The Y Relative To pop-up menu tells InDesign from where the horizontal location is calculated, using the following options: Line (Baseline), Line (Cap-height), Line (Top of Leading), Column Edge, Text Frame, Page Margin, and Page Edge.

     As you would expect, you can also indicate a specific amount of space to place between the chosen Y Relative To point and the anchored frame by typing a value in the Y Offset field.

9. No matter which position settings you apply, you can select the Prevent Manual Positioning option to ensure that the positions of individual frames can't be adjusted using InDesign's other frame-positioning controls (such as the Control panel's or Transform panel's X and Y fields). This forces users to use this dialog box to change the anchored frame's position.

10. Click OK to insert the anchored frame.

TIP To see the results of various position options as you work in the Insert Anchored Object dialog box, select the Preview check box. This greatly helps you to understand the results of various settings before you commit to them.

Converting existing frames to anchored frames

After you get the hang of when and how to use anchored frames, you'll likely want to convert some frames in existing documents to anchored frames. There's no direct way to do that in InDesign, but there is a more circuitous path you can take:

1. Use a selection tool to cut the existing frame you want to make into an anchored frame by choosing Edit ⇨ Cut or pressing ⌘+X or Ctrl+X. You can also copy an existing frame by choosing Edit ⇨ Copy or pressing ⌘+C or Ctrl+C.

2. Switch to the Type tool, and click in a text frame at the desired location to insert the text reference to the anchored frame.

3. Paste the cut or copied frame into that insertion point by choosing Edit ⇨ Paste or pressing ⌘+V or Ctrl+V. You now have an inline frame.

4. Choose Object ⇨ Anchored Object ⇨ Options to display the Anchored Object Options dialog box (which is nearly identical to the Insert Anchored Object dialog box shown in Figure 12.6).

5. Using the Position pop-up menu, choose Custom. This converts the frame from an inline frame to an anchored frame.

6. Adjust the position for the newly minted anchored frame as described in the previous section.

7. Click OK when done.

Adjusting anchored frames

After you create an anchored frame, you can adjust its position.

A quick-and-easy trick is simply to click and drag anchored frames or use the Control panel or Transform panel to adjust their position. If the text the frame is anchored to moves, however, InDesign, of course, overrides those changes. You can't manually move an anchored frame if the Prevent Manual Positioning option is selected in the Insert Anchored Object dialog box or Anchored Object Options dialog box. This option is not selected by default.

For the most control of an anchored frame's position, choose Object ➪ Anchored Object ➪ Options. The resulting Anchored Object Options dialog box is the same as the Insert Anchored Object dialog box covered previously in this section and shown in Figure 12.6, except that the Anchored Object Options dialog box does not have the Object Options section.

And, of course, you can adjust its other attributes as needed, such as strokes, fills, dimensions, rotation, and skew.

Releasing and deleting anchored frames

If you no longer want an anchored frame to be anchored to a text location, you can release the anchor. To do so, select the anchored frame and then choose Object ➪ Anchored Object ➪ Release.

It's also easy to delete an anchored frame: Select the frame and then choose Edit ➪ Clear or press Delete or Backspace. If you want to remove the object but keep it on the Clipboard for pasting elsewhere, choose Edit ➪ Cut or press ⌘+X or Ctrl+X.

Wrapping Text around Objects

In the days before personal computers and page-layout software, wrapping text around a graphic or other object was a time-consuming and expensive task. Text wraps were rare, found only in the most expensively produced publications.

Not any more. Not only do all page-layout programs let you create text runarounds, most programs, including InDesign, provide several options for controlling how text relates to graphics and other objects that obstruct its flow.

When a frame is positioned in front of a text frame, InDesign provides the following options. You can

- Ignore the frame and flow the text behind it
- Wrap the text around the frame's rectangular bounding box
- Wrap the text around the frame itself
- Jump the text around the frame (that is, jump the text from the top of the frame to the bottom)
- Jump the text to the next column or page when the text reaches the top of frame
- Specify the amount of distance between the text and the edge of the obstructing shape
- Flow text within the obstructing shape rather than outside it

TIP InDesign lets you wrap text around frames on hidden layers, as well as remove text wrap for objects on hidden layers. This is handy when you want to hide images or other distracting items but preserve the layout. See Chapter 5 for details on using layers.

If you want to wrap text around only a portion of a graphic — perhaps you need to isolate a face in a crowd — the best solution is to open the graphics file in its original program, create a clipping path around that portion and then resave the file and import it and its clipping path into an InDesign document (clipping paths are explained in Chapter 26). Another option is to use the Pen tool to create a free-form shape within InDesign and then use the shape as both a frame and a clipping path.

CAUTION InDesign does not properly align bulleted or numbered lists when the left side of the text frame they are in wraps around another object. Although InDesign should see the wrap boundary as the new left margin and thus adjust the list's indentation accordingly, it does not. Also, InDesign does not properly wrap text around inline graphics.

Using the Text Wrap panel

The controls in the Text Wrap panel (see Figure 12.9) let you specify how a selected object will affect the flow of text behind it. Remember, the flow of text around an obstructing object is determined by the text wrap settings applied to the obstructing object.

TIP You can override the text-wrap settings of objects that are in front of a text frame by telling the text frame to ignore them. To do so, click a text frame and then choose Object ➪ Text Frame Options or press ⌘+B or Ctrl+B. In the Text Frame Options dialog box's General pane, select Ignore Text Wrap and then click OK.

NOTE The Text Wrap panel has three options that may not display when you open it: Wrap Options; Contour Options; and Include Inside Edges. You can more easily hide/show these functions by double-clicking the double-arrow icon to the left of the Text Wrap label in the panel's tab or by choosing Hide Options/Show Options from the flyout menu.

Here's how to apply text-wrap settings to a frame or other object:

1. **If the Text Wrap panel is not displayed, choose Window ➪ Text Wrap or press Option+⌘+W or Ctrl+Alt+W.**

2. **Click any of the selection tools.** If the Type tool isn't selected, you can press V to select the Selection tool or press A to select the Direct Selection tool.

3. **Click the object to which you want to apply text-wrap settings.** The object can be anywhere, but you probably want to position it on top of a text frame that contains text so you can see the results of the settings you apply.

4. **Click one of the five text-wrap iconic buttons at the top of the Text Wrap panel.** Figure 12.9 shows how each of these options affects a graphics frame.

5. If you want, adjust the space between the surrounding text and the obstructing shape by typing values in the Top Offset, Bottom Offset, Left Offset, and Right Offset fields. (These fields are not available if you click the No Text Wrap iconic button.) If the object is a rectangle, all four fields are available if you click Wrap around Bounding Box or Wrap around Object Shape. Only the Top Offset field is available if you click the Wrap around Object Shape iconic button for a free-form shape or the Jump to Next Column button. The Top Offset and Bottom Offset fields are available if you click Jump Object.

FIGURE 12.9

Examples of the five text-wrap options (top to bottom) and their Text Wrap panel settings: No Text Wrap, Wrap around Bounding Box, Wrap around Object Shape, Jump Object, and Jump to Next Column. The sixth example shows the Invert option selected for the Wrap around Object Shape option.

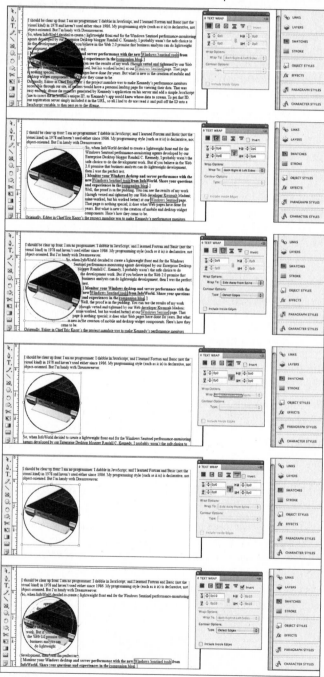

TIP The Text Wrap panel's Make All Settings the Same iconic button (the chain icon) determines how wrap margins are applied. If the chain is unbroken, changing any offset automatically changes the other offsets to the same value. If the chain is broken, you can adjust each offset independently. Click the button to toggle between the two modes.

NOTE A bounding box is the dimension of the graphic, whether or not it is wholly contained in its frame. You use a bounding box if you want to have the wrap follow the graphic's dimensions rather than that of the frame containing it.

   6. Select Invert if you want to flow the text inside the obstructing shape.

   7. If you choose the Wrap around Object Shape iconic button, you can also select from the Contour Options's Type pop-up menu. There are six options (Figure 12.10 shows examples of each):

   ▪ Bounding Box determines the dimensions of the bounding box — the uncropped image, which may be larger or smaller than the graphics frame containing it — and uses them for the wrap boundary.

   ▪ Detect Edges tries to determine the graphic's outside boundary by ignoring white space; you would use this for bitmapped images that have a transparent or white background.

   ▪ Alpha Channel uses the image's alpha channel, if any, to create a wrapping boundary.

   ▪ Photoshop Path uses the image's clipping path, if any, to create a wrapping boundary.

   ▪ Graphic Frame uses the frame's boundary rather than the bounding box.

   ▪ Same as Clipping uses the clipping path for the graphic created in InDesign.

User-Modified Path uses any modification to one of the above boundaries you have made by editing it with the Direct Selection tool. This option is grayed out unless you modify the wrap boundary yourself.

   8. **You can control how text wraps around an object that splits a column by choosing an option from the Wrap To pop-up menu.** The options are Right Side, Left Side, Both Left and Right Sides, Side Towards Spine, Side Away from Spine, and Largest Area. You rarely choose Both Left and Right Sides, because unless the object is small, readers' eyes stop at the interposed object and not see the rest of the text on the other side of it. Use either of the spine options to have the text stay on the outside or inside of a page, relative to the object, based on whether the page is right facing or left facing. You often want to choose Largest Area, because that gives the text the most space next to the interposed object, which tends to be what looks good in many situations.

   9. **By selecting the Include Inside Edges option, InDesign lets text appear inside any interior "holes" in the graphic.** Use this technique rarely because in most cases it's hard for the reader to follow text that wraps around an image, flows inside it, and then continues to flow outside it. But if the interior is large enough and not too distant from the text that flows on the outside, this effect might be readable.

FIGURE 12.10

The six contour options for text-wrap options (left to right, top to bottom): Bounding Box, Detect Edges, Alpha Channel, Photoshop Path, Graphic Frame, and Same as Clipping. The example at lower right shows the text wrap immediately above it modified by dragging and removing anchor points to create a user-adjusted path.

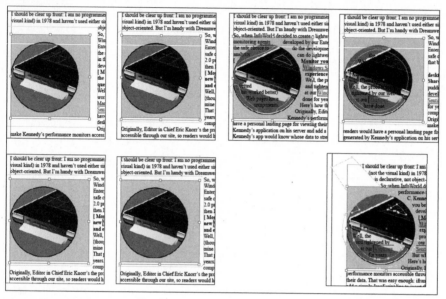

> **TIP** If you specify text-wrap settings when no objects are selected, the settings are automatically applied to all new objects.

> **TIP** To apply text-wrap settings to a master item on a document page, press and hold Shift+⌘ or Ctrl+Shift to select the item and then use the controls in the Text Wrap panel as just described. If you don't want the text wrap applied to existing document items, but do want it applied to new ones, choose Apply to Master Page Only in the Text Wrap panel's flyout menu.

Setting text-wrap preferences

There are several global text-wrap options you should be aware of, all of which are accessed via the Composition pane of the Preferences dialog box (choose InDesign ⇨ Preferences ⇨ Composition or press ⌘+K on the Mac, or choose Edit ⇨ Preferences ⇨ Composition or press Ctrl+K in Windows). Here are the options:

- **Justify Text Next to an Object:** This option is useful when you have left-aligned text that wraps around an object at the right. It also works if you have right-aligned text that wraps around an object at the left. This can lead to an awkward wrap, however, because

InDesign doesn't try to make the text align precisely to the wrap's contour (because the text isn't justified). Use this option to justify the text just around the wrap; then, continue using the text's specified nonjustified alignment.

- **Skip by Leading:** This option makes text wrap below or above an object based on the text's leading so that at least a full line space exists between the text and the object, even if the object's text-wrap settings would allow less space.

- **Text Wrap Only Affects Text Beneath:** This option, if selected, prevents text frames placed on top of an object from wrapping, while those behind the graphic frame are still allowed to wrap. This option allows some text to overlap the graphic and other text to wrap around it. Note this is a global setting, affecting all objects. To override wrap settings of individual text frames, choose Object ➪ Text Frame Options or press ⌘+B or Ctrl+B; then, select the Ignore Text Wrap option.

Changing the shape of a text wrap

When you specify text-wrap settings for an object, an editable shape is created. If the text-wrap shape is the same shape as the object, the text-wrap boundary is superimposed on the object. You can modify a text-wrap boundary by clicking it with the Direct Selection tool and then moving, adding, deleting, and changing the direction of anchor points and by moving direction lines. Figure 12.10 shows a text wrap before and after being manually reshaped.

CROSS-REF For more information about modifying free-form shapes, see Chapter 27.

Defining and Applying Object Styles

For many years, desktop-publishing programs have let designers save textual styles for easy reuse and application to text throughout a document. But of the major programs, only InDesign lets you create object styles so that you can ensure that multiple objects have the same attributes and that any changes to the style are made to all the objects using that style.

Designers should find the process of creating and applying object styles very familiar because the concept is the same as creating other types of styles, such as paragraph, character, and stroke styles.

CROSS-REF Paragraph and character styles are covered in Chapter 19. Stroke styles are covered in Chapter 11. Table and cell styles are covered in Chapter 21.

There are no hard-and-fast rules about how best to implement them. Like handwriting, you should develop your own style. How many styles you create, the names you use, and whether you apply them with keyboard shortcuts or through the Object Styles pane are all matters of personal taste. One thing is indisputable: You should use object styles whenever you're dealing with multiple objects that need to be formatted the same way.

Creating object styles

You create object styles using the Object Styles panel (choose Window⇨Object Styles or press ⌘+F7 or Ctrl+F7), shown in Figure 12.11. You can also click the New Object Style iconic button (the turned-page icon) at the bottom of the panel. New styles are added at the bottom of the style list or, if a group is selected, at the bottom of the group's list.

FIGURE 12.11

The Object Styles panel and its flyout menu

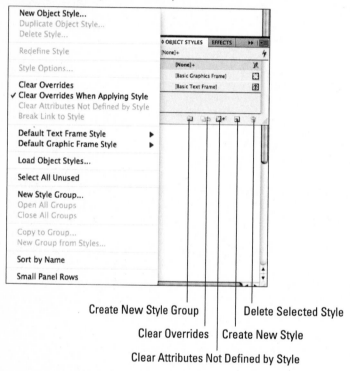

Create New Style Group

Delete Selected Style

Clear Overrides | Create New Style

Clear Attributes Not Defined by Style

> **TIP** The simplest way is to apply various attributes to an object (text frame, graphics frame, unassigned frame, or line) is to select it and then choose New Object Style from the Object Style panel's flyout menu. InDesign records all those settings automatically so that they're in place for the new object style.

Whether you start with an existing object or create a new object style completely from scratch, you use the New Object Style menu option that opens the New Object Style dialog box shown in Figure 12.12.

FIGURE 12.12

The New Object Style dialog box and its General pane

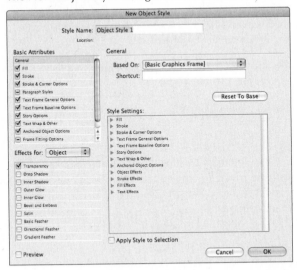

At the left side of the dialog box is a list of types of attributes that are or can be set. The selected items are in use for this style; you can deselect an item so that InDesign doesn't apply its settings to objects using the style. For example, if Fill is deselected, the object style won't apply any Fill settings to objects using that style.

> **NOTE** Because there are so many panes, the New Object Style dialog box breaks them into two sections: Basic Attributes and Effects. The Effects set of panes have the same functions as the Effects dialog box. For the details on the Effects panes' settings, see Chapter 11.

To switch from one type of attribute to another, simply click the item name in the list at left of the dialog box for the type of attributes on which you want to work, such as Stroke or Transparency.

> **TIP** Be sure to select the Preview check box to see the results of object styles on the currently selected object. Of course, you need to make sure the object is visible on-screen to see those effects.

The General pane

When you open the New Object Style dialog box, you see the General pane, which lets you create a style based on an existing object style (using the Based On pop-up menu), and which lets you assign a keyboard shortcut for fast application of this style (using the Shortcuts field).

You can use the Based On feature to create families of object styles. For example, you can create a style called Photo/Base for the bulk of your placed photographs and then create variations such as Photo/Sidebar and Photo/Author. The Photo/Base style might specify a hairline black stroke around the photo, while Photo/Sidebar might change that to be a white stroke. But if you later decide you want the stroke to be 1 point and change it in Photo/Base, Photo/Sidebar automatically gets the 1-point stroke while retaining the white color.

The General pane also lets you see the current style settings. Click any of the arrows in the Style Settings section to get more details on how they are set for this object style.

CROSS-REF   Chapter 7 covers the definition and application of colors, gradients, and tints.

The other options are grayed out because they do not apply to fills.

The Fill pane

Shown in Figure 12.13, the Fill pane of the New Object Style dialog box lets you set colors for fills using whatever colors are defined in the Swatches panel. You can also set the tint and, if you select a gradient fill, the angle for that gradient. Finally, you can choose to have the fill overprint the contents of the frame by selecting the Overprint Fill option.

FIGURE 12.13

The Fill pane of the New Object Style dialog box

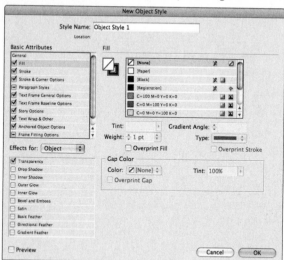

TIP   If you click the Stroke icon in the pane, you are taken to the Stroke pane of the New Object Style dialog box. This emulates the behavior of the Stroke and Fill iconic buttons in the Tools panel and the Swatches panel.

The Stroke pane

The Stroke pane in the New Object Style dialog box is identical to the Fill pane except that options specific to fills are grayed out and options available to strokes are made available. The color, tint, and gradient angle options are the same as for the Fill pane.

In the Stroke pane, you choose the type of stroke (solid line, dashed line, or dotted line) using the Type pop-up menu, and the thickness using the Weight field. You can also choose to overprint the stroke over underlying content by selecting the Overprint Stroke option. Finally, if your stroke is a dotted or dashed line, you can set the color, tint, and overprint for the gap in the Gap Color section.

> **TIP** If you click the Fill iconic button in the pane, you are taken to the Fill pane of the New Object Style dialog box. This emulates the behavior of the Stroke and Fill iconic buttons in the Tools panel and the Swatches panel.

> **CROSS-REF** Chapter 11 covers the use of strokes and settings such as gap.

The Stroke & Corner Options pane

Shown in Figure 12.14, the Stroke & Corner Options pane of the New Object Style dialog box lets you set stroke position and how corners and line ends are handled. It also lets you apply fancy corners to frames.

FIGURE 12.14

The Stroke & Corner Options pane of the New Object Style dialog box

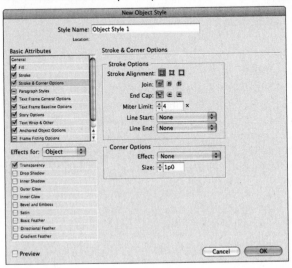

The Stroke Effects section is where you align the strokes to the frame edges, using the Stroke Alignment buttons. You also control how lines join at corners using the Join buttons. The End Cap buttons control how the lines end (such as immediately, or with a rounded or squared-off cap). You can also use the Miter Limit field to tell InDesign when a corner point should switch from *mitered* (squared off) to a beveled appearance, based on the sharpness of the corner's angle. Finally, you can select line endings such as arrowheads using the Line Start and Line End pop-up menus.

The Corner Options section is where you select from five fancy corners, such as Bevel and Rounded, using the Effect pop-up menu and where you specify the radius, or reach, of the corner using the Size field.

CROSS-REF Chapter 11 covers the use of strokes and settings such as alignment and line endings, as well as corner options.

The Paragraph Styles pane

The Paragraph Styles pane of the New Object Style dialog box controls which paragraph style, if any, is applied to text in the frame. It has just two options:

- You choose the style from the Paragraph Style pop-up menu that you want automatically applied to any text typed into the frame.

- If that style is set to invoke another style for the next paragraph, be sure to select the Apply Next Style option; otherwise, the object style insists on making every paragraph use the style specified in the pop-up menu.

NOTE Chances are you won't use the Paragraph Styles pane except for frames that contain only consistent, very simple text, such as pull-quotes or bios.

CROSS-REF Chapter 19 covers paragraph styles in detail.

The Text Frame General Options pane

Shown in Figure 12.15, the Text Frame General Options pane of the New Object Style dialog box controls how text is handled within a frame. This essentially replicates the controls in the General pane of the Text Box Options dialog box (choose Object ➪ Text Frame Options or press ⌘+B or Ctrl+B), including the number of columns, column width, gutter settings, inset spacing (how far from the frame edge text is placed), vertical justification (how text is aligned vertically in the frame), and whether text wrap settings are ignored when this frame overlaps other frames.

NOTE You can set text frame options even if the current object is not a text frame. That's so you can have a consistent style for multiple kinds of objects, with the text attributes coming into play only for objects that actually are text frames.

CROSS-REF Chapter 14 covers text frame options in detail.

The Text Frame General Options pane of the New Object Style dialog box

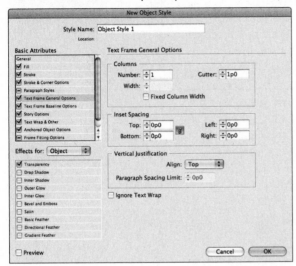

The Text Frame Baseline Options pane

The Text Frame Baseline Options pane of the New Object Style dialog box controls how text is handled within a frame. This essentially replicates the controls in the Baseline Options pane of the Text Box Options dialog box (choose Object ➪ Text Frame Options or press ⌘+B or Ctrl+B), including how the text baseline is calculated for the frame and whether the text frame gets its own baseline grid.

CROSS-REF These options are covered in Chapter 14.

The Story Options pane

The Story Options pane of the New Objects Style dialog box lets you enable optical margin alignment — its controls are the same as the Story panel (Type ➪ Story). Optical margin alignment adjusts the placement of text along the left side of a frame so the text alignment is more visually pleasing.

NOTE You can set optical margin alignment even if the current object is not a text frame. That's so you can have a consistent style for multiple kinds of objects, with the text attributes coming into play only for objects that actually are text frames.

CROSS-REF Chapter 18 covers optical margin alignment in detail.

The Text Wrap & Other pane

Shown in Figure 12.16, the Text Wrap & Other pane of the New Object Style dialog box lets you set text wrap — mirroring the features of the Text Wrap panel (choose Window ➪ Text Wrap or press Option+⌘+W or Ctrl+Alt+W), as well as make an object nonprinting (normally handled through the Attributes panel by choosing Window ➪ Attributes).

FIGURE 12.16

The Text Wrap & Other pane of the New Object Style dialog box

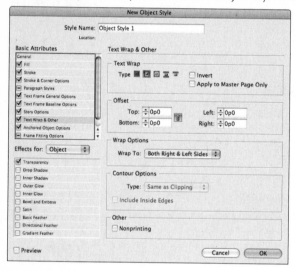

NOTE   You can set text wrap even if the current object is not a text frame. That's so you can have a consistent style for multiple kinds of objects, with the text attributes coming into play only for objects that actually are text frames.

CROSS-REF   Text wrap settings are covered earlier in this chapter. Chapter 9 covers nonprinting objects. Chapter 11 covers other Attributes panel options.

The Anchored Object Options pane

The Anchored Object Options pane of the New Object Style dialog box lets you set the attributes for inline and anchored frames, using the same settings as in the Anchored Object Options dialog box.

CROSS-REF   Anchored objects are covered previously in this chapter.

The Frame Fitting Options pane

The New Object Style dialog box's Frame Fitting Options pane lets you set the offset values for imported graphics, by entering values in the Crop Amount area. You select what those offset (crop) settings are calculated from by selecting one of the reference points in the Alignment area. And you select the default frame-fitting behavior for imported graphics in the Fitting pop-up menu: None, Fit Content to Frame, Fit Content Proportionally, or Fill Frame Proportionally. Figure 12.17 shows the pane.

CROSS-REF Reference points are covered in Chapter 2. Setting offset values for frames are covered in Chapter 19. Frame-fitting options are covered in Chapter 26.

FIGURE 12.17

The Frame Fitting Options pane of the New Object Style dialog box

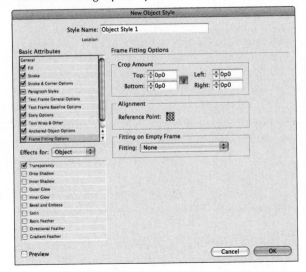

Managing object styles

The Object Styles panel's flyout menu of the New Object Style dialog box (refer to Figure 12.11) has several options for managing object styles:

- **Duplicate Style:** Click an object style's name and then choose this menu option to create an exact copy. If you want to create an object style that's similar to one you've already created, you might want to choose New Object Style rather than Duplicate Style and then use the Based On option to create a child of the original. If you choose Duplicate Style, the copy is identical to, but not based on, the original; if you modify the original, the copy is not affected. The panel also has the Create New Style iconic button (the turned-page icon) to create a new style.

- **Delete Style:** Choose this to delete selected object styles. To select multiple styles, press and hold ⌘ or Ctrl as you click their names. To select a range of styles, click the first one and then press and hold Shift and click the last one. You can also delete styles by selecting them in the pane and then clicking the Delete Selected Style iconic button (the trashcan icon) at the bottom of the panel.

- **Redefine Style:** This option lets you modify an existing object style by first making changes to an object that already has an object style defined for it and then choosing Redefine Style. The newly applied formats are applied to the object style.

- **Style Options:** This option lets you modify an existing object style. When a style is highlighted in the Object Styles panel, choosing Style Options displays the Object Style Options dialog box, which is identical to the New Object Style dialog box covered earlier.

- **Load Object Styles:** Choose this option if you want to import object styles from another InDesign document. You get a dialog box listing the styles in the chosen document so that you can decide which ones to import.

If you import styles whose names match those in the current document, InDesign gives you a chance to let the imported style overwrite the current style or to leave the current style as is and give the imported style a new name. If there is an entry in the Conflict with Existing Style, you can click that entry for a pop-up menu that provides two choices: Auto-Rename and Use Incoming Style Definition. Figure 12.18 shows this Load Styles dialog box.

Note that at the bottom of the dialog box is the Incoming Style Definitions window, which lists the style definitions to help you decide which to import, as well as which to overwrite or rename.

FIGURE 12.18

The Load Styles dialog box

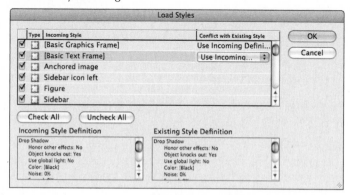

- **Select All Unused:** Select this option to highlight the names of all object styles that have not been applied to any objects. This is a handy way of identifying unused styles in preparation for deleting them (by choosing the Delete Style menu option).

- **Sort by Name:** This option alphabetizes your object styles.

- **Small Panel Rows:** Click this option to reduce the text size in the Object Styles panel. Although harder to read, a panel with this option selected lets you access more styles without having to scroll. To return the panel to its normal text size, deselect this option.

Using style groups

To help you find the desired style in documents that have dozens of them, InDesign lets you create style groups, which create a folder in the Object Styles panel's style list that you can open and close as desired. To create a group, choose New Style Group from the panel's flyout menu or click the Create New Style Group iconic button (the folder icon) on the bottom of the panel. Enter a name in the dialog box that appears and click OK.

To add styles to a group (which have a folder icon to the left of its name in the panel list), you have three options:

- You can drag any desired styles into the group.

- You can copy a selected style to the group by choosing Copy to Group and then selecting the target group in the dialog box that appears.

- If multiple styles are selected, you can create a group and move them into it in one fell swoop by choosing New Group from Styles in the flyout menu. (Note that this option is selected if any of the three predefined styles — [None], [Basic Graphics Frame], and [Basic Text Frame] — are selected.

 To quickly open all groups, choose Open All Groups in the panel's flyout menu. To quickly close them all, choose Close All Groups.

Understanding predefined styles

Note that InDesign comes with two predefined object styles — [Basic Text Frame], and [Basic Graphics Frame] — that you can modify as desired. Frankly, they're not necessary because it makes more sense for you to create object styles using your own naming conventions. Adobe's rationale is that at least one style should be defined so that if you delete all other styles, you still have a style that can be applied to objects. Although I don't buy that argument, the issue doesn't matter because you can easily ignore these default styles if you prefer.

You can set which object styles are automatically used for new text and graphics frames: In the Object Styles panel's flyout menu, choose Default Text Frame Style and then the desired style from the submenu to set a default text frame; choose Default Graphic Frame Style and then the desired style from the submenu to set a default graphics frame. To no longer have object styles automatically applied to new objects, choose [None] in the Default Text Frame and/or default Graphic Frame submenus.

Applying object styles

After you create an object style, applying it is easy. Just click an object and then click the object style name in the Object Styles panel, or press its keyboard shortcut. (Windows users must make sure Num Lock is on when using shortcuts for styles.)

CROSS-REF InDesign has a Quick Apply panel that lets you apply any style — object, paragraph, or character — as well as other saved settings from one location. Chapter 2 covers this panel.

Handling existing formatting

When you apply an object style to selected objects, all local formats are retained. All other formats are replaced by those of the applied style. That is, unless you do one of the following:

- If you press and hold Option or Alt when clicking a name in the Object Styles panel, any local formatting that has been applied to the objects is removed. You can achieve the same effect by choosing Clear Attributes Not Defined by Style from the Object Styles panel's flyout menu or by clicking the Clear Attributes Not Defined by Style iconic button at the bottom of the panel.

- To have any existing formatting automatically removed when applying a style, be sure that Clear Overrides When Applying Style is selected in the flyout menu.

- If you want to override any local changes with the settings in the object style, choose Clear Overrides in the flyout menu or click the Clear Overrides iconic button at the bottom of the Object Styles panel. The difference is that Clear Attributes Not Defined by Style removes all attributes for which the object style contains no settings, while Clear Overrides imposes the object style's settings over conflicting attributes that you set manually.

If a plus sign (+) appears to the right of an object style's name, it means that the object has local formats that differ from those of the applied object style. This can occur if you apply an object style to an object text to which you've done some manual formatting or if you modify formatting for an object after applying an object style to it. (For example, you may have changed the fill color; that is a local change to the object style and causes the + to appear.)

Removing an object style from an object

To remove a style from an object, choose Break Link to Style from the Object Styles panel's flyout menu. The object's current formatting won't be affected, but it will no longer be updated when the object style is changed.

Managing Links

The Links panel (choose Window ➪ Links or press Shift+⌘+D or Ctrl+Shift+D) is a handy place to manage the links to your graphics and text, particularly when you need to update them. Figure 12.19 shows the Links panel.

The Links panel and its flyout menu. Note the icons that indicate missing and modified source files.

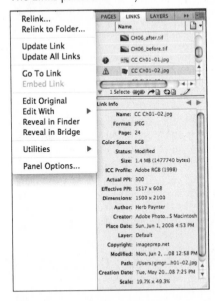

NEW FEATURE If you've used previous versions of InDesign, you'll note how different the Links panel is in InDesign CS4 — Adobe's given it a major overhaul.

InDesign always creates links for graphics files. But it will create links to source text files (including spreadsheets) only if the Create Links When Placing Text and Spreadsheet Files option is selected in the File Handling pane of the Preferences dialog box (choose InDesign ➪ Preferences ➪ File Handling or press ⌘+K on the Mac, or choose Edit ➪ Preferences ➪ File Handling or press Ctrl+K in Windows). This option is *not* selected by default because many designers don't want to have text files be easily updated in their layouts. That's because all the formatting they have done to the file in InDesign is removed when the link to the source file is updated, causing the text to be replaced. (Note that this option has moved from the Type pane of the Preference dialog box, where it resided in previous versions of InDesign.)

TIP If you can store all your linked files in a single location — not necessarily in a single folder, but perhaps within a folder hierarchy on your hard drive or a file server — you can minimize link problems. If you move, rename, or delete the original file after importing a graphic, you break the link, which causes printing problems. Keeping all graphics files in a single, safe place — a place that's backed up regularly — is a good idea.

NEW FEATURE You can see extensive information about the file in the Link Info section of the Links panel, containing all the attributes that are also available in Adobe's Bridge, such as file dimensions and color profile. To toggle this information off, just click the Show/Hide Item Information iconic button at the bottom left of the Links panel.

The first four sets of commands in the Links panel's flyout menu let you reestablish links to missing and modified files, display an imported graphic or text file in the document window, open the program used to create a graphic or text file, and work on copies and versions of the source graphics and text:

- **Relink:** This command, and the Relink iconic button (at the bottom of the panel), lets you reestablish a missing link or replace the original file you imported with a different file. When you choose Relink or click the button, the Relink dialog box is displayed and shows the original pathname and filename. You can enter a new pathname and filename in the Location field, but it's easier to click Browse, which opens a standard Open a File dialog box. Use the controls to locate and select the original file or a different file and then click OK. (You can also drag and drop a file icon from the Mac OS Finder or Windows Explorer directly into the Relink dialog box.) If you want to restore broken links to multiple files simultaneously, highlight their filenames in the scroll list and then choose Relink or click the Update Link button.

NEW FEATURE   InDesign lets you relink all instances of a file in your layout so that you have to do the operation only once. InDesign CS4 changes how this works: Be sure to hold Option or Alt when clicking the Relink command or Relink iconic button. Also, InDesign is now smarter about finding missing files when you open a file; if the Find Missing Links Before Opening Document option is selected in the File Handling pane of the Preferences dialog box, InDesign CS4 will search your drives for the files and automatically update them if it finds them.

- **Relink to Folder:** This new command lets you relink multiple files at the same time, and even change the type of graphic files to use at the same time. First, be sure to select all files in the panel you want to relink — only selected files will be updated. Then choose this option and navigate to the folder that has the files. If the filenames in the new folder match the filenames of the selected files in the panel, InDesign will update them. (It will leave alone any it cannot find.)

  You'll notice in the Open a File dialog box that appears when you choose this command that there's an option called Match This Filename But This Extension. Say that someone gave you JPEG files as placeholders for your layout and then delivered the final TIFF files for high-quality print output. Before, you would have to relink every single file manually. Now you can use this option and enter **TIFF** (or **TIF**, depending on the filename extension used) in the Match This Filename But This Extension field to substitute the high-quality TIFF files for the original low-quality JPEG files. That's a real timesaver! (Note that the new file can be any format supported by InDesign, not just TIFF.)

- **Update Link:** Choose this option or click the Update Link iconic button (at the bottom of the panel) to update the link to a modified graphic or text file. Highlight multiple filenames and then choose Update Link or click the Update Link button to update all those links simultaneously.

- **Update All Links:** Choose this option to update all files marked as modified without having to select individual files.

- **Go to Link:** Choose this option, or click the Go to Link iconic button (second from left) in the panel to display the highlighted file in the document window. InDesign will, if necessary, navigate to the correct page and center the frame in the document window. You can also display a particular graphic or text file by double-clicking its name in the scroll list while holding down the Option or Alt key.

- **Embed Link (for graphics only):** This option lets you embed the complete file of any imported graphics file. (InDesign normally imports only a low-resolution screen preview when you place a graphic that is 48K or larger.) If you want to ensure that the graphics file will forever remain with a document, you can choose to embed it; however, by embedding graphics, you'll be producing larger document files, which means that opening and saving them will take you longer. If you do use this option, InDesign displays an alert and informs you about the increased document size that will result. Click Yes to embed the file. Note that this menu option changes to Unembed File, so you can reenable the original link at any time.

- **Unlink (for text files only):** This option removes the link to the source text file so that it can't be updated. Note that you cannot undo this option from the Links panel; you have to choose Edit ⇨ Undo or press ⌘+Z or Ctrl+Z. Also, the option is available only if you enabled text linking via the Create Links When Placing Text and Spreadsheet Files option in the File Handling pane of the Preferences dialog box.

- **Edit Original:** If you want to modify an imported graphic or text file, choose Edit Original from the flyout menu or click the Edit Original button (far right) at the bottom of the panel. InDesign will try to locate and open the program used to create the file. This may or may not be possible, depending on the original program, the file format, and the programs available on your computer.

- **Edit With:** This new menu option lets you choose what program to edit a select object with.

- **Reveal in Finder (Macintosh) and Reveal in Explorer (Windows):** This menu option opens a window displaying the contents of the folder that contains the source file, so you can move, copy, or rename it if you want. (The Reveal in Bridge option is a similar feature for the expert Adobe Bridge companion program that is not covered in this book.)

NEW FEATURE The Relink to Folder menu option and the ability to change the file types of linked graphics are new to InDesign CS4. The Edit With menu option is new as well. And Gone is the Purchase This Image option because the Adobe Stock Photos service has been discontinued.

NOTE When you relink missing graphics and update modified ones, any transformations — rotation, shear, scale, and so on — that you've applied to the graphics or their frames are maintained, unless you've deselected the new Preserve Image Dimensions When Relinking option in the File Handling pane of the Preferences dialog box (choose InDesign ⇨ Preferences ⇨ File Handling or press ⌘+K on the Mac, or choose Edit ⇨ Preferences ⇨ File Handling or press Ctrl+K in Windows).

The new Utilities menu option in the flyout menu provides access to several additional functions:

- **Search for Missing Links**: Choose this menu option to look for missing files on your computer and networked drives.

- **Copy Link(s) To:** Choose this menu option to copy the source graphic or text file to a new location and update the link so that it refers to this new copy. (This is a new location for a function found in the Links panel's "main" flyout menu in previous versions of InDesign.)

- **XMP File Info:** This displays Extensible Metadata Platform (XMP) data, which is a way of labeling a file with relevant information, such as when a photograph was taken.

- **Copy Full Path:** This copies the file path so that you can use it in other applications.

- **Copy Platform Style Path:** This copies the file path in the native syntax of the operating system you are using (Mac OS X or Windows).

- **Check Out:** If you are using InCopy, this menu option lets you open an InCopy assignment file so that others cannot work on it at the same time. (This option, and the next two, existed in the "main" flyout menu of previous versions of InDesign.)

- **Cancel Check Out:** This menu option stops a linked file from being checked out if you just asked InDesign to check it out for you.

- **Check In:** This menu option checks the selected file back into InCopy so that others can use it.

- **Check in Link:** This menu option lets you check in to your layout the selected file in the Links panel, thus updating it. Typically, you would have first edited the file by choosing Edit ⇨ Edit Original and saved it in the application you edited it in.

- **Version:** This option lets you select an alternative version of an Adobe Creative Suite graphic file (if that graphic has been saved with at least one version). By default, a placed graphic displays the most recent version of itself in InDesign, so you would use this menu option to select a previous version of the file. (This option existed in previous versions of InDesign, in the "main" flyout menu.)

NOTE The Check Out, Cancel Check Out, and Check In menu options apply to InCopy assignments used in your document. The Check in Link and Version menu options apply to files created and updated by other Adobe applications using the Version Cue functionality.

CROSS-REF See Chapter 35 for more details in using InCopy. See Appendix C for more details on the Version Cue functionality.

You can control what appears in the Links panel using the Panel Options option in the flyout menu. This lets you specify what information appears with each filename, including whether icons of the file contents display. Figure 12.20 shows the dialog box.

You can set the row size by choosing an option from the Row Size pop-up menu, as well as determine whether and where thumbnail icons appear in the Links panel. You can also control what attributes are shown in the panel's list of linked items and what are shown in the Link Info area of the panel.

FIGURE 12.20

FIGURE 12.20

The Panel Options dialog box for the Links panel

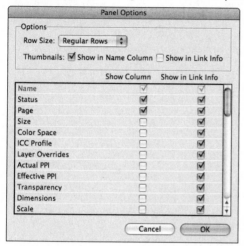

Although four sorting-oriented menu options — Sort by Name, Sort by Page, Sort by Type, and Sort by Status — have been removed from the flyout menu, these functions still exist. To sort, just click the column header you want to sort by.

NEW FEATURE The Panel Options dialog box is new to InDesign CS4, as are all its options except for Row Size, which has been enhanced in this version.

Summary

Most InDesign pages are made up of several objects. Each object occupies a separate level in a page's stacking order. The first object you place on a page occupies the bottom later, and each new object you create or place occupies a new layer that's on top of all other layers. You can change a page's stacking order by moving individual items forward or backward in the stacking order. InDesign also provides several options for working with several objects at one time. When multiple items are selected, you can combine them into a group that behaves like a single item. You can also place an object within a frame to create a nested object.

InDesign provides two ways to associate frames with text. One method lets you insert objects within a text thread to create inline frames that flow with the surrounding text. The other creates a link between a specific location in your text thread and an outside frame so that the frame moves along with that location as the text moves.

InDesign also lets you have text wrap around objects, with controls over the wrap's shape, location, and text flow.

InDesign lets you create object styles, which are named collections of attributes, that you can apply to objects to ensure consistent formatting and to easily update formatting across multiple objects, sort of the frame version of a paragraph style for text. You can also group frequently used styles into folders to make them easier to find in the Object Styles panel.

To manage the links to source files — such as to bring in an updated version or use a different version — use the Links panel. You can also get information about linked files.

Part IV

Text Fundamentals

Chapter 13

Importing Text Files

A lthough you can use InDesign as your primary word processor, doing so is a little like buying a Hummer for suburban errands — attention-getting but highly inefficient. (Especially these days!)

In publishing, at least the first draft of text is generally written in a word processor such as Microsoft Word. The key is to make sure you don't do work in your word processor that has no meaning to InDesign, resulting in wasted time or, worse, doing work in your word processor that requires extra effort in InDesign to undo or clean up.

Whether created in Word or not, text is imported into an InDesign publication to apply the layout and fine typographic formatting. Besides importing files into InDesign, you can drag text into your layout and, through the use of the Macintosh and Windows Clipboards (copy and paste), you can import file formats, to a limited degree, that are not directly supported by InDesign.

Determining Where to Format Documents

InDesign's import capabilities may tempt you to do a lot of your text formatting outside the program; however, it's not always wise to do so.

Because a word processor's formatting capabilities don't match all InDesign typographic features, it's often not worthwhile to do extensive formatting in your word processor. This is particularly true of layout-oriented formatting. Multiple columns and page numbers, for example, will be of a much higher standard in your final InDesign document than you could hope to create in a

IN THIS CHAPTER

Determining which formatting tasks to do in InDesign

Preparing files for import from word processors and spreadsheets

Pasting and dragging and dropping text from other programs

Importing text-only, Word, RTF, and Excel files

Exporting text

Working with tagged text

word processor. After all, even the sophisticated formatting features in today's word processors don't begin to approach those needed for true publishing.

It used to be true that layout programs ignored more sophisticated formatting, such as tables, during file import, but that's not true in InDesign. So you can produce your tables, footnotes, and even paragraph styles in Microsoft Word or in programs that can export their style-laden files to Word or RTF format. However, I would not spend much time on such complex formatting, because you'll want to use InDesign's more sophisticated tools.

Instead, use InDesign for your layout and complex text formatting (fonts, leading, and hyphenation) and use your word processor for the following tasks:

- Basic table setup (leave the high-end formatting to InDesign)
- Footnotes, basic text editing, paragraph style assignments (identifying headlines, body copy, and so forth)
- Basic character formatting (boldface, italic, and other meaning-oriented formatting)

Preparing Text Files

What preparation do you possibly need to do for your word processor files? They should just load into InDesign as is, right? This is not necessarily true, even if your word processor supports one of the InDesign text-import formats.

Limit your word processor formatting to the type of formatting that enhances reader understanding or conveys meaning. Such formatting may include using italic and boldface to emphasize a word, for example, or using styles to set headlines and bylines in different sizes and typefaces. (See Chapter 19 for tips on using styles in word processor text.) Let your editors focus on the words; leave presentation tasks to your layout artists.

One type of file preparation you may need to do is to translate text files into formats supported by InDesign. InDesign supports just Microsoft Word, Rich Text Format (RTF), and text-only (ASCII) formats. If you use Corel WordPerfect or Apple iWork Pages (or another word processor), you need to save in one of those other formats. Where possible, you should save in RTF or Microsoft Word format (up through the Office 12 version, better known as Office 2008 on the Mac and Office 2007 in Windows).

 InDesign supports both the traditional `.doc` and 2007/2008 `.docx` versions of Microsoft Word files.

InDesign also imports InCopy files. InCopy is an add-on program from Adobe meant for copy editors, editors, and other nonlayout artists that lets them do basic text editing of layout files without messing up the layout. Chapter 35 covers InCopy in more detail.

It's clear why you'd avoid text-only files in most cases — they carry no formatting. (That can be a useful feature when you have a document full of formatting that you don't want; saving to text-only format dumps it all.)

But how do you choose between Word and RTF formats? For most InDesign users, they are equivalent, supporting all the formatting you're likely to want to bring into your InDesign layouts. The real difference involves their capabilities in your word processor. The RTF format supports fewer features than Word; the one that matters to most people is that an RTF file cannot have tracked changes information, whereas a Word file can. If your editing workflow depends on tracked changes, saving to RTF is not an option. Chances are, though, that if tracked changes is a concern for you, you're using Microsoft Word anyhow, for which the Word file is native. If you're using an alternative word processor, chances are very high that you'll get the same formatting whether you save as RTF or Word.

Preserving special features in text files

Today's word processors let you do much more than type and edit text. You also can create special characters, tables, headers and footers, and other document elements. Some of these features work when imported into a publishing program, but others don't.

InDesign imports the following Word formatting (from Mac version 98 and later and from Windows version 97 and later):

- All caps
- Boldface
- Bulleted lists
- Color
- Column breaks
- Condensed/expanded spacing
- Double strikethrough
- Double underlines
- Drop caps
- Font
- Footnotes and endnotes
- Indents
- Index and table-of-contents text
- Inline graphics (if in an InDesign-supported format)
- Italic
- Numbered lists
- Outline

- Page breaks
- Paragraph and character style sheets
- Point size
- Redlining/revisions tracking (for use in InCopy, not InDesign)
- Small caps
- Strikethrough
- Subscripts and superscripts
- Tables
- Text boxes, including any follow-me links to them
- Underlines
- Underline options

CROSS-REF Support for automatic bulleted and numbered lists is covered in Chapter 17; support for Word's various underline options is covered in Chapters 17 and 18, and support for tracked changes is covered in Chapter 35.

The following formats are partially supported or are converted during import:

- Embossed text (made into paper color, usually white)
- Engraved text (made into paper color, usually white)
- Word-only underline (converted to single underlines, including for spaces and punctuation)

The following formats are *not* supported, and any text using them is imported as plain text:

- Highlighting
- Shadow
- Text effects, such as blinking and Las Vegas Lights

The following formats are not supported, and any text using them is removed during import:

- Annotations and comments
- Hidden text (deleted during import)
- Section breaks
- Subscribed/OLE items
- Text-wrapping breaks

Tables

Word processors have developed very capable table editors, letting you format tabular information quickly and easily, and often rivaling dedicated spreadsheet programs. InDesign can import tables created in Word or Excel, as well as tables in RTF documents.

 Chapter 21 covers tables in depth.

Headers and footers

Headers and footers are a layout issue, not a text issue, so there is no reason to include these elements in your word processor document. Because page numbers change based on your InDesign layout, there's no point in putting the headers and footers in your word-processor document anyway. Note that if you do use them, they do not import into InDesign.

CROSS-REF Chapter 5 explains how to add headers and footers to your layout.

Footnotes and endnotes

If you use a word processor's footnote or endnote feature and import the text file, InDesign correctly places footnotes at the bottom of the column and endnotes at the end of the imported text. The superscripted numerals or characters in the notes usually translate properly as well.

Hyperlinks

Modern word processors, such as Word, let you include hyperlinks in their text, so when you export to HTML or PDF formats, the reader can click the link and jump to a Web page or to another PDF or eBook file. When you import text files with such hyperlinks, InDesign retains their visual formatting — hyperlinks usually display as blue underlined text — as well as the actual link.

CROSS-REF InDesign retains hyperlinks for documents that are exported as PDF, eBook, Flash, or HTML files. Chapter 32 covers such documents in more detail.

Inline graphics and text boxes

Modern word processors typically support inline graphics, letting you import a graphic into your word processor document and embed it in text. Word, for example, lets you import graphics, and InDesign, in turn, can import the graphics with your text, as long as they are in formats supported by InDesign. But graphics embedded in your word processor document through Mac OS 9's Publish and Subscribe or through OLE (Object Linking and Embedding, available in both Windows and Mac OS) do not import into InDesign — both technologies are rare these days, so don't worry about them except for very old documents.

InDesign does import text boxes from a Word file (these are usually used for sidebars, captions, and pull-quotes) as separate text frames. If those Word text boxes are tied to a specific piece of text so that they flow with that text, InDesign honors those follow-me links and lets you adjust them.

CROSS-REF Chapter 13 covers follow-me links and related anchoring features in more detail.

Avoiding text-file pitfalls

Sometimes, issues not related to the contents of a word processor file can affect how files are imported into InDesign.

Fast save

Several programs (notably Microsoft Word) offer a fast-save feature, which adds information to the end of a word-processor document. The added information notes which text has been added and deleted and where the changes occurred. You can use this feature to save time because the program doesn't have to write the entire document to disk when you save the file. When you use the fast-save feature, however, text import into publishing programs — including InDesign — becomes problematic.

I suggest that you turn off fast save, at least for files you import into InDesign. With today's speedy hard drives, the time you gain by using fast save is barely noticeable anyway. The vast majority of file corruption problems and bugs in Word are related to the fast-save feature, and its use makes file recovery in the event of a crash problematic at best. To disable fast save in most versions of Word, choose Word ➪ Preferences on the Mac or Tools ➪ Options in Windows, go to the Save pane, and deselect the Allow Fast Saves option.

Software versions

Pay attention to the version number of the word processor you use. This caution may seem obvious, but the issue still trips up a lot of people. Usually, old versions (two or more revisions old) or new versions (newer than the publishing or other importing program) cause import problems. The import filters either no longer recognize the old format (something has to go to make room for new formats) or were written before the new version of the word processor was released. InDesign supports Microsoft Word for Windows versions 97, 2000, 2002/XP, 2003, and 2007, and Microsoft Word for Mac versions 98, 2001, X, 2004, and 2008, as well as the same-numbered versions of Excel.

Fixing Microsoft Word's Bad Dashes

Several versions of Word — including Word X for Mac and Word 97 and Word 2000 for Windows — have a default setting that converts two hyphens to an en dash (–) rather than an em dash (—), which is simply wrong typographically. (Word 98, 2004, and 2008 for Mac and Word 2002/XP and 2007 for Windows don't have this problem.)

To solve this problem, I recommend that you turn off Word's automatic conversion of two hyphens to a dash (choose Tools ➪ AutoCorrect ➪ AutoFormat as You Type and then deselect the Symbols option). Instead of using the incorrect automatic conversion, go to the AutoCorrect pane, type two hyphens in the Replace field, put an em dash (shortcut Option+Shift+– [hyphen] on the Mac or Alt+0151 in Windows) in the With field, and then click Add. This causes Word to substitute the correct dash when you type two consecutive hyphens.

Adding Text

No matter where your text originates — in your mind, in e-mail, on the Web, or in a word processor — you can add it to an InDesign publication easily. You can type text directly in InDesign, paste it, drag and drop it, or import it.

InDesign works with text inside *frames* — holders for the copy — that you can create in advance or let InDesign create for you when you import text. (Chapter 14 covers these frames in detail.)

　**If you click a frame that holds text or a graphic when importing text, the text replaces the existing text or graphic.**

　**All the text you import may not fit in the selected text frame. Chapter 14 explains how to make it flow to other text frames.**

Using the Type tool

First, you can't do anything with text without the Type tool. After you select the Type tool, as shown in Figure 13.1, you can click in an existing block of text or click and drag to create a new text frame. You can even click in any empty graphics frame or unassigned frame with the Type tool to convert it to a text frame.

You can't click in *master text frames* — text frames that are placed on the page by the master page in use — and simply start typing. To select a master text frame and add text to it, Shift+⌘+click or Ctrl+Shift+click it. (For more on master pages, see Chapter 6.)

NOTE　**What you can't do is simply click in your document and begin typing; any text must be in a frame. Fortunately, you can create that frame just by clicking and dragging with the Type tool.**

FIGURE 13.1

When the Type tool is selected, you can click in a text frame and start typing.

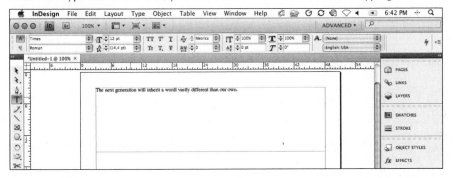

Keep Characters to a Minimum

If you're new to professional publishing, you have a few things to learn about the difference between typing on a typewriter or into a word processor and entering text for a high-end publication:

- Remember that you don't need to type two spaces after a period or colon (in either your word processor or InDesign). In fact, doing so causes awkward spacing and perhaps even text-flow issues.

- Don't enter extra paragraph returns for space between paragraphs, and don't enter tabs to indent paragraphs — you accomplish both more consistently with paragraph attributes (see Chapter 17).

- When you need to align text in columns, don't enter extra tabs; place one tab between each column and then align the tabs (see Chapter 21).

To see where you have tabs, paragraph breaks, spaces, and other such invisible characters, use the command Option+⌘+I or Ctrl+Alt+I, or choose Type ➪ Show Hidden Characters, or choose Hidden Characters from the View Options iconic pop-up menu in the new application bar. Chapter 15 shows the icons for each character.

From this point, start typing to enter text, or bring text in from other programs (as covered in the following sections). If you want to add placeholder text — random text that you might use to try out formatting on, for example — choose Type ➪ Fill with Placeholder Text. InDesign adds fake Latin text to the text frame until it is filled.

When you type new text, it takes on whatever style attributes are set for [Basic Paragraph Style], a predefined style in InDesign. You can modify this predefined style as you can any style you create.

CROSS-REF   **Chapter 19 covers styles in more detail.**

Pasting text

When text is on the Mac or Windows Clipboard and the Type tool is active in InDesign, you can paste the text at the location of the cursor (text-insertion pointer) or replace highlighted text with it. If no text frame is active, InDesign creates a new rectangular text frame to contain the pasted text.

InDesign uses standard menu commands and keyboard commands for cutting and copying text to the Clipboard and for pasting text. On the Mac, press ⌘+X to cut, ⌘+C to copy, and ⌘+V to paste. In Windows, press Ctrl+X to cut, Ctrl+C to copy, and Ctrl+V to paste.

By default, pasted text retains any formatting, such as boldface and font size, that it had in InDesign and in most other programs. (A few programs don't preserve that formatting when you paste text from them.) But InDesign lets you control whether pasted text retains its formatting as follows:

■ When pasting text from InDesign, you can strip out its formatting by choosing File⇨Paste without Formatting (or pressing Shift+⌘+V or Ctrl+Shift+V).

■ When pasting text from outside InDesign, you have the same Paste without Formatting option as when pasting text from InDesign and an option to always strip formatting automatically. To do enable this automatic formatting removal, go to the Clipboard Handling pane of the Preferences dialog box (choose InDesign⇨Preferences⇨Clipboard Handling or press ⌘+K on the Mac, or choose Edit⇨Preferences⇨Clipboard Handling or press Ctrl+K in Windows) and select the Text Only radio button for the Paste setting. Conversely, to ensure that formatting is retained in text copied from other applications, select the All Information (Index Marker, Swatches, Styles, Etc.) radio button.

Also, when you paste text, InDesign is smart enough to know to remove extra spaces or add them around the pasted text. You can disable this by deselecting the Adjust Spacing Automatically When Cutting and Pasting Words option in the Type pane of the Preferences dialog box.

Dragging and dropping text

You can also drag and drop text highlighted from text from another frame or document. If you press and hold Option or Alt while dragging, you drag a copy of the selected text rather than move the original text.

By default, InDesign allows drag and drop within the Story Editor. To enable drag and drop in your layout, go to the Type pane of the Preferences dialog box (choose InDesign⇨Preferences⇨Type or press ⌘+K on the Mac, or choose Edit⇨Preferences⇨Type or press Ctrl+K in Windows) and select the Enable in Layout View option. You can also drag and drop within the Story Editor by deselecting the Enable in Story Editor option.

CROSS-REF The Story Editor is covered in Chapter 15.

You can also drag text from external sources into InDesign:

■ You can drag the icon of a text file or a supported word processing file directly from the Windows Explorer (desktop or folder) or from the Mac Finder (desktop or folder) onto an InDesign page.

■ You can drag highlighted text from a document created with another program (Microsoft Word, for example) into an InDesign document window.

In both cases, a new text frame is created, and any styles in the source files are also brought into InDesign. Unlike importing a file through the Place command (covered later in this chapter), you have no control over how this formatting is imported; instead, all formatting is imported or none of it is, based on your InDesign preference settings.

NOTE You can drag in only files that are in one of the supported formats (Word, Excel, InCopy, RTF, and text-only).

As with copy and paste, InDesign lets you control whether formatting is retained in dragged text:

- When dragging text *within* InDesign, hold Shift to remove the text's formatting. The text will then take on the formatting of the text it is dragged in to.

- When dragging text from *outside* InDesign, use the Text Only option in the Clipboard Handling pane of the Preferences dialog box, as described in the previous section, to strip out formatting for all dragged text.

Importing text with the Place dialog box

The Place dialog box (choose File ➪ Place or press ⌘+D or Ctrl+D) gives you the most control over how text is imported. Figure 13.2 shows the dialog box.

FIGURE 13.2

The Place dialog box

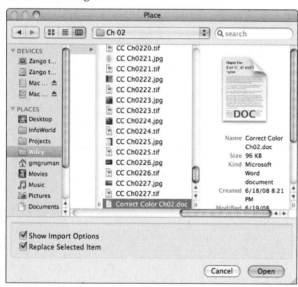

Text imported via the Place dialog box is placed according to your current selection:

- If the cursor (text-insertion pointer) is active within text in a text frame, the text is inserted at that location.

- If a text frame is selected but you have not clicked within the frame's text, the text is imported into the frame, replacing any existing text.

■ If two or more text frames are selected, a loaded-text icon appears. Chapter 14 explains the various forms this icon can take, but the basic form is of a paragraph icon with the first few words of the text displayed under it.

■ If no text frames are selected, a loaded-text icon lets you draw a rectangular text frame to contain the text, click in an existing empty frame, or click any empty area in your layout to create a text frame there with the text.

To place text:

1. **Choose File ➪ Place or press ⌘+D or Ctrl+D.**

2. **Locate the text file you want to import.**

3. **If you want to specify how to handle current formatting in the file, select the Place dialog box's Show Import Options option, shown in Figure 13.2, and click Open.** Doing so opens the appropriate Import Options dialog box for the text file's format. Then click OK to import the graphic. (I cover the Import Options dialog box a little later in this section.) If you don't select the Show Import Options option, clicking Open imports the graphic using default settings.

 If you prefer memorizing keyboard commands to selecting boxes, press Shift while you open the file to display the import options.

4. **If you had not selected a frame before starting the text import, specify where to place the text by clicking and dragging the loaded-text icon to create a rectangular text frame, clicking in an existing frame, or clicking in any empty frame.**

You can select multiple files — text and/or graphics — in the Place dialog box by Shift+clicking a range or by ⌘+clicking or Ctrl+clicking multiple files one by one. InDesign lets you place each file in a separate frame. Just click once for each file imported, or Shift+⌘+click or Ctrl+Shift+click to have InDesign place all files on the page in separate frames. If you place more than one file at the same time, the loaded-text icon displays the number of files to be placed, as well as a mini-preview of each file, as Figure 13.3 (in the upcoming subsection) shows.

 When you place multiple files at one time, you can place them in any order. Just move among them using the keyboard ← and → keys.

To cancel the entire text import, just select a different tool. To cancel a specific file in a multiple-file import, press Esc when that file's mini-preview is displayed. (The other files are still available to be placed.)

Import options for Microsoft Word and RTF files

InDesign offers a slew of options for controlling how Word and RTF files are imported through the Place dialog box. There are so many options that you can actually save your import preferences as a preset file for repeat use.

Figure 13.3 shows the Import Options dialog box for Microsoft Word. It has four groups of options. (The import options for RTF files are identical.)

FIGURE 13.3

The Microsoft Word Import Options dialog box

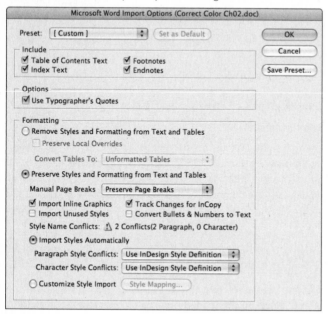

At the top of the pane is the Preset pop-up menu, which lets you select from saved sets of import options. If you change any options in this dialog box, the pop-up menu shows [Custom], so you know that any selected preset's settings have been altered for this specific file import. You can save settings by clicking Save Preset. And you can set a preset as the default import behavior by clicking Save as Default; these settings are used for all Word file imports unless you choose a new default or make changes in this dialog box. This feature lets you avoid using the Import Options dialog box for your routine imports.

The next section, Include, lets you strip out specific types of text from the Word file: Table of Contents Text, Index Text, Footnotes, and Endnotes. Any selected items are imported. It's common not to import table-of-contents or index text because you typically create your table of contents and indexes in InDesign.

The third section, Options, has just one option: Use Typographer's Quotes. If selected, it converts keyboard quotation marks (' and ") to the curly typographer quotation marks (', ', ", and "). Note that it will not convert two consecutive hyphens into an em dash, as some other programs do.

The fourth section, Formatting, is fairly complex.

To remove text formatting during import so that you have fresh text to which you can apply your InDesign styles, select the Remove Styles and Formatting option from Formatting section. Two additional controls become available if you select this option:

- **Preserve Local Overrides:** Selecting this option retains local formatting such as italic and boldface while ignoring the paragraph style attributes. You'd usually want this selected so that meaning-related formatting is retained.

- **Convert Tables To:** You can use this pop-up menu to choose how tables are unformatted during import. The Unformatted Tables menu item retains the table's cell structure but ignores text and cell formatting, whereas the Unformatted Tabbed Text menu item converts the table to tabbed text (with a tab separating what used to be cells and a paragraph return separating what used to be rows) and strips any formatting. If you intend to keep tables as tables but format them in InDesign, choose Unformatted Tables.

To retain text formatting during import so that the InDesign document at least starts out using the settings done in Word, select the Preserve Styles from Text and Tables option. There are two reasons to select this option. The most common reason is that you are using style sheets in Word with the same names as in InDesign. Doing so saves your designers from having to manually apply the correct styles when working on layouts. (The editors basically do it in Word when editing.) The other reason is that your Word file is really a rough template of your eventual InDesign file, so you want to keep all that Word effort and use it as the basis for refinement in InDesign.

The Preserver Styles from Text and Tables option has several controls:

- **Manual Page Breaks:** This pop-up menu lets you retain page breaks entered in Word, convert them to column breaks, or strip them out. The break option you choose depends on how your layout is structured compared to the Word file's layout.

- **Import Inline Graphics:** This option, if selected, imports graphics placed in the Word text. (Chapter 12 covers inline graphics in more detail.)

- **Import Unused Styles:** This option, if selected, loads all Word style sheets into InDesign, rather than just the ones you actually applied to text in the file. You normally would not want to import all of Word's styles because the program has dozens of predefined styles that could clog up your InDesign Paragraph Styles and Character Styles panels.

- **Track Changes:** This option, if selected, saves all changes tracked by Word and makes them available to InCopy users who work on the InDesign file (see Chapter 35). You cannot see these tracked changes within InDesign itself.

- **Convert Bullets & Numbers to Text:** This option, if selected, removes any automatic bullet and numbering lists in Word, converting the bullets and numbers into the actual characters. If you select this option and insert an item in an imported numbered list, the list doesn't renumber automatically, as it would if you leave this unselected. (In previous versions of InDesign, bullets and numbers were converted, eliminating the automatic aspect.)

- **Style Name Conflicts:** If InDesign detects that the Word file has styles with the same name as styles in your InDesign document, it notes how many duplicate style names it finds to the right of the Style Name Conflicts label. You then have two ways of handling these conflicts, with separate pop-up menus for paragraph styles and character styles:

  - If you select the Import Styles Automatically option, you get three options for both paragraph and character styles, using the two separate pop-up menus (Paragraph Style Conflicts and Character Style Conflicts). The Use InDesign Style Definition menu item preserves the current InDesign styles and applies them to any text in Word that uses a style sheet of the same name. This is the most common option because it lets your editors indicate what styles to use in InDesign but relies on InDesign's more precise typographic settings. If you choose the Redefine InDesign Style menu item, the Word style sheet's formatting permanently replaces that of InDesign's style. If you choose the Auto Rename menu item, the Word file's style sheet is renamed and added to the Paragraph Styles or Character Styles panel. This preserves your existing InDesign styles while also preserving the ones imported from the Word file.

  - If you select the Customize Style Import option, you can decide which specific InDesign styles override same-name Word styles, which Word styles override same-name InDesign styles, and which Word styles are renamed during import to prevent any overriding. Click Style Mapping to open the Style Mapping dialog box shown in Figure 13.4, where you make these decisions. You can also click Auto-rename Conflicts in that dialog box to rename all conflicting Word styles to new names. (Choosing this option is the same as choosing Auto Rename in the Import Styles Automatically pop-up menus.)

FIGURE 13.4

The Style Mapping dialog box

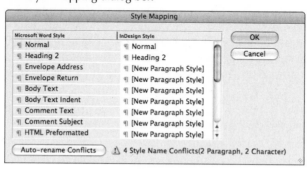

Exporting Text

Unfortunately, you can't export text from InDesign into the Word word processor format. You only options are RTF, InDesign Tagged Text, InCopy Document, InDesign Markup Language (IDML), and text-only formats. The best option is RTF if you want to send the file to someone using a word processor, and it's Tagged Text if you want to send it to another InDesign user with all InDesign settings retained.

After you click in a text frame with the Type tool, you export text by choosing File ⇨ Export, which provides a dialog box very much like the Save As dialog box. Here, you choose the file format, file-name, and file location. If you have selected a range of text in a text frame, only that text is exported; otherwise, the entire story is exported.

Be aware that if you export highly formatted InDesign files to RTF and then later reimport those RTF files into the same InDesign layout, you may get some odd effects, particularly around style names. That's because of how InDesign handles style names in groups versus how they are named during RTF export. The bottom line is that you may end up with several copies of the same style, perhaps with different settings, when you reimport that RTF file.

Note that you can export files to two InCopy formats: the new InCopy CS4 format (filename extension `.icml`), and the InCopy CS3 Interchange format (filename extension `.incx`) used in InCopy CS3.

Import options for text-only files

The options for text-only (ASCII) files are much simpler, as Figure 13.5 shows:

- **Character Set pop-up menu:** This menu lets you change the encoding type for the text file. The menu has 33 options, mainly for various languages and language groups such as Chinese, Central European, Turkish, Greek, Baltic, and Japanese. In most cases, you leave the menu at its default of Macintosh Roman (for North American Macs) or ANSI or one of the UTF formats (for North American PCs). Choose another option only if you know that the file is encoded in something else.

NEW FEATURE InDesign CS4 has added 15 options to the Character Set pop-up menu to expand the supported language encodings.

- **Platform pop-up menu:** This menu lets you choose between Macintosh and Windows. Choose whichever is appropriate for the source file. The biggest differences are in how paragraph returns are specified and in some supported special characters.

- **Set Dictionary To pop-up menu:** This menu lets you assign the default spelling and hyphenation dictionary language. Unless you're publishing in multiple languages or regions (such as in English for use in the U.K., Canada, and the United States), you can leave this at the default setting, which is based on the language you selected when you installed InDesign.

- **Extra Carriage Returns section:** In this section, you can control how carriage returns are handled. Select the Remove at End of Every Line option if the source file has a return at the end of each line (often the result of copying text from the Web or from a PDF file). Select the Remove Between Paragraphs option if the source file uses two hard returns to indicate new paragraphs. You can select neither, one, or both as appropriate to your source file.

- **Formatting section:** In this section, you can select the Replace option to have several consecutive spaces converted to a tab (you specify the minimum number of spaces in the field that follows). You can also select the Use Typographer's Quotes option to convert keyboard quotation marks (' and ") to the curly typographer quotation marks (', ', ", and "). This option is normally selected.

FIGURE 13.5

The Text Import Options dialog box for a text-only file

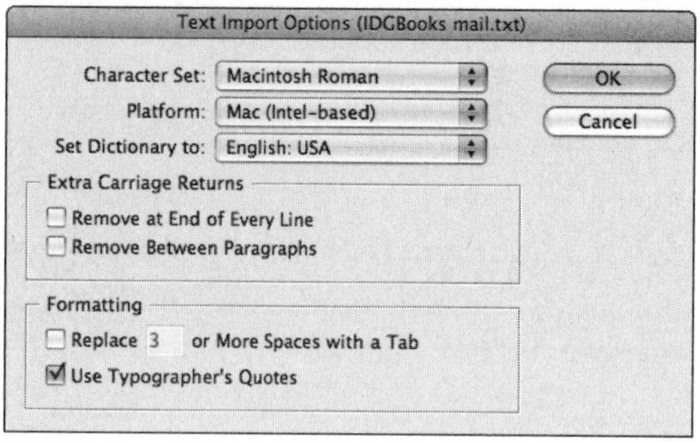

InCopy files

There are no options when importing InCopy files. Because they contain formatting applied as part of an InDesign layout, InDesign imports them as is.

Import options for Microsoft Excel files

When importing Excel spreadsheets, you have several options, as Figure 13.6 shows. In the Options section, you can control the following settings:

- **Sheet pop-up menu:** You can choose which sheet in an Excel workbook to import. The default is the first sheet, which is usually named Sheet1 unless you renamed it in Excel. (If you want to import several sheets, you need to import the same spreadsheet several times, choosing a different sheet each time.)

- **View pop-up menu:** You can import custom views you have defined in Excel for that spreadsheet. If the Excel document has custom views, you can ignore custom views by choosing [Ignore View] from the pop-up menu. If you have no custom views, this pop-up menu is grayed out.

- **Cell Range pop-up menu:** You can specify a range of cells using standard Excel notation *Sx:Ey*, where *S* is the first row, *x* the first column, *E* the last row, and *y* the last column, such as A1:G89. You can type a range directly in the pop-up menu, which also acts as a text-entry field, or you can choose a previously entered range from the pop-up menu.

- **Import Hidden Cells Not Saved in View:** By selecting this option, you import any hidden cells. Be careful when doing so because they're usually hidden for a reason (typically, they show noncritical data sources or interim calculations).

FIGURE 13.6

The Microsoft Excel Import Options dialog box

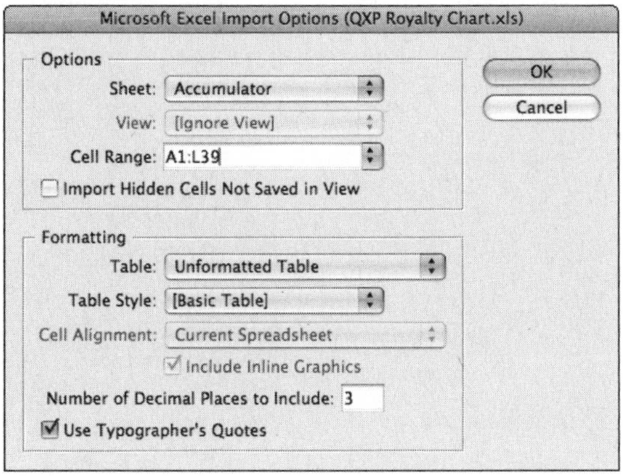

Microsoft Excel Import Options (QXP Royalty Chart.xls)

Options
Sheet: Accumulator
View: [Ignore View]
Cell Range: A1:L39
☐ Import Hidden Cells Not Saved in View

OK
Cancel

Formatting
Table: Unformatted Table
Table Style: [Basic Table]
Cell Alignment: Current Spreadsheet
☑ Include Inline Graphics
Number of Decimal Places to Include: 3
☑ Use Typographer's Quotes

In the Formatting section, you can control the following settings:

- **Table pop-up menu:** You choose the Formatted Table menu item, which imports the spreadsheet as a table and retains text and cell formatting; the Unformatted Table menu item, which imports the spreadsheet as a table but does not preserve formatting; or the Unformatted Tabbed Text menu item, which imports the spreadsheet as tabbed text (tabs separate cells and paragraphs separate rows) with no formatting retained.

- **Table Style pop-up menu:** Here, you can choose an InDesign table style to apply to the imported table, or leave it alone (by choosing [No Table Style]).

- **Cell Alignment pop-up menu:** You can tell InDesign how to align text within the cells. You can retain the spreadsheet's current alignments by choosing Current Spreadsheet or override them by choosing Left, Right, or Center.

- **Include Inline Graphics:** If selected, this option enables you to import any graphics placed in the Excel cells. (Chapter 13 covers inline graphics in more detail.)

- **Number of Decimal Places to Include:** In this field, type how many decimal places to retain for numbers. For example, if you type 4 in this field and have a cell that contains the value for π, InDesign imports the numeral 3.1415, even though the Excel spreadsheet displays 10 decimal places (3.1415926535). Note that InDesign does not import any formulas, just their numeric or textual results.

■ **Use Typographer's Quotes:** Select this option to convert keyboard quotation marks (' and ") to the curly typographer quotation marks (', ', ", and "). This option is normally selected.

Import options for Tagged Text files

InDesign offers a text-file format of its own: Adobe InDesign Tagged Text. Tagged Text actually is ASCII (text-only) text that contains embedded codes to tell InDesign which formatting to apply. You embed these codes, which are similar to macros, as you create files in your word processor.

CROSS-REF Chapter 4 explains how to export Tagged Text files. For a list of the Tagged Text codes themselves, check out the documentation that comes on the InDesign installation disc.

When importing Tagged Text files, you have a few options if you select the Show Import Options check box in the Place dialog box:

■ **Use Typographer's Quotes:** If selected, it converts keyboard quotation marks (' and ") to the curly typographer quotation marks (', ', ", and ").

■ **Remove Text Formatting:** If selected, all text formatting, including styles, is removed from the text.

■ **Resolve Style Conflicts Using:** With this pop-up menu, choose Publication Definition or Tagged Text Definition. The former applies the document's style formatting to any imported text that uses styles with the same names, overriding the formatting saved with the Tagged Text file; the latter applies the Tagged Text file's style definitions to any imported text that uses styles with the same names, overriding the formatting specified in the document.

■ **Show List of Problem Tags Before Place:** If selected, this option displays a dialog box listing any style sheets in the imported file whose names conflict with those in the document.

CROSS-REF See Chapter 22 for details on how to use the Tagged Text format to automate the creation of catalogs and other database-generated documents.

Summary

Because today's word processors are so powerful, people are tempted to do a lot of sophisticated, layout-oriented formatting in them before bringing the files into a layout program like InDesign. But don't. No word processor has the typographic or layout capability of InDesign, and doing a lot of work in your word processing file is simply a waste of time; you'd need to do it over again in InDesign in the context of your layout anyhow.

Focus on the meaning-oriented formatting in your word processor: use of style sheets to indicate headlines, bylines, quotation blocks, and so on, as well as local formatting such as italic, super-scripts, and font changes.

When you're done preparing your text, be sure to save it in a format compatible with InDesign. Even if your word processor format is not compatible with InDesign, chances are it can save in one that is.

InDesign provides a variety of methods for getting text into your documents, including importing files through the Place dialog box, dragging and dropping files generated in a word processor, and pasting text from other sources.

You can export text from InDesign for use in a word processor or another InDesign user. Your options are RTF, InDesign Tagged Text, InCopy, and text-only.

Chapter 14

Flowing Text through a Document

It doesn't take much experience with InDesign to discover that all your text doesn't fit into the finite space individual frames provide. Consider these scenarios:

- If you're laying out a newsletter, you might receive an article in the form of a Microsoft Word document that you need to flow into several columns across a spread.

- A magazine might have an article that starts on page 20 and then continues on page 198, with the text originating in Apple iWork Pages and saved as Rich Text Format (RTF) for import into InDesign.

- With catalogs, you might have a continuous file exported from a database that contains different product descriptions that are positioned below the items' pictures.

- In book publishing, each chapter may be imported as a separate word processing file and flowed continuously through many pages.

- The text of a simple advertisement, delivered by a client via e-mail, might flow through several text frames.

In all these cases, the benefits of frames — the ability to size, resize, reshape, and place them with precision — seem limiting. When the text doesn't fit in a frame, what are you supposed to do? Well, don't resort to cutting and pasting text into different frames. You need to keep the imported text together and link the frames that will contain the text. InDesign refers to the process of linking frames as *threading* and considers linked frames to be *threaded*. You can link frames on a single page, from one page to another no matter how many pages are in between, and automatically to quickly flow text while adding new pages with frames.

The text flowing through one or more threaded frames is considered a *story*. When you edit text in a story, the text reflows throughout the columns and threaded frames. You can also spell check and do search and replace for an entire story even though you have just one text frame active on-screen. Similarly, you can select all or some of the text in the story and change its formatting, copy it, or delete it.

CROSS-REF Chapter 8 explains how to create frames, and Chapter 13 describes what kind of text can be imported. Chapter 15 shows you how to select, spell check, and search and replace text. Chapters 16 through 19 explain how to format text.

Working with Text Frames

On a simple layout such as a business card or advertisement, you might simply create text frames as you need them. In a newsletter, you might drag text frames for an article in from a library. But with a book or even a text-heavy magazine, text frames are usually placed on master pages — a template for document pages — so they automatically appear on document pages. Many publications can combine master frames, individual frames, and threaded frames, as shown in Figure 14.1.

FIGURE 14.1

In this book spread, the how-to steps are in a master text frame, which is threaded to other master text frames as needed on subsequent pages. The folios at top are also defined on the master pages. The sidebar on the left page is placed in a text frame created on the document page.

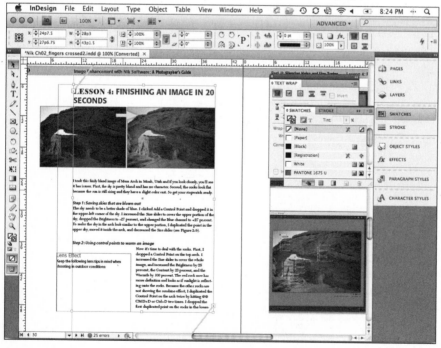

CROSS-REF For detailed information about using libraries and master pages, see Chapters 5 and 6.

Creating text frames on master pages

Master pages — predesigned pages that you can apply to other pages to automate layout and ensure consistency — can contain several types of text frames. You can have the following:

- Text frames containing standing text such as a magazine's folio.
- Text frames containing placeholder text for elements such as figure captions or headlines.
- An automatically placed text frame for flowing text throughout pages. The automatically placed text frame is called the *master text frame* and is created in the New Document dialog box (choose File ➪ New ➪ Document or press ⌘+N or Ctrl+N).

Creating a master text frame

A master text frame is an empty text frame on the default master page that lets you automatically flow text through a document. When you create a new document, you can create a master text frame, which fits within the margins and contains the number of columns you specify. Here's how it works:

1. **Choose File ➪ New ➪ Document or press ⌘+N or Ctrl+N.**
2. Select the Master Text Frame option at the top of the New Document dialog box, as shown in Figure 14.2.

FIGURE 14.2

Selecting the Master Text Frame option in the New Document dialog box places a text frame on the default master page within the margins you specify.

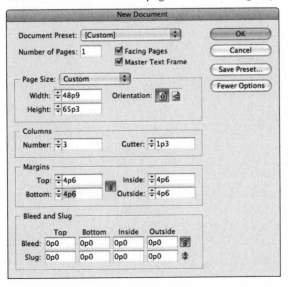

3. Use the Page Size area to set the size and orientation of the pages; select the Facing Pages option if your pages have a different inside and outside margin (as a book would).

4. Specify the size and placement of the master text frame by typing values in the Top, Bottom, Inside, and Outside fields (or the Left and Right fields if Facing Pages is deselected). InDesign places guides according to these values and places a text frame within the guides. The text frame fits within the boundaries of these values and the guides on the master page.

5. Type a value in the Number field in the Columns area to specify the number of columns in the master text frame. To specify the amount of space between the columns, type a value in the Gutter field. InDesign places guides on the page to indicate the columns.

6. Click OK to create a new document containing a master text frame.

After you create a document with a master text frame, you see guides on the first document page; these guides indicate the placement of the frame.

Modifying master text frames

Although you set up the master text frame in the New Document dialog box, you're not confined to those settings. As you design a publication, you may need to change the size, shape, and/or number of columns in the master text frame. To display the master page, choose Window ⇨ Pages or press ⌘+F12 or Ctrl+F12. In the Pages panel that appears, double-click the master page's icon. (That icon is usually in the upper portion of the panel; the default master page is called A-Master.)

CROSS-REF Chapter 5 covers the Pages panel in depth.

Use the Selection tool to click the master text frame within the guides and modify it using the following options:

■ The Control panel and Transform panel let you change the placement of a selected master text frame using the X and Y fields, the size using the W and H fields, the angle using the Rotation field, and the skew using the Shear X Angle field. You can also type values in the Scale fields to increase or decrease the width and height of the text frame by percentages. You can also use the mouse to resize and reposition the text frame.

■ The Text Frame Options dialog box (choose Object ⇨ Text Frame Options or press ⌘+B or Ctrl+B), shown in Figure 14.3, lets you change the number of columns and the space between them, specify how far text is inset from each side of the frame, specify how text aligns vertically within the frame, and specify the placement of the baseline grid. If you don't want text within this box to wrap around any items in front of it, select the Ignore Text Wrap option at the bottom of the dialog box.

- Paragraph styles, character styles, object styles, Story panel settings, and other text attributes are applied in the master text frame to the document text you flow into that frame. You can always override those attributes by applying other styles or formatting to the flowed text on your master text page.

- The Direct Selection tool lets you drag anchor points on the frame to change its shape.

FIGURE 14.3

To change the properties of a master text frame, select it on the master page and use the General pane of the Text Frame Options dialog box.

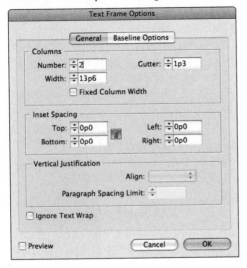

Drawing additional text frames

The master text frame is helpful for containing body text that flows through a document. You're likely to need plenty of other text frames on both master pages and document pages. Generally, these are smaller text frames intended to hold headlines, captions, or short paragraphs of descriptive copy.

Creating text frames on master pages

If you intend to add text frames to a master page for repeating elements such as headers and footers, you need to display the master page. Choose Window ➪ Pages or press ⌘+F12 or Ctrl+F12 to display the Pages panel. Then double-click the desired master page's icon. Any text frames you add to master pages appear on document pages based on that master page. To switch back to the document and view the text frames, double-click a page icon in the upper portion of the Pages panel.

Text Frame Anatomy

Before you start threading text frames, you need to understand what a text frame is trying to tell you about its text. To get the message, you need to select the text frames with one of the selection tools; when the Type tool is selected, all you can see is overset text. The text frame provides the following indicators, as shown in the figure:

- **In port (empty):** A small white square on the upper-left corner of a text frame is the in port, indicating where a story enters the frame.

- **In port (with arrow):** Within a chain of threaded text frames, the in port might contain a right-facing arrow indicating that the story is continuing into this frame from elsewhere.

- **Out port (empty):** A small white square on the lower-right corner of a text frame is the out port, indicating that the story fits comfortably within the frame.

- **Out port (with arrow):** Within a chain of threaded text frames, the out port might contain a right-facing arrow indicating that the story is continuing into another frame.

- **Out port (with plus sign):** A small red plus sign in the out port indicates that more of the story exists than can fit in the text frame and that there is no subsequent text frame for the text to flow into.

- **Threads:** When you choose View ⇨ Show Text Threads (or press Option+⌘+Y or Ctrl+Alt+Y), you can view threads, or lines, indicating the direction in which frames are threaded. (To see multiple text chains, Shift+click to select text frames from different threads.)

In the figure, the top text frame's in port (at the upper-right corner of the frame) is empty, indicating that the text starts in this frame rather than flows from another frame. An arrow icon in its out port (at the lower left of the frame) shows that the text flows elsewhere, and the thread from its out port shows that it flows to the frame below. That lower frame's in port shows an arrow icon, indicating that text is flowing to it. The out port of the lower frame shows the overset text icon (the red + symbol), indicating that all the text doesn't fit.

This spacious two-level condo, built in 1908 and extensively updated over the years, features 4 bedrooms and 2¼ bathrooms, with two bedrooms and one bathroom on each floor and an additional quarter bath on the main level.

Among the amenities in this light-filled home are:

- Flexible layout offers dining room or study off kitchen, plus living room with adjacent den or dining room as well as parlor/bedroom in front.
- Fireplace in living room.
- Close to Golden Gate Park.
- Hardwood floors throughout both levels.
- Period detail throughout.
- Modern amenities, including phone, Internet, and grounded electrical outlets.
- Open kitchen with plenty of storage, plumbed for gas.
- Kitchen appliances and in-unit washer and dryer are included.
- Recent remodeling of front exterior façade.
- Unit has deeded parking for two cars in shared garage, plus shared storage space.

- HOA dues of $220/mo.
- Shared backyard features brick patio, lush garden, and patio heater.
- Pets allowed (with size and number restrictions).
- Clean ($0) Markoff pest report provided by seller.
- Title records show living space of 1,818 square feet.
- Attic bedrooms and bath added by previous owner are unwarranted.

Offers as they come; no offers will be reviewed before April 28, 2007, at 5 p.m. E-mail agent for disclosure package. Include preapproval letter and disclosure acknowledgment with offers.

Showing Schedule	
Sun. 4/15, 4/22	2p-5p
Tue. 4/10, 4/17, 4/24	11:30a-1p
Thu. 4/19 *(by appt. only)*	6p-7p

Creating rectangular and variable-shaped text frames

To create rectangular text frames on document pages or master pages, select the Type tool. Click and drag to create text frames, and use the Control panel or Transform panel to fine-tune the placement and dimensions.

For variable-shaped text frames such as circles or Bézier shapes, use the Pen tool, Pencil tool, Ellipse tool, or Polygon tool to create an empty frame. Then convert the frame to a text frame by clicking it with the Type tool or a loaded text icon, or by choosing Object ⇨ Content ⇨ Text. (You get the loaded-text icon when you place a text file or when you flow text from an existing frame, which I describe later in this chapter.)

TIP If you're working on a document page and want to type in a text frame placed on the page by a master page, select the Type tool and Shift+⌘+click or Ctrl+Shift+click the frame.

CROSS-REF You can also edit an existing rectangular text frame with the Direct Selection tool as if it were a free-form shape, as described in Chapter 27.

Threading Text Frames

InDesign provides four options for *threading* (or linking) text frames: manual, semiautoflow, autoflow, and array. Each has its own icon, as shown later. The method you choose depends on how much text you're dealing with and the size and quantity of your text frames:

- You might use the manual method, in which you click the first text frame's out port and then the second text frame to link two text frames across several pages for an article continuation.

- The semiautoflow method lets you click a series of text frames to flow text. It works well for linking a succession of text frames in something such as a catalog layout.

- The autoflow method adds text frames and pages as you import text and is intended for flowing long text files such as a book chapter or annual report. A variation of it doesn't add new pages.

Here is what the various loaded-text icons mean:

- To flow a newly placed file into a text frame, or to link a text frames with text to another text frame, you might also use the manual method. For new text, just click in the frame you want to flow the text into. To flow to other frames, click the first text frame's out port and then click on the second text frame.

- To link two empty text frames across several pages (for example, for an article that starts on page 2 and continues on page 24) — for frames where you will *later* want to text to flow across — you might use the manual method, in which you click the first text frame's out port and then click the second text frame.

■ To link a succession of text frames, you might want to use the semiautoflow method, which allows you to click a series of text frames to flow text from one frame to the next. Hold the Option or Alt key when clicking the mouse during text placement. Remember that, as you're threading frames, Option+click or Alt+click each text frame, or you'll revert to manual threading.

■ To import text that is intended for long documents (such as a book chapter or brochure), you might want to use the autoflow method to add text frames and pages that accommodate the text you're importing. Hold the Shift key when clicking the mouse during text placement to fill all open master frames and create new ones as needed. Be sure to Shift+click near the upper-left corner of the master text frame so that InDesign uses that frame rather than creates a new one. Note that even if you've already placed a text file into a single text frame or a threaded chain of text frames, you can still autoflow text from the last text frame. To do this, click the out port and then Shift+click any page to indicate where to start the autoflow.

■ The second version of autoflow won't create new pages for the text being flowed; only open pages are used. Hold Option+Shift or Alt+Shift to use this option.

■ If you have selected multiple files for placement, you can hold Shift+⌘ or Ctrl+Shift when dragging the mouse in your document to place an array of the files, each in its own frame within the area defined when dragging the mouse. This new feature lets you place multiple text frames in a grid — such as for bios or other snippet-size text. InDesign CS4 will create as many frames as it can fit in that grid, placing the files into them. Any files not placed remain in the loaded-text icon for placement elsewhere. You can increase or reduce the number of rows in the grid by pressing ↑ or ↓ respectively. Likewise, you can increase or reduce the number of columns in the grid by pressing →or ← respectively.

NEW FEATURE The array placement option is new to InDesign CS4.

Also, InDesign CS4 now honors any Microsoft Word style settings and page break settings that assign text to flow to a right-hand page or left-hand page (which are called odd and even pages in both programs). So if you use those settings in Word, InDesign will retain and apply them as well.

Threading frames manually

To thread text frames manually, you simply use a selection tool to link out ports to in ports. You can prethread existing text frames by linking empty text frames and add text later, or you can create threads from a text frame that contains text.

TIP Linking manually from out port to in port works well for continuing a magazine article from one page to the next.

 Oddly, you cannot thread frames while the Type tool is selected, so remember to switch to a selection tool.

To thread text frames:

1. **Create a series of frames or shapes through which you intend to flow text.** (Any empty nontext frames are converted to text frames as soon as you thread to them from a text frame. Thus, at least the first frame in this chain must be a text frame.) The frames do not need to be on the same page.

2. **Click any of the selection tools.**

3. **Click the out port of the first text frame in the thread.** The pointer becomes the loaded-text icon.

4. **Click the in port of the second text frame in the thread.** You can also click any empty frame or click and drag to draw a new text frame. How text flow behaves depends on the text frame's status:

   ▨ If the first frame holds no text, when text is later placed or typed into it, any text that does not fit that first text frame flows into the second frame.

   ▨ If the first frame holds text but is not already linked to another text frame, any overset text flows into the text frame you just selected.

   ▨ If the first text frame is already linked to another text frame, the text is now redirected to the text frame you just selected.

5. **Use the Pages panel to add or switch pages as necessary while you continue clicking out ports and in ports until your chain of threaded text frames is complete.** You can also switch pages using the page controls at the bottom left of the document window. You do so by choosing Layout ➪ Go to Page or pressing ⌘+J or Ctrl+J, as explained in Chapter 5.

6. **When you finish threading text frames, select another object on the page or another tool.** When you import a story into any text frame in this chain, it starts in the upper-right corner of the first frame and flows through the frames in the same order as the threads.

 To see text threads easily while threading across pages, change the document view to 20 percent or so.

 Text flows in the order in which you select frames. If you move a frame, its order in the text flow remains unchanged, so if you're not careful, you could, for example, accidentally have text flow from a frame at the top of the page to one at the bottom of a page, and then to one in the middle of a page.

Threading frames semiautomatically

InDesign's semiautoflow method of threading text frames varies only slightly from the manual method. Follow the same steps as those for threading text frames manually, except press and hold Option or Alt each time you click in the next text frame. This lets you bypass the in ports and out ports and simply click from text frame to text frame to establish links. Note that if a text frame contains overset text, the overset text flows through the additional frames as you create the thread.

 Remember to Option+click or Alt+click each text frame, or you revert to manual threading.

 When you're first placing a word processing file, you can also Option+click or Alt+click in the first text frame to begin a semiautoflow process.

Threading frames and adding pages automatically

The autoflow method for threading frames is what lets you flow a lengthy story quickly through a document. You can either autoflow text into the master text frame or into automatically created text frames that fit within the column guides. InDesign flows the text into any existing pages and then adds new pages based on the current master page. You can initiate autoflow before or after placing a word processing file.

Placing text while autoflowing

If you haven't imported text yet, you can place a file and have it automatically flow through the document. This method works well for flowing text into pages that are all formatted the same way, such as a book. Here's how it works:

1. Confirm that the master page in use has a master text frame or appropriate column guides.

2. With no text frames selected, choose File ⇨ Place or press ⌘+D or Ctrl+D.

3. Locate and select the word-processing files you want to be placed in the same story and then click Open.

4. When the loaded-text icon appears, Shift+click in the first column that contains the text. Be sure to Shift+click within a few pixels of the upper-left corner of that column so that InDesign knows you want to place text in it; otherwise, InDesign will create a new text frame and place the text there instead of in your desired column. InDesign adds all the necessary text frames and pages, and flows in the entire story.

 To have InDesign flow text only into existing (blank) pages, hold Option+Shift or Alt+Shift instead of just Shift when clicking in the frame.

Autoflowing after placing text

If you've already placed a text file into a single text frame or even a threaded chain of text frames, you can still autoflow text from the last text frame. To do this, click the overset icon in the out port and then Shift+click on any page to indicate where to start the autoflow.

TIP You might use the autoflow-after-placing-text method if you're placing the introduction to an article in a highly designed opener page and then flowing the rest of the article into standard pages.

Using Smart Text Reflow options

InDesign CS4 offers a set of controls for what it calls *smart text reflow,* which lets you tell InDesign when to add and delete pages as you add and delete text. InDesign will add pages when your text won't fit in the current number of pages, and delete pages when empty ones result from your deleting text. Note that smart text reflow works with text you place, paste, or type in InDesign. You set these controls in the Type pane of the Preferences dialog box, in the Smart Text Reflow section.

NEW FEATURE The smart text reflow feature is new to InDesign CS4.

To turn on this feature, select the Smart Text Reflow option in the Type pane. Use the Add Pages To pop-up menu to tell InDesign where to add new pages: End of Story, End of Section, or End of Document. You have three additional controls available when smart text reflow is turned on:

- **Limit to Master Text Frames:** If selected, this option will add or delete pages only for text flowing through master text frames (covered in the "Creating text frames on master pages" section, earlier in this chapter).

- **Preserve Facing-Pages Spreads:** If selected, InDesign will not delete individual or add pages within existing spreads. That way, right-hand pages won't become left-hand pages and vice versa as pages are added and deleted.

- **Delete Empty Pages:** If selected, InDesign will delete pages when there is no longer any text on them. Note that it will not delete pages if they have other objects on them, except for objects created as part of master pages (see Chapter 6). Note that InDesign will *not* delete any pages that have master page objects that you later modified on the document page.

The smart text reflow feature can be a bit tricky to use. If you have a master text frame in your document, InDesign will automatically add pages (and delete them, if you selected the Delete Empty Pages option) — but only if you are working with text in a master text frame.

If you are working in a text frame other than the master text frame (or don't have a master text frame), InDesign may not automatically add pages for you. That's because InDesign will add pages only if the text frame you are adding text to is threaded to another text frame on another spread *and* if Limit to Master Text Frames is deselected in the Type pane of the Preferences dialog box.

Forcing Column and Other Breaks

Most of the time, you want text to flow naturally from column to column and page to page, but sometimes, you want to take over the flow and dictate exactly when text starts on a new column or page. InDesign provides several ways to do so:

- Choose one of the break options by choosing Type ⇨ Insert Break Character and then selecting the desired option from the submenu. The choices are Column Break (which makes the text start at the top of the next column), Frame Break (which starts the text at the top of the next frame in the story chain), Page Break (which starts the text at the next page containing a text frame in the story chain), Odd Page Break (which starts the next in the next odd-numbered page in the story chain), and Even Page Break.

- Use one of the keyboard shortcuts: keypad Enter for column break, Shift+keypad Enter for frame break, or ⌘+keypad Enter or Ctrl+keypad Enter for page break.

- Specify a break at the current text location using the Keep Options dialog box's Start Paragraph pop-up menu: In Next Column, In Next Frame, On Next Page, On Next Odd Page, or On Next Even Page. You can access the Keep Options dialog box by pressing Option+⌘+K or Ctrl+Alt+K, choosing Keep Options from the flyout menu of the Control panel's Paragraph (¶) pane, or choosing Keep Options from the flyout menu of the Paragraph panel (choose Type ⇨ Paragraph or press Option+⌘+T or Ctrl+Alt+T).

- Specify a break as part of the paragraph style, using the options in the Start Paragraph pop-up menu in the Keep Options pane of the New Paragraph Styles or Paragraph Style Options dialog box.

Note that if you apply a column break within a single-column text frame, InDesign considers the next frame in the story chain to be the next column. Likewise, if you apply a frame break within the sole text frame on a page, InDesign considers the next page that contains a frame in the story chain to be the next frame.

Breaking and rerouting threads

After text frames are threaded, you have three options for changing the threads: You can break threads to stop text from flowing, insert a text frame into an existing chain of threaded text frames, and remove text frames from a thread.

- To break the link between two text frames, double-click either an out port or an in port. The thread between the two text frames is removed and all text that had flowed from that point is sucked out of the subsequent text frames and stored as overset text.

- To insert a text frame after a specific text frame in a chain, click its out port. Then click and drag the loaded text icon to create a new text frame. That new frame is automatically threaded to the previous and next text frame.

■ To reroute text threads — for example, to drop the middle text frame from a chain of three — click the text frame with the Selection tool and press Delete or Backspace. The text frame is deleted and the threads are rerouted. You can Shift+click to multiple-select text frames to remove as well. Note that you cannot reroute text threads without removing the text frames.

Adjusting Columns

The placement of columns on the page and the amount of space between them has significant impact on readability. Column width, in general, works with type size and leading to create lines and rows of text that you can read easily. This means that you're not getting lost from one line to the next, accidentally jumping across columns, and getting a headache while squinting at the page.

> **TIP** **As a rule of thumb: As columns get wider, the type size and leading increase. For example, you might see 9-point text and 15-point leading in 2½-inch columns, whereas 15-point text and 13-point leading might work better in 3½-inch columns.**

InDesign lets you place columns on the page automatically, create any number of columns within a text frame, and change columns at any time.

Specifying columns in master frames

If you choose to create a *master text frame* — an automatically placed text frame within the margin guides — when you create a new document, you can specify the number of columns in it at the same time.

In the Columns area in the New Document dialog box shown previously in Figure 14.2, use the Number field to specify how many columns you need and the Gutter field to specify how much space to place between them. Whether or not you select the Master Text Frame option (which makes the frame appear on all pages), guides for these columns are still placed on the page and can be used for placing text frames and other objects.

Adjusting columns in text frames

After you create a text frame and flow text into it, you can still change the number of columns in it. First, select the text frame with a selection tool or the Type tool (or Shift+click to select multiple text frames and change all their columns simultaneously). Then choose Object ➪ Text Frame Options or press ⌘+B or Ctrl+B. You can also use the Control panel to quickly change the number of columns by entering a value in the Columns field when you've selected a text frame.

TIP   Although programs such as InDesign have long offered multiple-column text frames, many designers still draw each column as a separate frame. Don't do that! Creating individual frames for each column makes it all too easy to have columns of slightly different widths and slightly different positions, so you can wind up with text that doesn't align properly. Plus, if you use the Text Frame Options feature to create columns, you can easily change the number of columns; there's no need to resize existing text frames or relink them.

CROSS-REF   Chapter 15 covers other functions in the Text Frame Options dialog box.

Note that the options in the Columns area work differently depending on whether Fixed Column Width is selected or deselected:

- If it is not selected, InDesign subtracts from the text frame's width the space specified for the gutters. The program then divides the remaining width by the number of columns to figure out how wide the columns can be. For example, a 10-inch-wide text frame with three columns and a gutter of $1/2$ inch ends up with three 3-inch columns and two $1/2$-inch gutters. The math is $(10 - (2 \times 0.5)) \div 3$.

- If it is selected, InDesign resizes the text frame to fit the number of columns you selected at the indicated size, as well as the gutters between them. For example, if in a 10-inch-wide text frame you specify a column width of 5 inches and a gutter of $1/2$ inch, and you choose three columns, you end up with a 15-inch-wide text frame containing three 5-inch columns and two $1/2$-inch gutters. The math is $(5 \times 3) + (2 \times 2)$.

Select the Preview option to see the effects of your changes before finalizing them.

TIP   You can also use the Columns field in the Control panel to change the number of columns but not set any other options such as gutter size. The Columns field displays only if you have selected a frame with the Type tool and have the Control panel set to Paragraph view (the ¶ icon is selected).

Placing rules between columns

The use of vertical rules (thin lines) between columns — called *intercolumn rules* — is an effective way to separate columns with small gutters. This is often done in newspapers, in which columns and gutters are usually thin. It can also add visual interest and a sense of old-fashioned authority; it was a common technique for newspapers a century ago and is still used by the august *Wall Street Journal*, for example.

Unfortunately, InDesign does not provide an automatic method for creating intercolumn rules. To get around this lack, you need to draw lines on the page — in the center of the gutters — with the Line tool. Because you might resize text frames or change the number of columns while designing a document, you should add the vertical rules at the end of the process. In a document with a standard layout, such as a newspaper or magazine, you can place the rules between columns in text frames on the master page so that they're automatically placed on every page. As always with such objects, you can modify them on individual document pages as needed (just be sure to Shift+⌘+ click or Ctrl+Shift+click to select them when working in your document pages).

When drawing rules between columns, use the rulers to precisely position the lines. After you've drawn the lines, Shift+click to select all the lines and the text frames, and then choose Object ⇨ Group or press ⌘+G or Ctrl+G. When the lines are grouped to the text frame, you can move them all as a unit. Doing so also prevents someone from accidentally moving a vertical rule later.

> **TIP** Keep the width of intercolumn rules thin: usually a hairline (¼ point) or ½ point. Larger than that is usually too thick and can be confused with the border of a sidebar or other boxed element.

Managing Spacing and Alignment within Text Frames

The Text Frame Options dialog box lets you control several other key aspects of text placement within a frame, not just the number and size of columns. Two of these controls — both of which are in the General pane — affect the placement of text relative to the frame itself:

- The Inset Spacing options let you bring text in from the frame boundary. Rectangular frames have four options: Top, Bottom, Left, and Right. Other frames just have one option that applies to the entire frame: Inset. You typically use Inset Spacing when you have a stroke around or a background behind the text frame, so the text does not print at the very edge of the frame.

> **TIP** Use the Make All Settings the Same iconic button (the chain icon) in the area that contains the Inset Spacing fields in the Text Frames Options dialog box's General pane to make adjusting common offset values easier. If the chain is unbroken, changing any offset automatically changes the other offsets to the same value. If the chain is broken, you can adjust each offset independently of one another. Click the button to toggle between the two modes.

- The Vertical Justification section lets you specify how text aligns vertically within the frame, but only if the frame is rectangular. Use the Align pop-up menu to choose the desired alignment: Top, Center, Bottom, or Justify. If you choose Justify, InDesign spreads the text out so that it fills the frame from top to bottom, adding space between lines and paragraphs as needed to do so. You can control the maximum amount of space allowed between paragraphs by entering a value in the Paragraph Spacing Limit field, but note that doing so could result in InDesign's adding more space between lines than between paragraphs if that's what it takes to fill the frame.

> **CROSS-REF** For more details on the baseline grids options in the Text Frame Options, see Chapter 9. I cover the column settings in the previous section in this chapter. Chapter 15 covers the rest of the features of this dialog box.

Working with Overset Text

Even as you add text frames and pages, you can have more text than your layout has room for. Called *overset text*, this excess text doesn't appear anywhere in your layout. So how do you find overset text?

InDesign provides two ways:

- Look at the out port of the last text frame in a story chain. If it is a red cross, that means there is more text in the story that isn't placed in the layout. (If the out port is an empty black square, no unplaced text remains.)

- Open each story in the Story Editor and look at the ruler along the left side of the text, just to the right of the list of currently applied paragraph styles. Overset text is indicated by the *Overset* indicator and is furthermore noted with a red line to the right of the text. (Chapter 15 explains how to use the Story Editor.)

After you've identified your overset text, you then can edit the text to fit the space you do have; use tracking controls to tighten the spacing for a line here and there to get rid of widows that take up excess space; reformat text to fit the space you do have; add more space, such as through creating additional pages; or rebalance the space available by making some stories longer and others shorter. You can often use a combination of these techniques, in a process called *copyfitting*.

Summary

When text doesn't fit within a single text frame — as is the case in almost any multipage publication — you need to link (or *thread*) the text frames. You can do this manually, threading one text frame to the next, or you can have InDesign automatically add pages containing threaded text frames. After frames are threaded, you can still reflow text by breaking text threads and rerouting the threads.

In addition to flowing text through the threaded frames, you can flow it through multiple columns within each frame. You can change the number of columns or their widths within a frame at any time. To distinguish columns more visually, you can draw vertical lines between columns and group them with the text frames.

To control when text starts at the top of a column, frame, or page, InDesign offers both local and style-based options to force breaks.

When your story has more text than you have room for in your layout — something you can identify by looking at a story's last text frame's out port or by using the Story Editor — you need to use a combination of editing, formatting, and layout techniques to make everything fit.

Chapter 15

Editing and Formatting Text

Most users do the bulk of their writing and editing in a word processor before bringing the files into InDesign for layout.

But that doesn't mean you shouldn't perform word processor functions in InDesign. It makes a lot of sense to write captions, headlines, and other elements that need to fit a restricted area, as well as to take care of copy editing and minor revisions. InDesign lets you do such writing and editing in the actual layout, or in a built-in text editor that mimics the Mac's TextEdit or Windows' WordPad, except it does layout-specific things for you as well, such as tracking line counts.

Either way, you'll extensively use InDesign's editing, search-and-replace functions, and spell checker to refine your content.

Editing Text

When working in a layout, InDesign gives you the basic editing capabilities found in a word processor: cutting and pasting, and deleting and inserting text. These capabilities work very much like other text editors and word processors, so you should be able to use the techniques you already know to edit text within InDesign.

Controlling text view

But before you begin to edit text, you need to see it. In many layout views, the text is too small to work with. Generally, you zoom in around the block of text using the Zoom tool. For quick access to the tool, press Z. (Except

IN THIS CHAPTER

Editing text, including highlighting, cutting and pasting, and deleting

Using the Story Editor

Correcting mistakes as you type

Checking spelling as you type or all at one time

Customizing the spelling and hyphenation dictionaries

Searching and replacing words and formats

Adjusting text appearance within text frames

Placing notes in text

when the cursor is in a block of text! In that case, you need to click the Zoom tool.) Then click to zoom in. To zoom out, press and hold Option or Alt when clicking.

Another way to zoom in is to use the keyboard shortcut ⌘+= or Ctrl+=. Each time you use it, the magnification increases. Zoom out by pressing ⌘+– [hyphen] or Ctrl+– [hyphen].

It's best to use the ⌘+= or Ctrl+= method when your text cursor (text-insertion pointer) is already on or near the text you want to zoom into; the cursor location is the center point for the zoom. Use the Zoom tool when your pointer is not near the text you want to magnify and then move the Zoom pointer to the area you want to magnify and click once for each level of desired magnification.

TIP   It helps to memorize the zoom-in shortcut by thinking of it as ⌘++ (plus) or Ctrl++ (plus), but if you do, remember that you don't actually press the Shift key, which technically is what you would need to do to get a plus sign.

In addition to seeing the text at a larger size, it also helps you see the spaces, tabs, and paragraph returns that exist in the text. Choose Type ➪ Show Hidden Characters, choose Hidden Characters from the View Options iconic pop-up menu in the application bar, or press Option+⌘+I or Ctrl+Alt+I (refer to Figure 15.1).

FIGURE 15.1

To help you see spaces, breaks, and other control characters, special symbols can display on-screen (they do not print). Top row, from left to right: regular space, nonbreaking space, fixed-width nonbreaking space, em space, en space, thin space, hair space, punctuation space, quarter space, third space, figure space, and flush space. Second row: tab and right tab. Third row: discretionary hyphen and nonbreaking hyphen. Fourth row: forced line break (new line), discretionary line break, paragraph return, column break, frame break, page break, even page break, and odd page break. Fifth row: note, indent to here, end nested style here, non-joiner, and end-of-story marker.

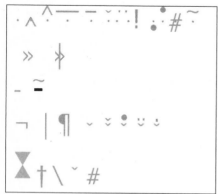

Navigating text

To work at a different text location, click in a different text frame or another location in the current text frame. You can also use the four arrow (cursor) keys on the keyboard to move one character to the right, one character to the left, one line up, or one line down. Add ⌘ or Ctrl to the arrow keys to jump one word to the right or left, or one paragraph up or down. The Home and End keys let you jump to the beginning or end of a line; add ⌘ or Ctrl to jump to the beginning or end of a story. (A *story* is text within a text frame or that is linked across several text frames, as described in Chapter 14.) Note that if your story begins or ends in a text frame on another page, InDesign brings you to that page.

Highlighting text

To highlight text, you can always use the old click-and-drag method. Or, you can add the Shift key to the navigation commands in the previous section. For example, while ⌘+→ or Ctrl+→ moves the cursor one word to the right, Shift+⌘+→ or Ctrl+Shift+→ highlights the next word to the right. Likewise, Shift+⌘+End or Ctrl+Shift+End highlights all the text to the end of the story.

For precise text selections, double-click to select a word and its trailing space (punctuation is not selected) and triple-click to select a paragraph. If you need the punctuation trailing a word, double-click and then press Shift+⌘+→ or Ctrl+Shift+→ to extend the selection. To select an entire story, choose Edit ⇨ Select All or press ⌘+A or Ctrl+A.

To deselect text, choose Edit ⇨ Deselect All, or press Shift+⌘+A or Ctrl+Shift+A. More simply, you can select another tool or click another area of the page.

Cutting, copying, and pasting text

After you've highlighted text, you can press ⌘+X or Ctrl+X to remove it from its story and place it on the Clipboard for later use. Use ⌘+C or Ctrl+C to leave the text in the story and place a copy on the Clipboard. Click anywhere else in text — within the same story, another story, or another document — and press ⌘+V or Ctrl+V. If you're menu driven, the Edit menu provides the equivalent Cut, Copy, and Paste commands as well.

The Paste without Formatting command (choose Edit ⇨ Paste without Formatting or press Shift+⌘+V or Ctrl+Shift+V) is handy when you have formatted text from another document or application that you want in your InDesign document without all that formatting applied. What you'll get is the raw text pasted in, with the current InDesign paragraph or character style applied to it — with "current" meaning whatever style is applied where you insert the text.

Deleting and replacing text

To remove text from a document, you can highlight it and choose Edit ⇨ Clear or press Delete or Backspace. Or you can simply type over the highlighted text or paste new text on top of it.

If text is not highlighted, you can delete text to the right or left of the cursor. On the Mac, press Delete to delete to the left and press Del (labeled Clear on some 1990s-era Mac keyboards and labeled Delete→ on Apple keyboards beginning in mid-2008) to delete to the right. In Windows, press Backspace to delete to the left and Delete to delete to the right.

> **TIP** If you double-click a text frame with any tool other than a drawing or frame tool, InDesign automatically switches to the Type tool and places the insertion point where you double-clicked. (This also works for text paths and table cells.) You can switch back to a selection tool by pressing Esc.

Undoing text edits

Remember to take advantage of InDesign's multiple undos while editing text. Choose Edit ➪ Undo and Edit ➪ Redo any time you change your mind about edits. The Undo and Redo keyboard commands are definitely worth remembering: ⌘+Z and Shift+⌘+Z or Ctrl+Z and Ctrl+Shift+Z.

Using the Story Editor

Editing in a layout can be difficult, such as having to scroll and up and down through multiple columns or change zoom levels based on the current text size. To let you get around that problem, InDesign offers the Story Editor. This window, shown in Figure 15.2, lets you edit text without the distractions of your layout. It presents your text without line breaks or other nonessential formatting. You just see attributes such as boldface and italics and, in a separate pane to the left, the names of the styles that have been applied.

After clicking in a text frame, you open the Story Editor by choosing Edit ➪ Edit in Story Editor or by pressing ⌘+Y or Ctrl+Y. The Story Editor will display all text in that story (all the frames that threaded to the one you selected).

> **TIP** In InDesign CS4, the Story Editor can appear in its own tab, making it easy to switch between the Story Editor and your layout views — just click the desired tab. (Chapter 2 explains the new tabs display for the document window.) Just drag the default, free-floating Story Editor window into the tabs at the top of the document window, and InDesign will convert it into a tabbed window. (Drag it out to make it free-floating again.)

> **NEW FEATURE** InDesign CS4 now displays the contents of tables in the Story Editor and lets you edit them. You can also insert tables when in the Story Editor. Previous versions showed just an indicator of where a table existed in the story.

In the Story Editor, you use the same tools for selecting, deleting, copying, pasting, and searching and replacing as you would in your layout. The Story Editor is not a separate word processor but is simply a way to look at your text in a less distracting environment for those times when your focus is on the meaning and words, not the text appearance.

FIGURE 15.2

The Story Editor in a tabbed window

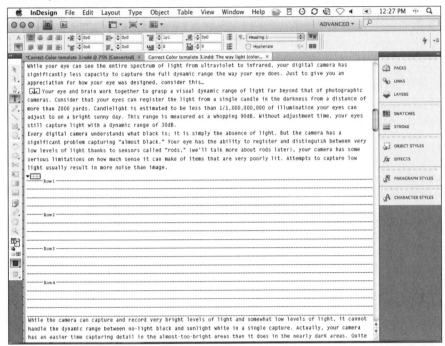

You set preferences for text size and font in the Story Editor Display pane of the Preferences dialog box (choose InDesign⇨Preferences⇨Story Editor Display or press ⌘+K on the Mac, or choose Edit⇨Preferences⇨Story Editor Display or press Ctrl+K in Windows), as detailed in Chapter 3. You can also set whether drag and drop is allowed for text within the Story Editor by using the Drag and Drop Text Editing controls in the Preference dialog box's Type pane. (By default, InDesign allows drag and drop within the Story Editor.)

The Story Editor can also identify overset text, as explained in Chapter 14.

Correcting Spelling Mistakes

Whether you're entering text directly in InDesign or importing text files from elsewhere, there are bound to be spelling mistakes. After all, we're all human. Fortunately, InDesign offers a few ways to take care of these misspellings.

InDesign's spell-check features flag three types of possible editorial problems: repeated words such as *an an,* words with odd capitalization such as the internal capitalization (called *intercaps*) in software and company names (such as *InDesign*), and words not found in the spelling dictionary that may be spelled incorrectly. You can customize the spelling dictionary, and you can purchase other companies' spelling dictionaries to add words from disciplines such as law and medicine, as well as add dictionaries for other languages.

Fixing spelling on the fly

In my word processor, I've long taken it for granted that text can be corrected as I type. Microsoft Word, for example, has a feature called AutoCorrect that lets you specify corrections to be made as you type, whether they are common typos or the expansion of abbreviations to their full words (such as having Word replace *tq* with *thank you*).

Now, InDesign offers the same functionality, which it calls Autocorrect (with a lowercase *c*). You enable Autocorrect in the Autocorrect pane of the Preferences dialog box (choose InDesign ➪ Preferences ➪ Autocorrect or press ⌘+K on the Mac, or choose Edit ➪ Preferences ➪ Autocorrect or press Ctrl+K in Windows), as Figure 15.3 shows.

 Autocorrect works only for text you type in InDesign after you've turned Autocorrect on; it does not correct imported or previously typed text.

It's easy to configure Autocorrect:

1. **In the Autocorrect pane, select the Enable Autocorrect option to turn on this feature.**

 You can also enable Autocorrect by choosing Edit ➪ Spelling ➪ Autocorrect.

2. **If you want InDesign to automatically fix capitalization errors, select the Autocorrect Capitalization Errors option.** Typically, this finds typos involving capitalizing the second letter of a word in addition to the first. For example, InDesign would replace *FOrmat* with *Format*.

3. **Choose the dictionary whose spelling and capitalization rules you want InDesign to use from the Language pop-up menu.** The default is based on the language you selected when you installed InDesign.

4. **To add your own custom corrections, click the Add button.** This opens the Add to Autocorrect List dialog box, also shown in Figure 15.3. Type the typo text or code you want InDesign to watch for in the Misspelled Word field and the corrected or expanded text you want InDesign to substitute in the Correction field. Click OK or press Enter when done, or click Cancel or press Esc to close the dialog box without adding anything.

 Oddly, you cannot use special symbols, not even InDesign's symbol codes (such as entering the ^+ code for an em dash), in the Correction field.

5. **Click OK to close the Preferences dialog box when done.**

FIGURE 15.3

The Autocorrect pane of the Preferences dialog box, as well as its Add to Autocorrect List dialog box

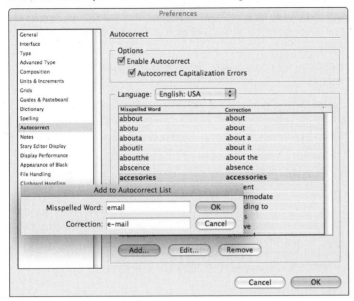

To remove an autocorrection, just select it in the Autocorrect pane's Misspelled Word list and click Remove.

NEW FEATURE InDesign CS4 adds the Edit button to the Autocorrect pane, so you can edit both the default autocorrections and any you added yourself. The Edit Autocorrect List dialog box is identical to the Add to Autocorrect List dialog box, shown in Figure 15.3. In previous versions, you had to remove an autocorrection and then add back the revised one to make changes.

Checking spelling as you type

You can have InDesign check your spelling as you type by simply choosing Edit ➪ Spelling ➪ Dynamic Spelling. You can also choose Spelling ➪ Dynamic Spelling from the contextual menu if you are using the Type tool. If that menu option is selected, InDesign checks the spelling as you type, as well as the spelling of any text already in the document. Suspected errors are highlighted with red squiggly underlining so that you can correct them as needed.

NOTE You can't have InDesign help you correct misspellings with as-you-type spell checking. If you want InDesign to suggest proper spelling, you need to use the Check Spelling dialog box, which I cover in the next section.

The Importance of Capitalization in Autocorrection

The Misspelled Word and Correction fields are case sensitive unless both entries are all lower-case. If you're not careful with how and when you capitalize text in these fields, you won't get the automated correction you expect.

The basic rule is this: Capitalize text in either field only if you are trying to fix capitalization errors. InDesign assumes you are fixing capitalization if you use any capital letters in these fields.

Thus, if you type **indesign** in the Misspelled Word field and **InDesign** in the Correction field, InDesign converts the *indesign, Indesign, inDesign*, and other miscapitalized variations to the properly capitalized *InDesign*. But if you type **Indesign** in the Misspelled Word field and **InDesign** in the Correction field, InDesign corrects only *Indesign*, not *indesign* and other miscapitalized variations.

Therefore, get in the habit of entering your text in lowercase in these fields. For example, if you type **portino** in the Misspelled Word field and **portion** in the Correction field, InDesign corrects *portino, Portino, POrtino*, and so on.

If you want to fix both spelling and capitalization errors at the same time, do it this way: Type the word in the Misspelled Word field in lowercase and the word in the Correction field as you want it capitalized. For example, type **indseign** in Misspelled Word and **InDesign** in Correction. This way, any instance of *indseign* — no matter how it is capitalized — is replaced with the properly spelled and capitalized *InDesign*.

Using the Check Spelling dialog box

The other method you can use to check spelling is the Check Spelling dialog box, which gives you more control. First, it lets you choose what part of the document to spell check. Second, it provides suggestions on correct spelling and lets you add correctly spelled words that InDesign doesn't know about to its spelling dictionary. So even if you use the new dynamic spell-checking feature, you still want to do a final spell-checking pass in the Check Spelling dialog box.

Specifying the text to check is a two-step process: First, set up the spell-check scope in the document; then, specify the scope in the Search menu.

To set up the scope, do one of the following: highlight text; click in a story to check from the cursor forward; select a frame containing a story; or open multiple documents. Just as in search and replace, what you choose to open and select determines what scope options InDesign has for spell checking.

Then, open the Check Spelling dialog box (choose Edit ⇨ Spelling ⇨ Check Spelling or press ⌘+I or Ctrl+I) and choose an option from the Search pop-up menu: Document, All Documents, Story, To End of Story, and Selection. Figure 15.4 shows the dialog box. How you set up the scope determines what options are available in the Search pop-up menu. For example, if you do not highlight text, the Selection option is not available. However, you can change the scope setup in the document while the Check Spelling dialog box is open. For example, you can open additional documents to check.

FIGURE 15.4

Use the Search pop-up menu in the Check Spelling dialog box to specify which text to spell check.

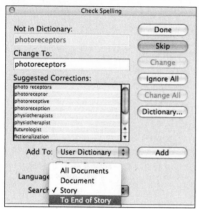

 To check the spelling of a single word, double-click to highlight it and then open the spell-checker. The Check Spelling dialog box's Search pop-up menu is automatically set to Selection.

TIP Control+click or right-click a word, range of text, or a point in a text frame (using the Type tool) to get the contextual menu from which you choose Check Spelling.

When you first open the Check Spelling dialog box and text is selected or the text cursor is active, it immediately begins checking the spelling, going to the first suspect word. You can change the scope of the search using the Search pop-up menu at any time.

If text is not selected or the text cursor is not active, the Check Spelling dialog box displays Ready to Check Spelling at the top. To begin checking the text scope you specified in the Search pop-up menu, click Start.

When adjusting the scope of the spell check in the Search pop-up menu, your choices are All Documents, Document, Story, and To End of Story. You can also make the spell check case sensitive by selecting the Case Sensitive check box.

When the spell checker encounters a word without a match in the dictionary or a possible capitalization problem, the dialog box displays Not in Dictionary at the top and shows the word. When the spell checker encounters repetition such as *me me,* the dialog box displays Duplicate Word and shows the repeated words. Use the buttons along the right side of the dialog box to handle flagged words as follows:

- To leave the current instance of a Not in Dictionary word or Duplicate Word unchanged, click Skip (which appears only after the spell check has started). To leave all instances of the same problem unchanged, click Ignore All.

- To change the spelling of a Not in Dictionary word, click a word in the Suggested Corrections list or edit the spelling or capitalization in the Change To field. To make the change, click Change.

- To correct an instance of a Duplicate Word, edit the text in the Change To field and then click Change.

- To change all occurrences of a Not in Dictionary word or a Duplicate Word to the information in the Change To field, click Change All.

- To add a word flagged as incorrect — but that you know is correct — click Add to add the word to InDesign's spelling dictionary. (If you have multiple user-created dictionaries, first choose the dictionary to add it to using the Add To pop-up menu.)

  To add a word flagged as incorrect to a specific dictionary, click Dictionary. The resulting Dictionary dialog box lets you choose which dictionary to add the word to, as well as what language to associate it with. You can also specify hyphenation settings. I cover the options in this dialog box later in this chapter.

- To close the Check Spelling dialog box after checking all the specified text, click Done.

While you're using Check Spelling, you can jump between the dialog box and the document at any time. This lets you edit a possibly misspelled word in context or edit surrounding text as a result of changed spelling. So if you find an instance of *a a* in front of *apple,* you can change the entire phrase to *an apple* rather than just replace the duplicate *a a* with *a* in the dialog box and have to remember to later change *a apple* to *an apple.*

Working with multiple languages

Each word in InDesign can have a distinct language assigned to it (English, French, Spanish, German, and so on). The word's language attribute tells InDesign which dictionary to consult when it's spell checking or hyphenating the word. For example, if you have the word *frères* in an English sentence, you can change the language of that word so that it is no longer flagged by the English spell checker — the French spell checker is used instead and recognizes that the word is correctly spelled.

Just because you have the ability to control language at the word level doesn't necessarily mean that you have to use it. In general, even when you're publishing for an international audience, full paragraphs or stories are in the same language. For example, if you have the same packaging for a product sold in the United States and France, you might have one descriptive paragraph in English and the other in French. The English dictionary also contains many common words with foreign origins such as *jalapeño, mélange,* and *gestalt.*

To assign a language to text, highlight the text and choose an option from the Language pop-up menu on the expanded Character panel, as shown in Figure 15.5. You can also set the language as part of a character or paragraph style (see Chapters 16 and 17 for more details). In the Check Spelling dialog box, a field above the Search menu shows the language of each word as it's checked. Unfortunately, you can't change the language in that dialog box.

 There's a language option called [No Language]; selecting it *prevents* spell checking and hyphenation.

FIGURE 15.5

The Language pop-up menu on the Character panel lets you choose a different language for hyphenating and spell-checking highlighted text.

Customizing the Spelling and Hyphenation Dictionaries

A spelling dictionary can never cover all the bases — you always have industry-specific words and proper nouns not found in the dictionary in use. In addition, copy editors tend to have their own preferences for how to hyphenate words. What they consider correct hyphenation may vary, and some word breaks are preferred over others. To solve both these problems, you can customize InDesign's dictionaries by adding words and specifying hyphenation. InDesign handles both spelling and hyphenation in one dictionary for each language, so you use the same controls to modify both.

Changes made to a dictionary file are saved only in the dictionary file, not with an open document. So if you add words to the English: USA dictionary, the modified dictionary is used for spell checking and hyphenating all text in documents that use the English: USA dictionary.

TIP   If you're in a workgroup, be sure to share the edited dictionary file so that everyone is using the same spelling and hyphenation settings. (The file is located in the `Dictionaries` folder inside the `Plug-ins` folder, which is inside your `InDesign` folder.) You can copy it for other users, who must then restart InDesign or press Option+⌘+/ or Ctrl+Alt+/ to reflow the text according to the new dictionary's hyphenation.

Customizing the spelling dictionary

While spell checking, you often find words that don't match those in the dictionary. If you know that the word is spelled correctly and likely to appear in your publications often, you might want to add it to the dictionary. After you add it, , that word is no longer flagged and you don't have to click Ignore to skip it; also, you can be sure that when it's used, it is spelled as it is in the dictionary.

When adding words to the dictionary, you can specify their capitalization. For example, InDesign's dictionary prefers *E-mail.* You can add *e-mail* if you prefer a lowercase *e,* or *email* if you prefer to skip the hyphen. If you're adding a word that may have variations (such as *e-mailing*) be sure to add those variations separately.

To add words to the dictionary:

1. **Choose Edit ⇨ Spelling ⇨ Dictionary.** The Dictionary dialog box shown in Figure 15.6 appears.

FIGURE 15.6

At left: Type a new term in the Word field and then click Add to include it in the spelling dictionary. Be sure to select the Case Sensitive option for proper names and acronyms. At right: Use tildes (~) to indicate hyphenation points and then click Add to include them in the spelling dictionary.

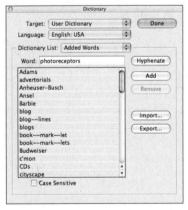

2. **Choose whether the addition to the dictionary affects just this document or all documents.** To do so, use the Target pop-up menu, which lists the current document name as well as User Dictionary (to change the dictionary file). The advantage of making the spelling specific to the document is that all users, such as service bureaus, have the same spellings; the disadvantage is that other documents won't share this spelling.

3. **Choose the dictionary that you want to edit from the Language pop-up menu.**

4. **Type or paste a word in the Word field.** The word can include special characters such as accents and hyphens, spaces, and a capitalization pattern to follow.

5. **If you want InDesign to accept only the added word with the capitalization typed in the Word field, select the Case Sensitive option.** This lets you add proper names, for example, but have them still flagged when typed in all lowercase or with extra capital letters. For example, if you type **Healdsburg** in the Word field and select Case Sensitive, InDesign doesn't flag *Healdsburg* but does flag *healdsburg* and *HEaldsburg*.

6. **If you want to edit the hyphenation, click Hyphenate.** You can add, remove, or modify the number of tildes to change the hyphenation rules for the word, as covered in the next section.

7. **Click Add.**

8. **If you want to import a word list or export one for other users to import into their copies of InDesign, click Import or Export as appropriate.** You navigate to a folder and choose a filename in a dialog box similar to the Open a File or Save dialog boxes. Note that when you click Export, InDesign exports all *selected* words from the list. If no words are selected, it exports all the words in the list.

9. **Continue to add words, and when you're finished, click Done.**

TIP When you're adding variations of words, you can double-click a word in the list to place it in the Word field as a starting place.

 **NEW FEATURE** InDesign CS4 adds an All Languages option for its list of dictionaries in the Languages pop-up menu. Words added to this dictionary are used for spell checking and hyphenation no matter what language you've set InDesign to use. It's a great way to make sure that universal terms — such as proper names or industry-specific jargon — are properly spelled no matter what language is in use.

In addition to adding words through the Dictionary dialog box, you can click Add in the Check Spelling dialog box when InDesign flags a word that you know is correct, as I cover earlier in this chapter.

To delete a word that you added to the dictionary, select it in the list and click Remove. To change the spelling of a word you added, delete it and then add it again with the correct spelling. You can see the words you've deleted since you opened the dialog box by choosing Removed Words from the Dictionary List pop-up menu, so you can add back any deleted by error.

Customizing hyphenation points

Industries and publications usually have internal styles on how words hyphenate, especially if the text is justified. For example, a bridal magazine that uses the term *newlywed* often may prefer that it break at the end of a line as *newly–wed*. But if that hyphenation would cause poor spacing, the publisher might let it break at *new–lywed* as well. InDesign lets you modify the hyphenation dictionary by specifying new, hierarchical hyphenation points.

NOTE   When you customize the hyphenation points, be sure to add variations of words (such as the plural form *newlyweds*). InDesign sees each word as wholly unrelated and therefore doesn't apply the hyphenation of, say, *newlywed* to *newlyweds*.

To specify hyphenation points:

1. Choose Edit ⇨ Spelling ⇨ Dictionary.

2. Choose from the Language menu the dictionary that you want to edit.

3. Type or paste the word in the Word field; you can also double-click a word in the list.

4. If you want, click Hyphenate to see InDesign's suggestions for hyphenating the word. You can then change the hyphenation according to Steps 5 and 6.

5. Type a tilde (~, obtained by pressing Shift+`, the open single keyboard quotation mark at the upper left of the keyboard) at your first preference for a hyphenation point. If you don't want the word to hyphenate at all, type a tilde in front of it.

6. Type tildes in other hyphenation points as well. If you want to indicate a preference, use two tildes for your second choice, three tildes for your third choice, and so on. InDesign first tries to hyphenate your top preferences (single tildes), and then it tries your second choices if the first ones don't work out, and so on. The right side of Figure 15.5 shows an example.

7. Click Add.

8. Continue to add words until you're finished and then click Done.

To revert a word to the default hyphenation, select it in the list and click Remove. To change the hyphenation, double-click a word in the list to enter it in the Word field, change the tildes, and then click Add. When you're adding variations of words, you can double-click a word in the list to place it in the Word field as a starting place.

TIP   If a word actually includes a freestanding tilde (not as an accent, as in ñ), type \~ to indicate that the character is part of the word. Freestanding tildes are rare and happen mostly in World Wide Web addresses.

Setting spelling and hyphenation dictionary preferences

By default, when spell checking and hyphenating text, InDesign consults dictionaries created by a company called Proximity. Because spelling and hyphenation points vary from dictionary to dictionary, and you may prefer one dictionary over another, you can purchase and install other companies' dictionaries to use instead of Proximity's. However, it's very hard to find commercial alternatives to the Proximity dictionaries, so most users use the ones that come with InDesign and update them as needed, or add their own user dictionaries to supplement them.

To replace a dictionary:

1. **Place the new dictionary file in the** `Dictionaries` **folder in the** `Plug-ins` **folder inside your InDesign folder.**

2. **Go to the Dictionary pane of the Preferences dialog box, shown in Figure 15.7.** (Choose InDesign ➪ Preferences ➪ Dictionary or press ⌘+K on the Mac, or choose Edit ➪ Preferences ➪ Dictionary or press Ctrl+K in Windows.)

FIGURE 15.7

If you purchase and install different hyphenation and spelling dictionaries, you can select them in the Dictionary pane of the Preferences dialog box. You can also add your own dictionaries.

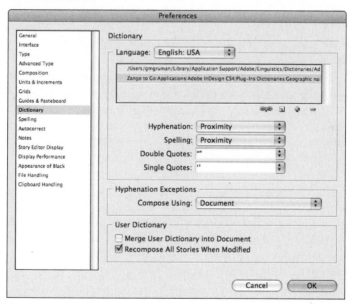

3. **From the Language pop-up menu, choose which language's dictionary you want to replace.** Dictionary files associated with that language appear in the list below the pop-up menu.

4. **Use the four buttons under the list of dictionary files to modify the dictionary files associated with the language.** They are, from left to right:

- **Relink User Dictionary:** This lets you select a replacement dictionary for the one selected in the list. Navigate to the folder and dictionary file you want to use and then click Open.

- **New User Dictionary:** This creates a new, empty dictionary file that you can then modify with the Dictionary dialog box, covered earlier in this chapter. The result is a custom dictionary.

- **Add User Dictionary:** This lets you add an existing dictionary to the selected language. Thus, you can have multiple dictionaries per language, which is very useful for handling industry-specific terms or trademarked terms, for example.

- **Remove User Dictionary:** This removes a dictionary associated to a language. Note that there must be at least one dictionary per language, so this button is grayed out when only one dictionary remains in the list.

TIP A fast way to fill a new custom dictionary with the desired words is to spell check a bunch of documents containing those special words. Add the words InDesign does not recognize to your custom dictionary, as I describe earlier in this chapter.

5. **If you have multiple rules engines for hyphenation and spelling, choose the referred rules engine from the Hyphenation and/or Spelling pop-up menu.** Such rules engines are rare, so you typically have only the default choice of Proximity for these two pop-up menus.

6. **If you don't want to use the language's standard quotation characters, you can change them in the Double Quotes and Single Quotes pop-up menus.** You might change the default quotation marks if you are publishing in one language but have extensive phrases from other languages in them. For example, a French book that extensively uses English passages (perhaps a literary article) might want to apply French quotation marks (« ») to text tagged with one of the English languages.

7. **To regulate how hyphenation is handled, use the Compose Using pop-up menu.** Your choices are the following: User Dictionary, which has InDesign ignore the hyphenation override settings that a user has made to this document (a great way to override someone's incorrect hyphenation changes); Document, which uses only the hyphenations specified in the document; and User Dictionary and Document, which uses hyphenation settings from the dictionary as well as any hyphenation specified in the document. This last setting is the default.

8. **To ensure consistent spelling and hyphenation, use the two options in the User Dictionary section:**

    - **Merge User Dictionary into Document.** If selected, this option copies the user dictionary into the document, so if the file is used by someone else who doesn't have that user dictionary, the spelling and hyphenation rules are nonetheless retained.

    - **Recompose All Stories When Modified.** If selected, this option rehyphenates and changes quotation mark settings for all stories in the document, even those created before the user dictionary was modified or added.

9. **Click OK.**

 **If you change Dictionary Preferences with no documents open, the new dictionary becomes a program default and applies to all new documents. If a document is open, the change applies only to that document.**

Searching and Replacing

InDesign's Find/Change dialog box (choose Edit ⇨ Find/Change or press ⌘+F or Ctrl+F) lets you do everything from, for example, finding the next instance of *curry* in an article so that you can insert *extra spicy* in red to finding all instances of a deposed chef's name in six different documents. If you know how to use the search-and-replace feature in any word processor or page-layout application, you should be comfortable with InDesign's Find/Change in no time.

CROSS-REF **The Find/Change dialog box lets you search for object attributes, not just text attributes. Chapter 10 covers object search and replace.**

Searching and replacing text

The Find/Change dialog box comes in two forms: reduced for finding and changing just text, and expanded for including attributes in a search. Click More Options to expand the dialog box to include formatting options for your search and replace, and Fewer Options to reduce it.

Before starting a Find/Change operation, determine the scope of your search:

- To search within a text selection, highlight it.

- To search from a certain location in a story to the end of it, click in that location using the Type tool to place the text cursor (also called the text-insertion point) there.

- To search an entire story, select any frame or click at any point in a frame containing the story.

- To search an entire document, simply have that document open.

- To search multiple documents, open all of them (and close any that you don't want to search).

To search for text:

1. **Determine the scope of your search, as just described, open the needed documents, and insert the text cursor at the appropriate location.**

2. **Choose Edit ⇨ Find/Change or press ⌘+F or Ctrl+F.** Go to the Text pane if it's not already displayed.

3. **Use the Search pop-up menu, as shown in Figure 15.8, to specify the scope of your search: Document, All Documents, Story, To End of Story, or Selection.** Options unavailable for the current search scope won't display.

FIGURE 15.8

At left: Use the Search pop-up menu in the Find/Change dialog box to specify the scope of the text to search. The buttons below also provide scope options. At right: Use the iconic pop-up menus to the right of the various fields for additional controls over special characters (the Special Characters for Replace iconic pop-up menu is shown here) and formatting.

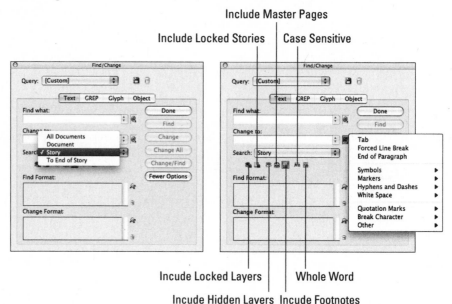

Include Master Pages

Include Locked Stories · Case Sensitive

Incude Locked Layers · Whole Word

Incude Hidden Layers · Incude Footnotes

> **TIP** As you're using the Find/Change dialog box to search and replace text, you can jump into a text frame (just click it with the Type tool) and edit it as you please, and then return to Find/Change by clicking the Find/Change dialog box.

4. **Type or paste the text you want to find in the Find What field.** To search for special characters, type their codes (see Table 15.1) or use the pop-up list (the right-facing arrow icon) to select from a menu of special characters. (If you type the codes, note that they are case sensitive.) To use special characters, use the Special Characters for Search pop-up list (the icon to the right of the Find What field) to select from a menu of special characters (refer to Figure 15.8).

5. **Type or paste the replacement text into the Change To field.** To use special characters, use the Special Characters for Replace pop-up list (to the right of the Find What field). Alternatively, type their codes (see Table 15.1).

6. **Specify the parameters for your search by selecting or deselecting the seven iconic buttons at the bottom of the pane: Include Locked Layers, Include Locked Stories, Include Hidden Layers, Include Master Pages, Include Footnotes, Case Sensitive, and Whole Word.** If an icon's background darkens, it is selected.

7. **Specify whether to consider capitalization patterns in the Find/Change operation by selecting or deselecting the Case Sensitive option.** When selected, Find/Change follows the capitalization of the text in the Find What and Change To fields exactly.

8. **If you want to search for or replace with specific formatting, use the Format buttons.** These buttons are available only if you have clicked More Options. (I cover these buttons later in this chapter.)

9. **Click Find to start the search.** Thereafter, click Find Next (it changes from the Find button after you start the search) to skip instances of the Find What text, and click Change, Change All, or Change/Find to replace the Find What text with the Change To text. (Change simply changes the found text; Change All changes every instance of that found text in your selection or story; and Change/Find changes the current found text and moves on to the next occurrence of it — it basically does in one click the actions of clicking Change and then clicking Find Next.)

10. **Click Done when you're finished.** Note that you can do several search-and-replace operations, which is why the dialog box stays open after completing a search.

> **NOTE** If you use the Change All feature, InDesign reports how many changes were made. If the number looks extraordinarily high and you suspect that the Find/Change operation wasn't quite what you wanted, remember that you can use InDesign's undo function (choose Edit ⇨ Undo or press ⌘+Z or Ctrl+Z) to undo the search and replace so that you can try a different replace strategy.

> **TIP** InDesign records your last 15 entries in the Find What and Change To fields so that you can repeat previous Find/Change operations. That's why each field is a pop-up menu. Click the menu to open it, and use the down-arrow key to scroll through those recorded operations.

> **NOTE** To search and replace regular spaces, type the number of spaces you want to find and change in the Find What and Change To fields, as if they were any other regular character.

If there are other characters not in InDesign's special-character menu that you want to search for or replace with, just type their keyboard codes (see Chapter 20) or paste them into the field. (You can paste them by first copying them to the Clipboard from your document text, or from a utility such as Character Palette on the Mac, Character Map in Windows, or PopChar in either platform, as Chapter 20 explains.)

InDesign also provides three wild cards — Any Character, Any Digit, and Any Letter — that let you search for unspecified characters, numbers, or letters in other text. For example, if you want to change all the numbered steps in a document to bulleted lists, you might search for Any Digit and replace it with a bullet. Or you can search for variations of a word to find, say, *cafe* and *café* at the same time (in this case, you would type **caf** and then choose Any Letter, or type **caf^$** if you prefer to use the codes).

TABLE 15.1

Text Codes for Search and Replace

Character	Code
Markers and Page Numbers	
Auto page number	^N
Next page number	^X
Previous page number	^V
Any page number*	^#
Anchored object market*	^a
Footnote reference marker	^F
Index entry marker*	^I
Section marker	^x
End nested style marker	^h
Inline graphic marker*	^g
Indent to here	^i
Symbols	
Bullet (•)	^8
Caret (^)	^^
Copyright (©) symbol	^2
Paragraph (¶) symbol	^7
Registered trademark (®) symbol	^r
Section (§) symbol	^6
Punctuation	
Double left quotation mark (")	^{
Double right quotation mark (")	^}
Double keyboard quote (")	^"
Any double keyboard quote*	"
Single left quotation mark (')	^[
Single right quotation mark (')	^]
Single keyboard quote (')	^'
Any single quote or apostrophe*	'
Em dash (—)	^_
En dash (–)	^=
Discretionary hyphen	^-
Nonbreaking hyphen	^~

Character	Code
Spaces	
Tab	^t
Right-indent tab	^y
Em space	^m
En space	^>
Flush space	^f
Nonbreaking space	^s
Nonbreaking fixed space	^S
Hair space	^|
Thin space	^<
Punctuation space	^.
Sixth space	^%
Quarter space	^4
Third space	^3
Non-joiner	^j
White space (any space or tab)*	^w
Breaks	
End of paragraph	^p
Forced line break	^n
Discretionary line break	^k
Column break	^M
Frame break	^R
Page break	^P
Odd page break	^L
Even page break	^E
Wild Cards	
Any character*	^?
Any digit*	^9
Any letter*	^$
Clipboard Contents	
Formatted contents**	^c
Unformatted contents**	^C

*Can be entered in the Find What field only

**Can be entered in Change To field only

What Is Grep?

In the Find/Change dialog box is a pane called Grep that looks to be the same as the Text pane. Grep is a utility in the Unix operating system (including variants such as Linux) that provides a powerful language for programming searches based on pattern matching. The Grep dialog box brings this language to InDesign's search-and-replace functions without having to know the Grep syntax or codes. It works just the same as the Text pane except that there are additional options in the Special Characters for Search and the Special Characters for Replace pop-up menus next to the Find What and Change To fields, respectively.

Under the hood, Grep uses complex codes to perform its pattern matching. Many of these codes are the same as internal InDesign codes, though with different meanings. To ensure that InDesign doesn't get confused as to what those codes mean, Adobe engineers had to create a separate Grep pane rather than add Grep features to the Text pane of the Find/Change dialog box.

In the Special Characters for Search pop-up menu, shown here, you can choose from several sub-menus: Location, Repeat, Match, Modifiers, and Posix. You can use as many of these as needed to define your search patterns.

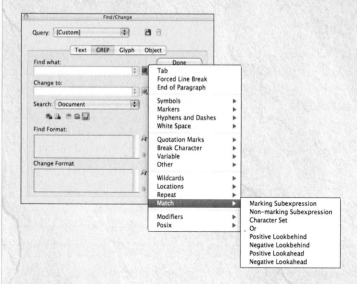

The Special Characters for Replace pop-up menu contains just one additional menu option — Found — which lets you select found text (from previous searches) to include in the replacement text.

Although InDesign simplifies access to Grep, using it still requires knowledge of what the Grep commands actually do and how they work (its syntax) — something that only a tiny minority of users will know, so don't feel bad if you don't end up using this feature. Adobe does include some documentation on Grep's syntax in its InDesign CD, and you can get an in-depth tutorial on Grep in many Unix books.

Changing special characters

InDesign also lets you replace special characters (called *glyphs* in InDesign) through a separate Glyph pane in the Find/Change dialog box, shown in Figure 15.9. This feature makes it easier to actually enter the desired characters. The process is mostly straightforward (just ignore the parts of the pane not described in this section):

FIGURE 15.9

The Glyph pane of the Find/Change dialog box, with a glyph selection dialog box and its Show pop-up menu displayed

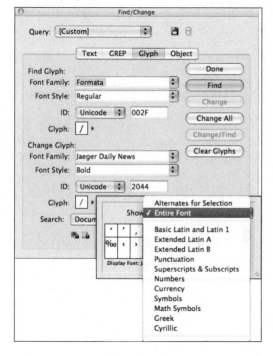

1. **In the Find Glyph section, choose the font of the desired character in the Font Family pop-up menu and choose the character's style in the Font Style pop-up menu.**

2. **To choose the character itself, click the pop-up menu icon to the right of the Glyph field.** You get a dialog box that mimics the Glyphs panel (see Chapter 20); choose the glyph from the dialog box by double-clicking it. You can display just subsets of that dialog box's glyphs using its Show pop-up menu.

3. **Repeats Steps 1 and 2 using the controls in the Change Glyph section to select the replacement glyph.**

4. **Set the scope of your search using the Search pop-up menu and the Include Locked Layers, Include Locked Stories, Include Hidden Layers, Include Master Pages, and Include Footnotes iconic buttons, as described earlier in this chapter.**

5. **Execute the search and/or replace using the Find, Change, Change All, and Change/ Find iconic buttons as described earlier in this chapter.**

6. **Click Done when done.**

 **If you want to quickly wipe out the selected glyphs, click the Clear Glyphs button.**

Searching and replacing formatting

To find and change formatting or text with specific formatting, you can use the expanded Find/ Change dialog box. For example, you might find all the blue words in 14-point Futura Extra Bold and change them to 12-point Mrs Eaves Bold. Or you might find all instances of the words *hot and spicy* in 15-point body text and then resize the text to 12 point and apply the font Chili Pepper.

To replace text formatting, follow these steps:

1. **To add formats to a Find/Change operation for text, click More Options in the Find/ Change dialog box (if it was not clicked earlier).** The dialog box expands to include the Find Format Settings (see Figure 15.10) and Change Format Settings areas.

2. **Use the Format buttons to display the Find Format Settings and Change Format Settings dialog boxes, which let you specify the formats you want to find.** The two dialog boxes are identical except for their names; refer to Figure 15.10 for the Find Format Settings dialog box.

FIGURE 15.10

Clicking More Options in the Find/Change dialog box displays the Find Format Settings and Change Format Settings areas. (More Options changes to Fewer Options.) Clicking Format opens either the Find Format Settings dialog box (shown here) or Change Format Settings dialog box, depending on whether you click Format in the Find Format Settings area or in the Change Format Settings area.

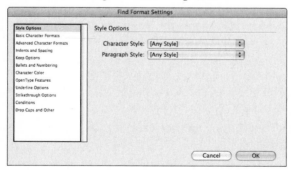

3. Use the menu at the top to specify the type of formatting: Style Options (paragraph and character styles), Basic Character Formats, Advanced Character Formats, Indents and Spacing, Keep Options, Bullets and Numbering, Character Color, OpenType Features, Underline Options, Strikethrough Options, and Drop Caps and Other. You can change multiple attributes at one time by making selections from as many panes as needed.

 **TIP** To search and replace formatting only — regardless of the text to which it is applied — leave the Find What and Change To fields blank.

Locating and specifying all the formatting you want to find and change requires you to dig deeper and deeper into the Find Format Settings and Change Format Settings dialog boxes. Unfortunately, you can't really get a picture of all the formats you're selecting at one time, and you have to keep jumping from one pane to the next. Fortunately, when you've finished selecting formats, the selected options are summarized in the Find Style Settings and Change Style Settings areas.

Changing fonts globally

Sometimes, you need to replace a font throughout your document. You can't use the Find/Change dialog box to do this because it requires that you specify specific text to find and replace. But you can choose Type ➪ Find Font and use the Find Font dialog box shown in Figure 15.11 to replace a specific font with another. The Fonts in Document section shows all fonts actually in use so that you can select the one you want to replace. You then choose the new font and style using the Font Family and Font Style pop-up menus in the Replace With section.

FIGURE 15.11

The Find Font dialog box with the More Info button clicked

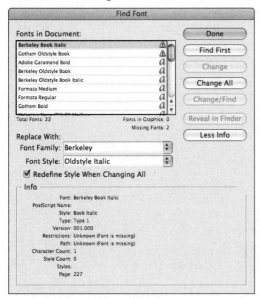

Managing Your Fonts

You typically replace fonts in your layout because you actually want to use a different font, not merely because you don't happen to have the fonts installed on your system that the document is using. After all, the design shouldn't change just because you don't happen to have the needed fonts on your computer.

In both Mac OS X 10.4 (Tiger) and 10.5 (Leopard), the easiest way to add fonts is by opening the Font Book program in the `Applications` folder and then choosing File⇨Add Fonts to install OpenType, Type 1 PostScript, and TrueType fonts. You can also do it manually by dragging fonts files to one of the following folders:

- `Fonts` **folder in the** `Library` **folder (**`Library:Fonts`**):** This is where you should place fonts that you want all users to have access to. Just drag them in, whether they're PostScript, TrueType, or OpenType.

- `Fonts` **folder in the user's** `Home` **folder's** `Library` **folder (**`Users/user name:` `Library:Fonts`**):** Any fonts dragged here are available only to that user.

- `Fonts` **folder in the** `System` **folder's** `Library` **folder (**`System:Library:Fonts`**):** This is where Apple places the default fonts for Mac OS X applications. You can add fonts here as well by dragging them, but I recommend that you leave this folder alone. You can create a horrible mess on your system if you place your own font files here.

Any fonts installed in the Mac OS X folders are not available to Mac OS 9 applications (which older PowerPC-based Macs can run under Classic mode). You need to also maintain fonts in the `System` `Folder`'s `Fonts` folder — note that the Mac OS 9 folder name is `System Folder` whereas the Mac OS X folder name is simply `System` — or use a Mac OS 9 font manager such as Adobe Type Manager.

In Windows XP and Vista, you add OpenType or TrueType fonts by opening the `Fonts` folder. In XP, choose Start⇨Settings⇨Control Panel and double-click the Fonts button; in Vista, choose Start⇨Control Panel and click Classic View in the right-hand pane, and then double-click the Fonts button. You can simply drag the new fonts into the window, or you can choose File⇨Install Fonts. (In Vista, you may have to press and release the Alt key to see the menus.)

Note that Windows XP has built-in support for TrueType and OpenType fonts, whereas Windows Vista has built-in support for PostScript Type 1, TrueType, and OpenType fonts.

If you're using a font management utility such as Insider Software's FontAgent Pro or Extensis's Suitcase for Mac, or Adobe's Type Manager or Extensis's Suitcase for Windows, use their tools to add fonts, as well as to activate and deactivate the fonts that are installed. Activation and deactivation let you turn fonts on and off without actually having to install or delete them. This is a great feature if your documents use different font sets, because you can then quickly turn on or off the correct fonts just for the job you happen to be working on at the moment.

 **Use the Redefine Style When Changing All check box to ensure that any font replacement updates all paragraph and character styles to use the new font.**

Two other buttons in the Find Font dialog box help you understand what font you're replacing:

- **Reveal in Finder (Mac) or Reveal in Explorer (Windows):** This button opens the folder that contains the font, which is handy if you have the same font in multiple folders and want to know which one InDesign is using.

- **More Info:** This button provides details on the selected font, such as any printing restrictions, the font version, the location, and the PostScript font name.

Working with saved search queries

If you plan to do the same search and/or replace operation repeatedly, you can save queries in InDesign. After entering the find and search information, click the Save Query iconic button, enter a name in the Save Query dialog box that appears, and click OK. That query will then appear in the Query pop-up menu in the Find/Change dialog box.

To run a saved query, just choose it from the Query pop-up menu. To delete a saved query, choose it from the Query pop-up menu and then click Delete Query iconic button.

Adjusting Text Appearance in Text Frames

Although most adjustments to text frames — such as frame size, shape, and location — affect the layout, not the text, there are several text-frame attributes that do affect your text's appearance.

Setting text frame options

Most of these adjustments reside in the General pane of the Text Frame Options dialog box, shown in Figure 15.12. You open the dialog box by selecting a frame and choosing Object ⇨ Text Frame Options or pressing ⌘+B or Ctrl+B.

FIGURE 15.12

The General pane (left) and Baseline Options pane (right) of the Text Frame Options dialog box

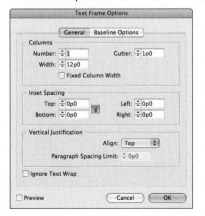

CROSS-REF   Chapter 8 covers the creation, modification, and deletion of text frames in more detail. Chapter 14 covers the Column settings in the Text Frame Options dialog box. The rest of Part IV covers formatting text.

These four sections of the General pane of Text Frame Options dialog box provide the following controls:

- **Columns:** This section lets you specify the number of columns, as well as column width and gutter settings, as explained in Chapter 14.

- **Inset Spacing:** This section creates an internal margin in the frame, putting space between the frame edge and the text. You can set the Top, Bottom, Left, and Right settings separately. To make the setting in one margin edge change the setting in all margin edges, be sure the Make All the Settings the Same iconic button appears as an unbroken chain; if the chain is broken, it is not enabled. Click the button to toggle between the two modes.

- **Vertical Justification:** This section controls the placement of text vertically in a text frame, similar to right-, center-, or left-aligning a paragraph horizontally. The Top, Center, and Bottom options in the Align pop-up menu move the text to the top, the center, or bottom of the text frame. The Justify option is a bit different: It permits variable spacing between paragraphs so that the text fits the full depth of the frame. If you choose Justify, the leading within paragraphs is unaffected, but InDesign adds as much space as needed between each paragraph — up to the value set in the Paragraph Spacing Limit field — to ensure that the last line of text in the frame is at the bottom of the frame. Because the default is 0p, text isn't vertically justified even if you choose Justify; you must also increase the Paragraph Spacing Limit value. Figure 15.13 shows some examples of working with vertical justification.

FIGURE 15.13

This brochure shows examples of vertical justification, showing how the spacing changes as the number of lines changes. (Normal, top-aligned text is at left.)

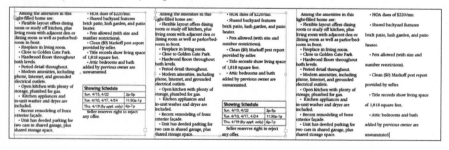

NOTE   In a multicolumn text frame, vertical justification applies only to the last column.

■ **Ignore Text Wrap:** This option is in its own untitled section. If selected, it lets text in the text frame overprint another object, even if text wrap is set for that object. You'll use this rarely. An example of when you might want to select this option is when you have a headline that you want to overprint a graphic that body text wraps around.

The Baseline Options pane provides controls for where text baselines begin relative to the frame's top:

■ **First Baseline:** This section lets you determine where the baseline for the first line of text in the frame rests. (The baseline is the invisible line on which characters rest and through which descenders, such as the lower portions of letters such as *p* and *g*, "poke through.") You have five options in the Offset pop-up menu. How you use each of them depends on your aesthetic goals:

  ▪ **Ascent:** This option puts the baseline as close to the top of the frame as possible so that the tops of characters graze the text frame's top (or the margin you set in the Inset Spacing section). This is the default.

  ▪ **Cap Height:** The Cap Height adjusts the baseline so that it is a cap height's distance from the frame top. The cap height is the height of a capital letter *C*, but some fonts have characters that extend above that location, and these fonts will have characters that rise above the top of the frame if you choose Cap Height here.

  ▪ **Leading:** This option places the baseline from the frame's top in the same amount as the text's leading. If leading is set to 13 points, for example, the baseline will be 13 points from the top of the frame, no matter if that makes characters rise above the frame top (such as if the text size is set at 15 points) or causes a gap (such as if the text size is set at 9 points).

  ▪ **x Height:** This adjusts the baseline so that it is an x height's distance from the frame top. The x height is the height of a lowercase letter *x*. Selecting x Height ensures that capital letters and letters with ascenders (such as *d* and *h*) poke through the top of the frame.

  ▪ **Fixed:** This option uses the value in the Min field to position the baseline. You use this if you want the baseline for all text frames to be the same no matter what the text size and appearance is. That's pretty rare. Standard practice is to have text positioned from the frame top relative to its size, which the other Offset options essentially do.

  You can override any of the settings described here by specifying an amount in the Min field. The Min field tells InDesign that the first baseline must be at least a specific distance from the frame top. InDesign first tries to position the baseline based on the Offset amount, but if that is closer to the frame top than the Min setting, the Min setting prevails.

■ **Baseline Grid:** This section lets you set a baseline grid just for the selected text frames. The baseline grid provides a set of guidelines for your text, which helps ensure that columns stay aligned. Note that you can have your paragraphs snap to these guidelines if you enable baseline grid alignment in your paragraph formatting or paragraph styles. Also note that your document can have its own universal baseline grid, and selected text frames can have their own independent ones. You set the document baseline grid in the Grids & Guides pane of the Preferences dialog box and the text-frame-specific baseline grids here, by selecting the Use Custom Baseline Grid option.

CROSS-REF The various baseline grid settings are covered in Chapter 3. Setting paragraphs to align to baseline grids is covered in Chapter 17.

The other frame-oriented action you can take that affects text is resizing (scaling). Normally, when you resize a text frame, the text size is unaffected, and the text simply reflows in the new frame's dimensions. But you can also have the text resized along the same percentages as the frame itself. Chapter 11 covers these techniques.

Working with Notes

Notes are very handy to leave yourself reminders or pass on instructions or explanations to other users.

NOTE Notes are inserted into text; you cannot add them to other objects.

You can add notes using any of three interface choices:

- Click the Notes tool in the Tools panel and then click at the text location where you want to insert a note.

- Using the Type tool, click in the text where you want to add a note and then choose Type ➪ Notes ➪ New Note to add a note.

- Using the Type tool, click in the text where you want to add a note and then open the Notes panel (Window ➪ Notes) and choose New Note from the flyout menu or click the New Note iconic button at the bottom of the panel.

NEW FEATURE In InDesign CS4, the Notes menu options have moved to a submenu of the Type menu; they are no longer available through a separate Notes menu.

However you add it, a note is indicated in the document with a golden yellow dual-triangle character that looks somewhat like an hourglass. Called a *note anchor*, it is shown in Figure 15.14. (That assumes, of course, you are displaying hidden characters by choosing Type ➪ Show Hidden Characters, choosing Hidden Characters from the View Options iconic pop-up menu in the application bar, or pressing Option+⌘+I or Ctrl+Alt+I.)

NOTE Of course, neither the note nor its anchor will print. These items also will *not* export to PDF files, as you might expect (because Adobe Acrobat has long had a similar notes capability).

If you select a string of text, InDesign won't display the New Note menu option; instead, it displays the Convert to Note option to make that text into a note. That's great if someone types a note directly into text, but it can be dangerous if you are trying to highlight an entire word, as you would do when adding notes in Adobe Acrobat. (If you accidentally convert a text select to a note, you can convert a note back to text by choosing Convert to Text from the Notes panel's flyout menu or from the Notes menu.)

FIGURE 15.14

The Notes panel and its flyout menu. In the text to the left of the Notes panel is the hourglass-shaped icon in text that indicates a note.

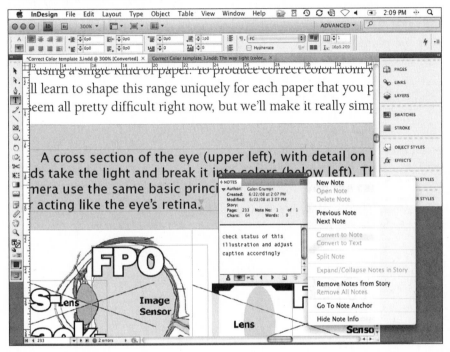

You can use the Notes panel's flyout menu or the Notes menu to navigate through notes (choose Previous Note or Next Note), control notes' display (Expand Notes in Story and Collapse Notes in Story), remove notes (choose Delete Note, Remove Notes from Story, or Remove All Notes), move to the note's anchor (choose Go to Note Anchor), or split a note into multiple notes (choose Split Note).

You can set note preferences in the Preference dialog box's Notes pane, as described in Chapter 3. (To open that pane, choose InDesign ➪ Preferences ➪ Notes or press ⌘+K on the Mac, or choose Edit ➪ Preferences ➪ Notes or press Ctrl+K in Windows.) In addition to changing the note anchor's color, you can also tell InDesign whether to spell check notes, search notes in find/change operations, and display a user color behind notes in text. (Each user who edits a file gets assigned a unique color for easy identification, à la Microsoft Word's Track Changes feature.)

Summary

InDesign provides a variety of methods for getting text into your documents, including typing directly into a text frame, placing or dragging and dropping files generated in a word processor, and pasting text from other sources. You can also edit and type text in the Story Editor window.

InDesign can check spelling as you type, correct some errors as you type, and spell-check high-lighted text, a whole story, a whole document, or a group of open documents as you prefer. You can customize the spelling and hyphenation dictionary to include industry-specific words or proper nouns and to specify your preferences for how certain words are hyphenated. InDesign provides dictionaries for many languages to support international publishing, and it lets you create your own dictionaries.

InDesign's Find/Change dialog box lets you search and replace not only text but also text formatting and special characters. The dialog box now has several new panes to give you finer controls over your searches, as well as the ability to save searches for reuse later.

The Text Frame Options dialog box lets you adjust the spacing of text within text frames, such as the distance from the frame edge and the alignment of paragraphs within the frame.

InDesign also lets you place notes in your files to act as reminders, instructions, or explanations for other people as well as for yourself.

Chapter 16

Specifying Character Attributes

ype is the visual representation of the spoken word. A typographer is a person who designs with type. As a user of InDesign, chances are you'll be making lots of decisions about the appearance of the text in the publications you produce. You are, whether you consider yourself one or not, a typographer. And not only are InDesign users typographers, they're typographers who have an extensive arsenal of text-formatting tools that let them tweak and polish their type in a nearly infinite variety of ways.

Of all the decisions an InDesign user makes when designing a publication, decisions about type are arguably the most important. Why? Because a publication can't be effective if the text is hard to read. The difference between good typography and bad typography is the same as the difference between clear speaking and mumbling. The intent of a clear speaker and a mumbler may be the same, but the effect on the listener is quite different. In publishing, the printed words are the containers in which the writer's message is transported to the reader. As the caretaker of those words, you hold great power. Whether the message is successfully transported depends largely on your typographic decisions.

As you learn to use InDesign's powerful type-formatting features, you should always remember the cardinal rule of typography: Type exists to honor content. By all means, you should take full advantage of the available tools, but sometimes knowing when not to use a fancy typographic feature is as important as knowing how to use the feature in the first place.

CROSS-REF This chapter focuses on modifying character-level typographic formats; Chapter 17 focuses on modifying paragraph-level formats.

IN THIS CHAPTER

Working with characters versus paragraphs

Changing font families, font styles, and font sizes

Applying other character formats

Controlling horizontal and vertical spacing

Working with Character Formats

Before you begin looking at InDesign's character-formatting features, you should be clear about a fundamental InDesign type-formatting concept: Using separate tools, InDesign lets you modify the appearance of highlighted characters or selected paragraphs:

- When characters are highlighted (or the text cursor is flashing), you can use the Character panel (choose Type ⇨ Character or press ⌘+T or Ctrl+T) shown in Figure 16.1 to change their appearance in several ways. (You can also choose Window ⇨ Type & Tools ⇨ Character.) If you choose Hide Options from the flyout menu, the Vertical Scale, Horizontal Scale, Baseline Shift, and Skew fields and the Language pop-up menu are not displayed. You can also use the double-arrow iconic button to the left of the panel name to toggle among showing the panel title, the basic options, and all options.

- When paragraphs are selected, the Paragraph panel (choose Type ⇨ Paragraph or press Option+⌘+T or Ctrl+Alt+T) lets you change how the paragraphs are constructed. (For more information about the Paragraph panel, see Chapter 17.)

FIGURE 16.1

The Character panel with all options shown, and its flyout menu

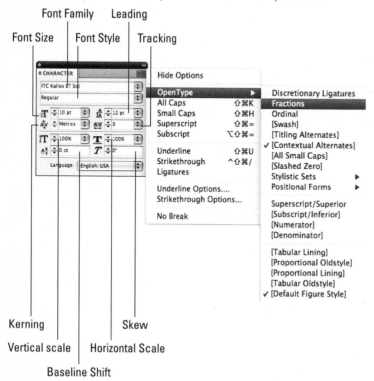

The Character panel provides access to most of InDesign's character-formatting options. Three of the options — Font Family, Font Style, and Font Size — are also available in the Type menu, and several options have keyboard shortcuts. The Control panel offers all the formatting options of the Character panel plus others, as shown in Figure 16.2. (If the Control panel doesn't show the character formatting options shown in the figure, be sure to select text and click the A iconic button on the panel. If the Control panel is not visible (it almost always is), display it by choosing Window ⇨ Control or pressing Option+⌘+6 or Ctrl+Alt+6.)

TIP If the Type tool is selected and no objects are active, the controls in the Character panel are still available. In this situation, any changes you make in the Character panel become the default settings for the document and are automatically used when you create new text frames. If you change character formats when the cursor is flashing and no text is selected, your changes are applied at the insertion point. When you begin typing, you see the results of your changes.

FIGURE 16.2

The character formatting options in the Character (A) pane of the Control panel and its flyout menu

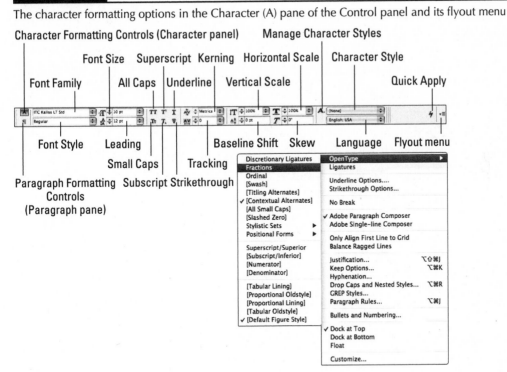

InDesign lets you apply character formats to highlighted text in two ways. You can:

- Use the local controls in the Character panel, the Control panel, or the Type menu; or use the keyboard shortcuts
- Create and apply character-level styles

Either way, you can apply the same formatting. The difference is that a character style's settings are stored, so you can apply the exact same settings easily to other text. Plus, if you change a character style's settings, any text based on it automatically changes to reflect the new settings.

If you're working on a simple, one-page publication, such as a business card, a poster, or an ad, you'll probably use the Character panel to format the text elements. However, if you're producing a multipage publication — a newsletter, magazine, catalog, or newspaper, for example — you should take advantage of styles. Using them saves you time and makes your job a whole lot easier.

CROSS-REF For details about creating and applying character and paragraph styles, see Chapter 19.

Even if you do use styles for a particular publication, you'll probably also do some local formatting. For example, you would probably use the Character panel to format the type on the opening spread of a feature magazine article and then use styles to quickly format the remainder of the article.

CROSS-REF Some of the object-level controls in the Control and Transform panels let you change the appearance of all the text within a text frame. For more information about these controls, see Chapter 10.

NOTE In InDesign (as with most programs), you can select only contiguous text. So if you have, for example, several subheads to which you want to apply local character formatting, you can't select them all and apply the formatting in one fell swoop. You have to do each text segment separately. (That's one reason to use character styles instead of local formatting.)

Changing Font Family, Font Style, and Font Size

These days, the terms *font, face, typeface, font family, font style,* and *type style* are often used interchangeably. When you're talking with friends or colleagues about typography, it doesn't matter which term you use as long as you make yourself understood, but if you'll be setting type with InDesign, you should be familiar with the font-related terms in the menus and panes.

The term *font,* or typeface, usually refers to a collection of characters — including letters, numbers, and special characters — that share the same overall appearance, including stroke width, weight, angle, and style. For example, Helvetica Plain, Arial Bold, Adobe Garamond Semibold Italic, and ITC New Baskerville Italic are well-known fonts. A *font family* is a collection of several fonts that share the same general appearance but differ in stroke width, weight, and/or stroke angle. Some examples of font families are Adobe Caslon, Berthold Baskerville, Times New Roman, and Tekton.

In InDesign, each of the fonts that makes up a font family is referred to as a *font style* (though most designers call these *type styles*). For example, the ITC Garamond font family is made up of 15 font styles, as shown in Figure 16.3. When you choose a font family from the Character panel's Font Family menu, InDesign displays the family's font style variations in the accompanying Font Styles pop-up menu.

FIGURE 16.3

The ITC Garamond font family includes 15 font styles; these are shown at left in the Character panel, at right in the Control panel.

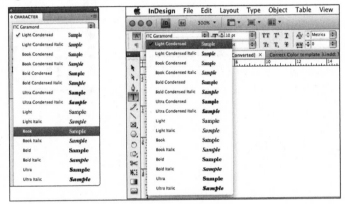

Unlike most word-processing and desktop-publishing programs, InDesign doesn't include built-in shadow and outline font styles. (These font styles are available only if a font includes them.) Most programs create these stylistic variations artificially by modifying plain characters. If you want to create outline text, you can use the Stroke panel (choose Window ⇨ Stroke or press ⌘+F10 or Ctrl+F10) to apply a stroke. If you want to create a drop shadow for text, you can do so using InDesign's lighting effects features. (Chapter 11 covers these features in detail.)

NEW FEATURE InDesign CS4 now lets you apply stroke cap, end join, miter limit, and stroke alignment to text as character formatting. Just select the character and apply the desired effects in the Stroke panel, as Chapter 11 explains how to do for frames. Note that stroke alignment is limited to center and outside for text.

Similarly, bold and italic variations are available only for font families that include these font styles. This prevents you from applying, for example, italic to Trajan, a font family that doesn't include an italic variation. (InDesign does let you create false italics by skewing text, which I cover later in this chapter. However, you should avoid such heavy-handed shape twisting unless it's absolutely necessary.)

When you change from one font to another in InDesign, you can choose a new font family and font style independently in the Character panel. For example, changing from Arial Bold to Times Bold or from Arial Regular to Berthold Baskerville Regular is a simple change of font family.

One Font, Many Names

InDesign sometimes displays a font name multiple times in various panes and dialog boxes, such as the Character panel. This occurs if you have multiple versions of a font on your computer — say, both a TrueType and PostScript version of Helvetica. (Version 2 and earlier of InDesign would show only one of these fonts, making the others inaccessible.) You can tell which is which by the code that InDesign appends to the font name: (TT) for TrueType, (T1) for PostScript Type 1, and (OTF) for OpenType.

You really shouldn't have multiple versions of a font on your computer because different versions can look dissimilar and be spaced differently, resulting in an inconsistent appearance that's hard to fix. If you notice such multiple versions because InDesign calls them to your attention, delete or deactivate the unneeded fonts. (Typically, you would keep the PostScript version — or the OpenType version, if it's supported by your service bureau.)

InDesign also shows icons next to the font names (whether or not you have multiple versions of any specific font) in its various font-related pop-up menus: a stylized "TT" for TrueType, a stylized "a" for PostScript Type 1, and a stylized "O" for OpenType, as shown in the following figure.

However, if you switch from Bookman Light to Century Schoolbook Bold Italic, you're changing both font family and font style.

> **NOTE** InDesign can display previews of fonts when you select fonts through the Control panel, various text-oriented panels, and the Type menu. You turn on this capability in the Type pane of the Preferences dialog box, as covered in Chapter 3. But it can make your menus unwieldy.

> **NOTE** When creating character styles, the font family, font style, and font size controls are available in the Basic Character Formats pane of the New Character Styles and New Paragraph Styles dialog boxes.

Selecting fonts

The Character panel and Control panel offer two methods for changing the font family applied to highlighted text. You can:

- Click the Font Family pop-up menu and then choose a name from the list of available font families.

- Click in front of or highlight the font name displayed in the Font Family field, type the first few letters of the font family you want to apply, and then press Return or Enter. For example, typing **Ari** selects Arial (if it's available on your computer).

If you use the Font submenu in the Type menu, you can type the first letter of a font to skip to font names beginning with that letter after you have highlighted any font in the submenu.

You can select just the font family, as Figure 16.3 shows. When you change the font family applied to selected text, InDesign tries to maintain the applied font style. If, for example, you switch from Adobe Garamond Bold Italic to Adobe Caslon, InDesign automatically uses Adobe Caslon Bold Italic, which is one of several font styles that make up this font family. But if you switch from Arial Bold Italic to Avant Garde, which doesn't include a bold italic variation, InDesign uses Avant Garde Book instead.

CAUTION When importing text into a layout and applying InDesign's style instead of the word processor's style (see Chapter 13) — or when you apply a new font family through, say, a paragraph style — InDesign may not be able to figure out a corresponding font style to apply to that original text. In that case, it will keep the original font style but put its name in brackets, so you know that font style doesn't exist in the new font family. If you don't correct these (as explained in Chapter 15), your document may not print correctly.

CROSS-REF See Chapter 15 for details on how to search and replace formatting such as font attributes, as well as how to replace a font completely throughout a document.

If a particular font family includes a submenu with font style variations, you can also choose a font style at the same time you choose a font family. If you choose only a font family when font styles are available in an accompanying submenu, no changes apply to the selected text. Figure 16.4 shows an example of choosing both at the same time.

FIGURE 16.4

You can select both the font family and the font style at the same time using the submenus in the Font Family menu in the Control panel (shown here), Character panel, or Character Styles panel, or in the Type menu's Font submenu.

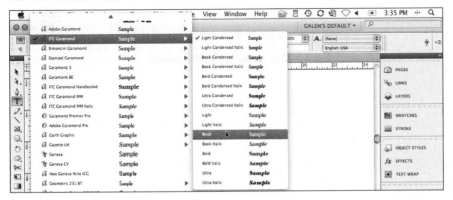

Changing font size

InDesign lets you specify font sizes (called *type sizes* by most publishers) from 0.1 point to 1,296 points (108 inches) in increments as fine as 0.001 point. Of course, even if it were possible to clearly print type as small as a thousandth of a point (that is, $\frac{1}{72,000}$ of an inch), which is beyond the capabilities of most printers, nobody could read it without a microscope anyway.

Use good judgment when choosing font sizes. For example, headlines should be larger than sub-heads, which in turn are larger than body text, which is larger than photo credits, and so on.

InDesign offers several methods for changing the font size of highlighted text. You can:

- Use one of several techniques in the Character panel and Control panel:
  - Choose one of the predefined sizes from the Font Size menu.
  - Highlight the currently applied font size displayed in the accompanying editable field, type a new size, and then press Return or Enter.
  - Use the up and down cursor keys to increase or decrease the size in 1-point increments. Pressing and holding Shift multiplies the increment to 10.
- Choose Type ⇨ Size and then choose one of the predefined sizes listed in the Size submenu. If you choose Other from the submenu, the Size field is highlighted in the Character panel. Type a custom size and then press Return or Enter.
- Control+click or right-click a text selection and then choose a size from the Size submenu. If you choose Other from the submenu, the Font Size field is highlighted in the Character panel. Type a custom size and then press Return or Enter.
- Use keyboard commands to adjust text size:
  - Press Shift+⌘+. (period) or Ctrl+Shift+. (period) to enlarge highlighted text in 2-point increments. (You can set a different increment in the Units & Increments pane in the Preferences dialog box, which you access by choosing InDesign ⇨ Preferences ⇨ Units & Increments or pressing ⌘+K on the Mac, or by choosing Edit ⇨ Preferences ⇨ Units & Increments or pressing Ctrl+K in Windows.)
  - Press Shift+⌘+, (comma) or Ctrl+Shift+, (comma) to reduce highlighted text.
  - Press Option+Shift+⌘+. (period) or Ctrl+Alt+Shift+. (period) to increase the text size in 10-point increments.
  - Press Option+Shift+⌘+, (comma) or Ctrl+Alt+Shift+, (comma) to decrease the text size in 10-point increments.

 It helps to think of these shortcuts as using the > and < characters, mnemonics for *more* and *less*, rather than as using the period and comma.

 If text is highlighted and the Font Size field is empty, it means that more than one font size is used in the selected text.

Labeling Paragraphs

Changing the formatting of the first few words in a paragraph can indicate the beginning of a story or a new topic. This is commonly used for *run-in heads* (short titles usually in boldface or italic, and often in a contrasting font) on the same line as the rest of the paragraph. Although you use this technique in paragraphs, you need to use local character formatting or character styles to change the look of the first part of each paragraph, so I'm explaining this technique here rather than in Chapter 17. You can also use the nested styles feature, described in this chapter, to apply the appropriate character style consistently to paragraphs that have such labels applied.

The following descriptions show frequently used label formatting. You use the appropriate controls in the Character panel or in the Character pane (press the A iconic button) of the Control panel.

- **Boldface:** Bold speaks the loudest and is generally used for subheads in magazines, newspapers, and reports.
- *Italic*: If bold shouts, italic tends to whisper. It's a good choice for tertiary heads and to label bulleted items within a list.
- <u>Underlines</u>: For a typewriter effect, you might underline the text of a label.
- SMALL CAPS: For a subtle, classic look that blends well with the rest of the document, use small caps on labels. However, don't use small caps if you're using labels as subheads that allow readers to skim through a document and read only relevant portions.
- **Typeface change:** Rather than rely on different variations of a font, you can use a different font altogether, such as Futura Heavy as used on this paragraph, for a label. To contrast with serif body text, you might choose a sans serif typeface that complements the look of your publication. Often, this will be a variation of your headline font.
- Scaled text: Scaling text horizontally — up 10 or 20 percent — quietly differentiates it from the remainder of the paragraph. (More severe scaling distorts the typeface and can look unprofessional.) In contrast to bold or underline, the text doesn't pop off the page at you, but it is visually distinct. Scaling text vertically, however, can be too subtle unless you combine it with boldface or another style.
- Size change: Creating a label by simply bumping the size up a point or two is another subtle design choice. The labels blend well with the body text, but they don't announce their presence enough to be used as subheads for scanning.

A tip: To provide a little more space between the label and the text, you might want to use an en space or em space rather than a normal space.

Applying Other Character Formats

Font family, font style, and font size are the most commonly modified character formats, but the Character panel and Control panel contain several other controls for managing the appearance of type. Some of these controls are displayed in the panel window; others are available in the panels' flyout menu. The Control panel offers more formatting options than the Character panel.

In the Control panel, you can adjust all caps, small caps, superscript, subscript, underline, strikethrough, kerning, tracking, horizontal and vertical scale, baseline shift, skew, character style, and language. Through the flyout menu, you can also set ligatures, modify underline and strikethrough settings, control whether text may break (be hyphenated), select its case (such as all caps and small caps), and select OpenType features. Figure 16.2 shows the flyout menu for the Control panel's character formatting (A) pane.

In the Character panel, you can adjust kerning, tracking, horizontal and vertical scale, baseline shift, skew, and language. Through its flyout menu (refer to Figure 16.1), you can also set all caps, small caps, superscript, subscript, underline, strikethrough, ligatures, and underline and strikethrough settings, as well as control whether text may break (be hyphenated) and select OpenType features.

> **NOTE** You must choose Show Options from the Character panel's flyout menu to display the Vertical Scale, Horizontal Scale, Baseline Shift, Skew, and Language options in the panel.

> **NOTE** When you create character styles, the kerning, tracking, subscript, superscript, case, ligature, underlining, break, and strikethrough controls are available in the Basic Character Formats pane of the New Character Styles and New Paragraph Styles dialog boxes. The scale, baseline shift, skew, and language controls are in the Advanced Character Formats pane. OpenType controls are in the OpenType Features pane. Custom underline and strikethrough options, as covered in Chapter 18, are available in the Underline Options and Strikethrough Options panes, respectively.

Figure 16.5 shows the various effects in action.

FIGURE 16.5

Various character-formatting options applied to text are illustrated here. Top row: The word *InDesign* has a different font style applied, *incredible* has been scaled horizontally, and *control* is in all caps, while *over* has had each letter's baseline shifted by a different amount. Middle row: The word *text* has been skewed, *with* is in small caps, a gradient and underline are applied to *typographic*, a custom underline has been applied to *capabilities, and formatting* has been vertically scaled. Bottom row: Compare the baseline shifts in the top row to the true superscript and subscript following the words *most* and *people*. The word *never* has a custom strikethrough applied, while *even* uses a standard one. The word *heard* has a colored stroke applied and a fill of white.

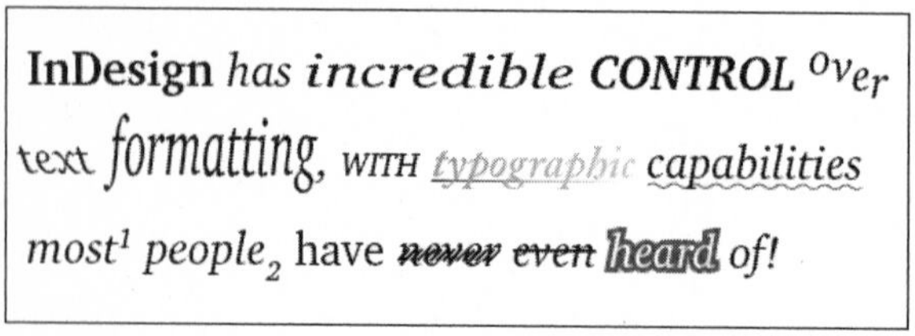

Horizontal Scale and Vertical Scale

Some font families include condensed (that is, slightly squeezed) and/or expanded (slightly stretched) stylistic variations, but most don't. InDesign's Horizontal Scale option lets you create artificially condensed and expanded type by squeezing or stretching characters. Similarly, the Vertical Scale option lets you shrink or stretch type vertically.

Among typographers, there are two schools of thought about scaling type. One camp contends that such distortions of letterforms are taboo and should be avoided. The other side contends that a small amount of scaling doesn't adversely affect the original font and is acceptable. There's general agreement that overscaling should be avoided. For the most part, if you need to make text bigger or smaller, you should adjust font size; if you need to squeeze or stretch a range of text a bit, it's better to use InDesign's kerning and tracking controls (covered later in this chapter) because the letterforms are not affected. Only the space between letters changes when you kern or track text.

Unscaled text has a horizontal and vertical scale value of 100 percent. You can apply scaling values between 1 percent and 1,000 percent. If you apply equal horizontal and vertical scale values, you're making the original text proportionally larger or smaller. In this case, changing font size is a simpler solution. Keep in mind that when you scale text, you are not changing the font size. For example, 24-point type scaled vertically to 200 percent is 48 points tall, but its font size is still 24 points.

To change the scale of highlighted text, enter new values in the Horizontal and/or Vertical Scale fields in the Character panel or Control panel. If a value is highlighted in the Horizontal Scale or Vertical Scale field, you can also use the up and down cursor keys to increase and decrease the scaling in 1 percent increments; press and hold Shift to increase or decrease in 10 percent increments.

Baseline Shift

The *baseline* is an invisible horizontal line on which a line of characters rests. The bottom of each letter (except descenders, such as in *y, p, q, j,* and *g*) sits on the baseline. InDesign's Baseline Shift feature lets you move highlighted text above or below its baseline. This feature is useful for carefully placing such characters as trademark and copyright symbols and for creating custom fractions. (In contrast to superscripts and subscripts, text whose baseline has shifted does not change size.)

To baseline-shift highlighted text, type new values in the Baseline Shift field in the Character panel or Control panel. You can also use the up and down cursor keys to increase the baseline shift in 1-point increments, or press and hold Shift when using the cursor keys to increase or decrease it in 10-point increments.

Skew (false italic)

For fonts that don't have an italic font style, InDesign provides the option to *skew*, or slant, text to create an artificial italic variation of any font. (You can also use it with fonts that have a natural italic; refer to Figure 16.5.) As with horizontal and vertical text scaling, skewing is a clunky way of creating italic-looking text. Use this feature to create special typographic effects, such as the shadow text shown in Figure 16.6, or in situations in which a true italic style is not available.

FIGURE 16.6

Skewing and shading a copy of the black text creates this backlit shadow effect.

Skewed shadow

NOTE Skewing as a form of italic typically works better for sans serif typefaces than for serif typefaces because the characters are simpler and have fewer embellishments that can get oddly distorted when skewed.

To skew highlighted text, you have two options:

- Type an angle value between –85 and 85 in the Skew field in the Character panel or Control panel. Positive values slant text to the left; negative values slant text to the right.

- Click the accompanying up or down cursors when the cursor is in the Skew field to skew text in 1-degree increments. Pressing and holding Shift while clicking the cursors changes the increment to 45 degrees.

TIP You can also skew all the text in a text frame using the Shear tool or by changing the value in the Shear X Angle field in the Control panel or Transform panel after selecting the frame. Slanting text by shearing a text frame does not affect the skew angle of the text. You can specify a skew angle for highlighted text independently from the frame's shear angle. Chapter 10 covers this effect in more detail.

Language

The ability to correctly hyphenate and check the spelling of text in several languages is one of InDesign's most powerful features. The program uses dictionaries to accomplish these tasks. These dictionaries, each of which contains several hundred thousand words, also let you specify a different language for text on a character-by-character basis, although chances are that a single word is the smallest text unit to which you would apply a separate language.

Typically, the language is specified at the paragraph level (see Chapter 17), but there are times you want to specify language at a more precise level, such as for specific words. For example, an article about traveling in France might include the word *tabac* (the French term for a kiosk or small store selling cigarettes, phone cards, and various sundries). By applying the French language to this word, InDesign does not flag it when you check spelling. However, if you were to apply U.S. English to *tabac*, it would show up as a misspelled word (unless you add it to your dictionary, as explained in Chapter 15).

To assign a different language to highlighted text, choose the appropriate language from the Language pop-up menu in the Control panel or from the Character panel's flyout menu.

 There's a language option called [No Language]; selecting it *prevents* spell checking and hyphenation.

All Caps and Small Caps

When you choose All Caps, the uppercase version of all highlighted characters is used: Lowercase letters are converted to uppercase, and uppercase letters remain unchanged.

Similarly, the Small Caps option affects just lowercase letters. When you choose Small Caps, InDesign automatically uses the Small Caps font style if one is available for the font family applied to the highlighted text (few font families include this font style). If a Small Caps font style is not available, InDesign generates small caps from uppercase letters using the scale percentage specified in the Advanced Type pane of the Preferences dialog box (choose InDesign ⇨ Preferences ⇨ Advanced Type or press ⌘+K on the Mac, or choose Edit ⇨ Preferences ⇨ Advanced Type or press Ctrl+K in Windows). The default scale value used to generate small caps text is 70 percent (of uppercase letters).

You should avoid typing text in all capital letters, even if you think you want all caps. If you type lowercase letters, you can easily change them to uppercase by applying the All Caps format, but if you type uppercase letters, you can't change them to lowercase or to small caps without retyping them or having InDesign retype them for you. To have InDesign do the work, select the text and then choose Type ⇨ Change Case ⇨ Lowercase. You can also choose Title Case (which capitalizes each word in the highlighted text) or Sentence Case (which capitalizes the first letter in each highlighted sentence) as appropriate to the text. (You can convert selected text to all uppercase by choosing Type ⇨ Change Case ⇨ Uppercase.)

TIP InDesign is smart enough to apply true small caps to OpenType fonts instead of the artificial small caps it normally uses when you apply Small Caps to text. (This is true whether you use the Small Caps options in the Control, Character, Character Style, or Paragraph Styles panel.) This is very handy in styles compared to using the OpenType Small Caps option, because when you select that option and then switch to a non-OpenType font, your text reverts to normal capitalization, which is probably not what you want. If you choose Small Caps instead, you always get the OpenType small caps when available and the regular small caps when not. (See Chapter 19 for more information on using styles and see the "OpenType details" section later in this chapter for more on OpenType small caps.)

Superscript and Subscript

When you apply the Superscript and Subscript character formats to highlighted text, InDesign applies a baseline shift to the characters, lifting them above (for Superscript) or lowering them below (for Subscript) their baseline, and reduces their size.

The amount of baseline shift and scaling that's used for the Superscript and Subscript formats is determined by the Position and Size fields in the Advanced Type pane of the Preferences dialog box (choose InDesign ⇨ Preferences ⇨ Advanced Type or press ⌘+K on the Mac, or choose Edit ⇨ Preferences ⇨ Advanced Type or press Ctrl+K in Windows). The default Position value for both formats is 33.3 percent, which means that characters are moved up or down by one-third of the applied leading value. The default Superscript and Subscript Size value is 58.3 percent, which means that superscripted and subscripted characters are reduced to 58.3 percent of the applied font size. The Advanced Type pane lets you specify separate default settings for Superscript and Subscript.

Why 58.3 percent for the default superscript and subscript size? There is a logical reason: That percentage happens to be $^7/_{12}$, or a nice round size of 7 points for 12-point text. In the days of metal- and photofilm-based typography, you couldn't have fractional point sizes, so your subscripts and superscripts were rounded to the nearest whole point. But today, with printers able to reproduce practically any size, that old-fashioned convention (which only works for text whose size is a multiple of 12, anyhow) makes no sense.

For most newspaper and magazine work, I prefer a size of 65 percent for superscripts and subscripts, as well as a position of 30 percent for subscripts and 35 percent for superscripts. To my eyes, these values work better than the InDesign defaults in the small text sizes and tight leading of such publications.

TIP   If you change these settings when no document is open, they become the default for all future new documents.

You can use the Superscript and Subscript formats to create, for example, custom fractions or numbers for footnotes or to reposition special characters such as asterisks. To apply the Superscript or Subscript format to highlighted text, choose the appropriate option from the Character panel's flyout menu. Figure 16.5 shows examples of text to which the default Superscript and Subscript settings have been applied.

Underline and Strikethrough

The Underline and Strikethrough formats are holdovers from the days of typewriters and are not typographically acceptable for indicating emphasis in text; it's better accomplished using bold and/ or italic font styles.

Underlines can be useful in kickers and other text above a headline, as well as in documents formatted to look as if they are typewritten. Strikethrough is rarely useful in a document, although in textbooks and other educational materials, you may want to use it to indicate incorrect answers, eliminated choices, or deleted text (when showing how to edit). A common use is in voter pamphlets showing deletions to laws that a successful citizen referendum would make.

If you do use underlines and strikethrough, InDesign lets you specify exactly how they look through the Underline Options and Strikethrough Options dialog boxes available in the flyout menus of the Character panel and Control panel.

CROSS-REF   Chapter 18 covers these custom underline and strikethrough settings in detail.

 If you don't set a specific size for underlines and strikethroughs, the weight of an underline or strikethrough line is relative to the font size.

Ligatures

A ligature is a special character that combines two letters. Most early typefaces included five ligatures: ff, fi, fl, ffi, and ffl. Many newer fonts — especially TrueType ones — include just two ligatures: fi and fl. (InDesign will use whatever of these five ligatures are available in your fonts.) When you choose the Ligature option, InDesign automatically displays and prints a font's built-in ligatures — instead of the two component letters — if the font includes ligatures.

One nice thing about the Ligature option is that, even though a ligature looks like a single character on-screen, it's still fully editable. That is, you can click between the two-letter shapes and insert text if necessary. Also, a ligature created with the Ligatures option does not cause InDesign's spell checker to flag the word that contains it.

To use ligatures within highlighted text, choose Ligatures from the Character panel's or Control panel's flyout menu (Ligatures is set to On by default). Figure 16.7 shows a before-and-after example of text to which the Ligature option has been applied.

FIGURE 16.7

Ligatures are used in the left two lines but not in the right two. Notice the difference in space between the *fi* and *fl* letter pairs in *finally* and *float*.

finally, I
can float!
finally, I
can float!

For most Mac fonts that include ligatures, pressing Option+Shift+5 inserts the fi ligature; Option+Shift+6 inserts the fl ligature. In Windows, you have to use a program such as Character Map that comes with Windows (usually available by choosing Start ⇨ All Programs ⇨ Accessories ⇨ System Tools ⇨ Character Map) to access the ligature characters in fonts that support them. Either way, if you type ligatures yourself, InDesign's spell checker flags any words that contain them. For this reason, you typically want to let the program handle the task of inserting ligatures itself.

OpenType options

InDesign takes strong advantage of OpenType, but only if you let it. The OpenType font standard has been around for several years, but it is still not used very much. One reason is that it requires publishers to replace their older fonts, which costs money for enhancements that everyone has lived without for years.

But OpenType offers compelling value, at least for some fonts. What OpenType provides is a greater variety of glyphs and glyph attributes than a standard font does. Small caps, old-fashioned numerals (the kinds with superiors and denominators), true fractions, true superiors (used for footnotes and mathematics), and true ordinals (the raised or superscript *th* in *4th*) are just some of the examples.

The key advantage here is that you don't have to manually style such attributes for every occurrence as you do with the so-called expert-collection fonts. Instead, InDesign automatically applies the available attributes to selected text or to text whose paragraph style or character style uses the specified OpenType features. (Note that any OpenType attributes in brackets are unavailable for the current font.)

There are several types of OpenType attributes:

- **Discretionary ligatures:** Creates ligatures beyond the standard fi, fl, ffi, and ffl that InDesign uses (when available) in TrueType, Type 1 PostScript, and OpenType fonts when ligatures are selected in the Character panel or in character styles.

- **Fractions:** Substitutes true fractions such as $\frac{1}{2}$ for the text *1/2*.

- **Ordinal:** Raises the *st*, *nd*, and *th* portions of ordinal numbers such as *1st*, *22nd*, and *345th*.

- **Swash:** Adds embellishments in front of the first character or at the end of the last letter of a word.

- **Titling Alternates:** Uses variants of a font for use in titles. These variants are usually a little clearer than the body-text version, so they work better as titles, whereas surrounding white space can make the normal variations within body text look strange.

- **Contextual Alternates:** Uses variants for specific characters to improve legibility in some contexts. For example, a contextual alternate for *t* might drop the left-side bar in the *t* so that it doesn't bump against an adjacent letter.

- **All Small Caps:** Replaces all the text with true small caps, not the scaled-down version that the standard InDesign small-caps feature uses. True small caps are usually a little thicker than their scaled-down version, so they have the same visual weight as lowercase letters.

- **Slashed Zero:** Adds a slash over a 0 character for fonts that support it. The slashed zero is often used in European writing to differentiate from the letter *O*.

- **Superscript/Superior:** Replaces scaled-down raised text that InDesign uses to create superscripts with thicker characters placed where the font designers think works best. As with true small caps, this feature results in superscripts that have more visual weight.

- **Subscript/Inferior:** Replaces scaled-down lowered text that InDesign uses to create subscripts with thicker characters placed where the font designers think works best. As with true small caps, this feature results in subscripts that have more visual weight.

- **Numerator:** Used to build the top part of a fraction when the font does not have predefined ones, such as for $\frac{n}{5}$.

- **Denominator:** Used to build the bottom part of a fraction when the font does not have predefined ones, such as for $^1/_n$.

- **Stylistic Sets:** Lets you choose which sets of variants within a font to use. A very few OpenType fonts, such as Poetica Std, use stylistic sets, which provide multiple variations of the same characters, letting you choose which variants to use.

- **Positional Forms**: Lets you choose which form of a character to use, for Arabic fonts and some Roman scripting fonts where the character's position within a word (beginning, middle, or end) determines its visual appearance.

- **Tabular Lining:** Uses standard numeric characters (which start on the baseline and have no descenders or ascenders) spaced evenly for proper alignment in tables.

- **Proportional Oldstyle:** Uses old-fashioned numerals with ascenders and descenders that are spaced in the same way as any other characters, based on their width, shape, and visual weight.

- **Proportional Lining:** Uses standard numerals spaced the same way as any other characters, based on their width, shape, and visual weight.

- **Tabular Oldstyle:** Uses old-fashioned numerals spaced evenly for natural alignment in tables.

- **Default Figure Style:** Does whatever the font's designers want it to do by default (one of the preceding four settings).

The results can be striking, as Figure 16.8 shows. Some things to notice in the text on the right in the figure as compared to the regular text on the left side are as follows:

- You can see contextual ligatures in many *st* and *sp* combinations, such as the word *Palestinian* on the third line.

- You can see the old-style numerals in the address and phone number in the second line.

- You can see a contextual alternate by looking at the word *Church* in the second line. Compare that embellished *C* and *h* with the same characters in the normal text at left.

- Many OpenType fonts display very oddly when you turn on Ordinal; they tend to take lots of seemingly random letters and essentially superscript them, not just do what you would expect and confine the style to forms like *24th* and *No. 1*. In this case, the font has an Ordinal screw-up just once: In Line 10 (begins with "meal"); note how *Not* is displayed as *Not*.

For the vast majority of fonts in use today, applying an OpenType feature has no effect because most fonts in use are standard Type 1 PostScript or TrueType. Among OpenType fonts, there is wide variation in what variations they support; InDesign indicates unavailable options by enclosing them in brackets in the menu.

FIGURE 16.8

The text at right has had several OpenType attributes enabled, as seen in the Character panel's flyout menu. The text at the left shows the same text with the normal attributes for the same font. Below the text are the Open Type menu options from the Character panel to show what features are selected.

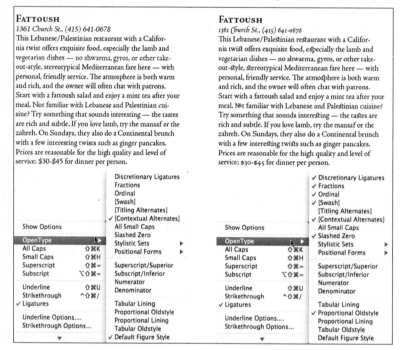

Expert Fonts Explained

There is a type of Type 1 PostScript font called an *expert font* that includes old-style numerals, fractions, true small caps, and other special characters. You can use it as an adjunct to the regular version of the font, which lets you manually apply the special characters.

For example, if you used Garamond as your font, you could apply Garamond Expert to the numerals to get old-style numerals. This is a lot of work, so most people don't bother except for typographically sophisticated — and short — documents, such as ads.

Unfortunately, InDesign doesn't detect the availability of expert fonts (for when you don't have OpenType fonts) and therefore doesn't use them to apply OpenType-like attributes such as old-style numerals, true small caps, and true fractions when they are available. Instead, you have to apply them manually — or buy and use OpenType fonts instead.

No Break

InDesign lets you prevent individual words from being hyphenated or a string of words from being broken at the end of a line. For example, you may decide that you don't want to hyphenate software names, such as InDesign, CorelDraw, or FreeHand. Or perhaps you don't want to separate the *J.* and the *P.* in *J. P. Morgan.* The No Break option was created for situations such as these.

To prevent a word or a text string from being broken, highlight it and then choose No Break from the Character panel's or Control panel's flyout menu.

CAUTION **If you apply the No Break option to a range of text that's longer than the width of the current column, InDesign tracks the text so that it fits on a single line — squeezing it unacceptably — and sometimes, InDesign refuses to display the rest of the text in the frame.**

TIP **You can prevent a word from being hyphenated by placing a discretionary hyphen (Shift+⌘+– or Ctrl+Shift+– in front of the first letter.**

Leaving Space between Characters and Lines

Typographers often pay as much attention to the space between characters, words, and lines of text as they do to the appearance of the characters themselves. Their concern about space is well justified. The legibility of a block of text depends as much on the space around it, called *white space,* as it does on the readability of the font.

InDesign offers two ways to adjust the space between characters — kerning and tracking — as well one way to adjust spacing between lines: leading.

CROSS-REF **InDesign also provides a way to adjust the space between paragraphs; see Chapter 17. It also explains how to control the spacing between words, which is part of paragraph formatting.**

Kerning

Kerning is the adjustment of space between a pair of characters. Most fonts include built-in kerning tables that control the space between pesky character pairs, such as *LA, Yo,* and *WA,* that otherwise could appear to have a space between them even when there isn't one. Particularly at small font sizes, it's safe to use a font's built-in kerning information to control the space between letter pairs. But for large font sizes, for example the front-page nameplate of a newsletter or a magazine headline, you may want to manually adjust the space between certain character pairs to achieve consistent spacing.

The Kerning controls in the Character panel and Control panel provide three options for kerning letter pairs: metrics kerning, optical kerning, and manual kerning:

- **Metrics kerning** uses a font's built-in kerning pairs to control the space between character pairs in the highlighted text.

- **Optical kerning** has InDesign look at each letter pair in highlighted text and add or remove space between the letters based on the shapes of the characters.

- **Manual kerning** is adding or removing space between a specific letter pair in user-specified amounts.

The kerning method you use depends on the circumstances. For example, some fonts include a large set of kerning pairs. Such fonts, especially at text font sizes (9 to 12 points) and lower, may look fine using the default metrics kerning option, which uses built-in kerning pairs. On the other hand, if the font applied to highlighted text has few or no built-in kerning pairs or if several different fonts are mixed together, the text may benefit from the optical kerning method. At display font sizes (36 points and larger), you may want to manually kern individual letter pairs to suit your taste.

When the flashing text cursor is between a pair of characters, the Kerning field displays the pair's kerning value. If metrics or optical kerning is applied, the kerning value is displayed in parentheses.

To apply metrics or optical kerning to highlighted text, choose the appropriate option from the Kerning pop-up menu. To apply manual kerning, click between a pair of letters and then type a value in the Kerning field or choose one of the predefined values. Negative values tighten; positive values loosen.

NOTE   InDesign applies kerning (and tracking) to highlighted text in $\frac{1}{1,000}$-em increments called *units*. An em is as wide as the height of the current font size (that is, an em for 12-point text is 12 points wide), which means that kerning and tracking increments are relative to the applied font size.

You can also use a keyboard shortcut to apply manual kerning. Press Option+← or Alt+← to decrease the kerning value in increments of 20 units. Press Option+→ or Alt+→ to increase the kerning value in increments of 20 units. If you add the ⌘ or Ctrl keys to these keyboard shortcuts, the increment is increased to 100 units. If you use the up and down cursor keys in the Kerning field in the Character panel or Control panel, you change the kerning in increments of 10; while pressing and holding Shift, the increments increase to 25.

CAUTION   A warning about kerning and tracking: InDesign happily lets you tighten or loosen text to the point of illegibility. If this is the effect you're after, go for it. But as a general rule, when letter shapes start to collide, you've tightened too far.

Tracking

Tracking is similar to kerning but applies to a range of highlighted text. Tracking is the process of adding or removing space among *all* letters in a range of text. You might use tracking to tighten character spacing for a font that you think is too spacey, or loosen spacing for a font that's too tight. Or you could track a paragraph tighter or looser to eliminate a short last line or a *widow* (the last line of a paragraph that falls at the top of a page or column).

To apply tracking to highlighted text, type a value in the Character panel's Tracking field or choose one of the predefined values. Negative values tighten; positive values loosen (in 0.001-em increments). Use the same keyboard techniques as for kerning.

Leading

InDesign's leading (rhymes with *sledding,* not with *heeding*) feature lets you control the vertical space between lines of type. In the days of metal type, typesetters would insert thin strips of metal — specifically, lead — between rows of letters to aid legibility. In the world of digital typography, *leading* refers to the vertical space between lines of type as measured from baseline to baseline.

In the publishing world, leading is traditionally an attribute of paragraphs, but InDesign takes a nonstandard, character-oriented approach. This means that you can apply different leading values within a single paragraph. InDesign looks separately at each line of text in a paragraph and uses the largest applied leading value within a line to determine the leading for that line.

That capability might have some utility in some cases, but for most publishers, the results are unevenly spaced lines that look unacceptably amateurish. Fortunately, you can make InDesign work the way the rest of the world does and apply consistent leading to entire paragraphs (using the largest leading value applied if several have been applied in a paragraph): Select the Apply Leading to Entire Paragraphs option in the Type pane of the Preferences dialog box (choose InDesign ⇨ Preferences ⇨ Type or press ⌘+K on the Mac, or choose Edit ⇨ Preferences ⇨ Type or press Ctrl+K in Windows).

Auto Leading Mysteries

In many ways, InDesign makes once-mystical typographic processes easy to use by designers, honoring the rules and intricacies of typography historically known only to typographers. But when it comes to auto leading, InDesign has gone off in a mysterious direction.

For example, why is something that InDesign treats as a character format setting accessed through the Paragraph panel? (Easy answer: Leading should be a paragraph attribute in the first place, and whoever put the Leading control in the Character panel missed the Auto Leading control!) A harder mystery: Why is the Auto Leading control offered as part of the justification controls, for which it has no relationship? (Maybe that's how it got missed when Leading was put in the Character panel!)

Another mystery is why you cannot specify Auto Leading amounts in anything other than percentages. This will cause many QuarkXPress documents imported into InDesign to flow incorrectly because QuarkXPress lets you set the Auto Leading to a specific value, such as +2 (which adds 2 points to the text size rather than use a percentage such as 120 percent that results in awkward leading amounts such as 14.4 points). Being able to specify a specific additive value such as +2 makes sense for many kinds of layouts, so the inability to specify such values is an unfortunate, continued omission in InDesign.

By default, InDesign applies Auto Leading to text. When Auto Leading is applied, leading is equal to 120 percent of the font size. For example, if Auto Leading is applied to 10-point text, the leading value is 12 points; for 12-point text, Auto Leading is 14.4 points; and so on. As long as you don't change fonts or font sizes in a paragraph, Auto Leading works pretty well. But if you do change fonts or sizes, Auto Leading can result in inconsistent spacing between lines. For this reason, it's safer to specify an actual leading value.

Generally, it's a good idea to use a leading value that is slightly larger than the font size, which is why Auto Leading works in many cases. When the leading value equals the font size, text is said to be *set solid*. That's about as tight as you ever want to set leading unless you're trying to achieve a special typographic effect or working with very large text sizes in ad-copy headlines. As is the case with kerning and tracking, when tight leading causes letters to collide — ascenders and descenders are the first to overlap — you've gone too far.

You can change InDesign's preset Auto Leading value of 120 percent. To do so, choose Type ➪ Paragraph or press Option+⌘+T or Ctrl+Alt+T to display the Paragraph panel. Choose Justification in the flyout menu, type a new value in the Auto Leading field and then click OK.

To modify the leading value applied to selected text, choose one of the predefined options from the Leading pop-up menu in the Character panel or Control panel, or type a leading value in the field. You can type values from 0 to 5,000 points in 0.001-point increments. You can also use the up and down cursor keys to change leading in 1-point increments.

Summary

As a user of InDesign, modifying the appearance of type is one of the more common tasks you'll perform. InDesign lets you modify the appearance of highlighted characters or selected paragraphs. When text is highlighted, you can use the controls in the Character panel or Control panel to change any of several character attributes: font family, font size, font style, leading, kerning, tracking, vertical and horizontal scale, baseline shift, and skew. You can also set the hyphenation and spell-checking language, apply all caps or small caps, superscripts or subscripts, underline, strikethrough, ligatures, and OpenType variations.

You also set line spacing (leading) as a character attribute, something that's normally applied to entire paragraphs in other programs. Setting it as a character attribute can lead to uneven line spacing, something that, fortunately, InDesign lets you override to get consistent leading throughout a paragraph.

Chapter 17

Specifying Paragraph Attributes

A s is an individual character, a paragraph in InDesign is treated like a basic typographic unit. When you create a new text frame and begin typing, you create a paragraph each time you press Return or Enter. A paragraph can be as short as one character or word on a single line or many words strung out over many lines. When you press Return or Enter, the paragraph formats of the preceding paragraph are automatically used for the subsequent paragraph (unless you create styles that automatically change paragraph formats).

In general, paragraph formats control how the lines of text in the paragraph are constructed. Changing paragraph formats doesn't change the appearance of the individual characters within the paragraph. To do that, you must highlight the characters and modify character-level formats.

CROSS-REF This chapter focuses on modifying paragraph-level typographic formats; Chapter 16 focuses on modifying character-level formats. Chapter 19 covers the creation and use of styles for both characters and paragraphs.

IN THIS CHAPTER

Understanding paragraph fundamentals

Changing basic and advanced paragraph formats

Applying automatic bullets and numbering

Working with hyphenation and justification

Modifying other paragraph formats

Understanding Paragraph Basics

To select a paragraph, simply click within it using the Type tool. Any change you make to a paragraph-level format applies to all the lines in the paragraph. (In contrast to how you modify character-level formats, you don't have to highlight all the text in a paragraph to modify a paragraph-level format.) If you need to change the paragraph formats of several consecutive paragraphs, you can highlight all the text in all the paragraphs, or you can click any-where in the first paragraph, drag anywhere within the last paragraph, and then release the mouse button.

Just as you can't apply two different colors to a single character, so you can't apply conflicting paragraph formats within a single paragraph. For example, you can't specify that one line in a paragraph be left-aligned and the rest right-aligned. All lines in a paragraph must share the same alignment, indents, tab settings, and all other paragraph-level formats.

As is the case with character formats, there are two ways to apply paragraph formats:

■ Use the controls in the Paragraph panel or Control panel's Paragraph (¶) pane, shown in Figures 17.1 and 17.2, or their keyboard shortcuts.

■ Create and apply paragraph styles.

FIGURE 17.1

The Paragraph panel and its flyout menu

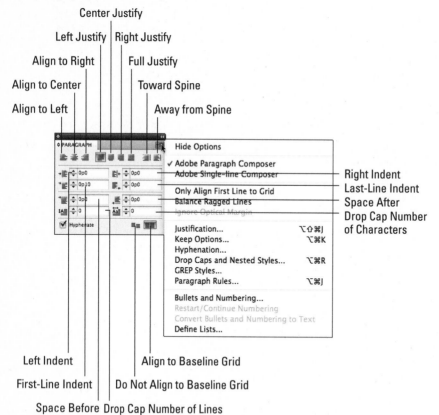

440

FIGURE 17.2

The Control panel's paragraph formatting options and flyout menu

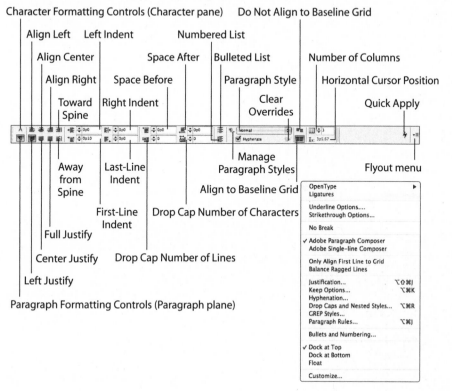

A paragraph style is essentially a text-formatting macro that lets you apply several paragraph formats to selected paragraphs in a single operation. If you're working on a multipage publication such as a book, newspaper, magazine, or catalog that repeatedly uses the same basic text formats, you definitely want to use paragraph styles to handle the bulk of your formatting chores. But even if you use styles, you probably also use the Paragraph panel to do some manual paragraph formatting.

CROSS-REF   Tab settings are also a paragraph-level format. See Chapter 21 for a detailed explanation of InDesign's tabs feature.

Figure 17.1 shows the Paragraph panel. There are three ways to open the Paragraph panel: Choose Type ➪ Paragraph, choose Window ➪ Type & Tables ➪ Paragraph, or press Option+⌘+T or Ctrl+Alt+T.

The panel can have two appearances: If you choose Hide Options from the pop-up menu, the Space Before, Space After, Drop Cap Number of Lines, Drop Cap Number of Characters, Hyphenate, and Align to Baseline Grid, and Do Not Align to Baseline Grid controls are not displayed. You can use the double-arrow iconic button to the left of the panel name to toggle among showing the panel title, the basic options, and all options.

You can also use the Control panel's paragraph formatting options, shown in Figure 17.2. (Be sure to click the ¶ iconic button to get the paragraph options.) These controls mirror those in the Paragraph panel, and using them instead of the Paragraph panel can reduce screen clutter. If the Control panel is not visible (it almost always is), display it by choosing Window ⇨ Control or pressing Option+⌘+6 or Ctrl+Alt+6.

In both the Paragraph panel and the Control panel, several of the options have keyboard shortcuts.

> **TIP**   If the Type tool is selected and no objects are active, any changes you make in the Control panel's Paragraph (¶) pane become the default settings for the document and are automatically used when you create new text frames.

Using leading

Leading (rhymes with *sledding*, not *heeding*), or the space between lines in a paragraph, is treated by InDesign as a character format through the Character panel or Control panel, even though it's traditionally an attribute of the paragraph. However, you can override InDesign's character-oriented approach so that it works like all other layout programs. To ensure that leading changes affect entire paragraphs, select the Apply Leading to Entire Paragraphs option in the Type pane of the Preferences dialog box (choose InDesign ⇨ Preferences ⇨ Type or press ⌘+K on the Mac, or choose Edit ⇨ Preferences ⇨ Type or press Ctrl+K in Windows).

> **CROSS-REF**   For more details on how to apply leading, see Chapter 16.

> **NOTE**   When creating paragraph styles, you set leading in the Basic Character Formats pane of the New Paragraph Styles dialog box.

Controlling alignment and indents

The nine alignment icons at the top of the Paragraph panel and the four fields are always displayed; the four additional fields, two icons, and the Hyphenate option are also displayed when you choose Show Options from the flyout menu. InDesign refers to the top set of options as Basic Paragraph Formats; the additional seven options are Advanced Paragraph Formats.

The top set lets you control a paragraph's alignment and indents (left, right, first line, and last line). The additional options control paragraph spacing and drop caps, as well as lock or unlock text baselines to the baseline grid.

> **NOTE**   When creating paragraph styles, you set alignments and indents in the Indents and Spacing pane of the New Paragraph Styles dialog box. Instead of buttons for aligning to the baseline grid, this pane has the Align to Grid pop-up menu, which has three options: None, All Lines, and First Line Only (this last option is also available in the Paragraph and Control panels' flyout menus).

The Paragraph Pane's Guest Functions

Two options in the Control panel's Paragraph (¶) pane are unrelated to paragraph formatting:

The Number of Columns field affects text frames and has the same effect as the same-named control in the Text Frame Options dialog box, as described in Chapter 14.

The Horizontal Cursor Position status indicator shows the horizontal position, relative to the frame's left inset, of the text cursor. This indicator can be helpful when you're trying to measure where to draw vertical rules, set tab stops, or otherwise understand where specific text sits within a line so that you can align or place something at the same horizontal location.

Alignment

The nine alignment icons at the top of the Paragraph panel control how line beginnings and endings in selected paragraphs are placed relative to the left and right margins. (All but one are also available in the Control panel's Paragraph [¶] pane.) Here's a description of each alignment option (the icons do a pretty good job of showing what they do):

- **Align Left (Shift+⌘+L or Ctrl+Shift+L):** Places the left edge of every line at the left margin (the margin can be the frame edge, frame inset, left indent, or column edge) and fits as many words (or syllables, if hyphenation is turned on) on the line as possible. When a word (or syllable) won't fit at the end of a line, it's placed (flush left) on the next line. In left-aligned paragraphs, the right margin is said to be *ragged* because the leftover space at the right end of each line differs from line to line and produces a jagged edge.

  Some designers prefer to use this alignment for columns of text because they like the irregular, somewhat organic shapes that result; others prefer to align both left and right edges by increasing spacing as needed between characters (called *justification*), which produces a more rigid, vertical look. Similarly, left-aligned text is sometimes hyphenated, sometimes not. (You can find more about hyphenation and justification later in this chapter.)

- **Align Center (Shift+⌘+C or Ctrl+Shift+C):** To create centered text, the leftover space of each line is divided in half. One-half of the leftover space is placed on the left end of the line; the other half is placed on the right end. The result is that both the left and right edges of the paragraphs are ragged, and the text is balanced along a vertical axis.

- **Align Right (Shift+⌘+R or Ctrl+Shift+R):** This is a mirror opposite of Align Left. The right edge is straight; the left edge is ragged. Columns of text are seldom set flush right because it's not as easy to read as flush-left text. Right-aligned text is sometimes used for such things as captions placed to the left of a picture, blurbs on magazine covers, and advertising copy.

- **Left Justify (Shift+⌘+J or Ctrl+Shift+J):** In justified text, the left and right ends of each line are flush with the margins. The flush-left/flush-right results are produced either by sprinkling the spaces of each line among characters and/or words or by reducing space between characters and/or words to accommodate additional characters (more about justification later in this chapter). Justified text is nearly always hyphenated (if you don't hyphenate justified text, spacing between letters and words is very inconsistent). Aligning the last line flush left is the traditional way of ending a paragraph, which is why Left Justify is the justified-text style most often used on paragraphs.

- **Center Justify:** This is the same as Left Justify except that the last line is center-aligned.

- **Right Justify:** This is the same as Left Justify except that the last line is right-aligned. Note that this iconic button is not available in the Control panel.

- **Full Justify (Shift+⌘+F or Ctrl+Shift+F):** This is the same as Left Justify except that the last line is also forcibly justified. This option can produce very widely spaced last lines. The fewer the characters on the last line, the greater the spacing.

  The previous three options are rarely used, and for good reason. People expect justified text to have the last line aligned left and the space at the end of the line to be a marker that the paragraph has ended. By changing the position of that last line, you can confuse your reader. So use Center Justify, Right Justify, and Full Justify options sparingly in special situations in which the reader won't be confused — typically in brief copy like ads and pull-quotes.

- **Align Towards Spine:** This is similar to Left Justify or Right Justify except that InDesign automatically chooses a left or right alignment based on where the spine is in a facing-pages document. Essentially, this automatically creates right-aligned text on left-hand pages and left-aligned text on right-hand pages.

- **Align Away from Spine:** This is the same as Towards Spine except that the alignment is reversed: text aligns to the left on left-hand pages and to the right on right-hand pages.

To apply a paragraph alignment to selected paragraphs, click one of the icons. (The hand pointer appears when the pointer is over a panel button.) You can also use the keyboard shortcuts in the preceding list.

NOTE Left-aligned and right-aligned paragraphs typically fit fewer characters per line than justified paragraphs. Most publications standardize on one of these two alignments for body copy; one factor is often how much copy needs to be squeezed in.

Indents

You can move the edges of paragraphs away from the left and/or right margins and indent the first line using the indent controls in the Paragraph panel or Control panel.

Left and right indents are often used for lengthy passages of quoted material within a column of text. Using indents is also handy way of drawing attention to pull-quotes and moving text away from a nearby graphic.

Spacing Guidelines for Indents

The easy part of creating first-line indents and hanging indents is using the software. The hard part can be deciding how much space to use. For example, how do you decide how deep to make a first-line indent? Amateur publishers or designers, who are likely to be thinking in inches rather than points or picas, are likely to use too much space. They're tempted to use 0.25", 0.125", or another nice dividend of an inch for spacing rather than a more appropriate value such as 6 points. When deciding on spacing, consider the following:

- First-line indents that indicate new paragraphs should generally be one or two em spaces wide. The width of an em space is equal to the point size in use — so 10-point text should have a 10- or 20-point first-line indents. Opt for less space in narrower columns to avoid awkward space and more space in wider columns so that the spacing is evident.

- As you remember from grade-school outlines, indents help organize information, with deeper indents indicating more detail about a topic. Professional publications, though, have many organizational options — such as headlines, subheads, and run-in heads — so they rarely have a need for more than two levels of indents. You might use indents on lengthy quotes, bulleted lists, numbered lists, kickers, and bylines. If you do, stick to the same amount of indent for each so that the readers' eyes don't wander.

Although these values give you a good starting point, you might need to modify them based on the typeface, font size, column width, design, and overall goals of the publication.

The options are:

- **Left Indent:** Type a value in this field to move the left edge of selected paragraphs away from the left margin. You can also use the up and down arrow keys. Each click increases the value by 1 point; pressing and holding Shift while clicking increases the increment to 1 pica.

- **Right Indent:** Type a value in this field to move the right edge of selected paragraphs away from the right margin. You can also use the up and down arrow keys.

- **First-Line Left Indent:** Type a value in this field to move the left edge of the first line of selected paragraphs away from the left margin. You can also press the up and down arrow keys. The value in the First-Line Indent field is added to any Left Indent value. For example, if you've specified a Left Indent value of 1 pica and you then specify a 1-pica First-Line Indent value, the first line of selected paragraphs is indented 2 picas from the left margin. If you've specified a Left Indent value, you can specify a negative First-Line Left Indent value to create a *hanging indent* (also called an *outdent*). But you cannot specify a First-Line Left Indent value that would cause the first line to extend past the left edge of the text frame (that is, the First-Line Left Indent value can't exceed that of the Left Indent value).

- **Last-Line Right Indent:** Type a value in this field to move the right edge of the last line of selected paragraphs away from the right margin. You can also press the up and down arrow keys. This function otherwise works just like the First-Line Left Indent function, so the Last-Line Right Indent value cannot exceed that of the Right Indent value.

Using a tab or spaces to indent the first line of a paragraph, which is what was done in the age of typewriters, is usually not a good idea. You're better off specifying a First-Line Indent. Similarly, you can indent an entire paragraph by inserting a tab or multiple word spaces at the beginning of every line in the paragraph, but both are typographic no-nos. Use the indent controls instead.

Hanging indents often have awkward measurements because they depend on the width of the bullet or other lead-in character. That can involve lots of experimentation to get the hang right. A simpler way is to insert the Indent Here character (choose Type ➪ Insert Special Character ➪ Other ➪ Indent to Here or press ⌘+\ or Ctrl+\). InDesign figures out the dimensions for you. Note that in this case, the Paragraph or Control panel will not show any indent values.

> **CAUTION**   There is a risk with using Indent Here: You can have inconsistent hanging indents if the lead-in characters or space differ in your paragraphs, or if tracking or kerning of text before the indent-to-here characters varies from paragraph to paragraph.

Lock to Baseline Grid

Every document includes a grid of horizontal lines, called the *baseline grid,* which can be displayed or hidden (choose View ➪ Grids & Guides ➪ Show/Hide Baseline Grid or press Option+⌘+' or Ctrl+Alt+') and used to help position objects and text baselines. A document's baseline grid is established in the Grids pane of the Preferences dialog box (choose InDesign ➪ Preferences ➪ Grids or press ⌘+K on the Mac, or choose Edit ➪ Preferences ➪ Grids or press Ctrl+K in Windows). Generally, a document's baseline grid interval is equal to the leading value applied to the body text.

You can ensure that lines of text align across columns and pages by locking their baselines to the baseline grid. To do so, click the Align to Baseline Grid iconic button in the Paragraph panel (the rightmost button on the bottom). To prevent such locking to the baseline, click the Do Not Align to Baseline Grid iconic button. These same buttons also exist on the right side of the Control panel's Paragraph (¶) pane.

You can also set individual baseline grids for specific text frames. You do so in the Baseline Options pane of the Text Frame Options dialog box (choose Object ➪ Text Frame Options or press ⌘+B or Ctrl+B). This is particularly handy for multicolumn text frames. InDesign aligns a paragraph to its text frame's baseline grid if it has one and to the document's baseline grid if not — assuming, of course, that Align to Baseline Grid option is selected.

> **CROSS-REF**   Chapter 9 covers how to set up baseline grids in more detail.

Although you can use InDesign's Lock to Baseline Grid feature to align text baselines across columns and pages (or within text frames), you can produce the same results by combining uniform body text leading with other paragraph formats (Space Before and Space After). Some designers like the certainty and simplicity of the Lock to Baseline Grid feature; others prefer to control text alignment across columns themselves. Whichever works best for you is fine.

Keep in mind that when paragraphs are aligned to the baseline grid, the applied leading values are ignored.

InDesign provides a way to change how the Lock to Baseline Grid feature works. Normally, every line in your text is aligned to the baseline grid when the feature is selected. But in some cases, you want only the first line of a paragraph to align to the baseline grid. For example, it's common to align just the first line in a multiline subhead to the baseline grid letting the extra lines fall naturally based on the paragraph's leading. InDesign gives you a control to get this behavior: The Only Align First Line to Grid option in the Paragraph panel's and Control panel's flyout menus. You can use this option for any paragraph that you want to be the reset point if your text gets off the baseline grid, without forcing every line to align to the grid. (Otherwise, every line in the subhead would be aligned to the baseline grid, essentially overriding your leading.)

Another option, Balance Ragged Lines, in the Paragraph panel's and Control panel's flyout menus ensures that the rag is balanced, which means that the lines of text alternate between short and long when possible, rather than fall in a seemingly random pattern. The purpose of this option is to make headlines and other large copy, such as in ads, more visually pleasing. You wouldn't use this option for body text; the use of small text size and the need for efficient spacing in body text make this feature irrelevant. Unfortunately, this setting also forces hyphenation to achieve the balanced rag, which may be contrary to your intent.

Adding Space between Paragraphs

When you choose Show Options from the Paragraph panel's flyout menu, four additional fields appear, as shown earlier in Figure 17.1. They're also always in the Control panel. Two of these fields let you insert space before and/or after paragraphs.

When you need to format a lengthy chunk of text with multiple paragraphs, there are two ways to indicate a new paragraph. You can:

- Indent the paragraph's first line (by specifying a First-Line Left Indent value).
- Insert some extra space between the new paragraph and the preceding one.

There's no rule that says you can't use both spacing methods, but generally you'll use one or the other. What you don't want to do is insert extra returns between a paragraph, which is what was done in the days of typewriters.

To insert space before selected paragraphs, type a value in the Space Before field in the Paragraph panel or Control panel. You can also use the up and down nudge buttons next to the fields, and you can use the ↑ and ↓ keys. (Just be sure you've selected the Space Before field first.) Each click of the nudge button or press of the ↑ or ↓ key increases the Space Before value by 1 point. If you hold Shift while using the nudge buttons or ↑ and ↓ keys, InDesign makes the spacing the nearest multiple of 10 points and then continues to increment your Space Before value 10 points at a time as long as hold Shift.

The Space After field works the same as the Space Before field but inserts space below selected paragraphs. Generally, you use Space Before or Space After to separate paragraphs. Combining both can be confusing.

 NOTE When creating paragraph styles, you set paragraph spacing in the Indents and Spacing pane of the New Paragraph Styles dialog box.

Using Drop Caps

A drop cap is created by *notching* a paragraph's first letter or letters into the upper-left corner of the paragraph. Drop caps are often used to embellish the first paragraph of a story, to draw attention to paragraphs, and to interrupt the grayness in columns of text.

Applying basic drop caps

In the Paragraph panel or Control panel, InDesign lets you specify the number of letters you want to include in a drop cap and the number of lines you want to notch them.

To add one or more drop caps to selected paragraphs, type a number in the Drop Cap Number field in the Paragraph panel or Control panel. That's how many characters will be made into drop caps. To specify the number of lines a drop cap extends into a paragraph, type a value in the Drop Cap Depth field.

If the first character in a paragraph is a quotation mark (" or '), it can look odd as a one-character drop cap. If you don't like this look, you have a couple of options: You can either delete the opening quotation mark, an acceptable but potentially confusing practice, or you can use the first two characters in the paragraph as drop caps instead. Some publications simply prefer not to start paragraphs with quotes, preventing the problem from the editorial side.

After you create a drop cap, you can modify it by highlighting it and then changing any of its character formats — font, size, color, and so on — using a character style, the Character panel or Control panel, and other panels (such as Stroke and Swatches). Figure 17.3 shows some examples of drop caps.

FIGURE 17.3

The first (leftmost) drop cap has a one-character drop cap three lines deep. In the second example, the font size of a one-letter, four-line drop cap has been enlarged to raise it above the first line of text. In the third example, a Left Indent value combined with a negative First-Line Left Indent value produced the one-character, three-line drop cap's hanging indent. The fourth (rightmost) example is of a two-line, four-character drop cap.

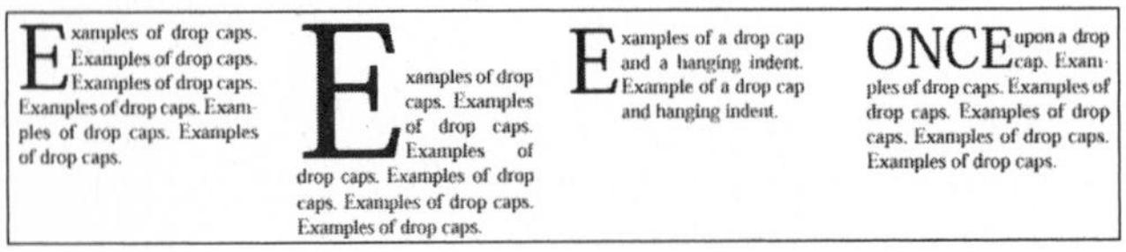

Using the Drop Caps and Nested Styles dialog box

A handy way to apply these settings is to use the Drop Caps and Nested Styles option in the Paragraph panel's or Control panel's flyout menu. You can also press Option+⌘+R or Ctrl+Alt+R. Figure 17.4 shows the dialog box.

FIGURE 17.4

The Drop Caps and Nested Styles dialog box

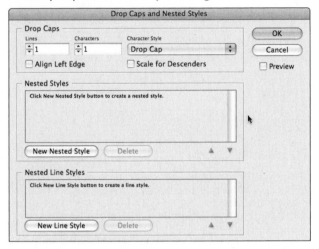

With this dialog box, you can set a character style that is applied to the drop cap, as well as set the number of lines and characters for that drop cap.

NEW FEATURE If you don't have a character style ready to use for your drop cap, InDesign CS4 now lets you create it by choosing New Character Style in the Character Style pop-up menu. In the previous version, you had to close the Drop Caps and Nested Styles dialog box, open the Character Styles panel and create the drop cap style there, and then close that panel and come back to the Drop Caps and Nested Styles dialog box to apply the new style.

You can also use this dialog box to apply another character style to other text in the paragraph. To do so, click New Nested Style and then choose from the three (unnamed) pop-up menus to specify how the style is to be applied. The first pop-up menu lets you choose the character style to apply, the second pop-up menu lets you choose Through or Up To (specify the number in the field to its right), and the third pop-up menu lets you determine what elements you're using, as the figure shows.

CROSS-REF Because the drop cap and nested style features are most useful when coupled with a paragraph style (otherwise, it's easier to simply highlight some text in a paragraph and apply a character style to it), Chapter 20 covers drop caps and other nested styles in more detail.

 When you're creating paragraph styles, you'll find the above controls available in the Drop Caps and Nested Styles pane of the New Paragraph Styles dialog box.

Using special initial cap techniques

The three-line, single-letter drop cap is used so often that it's almost a cliché. Serviceable, yes, but very commonplace. But you can create all sorts of initial caps — large first letters such as drop caps and raised caps — in InDesign, as Figure 17.5 shows:

FIGURE 17.5

Examples of special initial caps. From left to right: a raised cap, a drop cap created by converting a character into a graphic and then applying special effects to it, and a drop "cap" made up of a graphic.

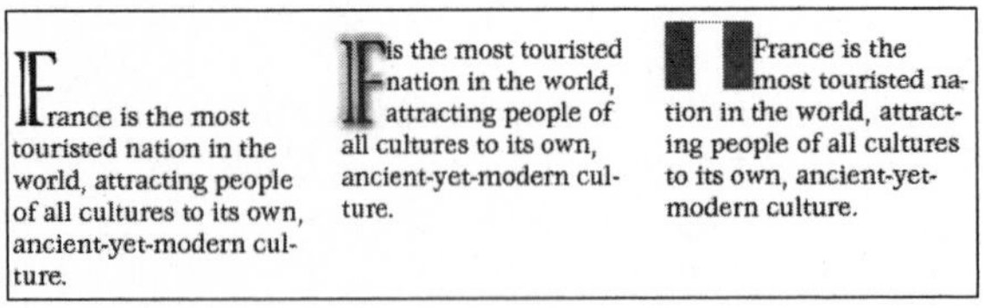

> France is the most touristed nation in the world, attracting people of all cultures to its own, ancient-yet-modern culture.
>
> Fis the most touristed nation in the world, attracting people of all cultures to its own, ancient-yet-modern culture.
>
> France is the most touristed nation in the world, attracting people of all cultures to its own, ancient-yet-modern culture.

Creating raised caps

Raised caps are an alternative to drop caps, created by enlarging and raising the first few characters of the paragraph above the first line in the paragraph. Creating raised caps is simple — highlight the characters you want to raise with the Type tool and enlarge them using the Font Size field in the Character panel (choose Type ➪ Character or press ⌘+T or Ctrl+T) or in the Character pane of the Control panel (press the A iconic button).

If you raise a word or phrase, you might need to track the raised words to tighten them. You also might need to kern between the raised text and the remainder of the line. Other options for raised caps include changing the font, color, and scale of the characters. If you plan to repeat the raised-cap formatting, save it as a character style.

You can also create partially raised caps by creating a drop cap and then enlarging the drop cap using the Character panel, the Character pane of the Control panel, or a character style.

Converting text to outlines for initial caps

You can convert drop caps, raised caps, or any character in any font to a graphic (actually, it's a frame, but you can work with it as if it were a graphic). You can then resize, scale, shear, fill, and stroke the character-shaped frame — even import a graphic into it. To do this, highlight the characters with the Type tool and then choose Type ➪ Create Outlines or press Shift+⌘+O or Ctrl+Shift+O. Frames are based on the size and outlines of the font in use and are automatically anchored in the paragraph so that they flow with the text.

Note that when you convert text to outlines, the characters no longer exist as text. If you converted part of a word, the remaining portions of the word may be flagged during a spelling check. If you need to edit the converted text, delete the outlines, retype the word, and convert the characters again.

Using graphics as initial caps

Rather than use text for initial caps, you can use graphics. You can purchase clip art collections that consist of nothing but ornate capital letters to use as initial caps. To use a graphic as an initial cap, first delete the character you will replace with a graphic. Then, use the Place command (choose File ➪ Place or press ⌘+D or Ctrl+D) to import the graphic.

Size the graphic as appropriate and then place it behind the paragraph, next to the paragraph, or anchored in the text of the paragraph. To anchor a graphic in text, select it with the Selection tool and choose Edit ➪ Cut or press ⌘+X or Ctrl+X. Select the Type tool and click at the beginning of the paragraph; then, choose Edit ➪ Paste or press ⌘+V or Ctrl+V. The graphic is now anchored to the text, and you can apply InDesign's Drop Cap settings to it as if it were text. Similarly, you can resize it to create a raised cap from it. (Chapter 12 covers anchoring in more detail.)

In addition to importing graphics for use as initial caps, you can create your own graphics in InDesign. For example, you can place the initial cap character in its own text frame and create reverse type from it, as I explain in this chapter. Or you can shade the character and place it slightly behind the paragraph.

Adding Automatic Bullets and Numbered Lists

Word processors have long been able to add automatic bullets and numbering to paragraphs. So it makes sense that a layout program can, too. In InDesign, automatic bullets and numbering are available as a paragraph-level format, accessed in the Paragraph panel's and Control panel's flyout menus by choosing Bullets and Numbering Options.

The simplest way to use these is to select the paragraphs that you want to be bulleted or numbered. Then click the appropriate button in the Paragraph (¶) pane of the Control panel. As you would expect, InDesign offers more than basic controls, which you can access via the Bullets & Numbering option in the Paragraph panel's flyout menu or via the submenu options when choosing Type ➪ Bulleted & Numbered Lists.

This bullets-and-numbering feature is most useful when coupled with a paragraph style; otherwise, you have to apply these settings for each selection of paragraphs you want to make into a list.

CROSS-REF Chapter 18 covers the setup, customization, and application of bullets and numbering in more detail. Chapter 19 covers styles in more detail.

Controlling Hyphenation and Justification

Hyphenation is the placement of hyphens between syllables in words that don't completely fit at the end of a line of text — a signal to the reader that the word continues on the next line. InDesign gives you the option to hyphenate or not hyphenate paragraphs, and if you choose to hyphenate, you can customize the settings that determine when and where hyphens are inserted.

As noted earlier, justification is the addition or removal of space between words and/or letters that produces the flush-left/flush-right appearance of justified paragraphs. InDesign's justification controls let you specify how space is added or removed when paragraphs are justified.

If your pages contain columns of text, you have to decide whether to use left-aligned or justified paragraphs and whether you want to hyphenate words that don't entirely fit at the end of a line. As mentioned earlier, if you justify paragraphs, you almost certainly want to hyphenate them, too. If you opt for left-aligned paragraphs, whether to hyphenate is a personal choice.

InDesign offers two hyphenation methods: manual and automatic.

NOTE When creating paragraph styles, all the hyphenation controls are available in the Hyphenation pane of the New Paragraph Styles dialog box — except for the composer setting.

Manual hyphenation

If you want to break a particular word differently from the way InDesign would normally break the word, you can place a *discretionary hyphen* in the word. If the word falls at the end of a line in a hyphenated paragraph, InDesign uses the discretionary hyphen to split the word if the first syllable fits on the line. To insert a discretionary hyphen, press Shift+⌘+– or Ctrl+Shift+– in the text where you want the hyphen to appear, or choose Type ➪ Insert Special Character ➪ Hyphens and Dashes ➪ Discretionary Hyphen.

You can prevent a particular word from being hyphenated either by placing a discretionary hyphen in front of the first letter or by highlighting the word and choosing No Break from the flyout menu of the Control panel or Character panel. (You need to select the A iconic button in the Control panel to get this option in its flyout menu.) But be careful: If you select more than a line's width of text and apply No Break, InDesign may not display the rest of the story's text.

TIP If you place a discretionary hyphen in a word, InDesign breaks the word only at that point (or does not break it at all). But you can place multiple discretionary hyphens within a single word; InDesign uses the one that produces the best results.

InDesign uses discretionary hyphens only if you select the Hyphenate option in the Paragraph panel or in the Control panel. If Hyphenate is not selected, neither manual nor automatic hyphenation is applied.

Likewise, if you want to force a hyphen that cannot be broken (meaning it cannot fall at the end of a line), insert the nonbreaking hyphen character (choose Type ➪ Insert Special Character ➪ Hyphens and Dashes ➪ Nonbreaking Hyphen or press Option+⌘+– or Ctrl+Alt+–).

Automatic hyphenation

To automatically hyphenate selected paragraphs, all you have to do is select the Hyphenate option in the Paragraph panel or Control panel. (The Hyphenate option appears only if you choose Show Options from the flyout menu.)

If you choose to hyphenate paragraphs, you can control how hyphenation is accomplished through the Hyphenation option in the flyout menu. When you choose Hyphenation, the Hyphenation Settings dialog box, shown in Figure 17.6, appears.

FIGURE 17.6

The Hyphenation Settings dialog box

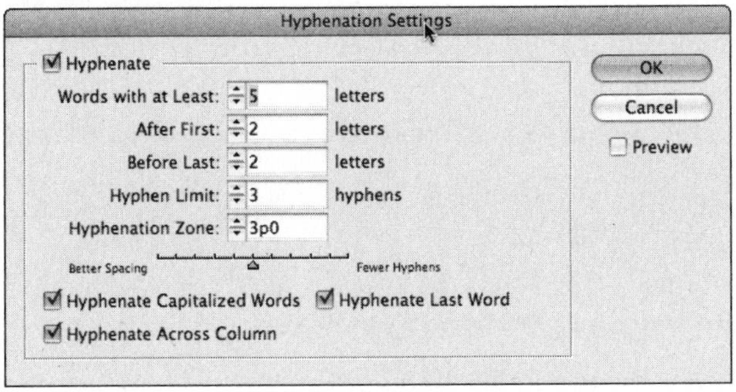

Here's a brief description of each option:

- **Hyphenate:** This is a duplicate of the Hyphenate option in the Paragraph panel and Control panel. If you didn't select it before opening the Hyphenation dialog box, you can select it here.

- **Words with at Least ___ Letters:** Here, you specify the number of letters in the shortest word you want to hyphenate. For example, if you specify four letters, *mama* can be hyphenated, but *any* can't be.

- **After First ___ Letters:** Here, you specify the minimum number of characters that can precede a hyphen. If you type **2**, for example, the word *atavistic* can be broken after *at*. If you specify 3, *atavistic* cannot be broken until after *ata*.

- **Before Last ___ Letters:** This field is similar to After First ___ Letters, but it determines the minimum number of characters that can follow a hyphen.

- **Hyphenation Limit ___ Hyphens:** Specify the number of consecutive lines that can be hyphenated in this field. Some designers limit the number of consecutive hyphens to two or three because they believe that too many consecutive hyphens produce an awkward, ladder-like look. If the Hyphenation Limit value you enter prevents hyphenation in a line that would otherwise be hyphenated, the line may appear more spaced out than surrounding lines.

- **Hyphenation Zone:** This field applies only to nonjustified text and only when the Adobe Single-Line Composer option is selected (in the Paragraph panel's or Control panel's fly-out menu). A hyphenation point must fall within the distance specified in this field to be used. Otherwise-acceptable hyphenation points that do not fall within the specified hyphenation zone are ignored. You can also click and drag the slider below the field to select a value rather than type a value in this field.

- **Hyphenate Capitalized Words:** Select this option to break capitalized words, such as proper names and the first word of sentences. If you don't select this check box, a capitalized word that would otherwise be hyphenated will get bumped to the next line, possibly producing excessive spacing in the previous line.

- **Hyphenate Last Word:** Select this option to break the last word in a paragraph. Otherwise, InDesign moves the entire word to the last line and spaces the preceding text as necessary. Some typographers don't like having a word fragment as the last line, arguing that there's no need to break a word in two because there is clearly enough space to keep it together. I'm not so dogmatic.

- **Hyphenate across Column:** Select this option to let text hyphenate at the end of a column.

When you're done specifying hyphenation settings in the Hyphenation Settings dialog box, click OK to close the dialog box and return to your document.

How Many Characters?

Consider changing the After First ___ Letters hyphenation setting to 2 if you have narrow columns or large text. Although many typographers object to two-letter hyphenation — as in *ab-dicate* or *ra-dar* — it often looks better than text with large gaps caused by the reluctance to hyphenate such words. Hyphenation also makes sense for many words that use two-letter prefixes such as *in-*, *re-*, and *co-*.

Although I advocate two-letter hyphenation at the beginning of a word, I prefer three-letter hyphenation at the end (set through Before Last ___ Letters). Except for words ending in *-ed* and sometimes *-al,* most words don't lend themselves to two-letter hyphenation at the end of the word. Part of this is functional, because it's easy for readers to lose two letters beginning a line. I prefer two-letter hyphenations at the end of a word only when the alternative is awkward spacing. As with all typography, this ultimately is a personal or house-style choice.

Although the use of two versus three letters is debated, everyone agrees that words broken using minimum settings of 1 look awful. They also go against reader expectations because the norm is to have several letters after a hyphen. Never use a minimum setting of 1 for After First ___ Letters. If you do, you get hyphenations such as *A-sia*, *a-typical*, and *u-niform* that simply look terrible in print. They also don't provide enough context for the reader to anticipate the rest of the word. Likewise, never use a minimum of 1 for Before Last ___ Letters because you get hyphenations such as *radi-o*.

Justifications controls

InDesign provides three options for controlling how justification is achieved. You can

- Condense or expand the width of spaces, or *spacebands,* between words
- Add or remove space between letters
- Condense or expand the width of characters, or *glyphs*

The options in the Justification dialog box, shown in Figure 17.7, let you specify the degree to which InDesign adjusts normal word spaces, character spacing, and character width to achieve justification. You access this dialog box through the flyout menu in the Control panel or in the Paragraph panel, or by pressing Option+Shift+⌘+J or Ctrl+Alt+Shift+J. Although you can use the Justification controls on selected paragraphs, in most cases you specify Justification settings when you create styles, particularly your body-text styles.

FIGURE 17.7

The Justification dialog box

Justification	Minimum	Desired	Maximum	
Word Spacing:	80%	100%	133%	OK
Letter Spacing:	0%	0%	0%	Cancel
Glyph Scaling:	100%	100%	100%	☐ Preview
Auto Leading:	120%			
Single Word Justification:	Full Justify			
Compose:	✓ Adobe Paragraph Composer			
	Adobe Single-line Composer			

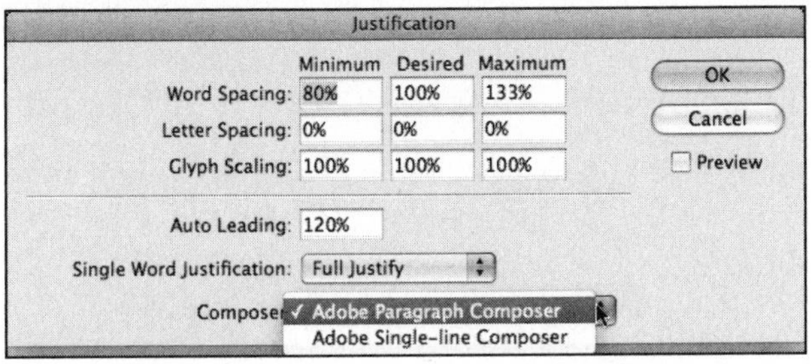

 **NOTE** When creating paragraph styles, all the justification controls are available in the Justification pane of the New Paragraph Styles dialog box.

Here's a brief description of each option:

- **Word Spacing:** Type the percentage of a spaceband character that you want to use whenever possible in the Desired field. (The default value is 100%, which uses a font's built-in width.) Type the minimum acceptable percentage in the Minimum field; type the maximum acceptable percentage in the Maximum field. The smallest value you can enter is 0%; the largest is 1000%. Some designers are adamant that only word spaces — not letter spaces — should be adjusted when justifying text. Others allow small adjustments to letter spacing as well.

- **Letter Spacing:** The default value of 0% in this set of three fields uses a font's built-in letter spacing. In the Desired field, type a positive value to add space (in increments of 1% of an en space) between all letter pairs; type a negative value to remove space. Type the minimum acceptable percentage in the Minimum field; type the maximum acceptable percentage in the Maximum field.

- **Glyph Scaling:** The default value of 100% uses a character's normal width. In the Desired field, type a positive value to expand all character widths; type a negative value to condense character widths. Type the minimum acceptable percentage in the Minimum field; type the maximum acceptable percentage in the Maximum field. Some designers adamantly contend that scaling characters is even more unacceptable than letter spacing, whereas others see no harm in scaling characters, as long as it's kept to a minimum. If you do apply glyph scaling, it's best to keep it to a range of 97 to 103 percent at most.

I suggest 85 percent minimum, 100 percent optimum, and 150 percent maximum for word spacing; and –5 percent minimum, 0 percent optimum, and 10 percent maximum for letter spacing. I prefer minimum settings that are less than the optimum because they help text fit more easily in narrow columns. These settings work well for most newsletters and magazines output on an imagesetter. At the same time, I usually leave the maximum word spacing at 150 percent.

 **When specifying values in the Justification dialog box, Minimum values must be smaller than Desired values, which in turn must be smaller than Maximum values.**

The Auto Leading field in the Justification dialog box lets you specify a custom value for Auto Leading. In InDesign, this is a character-level format, even though it rightfully should be a paragraph format. Although it's great that InDesign also makes it available in this paragraph-oriented dialog box, it's a bit hidden here. Plus, it's too bad that you can't specify an actual number of points (such as +2 to indicate 2 points of leading more than the text size), which is how leading is traditionally calculated.

CROSS-REF   **Leading is covered in detail in Chapter 16.**

InDesign also lets you control what happens to words that end up taking a full line's width. In the Single Word Justification pop-up menu, you would normally keep the default Full Justification option, which spaces the word to fill the line. You could also choose Align Left, Align Center, or Align Right to avoid spacing out the word to fit. But that's a cure worse than the problem: Having a line of a different width than the others looks like either a new paragraph or a mistake, and both appearances are sure to confuse readers.

About Word Spacing

Word spacing — the space between words — is another important contributor to the aesthetics of a document. Think about it: If the words in a sentence are too close to one another, comprehension may be affected because of the difficulty in telling where one word ends and another begins. If the words are too far apart, the reader might have a difficult time following the thought that's being conveyed.

Here's a design rule I like to follow: The wider the column, the more space you can add between words. This is why books tend to have more word spacing than magazines. Like all other typographic issues, there's a subjective component to picking good word spacing. Experiment to see what works best in your documents.

If you use the Adobe Paragraph Composer option (explained in the next section) for justified paragraphs, specifying a narrow range between minimum and maximum Word Spacing, Letter Spacing, and Glyph Scaling generally produces good-looking results. However, if you choose the Adobe Single-Line Composer option, a broader range between Minimum and Maximum gives the composer more leeway in spacing words and letters and hyphenating words and can produce better-looking results. The best way to find out what values work best for you is to experiment with several settings. Print hard copies and let your eyes decide which values produce the best results.

NOTE **A paragraph's justification settings are applied whether the paragraph is justified or not. However, for nonjustified paragraphs, only the Desired values for Word Spacing, Letter Spacing, and Glyph Scaling are used.**

Composing text

The Paragraph panel's — as well as the Control panel's — flyout menu offers two choices for implementing the hyphenation and justification settings you've established: the Adobe Single-Line Composer and the Adobe Paragraph Composer. (These are also available in the Justification dialog box I cover in the previous section.)

Adobe Single-Line Composer

Old-school programs such as QuarkXPress and PageMaker use single-line composition methods to flow text. This method marches line by line through a paragraph and sets each line as well as possible using the applied hyphenation and justification settings. The effect of modifying the spacing of one line on the lines above and below is not considered in single-line composition. If adjusting the space within a line causes poor spacing on the next line, tough luck.

InDesign offers this traditional approach to composing text; just choose Adobe Single Line Composer in the Justification dialog box's Compose pop-up menu. When you use the Adobe Single-Line Composer, the following rules apply:

- Adjusting word spacing is preferred over hyphenation.
- Hyphenation is preferred over glyph scaling.
- If spacing must be adjusted, removing space is preferred over adding space.

Adobe Paragraph Composer

InDesign's Adobe Paragraph Composer (called the Multi-Line Composer in some earlier versions) is enabled by default. It takes a broader approach to composition by looking at the entire paragraph at one time. If a poorly spaced line can be fixed by adjusting the spacing of a previous line, the Paragraph Composer reflows the previous line. The Paragraph Composer is governed by the following principles:

- The evenness of letter spacing and word spacing is the highest priority. The desirability of possible breakpoints is determined by how much they cause word and letter spacing to vary from the Desired settings.

- Uneven spacing is preferred to hyphenation. A breakpoint that does not require hyphenation is preferred over one that does.

- All possible breakpoints are ranked, and good breakpoints are preferred over bad ones.

The paragraph-level composer is more sophisticated than the single-line option, offering generally better overall spacing because it sacrifices optimal spacing a bit on one line to prevent really bad spacing on another, something the single-line method does not do.

However, there is one frustration in dealing with the paragraph-level composer: When you try to edit text or play with tracking to get rid of an orphan or widow, the Paragraph Composer keeps adjusting the text across several lines, often counteracting your nips and tucks. The Single-Line Composer doesn't do that.

 When creating paragraph styles, the composition controls are available in the Justification pane of the New Paragraph Styles dialog box.

Setting Other Paragraph Formats

The Paragraph panel's and Control panel's flyout menus contain two additional paragraph-formatting options:

- **Keep Options:** This option lets you determine how and when paragraphs can be split when they fall at the bottom of a column or page.

- **Paragraph Rules:** This option lets you place a horizontal line in front of or after a paragraph. Lines placed using the Paragraph Rules feature become part of the text and move along with surrounding text when editing causes text reflow.

Keep Options

A *widow* is the last line of a paragraph that falls at the top of a column (the poor thing has been cut off from the rest of the family). An *orphan* is the first line of a paragraph that falls at the bottom of a column (it, too, has become separated from its family). InDesign's Keep Options feature lets you prevent widows and orphans; it also lets you keep paragraphs together when they would otherwise be broken at the bottom of a column.

When you choose Keep Options from the Paragraph panel's or Control panel's flyout menu — or when you use the shortcut Option+⌘+K or Ctrl+Alt+K — the Keep Options dialog box, shown in Figure 17.8, appears.

The Keep Options dialog box provides several options for how paragraphs are managed as text breaks across columns and pages:

- **Keep with Next ___Lines:** This option applies to two consecutive paragraphs. Specify the number of lines of the second paragraph that must stay with the first paragraph if a column or page break occurs within the second paragraph. This option is useful for preventing a subhead from being separated from the paragraph that follows.

- **Keep Lines Together:** Select this option to prevent paragraphs from breaking and to control widows and orphans. When this box is selected, the two options below it become available. (The radio buttons present an either/or choice. One must be selected; At Start/End of Paragraph is selected by default.)

- **All Lines in Paragraph:** Select this option to prevent a paragraph from being broken at the end of a column or page. When a column or page break occurs within a paragraph to which this setting has been applied, the entire paragraph moves to the next column or page.

- **At Start/End of Paragraph:** Select this option to control widows and orphans. When this option is selected, the two fields below it become available:

  - **Start ___ Lines:** This field controls orphans. The value you type is the minimum number of lines at the beginning of a paragraph that must be placed at the bottom of a column when a paragraph is split by a column ending.

  - **End ___ Lines:** This field controls widows. The value you type is the minimum number of lines at the end of a paragraph that must be placed at the top of a column when a paragraph is split by a column ending.

CAUTION   Keep in mind that when you eliminate an orphan or widow using Keep Options, the line that precedes the widow line is bumped to the next column or page, which can produce uneven column endings on multicolumn pages.

- **Start Paragraph:** From this pop-up menu, choose In Next Column to force a paragraph to begin in the next column; choose In Next Frame to force a paragraph to begin in the next frame; choose On Next Page to force a paragraph to begin on the next page (such as for chapter headings). Your other choices are similar: On Next Odd Page and On Next Even Page. Choose Anywhere to let the paragraph begin where it would fall naturally in the sequence of text (no forced break).

FIGURE 17.8

The Keep Options dialog box

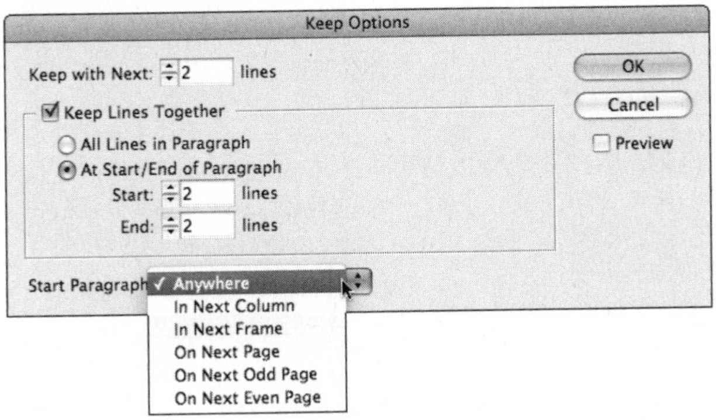

 When creating paragraph styles, all the above controls are available in the Keep Options pane of the New Paragraph Styles dialog box.

Paragraph rules

Usually, the easiest way to create a horizontal line is to use the Line tool. But if you want to place a horizontal line within text so that the line moves with the text when editing causes the text to reflow, you need to create a paragraph rule. A paragraph rule looks much like a line created with the line tool but behaves like a text character. Paragraph rules have many uses. For example, you can place one above or below a subhead to make it more noticeable or to separate the subhead from the paragraph that precedes or follows it. Or you can place paragraph rules above and below a pull-quote so that the rules and the pull-quote text move if editing causes text reflow.

Here's how to place a paragraph rule:

1. **Select the paragraphs to which you want to apply a rule above and/or a rule below and then choose Paragraph Rules from the Paragraph panel's or Control panel's fly-out menu or press Option+⌘+J or Ctrl+Alt+J.** You can also specify this as part of a paragraph style. The Paragraph Rules dialog box, shown in Figure 17.9, is displayed.

FIGURE 17.9

The Paragraph Rules dialog box

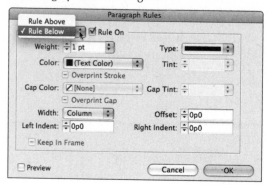

2. **Choose Rule Above or Rule Below and then select the Rule On option.** You can add a rule above, below, or both. If you want to add rules above and below, you must select Rule On for both options and specify their settings separately. If you want to see the rule as you create it, select the Preview option.

3. **For Weight, choose a predefined thickness from the pop-up menu or type a value in the field.**

4. **Choose a rule type from the Type pop-up menu.** Typically, you'd use just a simple line, but InDesign offers 17 types of lines, including dashed, striped, dotted, and wavy.

Any custom stroke styles you create (see Chapter 11) also show up as options in the Type pop-up menu.

5. **Choose a color from the Color pop-up menu, which lists the colors displayed in the Swatches panel (choose Window ⇨ Swatches or press F5).** If you choose (Text Color), InDesign automatically uses the color applied to the first character in the paragraph. If your ruling line is not a plain line, you can also choose the Gap Color to determine what color goes between dashes, stripes, dots, and so on in your line. For both the Color and Gap Color options, you can specify a corresponding tint (shade) with the Tint and Gap Tint pop-up menus, respectively.

6. **From the Width pop-up menu, choose an option.** Choose Column if you want the rule to extend from the left edge of the column to the right edge of the column; choose Text if you want the rule to extend from the left edge of the frame or column to the line ending on the right.

7. **To indent the rule from the left and/or right edges, type values in the Left Indent and/or Right Indent fields.**

8. **To control the vertical position of the rule, type a value in the Offset field.** For a rule above, the offset value is measured upward from the baseline of the first line in a paragraph to the bottom of the rule; for a rule below, the offset is measured downward from the baseline of the last line in a paragraph to the top of the rule.

9. **Click the Overprint Stroke option if you want to print a rule on top of any underlying colors.** This ensures that any misregistration during printing does not result in white areas around the rule where the paper shows through. You typically use this for black or other dark colors. There's a similar Overprint Gap option for lines that have a Gap Color.

10. **To ensure that a rule over a paragraph at the top of a frame displays within the text frame, select the Keep in Frame option.**

11. **Click OK to close the dialog box, implement your changes, and return to your document.**

To remove a paragraph rule, click in the paragraph to which the rule is applied, choose Paragraph Rules from the Paragraph panel's flyout menu, deselect the Rule On option, and then click OK.

TIP You can use the Paragraph Rules feature to place a band of color behind text by specifying a line thickness at least 2 points larger than the text size and offsetting the rule so that it moves up behind the text.

NOTE When you're creating paragraph styles, all the preceding controls are available in the Paragraph Rules pane of the New Paragraph Styles dialog box.

Optical margin override

Additionally, the Paragraph panel's flyout menu contains a third option not available in the panel itself: Ignore Optical Margin, which tells InDesign not to apply optical margin alignment for specific paragraphs in a story that has optical margin alignment applied. (Chapter 18 explains this feature in depth.)

You can also control ignore optical margin alignment as a paragraph style setting, so any paragraphs with a certain style applied ignore the optical margin alignment set for the story. To do so, select the Ignore Optical Margin check box in the Indents and Spacing pane of the New Paragraph Style or Paragraph Style Options dialog box. (Chapter 19 explains how to create and edit styles.)

Summary

Just as character formats let you control how selected characters look, InDesign's paragraph formats let you control the appearance of selected paragraphs. For example, you can control a paragraph's alignment and specify left, right, and/or first-line indents, and you can use drop caps to add space between paragraphs. If you want to hyphenate a paragraph, you can add hyphenation points manually to individual words, or you can have InDesign automatically hyphenate words as appropriate.

If you choose to use InDesign's justification controls to specify how space is added or removed between characters and/or words to achieve justification, you also have two options for composing text (controlling the spacing approach): the full-paragraph composition method that looks at several lines of text at one time, and the single-line method that looks at each line in isolation.

Chapter 18

Creating Special Text Formatting

After you learn the basics of typefaces, character formats, and paragraph formats, you can achieve just about any look with text. The trick is combining and applying the skills you've learned to produce special effects that not only look professional but also enhance the meaning of the text.

Glance at any professional publication — a national magazine, direct-mail catalog, cookbook, or product brochure — and you see typographic techniques that set the publication apart from anything that can be easily produced in a word processor. (Even when word processors do offer a feature, they often lack the control necessary to really fine-tune an effect.) And skilled designers use these effects with a purpose — special bullet characters emphasize a theme, drop caps draw readers in, and pull-quotes tantalize the audience, for example.

Throughout this chapter, you learn how InDesign can produce special typographic effects and, more important, when to use them.

You can apply all sorts of formatting to text beyond those described here. For example, by using InDesign's object transformation tools, as covered in Chapter 10, you can change the look of entire text blocks such as through rotation and scaling.

By applying special object effects such as transparency and embossing — covered in Chapter 11 — you can really jazz up your layouts. InDesign's text-wrap feature (covered in Chapter 12) also lets you make text interact with surrounding objects.

And for text selections, you can apply color (see Chapter 7), strokes (see Chapter 11), and various character and paragraph formatting (see Chapters 16 and 17).

IN THIS CHAPTER

Working with bulleted and numbered lists

Formatting fractions

Creating reverse type

Adding sidebars and pull-quotes

Specifying optical margin alignment

Creating custom underlines and strikethroughs

Converting text to graphics

Running text along a path

Using Bulleted and Numbered Lists

Automatic bullets and numbering are available as a paragraph-level format in InDesign, accessed in the Paragraph panel's and Control panel's flyout menus by choosing Bullets and Numbering Options. (Figure 18.1 shows the resulting dialog box.) There are additional bullet and number controls in the Type menu. You can also apply these lists via paragraph styles.

FIGURE 18.1

Note that in the Bullets and Numbering dialog box, the top part changes based on whether you are formatting bullets (left) or numbered lists (right).

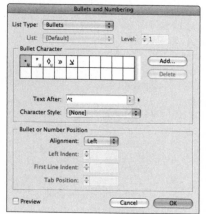 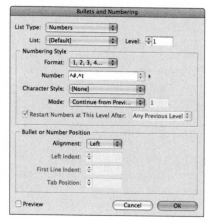

Defining lists

The process for setting automatic bullets and numbered lists is almost identical; only the top part of the Bullets and Numbering dialog box differs, based on whether you select Bullets or Numbers from the List Type pop-up menu. (Choose None to remove the automatic bullets or numbers.)

Follow these steps to set up a list (select the Preview option if you want to see the results of your choices before you finalize them):

1a. **For a bulleted list, choose a bullet character from the Bullet Character area.** The area shows bullet characters available for the current font; you can change the selection by changing the selected font or by clicking Add, which opens a dialog box similar to the Glyphs panel (see Chapter 20).

1b. **For a numbered list, choose a numbering style in the Format pop-up menu and go through the following options.**

    i. Specify the number's formatting in the Number field (you can select special characters and placeholder numbers in the pop-up menu to its right) and choose whether the numbers continue or start anew at this paragraph through the Mode pop-up menu (your choices are Continue from Previous Number and Start At).

ii. In the Format pop-up menu, your options are 1, 2, 3, 4 . . .; 01, 02, 03, 04 . . .; I, II, III, IV . . .; i, ii, iii, iv . . .; A, B, C, D . . .; a, b, c, d . . . .; 001, 002, 003, 004 . . .; and 0001, 0002, 0003, 0004 . . . .

NEW FEATURE The 001, 002, 003, 004 . . . and 0001, 0002, 0003, 0004 . . . options for numbering are new to InDesign CS4.

iii. If you are using defined lists (covered later in this section), select the appropriate list type from the List Type pop-up menu. You can also choose New List to create a new list type.

iv. If you are using sublists, also called *nested lists,* specify the current paragraph's list level by entering a value between 1 and 9 in the Level field. (This paragraph is part of a sublist under the paragraph 1b in the main list.) If you do use sublists, select the Restart Numbers at This Level After check box and enter a level — it must be higher than the current level — in the adjacent field or choose the Any Previous Level option from the adjacent pop-up menu to reset the numbering if this paragraph is at a different numbering level from previous ones in the list. Specifying a specific level means that the numbering will restart only if the previous numbered paragraph was at the specified level. Choosing Any Previous Level resets the numbering if the previous numbered paragraph was at any other level than this paragraph's.

v. In the Number field, you can insert all sorts of special spaces and characters, giving you broad control, through the Insert Special Characters submenu, over how numbers display. You can also choose number placeholders, which tell InDesign what numbers to insert in the list. For simple lists, choose Current Level from the Insert Number Placeholder pop-up submenu — the default. The other levels are used when you have sublists within lists. You can also choose Chapter Number to insert the chapter's number as part of the list item's placeholder number. (See Chapter 24 for more on specifying the chapter number.)

2. **Set the font settings for the bullet or numbers using the Character Style pop-up menu to choose a character style.** The default setting of [None] uses the paragraph's current formatting. Note that the look of the numerals is more a design decision than an editorial decision. If numerals are in a different typeface and/or in a different color, a period following the numeral might just look cluttered.

3. **In the Bullet or Number Position section of the dialog box, set the indents for the list.** Using the Alignment pop-up menu, choose Left, Center, or Right to determine where the bullet or numeral is positioned within its tab. You can set the hanging indent amount and the bullet's or numbers overhang by using the Left Indent, First Line Indent, and Tab Position fields.

4. **Click OK when you are done with the settings.**

Spacing Guidelines for Lists

The easy part of creating bulleted lists and numbered lists in InDesign is using the software. The hard part can be deciding how much space to use. For example, how much space goes between a bullet and the text following it? Amateur publishers or designers, who are likely to be thinking in inches rather than points or picas, are likely to use too much space. They're tempted to use 0.25", 0.125", or another nice fraction of an inch for spacing rather than a more appropriate value such as 6 points. When deciding on spacing, consider the following:

- In bulleted lists, use a hanging indent for a succession of two- or three-line bulleted paragraphs in wider columns. If your bulleted items are five or six lines long, especially in narrow columns, it might work better to use run-in heads to break up the information.

- Generally, the amount of space between a bullet and its text is equal to half the point size of the text. So if you're working with 11-point text, place 5.5 points between the bullet and text.

- When it comes to numbered lists, you need to decide whether you're going to include a period or other punctuation after the number and whether you'll ever have two-digit numbers. Numerals in most typefaces are the width of an en space, and they should be followed by the same amount of space that the numbers and their punctuation take up. If you have a two-digit numeral, the numbers take up one em space and so should be followed by one em space.

Although these values give you a good starting point, you might need to modify them based on the typeface, font size, column width, design, and overall goals of the publication.

InDesign gives you even more control over bulleted and numbered lists through the options you get by choosing Type ⇨ Bulleted & Numbered Lists:

- The Apply/Remove Bullets and Apply/Remove Numbers submenu options quickly let you turn on or off the bullets or numbering for selected paragraphs. You can also use the iconic buttons for these controls on the Control panel.

- The Restart/Continue Numbering option is a handy way to control which paragraphs are numbered, such as when you have an unnumbered paragraph within a list. (This option is also available in the flyout menu of the Paragraph panel and Control panel.)

- The Convert Bullets to Text and Convert Numbering to Text options remove the automatic bullets or numerals in a paragraph but leave an actual bullet character or numeral at the beginning of the paragraph for you to do as you please. (These options are also available in the flyout menu of the Paragraph panel and Control panel.)

A more advanced option is the Define Lists option (available in three places: by choosing Type ⇨ Bulleted & Numbered Lists ⇨ Define Lists, by choosing Define Lists from the Paragraph panel's flyout menu, or by choosing New List in the List Type pop-up menu in the Bullets and Numbering dialog box). Here, you create list types with just two options: Continue Numbers across Stories and Continue Numbers from Previous Document in a Book. You access these list types when you create or edit paragraph styles using the style dialog boxes' Bullets and Numbering pane, or when you apply bullets and numbering through the Paragraph panel's or Control panel's flyout menu. (Either way, choose the appropriate style in the List Type pop-up menu.)

When you select Continue Numbers across Stories, InDesign continues numbering text based on the last number used in the previous story rather than restart the numbering at each story (the normal behavior). When you select Continue Numbers from Previous Document in a Book, InDesign continues numbering text based on the last number used in the previous chapter of a book (see Chapter 22) rather than start over again with this document (the normal behavior).

Applying lists

When you specify numbered or bulleted list settings in the Paragraph panel, these settings are immediately applied to any selected paragraphs. Likewise, any list settings specified in paragraph styles are automatically applied to any paragraphs using those styles.

But you can quickly default bulleted or numbered lists to selected paragraphs using these techniques:

- Click the Bulleted List or Numbered List iconic button in the Control panel.
- Choose Type ⇨ Bulleted & Numbered Lists ⇨ Apply Bullets or choose Type ⇨ Bulleted & Numbered Lists ⇨ Apply Numbers.

You can also unapply (remove) a bulleted list or numbered list from selected paragraphs by using the preceding formatting commands. For example, to make a bulleted list normal (no bullets or numbers), click the Bulleted List iconic button or choose Type ⇨ Bulleted & Numbered Lists ⇨ Apply Bullets. These commands act as toggles, turning the lists off and on.

CAUTION InDesign does not properly align bulleted or numbered lists when the left side of the text frame they are in wraps around another object. Although InDesign should see the wrap boundary as the new left margin and thus adjust the list's indentation accordingly, it does not.

Working with imported lists

But chances are you're not writing the bulk of your text in InDesign. Instead, the text was delivered in the form of a word processing file, and the writer or editor made some decisions about bullets or numerals. A lot of times, writers simply type an asterisk followed by a space to indicate a bullet. Or maybe an editor typed a numeral followed by a parenthesis in front of each step. Other times, writers or editors use their word processor's automatic bullet or numbering feature.

If the writer used manual numerals or bullets, that's what you get. If the writer used automatic bullets or numbers, that's also what you get, unless you told InDesign to override them, as I cover in Chapter 13.

Bullet Character Options

Although you may not know what they're called, you're used to seeing *en bullets*, the small round bullet (•) included in most typefaces. But you're not limited to using this character. You can use any character in the body text font, or you can switch to a symbol or pi font and choose a more decorative character.

Zapf Dingbats and Wingdings are the most common symbol fonts, offering an array of boxes, arrows, crosses, stars, and check marks. These can be cute and effective, but cute isn't always a good thing. If you opt for a different bullet character, make sure you have a reason and that it works well with the rest of the design. Check-mark bullets in an election flyer might make sense; bulky square bullets in a to-do list for a wedding caterer might not make sense.

Note that you might want to reduce the size of the symbol slightly and that you might need to use different spacing values than you would use with an en bullet.

Don't limit yourself to these two common fonts either. You can purchase many different symbol fonts to support different content. For example, you might see leaf-shaped bullets in an herb article and paw-print bullets in a pet training article. To use your own drawing or a logotype as a bullet, convert the drawing to a font using a utility such as FontLab Studio (see the companion Web site www.InDesignCentral.com for links to this and other font utilities).

Formatting Fractions

Creating fractions that are formatted correctly can be handy. Compare the left fraction in Figure 18.2, which is not formatted appropriately, to the other fractions in the figure, which are correctly formatted. Although InDesign doesn't provide an automatic fraction maker, you can use OpenType typefaces, expert typefaces, or character formats to achieve professional-looking fractions.

FIGURE 18.2

From left to right: The ⅞ fraction unformatted, formatted via OpenType, formatted via an Expert Collection font, and formatted manually. Note that the rightmost fraction uses a regular slash, whereas the middle two use virgules. Also shown is the Glyphs panel used to select the Expert Collection symbol.

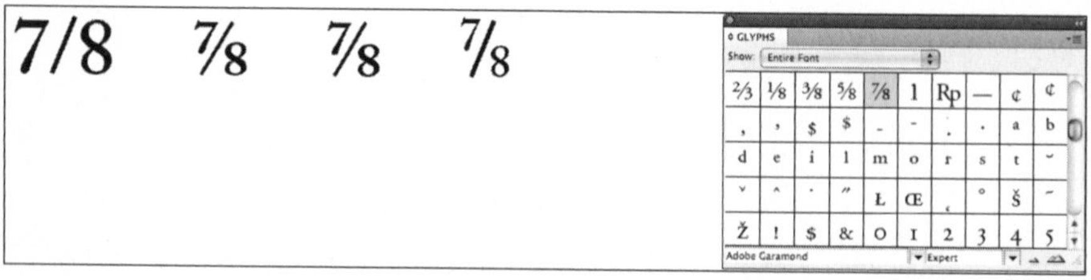

Applying a fraction typeface

Some expert typefaces include a variation, appropriately called *Fractions*, that includes a number of common fractions, such as ¹/₂, ¹/₃, ¹/₄, and ³/₄. Adobe has Expert Collection variants for many of its popular Type 1 PostScript fonts; these collections include true small caps, true fractions, and other typographic characters. You can also use a symbol font, though the numerals may not exactly match the appearance of numerals in the rest of your text because symbol fonts typically use plain fonts such as Helvetica as their basis.

OpenType fonts also typically contain these special symbols (called *glyphs*), with the convenience that they aren't separate fonts from the "regular" alphanumeric characters, so it's easier to access them in InDesign.

To use a true fraction from an Expert Collection or OpenType font, choose Type ⇨ Glyphs, select the font and face from the pop-up menus at the bottom of the panel shown in Figure 18.2 and then select the fraction you want to use.

If you have OpenType fonts, the process can also be automated: Be sure that the Fraction option is enabled for the selected text, either as part of its character or paragraph style or by highlighting the text and adjusting the OpenType options directly:

- For styles, go to the OpenType Features pane when creating or modifying a paragraph or character style and select Fractions.

- For local formatting, highlight the text containing the fraction and then choose OpenType ⇨ Fraction from the flyout menu of the Character panel or Control panel — and be sure that Fraction is select in the menu (choose it if not).

 These OpenType options have no effect on non-OpenType fonts.

 Chapter 16 covers the various options available in OpenType fonts.

Formatting fractions manually

If you're dealing with a wide range of fractions in something like a cookbook, you probably won't find all the fractions you need in your Expert Collection font. Regular Type 1 Postscript and TrueType fonts certainly don't have the desired fractions. And although OpenType fonts have the necessary characters to create almost any fraction, many fonts are not available in OpenType format — and even when they are available, many publishers have not spent the money to replace them all. Therefore, most organizations opt for formatting all the fractions manually. But if you are a frequent fraction user, I strongly encourage you to switch to OpenType fonts.

The built-in fractions in expert fonts and the fractions generated by OpenType fonts are approximately the same size as a single character in that font; this size should be your goal in formatting a fraction manually. Usually, you achieve this by decreasing the size of the two numerals (perhaps by using the subscript and superscript formats), raising the numerator (the first, or top, number in the fraction) using the baseline shift feature, and kerning on either side of the slash as necessary. (Chapter 16 covers these controls.)

InDesign's default superscript and subscript size is 58.3 percent of the character's size (this odd value actually equals $7/12$, in keeping with typography's standard of using points, of which there are 12 in a pica, for text measurement). The numerator and denominator in a fraction should be the same size, so if you use InDesign's superscripts at its default settings, multiply the text's point size by 0.583 (just highlight the denominator text, go to the Font Size field in the Character panel or Control panel, and type *0.583 after the current size value). I recommend changing InDesign's superscript and subscript font styles to 65 percent to improve readability, especially at smaller sizes. You can change these default settings in the Advanced Type pane of the Preferences dialog box (choose InDesign ⇨ Preferences ⇨ Advanced Type or press ⌘+K on the Mac, or choose Edit ⇨ Preferences-Advanced Type or press Ctrl+K in Windows).

PLATFORM DIFFERENCES Macintosh fonts provide another option for refining fractions: a special kind of slash called a *virgule,* which is smaller and at more of an angle than a regular slash. Press Option+Shift+1 to enter a virgule, and then kern around it as you would a slash. Expert fonts and OpenType fonts also come with virgules, which they use in their fractions; Figure 18.2 shows the difference.

Unless you rarely use fractions, by all means save your manual formatting as character styles: one for the numerator, one for the denominator, and perhaps one for the slash or virgule. You can apply the formats with a keystroke or use Find/Change (choose Edit ⇨ Find/Change or press ⌘+F or Ctrl+F) to locate numerals and selectively apply the appropriate character style.

Reversing Type out of Its Background

This is the reverse of what you usually see — rather than black type on a white background, white type appears on a black background. Of course, reverse type doesn't have to be white on black; it can be any lighter color on a darker color. You can often see reverse type in table headings, kickers (explanatory blurbs following headlines), and decorative elements. Reverse type, which brightens text and pulls readers in, works best with larger type sizes and bold typefaces so that the text isn't swallowed by the background.

InDesign doesn't have a reverse type command or font style — but using this effect involves just a simple combination of basic InDesign skills. To lighten the text, highlight it with the Type tool, click the Fill iconic button on the Tools panel or Swatches panel, and choose a light color from the Swatches panel (choose Window ⇨ Swatches or press F5). For a dark background, you have three options: filling the text frame with a darker color, making the text frame transparent and placing it on top of darker objects, or using a ruling line behind the text.

For the first two options, select the text frame with any selection tool, and then click the Fill iconic button on the Tools panel. To fill the text frame with a color, click a darker color on the Swatches panel. To make the text frame transparent, click the Apply None iconic button on the Tools panel. Then place the text frame in front of a darker object or graphic.

For reverse-out type that is not in its own text frame, you use a ruling line of the appropriate width (at least a couple points larger than the text size) and move it into the text. If you use Rule Above, you move the line down behind the text; if you use Rule Below, you move it up. Figure 18.3 shows reversed-out type used as description headings, as well as the Paragraph Rules dialog box and the settings used to create the effect. (To access this dialog box, choose Paragraph Rules from the fly-out menu of the Control panel or Paragraph panel or press Option+⌘+J or Ctrl+Alt+J.)

FIGURE 18.3

This product guide uses reversed-out text created with ruling lines for its description titles, as well as for its colored section titles.

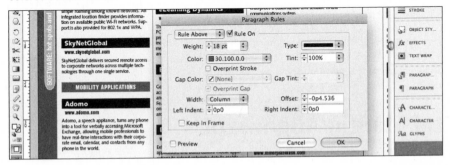

When designing elements with reverse type, make sure the point size of the text is large enough to print clearly on the darker background. Consider the thinnest part of characters, especially in serif typefaces, when judging the size and thickness of reverse type. You often want to use a semibold or bolder version of a font so the text maintains its visual integrity.

 **All paragraph formatting options in the Control panel are in the paragraph pane; be sure the ¶ iconic button is selected to display them.**

Creating Sidebars and Pull-Quotes

Pick up almost any publication, from *Newsweek* magazine to your neighborhood newsletter, and you're almost guaranteed to see sidebars and pull-quotes. So basic that you can even create them with a modern word processor, these treatments aren't really typographic treatments — they're just page-layout techniques involving text elements you create by applying simple InDesign skills.

A *sidebar* is supplemental text, formatted differently and often placed within a shaded or outlined box. Sidebars help break up text-heavy pages and call attention to information that is often interesting but not essential to the main story. Even in technical publications, it's helpful to pull in-depth information or related text into sidebars to provide visual relief. To create a sidebar, you usually place the text in its own frame, apply a stroke to the frame, and optionally fill it with a tint, as I cover in Chapters 7 and 11. To inset the text from the edges of the frame, use the Text Frame

Options dialog box (choose Object ⇨ Text Frame Options or press ⌘+B or Ctrl+B), as I cover in Chapter 14.

A *pull-quote* is a catchy one- or two-line excerpt from a publication that is enlarged and reformatted to achieve both editorial and design objectives. On the editorial side, pull-quotes draw readers into articles with excerpts that do everything from summarize the content to provide shock value. On the design side, pull-quotes break up staid-looking columns and offer opportunities for typographic treatment that emphasize the content (such as colors and typefaces that reflect the mood of an article). Although the design often dictates the use of and length of pull-quotes, an editorial person should select the text and indicate it on hard copy or within text files. To create a pull-quote, copy and paste the relevant text into its own text frame and then reformat the text and frame as you want. Use the Text Wrap panel (choose Window ⇨ Text Wrap or press Option+⌘+W or Ctrl+Alt+W) to control how text in columns wraps around the pull-quote.

CROSS-REF InDesign lets you anchor a sidebar, pull-quote, or other frame to a specific spot in the text so that it follows that text as the text reflows. Chapter 12 covers this capability in detail. It also covers text wrap in detail.

Optical Margin Alignment

When display type such as a pull-quote or a headline in ads is left-aligned or justified, the edges can look uneven due to the gaps above, below, or next to quotation marks, punctuation, and some capital letters, as shown in the text frame at right in Figure 18.4. To correct the unevenness, graphic designers use a technique called *hanging punctuation* — which InDesign calls *optical margin alignment* — in which they extend the punctuation slightly beyond the edges of the rest of the text, as shown in the text frame at left in Figure 18.4.

NOTE The *edge* of text is defined by the edges of the text frame or any Inset Spacing specified in the Text Frame Options dialog box (choose Object ⇨ Text Frame Options or press ⌘+B or Ctrl+B).

InDesign's Optical Margin Alignment option automates hanging punctuation, extending punctuation and the edges of some glyphs (such as a capital *T*) slightly outside the edges of the text.

Unfortunately, you can't control how much the characters "hang" outside the text boundaries — InDesign decides that for you. And optical margin alignment applies to all the text frames in a story rather than to just the highlighted text. This means you need to isolate into its own story any text for which you want hanging punctuation.

To specify optical margin alignment, select any text frame in a story and choose Window ⇨ Type & Tables ⇨ Story to open the Story panel. Select the Optical Margin Alignment option, as shown in Figure 18.4.

NOTE In general, optical margin alignment improves the look of display type whether it's left-aligned, centered, justified, or even right-aligned. However, optical margin alignment actually causes columns of body text to look uneven (because they are).

Notice the difference between the text frame at right with Optical Margin Alignment enabled and the text frame at left with standard alignment.

You can disable optical margin alignment for specific paragraphs while keeping it applied to the rest of the story's text by using either of the following techniques:

- For selected paragraphs, choose Ignore Optical Margin in the Paragraph panel's flyout menu.
- For all paragraphs using a specific paragraph style, enable the Ignore Optical Margin check box in the Indents and Spacing pane of the New Paragraph Style or Paragraph Style Options dialog box. (See Chapter 19 for details on creating and editing styles.)

End-of-Story Markers

In magazines, newsletters, and other publications with multiple stories, the text often continues from one page to the next. In a new magazine, a story might meander from page to page, interrupted by sidebars and ads. In a fashion magazine, stories generally open on a splashy spread and then continue on text-heavy pages at the back of the magazine. In either case, readers can get confused about whether a story has ended. Designers solve this by placing a *dingbat* (a special character such as a square) at the end of each story.

You can use any dingbat character — in Zapf Dingbats, DF Organics, Woodtype, or Wingdings, for example — or an inline graphic to mark the end of a story. The end-of-story marker should reflect the overall design and feel of a publication or emphasize the content. You might see a square used in a financial publication, a heart in a teen magazine, or a leaf in a gardening magazine. A derivative of the company's logo might even be used to mark the end of a story — you can easily envision the Nike swoosh used in this way.

To place a dingbat, first decide on the character and create a character style for it. If you're using a graphic, you might consider converting it to a font with a utility such as FontLab Studio so that you can insert it as text at the end of your text and use a character style to format it consistently. If you're using an inline graphic, you might store it in an InDesign library (see Chapter 6) so that it's easily accessible. Make sure everyone working on the publication knows the keystroke for entering the dingbat or the location of the graphic.

When you have the character established, you need to decide where to place it. Generally, the dingbat will be flush with the right margin or right after the final punctuation in the last line:

- To place the dingbat flush with the right margin, there are two ways to set a right-aligned tab:

  - One is to choose Type ⇨ Insert Special Character ⇨ Other ⇨ Right Indent Tab or just press Shift+Tab.

  - The other way is to set a tab stop in the paragraph style you use for final paragraphs (see Chapter 21 for more details on setting tabs). Because InDesign offers an easier method to right-indent a dingbat, you should use this method only if you want to right-align the dingbat to a place in the column other than at the right margin — essentially, if you want to have it indented a little from the right margin.

- When you're placing the dingbat after the final punctuation, I recommend clearly separating the two with an en space by typing Shift+⌘+N or Ctrl+Shift+N, or with an em space by typing Shift+⌘+M or Ctrl+Shift+M.

Underline and Strikethrough Options

InDesign lets you create custom underlines and strikethroughs. Although you'll use these sparingly, they can be effective for design-oriented text presentation, such as in the examples shown in Figure 18.5.

The Character panel's and Control panel's flyout menus provide the Underline Options and Strikethrough Options menu items to create custom versions. (You must have the Character pane of the Control panel selected to get these options; click the A iconic button to display it.) The process for the two is similar:

1. **Highlight the text to which you want to apply the custom underline or strikethrough.**

2. **Specify the thickness, type, color, and other settings for the line that makes up the underline or the strikethrough line.** Note that if you choose a line type that has gaps — such as dashed, dotted, or striped lines — you can also choose a gap color, such as was done for the top example in Figure 18.5. Figure 18.6 shows the Strikethrough Options and Underline Options dialog boxes.

FIGURE 18.5

Examples of custom underlines and strikethroughs

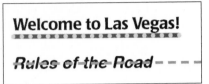

3. **Apply the underline style through the Control panel or Character panel or use the keyboard shortcut (Shift+⌘+U or Ctrl+Shift+U).** Apply the strikethrough style through the Control panel or Character panel or use the keyboard shortcut (Shift+⌘+/ or Ctrl+Shift+/).

A custom underline or strikethrough created and applied this way is in effect only for the first text to which an underline or a strikethrough is applied. InDesign reverts to the standard settings the next time you apply an underline or strikethrough using the Character panel or Control panel or by using the shortcuts Shift+⌘+U or Ctrl+Shift+U for underlines and Shift+⌘+/ or Ctrl+Shift+/ for strikethroughs.

CROSS-REF   If you want to use a custom underline or strikethrough setting repeatedly, you should define the setting as part of a character style, as described in Chapter 19.

FIGURE 18.6

The Underline Options (left) and Strikethrough Options (right) dialog boxes. In both, the Type pop-up menu at the right provides the list of line types available.

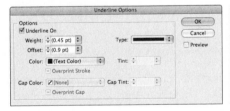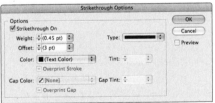

Adjusting character strokes

InDesign CS4 lets you adjust the strokes that make up characters, as Figure 18.7 shows. This is a design effect you'll use rarely. To change the stroke, select the text you want to adjust and then go to the Stroke panel (choose Window ➪ Stroke or press ⌘+F10 or Ctrl+F10) and adjust any of the following settings: Join, Miter Limit (if Miter Join is the selected Join), and Align Stroke. Note that for text, you get only the Center and Outside options, not Inside, for Align Stroke. (Chapter 11 covers strokes in more detail.)

FIGURE 18-7

Compare the adjusted stroke at left (it aligns the stroke to center) to the regular stroke at right (it aligns the stroke to the outside).

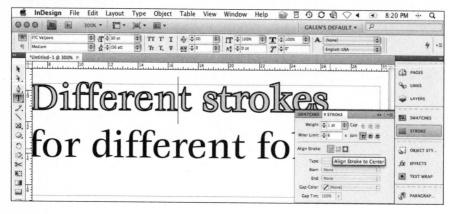

NEW FEATURE The ability to adjust text's strokes is new to InDesign. In previous versions, you had to first convert the text to an outline, as described in the next section.

Converting text into shapes

If you want to use the shape of a letter or the combined shapes of several letters as a frame for text or a graphic, you can test your skill with the Pen tool and create the letter shapes yourself. But getting hand-drawn characters to look just the way you want them to can take lots of time. A quicker solution is to use the Create Outlines command to convert text characters into editable outlines. The Create Outlines command is particularly useful if you want to hand-tweak the shapes of characters, particularly at display font sizes, or place text or a graphic within character shapes.

TIP If all you need to do is apply a stroke or fill to characters within text, you don't have to convert the characters into outlines. Instead, use the Stroke panel, as I explain in Chapter 11.

When you use the Create Outlines command, you have the choice of creating an inline compound path that replaces the original text or an independent compound path that's placed directly on top of the original letters in its own frame. If you want the text outlines to flow with the surrounding text, create an inline compound path. If you want to use the outlines elsewhere, create an independent compound path.

To convert text into outlines:

1. **Use the Type tool to highlight the characters you want to convert into outlines.** Generally, this feature works best with large font sizes.

2. **Choose Type ⇨ Create Outlines or press Shift+⌘+O or Ctrl+Shift+O (that's the letter *O*, not a zero).** If you hold down the Option or Alt key when you choose Create

Outlines, or if you press Shift+Option+⌘+O or Ctrl+Alt+Shift+O, a compound path is created and placed in front of the text. In this case, you can use either of the selection tools to move the resulting compound path. If you don't hold down Option or Alt when you choose Create Outlines, an inline compound path is created: This object replaces the original text and flows with the surrounding text.

When you create outlines out of a range of highlighted characters, a compound path is created, and each of the characters becomes a subpath. You can use the Release (Compound Path) command (choose Object ⇨ Paths ⇨ Release Compound Path or press Option+Shift+⌘+8 or Ctrl+Alt+Shift+8) to turn each of the subpaths into independent paths, as described in Chapter 27.

After you create text outlines, you can modify the paths the same as you can modify hand-drawn paths — by selecting them with the Direct Selection tool and then adding, deleting, or moving anchor points; clicking and dragging direction handles; and converting smooth points to corner points and vice versa. You can also use the transformation tools, the Control panel (choose Window ⇨ Control or press Option+⌘+6 or Ctrl+Alt+6), and the Transform panel (Window ⇨ Transform) to change the appearance of text outlines. You cannot, however, edit text after converting it to outlines.

Additionally, you can use the Place command (choose File ⇨ Place or press ⌘+D or Ctrl+D) or the Paste Into command (choose Edit ⇨ Paste Into or press Option+⌘+V or Ctrl+Alt+V) to import text or a graphic into the frames created by converting text to graphics.

Making Text Follow a Path

InDesign lets you have text follow any open or closed path, such as a line or frame. Simply select the path or shape with the Type on a Path tool, which is available from the Type tool's pop-out menu. Now start typing (or paste or place) your text.

After you have entered the text and formatted it with font, size, color, and so forth, you can apply special effects to it using the Type on a Path Options dialog box, which you access by choosing Type ⇨ Type on a Path ⇨ Options and then selecting from its options.

Figure 18.8 shows the dialog box and several examples of its formatting. In the dialog box:

- Use the Effect pop-up menu to choose an effect (the options show previews of each one).
- Use the Align pop-up menu to choose what part of the text is aligned (Baseline, Center, Ascender, or Descender).
- Use the To Path pop-up menu to choose whether to align to the center, bottom, or top of the path.
- Flip the text by selecting the Flip option.
- Change the text's spacing by entering a value in the Spacing field. (Positive numbers space out the text; negative ones contract it.)

FIGURE 18.8

The Type on a Path Options dialog box lets you apply special effects and alignment, and flip to text following a path.

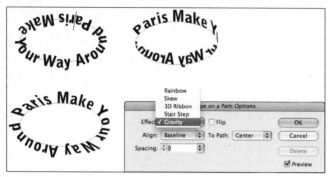

Summary

InDesign gives you the power to embellish and manipulate text in almost infinite ways. It's your responsibility to format text in ways that clarify and reinforce the content rather than simply decorate it.

Bulleted lists — often created with special character bullets — help break out information. So do numbered lists.

If your text uses fractions, you have several ways to format them, depending on the fonts you have: automatically with OpenType, by selecting the specific fraction in an Type 1 PostScript Expert Collection font or by manually creating the fraction using baseline shifts, size changes, and kerning on each character.

You can pull readers into a story with sidebars and pull-quotes, which also break up text-heavy areas. For display type, InDesign provides an automatic method for hanging punctuation outside the margins. The use of special characters at the end of the story is an effective way to let the reader know the story is complete; you can help these dingbats' visual appearance by preceding them with a special space or a right tab.

Underline and strikethroughs need not be the standard lines everyone uses; InDesign lets you create custom lines — dotted, dashed, multiline, and others — for a little extra pizzazz.

Desktop publishing has blurred the line between text and graphics, so it's no surprise you can convert text to frames, which lets you treat them as graphics. You can also have text follow the contours of a shape or line.

Chapter 19

Setting Up Styles

IN THIS CHAPTER

Creating and applying
paragraph and character styles

Working with nested styles

Modifying style-formatted text

Modifying styles

Importing styles

If you were assigned the task of making 500 star-shaped cookies, the first thing you'd do is find a star-shaped cookie cutter. Of course, you could shape each cookie by hand, but this would take considerably more time than using a cookie cutter, plus no two cookies would look exactly the same. Think of styles as cookie cutters for formatting text. They save you time and ensure consistency. If you'll be using InDesign to create long documents that require considerable text formatting, styles are indispensable.

InDesign lets you create two types of textual styles:

- A *character style* is a set of character-level formats you can apply to range of highlighted text in a single step.

- A *paragraph style* is a set of both character- *and* paragraph-level formats you can apply to selected paragraphs in a single step.

NOTE InDesign calls these *styles*, not *style sheets* as other programs such as Microsoft Word and QuarkXPress do. I personally prefer *style sheet* because that term has a longer history in publishing terminology and because *style* is also used to indicate font styles such as boldface and italics. But in this book, I'm sticking with the InDesign term *style*.

CROSS-REF InDesign also lets you create styles for objects such as frames and lines, as Chapter 12 explains. And you can create styles for tables and cells, as covered in Chapter 21.

In one respect, styles are far superior to cookie cutters. If you use a cookie cutter to create hundreds of cookies and then find out your cookies are the wrong shape, you're out of luck. But if you use a style to format hundreds of pieces of text and then decide you don't like the look of the formatted text, you can simply modify the style. Any text you've formatted with a style is automatically updated if you modify the style.

When it comes to using styles, it's as important to know when *not* to use them as it is to know *when* to use them. For short documents — especially one-pagers such as business cards, ads, and posters — that contain relatively little text and don't use the same formats repeatedly, you're probably better off formatting the text by hand.

Creating and Applying Styles

Before you can use a style to format text, you must create it. You can create styles whenever you want, but usually, creating styles is one of the first tasks you tackle when working on a long document. Also, you may want to create your paragraph styles first and then, if necessary, add character styles. In many cases, character styles are used to format text within paragraphs to which paragraph styles have already been applied.

Note that InDesign comes with a predefined default paragraph style called [Basic Paragraph] that text in a new frame automatically has applied to it. You can edit [Basic Paragraph] like any other style. Similarly, there's a predefined character style called [Basic Character].

Note that this chapter assumes you know how to use the character and paragraph formatting tools covered in Chapters 16 and 17, respectively. Also, text in your layout may already have styles applied, using styles defined in Microsoft Word, as explained in Chapter 13.

Paragraph styles

Let's say you've been given the job of creating a newsletter. It will be several pages long and contain several stories. Each story will have the same text elements: a big headline, a smaller headline, an author byline, and body text. The stories will also include pictures, and each picture requires a caption and a credit line. Before you begin laying out pages and formatting text, you should create styles for all these repetitive text elements. The Paragraph Styles panel (choose Type ⇨ Paragraph Styles or press ⌘+F11 or Ctrl+F11), shown in Figure 19.1, is where you need to go for both creating and applying styles.

Creating paragraph styles

The easiest way to create a paragraph style is to manually apply character- and paragraph-level formats to a sample paragraph and then — with the sample paragraph selected — follow the next set of steps. If no text is selected when you create a style, you'll have to specify character- and paragraph-level formats as you create the style, which is more difficult than formatting a paragraph in advance. Here's how you create a paragraph style from a preformatted paragraph:

The Paragraph Styles panel and its flyout menu

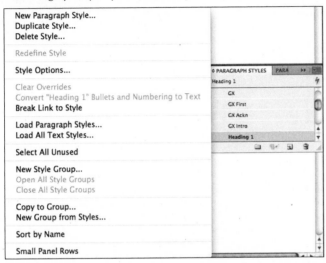

1. **If it's not displayed, show the Paragraph Style panel by choosing Type ⇨ Paragraph Styles or pressing ⌘+F11 or Ctrl+F11.** You can also choose Window ⇨ Type & Tables ⇨ Paragraph Styles.

2. **Make sure you highlight a paragraph that's been styled with all the character and paragraph formats you want to include in your style; then, choose New Style from the Paragraph Styles panel's flyout menu, as shown in Figure 19.1.** The New Paragraph Style dialog box, shown in Figure 19.2, appears. You can also create a new style by clicking the Create New Style button (the page icon) at the bottom of the Paragraph Styles panel. When you click this button, a new style with a default name (Paragraph Style 1, Paragraph Style 2, and so on) is added to the list. The formats applied to the selected paragraph are included in the new style; the New Paragraph Style dialog box is not displayed.

3. **Type a name for the style in the Style Name field.** Assign your style names with care; be descriptive. Imagine that somebody else will be using the document, and assign a name that conveys the purpose of the style. For example, anybody will know what a style called Body Copy is used for, but a style called Really Cool Style won't mean anything to anybody but you.

4. **Change character- or paragraph-level formats.** The scroll list to the left of the dialog box shows 16 options, as shown in Figure 19.2. If you want to change any character- or paragraph-level formats, choose the appropriate option to switch to the relevant pane and then make your changes.

FIGURE 19.2

The New Paragraph Style dialog box

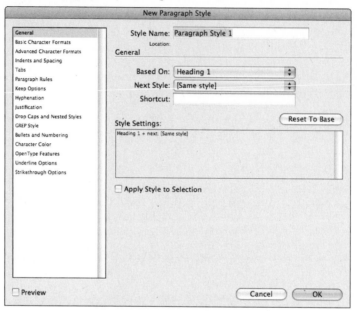

5. **Use the Based On pop-up menu, which displays the names of other paragraph styles, to create families of styles.** For example, you could create a style called Body Copy/Base for the bulk of your body text and then create variations such as Body Text/ Drop Cap, Body Text/No Indent, and Body Text/Italic. If you use the Based On pop-up menu to base each of the variations on Body Text/Base and you then modify this parent style, your changes are applied to all the variations. By default, a new style is not based on anything, so [No Paragraph Style] displays in this pop-up menu.

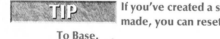

TIP If you've created a style based on another and you don't like the changes you've made, you can reset the style to be the same as its based-on style by clicking Reset To Base.

6. **To automatically switch from the style you are creating to another style as you type text, choose a style from the Next Style pop-up menu.** If you specify a Next Style for a style, it's automatically applied to a new paragraph when you press Return or Enter. If you choose [Same Style] (the default), the style you're creating continues to be applied to new paragraphs when you press Return or Enter while typing. Typically, you'd use the Next Style feature for things such as headlines that are always followed by a specific kind of paragraph (such as a byline). And you'd typically use [Same Style] for body text, because the next paragraph usually has the same formatting.

7. **Assign a keyboard shortcut.** If you want to (and you often should), you can assign a keyboard shortcut to a style (Windows users must make sure Num Lock is on). Press and hold any combination of ⌘, Option, and Shift, or Ctrl, Alt, and Shift, and press any number on the keypad. (Letters and nonkeypad numbers cannot be used for keyboard shortcuts.)

8. **When you're done specifying the attributes of your style, click OK.**

 **If you want to apply a new style to text that is selected, be sure to select the Apply Style to Selection check box before clicking OK to save the new style.**

 **Grep styles, a new option in InDesign CS4's New Paragraph Style dialog box, are covered in Chapter 22.**

Applying paragraph styles

After you create a paragraph style, applying it is easy. Just click within a paragraph or highlight text in a range of paragraphs, and then click on the style name in the Paragraph Styles panel or press its keyboard shortcut. (Windows users must make sure Num Lock is on when using shortcuts for styles.)

 **If your selected paragraphs have more than one paragraph style applied within the group, the Paragraph Styles panel displays the text *(Mixed)* at the lower left.**

When you apply a style to selected paragraphs, all local formats and applied character styles are retained. All other formats are replaced by those of the applied style.

CROSS-REF **InDesign has a Quick Apply panel that lets you apply any style — object, paragraph, or character — as well as other saved settings from one location. Chapter 2 covers this panel.**

Overriding existing formatting

If you press and hold Option or Alt when clicking a name in the Paragraph Styles panel, any character styles that have been applied within selected paragraphs are retained, as are the following character formats: Superscript, Subscript, Underline, Strikethrough, Language, and Baseline Shift. If you press and hold Option+Shift or Alt+Shift when clicking a style name, all local formatting, including any character styles, within the selected paragraphs is removed.

You can also use the Clear Overrides button at the bottom of the panel or the Clear Overrides option in the flyout menu. Either way, you remove all formatting that conflicts with the style's formatting — unless you press and hold ⌘ or Ctrl, which clears character formatting only, or Shift+⌘ or Ctrl+Shift, which clears paragraph formatting only.

If you want to remove a style from a paragraph so that it's not changed if the style is later changed, choose Break Link to Style from the flyout menu. The upper left of the panel displays the text *(No Style)*.

A few last words about paragraph styles: There are no hard-and-fast rules about how best to implement them. As with handwriting, you should develop your own style. How many styles you create, the names you use, whether you apply them with keyboard shortcuts or through the Paragraph Styles panel, and whether you use paragraph styles, character styles, or both are all matters of personal taste. One thing is indisputable: You should use styles whenever possible; they are a layout artist's best friend.

Managing paragraph styles

The Paragraph Styles panel's flyout menu, shown in Figure 19.1, displays 18 options for managing styles; three iconic buttons at the bottom of the panel let you reapply, create, and delete paragraph styles. Here's a brief description of each option:

- **New Paragraph Style:** This option creates a new paragraph style. When you choose New Paragraph Style, the New Paragraph Style dialog box appears. The panel also has an iconic button to create a new style.

- **Duplicate Style:** Click a style name and then click this button to create an exact copy. If you want to create a style that's similar to one you've already created, you can choose New Paragraph Style rather than Duplicate and then use the Based On option to create a child of the original. If you choose Duplicate, the copy is identical to but not based on the original; if you modify the original, the copy is not affected.

- **Delete Style:** Choose this option to delete highlighted styles. To select multiple styles, press and hold ⌘ or Ctrl as you click their names. To select a range of styles, click the first one and then press and hold Shift and click the last one.

> **NOTE**   InDesign gives you the option of replacing a deleted style with another style. You can also choose [No Paragraph Style] if you no longer want a style applied. In that case, select the Preserve Formatting option to convert the unapplied style's formatting to local formatting, or deselect it to make the text lose that formatting as well as its style.

- **Redefine Style (Option+Shift+⌘+R or Ctrl+Alt+Shift+R):** This option lets you modify an existing style. Highlight text to which the style you want to modify has been applied, change the formats as desired, and then click Redefine Style. The newly applied formats are applied to the style.

- **Style Options:** This option lets you modify an existing style. When a style is highlighted in the Paragraph Styles panel, choosing Style Options displays the Paragraph Style Options dialog box, which is identical to the New Paragraph Style dialog box.

- **Clear Overrides:** This option removes any local formatting such as boldface or small caps applied to the selected paragraphs. Note that the text within the paragraph that has the local overrides must be selected; you cannot just click anywhere in the paragraph. Choosing this option does the same as pressing and holding Option or Alt to remove local formatting (but to retain any character styles applied) for styles selected in the panel. Note that you can press and hold Option+Shift or Alt+Shift to remove *both* local formatting and applied character styles at the same time.

- **Convert "*current style name*" Bullets and Numbering to Text:** This option removes any automatic bullets or numbering defined through InDesign's bulleted and numbered lists feature from selected paragraphs (see Chapter 18). The paragraphs that this option is applied to still have bullets and numbers, but they are no longer updated if the style is changed or if paragraphs are added or deleted. (Adding paragraphs would normally add bullets or adjust numbering.)

- **Break Link to Style:** This option removes the style from the paragraph but leaves it with the formatting, now converted to local formatting. That way, the selected paragraph won't be changed if the paragraph style is later changed. After you remove a style from a paragraph, InDesign displays (*No Style*) at the bottom of the Paragraph Styles panel when the paragraph is selected.

- **Load Paragraph Styles:** Choose this option if you want to import styles from another InDesign document. (I discuss importing styles in detail later in this chapter.)

- **Load All Text Styles:** This option lets you import both paragraph and character styles from another InDesign document. (I cover importing styles in detail later in this chapter.)

- **Select All Unused:** Select this option to highlight the names of all paragraph styles that have not been applied to any paragraphs. This is a handy way of identifying unused styles in preparation for deleting them (by choosing the Delete Style option).

- **The five style group options:** I cover these in the next section.

- **Sort by Name:** Normally, styles are added to the panel in the order you create them. To alphabetize the list, select this option.

- **Small Panel Rows:** Click this option to reduce the text size in the Paragraph Styles panel. Although harder to read, a panel with this option set lets you access more styles without having to scroll. To return the panel to its normal text size, select this option again.

Applying a Sequence of Styles All at One Time

InDesign has a neat capability that lets you apply multiple styles to selected text.

First, define the various styles, and be sure that each style has a different style selected in the Next Style pop-up menu in the Paragraph Style Options or New Paragraph Style dialog boxes. For example, if you have Headline, Byline, and Body Copy styles, make sure that Headline has Byline selected in Next Style and that Byline has Body Copy selected in Next Style.

Then highlight all the text that uses this sequence of styles. Now Control+click or right-click Headline and select Apply "Headline" + Next Style from the contextual menu. InDesign will apply Headline to the first paragraph, Byline to the second paragraph, and Body Copy to the rest.

Using style groups

To help you find the desired style in documents that have dozens of them, InDesign lets you create style groups, which create a folder in the styles panel's style list that you can open and close as desired. To create a group, choose New Style Group from the panel's flyout menu or click the Create New Style Group iconic button (the folder icon) on the bottom of the panel.

Or you can select multiple styles in the panel and choose New Group from Styles in the flyout menu. (Note that this option is grayed out if you have selected any of the predefined styles — [None] and either [Basic Paragraph] or [Basic Character].)

Enter a name in the dialog box that appears and click OK.

To add styles to an existing group (which will have a folder icon to the left of its name in the panel list), you have two options:

- You can drag any desired styles into the group.
- You can copy a selected style to the group by choosing Copy to Group and then selecting the target group in the dialog box that appears.

To quickly open all groups, choose Open All Groups in the panel's flyout menu. To quickly close them all, choose Close All Groups.

Character styles

Character styles are nearly identical in every respect to paragraph styles, but instead of using them to format selected paragraphs, you use character styles to apply character-level formats to a highlighted range of text. For example, you can use a character style to

- Modify the appearance of the first several words in a paragraph. For example, some publications, particularly magazines, use a type-style variation such as small caps as a lead-in for a paragraph. You can use a character style not only to switch the type style to small caps but also to change size, color, font family, and so on.
- Apply formatting to part of a paragraph via a paragraph style. The paragraph style controls for drop caps, nested styles, automatic bullets, and automatic numbering all rely on character styles.
- Apply different formatting to such text elements as Web site, e-mail, and FTP addresses within body text.
- Create other body text variations for such things as emphasis, book and movie titles, product and company names, and so on.

Creating and applying character styles

Using character styles is much the same as using paragraph styles. First you create them and then you apply them. And you use the Character Styles panel (choose Type ⇨ Character Styles or press Shift+⌘+F11 or Ctrl+Shift+F11), shown in Figure 19.3, to do both. As is the case with paragraph styles, the easiest way to create a character style is to apply the character-level formats you want to use in the style to some sample text and then follow the steps in this section. You can create a character style from scratch (that is, without preformatting any text), but if you do, you'll have to set all the character formats when you create the style.

The Character Styles panel and its flyout menu

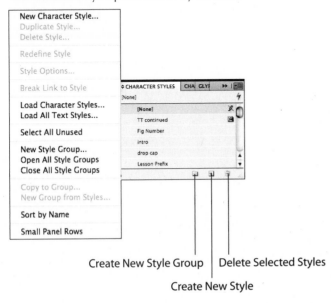

Create New Style Group | Delete Selected Styles

Create New Style

NOTE If your selected text has more than one character style applied within the selection, the Character Styles panel displays the text *(Mixed)* at the lower left.

To create a character style from highlighted text:

1. **If it's not displayed, show the Character Style panel by choosing Type ⇨ Character Styles or pressing Shift+⌘+F11 or Ctrl+Shift+F11.** You can also choose Window ⇨ Type & Tables ⇨ Character Styles.

2. **Make sure you highlight text that's been styled with all the character formats you want to include in your style; then, choose New Style from the Character Styles panel's flyout menu.** The New Character Style dialog box, shown in Figure 19.4, appears.

   You can also create a new style by clicking the Create New Style iconic button (the page icon) at the bottom of the panel. When you click this button, a new style with a default name (Character Style 1, Character Style 2, and so on) is added to the list. The formats applied to the selected text are included in the new style; the New Character Style dialog box is not displayed.

FIGURE 19.4

The New Character Style dialog box

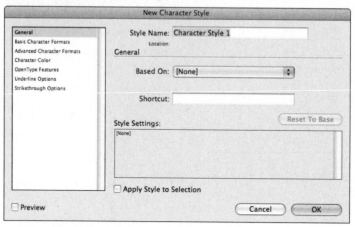

3. Type a name for the style in the Style Name field.

4. **Choose the appropriate option from the scroll list to the left of the Style Name field to open the relevant pane if you want to change any character-level formats.** The list displays seven options: General, Basic Character Formats, Advanced Character Formats, Character Color, OpenType Features, Underline Options, and Strikethrough Options.

5. **Use the Based On pop-up menu to create families of styles.** This menu displays the names of other character styles. For example, you could create a style called Body Copy/ Base Character that uses the same character attributes as your base Body Copy paragraph style and then create variations such as Body Text/Emphasis, Body Text/URLs, and so on. If you use the Based On pop-up menu to base each of the variations on Body Text/Base Character and you modify this parent style, your changes are applied to all the variations.

 If you've created a style based on another, and you don't like the changes you've made, you can reset the style to be the same as its based-on style by clicking Reset To Base.

6. **If you want (and you should), you can assign a keyboard shortcut to a style (Windows users should make sure that Num Lock is on).** Press and hold any combination of ⌘, Option, and Shift, or Ctrl, Alt, and Shift, and press any number on the keypad. (Letters and nonkeypad numbers cannot be used for keyboard shortcuts.)

7. When you're done specifying the attributes of your style, click OK.

 If you want to apply a new style to text that is selected, be sure to select the Apply Style to Selection check box before clicking OK to save the new style.

Overriding character styles

Overriding existing formatting via character styles does work differently than overriding formatting in paragraph styles in two ways.

First, when you remove the link to a character style, the Character Styles panel displays [None] as the current style in its style list. When you remove the link to a paragraph style, the Paragraph Styles panel shows no style in the style list but instead displays (*No Style*) at the bottom of the panel.

Second, there is no Clear Overrides iconic button in the Character Styles panel (nor does the shortcut of Option+Shift+clicking or Alt+Shift+clicking perform this function). Instead, you apply the [None] style to clear a character style from text. Note that if you later apply a paragraph style to text with [None] character style, the text will take on the paragraph style's formatting rather than retain its local formatting.

But as with paragraph styles, you can break the link of text to its character style by choosing Break Link to Style from the flyout menu.

Managing and grouping character styles

The options displayed in the Character Styles panel's flyout menu are the same as those for the Paragraph Styles panel's flyout menu, which are explained earlier in this chapter.

Similarly, style groups work the same way for character styles as they do for paragraph styles.

Working with Nested Styles

Often, you'll want to apply character formatting in a consistent manner to many paragraphs. For example, you may want to change the font for the first character in a bulleted list so that the correct symbol appears for the bullet. Or you might want to italicize the numerals in a numbered list. Or you might want the first four words of body text that appear after a headline to be boldface and in small caps. Or you might want the first sentence in instructional paragraphs to be italic. InDesign lets you automate such formatting through the nested styles feature.

NEW FEATURE InDesign CS4 adds a new form of nested style: nested line styles. It works just the same as other nested styles (explained next) except that it lets you apply a character style to a certain number of lines in a paragraph. This is a popular design approach, such as having the first line in small caps. You specify the desired character style and how many lines you want it applied to, and InDesign does the rest. (In the previous version of InDesign, you had to use the End Nested Style Character at the end of the line and then hope that the line ending didn't change due to text or other alterations in your file.) Figure 19.5 shows a nested line style in use.

Figure 19.5 shows an example of nested styles in use, along with the Paragraph Style Options dialog box's Drop Caps and Nested Styles pane in which you create them. Here, you can see that the first sentence of the introductory paragraph's text is set to appear in red.

FIGURE 19.5

You can use a nested style to set the first line (for example) to use a specific character style. Essentially, you create a set of rules as to how much text gets a specific character style applied using the scope options, shown in the pop-up menu, for a nested style to determine what text receives the specified formatting, such as two sentences or all words until an em space. A nested line style does the same for lines of text.

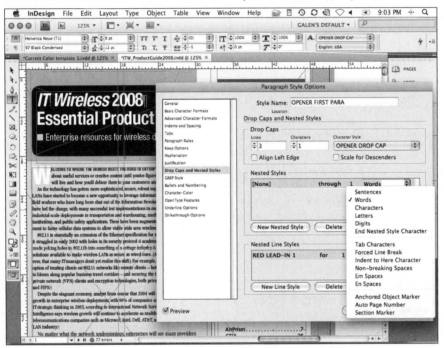

> **NOTE**   The Nested Styles feature is included in the same dialog box as the Drop Caps feature. That's because a drop cap would be the first nested style in a paragraph and can never be anything but the first style. By combining the two into one dialog box, InDesign lets you treat a drop cap as part of a series of styles to be applied to a paragraph. If you want only a drop cap, you simply don't create a nested style.

Here's how the nested styles work:

1. **Define any character styles that you'll apply to text through a nested style.** Even if all you're doing is making text italic, you need to define a character style to do so. The nested styles feature cannot apply any attributes other than those available in a character style.

2. **Open the Paragraph Styles panel (choose Type ⇨ Paragraph Styles or press ⌘+F11 or Ctrl+F11), choose Style Options from the flyout menu to open the Paragraph Style Options dialog box, and go to the Drop Caps and Nested Styles pane.**

3. **Click New Nested Style.** An entry appears in the Nested Styles section of the dialog box. This is what will be applied to text.

4. **Click the style name in the Nested Styles section of the pane to choose from an existing character style.** When you click the style name, a list of other styles appears, including [None], which uses the paragraph style's default formatting.

 You also have the [Repeat] option, which if selected lets you repeat a sequence of previous styles. (You choose the number in the third column.)

5. **Click in the second column to determine the scope end point.** Your choices are Through or Up To. For example, if you choose Through for a nested style that is set for four words, all four words will get the nested style. If you choose Up To, the first three words get the style and the fourth doesn't.

6. **In the third column, specify how many items you want InDesign to count in determining the scope's endpoint.** For example, if you want the first seven characters to have the style applied, type 7. If you want to have the style applied up to the first tab, type 1.

7. **Click the item in the fourth column to specify the scope of text to which you're applying the nested styles.** Figure 19.5 shows the options. They break into three groups: a number of items (characters, words, and so on), a specific character (tab, em space, and so on), and a specific marker character (inline graphic marker, auto page number, and section marker). Whatever you choose needs to be consistent in all your text because InDesign will follow these rules slavishly.

8. **Create multiple nested styles in one paragraph with different rules for each.** Obviously, you may not need to do this, but the option exists. InDesign applies the styles in the order in which they appear in the dialog box, and each starts where the other ends. Use the up and down arrow iconic buttons at the bottom of the section to change the order of nested styles.

9. **Create any desired line styles in the Nested Line Styles section of the pane.** It works just like the Nested Styles section except that there are just two pop-up menus: one for the character style you want to apply and one for the number of lines you want it to applied to. If you create more than one nested line style, they are applied in the order displayed in the pane. Use the up and down arrow iconic buttons at the bottom of the section to change the order of nested line styles.

10. **Select the Preview option to preview the formatting if you selected sample text before opening the dialog box.**

11. **Click OK when you're done.**

NEW FEATURE If you don't have a character style ready to use for your drop cap, nested style, or nested line style, InDesign CS4 now lets you create it by choosing New Character Style in each of the Character Style pop-up menus. In previous versions, you had to close the Drop Caps and Nested Styles dialog box, open the Character Styles panel and create the drop cap style there, and then close that panel and come back to the Drop Caps and Nested Styles dialog box to apply that new style.

Changing Styles

If you scratch your name into wet cement, you have only a few minutes to change your mind. After that, your formatting decisions are cast in stone, so to speak. Fortunately, styles are much more forgiving. Not only can you modify a style whenever you want, you're free to manually modify text to which styles have been applied.

Modifying styles

The most important thing to know about modifying a style is that all text to which a modified style has been applied is automatically updated. Additionally, if you modify a parent style, all children styles that were created by choosing Based On are also automatically updated.

There are three ways to modify an existing style. You can

- **Click the style name in the Character Styles or Paragraph Styles panel and then choose Style Options from the panel's flyout menu.** The Character Style Options or the Paragraph Style Options dialog box appears.

- **Double-click a style name to display the Character Style Options or Paragraph Style Options dialog box.**

- **Control+click or right-click a style name and choose Edit "*style name*" from the contextual menu to display the Character Style Options or Paragraph Style Options dialog box.**

Either way, these dialog boxes are the same as the New Character Style and New Paragraph Style dialog boxes, respectively. Make whatever changes you want and then click OK. Any text with the styles applied will be updated automatically with the new formatting.

Modifying text that's been styled with a style

If you need to change the appearance of text that's been formatted using a style, all you have to do is highlight the text — characters or paragraphs — and then use the Control panel, Character panel (choose Type ⇨ Character or press ⌘+T or Ctrl+T), or Paragraph panel (choose Type ⇨ Paragraph or press Option+⌘+T or Ctrl+Alt+T) to change the formats.

When you change any formats in text to which a style has been applied, you are making local changes. (To make global changes, you would modify the style.) When you change formatting in style-formatted text, a plus sign (+) appears next to the style name in the Character Styles or Paragraph Styles panel, as shown in Figure 19.6.

FIGURE 19.6

The plus sign (+) next to the style name in the Paragraph Styles panel (left) indicates that local formatting has been applied within a paragraph, overriding the style's attributes. The Character Styles panel (right) uses the same symbol to indicate the use of local formatting as well.

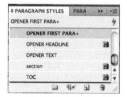 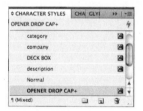

Importing Styles

If you create a style, you never have to re-create it, assuming you save the document that contains the styles. InDesign lets you import character and paragraph style from one document into another. Also, when you import text files from word processing programs that use style sheets, you can import the style sheets along with the text.

Importing styles from InDesign documents

The Paragraph Styles and Character Styles panels' flyout menus contain commands that let you move styles between documents. The Paragraph Styles panel lets you import only paragraph styles or both paragraph and character styles; the Character Styles panel lets you import only character styles or both character and paragraph styles. Here's how you do it:

1. **If it's not displayed, show the Paragraph Styles panel by choosing Type ⇨ Paragraph Styles or pressing ⌘+F11 or Ctrl+F11; or show the Character Styles panel by choosing Type ⇨ Character Styles or pressing Shift+⌘+F11 or Ctrl+Shift+F11.**

2. **Choose Load Paragraph Styles from the Paragraph Styles panel's flyout menu if you want to import selected paragraph styles. Likewise, choose Load Character Styles from the Character Styles panel's flyout menu if you want to import selected character styles.** You can also choose Load All Text Styles from either panel's flyout menu if you want to import both character and paragraph styles from that other document. Regardless of what kind of types of styles you choose to import, the Open a File dialog box appears.

3. **Use the controls in the Open a File dialog box to locate the InDesign document that contains the styles you want to import.**

4. **Double-click the document name or click the document name once and then click Open.** The Load Styles dialog box, shown in Figure 19.7, appears and lists the styles in the chosen document so that you can decide which ones to import.

FIGURE 19.7

The Load Styles dialog box

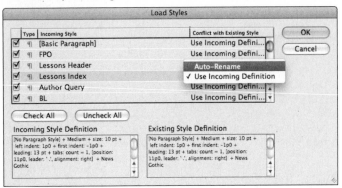

If you import styles whose names match those in the current document, InDesign gives you a chance to allow the imported style to overwrite the current style or to leave the current style as is and rename the imported style. If there is an entry in the Conflict with Existing Style column, you can click that entry for a pop-up menu that provides two choices: Auto-Rename and Use Incoming Definition (the default). If you choose Use Incoming Style Definition, the imported style overwrites the current document's style.

Note that there are two windows at the bottom of the dialog box that list the style definitions for the currently selected style to help you decide which styles to import, as well as which ones to overwrite or rename.

You can also use the Copy (choose Edit ⇨ Copy or press ⌘+C or Ctrl+C) and Paste commands (choose Edit ⇨ Paste or press ⌘+V or Ctrl +V) to move a style from one document to another. Simply copy some text in the source document to which the style you want to move has been applied. Then display the target document and use the Paste command to place the copied text into a text frame. The Character Styles and/or Paragraph Styles panels in the target document display the names of the new, "imported" styles.

Working with style sheets in imported text files

In most workgroup publishing environments, writers generate text using Microsoft Word, and InDesign users place the text in a layout and add other design elements — imported pictures, illustrations, lines, and so on — to create a finished publication. Whether writers are producing short magazine articles or lengthy book chapters, chances are they're doing some text formatting as they write — perhaps as little as applying occasional bold or italic styles or as much as using a complete set of style sheets, if their word processor supports them.

NOTE I use the term *style sheet* to refer to the formatting capability in Microsoft Word, following Word's naming convention. And I use *style* when referring to the formatting capability in InDesign, per its naming convention. In the rest of this section, the use of the two terms should help you keep track of when I mean the style sheets from Word versus the styles in InDesign.

When you import a word processing file into InDesign, you can bring the formatting and style sheets along with the text.

A writer might use isolated formatting to indicate which styles should be applied in InDesign — for example, she might apply bold to one-line paragraphs that should be formatted as a subhead. However, if the writer applies appropriate paragraph styles to text in her word processor, much of the formatting in InDesign can be automated by importing the style sheets. To import style sheets with a word processing file, select the Retain Format option in the Place dialog box (choose File ➪ Place or press ⌘+D or Ctrl+D). You can determine which style sheets import and how to handle any conflicts between style names if you select the Show Import Options option in the Place dialog box.

CROSS-REF See Chapter 13 for a complete list of formatting options that will import from Word, as well as for more information about using the Place command to import text files and managing style-sheet import.

After you place a text file that contains style sheets, the Paragraph Styles panel and Character Styles panel display the names of all the imported styles.

Editing imported paragraph style sheets

If you import paragraph style sheets with text, you can simply use the style sheets specified in the word processor to format the text. This method works well for designs that do not follow a template — for example, brochures or feature stories. You might import the text, experiment with formatting it, and then edit the imported style sheets now available as styles in InDesign to reflect your design.

For example, say you import a magazine feature article that is formatted with three paragraph style sheets (Headline, Byline, and Body Copy) into an InDesign document that does not contain styles with those names. The three styles are added to InDesign's Paragraph Styles list and have similar specifications to what the same-named style sheets had in the word processor. However, because InDesign offers more formatting options, you might modify those styles to fine-tune the text formatting. To edit a paragraph style, select it in the Paragraph Styles panel, choose Style Options from the panel's flyout menu, and then make your changes in the Modify Paragraph Style Options dialog box.

Overriding imported paragraph styles

In documents that follow a template, you can provide writers with style-sheet names that must be applied to their text. For example, say you're working on a tri-fold brochure that is part of an entire series of similar tri-folds. The writer might format the text with five paragraph style sheets that also exist as styles in your InDesign document: Heads, Subheads, Body Copy, Bullets, and Quotes. The style-sheet specifications in the word processor don't matter — only the name counts — because the styles in an InDesign document override same-name style sheets in imported text files.

For example, the writer's style sheets use standard fonts such as Times and Helvetica along with bold and italic typestyles to distinguish the types of text. But when the word processing file is imported into InDesign, the style sheets are overridden with InDesign styles that have the same name but specify the actual fonts used by the designer and the many formatting options available in InDesign.

You can supply writers either with actual style sheets or with only style-sheet names:

- To supply style sheets, export text in InDesign from a similar story as a Rich Text Format (RTF) file, which writers can open in their word processor; the word processor adds the style-sheet names in the RTF file to its own style-sheet list. The writers can then save these style-sheet names to a template file and use that template for future documents. To export text, use the Export dialog box (choose File ➪ Export or press ⌘+E or Ctrl+E) and choose Rich Text Format from the Format pop-up menu (called Save as Type in Windows).

- Or, you can simply give writers a list of style-sheet names that they can create themselves to their own specifications. In this case, it's particularly important that the style sheets created in the word processor have exactly the same names as those styles in the InDesign document.

Exporting styles

Although InDesign lets you export text (through the File ➪ Export command), only a few file formats are supported: Text-only (ASCII), RTF, InCopy, and InDesign Tagged Text.

An exported RTF file keeps the style names but not the actual formatting, which can make further editing difficult in a word processor. An InDesign Tagged Text file retains the style definitions, but it does so as codes, so again it's hard to deal with in a word processor. So you really can't export styles to word processor users, just to other InDesign users.

Summary

If you're working on a document that uses the same text formats repeatedly, you can save time and ensure consistency by using styles. A style is essentially a macro for formatting text. InDesign lets you create character-level styles and paragraph-level styles. Character styles let you apply several character attributes — such as font, size, leading, kerning, and tracking — to highlighted text at one time. Similarly, you can use paragraph styles to apply several paragraph formats — alignment, indents, drop caps, space before or after, and so on — simultaneously to selected paragraphs.

After you apply a style sheet to text, you can still manually modify the text by highlighting it and overriding the style's formats. And any modifications you make to the style are automatically applied to any text using it.

If you're importing a text file from Microsoft Word, you can import any applied styles along with the text, making them available as InDesign styles.

Chapter 20

Using Special Characters

I nDesign is a real internationalist, supporting 27 languages and 12 variants in its spelling and hyphenation dictionaries and providing easy access to foreign characters.

Even if you publish everything in English, InDesign's linguistic flexibility is quite useful, as the same mechanism that gives you easy access to foreign characters also gives you easy access to all sorts of special symbols — such as ¢, £, ©, and • — used in finance, mathematics, physics, and so on.

These symbols — whether regular letters, foreign characters, or special symbols — are called *glyphs*. InDesign offers menu options and keyboard shortcuts to use common glyphs, and the Glyphs panel to access specialty glyphs. Do note that many fonts have lots of glyphs available, which the Glyphs panel will reveal, but you'll likely need to buy fonts, called *pi fonts*, to handle special characters used in specific fields.

PLATFORM DIFFERENCES Macintosh and Windows fonts come with a wealth of special characters called glyphs, and Mac OS and Windows fonts often have different glyph collections. If you work across platforms, this makes it important to use the same symbol fonts on both platforms and to be sure that you know the glyphs you use are available in all the fonts you use.

CROSS-REF Fonts in the OpenType format typically have many more glyphs and non-Roman alphabetic characters than do fonts in PostScript Type 1 and TrueType fonts. OpenType fonts also often support variations of characters, such as swashes and expert characters. Chapter 16 explains how to work with these other OpenType fonts' capabilities.

IN THIS CHAPTER

Inserting special characters via menus, shortcuts, and the Glyphs panel

Creating and sharing glyphs sets

Using other tools for accessing special characters

Understanding special spaces, dashes, and quotes

Working with foreign languages

Inserting Glyphs

InDesign provides three ways to insert glyphs into your text: using menus, using the Glyphs panel, and using keyboard shortcuts. Typically, you use keyboard shortcuts for the symbols you use repeatedly, the menus for ones you use less frequently (given that they're organized into common usages such as spaces and dashes), and the Glyphs panel for those you use the least or that you can't access via shortcuts or menus.

Using keyboard shortcuts

Symbols are commonly used in all sorts of documents, from legal symbols to scientific ones. That's why most fonts have a selection of popular symbols built in that you can access via keyboard shortcuts. Table 20.1 shows the common symbols for Windows and Macintosh fonts. (Table 20.2, later in this chapter, shows the shortcuts for foreign characters such as accented letters.)

CROSS-REF   When you're searching and replacing text via the Find/Change dialog box, InDesign uses codes to indicate special symbols, as well as lets you paste the symbol into its Find What and Change To fields. Chapter 15 covers this in more detail.

TABLE 20.1

Shortcuts for Common Symbols

Character	Mac Shortcut	Windows Shortcut
Legal		
Copyright (©)	Option+G	Shift+Alt+C *or* Ctrl+Alt+C *or* Alt+0169
Registered trademark (®)	Option+R	Shift+Alt+R *or* Alt+0174
Trademark (™)	Option+2	Shift+Alt+2 *or* Alt+0153
Paragraph (¶)	Option+7	Shift+Alt+7 *or* Ctrl+Alt+; *or* Alt+0182
Section (§)	Option+6	Shift+Alt+6 *or* Alt+0167
Dagger (†)	Option+T	Shift+Alt+T *or* Alt+0134
Double dagger (‡)	Option+Shift+T	Alt+0135
Currency		
Cent (¢)	Option+4	Alt+0162
Euro (€)	Option+Shift+2	Alt+Ctrl+5
Pound sterling (£)	Option+3	Alt+0163
Yen (¥)	Option+Y	Ctrl+Alt+– (hyphen) *or* Alt+0165
Punctuation		
En bullet (•)	Option+8	Alt+8 *or* Alt+0149
Thin bullet (·)	*Not supported*	Alt+0183
Ellipsis (...)	Option+; (semicolon)	Alt+0133

Character	Mac Shortcut	Windows Shortcut
Measurement		
Foot (')	Control+'	Ctrl+'
Inch (")	Control+Shift+'	Ctrl+Alt+'
Mathematics		
One-half fraction (½)	*Not supported*	Ctrl+Alt+6 *or* Alt+0189
One-quarter fraction (¼)	*Not supported*	Ctrl+Alt+7 *or* Alt+0188
Three-quarters fraction (¾)	*Not supported*	Ctrl+Alt+8 *or* Alt+0190
Infinity (∞)	Option+5	*Not supported*
Division (÷)	Option+/	Alt+0247
Root (√)	Option+V	*Not supported*
Greater than or equal to (≥)	Option+>	*Not supported*
Less than or equal to (≤)	Option+<	*Not supported*
Inequality (≠)	Option+=	*Not supported*
Rough equivalence (≈)	Option+X	*Not supported*
Plus or minus (±)	Option+Shift+=	Alt+0177
Logical not (¬)	Option+L	Ctrl+Alt+\ *or* Alt+0172
Per mil (‰)	Option+Shift+R	Alt+0137
Degree (°)	Option+Shift+8	Alt+0176
Function (*f*)	Option+F	Alt+0131
Integral (∫)	Option+B	*Not supported*
Variation (∂)	Option+D	*Not supported*
Greek beta (β)	Option+S	*not supported*
Greek mu (μ)	Option+M	Alt+0181
Greek Pi (Π)	Option+Shift+P	*Not supported*
Greek pi (π)	Option+P	*Not supported*
Greek Sigma (Σ)	Option+W	*Not supported*
Greek Omega (Ω)	Option+Z	*Not supported*
Miscellaneous		
Apple logo ()	Option+Shift+K	*Not supported*
Light (◻)	*Not supported*	Ctrl+Alt+4 *or* Alt+0164
Open diamond (◊)	Option+Shift+V	*Not supported*

On-Screen Special Characters

When you use special characters such as em spaces and nonbreaking hyphens, it can be hard to tell them apart from regular characters. That's why InDesign lets you display these spaces, tabs, hyphens, breaks, paragraph returns, and other control characters that exist in the text. Choose Type ➪ Show Hidden Characters or press Option+⌘+I or Ctrl+Alt+I to turn on this display. (Note that these on-screen symbols will not print.)

Here's what the symbols look like for the various control characters. Top row, from left to right: regular space, nonbreaking space, fixed-width nonbreaking space, em space, en space, thin space, hair space, punctuation space, quarter space, third space, figure space, and flush space. Second row: tab and right tab. Third row: discretionary hyphen and nonbreaking hyphen. Fourth row: forced line break (new line), discretionary line break, paragraph return, column break, frame break, page break, even page break, and odd page break. Fifth row: note, indent-to-here, end-nested-style, non-joiner, and end-of-story markers.

Using menus

InDesign provides a set of menus to insert commonly used special characters, such as special spaces and dashes, as well as internal control characters such as Indent to Here and Column Break. There are three menu options, all in the Type menu, for inserting special characters:

- **Insert Special Characters:** This option has five submenus: Symbols, Markers, Hyphens and Dashes, Quotation Marks, and Other. The Symbols submenu includes items such as ® and ©; the Markers submenu includes automatic page numbers, section markers, and footnote numbers; and the Other submenu includes tabs, Indent to Here, End Nested Style Here, and Non-joiner.

- **Insert White Space:** This option's submenu offers 12 types of fixed-size spaces as well as a nonbreaking version of variable-sized (regular) space.

- **Insert Break Character:** This option's submenu offers six types of break characters (such as column breaks and page breaks), a paragraph break (it's easier just to press Return or Enter to get this), and two types of line breaks (forced and discretionary).

CROSS-REF The spaces, dashes, and quotation marks characters are covered in this chapter. The hyphen and Indent to Here characters are covered in Chapter 17. The break characters are covered in Chapter 14. The End Nested Style Here character is covered in Chapter 19. Automatic page and section markers are covered in Chapter 6. Footnotes are covered in Chapter 23. Tabs are covered in Chapter 21.

Using the Glyphs panel

Inspired by Microsoft Word's Symbol dialog box (choose Edit ⇨ Insert Symbol), InDesign's creators have created a flexible panel, the Glyphs panel, to access special symbols and characters in any font.

To open the panel, choose Type ⇨ Glyphs or press Option+Shift+F11 or Alt+Shift+F11. The Glyphs panel, shown in Figure 20.1, displays. By default, the panel shows available characters for the current font, but you can change the font using the Font Family and Font Style pop-up menus at the bottom of the panel.

It's unlikely that the Glyphs panel will show all available characters in its window, so use the scroll bar at right to move through all the characters. To show a subset of the font's characters, choose an option such as Entire Font or Currency from the Show pop-up menu (the options will depend on how the font file is organized internally); Figure 20.1 shows an example. You can also make the characters larger or smaller by clicking the Zoom Out or Zoom In iconic buttons at the panel's bottom right.

FIGURE 20.1

The Glyphs panel and its flyout menu (left). The panel and its Show pop-up menu for an OpenType font (right).

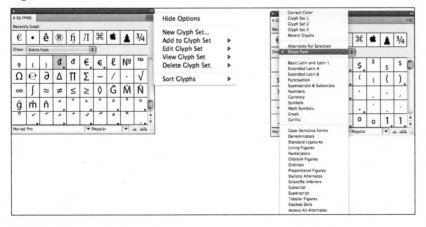

NOTE Recently used glyphs display at the top of the Glyphs panel, making it easier to use them. (If they don't appear, choose Show Options from the flyout menu or click the double-arrow icon in the tab to the left of the panel's name. These two methods will also hide the recently used glyphs if they are already visible.)

InDesign also lets you change how the glyphs are sorted in the panel. Choose Sort Glyphs ⇨ By Unicode (the default) from the flyout menu to have them appear in order of the international Unicode standard's numbering scheme, or choose Sort Glyphs ⇨ By CID/GID to sort them based on the font's internal character and glyph IDs. There's really no reason to change this sort option from the Unicode default.

Creating glyph sets

For quick access to frequently used glyphs (from multiple fonts), InDesign lets you create glyph sets.

To create glyph sets:

1. **Click New Glyph Set from the Glyphs panel's flyout menu.** Choose Type ⇨ Glyphs or press Option+Shift+F11 or Alt+Shift+F11, to open the panel. You can also choose Window ⇨ Type & Tables ⇨ Glyphs.

2. **Type a name in the New Glyph Set dialog box, and click OK.** You now have a new, empty glyph set on your computer, although it won't show on-screen. (Before you click OK, you can use the Insert Order pop-up menu and choose the order in which you want added glyphs to appear. Your choices are Glyph Value Order (such as the Unicode value), Insert at Front, or Insert at End.)

3. **In the Glyphs panel, select the special character you want to add to your new set.** You may need to change the font and style using the pop-up menus at the bottom of the panel.

4. **In the panel's flyout menu, choose Add to Glyph Set ⇨ set name to add the symbol to the chosen set.**

5. **Repeat Steps 4 and 5 for each glyph you want to add.**

You could end the process there, but InDesign provides a few more controls for your new (or existing) glyph set that you may want use. To edit a glyph set, choose Edit Glyph Set ⇨ set name, make your changes, and click OK when done. The resulting Edit Glyph Set dialog box is shown in Figure 20.2. Your options include:

- You can change the name and the glyph insertion order, using the Name field and the Insertion Order pop-up menu, respectively.

- If you want a specific font to be used for a glyph (which you need to do for symbols chosen from pi fonts, as opposed to common symbols such as ™ available in most fonts), make sure that the Remember Font with Glyph option is selected. You can also choose or change the font using the Font and Style pop-up menus in the dialog box.

- To delete a glyph, select it in the Edit Glyph Set dialog box and then click Delete from Set.

FIGURE 20.2

Editing a glyph set

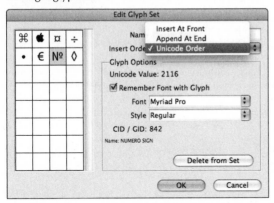

> **NOTE** InDesign automatically creates a glyph set called Recent Glyphs, which are glyphs you've selected recently. You can edit and otherwise work with this automatic set just as you can with any other set.

To access a glyph set, simply click the desired glyph set from the Show pop-up menu in the Glyph panel. Make sure the Type tool is active and that the text cursor (text-insertion point) is active in a text frame or path. Double-click the desired glyph in the Glyphs panel; InDesign will insert it at the text cursor location.

Sharing glyph sets

You can share glyph sets with other users. When you create a glyph set, InDesign creates a file in the `Glyph Sets` folder within the `Presets` folder that in turn resides within the folder containing the InDesign application. Just copy these files to other users' `Glyph Sets` folders to give them access to them.

Using Other Tools to Access Special Characters

Besides using the built-in InDesign tools for special characters, you can also use utility programs. You might do this because you want to use the same consistent tool for all your applications.

Mac OS X 10.4 (Tiger) and Mac OS X 10.5 (Leopard) each comes with two tools that are like a simple version of InDesign's Glyphs panel, as shown in Figure 20.3: the Keyboard Viewer and Character Palette. Both are available under the Keyboard Input menu item. Note that you might need to turn on the Keyboard Input menu item by choosing ⌘ ⇨ System Preferences and then going to the International control panel's Input Menu pane. Select the Show Input Menu in Menu Bar option.

Similarly, Windows has a tool to access special symbols, as shown in Figure 20.4: In both
Windows XP and Windows Vista, use the Character Map utility that comes with Windows.
Character Map is usually installed in the Windows Start menu; choose Start ➪ All Programs ➪
Accessories ➪ System Tools ➪ Character Map. (If you use the Classic Start Menu interface, choose
Start ➪ Accessories ➪ System Tools ➪ Character Map.)

FIGURE 20.3

Mac OS X's Character Palette and Keyboard Viewer

FIGURE 20.4

Windows XP's Character Map utility (the Windows Vista version is identical).

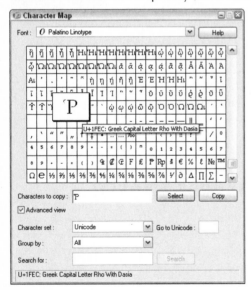

On both platforms, you can also use a utility like Ergonis's PopChar, which adds a quick-access icon to the Mac and Windows menu bars. Figure 20.5 shows the Mac and Windows versions. Notice how the keyboard shortcut for each special character is shown at the bottom as a character is highlighted. (This book's companion Web site, www.InDesignCentral.com, has links to this and other utilities.)

FIGURE 20.5

The PopChar utility for Mac OS X (top) and Windows (bottom)

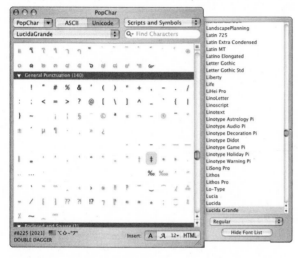

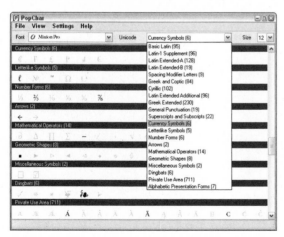

If you don't want to use one of these utilities in all your applications but instead want to take advantage of your word processor's tools, note that the popular word processors have their own feature for special character access, as shown in Figure 20.6:

- In Microsoft Word (Mac or Windows), choose Insert ⇨ Symbol. (It may also be accessible through the toolbar if you added this command to your toolbar; look for the button with the Ω character.)

- In Corel WordPerfect, choose Insert ⇨ Symbol. (Use the Set pop-up menu to switch among different types of symbols.)

- In Apple iWork Pages, choose Edit ⇨ Special Characters. (Use the list of symbol categories at left to switch among different types of symbols.)

FIGURE 20.6

The tools for inserting special characters in Microsoft Word (top), Corel WordPerfect (bottom left), and Apple iWork Pages (bottom right)

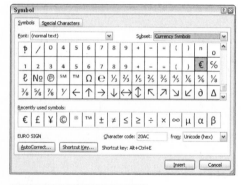

Understanding Special Spaces, Dashes, and Quotes

Typographers have long had a wide arsenal of spaces, dashes, and hyphens to control text appearance. Although word processors offer some of these characters, InDesign goes way beyond what most people even know exist.

Using special spaces

One way to carefully fine-tune spacing is to literally replace individual spaces with special spaces. Instead of narrowing and widening with tracking and justification settings, these special spaces maintain their widths. InDesign provides 13 special space options in two categories: nonbreaking spaces and fixed-width spaces.

Nonbreaking spaces

A *nonbreaking space* glues two words together, ensuring that a line doesn't wrap between two words if you don't want it to. For example, you might want to use a nonbreaking space in *OS X* so that *OS* doesn't end on one line with *X* starting on the next line. Nonbreaking spaces are also handy if you put spaces on either side of your dashes; they make sure that a dash is glued to the word before it. All are available by choosing the desired space from Type ⇨ Insert White Space's submenu.

InDesign has two types of nonbreaking spaces: the regular one, whose size is variable and thus can be adjusted the way any other regular space in a line can be; the fixed-width one, which essentially is a nonbreaking en space. The regular nonbreaking space is the one you'll use 99 percent of the time.

Fixed-width spaces

Fixed-width spaces keep their size intact no matter how much InDesign adjusts regular spaces elsewhere in your text as part of its text-flow and composition decisions.

The three most common fixed-width spaces are the em space (the width of a capital *M*, which also happens to be the same width as the type size), the en space (the width of a capital *N*, which happens to be half the width of an em space), and the thin space (the width of a lowercase *t*, which happens to be a quarter the width of an em space).

But InDesign's creators are control freaks, so they offer a lot more fixed-width space options than just the common em, en, and thin spaces, as Table 20.2 shows:

- A punctuation space is the width of a comma or period, useful in aligning text in tables.
- A figure space is the width of a standard (tabular lining) numeral, also useful in aligning text in tables.
- A flush space is used to fill out a line between an end-of-story character and the text on the rest of line. But it works only if the paragraph is set to Full Justify. Frankly, it's easier to use a right tab character (press Shift+Tab), which does the same thing no matter what justification is applied to your paragraph.
- A hair space is essentially half a thin space and is typically used instead of kerning to nudge slightly overlapping characters away from each other.
- The other spaces — third space, quarter space, and sixth space — are the specified fractions of an em space's width.

The non-joiner character is a zero-width "space" character that you'll hardly use because it's really designed for languages such as Arabic and Devanagari, in which letterforms get joined in some circumstances but not others. The non-joiner prevents the characters from being joined, overriding any automatic font options. In English, you might use this character to manually prevent automatic ligatures (the only circumstance in which characters are joined together in American English).

TABLE 20.2

Shortcuts for Spaces, Dashes, Hyphens, and Quotes

Character	Mac Shortcut	Windows Shortcut
Em space ( )	Shift+⌘+M	Ctrl+Shift+M
En space ( )	Shift+⌘+N	Ctrl+Shift+N
Thin space ()	Option+Shift+⌘+M	Ctrl+Alt+Shift+M
Nonbreaking space	Option+⌘+X	Ctrl+Alt+X
Em dash (—)	Option+Shift+–	Alt+Shift+– *or* Alt+0151
En dash (–)	Option+–	Alt+– *or* Alt+0150
Nonbreaking hyphen	Option+⌘+–	Ctrl+Alt+–
Discretionary hyphen	Shift+⌘+–	Ctrl+Shift+–
" (open double quote)	Option+[	Shift+Alt+[
" (closed double quote)	Shift+Option+[	Shift+Alt+]
' (open single quote)	Option+]	Alt+[
' (closed single quote)	Shift+Option+]	Alt+]
" (keyboard double quote)	Option+shift+'	Ctrl+Alt+'
' (keyboard single quote/apostrophe)	⌘+'	Ctrl+'
` (keyboard open single quote)	`	`

Using dashes

Many people confuse the two types of dashes used in typography: the em dash and en dash.

All about em dashes

An em dash (so called because it is the width of a capital *M*) is the most common dash and is used to indicate a break in sentence flow, either for an inserted phrase (sort of a supersize parenthesis) or to indicate a complete change in thought (which typically occurs in transcribed text).

When you import text from a word processor, InDesign converts two consecutive hyphens — the way you indicate a dash in a typewriter — to a real em dash. But InDesign doesn't do this when you type, so you must specify the em dash through the torturous menu command Type ⇨ Insert Special Character ⇨ Hyphens and Dashes ⇨ Em Dash or know its keyboard shortcut (Option+ Shift+– [hyphen] or Alt+Shift+– [hyphen]).

Spacing Em Dashes — or Not

Typographers are divided over whether you should put spaces around em dashes — like this — or not—like this. Traditionally, there is no space. But having space lets the publishing program treat the dash as a word, thereby creating an even amount of space around all words in a line. Not having a space around dashes means that the publishing program sees the two words connected by the em dash as one big word. So the spacing added to justify a line between all other words on the line may be awkwardly large because the program doesn't know how to break a line after or before an em dash that doesn't have space on either side. Still, whether to surround a dash with space is a decision in which personal preferences should prevail.

PLATFORM DIFFERENCES Note that most Windows programs don't use the Alt+Shift+– shortcut for an em dash; if they don't have their own shortcut, you can use the universal Windows shortcut Alt+0151 (be sure to type the numbers from the numeric keypad, not from the keyboard). By the way, the universal Windows shortcut for an en dash is Alt+0150.

CAUTION Several versions of Word — including Word 97 and Word 2000 for Windows and Word X for Mac — have a default setting that converts two hyphens to an en dash (–) rather than an em dash (—), which is simply wrong typographically. Chapter 13 explains how to handle this.

All about en dashes

The en dash, so called because it is the width of a capital *N*, is traditionally used to

- Separate numerals, as in a range of values or dates (pages 41–63)
- Label a figure (Figure 20–1), although publishers are divided on whether to do this (some just use a regular hyphen)
- Indicate a negative value (–45) as a minus sign
- Indicate an interrupted hyphenation (first– and business-class passengers)
- Indicate a multiple-word hyphenation (Civil War–era rifle)

Of course, many people don't use an en dash at all — or incorrectly use it instead of an em dash. Although desktop publishing has made it easy for almost anyone to produce good-looking documents, most people have no clue about the use of special characters that typographers and copy editors have traditionally applied to final documents.

Using quotation marks and apostrophes

By default, InDesign replaces the keyboard's typewriter-style, straight quotation marks (" and ') and apostrophe (') with the typographic, curly quotation marks — that is, as long as Use Typographer's

Quotes is enabled in the Type pane of the Preferences dialog box (choose InDesign ⇨ Preferences ⇨ Type or press ⌘+K on the Mac, or choose Edit ⇨ Preferences ⇨ Type or press Ctrl+K in Windows). InDesign handles both quotation marks in imported text and as you type.

You can change the quotation marks that InDesign uses in the Dictionary pane of the Preferences dialog box, as Chapter 3 explains.

CAUTION **Do not use the keyboard open single quotation mark key (`), in the upper-left corner of your keyboard to the left of the 1, as an open single quotation mark. Instead, use the keyboard apostrophe (') key. If you use the open single quotation mark keyboard key, you will get a different open single quotation mark character from the standard typographic version.**

Entering keyboard quotes

When Use Typographer's Quotes is enabled, you can enter the keyboard quotation marks — perhaps for use as foot marks (') and inch marks (") — by using keyboard shortcuts. Press Option+⌘+' or Ctrl+Alt+' for double quotation marks and ⌘+' or Ctrl+' for single quotation marks. They're also available by choosing Type ⇨ Insert Special Character ⇨ Quotation Marks.

Typing reverse single quotation marks

A reverse single quotation mark — a close single quotation mark, really — is often used to indicate an omission — for example, in '*80s* to mean the 1980s or in '*burbs* to mean suburbs. You need to enter this type of reverse quote manually at all times (whether or not Smart Quotes is in use) by typing Option+] or Alt+].

Handling adjacent single and double quotation marks

When a single quotation mark is followed immediately by a double quotation mark, or vice versa, separate the two with your choice of a nonbreaking space, thin space, or punctuation space. For most fonts, I think the thin space provides the best visual result. For example:

- He told me, "I asked, 'Do you have time to help?'"
- "'I am too busy' was her answer," he sighed.

Working with Foreign Languages

Adobe offers 18 language versions of InDesign, covering Brazilian Portuguese, Chinese (in both simplified and traditional versions), Czech, Danish, Dutch, English (providing both American and British English in the same version), Finnish, French, German, Greek, Italian, Japanese, Korean, Norwegian, Polish, Spanish (Castilian), and Swedish. WinSoft sells versions of InDesign in several other languages, including Arabic (both Middle Eastern and North African forms), Hebrew, Hungarian, Russian, and Turkish.

But you don't need one of those editions to work with these languages' characters and symbols. InDesign supports 27 languages and 12 additional variants no matter which version you use.

Those language-specific editions from Adobe and WinSoft provide the user interface in a local language, but all are multilingual when it comes to the text they handle.

Many languages use the Roman alphabet, often with accent marks added. Western and Eastern European languages, for example, use the Roman alphabet, although some languages have extra characters such as the German ß, the Icelandic Þ, the French «, and the Spanish ¡. For Western European languages, the majority of Roman-based fonts include these extra characters — but not all do, so do check before relying on a specific font. Fewer Roman-based fonts have the special accented letters common in Eastern European and Turkish languages such as the Ł and Ğ — so chances are you need to buy fonts designed specifically for these languages. And for languages with non-Roman scripts — such as Arabic, Chinese, Greek, Hebrew, Japanese, Korean, Thai, and Vietnamese — it's a sure bet you need to get language-specific fonts.

CROSS-REF InDesign comes with spelling and hyphenation dictionaries for the 27 languages it supports. Chapter 15 covers how to work with these dictionaries in more detail, as well as how to let InDesign know which language specific text is in, so that it knows which dictionaries to use with it.

Although most American publishers don't produce work in other languages, they may still use accents in their work. (Canadian publishers, of course, often publish in English and French.) And, of course, many publishers do publish in other languages, such as Spanish, French, German, and Portuguese, because they do business with customers in multiple countries. Even all-English publishers may choose to use accents in foreign words such as *café* to help pronunciation and show a bit of international flair.

See Table 20.3 for foreign-language characters used in Western European languages — the ones that most North American publishers are apt to use occasionally, without resorting to fonts designed for these languages. Note that Windows shortcuts involving four numerals (such as Alt+0157) should be entered from the numeric keypad while holding the Alt key.

TIP If your font doesn't have the accented characters you need, you may be able to create them by kerning accent marks over the letters. See Chapter 16 for detailed information on kerning.

TABLE 20.3

Shortcuts for Western European Accents and Foreign Characters

Character	Mac Shortcut	Windows Shortcut
acute (´)*	Option+E *letter*	' *letter*
cedilla (ç)*	*see* Ç *and* ç	' *letter*
circumflex (^)*	Option+I *letter*	^ *letter*
grave (`)*	Option+` *letter*	` *letter*

continued

TABLE 20.3 *(continued)*

Character	Mac Shortcut	Windows Shortcut
tilde (~)*	Option+N *letter*	~ *letter*
trema (¨)*	Option+U *letter*	" *letter*
umlaut (¨)*	Option+U *letter*	" *letter*
Á	Option+E A	' A *or* Alt+0193
á	Option+E a	' a *or* Alt+0225
À	Option+` A	` A *or* Alt+0192
à	Option+` a	` a *or* Alt+0224
Ä	Option+U A	" A *or* Alt+0196
ä	Option+U a	" a *or* Alt+0228
Ã	Option+N A	~ A *or* Alt+0195
ã	Option+N a	~ a *or* Alt+0227
Â	Option+I A	^ A *or* Alt+0194
â	Option+I a	^ a *or* Alt+0226
Å	Option+Shift+A	Alt+0197
å	Option+A	Alt+0229
Æ	Option+Shift+`	Alt+0198
æ	Option+`	Alt+0230 *or* Ctrl+Alt+Z
Ç	Option+Shift+C	' C *or* Alt+0199
ç	Option+C	' c *or* Alt+0231 *or* Ctrl+Alt+,
Ð	*Not supported*	Alt+0208
ð	*Not supported*	Alt+0240
É	Option+E E	' E *or* Alt+0201
é	Option+E e	' e *or* Alt+0233
È	Option+` E	` E *or* Alt+0200
è	Option+` e	` e *or* Alt+0232
Ë	Option+U E	" E *or* Alt+0203
ë	Option+U e	" e *or* Alt+0235
Ê	Option+I E	^ E *or* Alt+0202
ê	Option+I e	^ e *or* Alt+0234
Í	Option+E I	' I *or* Alt+-205
í	Option+E i	' i *or* Alt+0237
Ì	Option+` I	` I *or* Alt+0204
ì	Option+` i	` i *or* Alt+0236
Ï	Option+U I	" I *or* Alt+0207

Character	Mac Shortcut	Windows Shortcut
ï	Option+U i	" I or Alt+0239
Î	Option+I I	^ I or Alt+0206
î	Option+I i	^ I or Alt+0238
Ñ	Option+N N	~ N or Alt+0209
ñ	Option+N n	~ n or Alt+0241
Ó	Option+E O	' O or Alt+0211
ó	Option+E o	' o or Alt+0243 or Ctrl+Alt+O
Ò	Option+` O	` O or Alt+0210
ò	Option+` o	` o or Alt+0242
Ö	Option+U O	" O or Alt+0214
ö	Option+U o	" o or Alt+0246
Õ	Option+N O	~ O or Alt+0213
õ	Option+N o	~ o or Alt+0245
Ô	Option+I O	^ O or Alt+0212
ô	Option+I o	^ o or Alt+0244
Ø	Option+Shift+O	Alt+0216
ø	Option+O	Alt+0248 or Ctrl+Alt+L
Œ	Option+Shift+Q	Alt+0140
œ	Option+Q	Alt+0156
Þ	*Not supported*	Alt+0222
þ	*Not supported*	Alt+0254
ß	Option+S	Ctrl+Alt+S or Alt+0223
ī	Option+B	*Not supported*
Š	*Not supported*	Alt+0138
š	*Not supported*	Alt+0154
Ú	Option+E U	' U or Alt+0218
ú	Option+E u	' u or Alt+0250 or Ctrl+Alt+U
Ù	Option+` U	` U or Alt+0217
ù	Option+` u	` u or Alt+0249
Ü	Option+U U	" U or Alt+0220
ü	Option+U u	" u or Alt+0252
Û	Option+I U	^ U or Alt+0219
û	Option+I u	^ u or Alt+0251

continued

TABLE 20.3   *(continued)*

Character	Mac Shortcut	Windows Shortcut
Ý	*Not supported*	' Y *or* Alt+0221
ý	*Not supported*	' y *or* Alt+0253
Ÿ	Option+U Y	" Y *or* Alt+0159
ÿ	Option+U y	" y *or* Alt+0255
Ž	*Not supported*	Alt+0142
ž	*Not supported*	Alt+0158
Spanish open exclamation (¡)	Option+1	Ctrl+Alt+1 *or* Alt+-0161
Spanish open question (¿)	Option+Shift+/	Ctrl+Alt+/ *or* Alt+0191
French open double quote («)	Option+\	Ctrl+Alt+[*or* Alt+0171
French close double quote (»)	Option+Shift+\	Ctrl+Alt+] *or* Alt+0187

* On the Mac, enter the shortcut for the accent and then type the letter to be accented. For example, to get é, type Option+E and then the letter e. In Windows, if the keyboard layout is set to United States-International — via the Keyboard icon in the Windows Control Panel — you can enter the accent signifier and then type the letter (for example, type ` and then the letter e to get è). To avoid an accent (for example, if you want to begin a quote — such as *"A man"* rather than have *Ä man"* — type a space after the accent character — for example, type " and then a space, and then A, rather than typing " and then A.

European Languages and Accented Characters

Using accents in foreign words is great, but many Americans use them incorrectly, which is embarrassing. Although I can't tell you how to properly spell and accent every foreign word (a good dictionary for that language can!), I can tell you which accented characters are used in European languages. If you're using a word from one of the languages here and that word uses an accented character not shown for the language, you either have the wrong accent or that word is actually from a different language. I've also indicated which countries use the euro currency symbol (€) by including that symbol in their lists, and I've indicated special currency symbols for other nations.

Many of the characters shown here are not available in standard PostScript and TrueType fonts. Most are available in OpenType fonts, though not in every case. You may need a special font for the specific language to get all the characters.

Albanian: ç, ë

Basque (Euskara): ñ; €

Breton: â, ê, è, ñ, ô, ù, ü; €

Catalan: à, ç, è, é, í, ï, ï, ò, ó, ú, ü; €

Croatian: ć, č, đ, š, ž

Czech: á, č, ď, é, ě, í, ň, ř, š, ť, ú, ů, ý, ž

Danish: å, æ, é, ø, ú

Dutch: á, â, è, é, ê, ë, í, ï, ij, ó, ô, ö, ú, û; €

English, American and Canadian: $, ¢

English, British: ö; £

English, Old: ð, þ

Estonian: ä, õ, ö, š, ž

Faroese: á, æ, ð, í, ó, ø, ú, ý

Finnish: ä, ö; €

French: à, â, æ, è, é, ê, ë, ç, î, ï, ô, ö, œ, ù, û, ü; ÿ, «, »; €

Frisian: â, ê, î, ô, ú, û

Gaelic (Irish): á, é, í, ó, ú; €

Gaelic (Scots): à, á, è, é, ì, ò, ó, ù; £

German: ä, ö, ß, ü; €

Hungarian: á, é, i', ó, ö, ő, ú, ü, ű

Icelandic: á, æ, é, ð, í, ó, ö, þ, ú, ý

Italian: à, è, ì, í, ò, ó, ù; €

Latvian: ā, č, ē, ġ, ī, ļ, ņ, š, ū, ž

Lithuanian: ą, č, ę, ė, į, š, ų, ū, ž

Luxembourgean: ä, ë, é, ï, ö, ü; €

Maltese: à, ċ, è, ġ, ħ, î, ì, ò, ù, ż; €

Norwegian: å, ø, æ

Occitan (Provençal): á, à, ç, é, è, í, ó, ò, ú; €

Polish: ą, ć, ę, ł, ń, ó, ś, ź, ż

Portuguese: à, á, â, ã, é, ê, ç, í, ñ, ó, ô, ô, õ. Ú, ü; €

Rhaeto-Roman: à, è, é, ì, î, ò, ù

Romanian: â, ă, î, ş, ţ

Slovak: á, ä, č, ď, é, í, Í, ľ, ń, ó, ô, ŕ, š, ť, ú, ý, ž; €

Slovenian: č, š, ž; €

Spanish (Castilian, Galician): á, é, í, ñ, ó, ú, ü; ¿ ¡; €

Swedish: å, ä, é, ö

Turkish: â, ç, ğ, î, ı, ö, ş, û, ü

Welsh: à, á, â, ä, è, é, ê, ë, ì, í, î, ï, ò, ó, ô, ö, ù, ú, û, ü, ŷ, ý, ŷ, ÿ; £

Summary

A multitude of special characters is available for your documents. You can access common ones via keyboard shortcuts, less common ones through InDesign's Type menu, and all available characters through the Glyphs panel.

InDesign also automatically converts keyboard quotes into their typographic counterparts, plus it lets you select the quotation mark style to be used so that you can use the right style for the language you are publishing in.

Part V

Business Document Fundamentals

Chapter 21

Setting Up Tabs and Tables

I f you ever used a typewriter, you may remember pressing the Tab key to indent each paragraph. And you may have pounded on it repeatedly to align columns of data. In InDesign, you use first-line indents to distinguish the first line of a new paragraph, and you reserve tabs for separating columns of data. Although InDesign has a built-in table editor, you can create simple tables using regular tabs quickly with the tabs feature. For more sophisticated tables, use the table editor.

In InDesign, tabs are part of paragraph formats — meaning that when you set them, they apply to all the text in selected paragraphs rather than to selected characters within a paragraph. By default, when you start typing in a paragraph or you create a new paragraph style, there are invisible, automatic tab stops every half-inch. Regardless of the measurement system your rulers are set to use, when you press Tab you jump to the next 0.5-inch increment on the ruler.

As soon as you set a tab stop of your own, it overrides any of the automatic tab stops to its left. The automatic tab stops remain to the right until you override all of them.

Preparing Text Files for Setting Tabs

When designers import text, the most common problem they encounter is that writers try to line up the text on their screens by using multiple tabs between columns rather than setting appropriate tab stops in the first place and having one tab between each "cell." That's because word processors also have default tab stops of 0.5", and most users use those defaults — adding as many tabs as needed to align their text — rather than figure out how to set the needed tabs themselves. When you import the file with these tabs, the chances of items lining up in InDesign as they do in the word processor are pretty close to zero. That means a lot of clean-up work for the designers.

Before you start setting tabs in InDesign, take a look at the tabs already entered in the text. You can check this out in your word processor or in text that has been placed in InDesign. To view tab characters in InDesign, choose Type➪Show Hidden Characters, choose Hidden Characters from the View Options iconic pop-up menu in the application bar, or press Option+⌘+I or Ctrl+Alt+I. The light-blue double French close-quotation mark symbols (») are tabs.

To set effective tabs for columns of data, each line or row of information should be its own paragraph, and each column of data should be separated by only one tab character. If there's only one tab between each column, you need to set only one tab stop per column, and you can more carefully control a single tab stop rather than several.

Because the text is not in its final font or text frame, the current tab placement does not matter. But if necessary, the writer can change tab settings in Word to align the columns for proofreading or editing purposes.

As with multiple tabs stops, if there are extra paragraph returns between the rows or information, or if each line ends in a soft return or line break (press Shift+Return or Shift+Enter) rather than a paragraph return (press Return or Enter), you should fix these with search and replace in your word processor or by using the Find/Change dialog box (choose Edit➪Find/Change or press ⌘+F or Ctrl+F) in InDesign, as described in Chapter 15.

It's best to insist that any word processor documents imported into InDesign be created so that there is only one tab between each entry on a line, no matter how it looks in the word processor. Then you can set up the appropriate tab stops in InDesign.

InDesign provides four different types of tabs so that you can:

- Left-align text to the left at a tab stop (the default setting, and the one you'll use most often)
- Center text on either side of the tab stop (very useful in column headers)
- Right-align text at a tab stop (useful for columns of integers)
- Align a specific character in the text with the tab stop (such as a comma or period in a number)

Figure 21.1 shows examples of tabs.

FIGURE 21.1

Under the Item column, Trifle and Whip Cream are positioned with right-aligned tabs. The three other column headings — Ingredient, Amount, and Price — are positioned with center tabs. In the chart, the ingredients are left-aligned, the amounts are center-aligned, and the prices are aligned on the dollar sign (top chart) and the decimal point (lower chart).

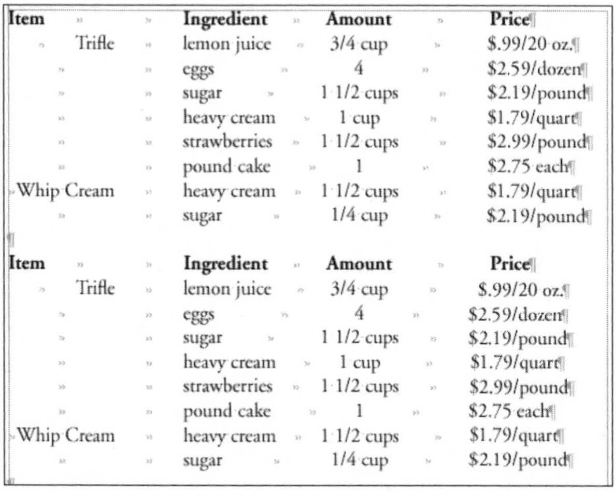

Item			Ingredient		Amount		Price
	Trifle		lemon juice		3/4 cup		$.99/20 oz.
			eggs		4		$2.59/dozen
			sugar		1 1/2 cups		$2.19/pound
			heavy cream		1 cup		$1.79/quart
			strawberries		1 1/2 cups		$2.99/pound
			pound cake		1		$2.75 each
Whip Cream			heavy cream		1 1/2 cups		$1.79/quart
			sugar		1/4 cup		$2.19/pound

Item			Ingredient		Amount		Price
	Trifle		lemon juice		3/4 cup		$.99/20 oz.
			eggs		4		$2.59/dozen
			sugar		1 1/2 cups		$2.19/pound
			heavy cream		1 cup		$1.79/quart
			strawberries		1 1/2 cups		$2.99/pound
			pound cake		1		$2.75 each
Whip Cream			heavy cream		1 1/2 cups		$1.79/quart
			sugar		1/4 cup		$2.19/pound

Using the Tabs Panel

To set tabs in InDesign, you use the Tabs panel, which floats above your text so that you can keep it open until you're finished experimenting with tabs. To open the Tabs panel, choose Type ➪ Tabs or press Shift+⌘+T or Ctrl+Shift+T. Figure 21.2 shows the Tabs panel along with a simple table created using one tab stop.

Tab style buttons

Four buttons on the Tabs panel let you control how the text aligns with the tab you're creating:

- **Left:** The default tab stops are left-aligned, which means that the left side of the text touches the tab stop as if it were a left margin. Most tabs you create for text will be left-aligned.

- **Center:** Centered tab stops are like the centered paragraph alignment, with text balanced evenly on either side of the tab stop. Center tabs are often used for table headings.

- **Right:** When you set right-aligned tabs, the right edge of text touches the tab stop. This is commonly used for aligning numbers that do not include decimals or for the last column in a table.

FIGURE 21.2

Top: The Tabs panel and a simple table created with several tab stops. Bottom: A table that has leaders (in this case, a row of periods) applied to the right-aligned tab stop.

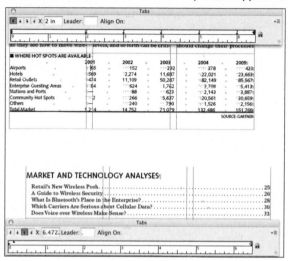

- **Align On:** By default, the last tab style button is for decimal tabs, which means that a period in the text aligns on the tab stop. If there's no period in the text, InDesign pretends that there is one after the last character. Instead of aligning on a period, you can specify a different character, such as a comma or dollar sign, for an Align On tab, and text aligns to that character. You do this using the Align On field, which is covered later in this section.

TIP If you need a tab flush with the right margin, for example, to position a dingbat at the end of the story, click the Right Tab iconic button and position it on the right side of the tab ruler. Then drag the right-aligned tab on top of the right indent arrow. (You can't actually click to place a tab on top of the arrow, but you can drag a tab on top of it.) An even faster way is to choose Type ➪ Special Character ➪ Other ➪ Right Indent Tab or press Shift+Tab.

X field

The X field of the Tabs panel lets you specify a position for a new tab stop. You can type a value in this field in 0.01-point increments and then press Shift+Enter or Shift+Return to create a tab. InDesign positions tabs relative to the left edge of the text frame or column. Or you can just click the mouse on the ruler where you want the tab to be, as described later.

If a text frame has Inset Spacing specified for its left edge in the General pane of the Text Frame Options dialog box (choose Object ➪ Text Frame Options or press ⌘+B or Ctrl+B), InDesign measures tabs from the text inset rather than from the frame.

TIP Why type numbers when you can just use the mouse? The reason is to get more accurate positioning than using the mouse usually allows, especially when you know exactly where the tab stop should be. Of course, you can add a tab by using the mouse and then click the field and type a more precise value in the X field.

As with other fields in InDesign, the X field can perform mathematical computations for you. So you can set a tab at half of 0.125" without figuring out that value, or you can move a tab by adding to or subtracting from its current value. It may seem unlikely that you would ever do this, but it's extremely handy for changing tab settings so that they're, say, half as far apart as they used to be, or half as far apart plus 2 points to the right.

The operands for performing math in fields are + (addition), – (subtraction), * (multiplication), and / (division). If you want to combine these operands — for example, add 5 and then subtract 2 — you have to remember back to middle school and Algebra I to type the operands in the correct order: multiply, divide, add, and then subtract.

Leader field

A tab leader is a character or series of characters that fills the white space between tabs, such as the periods you see between a table of contents entry and its page number. They got the name *leader* because they lead your eyes across the page. Figure 21.2 shows a dot leader in use between the section title and the page number.

InDesign lets you specify up to eight characters, including special characters that repeat to fill any white space. When you set a leader for a tab stop, the leaders actually fill any space prior to that tab stop (between the previous text and the tab location).

To spread out the leader characters, type spaces between the characters you enter. Don't enter spaces before and after a single character, though, because doing so results in two spaces between the characters when the pattern repeats. (You can, of course, do this if that's the look you're going for.) You can't enter special types of spaces — such as thin spaces or hair spaces — in the Leader field; you always get em spaces.

NOTE The reason to use tab leaders is to help the reader. Unless the design is more important than the content, you probably shouldn't use eight-character tab leaders even though you can. A cacophony of characters draws too much attention and can be confusing. Because the pattern of leaders repeats, one space and a period are usually sufficient.

To enter special characters in the Leader field, use keyboard commands, InDesign's Glyphs panel, or a utility such as PopChar, Mac OS X's Character Palette, or Windows's Character Map. If you use InDesign's Insert Special Character menu option (choose Type ➪ Insert Special Character) or the Glyphs panel (choose Type ➪ Glyphs), you insert a character into your text, which you have to cut and paste into the Leader field. It isn't inserted directly in the Leader field as you would expect.

Align On field

The Align On tab style defaults to a period, but you can replace the period with any character, including special characters. When that character is found in tabbed text, it aligns on the tab stop. If that character is not found, InDesign pretends that it follows the last character in the tabbed string. The most common characters entered in the Align On field include a comma (,), dollar sign ($), cents symbol (¢), and open and close parentheses, that is, (and).

 If the Align On field is not visible in the Tabs panel, just widen the panel by dragging one of its sides so that the field displays.

Tab ruler

Rather than type values in the X field, you can position tabs by clicking the ruler at the bottom of the Tabs panel. The Tab ruler has the following characteristics:

- **It displays in the same measurement system as the document, with 0 specifying the edges of the column.** If Inset Spacing is specified for the left edge of the text frame in the Text Frame Options dialog box (choose Object ➪ Text Frame Options or press ⌘+B or Ctrl+B), the ruler starts after the text inset in the first column.

- **The ruler provides arrows for controlling and displaying the selected paragraph's first-line, left, and right indents.** Dragging the two left arrows changes both the paragraph's first-line and left indents, whereas dragging the top arrow changes only the first-line indent. Dragging the arrow at right changes the right indents. These arrows help you see indents in relation to tabs that you're setting. (They have the same effect as changing the indent settings in the Paragraph or Paragraph Styles panels, as covered in Chapter 17.)

- **Icons that match the tab styles display on the rulers to show you where and what type of tabs are already set.** You can drag these around to reposition existing tabs, and you can drag them off the ruler to delete tabs.

- **You can scroll through the ruler by clicking it and dragging to the left or right.** This lets you set tabs beyond the current column or text frame width, such as for text that flows into text boxes of different widths.

Position Panel above Text Frame button

Under the right circumstances, clicking the Position Panel above Text Frame iconic button (the magnet icon) in the lower-right corner of the Tabs panel snaps the panel and the ruler to the selected text frame or column. The idea is to make it easier to see the tab stops in relation to an actual area of text.

For this to work, you need to make sure the top of the text frame is visible on-screen, the Type tool is selected, and you've placed the cursor in text or highlighted text. If you don't meet all these prerequisites, nothing happens.

After you manage to get the Tabs panel positioned correctly, it's quite useful. You can add and adjust tabs in relation to the text (provided that the text is at the top of the text frame!) and you can always see from where the tabs are measured. Even better, if you move the cursor to another column in the text frame, you can click the Position Panel above Text Frame iconic (magnet) button again to position the Tabs panel over that column.

Flyout menu

In addition to setting tabs and indents in the Tabs panel, InDesign provides four additional options through the flyout menu:

- **The Clear All menu option deletes any tabs you've created.** Any text positioned with tabs reverts to the position of the default tab stops. (You can delete an individual tab stop by dragging its icon off the ruler.)

- **The Delete Tab menu option deletes the currently selected tab.** (Just click it first in the tab ruler.)

- **The Repeat Tab menu option lets you create a string of tabs across the ruler that are all the same distance apart.** When you select a tab on the ruler and choose this menu option, InDesign measures the distance between the selected tab and the previous tab (or, if it's the first tab on the ruler, the distance between the selected tab and the left indent/ text inset). The program then uses this distance to place new tabs, with the same alignment, all the way across the ruler. InDesign repeats tabs only to the right of the selected tab, but it inserts tabs between other tab stops.

- **The Reset Indents menu option removes any changes to the left indent, right indent, or indent hang settings defined in the paragraph style currently applied to the text.**

 You can also delete tabs by dragging them off the tab ruler using the mouse.

Creating Tables

Whether you're working on yesterday's box scores for the sports pages, an annual report, or a fun little parenting magazine, you've got numbers — numbers with dollar signs, numbers with decimals, numbers intermixed with text. You have to line the columns up correctly, not only so that the information looks good but also to make it easy to read. Then you often need to add ruling lines to separate the material visually for the reader.

You can do all this with tab stops, ruling lines, and other InDesign tools. Or you can make your life easier and use InDesign's table editor, which lets you specify almost any attribute imaginable in a table through the Table panel and the Table menu.

CROSS-REF InDesign lets you import tables from Microsoft Word, RTF, and Microsoft Excel files, including some of their cell formatting. Likewise, you can convert their tables to tabbed text using the options in the Import Options dialog box that's accessible when you place a file through the Place dialog box, as covered in Chapter 13.

Figure 21.3 shows the Table panel and Table menu, as well as a table. You access the Table panel by choosing Window ➪ Type & Tables ➪ Table or pressing Shift+F9.

Creating a table

To create a table in InDesign, you first create or select a text frame with the Type tool and then choose Table ➪ Insert Table or press Option+Shift+⌘+T or Ctrl+Alt+Shift+T. If you select an existing text frame, the table will be inserted at the text cursor's location in the existing text.

FIGURE 21.3

The Table panel, the Table menu, and the Control panel when a cell is selected. This figure also shows the table that appears at the top of Figure 21.2; however, this time it's been created using the table tools rather than via tabs.

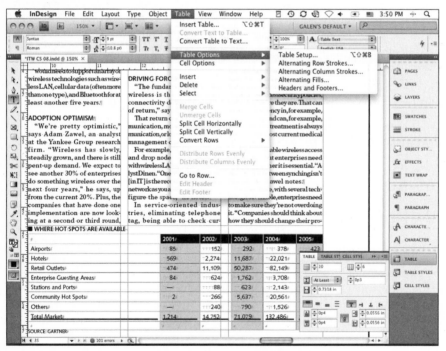

Choosing Table ⇨ Insert Table or pressing Option+Shift+⌘+T or Ctrl+Alt+Shift+T produces the Insert Table dialog box, in which you type the number of body rows and columns and the number of header and footer rows. (Header and footer rows repeat on each page for tables that go across multiple pages.) Click OK to have InDesign create the basic table, which is set as wide as the text frame. The depth is based on the number of rows, with each row defaulting to the height that will hold 12-point text.

You can also apply a table style to the new table by selecting one from the Table Style pop-up menu. I cover how to create these styles later in this chapter.

With the basic table in place, you now format it using the Table panel and the Table menu. You can increase or decrease the number of rows and columns, set the row and column height, set the text's vertical alignment within selected cells (top, middle, bottom, and justified), choose one of four text-rotation angles, and set the text margin within a cell separately for the top, bottom, left, and right. Note that all the Table panel's options affect only the currently selected cells, except for the Number of Rows and Number of Columns fields. Figure 21.4 shows the Table panel with its flyout menu.

FIGURE 21.4

The Table panel and its flyout menu

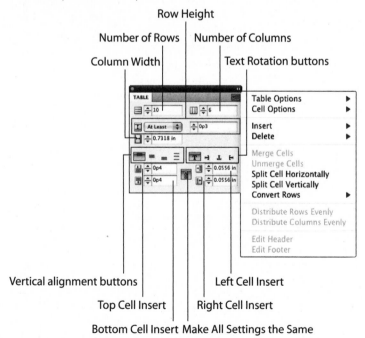

527

CROSS-REF You set cell text's horizontal alignment using the paragraph formatting controls covered in Chapter 17. You can apply other paragraph and character formatting to cell text as described in Chapters 16 and 18. You can also apply tabs within cells using the Tabs panel covered earlier in this chapter.

For more sophisticated table attributes, use the Table Options dialog box and its five panes, as shown in Figures 21.5 through 21.8. Access this dialog box using the Table Options menu item in the Table panel's flyout menu or by choosing Table ➪ Table Options ➪ Table Setup or pressing Option+Shift+⌘+B or Ctrl+Alt+Shift+B. In both menus, you can select a specific pane using a submenu from the Table Options menu item.

To add items to a table, you can type text in any cell, paste text or graphics into a cell, or place text or graphics into a cell by choosing File ➪ Place or pressing ⌘+D or Ctrl+D. Note that if you paste tabbed text into tables, the tabs are retained and all the text is pasted into the same cell.

NEW FEATURE InDesign CS4 lets you edit table contents using the Story Editor (see Chapter 15). It also tracks any changes to the table's contents so that you can see exactly what has changed and decide whether to accept those changes if you use the companion InCopy software (see Chapter 35).

Table Setup pane

The Table Options dialog box's Table Setup pane is the default pane for this dialog box. As shown in Figure 21.5, it lets you adjust the rows and columns, as you can do in the Table panel. It's also where you specify the table border's weight, line type, color, tint, gap color and tint (if you choose a dashed, dotted, or striped line for the border), the space before and after the table, and whether row lines (which InDesign calls *strokes*) are placed on top of column lines or vice versa. If your table has cells with different line settings that would be overridden by the table border, you can preserve those cell settings by selecting the Preserve Local Formatting option.

You also can set how strokes draw in the Draw pop-up menu at the bottom of the pane; note that the InDesign 2.0 compatibility option essentially places rows in front but has them end inside the outside border, while the Row Strokes in Front has those strokes overprint the table border as well.

Row Strokes and Column Strokes panes

InDesign lets you have the lines between columns and rows alternate color, thickness, and even type. Figure 21.6 shows the Row Strokes pane; the Column Strokes pane is identical, except that it applies to column (vertical) strokes rather than to row (horizontal) strokes.

You can choose a predefined alternate pattern by using the Alternating Pattern pop-up menu, or by simply typing a number in the First and Next fields. The First field at the left of the pane specifies how many row strokes (or column strokes) get the formatting specified on the left side of the pane, while the Next field at the right side specifies how many get the formatting specified at the right. InDesign applies the formatting at left to the number of rows specified in its First field and then switches to the formatting at right for the number of rows specified in that First field. If there are still more rows, InDesign switches back to the left side's formatting, repeating the alternating pattern until it runs out of rows. The Column Strokes pane works the same way.

FIGURE 21.5

The Table Setup pane of the Table Options dialog box

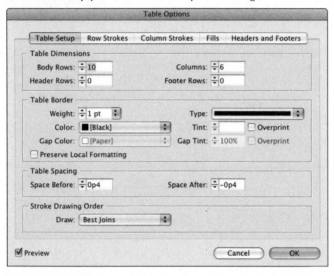

FIGURE 21.6

The Row Strokes pane of the Table Options dialog box. (The Column Strokes pane is identical except that columns replace rows in its options.)

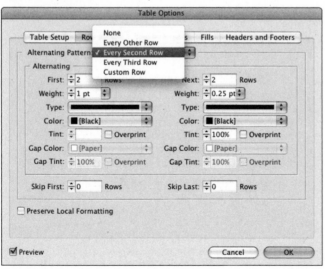

In addition to specifying the line attributes, you can also have InDesign skip a specified number of top and bottom rows (or columns) using the Skip First and Skip Last fields. You can specify these so that header and footer rows are excluded from the pattern.

Fills pane

The Fills pane, shown in Figure 21.7, is similar to the Row Strokes and Column Strokes panes. You set the color, tint, alternation pattern, and any skipped rows or columns — but not both — for fills you want applied to your table. The Alternating Pattern pop-up menu lets you pick from predefined numbers of columns or rows, depending on whether you want the fills to alternate from left to right or from top to bottom across the table.

FIGURE 21.7

The Fills pane of the Table Options dialog box

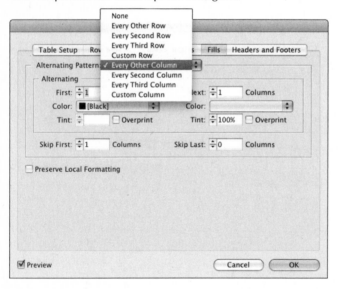

If you choose Custom Row, InDesign uses the alternation settings in the Row Strokes pane; if you choose Custom Column, InDesign uses the alternation settings in the Column Strokes pane. This approach ensures that the line color and other settings change with the fills.

Headers and Footers pane

The Headers and Footers pane, shown in Figure 21.8, lets you change the number of header and footer rows, as well as specify how often the header and footer repeats. (If your Word or RTF file's table uses a heading row, InDesign designates it as a header row.) Your options are Every Text Column, Once per Frame, and Once per Page. You'll usually use one of the latter options because it automatically repeats the header row for tables that break across text frames and/or pages.

FIGURE 21.8

The Headers and Footers pane of the Table Options dialog box

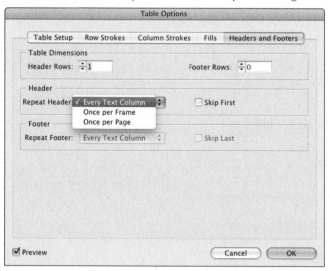

Working with rows and columns

InDesign's table editing tools work very much like those in Microsoft Word. To select a row or column, click an outside edge; you can also click in a cell with the Type tool and choose Table ⇨ Select ⇨ Row or press ⌘+3 or Ctrl+3, or choose Table ⇨ Select ⇨ Column or press Option+⌘+3 or Ctrl+Alt+3. The submenu in Table ⇨ Select also lets you select all header rows, all footer rows, and all body (regular) rows.

To move to a specified row, you can choose Table ⇨ Go to Row and type the row's number, but it's usually easier to use your mouse to move to the desired row. After all, how often do you know the row's number?

To quickly select header rows or footer rows, choose Table ⇨ Edit Header or Table ⇨ Edit Footer.

 Choose Table ⇨ Select ⇨ Table or press Option+⌘+A or Ctrl+Alt+A to select an entire table. Choose Table ⇨ Delete ⇨ Table to delete an entire table.

Adding and deleting

Insert or delete rows and columns using the Table menu or the Table panel's flyout menu. Both have Insert and Delete menu options. Selected rows or columns are deleted, and new rows or columns are inserted before any selected row or column. You can also use the shortcuts in Table 21.1.

Manipulating rows and columns

You can make the space between rows or columns even by choosing Table ⇨ Distribute Rows Evenly or Table ⇨ Distribute Columns Evenly, respectively. But be careful: Merging several cells increases the perceived column or row size and causes InDesign to excessively space rows or columns based on those merged cells' size.

You can also resize rows and columns by clicking any of the cell boundaries and dragging them — similar to how you can resize columns and rows in Microsoft Word's table editor.

InDesign also lets you control how rows break across frames and pages, and whether rows must be kept together. But to do so requires a dialog box oriented to cell formatting, which is covered later in this chapter.

TIP   InDesign can convert regular (body) rows to header and footer rows, or vice versa. Select the rows you want to convert; next, choose Table ⇨ Convert Rows and then choose To Header, To Body, or To Footer as appropriate.

NOTE   All the row and column options are available in both the Table menu and the Table panel's flyout menu, as well as through the contextual menu that appears when you select one or more cells and Control+click or right-click.

TABLE 21.1

Table-Editing Shortcuts

Command	Mac Shortcut	Windows Shortcuts
Select cell	⌘+/	Ctrl+/
Select row	⌘+3	Ctrl+3
Select column	Option+⌘+3	Ctrl+Alt+3
Select table	Option+⌘+A	Ctrl+Alt+A
Insert cell	Option+⌘+9	Ctrl+Alt+9
Insert row	⌘+9	Ctrl+9
Delete cell	Shift+Delete	Shift+Backspace
Delete row	⌘+Delete	Ctrl+Backspace

Working with cells

InDesign offers the Cell Options dialog box to manage the formatting of cells. It's accessible by choosing Cell Options from the Table menu or from the Table panel's flyout menu. Four panes are available, as shown in Figures 21.9 through 21.12.

Text pane

The Cell Options dialog box's Text pane, which is accessible through the shortcut Option+⌘+B or Ctrl+Alt+B and shown in Figure 21.9, addresses several options available in the Table panel covered earlier in this chapter, including the top, bottom, left, and right cell insets (margins), as well as vertical text alignment and text rotation. But it has several other options:

- **Paragraph Spacing Limit:** This option determines the maximum space between paragraphs in a cell when you choose Justify from the Align pop-up menu. This prevents too much space between paragraphs in a cell.

- **First Baseline:** This option determines how the text baseline is positioned from the top of a cell. The options are Ascent, Cap Height, Leading, x Height, and Fixed.

> **CROSS-REF** Vertical alignment and baseline positioning work the same as they do for text frames, as covered in Chapters 14 and 9, respectively.

- **Clip Contents to Cell:** This option displays only the amount of text that fits in the cell's current size. If selected, it prevents the cell from expanding to accommodate the text.

FIGURE 21.9

The Text pane of the Cell Options dialog box

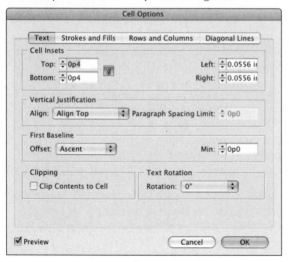

Strokes and Fills pane

Shown in Figure 21.10, the Strokes and Fills pane lets you choose the weight, type, color, and tint of the strokes around a cell, as well as any gap color and tint (if you choose a striped, dashed, or dotted line as the stroke type).

FIGURE 21.10

The Strokes and Fills pane of the Cell Options dialog box

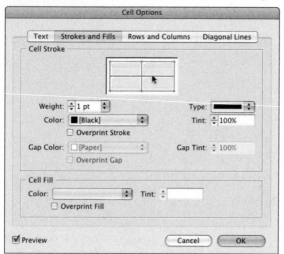

At the top of the pane is the representation of the selected cells, depending on whether you've highlighted one or multiple cells when you open this pane. Figure 21.10 shows the representation when multiple cells are selected across more than one row and more than one column. (If you select multiple cells in one row, you get two cells shown side by side; if you select multiple cells in one column, you get two cells, one on top of the other.)

Click the cell boundary to which you want to apply the stroke formatting and then choose the formatting you want. You can have different formatting for each of the left, right, top, and bottom outside cell boundaries, as well as different formatting for the horizontal boundary between selected cells and for the vertical formatting for the vertical boundary between selected cells. Usually, you select all outside boundaries and apply stroke formatting to all of them simultaneously, and you may do the same for the interior boundaries.

NOTE InDesign does not show you the stroke formatting applied to the representation's segments, so you may not realize that different segments have different settings. Therefore, it's best to make sure the selected cells are visible and that you've selected the Preview option so that you can see what you're actually applying to the cells.

In this pane, you can also select a fill color for the selected cells, based on existing color swatches, as well as a tint.

You can set both cell strokes and fills as Overprint, which means that the color prints on top of any underlying color rather than knocks out that color. Overprinting can change the color the reader sees because it essentially mixes inks. Overprinting a blue fill on a yellow background, for example, results in a green fill.

Rows and Columns pane

The Row and Columns pane (see Figure 21.11) sets row height and column width, as well as keeps options for rows:

FIGURE 21.11

The Rows and Columns pane of the Cell Options dialog box

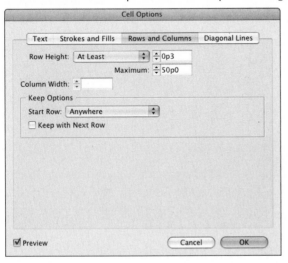

- **Row Height pop-up menu:** Use this to specify the height as either Exactly or At Least the measurement to the right of the menu. This is the same as what you can specify in the Table pane.

- **Column Width field:** This field is also the same option you have in the Table pane to set the column width.

- **Keep Options:** Use the Start Row pop-up menu to determine where the selected row starts. You can choose Anywhere, which means after the previous row (space permitting in the text frame, of course); In Next Text Column; In Next Frame; On Next Page; On Next Odd Page; or On Next Even Page. Select the Keep with Next Row option to keep rows together.

Diagonal Lines pane

A unique InDesign feature is the ability to place diagonal lines in table cells. Figure 21.12 shows the Diagonal Lines pane. It's similar to other panes involving strokes except for two specific options:

- You choose the type of diagonal line — top left to bottom right, bottom left to top right, or both — using the iconic buttons at the top of the pane.

- You determine whether the diagonal line appears on top of the cell contents or vice versa using the Draw pop-up menu.

FIGURE 21.12

The Diagonal Lines pane of the Cell Options dialog box

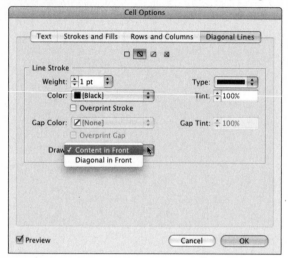

Other cell options

Most of the work you do with cells involves typing and editing text (or graphics), applying fills and strokes, and setting margins (as covered earlier in this chapter), as well as formatting text (as covered in Chapters 15 through 19) and formatting frames (as covered in Chapters 10 and 11). After all, a cell is essentially just a text or graphics frame that's contained in a table with other frames. But there are a few other things to know about working with cells:

■ You can merge and unmerge cells by highlighting the cells and choosing Table ⇨ Merge Cells or Table ⇨ Unmerge Cells.

■ You can split cells by highlighting the cells and choosing Table ⇨ Split Cell Horizontally or Table ⇨ Split Cell Vertically. To unsplit cells, you must merge them. (You can also choose Edit ⇨ Undo or press ⌘+Z or Ctrl+Z before taking another action.) Cells that are split take on the cell's current settings for text formatting, fill color, size, margins, and strokes.

■ InDesign indicates text that does not fit in a cell with a large red dot in the cell.

■ You can apply colors and gradients to cells, as well as strokes, using the standard InDesign Swatches, Gradient, and Stroke panels (all accessible through the Window menu). These have the same effect as using the equivalent Table menu and Table panel options.

■ The Control panel offers easy access to several cell and table features, as Figure 21.13 shows. Note that these options appear only if at least one cell is selected — meaning the entire cell, rather than just some of its contents. Figure 21.13 also calls out table- and cell-specific controls.

FIGURE 21.13

The Control panel and its flyout menu when table cells are selected

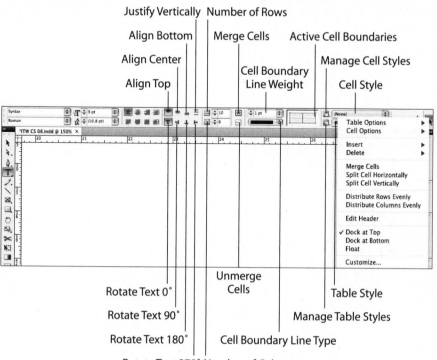

Justify Vertically   Number of Rows

Align Bottom   Merge Cells   Active Cell Boundaries

Align Center   Manage Cell Styles

Cell Boundary
Line Weight   Cell Style

Align Top

Rotate Text 0°   Unmerge
Cells   Table Style

Rotate Text 90°   Manage Table Styles

Rotate Text 180°   Cell Boundary Line Type

Rotate Text 270°   Number of Columns

TIP   You can apply strokes to cells through the Stroke panel (choose Window ⇨ Stroke or press ⌘+F10 or Ctrl+F10). Use its flyout menu to select the Stroke Styles menu option, which provides a list of styles and the ability to create your own, as Chapter 11 explains.

Using table and cell styles

To make it easy to apply and update table formatting across a document, InDesign provides table and cell styles. They work like paragraph, character, and object styles, taking the table formatting features covered earlier in this section and bringing them together into the New Table Style and New Cell Style dialog boxes.

To work with table styles, open the Table Styles panel by choosing Window ⇨ Type & Tables ⇨ Table Styles. To work with cell styles, open the Cell Styles panel by choosing Window ⇨ Type & Tables ⇨ Cell Styles. Choose New Table Style or New Cell Style from the appropriate panel's flyout menu and then use the various panes to specify the desired formatting. The panes, and their options, are the same as described earlier in this chapter.

TIP Whether creating a new table style or a new cell style, the easiest method is to format an existing table or cell the way you want it, select it, and then create a new table or cell style — InDesign picks up the existing formatting for the new style. Otherwise, you have to specify everything in the New Table Style or New Cell Style dialog box, where it's harder to see the effects of your settings.

There are a few notes about creating table and cell styles — in the General pane of the New Table Style and New Cell Style dialog boxes, shown in Figures 21.14 and 21.15, respectively — that you should know before getting too far in to them:

- You give each style its own name. Choose names that should make sense a week or a month later so that you know what they are meant to be used for!

- You can base a new table style on an existing one so that changes to the parent style are automatically reflected in the children styles based on it.

- You can assign a keyboard shortcut to styles you use frequently.

When creating table styles, you can also have the table style automatically apply the cell styles of your choosing to the following table elements: header rows, footer rows, body rows, the leftmost column, and the rightmost column.

When creating cell styles, you can choose a paragraph style to be automatically applied to text in cells using the style.

FIGURE 21.14

The General pane of the New Table Style dialog box

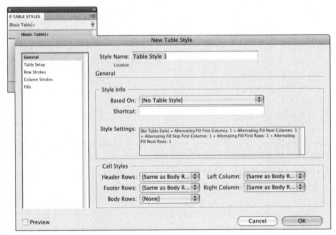

CROSS-REF The controls for applying, modifying, and managing table and cell styles are the same as for paragraph and character styles, so refer to Chapter 19 for details on these common functions.

The General pane of the New Cell Style dialog box

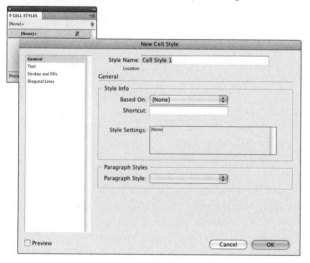

Converting Tabs to Tables

Often, you'll have a table done using tabs — whether imported from a word processor or originally created in InDesign with tabs — that you want to convert to a real InDesign table. That's easy. Select the tabbed text you want to convert and choose Table ➪ Convert Text to Table. You get the Convert Text to Table dialog box shown in Figure 21.16.

Left: The Convert Text to Table dialog box. Right: The Convert Table to Text dialog box.

In the Convert Text to Table dialog box, you can choose a Column Separator (Tab, Comma, Paragraph, or a text string you type in the field) or a Row Separator (same options). Although most textual data uses tabs to separate columns and paragraphs to separate rows, you may encounter other data that uses something else. For example, spreadsheets and databases often save data so that commas separate columns rather than tabs. That's why InDesign lets you choose the separator characters before conversion. You can also apply a table style to apply to the converted text.

During the conversion, InDesign formats the table using the standard settings, and the current text formatting and the default cell insets and stroke types. You can then adjust the table using the tools covered earlier in this chapter. Note that the conversion treats all rows as body rows.

You can also convert a table to text by selecting multiple cells or an entire table, as described earlier, and choosing Table ➪ Convert Table to Text. As Figure 21.16 shows, InDesign presents essentially the same options as it does in the Convert Text to Table dialog box so that you can determine how the converted data appears.

Summary

Unlike the typewriter days, creating tabs in a page-layout application provides various options for aligning text with a tab and creating tab leaders. The Tabs panel (choose Type ➪ Tabs or press ⌘+Shift+T or Ctrl+Shift+T) provides an interactive ruler for positioning tabs along with all the other controls you need. Your ultimate success with using the tabs feature depends on how well you prepared the text in the first place. The key is to position one tab correctly rather than entering several tabs to achieve the correct placement.

To create tables in InDesign, you use the Table panel (choose Window ➪ Type & Tables ➪ Table or press Shift+F9) to create the table outline, format cells, merge and split cells, apply colors and ruling lines, and do other complex table editing. Table and cell styles let you apply this formatting consistently across multiple tables, as well as update multiple tables simultaneously as formatting changes.

You can also convert tabbed text into a table and vice versa.

Chapter 22

Using Automatic and Custom Text

A key area of improvement over the years in InDesign is the increased use of text automation. From the very beginning, InDesign offered automatic page numbers so that your folios and cross-references would reflect the current pages as your layout changed. Later versions enhanced this with section markers, which let you create variable names in folios for your section titles. Still later came the ability to use data files and merge their contents into a layout to customize your output, similar to how word processors let you customize labels with their mail-merge feature. Then came variable text, which gives you more flexibility in where and how you can have InDesign update text automatically throughout a document. Now, InDesign CS4 adds automatically updating cross-references, conditional text, and a method to apply text formatting using the rules of the Unix Grep syntax.

Although not designed specifically for variable or custom text, another long-standing InDesign feature helps automate the creation of documents from sources such as databases. The Tagged Text format is a powerful way to create catalogs and other such layouts that have consistent formatting for content that varies from each edition — or even from entry to entry within a layout.

Altogether, these features have helped InDesign stake significant ground in reducing the labor and time of manual processes, such as search and replace, for text that changes predictably throughout the document.

Automating Page Numbers

You may often want page references in text — the current page number in a folio, for example, or the target page number for a "continued on" reference. You could type in a page number manually on each page of a multipage

IN THIS CHAPTER

Using automatic page numbers and section names

Working with text variables

Cross-referencing text

Using conditional text

Working with Grep styles

Creating mail-merged and other customized documents

Creating catalogs and other structured documents with Tagged Text files document, but that can get old fast. As I mention earlier in this book (see Chapters 5 and 6), if you're working on a multipage document, you should be using master pages. And if you're using master pages, you should handle page numbers on document pages by placing page-number characters on their master pages.

If you want to add the current page number to a page, choose Type ⇨ Insert Special Character ⇨ Markers ⇨ Current Page Number or press Option+Shift+⌘+N or Ctrl+Shift+Alt+N, whenever the Type tool is active and the text cursor (text-insertion point) is flashing. If you move the page or the text frame, the page-number character is automatically updated to reflect the new page number.

To create "continued on" and "continued from" lines, choose Type ⇨ Insert Special Character ⇨ Markers ⇨ Next Page Number to have the next page's number inserted in your text, or choose Type ⇨ Insert Special Character ⇨ Markers ⇨ Previous Page Number to have the previous page's number inserted. That next or previous page is the next or previous page in the story. (There are no shortcuts for these complex menu sequences — unless you assign your own, as explained in Chapter 3.)

One flaw in InDesign's continued-line approach is that the text frames must be linked for InDesign to know what the next and previous pages are. Thus, you're likely to place your continued lines in the middle of your text. But if the text reflows, so do the continued lines. Here's a way to avoid that: Create separate text frames for your continued-on and continued-from text frames. Now link just those two frames, not the story text. This way, the story text can reflow as needed without affecting your continued lines.

Using Section Markers

InDesign offers another marker called the section marker that lets you insert specific text into your document and update it by just changing the marker text.

The section marker is defined as part of a section start (see Chapter 5), and it's meant to be used in folios for putting in the section name or chapter name. But you can use it anywhere you want and for anything you want, not just for section or chapter labels.

To define a section marker (there can be only one per section, of course), open the Pages panel (choose Window ⇨ Pages or press ⌘+F10 or Ctrl+F10) and choose Numbering & Section Options from the panel's flyout menu. In the resulting dialog box, type a text string in the Section Marker field. Then click OK.

To use the marker, have the text insertion point active in whatever text frame you want to insert it and then choose Type ⇨ Insert Special Character ⇨ Markers ⇨ Section Marker. That's it!

Using Text Variables

The section marker was clearly the inspiration for the new text-variable feature. Why stop at section markers? With text variables, you can define an unlimited number of text variables that InDesign happily updates across your documents whenever you change them, or they change with your layout.

Creating text variables

To create a text variable, choose Type ➪ Text Variables ➪ Define. You'll get the Text Variables dialog box shown in Figure 22.1. It lists existing text variables, including the seven variables predefined in InDesign: Chapter Number, Creation Date, File Name, Last Page Number, Modification Date, Output Date, and Running Header. Any text variables you create are added to this list.

Note that the source of the number used in the Chapter Number text variable is something you define as part of a book. For each document in a book, you can specify its chapter number using the Document Numbering Options dialog box accessed from the book panel's flyout menu.

CROSS-REF   Chapter 24 explains books and how to set the chapter number.

To create a new text variable, click New. You get the New Text Variable dialog box shown in Figure 22.1. Give the variable a name in the Name field and choose the type of variable you want from the Type pop-up menu. Your choices are the eight predefined types — Chapter Number, Creation Date, File Name, Last Page Number, Modification Date, Output Date, Running Header (Character Style), and Running Header (Paragraph Style) — plus Custom Text, which lets you enter any text of your choosing.

Note that you can create more than one variable for, say, File Name or Modification Date — just give each its own name. You might do this because you want them formatted differently in different contexts. For example, you might want the modification date formatted as "Published on March 27, 2009" on a title page but as "Mod. Date: 03/27/09" in a footnote. Having two text variables using the Modification Date type lets you do this.

Also note that there are two types of running header text variables. You choose Running Header (Character Style) if you want to insert text derived from text using a certain character style; you choose Running Header (Paragraph Style) if you want to insert text derived from text using a certain paragraph style. The idea of a running header is to give the reader context for the current contents of a page as part of a folio. For example, an encyclopedia might display the name of the page's first entry in its left page folios and the name of the page's last entry in its right page folios to help the reader quickly zero into a specific topic as she thumbs through the pages. The options for formatting a text variable varies based on the type of variable it is.

TIP   If you create text variables when no document is open, these text variables will be available in all new documents you later create. You can also load text variables from other documents, as described later in this chapter.

FIGURE 22.1

Left: The Text Variables dialog box. Right: The New Text Variable dialog box, for a running header.

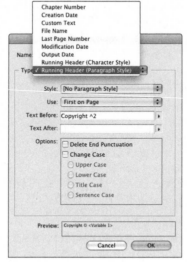

Formatting text variables

Three formatting options are available for more than one type of text variable:

- **Text Before and Text After:** These two fields — available for all types except Custom Text — let you add any text you want before or after the variable. For example, you might enter the word *Chapter* in the Text Before field for a Chapter Number variable. Note that both fields have an unnamed pop-up menu to their right from which you can select a variety of common symbols and spaces.

 Don't forget to add any needed leading or trailing spaces in the Text Before and Text After fields.

- **Style:** This pop-up menu lets you select the numbering style to apply in the Chapter Number and Last Page Number types, the character style for the Running Header (Character Style) type, and the paragraph style for the Running Header (Paragraph Style) type of text variables.

- **Date Format:** This field and its associated pop-up menu lets you choose the desired date and time formats for the Creation Date, Modification Date, and Output Date text variables. Examples include *MM/dd/yy* to get a date such as 05/08/62 and *MMMM d, yyyy* to get a date such as August 15, 1962. Don't worry about memorizing codes — just pick the desired options from the pop-up menu to the right of the Date Format field.

Several other variables have unique options:

- **Custom Text:** This has the fewest options. Just enter the desired text, including choosing special characters such as spaces and dashes from the unnamed pop-up menu to the right of the Text field. That's the only field to adjust for this text variable.

- **Last Page Number:** In addition to the Text Before, Text After, and Style formatting controls, this type includes one unique control: the Scope pop-up menu. Here, you choose between Section and Document to tell InDesign what you mean by last page number: if it's the section's last page or the document's last page.

- **File Name:** In addition to Text Before and Text After formatting controls, this type has two unique check boxes — Include Entire Folder Path and Include File Extension — to tell InDesign exactly how much of the filename to include. If both are unselected, InDesign includes just the core filename, such as Jan 09 TOC. Selecting the Include Entire Folder Path adds the file location before the core filename, such as MacintoshHD:Projects: Jan 09 TOC or C:\Projects\Jan 09 TOC. Selecting the Include File Extension appends the filename extension, such as Jan 09 TOC.indd.

- **Running Header:** The formatting options for these two types are the most complex, as shown in Figure 22.1. The two Running Header menu options have two options not available to other Type pop-up menu options:
  - **Use:** Here, you determine which text to use: First on Page uses the first text on the page that has the specific style applied, and Last on Page uses the last text on the page that has the specific style applied.
  - **Options:** Here, you can control whether the punctuation of the source text is retained or not in the running header (select Delete End Punctuation to remove it) and whether the running header overrides the text of the source text's capitalization (select Change Case and then choose the appropriate capitalization option: Upper Case, Lower Case, Title Case, or Sentence Case).

Editing and managing text variables

Editing text variables is very much like creating them: Just select the variable to change in the Text Variables dialog box and click Edit. You get the Edit Text Variable dialog box, which is identical except for its name to the New Text Variable dialog box covered in the previous section.

You format text variables the same as you do any other text, applying styles and local formatting as you would with any other text.

You can also import text variables from other documents by clicking Load in the Text Variables dialog box and then choosing the document to import the variables from. After choosing a document, you get the Load Text Variables dialog box, shown in Figure 22.2, in which you can select which variables are imported and handle name conflicts.

Linguistic Smarts

InDesign's text-variable feature is smart enough to translate names of days and months into whatever language you've specified for the text (using the Language option in the Character panel or in your character or paragraph style). For example, Monday, May 11, 2009 AD becomes mardi, mai 11, 2009 apr. J.-C. in French and Τρίτη, Μαΐου 11, 2009 μ.Χ. in Greek.

But it is not smart enough to change the date format for the target language, such as changing the American English notation of 05/11/2009 to 11/05/2009 for most European languages.

To get rid of a text variable, select it from the list in the Text Variables dialog box and click Delete.

To convert a text variable in your document to the actual text, highlight it using the Type tool and either choose Type ⇨ Text Variables ⇨ Convert Variable to Text or, if you happen to be in the Text Variables dialog box, click Convert to Text.

FIGURE 22.2

The Load Text Variables dialog box

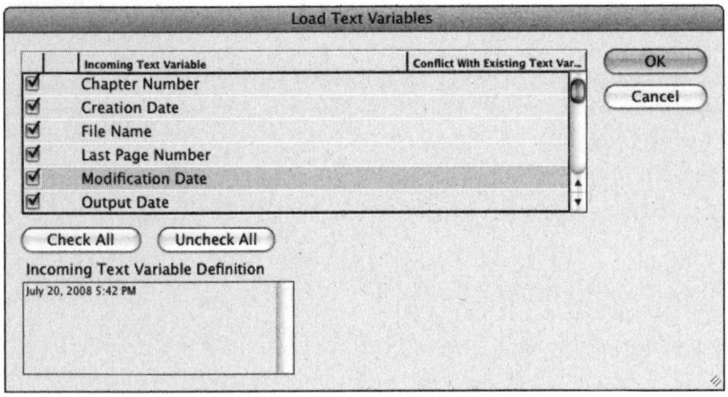

Inserting text variables

Inserting text variables in your document uses the same essential process as inserting a special character such as a section market, except you use the Text Variable menu option: Choose Type ⇨ Text Variables ⇨ Insert Variable and then choose the desired variable from the submenu. If you happen to be in the Text Variables dialog box, select the desired text variable from the list and click Insert.

Working with Cross-References

InDesign CS4 uses the Hyperlinks panel to add a related capability: cross-references. Automated cross-references are used just for text, such as to automatically keep page numbers and chapter titles updated in text such as *see page 227* and *Learn more about color in the chapter "All about Color."*

NEW FEATURE   The cross-references features are new to InDesign CS4. They use an extended version of the hyperlinks feature, covered in Chapter 32.

Adding and editing cross-references

To work with cross-references, you have two choices for their "to" locations. You can specify locations by adding text anchors in your documents using the hyperlinks destination feature described in the previous section and then selecting that text anchor in the New Cross-Reference dialog box. Or you can just choose from a list of paragraphs and make the cross-reference link to that selected paragraph in the New Cross-Reference dialog box.

You open the New Cross-Reference dialog box, shown in Figure 22.3, by choosing Type ⇨ Hyperlinks & Cross-References ⇨ Insert Cross-Reference, by choosing Insert Cross-Reference from the Hyperlinks panel's flyout menu, or by clicking the Create New Cross-Reference iconic button at the bottom of the Hyperlinks panel. (To open the Hyperlinks panel, choose Window ⇨ Interactive ⇨ Hyperlinks or choose Window ⇨ Type & Tables ⇨ Cross-Reference.)

FIGURE 22.3

The New Cross-Reference dialog box and a cross-reference in text (to its left)

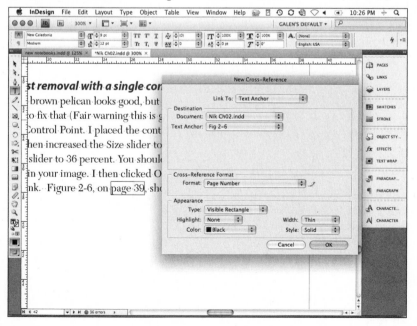

NOTE **To edit an existing cross-reference, choose Cross-Reference Options from the Hyperlinks panel's flyout menu, or choose Type ⇨ Hyperlinks & Cross-References ⇨ Cross-Reference Options. Either way, you get the Cross-Reference Options dialog box, which is identical to the New Cross-References dialog box shown in Figure 22.3.**

In the Linked To pop-up menu, choose Text Anchor if your "to" destination is a text anchor. If you want to select a specific paragraph instead, choose Paragraph; InDesign will show all the first words of each paragraph in the document so that you can scroll through the list and choose the desired one. You can also filter that list by choosing from the styles at left; only paragraphs with the selected style will appear. (So, for example, you can see just headings by choosing the paragraph style for your headings.)

You control how the cross-reference appears using the Appearance section's controls:

- Use the Type pop-up menu to choose Invisible Rectangle or Visible Rectangle. The Invisible Rectangle option gives no visual indication that the text contains a hyperlink, except that the mouse pointer becomes a hand icon when the reader maneuvers through the document. (You would typically pick this option when you've used blue underline as a character attribute for the hyperlink text to mirror the standard Web way of indicating a hyperlink.) The Visible Rectangle option puts a box around the text using the four settings below. (They are grayed out if Invisible Rectangle is selected.)

- The Highlight pop-up menu lets you choose how the source text or frame is highlighted: None, Invert (reserves the foreground and background colors), Outline (places a line around the source), and Inset (places a line around the source, but inside any frame stroke; for text, it's the same as Outline).

- The Color pop-up menu displays Web-safe colors as well as any colors you defined in the document.

- The Width pop-up menu lets you choose the thickness of the line used in the Outline and Inset options from the Highlight pop-up menu. The choices are Thin, Medium, and Thick.

- You can choose the type of line in the Style pop-up menu: Solid or Dashed.

NOTE **The Highlight, Color, Width, and Style options are meant for PDF documents, not printed documents, but they can be used in print documents. Highlight, Width, and Style have no effect in documents exported to the Web; instead, the Web document will use either the standard HTML hyperlink display (underlined blue text) or whatever active hyperlink style you set in your Web editor.**

To determine what cross-reference text displays in your cross-references (such as *please refer to Chapter 4* or *Find more details in the "History of Mac OS X" section in the* Operating System Essentials *book*), choose a cross-reference format in the Format pop-up menu. You can also edit or create a new one by clicking the pencil iconic button to the right of the pop-up menu. (See the next section for how to work with cross-reference formats.)

Working with cross-reference formats

Use the Cross-Reference Format section of the New Cross-Reference dialog box to control what text displays for that cross-reference. You can be as basic as the page number (note that the word *page* will appear with it automatically) or as complex as, for example, showing the full paragraph text (such as a heading) and the page number.

You can create your own cross-reference formats, and modify the existing ones, using the Cross-Reference Formats dialog box, shown in Figure 22.4.

To open that dialog box, click the button to the right of the Format pop-up menu in the New Cross-Reference dialog box (handy when you want to create a new format as you are adding a cross-reference) or choose Define Cross-Reference Formats from the Hyperlinks panel's flyout menu. You can also edit an existing format this way.

The procedure for adding or editing a cross-reference format is as follows:

1. **Click the + iconic button at the lower left of the dialog box to add a new format.** Note that when you add a new format, whatever format is selected in the list at left becomes the basis for your new format. (You can also just select an existing format from the list at left to modify it.) Click the – iconic button to delete a format.

2. **In the Name field, be sure to change the name of your new format to something meaningful to you.**

3. **In the Definition section, edit, delete, and add the text you want to appear in the cross-reference.** Note that special codes are surrounded by < and > characters. You don't need to memorize them; just use the first iconic pop-up menu (the + symbol) shown in Figure 22.4 to select those codes, and use the second iconic pop-up menu (the @ symbol) below to choose special characters such as em spaces.

4. **If you want, select a character style to be applied to the cross-reference text as part of the format.** To do so, select the Character Style for Cross-Reference check box and then choose a character style from the pop-up menu to its right.

5. **Click Save to save the format and then add or delete another one. Click OK when you're done adding and editing formats.**

The Cross-Reference Formats dialog box.

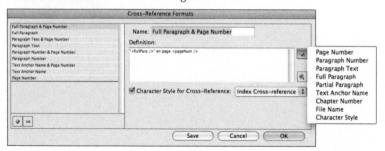

Using Conditional Text

Have you ever worked on a document that has variations, forcing you to create separate copies that you must then ensure have any changes applied to all copies? Perhaps you used the layers feature (see Chapter 5) to restrict the unique content to its own layer so that you could make visible each version's layer when you wanted to print that specific version. But you realized that this technique doesn't work well for text inside paragraphs because changes to the text mean that whatever you placed in layers won't be at the right location if your text changes move the text's locations in the "main" layer.

NEW FEATURE InDesign CS4 offers a new way to have multiple versions of text in a document that gets around these issues: conditional text. You can think of conditional text as sort of a layer that works within text, so if the text moves, the conditional "layers" do, too.

For example, say you have a publication that is distributed in Canada, Ireland, and the U.K., where pricing is different (dollars, euros, and pounds, respectively). You can't really have the main layer for the prices in dollars, one for the prices in euros, and one for the prices in pounds, because if you changed the text in the main layer that includes the dollar prices, the pounds and euros layers would either have the old text and need to be changed also (a management nightmare) or the individual text frames you set up for their prices would now be nowhere near the text they belong with.

With conditional text, you instead have just one layer for your text, and where the text may need to change (such as for pricing), you insert conditional text. Then, if you want to display the price in dollars, you select the dollars condition, and the right text appears no matter how the text is flowing. When you want to display the price in euros, you select the euros condition. Ditto for pounds.

Here's how to create and apply conditional text:

1. **In your text, enter each of the text variations you want.** For example, as you can see in Figure 22.5, if you have three prices, enter all three in sequence as if they were one piece of text. Apply any formatting desired. Don't worry for the moment that you don't want them all to display or print at the same time.

2. **Open the Conditional Text panel (choose Window ⇨ Type & Tables ⇨ Conditional Text) and choose New Condition from the flyout menu.**

3. **In the New Conditions dialog box, give the condition a name and assign it a color and a line type, as shown in Figure 22.5.** You can modify conditions later by choosing Condition Options from the Conditional Text panel's flyout menu. (That dialog box is identical to the New Conditions dialog box.)

4. **In the text, highlight a piece of text (such as the euro price) and then click the related condition to apply that condition to the selected text.** A check mark appears to the immediate left of the active condition for whatever text is selected or in which your text cursor is active. In your layout, the text will also have whatever line type in whatever color you specified in the New Conditions dialog box, so you have a visual guide as to what conditions are applied to what text.

   Add as many conditions using Steps 3 and 4 as you will need. In the figure's example, there are three: one for each price. (Note that the [Unconditional] condition is just your regular text, which always will display and print.)

5. **Now, click the squares in the Conditional Text panel to the far left of the various conditions.** If the square shows an eye, any text tagged with that condition *will* be visible. If the square is empty, any text tagged with that condition will *not* display. By controlling which conditions are active (eye icons), you determine what displays and prints in your document. (This is exactly how you make layers visible and invisible in the Layers panel, as Chapter 5 explains.) The bottom of Figure 22.5 shows the same text as in the top of Figure 22.5 but with just the [Unconditional] and the euros text visible.

Pretty easy, isn't it? Just turn off and on the text you want to display and print by hiding and showing the appropriate conditions.

FIGURE 22.5

Top: The Conditional Text panel and its New Condition dialog box. Above them is the text to which the conditions are be applied (the three prices). Bottom: The same text as at top, but with the dollars and pounds conditions turned off in the Conditional Text panel so that only the euro pricing displays and prints.

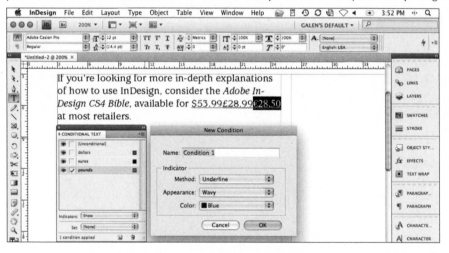

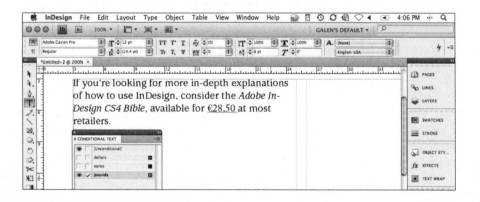

What Are Grep Styles?

Another way of applying conditions to text is by using Grep styles, which are handled through InDesign's paragraph styles feature, in the Grep Style pane. Grep is a Unix language for applying conditions based on pattern-matching, as the sidebar "What Is Grep?" in Chapter 15 explains. (Chapter 19 explains how to create and apply styles.)

If you create a Grep style as part of a paragraph style, you're setting up a condition that has InDesign apply a character format to text that matches whatever pattern you set in the Grep pane. What's cool about this is that InDesign will automatically apply the Grep style when you add (by typing, pasting, or placing) any text that matches that condition; you don't need to "tag" the text with the style to apply it.

The figure below shows the Grep pane with a sample Grep condition (/d means any digit, while + means one or more times — in other words, apply the character style Copyright to any digit as many times as one appears in the paragraph.

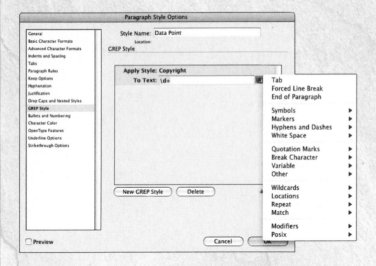

To take full advantage of Grep styles, you need to know how to construct the desired conditions using the Grep language. But there is one very easy use of Grep styles that anyone can take advantage of even knowing not a whit of the Grep language. If you create a Grep style that simply replaces specific text with a formatted version of that text, InDesign will automatically format that text for you as you enter, paste, or place it in your document. For example, if you replace the text "The Zango Group" with the text "The Zango Group" that has the character style Bold Red applied, any time you enter, paste, or place the text "The Zango Group," InDesign will automatically apply the Bold Red character style to it.

Working with Merged Data

Word processing programs such as Microsoft Word have long let you create forms with mail merge so that you can send a letter to lots of people, letting Word automatically print a copy for all recipients and insert their names, addresses, and so forth into their copies. (Some programs have called this capability *variable text*.) A decade ago, PageMaker 7 added a similar capability called *data merge*, which uses the same principle to handle variable text for form letters, catalogs, and other documents for which the layout is identical but specific pieces are customized. InDesign's approach is based on the old PageMaker tool.

Merged-data documents fall into two basic classes, as Figure 22.6 shows:

■ Form letters, for which one layout is printed multiple times, with each copy having personalized information.

■ Labels, for which layout components are repeated several times in the same layout but with different information. Usually just one copy is printed.

What InDesign's data-merge feature cannot do is let you create catalogs in which you have different, variable-sized records on one page. You can use the data-merge feature for catalog-type documents if your layout is highly structured and each record takes exactly the same amount of space (as address labels do).

CROSS-REF If you want to create catalogs or other documents with variable-sized records from databases or similar sources, use InDesign Tagged Text, as described later in this chapter.

Setting up merged data

Regardless of which kind of merged documents you are creating, the setup is the same. Create a text file with the various data separated either by tabs or commas (use just one as your separator in the file, rather than mix the two). Start a new record by pressing Enter or Return (a new paragraph). The first row should contain the names of the fields. For example, for a local guidebook listing cafés, your data might look like this (I've put → characters to indicate the tabs):

```
name→address→phone
Martha & Bros.→3868 24th St.→(415) 641-4433
Martha & Bros.→1551 Church St.→(415) 648-1166
Martha & Bros.→745 Cortland St.→(415) 642-7585
Martha & Bros.→2800 California St.→(415) 931-2281
Diamond Corner Café→751 Diamond St.→(415) 282-9551
Farley's Coffeehouse→1315 18th St.→(415) 648-1545
```

This simple file has three fields per entry: the café name, its address, and its phone number. The file uses tabs as the separators.

 **NOTE** Because the source file is a text-only file, it cannot contain any formatting such as boldface or italic.

FIGURE 22.6

Two types of merged-data documents: a form letter (left) and a set of mailing labels (right)

To import graphics as inline graphics, precede the field name with @, such as *@photo*. The record fields need to provide the complete path to the graphic file, which must be in a supported format. For example, a file's complete path could be `MacintoshHD:Images:myphoto.tiff` on the Mac or `C:\Images\myphoto.tif` in Windows.

Creating pages with merged data

With the source file ready, create or go to the text frame in which you want to flow your data, selecting the text-insertion point with the Type tool.

> **TIP**   There's a real benefit to putting your fields on master pages: You can then update the layout if the source data file changes (choose Update Data Fields from the Data Merge panel's flyout menu). You cannot do this if you place the fields on a regular document page because InDesign would have created a new document containing the merged data.

Now follow these steps to insert the fields in that frame:

1. Open the Data Merge panel by choosing Window ➪ Automation ➪ Data Merge.

2. **Choose Select Data Source from the Data Merge panel's flyout menu, navigate to the desired file using the resulting dialog box, and click Open.** If your data file changes, you

can import the most current version by choosing Update Data Source from the Data Merge panel's flyout menu. Choose Remove Data Source to remove a data file from the panel.

3. **The Data Merge panel now lists the data file and the fields it contains, as Figure 22.7 shows.**

4. **Click and drag the fields to the appropriate spots in your layout, or double-click a field name to insert it at the current text-insertion point.** For example, in a form letter, you might click and drag the Name field to a point right after the text *Dear* and before the comma in the salutation. The field names are enclosed in French quotation marks (« »). In your layout, this would look like

   ```
   Dear «Name»,
   ```

   You can use a field more than once in the layout. The panel shows which page numbers each field is used in (to the right of the field name).

FIGURE 22.7

The Data Merge panel and its flyout menu

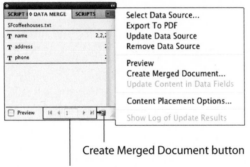

Create Merged Document button

Controls for moving through records
if Preview is enabled

5. **Format the fields as desired.** They take on any paragraph formatting applied to the paragraphs containing them. You can use character styles and/or other local formatting on the fields as desired.

6. **Click the Create Merged Document iconic button at the bottom right of the panel or choose Create Merged Document from the flyout menu to import the entire data file's contents into your layout.** The Create Merged Document dialog box shown in Figure 22.8 opens with the Records pane. In this pane, you have the following options:

FIGURE 22.8

Left: The Records pane of the Create Merged Document dialog box. Right: The Options pane of the Create Merged Document dialog box (upper right) and the Content Placement Options dialog box (lower right) offer the same options.

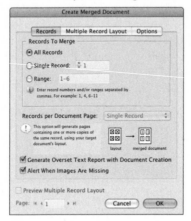
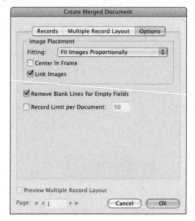

- In the Records to Merge section, choose which records to import. You can choose All, Single Record, or Range.

- In the Records per Document Page pop-up menu, choose Single Record if you want a new page output per record (such as in a form letter) or Multiple Records if you want to print multiple copies of the same record on a page (such as for business cards). Note that InDesign copies the entire text frame containing the data fields when you choose Multiple Records. (See the next section for more details on placing multiple records per page.)

7. Go to the Options pane and verify that the placement options work for your document. Figure 22.8 shows the Options pane, whose options are as follows:

   - In the Image Placement section, choose how to fit any imported graphics by choosing an option in the Fitting pop-up menu. You typically pick Fit Images Proportionally, which is the default setting. You can also select the Center in Frame option to center the imported graphics, and the Link Images option to link to the source graphics files rather than embed the graphic into the InDesign layout.

   - In the lower section of the pane, you can have InDesign remove blank lines created by empty fields by selecting the Remove Blank Lines for Empty Fields option. This is handy, for example, if your layout permits two address lines per recipient. Anyone with a single address line has no space between that address and the city name if this option is selected. You can also limit the number of pages in the merged document by selecting the Page Limit per Document option and typing a value in its field.

NOTE You can set placement options before creating a merged document by choosing Content Placement Options from the Data Merge panel's flyout menu. Figure 22.8 shows the Content Placement Options dialog box, which has the same options as the Options pane of the Create Merged Document dialog box.

8. **Click OK. InDesign creates a new document based on the original layout and merged data.** The merged text is now editable and is no longer linked to its source data, so to update the document you need to regenerate it from the document that contains the data-merge records. (That's why InDesign creates a new document for the resulting data rather than replacing the source file.)

There is a key exception: If you place the records on a master page, the data-merge feature creates document pages based on the imported data within the current document, rather than creating an entirely new document. If you place the records on a master page, you can later update the records through the Data Merge panel and have the document pages updated as well.

TIP You can preview the data in your fields by selecting the Preview check box in the Data Merge panel (or choosing Preview from its flyout menu). You can go through the actual data by using the arrow buttons to the right of the Preview option or by typing a record number in the preview field.

NEW FEATURE InDesign CS4 now lets you export your merged-data document straight to a PDF file, using the Export to PDF option in the Data Merge panel's flyout menu. This saves you the step for creating the merged document as an InDesign file and then exporting that to PDF.

Working with multiple records per page

As I describe in the previous section, you can have InDesign create a new page for each record or place multiple records on the same page. Although the process for both adding fields and generating the pages via the Data Merge panel is the same for both, note that creating multiple records on a page may not quite work as you might expect:

- The various options pertaining to multiple records are grayed out if your document has other pages with content already placed on them. So if you want to have pages that contain other information, such as a title page, you need to create those pages after you have created the multiple records. Note that you can have other objects on the master page or document page that contains the frame from which the multiple records will be based, but not content on any other page.

- Keep in mind that InDesign copies the entire frame that your merged data is in, one for each of the record — *don't* copy the frames containing the data-merge text in your layout to fill out your page. So be sure you want everything in that frame copied and that the frame is as large as needed to hold the records but no larger (otherwise, you will get excessive white space). And be sure that this "master" frame should be placed at the top-most and leftmost position in your layout.

■ Be sure that you leave blank the space in which the labels' fields are copied — the data-merge feature won't work around objects in the layout. Instead, it blindly follows the specs in the Multiple Record Layout pane, repeating fields until the page is full or until it runs out of fields.

Figure 22.9 shows a simple layout that is a typical example of where you would use the Multiple Records option. You set up the placement of these records in the Multiple Record Layout pane, as the figure shows.

FIGURE 22.9

Top: A layout with one record that will be copied multiple times on the page using the Data Merge panel's Multiple Record Layout functions (see the Multiple Record Layout pane at right). Bottom: A page created with six records from the frame at top.

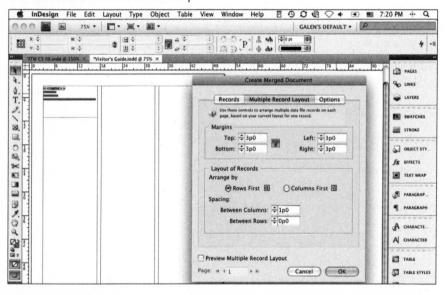

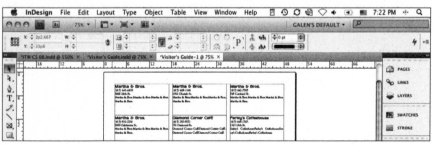

Using Tagged Text for Database Publishing

The InDesign Tagged Text format can be very handy as a start to database publishing. Its markup codes let you specify and even define the formatting in a document, so you can create a text file with the InDesign commands embedded in them. When InDesign imports the file, it applies all the formatting specified. If you can generate these codes from a database or other automation system, you can automate much of the creation of complex documents such as catalogs whose content changes frequently.

CROSS-REF Chapter 4 explains the Tagged Text format in more detail.

For example, say you have a product directory that lists the company name, URL, and product description. You'd have a text file with entries that look something like this:

```
<ASCII-WIN>
<pstyle:Company>Name 1
<pstyle:URL>Web address 1
<pstyle:Description>Descriptive text 1 goes here.
<pstyle:Company>Name 2
<pstyle:URL>Web address 2
<pstyle:Description>Descriptive text 2 goes here.
```

The <ASCII-WIN> (or <ASCII-MAC> if the file was created on a Mac) code appears only at the top of the file. The code <pstyle:style name> specifies the paragraph style to apply (for character styles, the code is <cstyle:style name>). Be sure that the name is an exact match, including any capitalization; otherwise, InDesign doesn't recognize the style you want to use.

The trick is to have your database or other information source add the codes before the content they export. Typically, you'd do this using a programming language that comes with or is compatible with your database or content source.

To use text coded this way, you open an existing document that is already set up with text frames and styles and then you place the Tagged Text file into the document. The coded text takes on the designated styles, making it easy, for example, to flow an updated catalog into a template. Figure 22.10 shows a document created this way.

FIGURE 22.10

A catalog created by importing a Tagged Text file

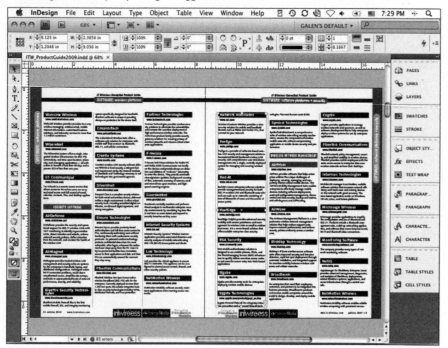

Summary

It's a lot of work to track page number references in a document as text reflows and the number of pages changes. The automatic page numbering characters in InDesign resolve that burden, tracking the current page numbers and the page numbers used in continued lines for you.

InDesign lets you specify all sorts of text variables — such as section names, current date, chapter numbers, and text you specify — to likewise remove the manual effort in keeping text that changes predictably up-to-date.

InDesign CS4 offers several new automated-text capabilities. Cross-references let you insert *see page x* and *refer to Chapter x, "title goes here"* references in text and have InDesign make sure they refer to the current page numbers, chapter numbers, chapter titles, and the like automatically for you. Conditional text lets you turn specific text on throughout a document, such as euro pricing versus dollar pricing, so that you can handle predictable variations without having to create a separate layout. And the Grep styles feature within paragraph styles let you apply formatting via character styles to text based on pattern matching.

To help reduce labor, InDesign also lets you produce data-merge documents. Such documents contain variable text, such as the address in a form letter or pricing and names in a catalog.

Finally, consider using the InDesign Tagged Text format to specify sophisticated formatting, such as defining paragraph and character styles in InDesign, in your word processor or database. This requires a familiarity with programming or coding in formats such as HTML but can be a powerful way to add formatting for highly predictable, structured documents in your word processor before you import the file into InDesign. Using it just to specify paragraph and style sheets is a great way to bring database-oriented data, such as catalogs, into an InDesign template.

Chapter 23

Working with Footnotes, Indexes, and TOCs

M any business documents — books, reports, white papers, and so on — use features traditionally associated with academic book publishing: footnotes to cite sources, indexes to provide a map to where specific content is located in the document, and tables of contents (TOCs) to provide an overview of the document's structure and contents.

When you're working on any type of document — a report, a magazine, a textbook — you can easily spend more time manually creating tables of contents, keeping footnotes updated, and laboriously managing indexes than you spend designing the publication. InDesign helps reduce this labor while also ensuring that your footnotes, indexes, and TOCs stay automatically updated as your document is revised.

CROSS-REF Although you can use the footnote, index, and TOC features in individual documents, they're also designed to work across multiple documents such as books. Chapter 24 covers how to manage such multidocument projects.

IN THIS CHAPTER

Adding footnotes

Indexing documents and books

Creating tables of contents and lists

Working with Footnotes

Many kinds of document use footnotes — academic articles and journals, books, manuals, and even some magazines. So it makes sense for InDesign to support them as well.

InDesign imports footnotes from Microsoft Word files (see Chapter 13) as well as lets you add footnotes directly. The process is simple: Choose Type ➪ Insert Footnote, and InDesign adds a footnote to the bottom of the column that contains the footnote entry, as Figure 23.1 shows. InDesign handles the footnote numbering as you add and delete footnotes; you type the footnote text.

InDesign can help you find the footnoted text in your document. Using the Type tool, select all or part of the desired footnote text at the bottom of a column or text frame and then choose Type ⇨ Go to Footnote Reference. InDesign then goes to the page containing the original footnote reference, placing that text near the center of the window.

But footnotes are more complicated than that, so InDesign lets you control much of the appearance of footnotes by choosing Type ⇨ Document Footnote Options to open the Footnote Options dialog box, whose two panes are shown in Figure 23.2.

FIGURE 23.1

A three-column text box with a footnote in the first column

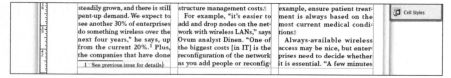

FIGURE 23.2

The Footnote Options dialog box's two panes: Numbering and Formatting (left) and Layout (right)

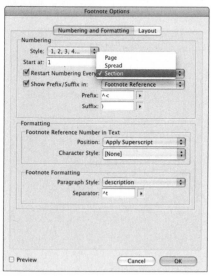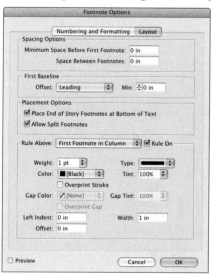

CAUTION InDesign also inserts footnotes at the bottom of a text frame, even if there are other frames overlapping that text frame with text wrap turned on. This means that you can inadvertently obscure a footnote under another frame because you understandably — but mistakenly — think that turning on text wrap causes InDesign to keep the footnote outside that other frame.

564

CAUTION You cannot insert footnotes into tables. Instead, you have to handle them the old, manual way: inserting a footnote character as needed and typing your footnotes below the table, and updating the footnote as needed manually.

Numbering and Formatting pane

Use the Numbering and Formatting pane of the Footnote Options dialog box to control the formatting of the footnote text and footnote character in the current InDesign document. (To change these settings for future documents, open the dialog box with no document open and set your new defaults.)

You have these options in the Numbering section:

- **Style:** Choose the numbering style through the Style pop-up menu, which gives you seven numbering options:

  - *, **, *** . . .
  - a, b, c, d, . . .
  - A, B, C, D, . . .
  - *, †, ‡, §, ¶ . . .
  - i, ii, iii, iv . . .
  - I, II, III, IV . . .
  - 1, 2, 3, 4 . . .
  - 01, 02, 03, 04 . . .
  - 001, 002, 003, 004 . . .

NEW FEATURE The 01, 02, 03, 04 . . . and 001, 002, 003, 004 . . . numbering styles are new to InDesign CS4.

- **Start At:** Choose the starting number by typing a value in the Start At field (the default is 1).

- **Restart Numbering Every:** If you want the numbering to restart on each page, spread, or section, select the Restart Numbering Every option and then choose Page, Spread, or Section from its pop-up menu.

- **Show Prefix/Suffix In:** If you want a prefix and/or suffix with the footnote number, select the Show Prefix/Suffix In option. Then choose where the prefix and/or suffix should be displayed with the adjoining pop-up menu. Its choices are Footnote Reference (that's the footnote in the text), Footnote Text (the actual footnote at the bottom of the column), and Both Reference and Text (at both locations).

  Type your prefix characters in the Prefix field and your suffix characters in the Suffix field. Use the pop-up menu to the right of the Prefix field to insert any of several special characters into the Prefix field: (, [, a hair space, and a thin space. All characters in the Prefix field precede the footnote character. Likewise, with the pop-up menu to the right of the Suffix field, you can insert a) or] in the Suffix field. All characters in the Suffix field follow the footnote character.

CROSS-REF See Chapter 20 for details on special spaces such as hair spaces.

In the Formatting section, there are two subsections: Footnote Reference Number in Text and Footnote Formatting.

In the Footnote Reference Number in Text subsection, you have two options:

- **Position:** Using the Position pop-up menu, specify how the footnote character is formatted; your options are Apply Superscript, Apply Subscript, and Apply Normal. Most documents use superscripts and don't have any suffixes or prefixes. But some documents enclose their footnotes in parentheses or brackets rather than superscript them; if that is your style, you would choose Apply Normal and type [in the Prefix field and] in the Suffix field in the Numbering section above.

- **Character Style:** If you want to apply a character style to the footnote character in text, select the Apply Character Style option and then choose the style in the adjoining pop-up menu.

In the Footnote Formatting subsection, you have these options:

- **Paragraph Style:** You can apply a specific paragraph style to the footnote text by choosing a style in the Paragraph Style pop-up menu. You typically should have a specific style for your footnotes.

- **Separator:** Type in the Separator field the characters you want to separate the footnote number and its text. (This follows any text you typed in the Suffix field.) These are often various spaces, but they can also be a period or colon followed by a space. The pop-up menu below the field lets you choose several kinds of spaces (tab, em space, and en space).

NOTE You can use the codes for various space characters in the Prefix, Suffix, and Separator fields. Common ones are ^t for a tab, ^m for an em space, ^> for an en space, ^< for a thin space, and ^\ for a hair space.

Layout pane

Use the Layout pane to control the placement of the footnote relative to the rest of the document.

In the Spacing Options section, you have these options:

- **Minimum Space before First Footnote:** Set the space between the bottom of the column and the first footnote by typing a value in the Minimum Space before First Footnote field.

- **Space Between Footnotes:** Set the space between footnotes by typing a value in the Space Between Footnotes field. You typically do not add a value here because you can better control spacing with your paragraph style used by the footnote text.

In the First Baseline section, you have these options:

- **Offset:** Set how the footnote's baseline should be determined; your options are Ascent, Cap Height, x Height, and Fixed.
- **Min:** You also can set the minimum distance from that location to the baseline by entering a value in the Min field.

CROSS-REF See Chapter 15 for more on setting baselines.

In the Placement Options section, you have these options:

- **Place End of Story Footnotes at Bottom of Text:** Select the Place End of Story Footnotes at Bottom of Text option to override end-of-story footnotes (endnotes) generated in Microsoft Word so that they appear at the bottom of text columns in InDesign.
- **Allow Split Footnotes:** If you don't want footnotes to break across columns, deselect the Allow Split Footnotes option.

In the Rule Above section, you have these options:

- **Rule On:** Select the Rule On option to place a ruling line above the footnotes. In the Rule Above pop-up menu to its left, choose First Footnote in Column or Continued Footnotes to determine which footnotes get the ruling line above them.
- **Weight, Color, Type, Tint, Overprint Stroke, Gap Color, Gap Tint, and Overprint Gap:** Use these controls to format the stroke that is used as the ruling line. (Chapter 11 covers these settings in detail.)
- **Left Indent, Width, and Offset:** Use these fields to control how the line is positioned relative to the text frame.

Indexing Documents and Books

If you've ever been unable to find information in a book that you knew was there, you can appreciate how important a good index can be. Short, simple documents can get by fine without indexes. But long books almost always need indexes to help the reader locate specific information. Indexing used to be a laborious process, involving lots of index cards. InDesign makes indexing much easier, although it relies on you to make key decisions about how the index will be formatted. The following sections show you how to do your part.

CROSS-REF After reading this chapter, you may find that you need a more sophisticated indexing tool than InDesign provides. Check out Sonar Bookends InDex Pro by Virginia Systems, to which I have a link on the plug-ins page on the companion Web site (www.InDesign Central.com). In addition, the company offers Sonar Bookends InXref for creating cross-references in text that update automatically.

Nested or Run-in Index?

There is no right way to index, but common sense should be a guide. Determine which index format you use by the number of levels in the index's hierarchy. If the index has only two levels, a run-in format works well, but an index with three or more levels requires a nested format for the sake of clarity.

Nested indexes look like this:

Kitchen Hardware

Buying, 191

Cost estimates, 242–248

Design guidelines 92–94, 96, 99–101

Hiring contractors, 275–284

Installation, 180–195

Sizing, 91–99

Standards, 24–28, 98, 133

Tools, 199–203, 224, 282–283

Run-in indexes look like this:

Kitchen Hardware: Buying, 191; Cost estimates, 242–248; Design guidelines 92–94, 96, 99–101; Hiring contractors, 275–284; Installation, 180–195; Sizing, 91–99; Standards, 24–28, 98, 133; Tools, 199–203, 224, 282–283

Although InDesign doesn't force you to make this decision until you actually build the index, you really need to make it before you get started. If you tag words for a four-level nested index, but then build a run-in index, your index will be too confusing for readers to make sense of trying to follow all those levels in a string of text.

Choosing an indexing style

Your approach to developing an index depends on the indexing style you want to use. Large publishers usually have their own house style guides for indexes. If you don't have a style guide for indexes, I recommend that you read through the indexing guidelines in *The Chicago Manual of Style*. Another option is to use an index you like as a model and then take the steps necessary in InDesign to achieve that index style. Before you begin indexing your document, ask yourself the following questions:

- Do you want to capitalize all levels of all entries, or do you just want sentence-style caps?
- Should headings appear in boldface?

- What type of punctuation will you use in your index?
- Should the index be nested or run-in style (see the sidebar "Nested or Run-in Index?")?

After you make these decisions, it's a good idea to make a small dummy of your index. From the dummy, create a master page for index pages, paragraph styles for letter headings (A, B, C, and so on in the index), paragraph styles for each level of the index (including indents as appropriate), and character styles for any special formatting you want on page numbers or cross-reference text. InDesign doesn't do any of this for you — if you don't set up styles for your index, your multilevel index will simply look linear when it's built.

Using the Index panel

When a chapter or document is ready to be indexed, open the Index panel (choose Window ↬ Type & Tables ↬ Index or press Shift+F8). You use this panel to add words to the index in up to four indent levels, edit or delete index entries, or create cross-references. The Index panel appears in Figure 23.3.

Understanding Reference and Topic modes

The Index panel has two modes, indicated by the radio buttons at the top: Reference and Topic. Reference mode is the mode you should be in when adding and editing entries from selected text.

NOTE If you're creating an index in a book (see Chapter 24), be sure to select the Book check box in the Index panel.

The Topic mode is meant to give you a clean environment in which to enter the topic names and levels that you want your index to have. Then, when an indexer adds an index entry, she can use the topics that appear in the bottom of the New Page Reference dialog box and double-click the topic to use that topic definition rather than whatever she might enter herself in the dialog box. You don't have to use Topic mode if you don't want to — all index entries create *topics* (InDesign-speak for the entry text). Although a well-intentioned feature meant to help standardize index entries, the Topic mode's use is not intuitive, and most indexers simply ignore it, adding entries manually from selected text or by typing phrases into the Index panel when in Reference mode.

Note that only topics that have actual references (where text occurs on actual pages, not in the pasteboard, on a master page, or in overset text) or cross-references will appear in the final index. So don't worry about unused topic text appearing in your index.

The Index panel has the Book option. Select this check box if you are creating an index for multiple chapters in a book. You must have a book open for this option to be available. If you do have a book open and do not select it, the index is saved with the current document and not opened with any chapter of the book. If it is selected, you can see all topics indexed across a book if you select the Topic radio button.

FIGURE 23.3

The Index panel and its flyout menu

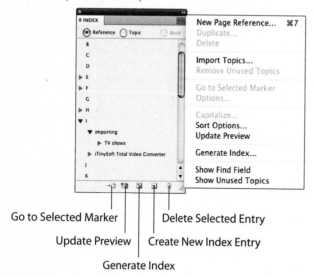

Go to Selected Marker

Update Preview

Generate Index

Delete Selected Entry

Create New Index Entry

Entering index items via the Index panel

To add entries to your index, choose New Page Reference from the Index panel's flyout menu, or press ⌘+7 or Ctrl+7, to get the dialog box shown in Figure 23.4. Here's how the controls work:

NEW FEATURE   The shortcut for adding entries has changed from ⌘+U or Ctrl+U in previous versions to ⌘+7 or Ctrl+7 in InDesign CS4.

- If you selected text first in your document, the text is entered automatically into Topic Level 1. Otherwise, type the text that you want to add to the index. The text is added to the Topic list and, if it is in the document, also to the list of index entries.

- You can type text that controls how the entry is sorted in the Sort By column. For example, if the highlighted text is *The Zango Group,* but you wanted it sorted as if it were *Zango Group, The* (so it appears with the *Z* entries in the index), type *Zango Group, The* in the Sorted By column. Similarly, you might have the movie title *2001: A Space Odyssey* sorted as *Two Thousand and One: A Space Odyssey* so that the listing appears properly with the *T* entries in the index.

- More complex indexes take advantage of the four possible entry levels. You may want an index entry to appear under a higher-level topic. For example, you may want *2001: A Space Odyssey* to appear in the index under *Classic Science Fiction,* in which case you would enter *Classic Science Fiction* in the Topic Level 1 field and *2001: A Space Odyssey* in the Topic Level 2 field.

FIGURE 23.4

The New Page Reference dialog box. The middle portion changes if you select one of the cross-reference options such as See or [Custom Cross-Reference] in the Type pop-up menu, as shown in the dialog box on the right.

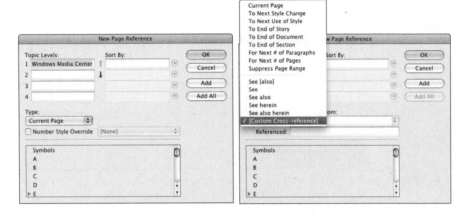

- You can apply a specific character style to an index entry's page number by selecting the Number Style Override check box and then choosing a character style from the pop-up menu to its right. InDesign lets you apply consistent formatting to all page numbers in an index, but this option is handy when you want to highlight specific page numbers to call special attention to them, such as having the definitional reference's page number appear in boldface.

- Use the Type pop-up menu to determine the page entries for the index entry. The pop-up menu has two basic sections, shown in Figure 23.5.

  - One section covers the entry's range — typically, you just want the current page number on which the text appears, but in some cases, you might want to indicate that a topic spans a number of pages, a document section, all text with a specific style, or one of the other options. For example, if you have a section about France in a world history book, you might want the main entry to indicate the whole section — such as *France, 167–203*, while leaving references in other sections (such as references in a section on Germany) to be for just the page on which it appears. If you choose For Next # of Pages or For Next # of Paragraphs, the dialog box displays the Number field for you to enter how many paragraphs or pages you want the index entry's range to span. Note that you can apply a character style to the page number generated in the index by selecting the Number Style Override option and choosing a character style in the pop-up menu to its right.

  - The other section covers cross-references, letting you choose from several types. The dialog box changes slightly, as shown in Figure 23.4, if you choose a cross-reference entry. It adds the Referenced text field for you to type the text that the index contains after the cross-reference. For example, you might choose a See reference so that an entry for *secure login* appears in the index as *Secure login: See login ID.* You can create your own custom cross-references by choosing [Custom Cross-Reference]; InDesign displays the Custom text field and pop-up menu in which you type (or select from previously typed) text that you want InDesign to use. For example, you might want the cross-reference to say *Go to* rather than one of the defaults such as *See.*

NOTE Use *See* to point readers to the appropriate index entry; use *See Also* to point the readers to additional useful information elsewhere in the index; use *See Herein* to point readers to a subentry for this index entry; and use *See Also Herein* to point readers to additional useful information in a subentry to this index entry.

- To add text within the range specified, click Add. (If the text entered is not in the specified range, the text will be added to the Topic list, but no index entry will appear for the text.) To add all occurrences of the text in the document (or book), click Add All.

FIGURE 23.5

The Type pop-up menu's options in the Page Reference Options dialog box (The New Page Reference dialog box is identical except for the name.)

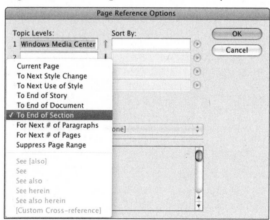

- To change previously defined index entries, choose Page Reference Options in the Index panel's flyout menu.

NOTE In multiparagraph text selections, InDesign indexes each paragraph in that selection. The idea is that you can create lists this way.

At the bottom of both the New Page Reference and Page Reference Options dialog boxes is a list of letters as well as the entry Symbols. You can scroll through this list of headings to see what is already indexed under each letter. Although you might think clicking a letter forces the current index entry to appear in that letter's section of the index, it does not.

To see which text in your document is indexed, choose Type ➪ Show Hidden Characters or press Option+⌘+I or Ctrl+Alt+I, or choose Hidden Characters from the View Options iconic pop-up menu in the application bar. Index entries will have a wide, light-blue caret symbol before them, as Figure 23.6 shows.

FIGURE 23.6

If hidden characters are displayed, you can identify index entries by the wide, light-blue caret in front of the indexed text ("Keyboard," in this example).

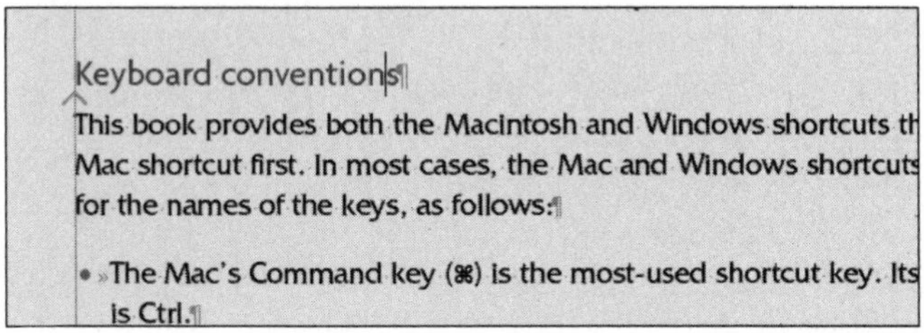

Keyboard conventions¶
This book provides both the Macintosh and Windows shortcuts th
Mac shortcut first. In most cases, the Mac and Windows shortcuts
for the names of the keys, as follows:¶

• The Mac's Command key (⌘) is the most-used shortcut key. Its
  is Ctrl.¶

Entering index items using keyboard shortcuts

To quickly add a word or text selection to an index, highlight the text and press ⌘+7 or Ctrl+7; doing so adds the text to the New Page Reference dialog box (refer to Figure 23.4).

To index a word without opening that dialog box, just press Option+Shift+⌘+[or Ctrl+Alt+Shift+[. This action adds the text to the index using the index's default settings. (You can always edit those settings later, as I describe in the next section.) And to enter an index entry as a proper name (last name, first name), use the shortcut Option+Shift+⌘+] or Ctrl+Alt+Shift+].

Editing index entries

You can edit an index entry by double-clicking its page number in the Index panel or by selecting a page number and choosing Page Reference Options from the flyout menu. The Page Reference Options dialog box, shown previously in Figure 23.5, appears. Except for its name, this dialog box is identical to the New Page Reference dialog box (refer to Figure 23.4). To change the entry, just change the desired attributes in this dialog box and click OK.

Working with the index

The Index panel's flyout menu has several options useful for fine-tuning and generating the index:

■ **Duplicate Topic:** This option lets you duplicate a topic entry so that you can use the settings in one entry without having to reselect them all.

■ **Delete Topic:** This option removes a topic (and any associated entries) from the index.

■ **Import Topics:** This option lets you import topic lists from other InDesign documents — a very handy way to ensure consistent entry labels from chapter to chapter in a book, for example.

- **Go to Selected Marker:** This option causes InDesign to jump to the text that contains the selected index entry in the Index panel. This is a handy way of seeing whether the reference in the text truly merits being listed in the index.

- **Topic Options:** This lets you edit the Level and Sort By settings for topic entries; these affect all index entries that use them. Note that this menu option becomes Page Reference Options if you have selected a specific entry's page number in the Index panel. And if the Topics radio button is selected in the Index panel, the Topic Options menu is renamed simply Options.

- **Capitalize:** This option lets you standardize the capitalization of topic entries — you can choose Selected Topic, Selected Topic and All Subtopics, All Level 1 Topics, and All Topics.

- **Update Preview:** This option updates the index entries in the Index panel to reflect page-number changes, new occurrences of index text occurrences, and deleted occurrences of indexed text. It does not change the actual index.

- **Generate Index:** This creates the actual index in your document, via the dialog box shown in Figure 23.7. Here, you specify the following: the title for the index; the paragraph style for that title; whether a selected index is replaced with the new one; whether an entire book is indexed; whether layers on hidden layers are indexed; whether the index is nested or run-in (see the sidebar "Nested or Run-in Index?" earlier in the chapter); whether empty index headings and sections are included; what paragraph styles are applied to each level of index entry and what character styles are applied to different portions of index entries; and, finally, the characters used as separators within index entries. (Click More Options to see the nested/run-in and later options.) After you generate an index, you get the standard InDesign loaded-text pointer (the paragraph icon). Click an existing text frame into which you want to flow the index, or click anywhere in a document to have InDesign create the text frame for you and flow the index text into it.

> **TIP**   Each time you edit text in a document or book chapter, it's a good idea to rebuild the index so that the page numbers in it are updated. There is no dynamic link between a flowed and formatted index and the index markers in text.

- **Sort Options:** This lets you determine which alphabets — such as Roman, Cyrillic, and Greek — should be indexed and in what order they should appear in your index. This is quite handy for documents that use multiple alphabets. (Without this option, entries using foreign alphabets were grouped into the Symbols category in the index.)

- **Show Find Field:** This lets you find text within the entries and topics in the Index panel — it adds a Find field and ↓ (Search Forward) and ↑ (Search Backward) iconic buttons to the Index panel.

- **Show Unused Topics:** This highlights topics for which there are no index entries, so you can easily delete them.

> **NOTE**   For documents that contain foreign alphabets that you nonetheless want indexed all in one alphabet (such as Roman), be sure to use the desired alphabet's transliteration for the foreign term's entry in the index's topic list. For example, if your text uses the Greek letters for a fraternity name, such as ΦΓΔ, you would enter Phi Gamma Delta as the index entry.

Incorporating Indexing into a Workflow

If you're working on a document by yourself, or you're creating a fairly simple index in a workgroup, you can pretty much index as you go. Or you can plan some time at the end of the editorial cycle to go through a document or chapters to index them.

But if your publication requires professional indexing — as would be the case for the multilevel index of a long book such as this one — deciding when to send your original InDesign files out for indexing is difficult. You might do it one chapter at a time, right after editorial approval and right before the file goes to production. Or you might send each chapter out for indexing before the last round of edits.

What you can't do is continue working on one copy of your InDesign documents while another copy is being indexed. There is no way to move the index tags to another file.

If you're on a tight schedule, you may be tempted to move your InDesign documents into production while another copy of your files is indexed. You then generate the index, send that file to production, and then send the whole thing to print. The index is trapped in InDesign documents that aren't final — which is unfortunate because the next time you edit the document, you would like to have the index tags in it. If you have to work this way, you need to decide whether to re-index the publication or redo the production work.

FIGURE 23.7

The Generate Index dialog box, with all options displayed

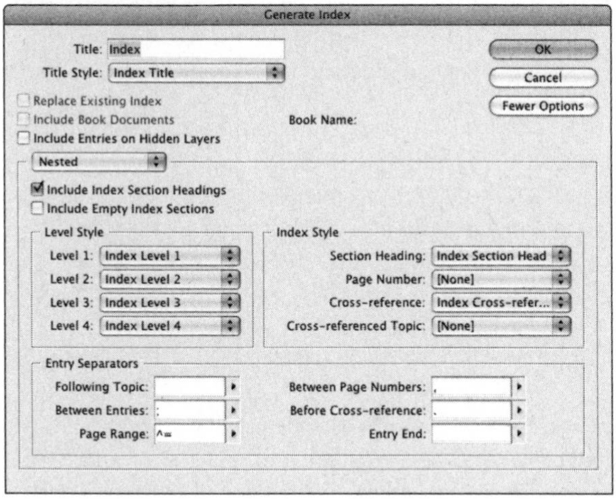

Creating Tables of Contents

Long documents such as books and catalogs lend themselves to tables of contents (TOC) to give the reader a summary of the content and the locations for each section. In InDesign, a TOC is simply a list of paragraphs that are formatted with the same styles. After you create a book (or even a single document), InDesign can build a TOC by scanning the chapters for the paragraph styles you specify. For example, if you create a book, you might have paragraph styles named Chapter Title, Section, and Subsection that you apply to chapter titles, chapter sections, and chapter subsections. Using the Table of Contents feature, InDesign can generate a TOC that has all three levels.

If you want to use the Table of Contents feature, you have to use styles. Not only do styles guarantee consistent formatting, but they also tell InDesign what text you want to include in your TOC. The other thing to keep in mind for TOCs: They are linear, either listing from top to bottom the text in the order it appears in a document or in alphabetical order.

CROSS-REF   TOCs rely on paragraph styles. For more on styles, see Chapter 19.

Planning a TOC

Before you start whipping up a TOC in InDesign, decide what the content of your TOC will be: Is all the text tagged with Head and Subhead paragraph styles? (Be sure you apply styles consistently to generate an accurate TOC, so if you're not sure about that, look through the documents or chapters.)

You also need to create paragraph styles for the TOC itself. It's easy to forget that because TOCs usually have several levels themselves (a title, as well as formatting specific to each level of listing), and each level should usually have its own paragraph style. You likely also need some character styles for your TOC; for example, you might want the page numbers to be bold, in which case you'd need a character style that applies boldface to them.

After you decide what goes in your TOC, use a little bit of dummy text to format a sample TOC before you create the styles that will format the TOC itself. Your formatting should include any indents for different levels in your list and should include tabs and fill characters as necessary. When you're satisfied with the formatting of your sample TOC, create the TOC paragraph and character styles from it. Be sure to use clear names such as TOC-Level 1.

Defining a TOC

InDesign uses TOC styles to manage the formatting of TOCs. A TOC style defines the text you want in a TOC, in what order it appears, how page numbers are added, and how the various TOC elements are formatted. To create a TOC style, you choose the Layout ➪ Table of Contents Styles, which opens Table of Contents Styles dialog box.

Creating Other Lists

Although InDesign calls its list-generation feature the Table of Contents feature, you can use it for other kinds of lists. Basically, anything that is tagged with a paragraph style can be used to create a list. For example, if your captions all have titles that use their own paragraph style, you can generate a list of figures by creating a TOC style that includes just, say, the Caption Title paragraph style. An InDesign document can have more than one TOC, so you can have multiple lists in your document.

What InDesign cannot do is create a list based on *character* styles, so you can't create a list based on, say, names in a gossip column where the names use a character style to make them bold and perhaps change font as well. Nor can you create a list based on caption titles that are part of a paragraph also containing the caption; if you try to do so, your list will include the complete text of the captions as well as the embedded title.

But you may have to create your lists this way, getting the entire paragraph of, say, a caption, using the TOC feature to gather all those captions into a TOC-built list, and then removing all the text that you don't need. That still saves you time and gives you a better shot at having a complete list than finding and entering all that text manually.

In the Table of Contents Styles dialog box, click New to create a new TOC style. You can also edit an existing style by clicking Edit, delete one by clicking Delete, and import one from another InDesign document by clicking Load.

Here's how to create a TOC style after clicking New and getting the dialog box shown in Figure 23.8 (be sure to click More Options to see everything in the figure):

1. **Type a name for the TOC style in the TOC Style field.** The default is TOC Style 1.

2. **In the Title field, type a heading for the TOC.** This is the actual text that will appear in your TOC.

3. **Use the Style pop-up menu to its right to choose the paragraph style that this title will have.** If you don't want a title, leave the Title field blank, but note that you still get an empty paragraph at the top of your TOC for this title. You can always delete that paragraph.

4. **In the Styles in Table of Contents section of the dialog box, click a paragraph style from the Other Styles list on the right that you want to appear in your TOC.** For example, you might click Chapter Title in a book. Click <<Add to add it to the Include Paragraph Styles list at left. (Click Remove>> to remove any paragraph styles you don't want to be used in the TOC generation.)

FIGURE 23.8

The New Table of Contents Style dialog box

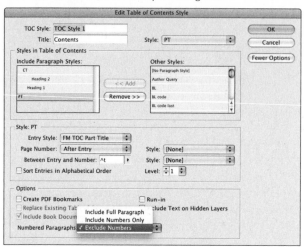

5. **Now choose the formatting for the TOC entries that come from the selected paragraph style, using the Style section of the dialog box.** Here's where you apply the formatting to the text that appears in the TOC:

   ■ Use the Entry Style pop-up menu to select the paragraph style for the current TOC level.

   ■ Use the Page Number pop-up menu to determine how page numbers are handled: After Entry, Before Entry, and No Page Number. (You might use this last option for alphabetically arranged categories in a catalog, where you want to list page numbers only for product classes and specific products.) If you want the page numbers to have a character style applied, choose that style from the Style pop-up menu to the right of the Page Number pop-up menu. Use the Between Entry and Number field and pop-up menu to choose what appears between the TOC text and the page number. You can type any characters you want, as well as have multiple characters; use the pop-up menu to select special characters such as bullets and tabs. In most cases, you would select a tab; the paragraph style selected earlier for the TOC entry would include leader information, such as having a series of periods between the text and the number. You can also apply a character style to the characters between the text and the page numbers through the Style pop-up menu at right.

   If the Entry Style, Page Number, and other options don't appear, click More Options to see them.

■ If you want the entries at this level to be sorted alphabetically, such as for a list of companies in a magazine article, select the Sort Entries in Alphabetical Order option.

TIP   Before having InDesign generate the TOC (described later in this chapter), you can change the alphabetization order by changing the Language option in the Character panel's flyout menu when no text or text frame is selected. The TOC will then take on the chosen language's rules for alphabetizing.

■ If you want to change the level of the current TOC entry, use the Level pop-up menu. Note that you do not have to manually rearrange the order of items in the Include Paragraph Styles list by clicking and dragging them if you change the level of entries — InDesign correctly sorts them when it creates the TOC, even if the levels seem out of order in the Include Paragraph Styles list.

■ Choose the appropriate options from the Options section of the dialog box. Select the Create PDF Bookmarks option if you're exporting the document as a PDF file and want the file to have *bookmarks* (which is essentially a clickable set of TOC links). Select the Run-in option if you want all entries at the same level to be in one paragraph; this is not common for TOCs but is used in indexes and lists of figures. Select the Replace Existing Table of Contents option if you want InDesign to automatically replace an existing TOC if the TOC style is changed. Select the Include Text on Hidden Layers option if you want text on hidden layers to be included in the TOC. Finally, select the Include Book Documents option if you have a book open and want InDesign to generate a TOC based on all chapters in that book. (InDesign shows the current open book's name.) You can control how numbered paragraphs are treated in the TOC by choosing an option from the Numbered Paragraph pop-up menu: Include Full Paragraph, Include Numbers Only, and Exclude Numbers.

6. **Continue this process for each paragraph style whose text should be in the TOC, such as Section and Subsection in a book.** Note that the order in which you add these styles determines the initial levels: The first paragraph style added is level 1, the second is level 2, and so on. But you can change the order by changing the Level setting, as I describe earlier.

After you define a Table of Contents style, you can go to the Edit TOC Style dialog box — it's identical to the New Table of Contents Styles dialog box — and make any changes. Just choose Layout ➪ Table of Contents Styles, select the TOC style to edit, and click Edit.

With a TOC style in place and your document properly formatted with the paragraph styles that the TOC style looks for when generating a TOC, you're ready to have InDesign create the actual TOC for you. But before you do this, make sure you've saved space in the document for the TOC. This could consist of a single text frame or a series of linked text frames, or simply an empty page or set of pages (depending on how long your TOC is). When you're creating a TOC for a book, it might be useful to flow it into its own chapter.

To generate a TOC, choose Layout ➪ Table of Contents. A dialog box appears that is identical to the New Table of Contents Style dialog box, shown previously in Figure 23.8. If desired, you can make changes to the TOC style settings. (If you want to save those changes for future TOCs generated by the TOC style, be sure to click Save Style.) Then click OK to have InDesign generate the TOC. You may also get a dialog box asking whether you want to include items in *overset text* (text that didn't fit in your document after you placed it); click Yes or No as appropriate. It may take a minute or two for the program to generate the TOC. If you've selected a text frame (with or without text in it), InDesign places the TOC text in it. If no text frame is selected, InDesign displays the familiar text-insertion icon (the paragraph pointer) that it displays when you place a text file. Either click a text frame to insert the TOC text in that frame or click your document to have InDesign create a text frame in which to flow the TOC text.

You might need to generate a TOC just to see how long it really is and then make the necessary space available in your document. If your TOC has its own set of page numbers, such as using Roman numerals in a separate section (as this book does), this is not an issue. But if the TOC's page numbers affect the numbering for the pages that follow, it's imperative that you generate a TOC and add the necessary pages, and then generate the TOC again. Otherwise, if you have to add or delete pages based on the TOC length, the TOC will have the old page numbers, not the current ones. If you do need to update page numbering after flowing a TOC, simply rebuild the TOC by selecting the text frame holding the TOC and then choosing Layout ➪ Update Table of Contents. (Doing so skips the Table of Contents dialog box.)

NOTE If you applied local formatting to the TOC after it was generated and then later regenerate that TOC for any reason, you may need to reapply that local formatting to the updated TOC.

Summary

InDesign's book, TOC, and indexing features can significantly streamline your efforts when using these features in all sorts of business documents.

InDesign supports footnotes, both those imported from Microsoft Word and those created in InDesign. You have several options to control the formatting of the footnote text and its placement in your document.

InDesign also provides the ability to index your document, and control the formatting of those indexes. Although most users can make use of the simpler features — such as adding a First Level entry that consists of text highlighted in the document — the more complicated your index, the more you may need a professional indexer, even if he or she does the work in InDesign. If you do need a professional, be sure your schedule allows time for the indexer to take possession of your InDesign files.

The Table of Contents feature makes it easy to generate TOCs, and you can also use it for some other kinds of lists, as long as you tag the source text with consistent paragraph styles.

Chapter 24

Creating Multidocument Projects

onger projects such as books, catalogs, and magazines often consist of multiple InDesign documents, so multiple users can work on different pieces of the project simultaneously. Breaking up these projects into several documents also results in smaller, more manageable documents. If you're working on this type of document, by yourself or in a workgroup, InDesign provides the book feature for managing the document files, updating page numbers across documents, and ensuring consistency in the book.

In InDesign, a *book* is a special type of file that you create to track multiple documents for yourself or for a workgroup. A book file displays as a panel, and it lists each InDesign document — let's call them *chapters* to distinguish them from stand-alone documents — that you add to the book. Using these book panels, you can add, open and edit, rearrange, and print chapters of the book.

CROSS-REF Books are a natural venue for using the index and table of contents (TOC) features, given you can create a unified index or TOC across all chapters within a book in one fell swoop. Chapter 23 covers how to create indexes and TOCs. Books are also a natural way to contain files in a workgroup environment. See Chapter 34 for more details on workgroup workflow techniques.

IN THIS CHAPTER

Planning your multiple-document book project

Creating and opening books

Adding chapters to books

Managing style sources across chapters

Controlling page numbering, section variables, and chapter numbering

Printing and exporting books

Planning Your Book

Be sure to do some planning before you even create a book so that you use the feature efficiently and effectively. I recommend you do the following before you begin building your book in InDesign:

- Organize your chapters in advance by deciding on the number, names, and order of the chapters. You can make changes to a chapter's number, name, and order at any time, but figuring out these basics ahead of time will save you time in the long run.

- Make decisions about the format of the book (styles, swatches, pagination style, and so on) at the chapter level, beginning with the first chapter.

- Pay attention to formatting. Formatting is important because if your chapters use different color swatch names, style names, and so on, synchronizing the formatting across the chapters will be difficult.

- Use templates and styles to format the chapters uniformly.

- Decide where to store the book file itself (this must be a shared server for a workgroup) and store the documents in this folder as well. Set up the appropriate sharing through your operating system.

- Make sure members of the workgroup have access to any templates, libraries, graphics, fonts, plug-ins, and so on that are necessary to work on the project.

Creating and Opening Books

To create a new book, choose File ➪ New ➪ Book. The New Book dialog box lets you specify a location for the book and give it a name — it works just like the familiar Save As and Export dialog boxes. If you're on a Mac and creating a book that may be used in Windows, you'll notice that InDesign automatically adds the .indb extension to the filename. Click OK to create and open the book.

To open an existing book, choose File ➪ Open command or press ⌘+O or Ctrl+O. Each book appears in its own panel. If several books are open, the panels are contained in a free-floating panel group.

If you're opening a book from a shared server, make sure to mount the server on your desktop first. You can also double-click a book's icon, which also shows the open book's panel. To close a book's panel, and any book documents that are in it, simply click its Close box.

TIP Multiple users on the same platform (Mac or Windows) — but not users from multiple platforms — can open the same book panel at the same time. If another user makes changes to the book, those changes appear in your copy of the book when you click the panel.

TIP You can add several documents at one time. If they are in the same folder, just click the first document and Shift+click the last to select all documents between them, or ⌘+click or Ctrl+click the individual documents if they are not listed contiguously.

Adding chapters to books

New book panes are empty — you need to add your carefully prepared documents to them. To do this, click the Add Document iconic button (the + icon on the bottom right of your book's panel) shown in Figure 24.1, or choose the Add Document menu option in the book panel's flyout menu. Either way, Use the Add Documents dialog box to locate and select the first document — or "chapter" — you want to add. Click the Open button to make this the first chapter in the book. Repeat this process to add to the book all the chapters you have ready. (You can also add more later.)

Opening and editing chapters

To work on a chapter in a book, first open the book. Then double-click the chapter name in the book's panel. The chapter opens in InDesign the same way any other InDesign document opens. Note that to open a chapter, it must be available, as I discuss in the next section. When you finish editing a chapter, save and close it as usual. (Any open chapter documents will remain open in InDesign even if you close the book's panel.)

If you need to take a chapter home and work on it, you can edit a chapter outside the book. To do this, first move (not copy) the chapter's file to a different folder or disk so that the chapter displays as Missing in the book panel. Doing so keeps other users from editing it while you have it. When you finish editing the file, move the edited file back in its original location. The book panel shows this chapter as Modified. (To move a file across disks on the Mac, hold ⌘ when dragging it to its new location; in Windows, hold Shift.)

You can replace an existing chapter with another document by selecting the chapter in the book panel and then choosing Replace Document from the flyout menu. Navigate to a new document, select it, and click the Open button. InDesign replaces the selected chapter with the new document.

You can delete chapters from a book by choosing Remove Document from the flyout menu or by clicking the Remove Document iconic button (the – icon) from the bottom of the panel.

Finally, there are three other menu options in the flyout menu that come in handy for managing the book: You can save books by choosing Save Book, save to a new name by choosing Save Book As, and close the book by choosing Close Book. (Any changes to the book are not saved, although you get a warning box giving you the chance to save any unsaved books.)

Saving a book is separate from saving a document in a book. Any changes made to an open document are saved only if you save that document. But any changes you make through the book panel's flyout menu, such as synchronizing styles (covered in the next section), are automatically saved in the affected documents.

FIGURE 24.1

A book panel and its flyout menu. The icon to the left of a chapter's filename indicates the style source. The status column shows which chapters are open on your computer, which are in use by others, which are available to be opened, and which are missing.

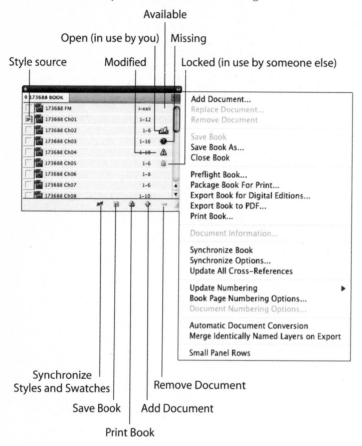

If the Automatic Document Conversion menu option is selected in the book panel's flyout menu, InDesign converts all chapters created in earlier versions of InDesign to the InDesign CS4 format. Otherwise, if this menu option is not selected, InDesign will ask you to save any previous-version chapters to new InDesign CS4-format files with new names, leaving the originals untouched, whenever you first synchronize chapters or update page numbering for the book.

Understanding a book panel's status reports

If you're using a book panel in a workgroup, it provides helpful status reports about each chapter, as shown in Figure 24.1. The statuses include:

- **Available:** The chapter can be opened, edited, or printed. Only one user at a time can open a chapter.

- **Open:** You have the chapter open and can edit it or print it. Nobody else can open the chapter at this time.

- **Locked:** Another user has the chapter open. In this case, you cannot edit or open the chapter.

- **Modified:** The chapter has been changed since the last time you opened the book panel. Simply click the book panel to update it.

- **Missing:** The chapter's file has been moved, renamed, or deleted since it was added to the book. Double-click the chapter name to open a Find File dialog box and locate it.

There's also the Document Information menu option in a book panel's flyout menu. When you select a chapter and choose this option, InDesign shows you the file's modification date, location, and page range, as well as lets you replace it with a different document.

Working with Style Sources

The first chapter you add to the book is, by default, the style source, as indicated by the icon to the left of its filename. If the chapters of your book don't share common formatting, you don't need to worry about this feature. But with a book, that's rarely the case — usually you want the styles, swatches, and so on to remain the same. The style source in an InDesign book defines the styles and swatches that are common to all the chapters in the book. When you use the Synchronize feature, discussed in the next section, InDesign makes sure that the paragraph styles, character styles, object styles, table styles, cell styles, trap presets, TOC styles, master pages, numbered lists, text variables, and swatches in each chapter in the book match those in the style source.

NEW FEATURE InDesign CS4 adds the ability to synchronize conditional text definitions and cross-reference formats, both of which are new capabilities in InDesign CS4 and covered in Chapter 22. Also new is the ability to update cross-references throughout a book, using the Update All Cross-References option in a book panel's flyout menu.

If you decide to make a different chapter the style source, all you need to do is click in the column to the left of that chapter's filename. This moves the icon indicating the style source to that chapter (refer to Figure 24.1).

To help you make sure that common formatting remains consistent across the document, the book panel provides a Synchronize Styles and Swatches iconic button, as well as a Synchronize Selected Documents or Synchronize Book menu item (based on whether documents are selected in the book panel) in the flyout menu. Follow these steps to synchronize:

1. **Be sure you're satisfied with the styles in the style source and that all chapters are available for editing.**

2. Choose the style source (the document whose styles you want to be used everywhere) by clicking the box to the left of the source chapter so that the style-source icon appears.

3. **Choose Synchronize Options from the book panel's flyout menu, which opens the dialog box shown in Figure 24.2.** Make sure every type of item you want synchronized — Object Styles, TOC Style, Character Styles, Paragraph Styles, Trap Presets, Swatches, Master Pages, and so on — is selected.

NEW FEATURE New to InDesign CS4 is the ability to compare style groups across documents and figure out which contain the same styles so that the style groups are also kept consistent. To enable this feature, be sure the Smart Match Style Groups check box is selected in the Synchronize Options dialog box.

FIGURE 24.2

The Synchronize Options dialog box

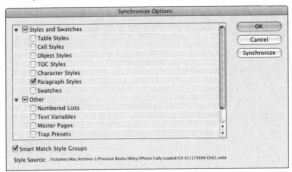

4. **Select the chapters you want to synchronize and click Synchronize Styles and Swatches or choose Synchronize Selected Documents from the flyout menu.** If no chapters are selected, InDesign assumes you want to synchronize all chapters; you'll see the Synchronize Book menu option in the flyout menu rather than Synchronize Selected Documents menu option in that case.

5. **Now compare the styles (character, paragraph, object, table, cell, and TOC), swatches (color, tint, and gradient), trap presets, master pages, and so on in the style source to those in each chapter.** If anything is different, the information in each chapter is updated to match the style source. This means that if someone changes the typeface in a style in a chapter, it reverts to the typeface specified in the style source. If anything is missing from a chapter — for example, if you just added a swatch to the style source but not to other chapters — that information is added to each chapter.

By using the synchronization feature, each chapter has the same basic set of styles and swatches as the style source. I say "basic set" because you can still add more of these specifications to each chapter. When using the synchronization feature, you need to keep in mind the following:

- Synchronizing will *not* remove unique paragraph styles, character styles, object styles, TOC styles, swatches, trap presets, and so on from your chapters — as long as their names don't match those in the style-source document, of course. Therefore, you can implement special formatting needs in a chapter by creating unique styles in that chapter.

- Synchronizing cannot solve any problems related to using the template or styles incorrectly, or change any local formatting applied to text (such as font changes or italic) or local changes to master page items.

Clearly, synchronizing is no cure-all for the renegade formatting that often occurs when multiple users work on the same project. Be sure everyone knows what the standards are for the design, how to implement the standards properly, and how to make local changes appropriately.

Working with Page Numbers and Sections

A key reason to use the book feature is to let InDesign handle the page numbering within your book's chapters and sections, for folios, cross-references, index entries, and tables of contents.

When working with books, you have two choices for numbering pages: You can let the book panel number pages consecutively from one chapter to the next or you can add sections of page numbers, which carry through the book until you start a new section. In long documents, section page numbering is common because it lets you have page numbering such as 2.1–2.14 in, say, Chapter 2. (Plus, as Chapter 5 explains, creating a section start is the only way to start a document on a left-facing page, which is often necessary in magazines.)

Numbering pages consecutively

If the chapters you add to a book have no sections in them, you end up with consecutive page numbering: The first page number of each chapter follows the last page number of the previous chapter (so if one chapter ends on page 16, the next chapter starts on page 17). When working in a chapter, if you open the Section dialog box (choose Numbering & Section Options in the Pages panel's flyout menu), you see that Automatic Page Numbering is selected by default.

The consecutive page numbering works as follows:

- Whenever you add a chapter with no sections to a book, InDesign numbers pages consecutively throughout the book.

- As you add and delete pages from chapters, the page numbers are also updated.

- You can force repagination by choosing Update Numbering from the book panel's flyout menu.

- You control the page numbering using the Book Page Numbering Options dialog box (choose Book Page Numbering Options from the book panel's flyout menu), shown in Figure 24.3. You can have the numbering pick up after the previous chapter's page number, skip to the odd page number that would follow the previous chapter's page number, or skip to the even page number that would follow the previous chapter's page number. These last two options are meant when you have chapters that always start on a right or left page (respectively) no matter where the previous chapter's last page falls. (You can also have InDesign automatically add a blank page as needed in these cases.) In this dialog box, you also can tell InDesign to update all page and section numbers for you to reflect any changes to the book's chapters, by selecting the Automatically Update Page & Section Numbers option.

FIGURE 24.3

The Book Page Numbering Options dialog box

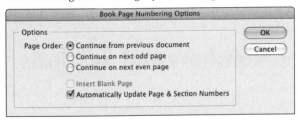

InDesign lists chapters alphabetically by filename in a book panel, so if your chapters don't have section starts, the automatic page numbering may not follow your desired chapter order. To fix this, click and drag the chapters within the book pane to the desired location in the pane so that the first chapter is in the top position, the next chapter is in the second position, and so on.

Numbering pages with sections

If any chapters you add to books already contain sections of page numbers (implemented through the Section dialog box, which you access via the Numbering & Section Options menu option in the Pages panel's flyout menu), the section page numbering overrides the book's consecutive page numbering.

The section page numbering carries through chapters of the book until InDesign encounters a new section start. So if one chapter ends on page *iv*, the next page starts on page *v* unless you start a new section. Note that it's fairly typical in magazines to assign the page number in each article's document file because there are usually ads between articles that are inserted later in the printing process.

 Using the options in the Section dialog box is covered in Chapter 5.

Sometimes, having InDesign automatically update page and section numbering is a real pain, as you must wait for it to grind through all the chapters when you, for example, add or update a chapter near the beginning of the book's chapter list. In that case, deselect the Automatically Update Page & Section Numbers in the Book Page Numbering Options dialog box, accessible from the book panel's flyout menu.

When it is time to repaginate the book, choose Update Numbering from the panel's flyout menu and then choose the appropriate option from its submenu: Update Page & Section Numbers, Update Chapter & Paragraph Numbers, or Update All Numbers. Also be sure to update all the cross-references in your book by choosing Update All Cross-References from the flyout menu.

 **CROSS-REF** Paragraph numbers refers to the new numbered lists capability described in Chapter 18. Section numbers are covered in Chapter 5. Chapter 22 covers cross-references.

Specifying chapter numbers

You can see and modify any chapter's page numbering settings by selecting the chapter in the book panel and then choosing Document Numbering Options from the flyout menu. Figure 24.4 shows the dialog box. The top half of the dialog box is the same as the Pages panel's Section dialog box, and the bottom half — the Document Chapter Numbering area — lets you control the chapter numbering style and the chapter number itself.

You can force a chapter to have a specific number by selecting the Chapter Number option, have the chapter use the same chapter number as the previous document (such as when you break a chapter into two documents), and have InDesign automatically number the current document by incrementing from the previous document's chapter number.

CROSS-REF The chapter number defined here — whether manually overridden or automatically adjusted — is what the Chapter Number text variable uses, as explained in Chapter 22.

FIGURE 24.4

The Document Numbering Options dialog box

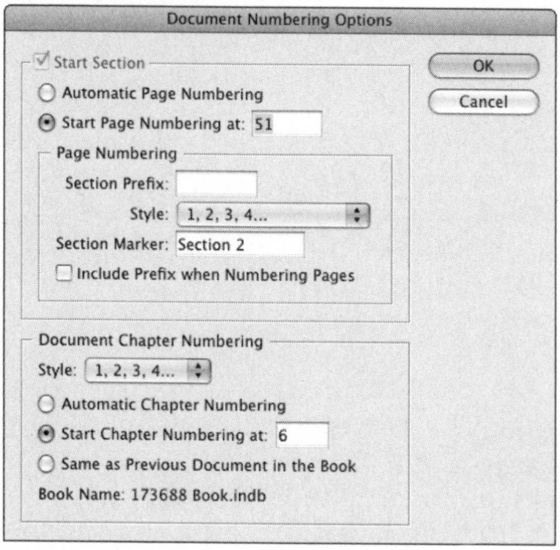

> **Document Numbering Options**
>
> ☑ Start Section
> ○ Automatic Page Numbering
> ● Start Page Numbering at: 51
>   Page Numbering
>   Section Prefix: [   ]
>   Style: 1, 2, 3, 4...
>   Section Marker: Section 2
>   ☐ Include Prefix when Numbering Pages
>
> Document Chapter Numbering
> Style: 1, 2, 3, 4...
> ○ Automatic Chapter Numbering
> ● Start Chapter Numbering at: 6
> ○ Same as Previous Document in the Book
> Book Name: 173688 Book.indb
>
> OK
> Cancel

Printing Chapters and Books

If you want to print multiple chapters in the book with the same settings, you can print through the book panel. You can print any chapters with the status of Available or Open. Here's how:

1. **To print the entire book, make sure no chapters are selected.** To print a continuous range of chapters, Shift+click them. To print noncontiguous chapters, ⌘+click or Ctrl+click the chapters to select them.

2. **Click the Print Book iconic button or choose Print Book or Print Selected Documents in the book panel's flyout menu (the option displayed depends on whether chapters are selected in the book panel).** The standard InDesign Print dialog box opens. Note that the option to choose all pages or a range of pages is grayed out — you must print all chapters in the selected chapters.

3. **Make any adjustments in the Print dialog box.**

4. **Click Print to print the chapters.**

A related set of features includes the capability to output a book to PDF, using the Export Book to PDF or Export Selected Documents to PDF menu options in the flyout menu. They work the same as their equivalent Print menu options. You can also preflight a book or selected chapters and package a book or selected chapters for a service bureau. The Preflight Book/Preflight Selected Documents menu options in the book panel work the same as their equivalent menu options in the File menu.

> **NOTE** If the Merge Identically Named Layers on Export option in the book panel's flyout menu is selected, InDesign unifies layers with the same name into one layer for exported PDF files generated from multiple documents in the same book, rather than create separate layers for each chapter's layer.

> **CROSS-REF** For more on preflighting, packaging, printing, and output settings, see Part VII.

Summary

InDesign lets you control how page numbering, chapter numbering, and section numbering are handled and updated across multiple documents that comprise a book via the book panel's flyout menu. It also lets you control which chapters are printed or exported to PDF.

Part VI

Graphics Fundamentals

Chapter 25

Importing Graphics

You can import graphics of all sorts into your InDesign documents several ways. InDesign is particularly adept at importing graphics created in popular Macintosh and Windows formats. And through the Mac and Windows Clipboards (copy and paste), you can import file formats — to a limited degree — that InDesign doesn't directly support.

Because InDesign has some built-in graphics features, as I describe in Chapters 26 and 27, you may be tempted to use InDesign as your graphics program. Don't. Its tools are fine for some work, such as creating shapes that text wraps around, borders, and gradations of color — but InDesign is not meant to be a professional graphics-creation tool. In fact, it's designed to work closely with such professional tools, especially Adobe's Illustrator and Photoshop.

Particularly for bitmap images such as scanned files and photographs, InDesign has few capabilities to apply special effects or otherwise manipulate the image's content, so you should do as much work as possible in your image editor before importing the file into InDesign. For example, you can resize, crop, rotate, and slant an imported image in InDesign, but you can't convert it from a full-color image into a duotone or change its line screen or brightness and contrast.

The bottom line is this: Use your graphics program for creating and editing original images and photos. Use InDesign's graphics features to embellish your layout, rather than create original artwork.

InDesign lets you easily open a graphics program to edit placed images from within InDesign. You can select the image and choose Edit ➪ Edit Original, or you can press and hold Option or Alt and then double-click the image. InDesign launches the program that created the graphic; if you don't own

593

that program, InDesign launches a compatible program if you have one. For example, if you Option+double-click or Alt+double-click an Encapsulated PostScript (EPS) file in your layout that was created in Adobe Illustrator, but you use CorelDraw instead, InDesign launches CorelDraw on your system.

NEW FEATURE InDesign CS4 lets you specify what program you want to edit a graphic in — not have InDesign choose for you — by selecting the graphic and then choosing Edit ⇨ Edit With. The submenu that appears will list all the programs that InDesign thinks can edit the graphic. Pick one or choose Other to browse your computer for a different application.

CROSS-REF Transformations such as resizing, flipping, rotating, and skewing that you're likely to apply to imported graphics use the same tools as for any InDesign objects, so I cover all these transformations in one place: Chapter 10. I cover the effects that you can apply to any object, including graphics, in Chapter 11.

Preparing Graphics Files

InDesign offers support for many major formats of graphics files. Some formats are more appropriate than others for certain kinds of tasks. The basic rules for creating your graphics files are as follows:

- **Save line art in a format such as EPS, PDF, Adobe Illustrator, Windows Metafile (WMF), Enhanced Metafile (EMF), or PICT.** (These object-oriented formats are called *vector* formats. Vector files are composed of instructions on how to draw various shapes.) InDesign works best with EPS, PDF, and Illustrator files.

- **Save bitmaps (photos and scans) in a format such as TIFF, Adobe Photoshop, PNG, JPEG, PCX, Windows Bitmap (BMP), GIF, Scitex Continuous Tone (SCT), or PICT.** (These pixel-oriented formats are called *bitmap* or *raster* formats. They are composed of a series of dots, or pixels, that make up the image.) InDesign works best with TIFF and Photoshop files.

Note that PICT files can be in vector or bitmap format depending on the original image and the program in which it was created or exported from. If you enlarge a PICT image and it begins to look blocky, it's a bitmap. Similarly, EPS and PDF files can contain bitmap images as well as vector ones.

InDesign can import InDesign files as if they were graphics; when importing a multipage document, you choose the page you want to import, as you can with PDF files. Note that InDesign files imported as graphics cannot be edited directly in the InDesign layout they were placed in; you must update the original file instead in a separate window.

I suggest that you make EPS and TIFF formats your standards because these have become the standard graphics formats in publishing. If you and your service bureau work almost exclusively with Adobe software, you can add the PDF, Illustrator, and Photoshop formats to this mix. (The Illustrator and PDF formats are variants of EPS.) If you use transparency in your graphics, it's best to save them in Photoshop, Illustrator, or PDF formats because other formats (particularly EPS and TIFF) remove much of the transparency layering data that will help an imagesetter optimally reproduce those transparent files.

Graphics embedded in text files

Modern word processors typically support inline graphics, letting you import a graphic into your word processor document and embed it in text. Word, for example, lets you import graphics, and InDesign, in turn, can import the graphics with your text. But graphics embedded in your word-processor document though Mac OS 8 and 9's Publish and Subscribe or Windows' OLE do not import into InDesign. These technologies are rarely used today, so you'll encounter this issue only with old images.

Inline graphics import exactly as their preview images, not as the original formats. This means that in most cases, you get a much lower-resolution version in your InDesign layout. Despite their limitations, using inline graphics in your word processor can be helpful when you're putting together an InDesign document: Use the inline graphics whose previews are imported into InDesign as placeholders so that the layout artist knows you have embedded graphics. The artist can then replace the previews with the better-quality originals.

> **TIP** If you find yourself using several graphics as characters (such as a company icon used as a bullet), use a font-creation program such as FontLab Studio or FontLab Fontographer to create a symbol typeface with those graphics. Then both your word processor and layout documents can use the same high-quality versions. Go to `www.InDesignCentral.com` for links to these programs.

InDesign imports many file formats. If your graphics program's format is not one of the ones listed here, chances are it can save as or export to one. In the following list, the text in monofont and parentheses is the filename extension common for these files on PCs.

The file formats InDesign imports include:

- **BMP:** The native Windows bitmap format (`.bmp`, `.dib`).

- **EPS:** The Encapsulated PostScript file format favored by professional publishers. A variant is called DCS, a color-separated variant whose full name is Desktop Color Separation (`.eps`, `.dcs`).

- **Flash animation:** For use in interactive documents, InDesign supports this Adobe-owned, cross-platform format (`.swf`). Chapter 32 covers the use of multimedia elements in more detail.

- **GIF:** The Graphics Interchange Format common in Web documents (`.gif`).

- **JPEG:** The Joint Photographic Expert Group compressed bitmap format often used on the Web (`.jpg` or `.jpeg`).

- **Illustrator:** The native format in Adobe Illustrator 5.5 through CS4 is similar to EPS (`.ai`).

- **PCX:** The PC Paintbrush format that was very popular in DOS programs and early version of Windows; other formats have now largely supplanted it (`.pcx`, `.rle`).

- **PDF:** The Portable Document Format that is a variant of PostScript (as EPS is) and is used for Web-, network-, and CD-based documents. InDesign CS4 supports PDF versions 1.3 through 1.8 (the formats used in Acrobat 4 through 9) (`.pdf`).

- **Photoshop:** The native format in Adobe Photoshop 5.0 through CS4. (`.psd`) Note that InDesign cannot import the Photoshop Raw format (`.raw` files).

- **PICT:** Short for *Picture*, the Mac's native graphics format until Mac OS X (it can be bitmap or vector) that is little used in professional documents and is becoming rare even for inexpensive clip art (`.pct`).

- **PNG:** The Portable Network Graphics format introduced several years ago as a more capable alternative to GIF (`.png`).

- **QuickTime movie:** For use in interactive documents, InDesign supports this Apple-created, cross-platform format. (`.mov`) Chapter 32 covers the use of multimedia elements in more detail.

- **Scitex CT:** The continuous-tone bitmap format used on Scitex prepress systems (`.ct`).

- **TIFF:** The Tagged Image File Format that is the bitmap standard for professional image editors and publishers (`.tif` or `.tiff`).

- **Windows Metafile:** The format native to Windows but little used in professional documents. Since Office 2000, Microsoft applications create a new version called Enhanced Metafile (`.wmf`, `.emf`).

NOTE   Spot colors (called *spot inks* in Photoshop) are imported into InDesign when you place Photoshop, Illustrator, and PDF images into InDesign, as well as for InDesign documents imported as graphics. They appear in the Swatches panel, which I cover in Chapter 7.

InDesign does not support a few somewhat popular formats: AutoCAD Document Exchange Format (DXF), Computer Graphics Metafile (CGM), CorelDraw, Eastman Kodak's Photo CD, and Scalable Vector Graphics (SVG). DXF and CGM are vector formats used mainly in engineering and architecture, CorelDraw is the native format of the leading consumer-oriented Windows illustration program, Photo CD is a bitmap format meant for electronically distributed photographs, and SVG is a Web-oriented format for rich vector graphics.

CROSS-REF   InDesign can export JPEG, EPS, and PDF files. (Chapter 31 covers EPS and PDF export; Chapter 4 covers JPEG export.)

Issues with vector files

Vector images are complex because they can combine multiple elements — curves, lines, colors, fonts, bitmap images, and even other imported vector images. This means that you can unknowingly create a file that can cause problems when you try to output an InDesign layout file using it. Thus, when dealing with vector formats, you'll need to keep several issues in mind.

Embedded fonts

When you use fonts in text included in your graphics files, you usually have the option to convert the text to curves (graphics). This option ensures that your text prints on any printer. (If you don't use this conversion, make sure that your printer or service bureau has the fonts used in the graphic. Otherwise, the text does not print in the correct font; you likely get Courier or Helvetica instead.)

If your graphic has a lot of text, don't convert the text to curves — the image could get very complex and slow down printing. In this case, make sure that the output device has the same fonts as are in the graphic.

PostScript files: EPS, DCS, Illustrator, and PDF

PostScript-based files come in several varieties — EPS, DCS, Illustrator, and PDF — and because the format is a complex one, there are more issues to be aware of up front.

EPS

The usual hang-up with EPS files is the preview header. The preview is a displayable copy of the EPS file. Because EPS files are actually made up of a series of commands that tell the printer how to draw the image, what you see on-screen is not the actual graphic. Most programs create a preview image for EPS files, but many programs have trouble reading them, especially if the EPS file was generated on a different platform. In those cases, they display an X or a gray box in place of the image. (The EPS file prints properly to a PostScript printer.) That's why InDesign creates its own preview image when you import EPS files, lessening the chances of your seeing just an X or a gray box in place of the EPS preview.

When you import EPS files, InDesign lets you control some settings if you select Show Import Options in the Place dialog box, as covered later in this chapter. You can apply Photoshop clipping paths in the file (see Chapter 26), choose the preview format, convert the PostScript vector information into a bitmap (a process called *rasterization*), or embed links to OPI high-resolution source images (see Chapter 30 for details on OPI).

> **TIP** In CorelDraw 6.0 and later, and in Adobe Illustrator 6.0 and later, be sure to set the EPS creation options to have no preview header. This keeps your files smaller. (In CorelDraw, export to EPS. In Illustrator 6.0 and later, save as Illustrator EPS. Note that Illustrator 5.x's native format is EPS, so don't look for an export or save-as option.)

> **CAUTION** If you use transparency in your graphics, it's best to leave the files in Adobe Illustrator format rather than save them to EPS. Chapter 30 explains the issues in more depth.

DCS

The DCS variant of EPS is a set of five files: an EPS preview file that links together four separation files (one each for cyan, magenta, yellow, and black). Using this format ensures correct color separation when you output negatives for use in commercial printing. Service bureaus that do color correction often prefer these files over standard EPS files. One variation of the DCS file format, DCS 2.0, also supports spot color plates in addition to the standard plates for cyan, magenta, yellow, and black.

You should not use DCS files if you intend to create composite proof files or in-RIP separations from InDesign — InDesign will ignore the DCS separation files and just use the preview file for output. (RIP stands for raster-image processor.) Only use DCS files if you're outputting separations (but not in-RIP separations). Chapter 30 covers this in detail.

Illustrator

Adobe Illustrator files are very similar to EPS files except that they don't have a preview header and they better support transparency settings in graphics. There are no special concerns for Illustrator files; just be sure to note the font and color issues I mentioned previously in this section. As I describe later in this chapter, InDesign can differentiate layers in an Illustrator file, letting you decide which ones to display in your layout.

PDF

PDF files can contain all sorts of elements — text, graphics, sounds, hyperlinks, and movies — presented as one or more pages with the visual richness of a print document. When you import a PDF file, InDesign treats it as a graphic and can place one or more of the PDF file's pages (if it has more than one page) into your document as an uneditable graphic. You can crop, resize, and do other such manipulations common to any graphic, but you can't work with the text or other imported PDF file's components.

 Special PDF features, such as sounds, movies, hyperlinks, control buttons, and annotations, are ignored in the imported file.

Other vector formats

If you're outputting to negatives for professional printing, you should avoid non-PostScript vector formats. But they're fine for printing to inkjet and laser printers.

PICT

The standard Macintosh format for drawings, PICT also supports bitmaps and was the standard format for Mac OS 8 and 9 screen-capture utilities. InDesign imports PICT files with no difficulty, but it cannot color-separate them for output to negatives. Because fonts in vector PICT graphics are automatically translated to curves, you need not worry about whether fonts used in your graphics reside in your printer or are available at your service provider.

Windows Metafile

The standard Windows format for drawing, Windows Metafile is similar to PICT in that it can contain bitmap images as well as vector drawings. But InDesign will ignore bitmap information in Windows Metafiles, stripping it out during import. Microsoft Office 2000 introduced a new version of this format, called *Enhanced Metafile*, which InDesign also supports.

Issues with bitmap formats

Bitmap (also called *raster*) formats are simpler than vector formats because they're made up of rows of dots (*pixels*), not instructions on how to draw various shapes. But that doesn't mean that all bitmaps are alike.

Professional-level bitmap formats

Although InDesign supports a wide variety of bitmap formats, there is usually just one to worry about if you're producing professional documents for output on a printing press: TIFF. (You may also use the Scitex CT format if you're using Scitex output equipment to produce your negatives.) I suggest you convert other formats to TIFF using your image editor (Corel Photo-Paint and Adobe Photoshop, the two top image editors, import and export most formats, as do other modern image-editing programs) or a conversion program such as the Mac shareware program GraphicConverter, Equilibrium's DeBabelizer for Macintosh, the shareware program Advanced Batch Converter (for Windows), or DataViz's Conversions Plus (for Windows) and MacLinkPlus (for Macintosh).

CROSS-REF For links to graphics conversion tools, go to this book's companion Web site at www.InDesignCentral.com.

Photoshop

InDesign can import version 4.0 and later of this popular image editor's file format. When you place Photoshop files in InDesign, you can control how the alpha channel is imported — be sure to select Show Import Options in the Place dialog box to get this control. You also can apply any embedded clipping paths (see Chapter 26) and import or exclude any embedded color profile. As I describe later in this chapter, InDesign can differentiate layers in a Photoshop image, letting you decide which ones to display in your layout.

CROSS-REF The Photoshop format also supports transparency very well, which helps avoid later printing problems, as Chapter 30 explains.

Scitex CT

The continuous-tone Scitex CT format is used with Scitex output high-resolution devices and is usually produced by Scitex scanners. If you're using this format, you should be outputting to a Scitex system. Otherwise, you're not going to get the advantage of its high resolution.

TIFF

The most popular bitmap format for publishers is TIFF, developed by Aldus (later bought by Adobe Systems) and Microsoft. TIFF supports color up to 24 bits (16.7 million colors) in both RGB and CMYK models, and every major photo-editing program supports TIFF on both the Macintosh and in Windows. TIFF also supports grayscale and black-and-white files.

The biggest advantage to using TIFF files rather than other formats that also support color, such as PICT, is that InDesign is designed to take advantage of TIFF. For example, in an image editor, you can set clipping paths in a TIFF file, which act as a mask for the image. InDesign sees a path and uses it as the image boundary, making the area outside of it invisible. That in turn lets you have nonrectangular bitmap images in your layout — the clipping path becomes the visible boundary for your TIFF image. InDesign also supports embedded alpha channels and color profiles in TIFF files.

CAUTION TIFF files do not handle images with transparency well. Even though the files will look okay on-screen, they may not print well or may cause printer errors. It's best to stick with the Adobe Photoshop format if you use transparency.

TIFF files have several variations that InDesign supports. But because other programs aren't as forgiving, follow these guidelines to ensure smooth interaction:

- You should have no difficulty if you use uncompressed and LZW-compressed TIFF files supported by most Mac and Windows programs. InDesign even supports the less-used Zip compression method for TIFF files. You should be safe using LZW-compressed TIFF files with any mainstream program, but if you do have difficulty, I recommend that you use uncompressed TIFF files. Also, always talk to your service bureau about LZW support before sending files for output. Many older imagesetters do not handle LZW compression and fail to output images that use it.

- Use the byte order for the platform for which the TIFF file is destined. Macs and PCs use the opposite byte order — basically, the Mac reads the eight characters that comprise a byte in one direction and the PC reads it in the other direction. Although InDesign reads both byte orders, other (typically older) programs may not, so why invite confusion? Of course, if only InDesign and Photoshop users will work on your TIFF files, the byte order doesn't matter.

Web-oriented bitmap formats

In recent years, several formats have been developed for use in the Hypertext Markup Language (HTML) documents found on the Web. These formats — GIF, JPEG, and PNG — achieve small size (for faster downloading and display on your browser) by limiting image and color detail and richness.

Although you can use any supported graphics format for documents you expect to export to the Web's XHTML document format, if you know your document is bound for the Web, you might as well use a Web graphics format from the start. (Note that InDesign converts all images to GIF or JPEG when you export to XHTML.)

GIF

GIF is the oldest Web format. To help keep file size down, it is limited to 256 colors. This reduces file size but also makes it unsuitable for photographs and graphics with color blends. But its compression approach doesn't lose any image detail, so it works well for sketches, cartoons, and other simple images with sharp details.

JPEG

The JPEG compressed color-image format is used for very large images and the individual images comprising an animation or a movie. Images compressed in this format may lose detail, which is why publishers prefer TIFF files. JPEG can even be used effectively on documents output to an inkjet printer because you can set the level of loss to none during export. But in professional printing, don't use JPEG images. That's because JPEG images use the RGB color model, not the CMYK model of standard printing. Although creating CMYK JPEG files with Photoshop is possible, those CMYK JPEGs won't display in and may even crash other applications and Web browsers.

600

When importing JPEG files, InDesign automatically scales the image to fit in the page. This helps deal with digital-camera graphics that tend to be very large and that, when imported, end up taking much more than the width of a page. Although you likely still need to scale the image to fit your layout, you can at least see the whole image before doing so.

JPEG is more useful on the Web, where the limited resolution of a computer monitor makes most of JPEG's detail loss hard to spot and provides an acceptable trade-off of slightly blurry quality in return for a much smaller file size. It's particularly well suited for photographs because the lost detail is usually not noticeable because of all the other detail surrounding it.

If you do use JPEG for print work, note that you can provide a clipping path for it in programs such as Photoshop. The clipping path lets the image have an irregular boundary (rendering the rest of its background transparent) so that you can use InDesign effects such as text wrap.

PNG

The PNG format is meant to provide GIF's no-loss compression but support 24-bit color so that it can be used for photography and subtly colored illustrations on the Web. The PNG format's other significant attribute is full transparency support with an embedded alpha channel. (That is why InDesign lets you replace the transparency with white or keep the background color in the Image Import Options dialog box, as I cover later in this chapter.) The transparency also works in most recent Web browsers.

Other bitmap formats

The other supported formats are ones that you should avoid, unless you're printing to inkjet or laser printers. If you have images in one of these formats and want to use the format for professionally output documents, convert the images to TIFF before using them in InDesign.

- **BMP:** As does TIFF, the BMP Windows bitmap format supports color, grayscale, and black-and-white images.
- **PCX:** As does TIFF, PCX supports color, grayscale, and black-and-white images.
- **PICT:** PICT, the old standard Macintosh format for drawings, also supports bitmaps. InDesign imports PICT files with no difficulty.

Identifying Color Issues

It used to be that importing color from graphics files into publishing programs was an iffy proposition: Colors would often not print properly even though they appeared to be correct on-screen. Those nightmares are largely a thing of the past because modern page-layout software such as InDesign accurately detects color definitions in your source graphics, and modern illustration and image-editing programs are better at making that information accessible to page-layout programs. So, just note the following advice to ensure smooth color import.

If you create color images in an illustration or image-editing program, make sure that you create them using the CMYK color model or using a named spot color. If you use CMYK, the color is, in effect, preseparated. With InDesign, any spot colors defined in an EPS file are automatically added to the Swatches panel for your document and set as spot colors.

CROSS-REF See Chapter 7 for more on creating and editing colors.

If your program follows Adobe's EPS specifications (Adobe Illustrator, CorelDraw, and the discontinued Macromedia FreeHand all do), InDesign color-separates your EPS file, no matter whether it uses process or spot colors. Canvas automatically converts Pantone spot colors to process colors in your choice of RGB and CMYK models. For other programs, create your colors in the CMYK model to be sure they print as color separations from InDesign.

Color systems

There are several color systems, or models, in use, and InDesign supports the common ones, including CMYK (process), RGB, Pantone, Focoltone, Dainippon Ink & Chemical (DIC), Toyo, Trumatch, and Web. A color system defines either a set of individual colors that have specially mixed inks (shown on swatchbooks, which have small samples of each color) or a range of colors that can be created by combining a limited number of inks (such as RGB for red, green, and blue and CMYK for cyan, magenta, yellow, and black).

Chapter 7 describes the various color models, but for file import, it's best to use just three — CMYK (process), RGB, and the Pantone Matching System — because they're universally used and tend to be the most reliable when passing information from one system to another.

NOTE The advice on color systems applies to just vector images because bitmap programs use CMYK or RGB as their actual color models, even if they offer swatchbooks of other models' colors.

Most layout artists use Pantone to specify desired colors, so keep a Pantone swatchbook handy to see which CMYK values equal the desired Pantone color. (One of the available Pantone swatchbooks, *The Pantone Process Color Imaging Guide CMYK Edition*, shows each Pantone color next to the CMYK color build used to simulate it.) This book's companion Web site (www. InDesignCentral.com) provides links to Pantone and other color swatchbooks.

Of course, you can simply pick a Pantone color from the electronic swatchbook in InDesign, and InDesign converts it to CMYK if you specify it to be a process color (the default setting). Many high-end illustration programs, including Adobe Illustrator, support Pantone and can do this instant conversion as well. If available (as it is in InDesign), use the Pantone Process Coated color model because it is designed for output using CMYK printing presses. But remember: What you see on-screen won't match what you get on paper, so it's a good idea to have the printed Pantone swatchbook.

Calibrated color

With InDesign's color management system (CMS) feature enabled, the program calibrates the output colors (whether they're printed to a color printer or color-separated for traditional printing) based on the source device and the target output device in an attempt to ensure that what you see on-screen comes close to what you'll see on the printed page. Although color calibration is a tricky science that rarely results in exact color matches across all input and output devices, it can help minimize differences as the image travels along the creation and production path.

Today, most image-editing programs let you apply color profiles that conform with the International Color Committee (ICC) standards. If you use color calibration, applying these ICC profiles in the images when you create them is best.

If you can't — or forget to — apply an ICC profile when creating your image, don't worry. You can add a profile (if you're creating images in a program that doesn't support ICC profiles) or apply a different one from InDesign.

CROSS-REF Chapter 28 covers color calibration in depth.

Exploring Methods for Importing Graphics

You can import a graphic into any kind of frame or shape (including a curved line created with the Pen tool) except a straight line, using the Place command, copy and paste, or drag and drop.

CAUTION But be careful: If the Type tool is selected when you use the Place dialog box to import a graphic into a selected text frame, you create an inline graphic at the text-insertion point (see Chapter 12 for information about creating and managing inline graphics).

When it's time to import a graphic, you're responsible for knowing where the file is — whether it's stored on a floppy disk that your friend gave you, on your hard drive, on a networked file server, or on a local or networked CD-ROM.

If you import a graphics file that's stored on any kind of removable media, such as a floppy disk, Zip disk (remember those?), thumb drive, or CD, the link between the document and the graphics file will be broken when the media is removed. Generally, it's best to copy graphics files to your hard drive or to a networked file server before importing them into an InDesign document.

CROSS-REF Chapter 12 covers how to work with linked source files, such as how to update an imported file in InDesign if it is changed in another program.

Using the Place dialog box

Although InDesign provides several ways to add a graphics file to a document (all of which I explain in this chapter), the Place dialog box (choose File ⇨ Place or press ⌘+D or Ctrl+D) is the method you should use most often. When you use the Place dialog box, InDesign offers import options for various graphics file formats that are not available if you use other import methods.

When importing images, make sure Show Import Options is selected in the Place dialog box. Even if you're happy with the default import options, it's good to see what the import options are so that when a nondefault option does make sense, you're aware you have access to it.

Here's how to use the Place dialog box to import a graphic:

1. **Choose File ⇨ Place or press ⌘+D or Ctrl+D.** If you want to import a graphic into an *existing frame*, select the target frame using either of the selection tools (either before you choose File ⇨ Place or afterward). If you want InDesign to create a *new frame* when you import the graphic, make sure no object is selected when you choose Place. Either way, the Place dialog box appears.

2. **Use the controls in the Place dialog box to locate and select the graphics file you want to import.**

3. **If you want to display import options that let you control how the selected graphics file is imported, do one of the following: select Show Import Options and then click Open; press and hold Shift and double-click the filename; or Shift+click Open.** If you choose Show Import Options, the EPS Import Options, Place PDF, Place InDesign Document, or Image Import Options dialog box — depending on what kind of graphic you are importing — appears.

4. **Specify the desired import options, if any are applicable, and then click OK.** (I cover these options later in this chapter.)

5. **You can place the graphic in an existing frame or in a new frame, as follows:**

   - If an empty frame is selected, InDesign automatically places the graphic in the frame. The upper-left corner of the graphic is placed in the upper-left corner of the frame, and the frame acts as the cropping shape for the graphic.

   - If a frame already holding a graphic is selected, InDesign replaces the existing graphic with the new one if you selected the Replace Selected Item option in the Place dialog box. Otherwise, InDesign assumes that you want to put the new graphic in a new frame.

   - To place the graphic into a new frame, click the loaded-graphic icon (shown in Figure 25.1) on an empty portion of a page or on the pasteboard. The point where you click establishes the upper-left corner of the resulting graphics frame, which is the same size as the imported graphic and acts as the graphic's cropping shape.

   - To place the graphic in an existing unselected frame, click in the frame with the loaded-graphic icon. The upper-left corner of the graphic is placed in the upper-left corner of the frame, and the frame acts as a cropping shape.

   - InDesign CS4 lets you draw a frame when placing graphics. InDesign will make the frame proportional to the graphic's proportions — unless you hold Shift, in which case the frame may have any dimensions you want. Either way, the current graphic will then be fitted proportionally within that rectangle. When importing multiple graphics, you can draw a separate frame for each, as well as for some and not others.

NEW FEATURE   The ability to draw a frame for fitting a graphic into is new to InDesign CS4.

FIGURE 25.1

The loaded-graphic icon displays a preview image of the imported graphics, as well as the number of graphics ready to be placed (10, in this case).

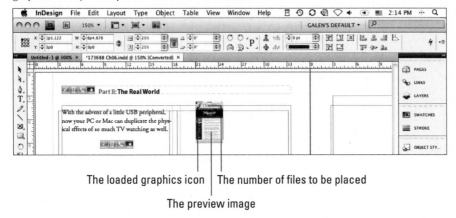

The loaded graphics icon | The number of files to be placed

The preview image

You can select multiple files — graphics and/or text — in the Place dialog box by Shift+clicking a range or by ⌘+clicking or Ctrl+clicking multiple files one by one.

To cancel the entire graphics import, just select a different tool. To cancel a specific file in a multiple-file import, press Esc when that file's mini-preview is displayed. (The other files are still available to be placed.)

After you place a graphic, it's displayed in the frame that contains it, and the frame is selected. If the Selection tool is selected, the eight handles of its bounding box are displayed; if the Direct Selection tool is selected, handles are displayed only in the corners. At this point, you can modify either the frame or the graphic within, or you can move on to another task.

When placing multiple graphics at one time, InDesign will let you place each file in a separate frame. Just click once for each file imported, or Shift+⌘+click or Ctrl+Shift+click to have InDesign place all files on the page in separate frames. If you place more than one file at the same time, the loaded-text icon displays the number of files to be placed, as well as a mini-preview of each file (refer to Figure 25.1).

 When you place multiple files at one time, you can place them in any order. Just move among them using the keyboard ← and → keys.

If you hold Shift+⌘ or Ctrl+Shift when placing multiple images, InDesign CS4 places as many as will fit on to the page below the mouse pointer's location, arranging them in a grid. If you draw a frame when placing graphics and also use the Shift+⌘ or Ctrl+Shift option, InDesign then places the images in a grid that fits within the frame you drew. You can increase or reduce the number of rows in the grid by pressing ↑ or ↓, respectively, after the loaded-graphics icon appears. Likewise, you can increase or reduce the number of columns in the grid by pressing → or ←, respectively.

NEW FEATURE The ability to place multiple files simultaneously in a grid of frames is new to InDesign CS4. (Previous versions used the Shift+⌘ or Ctrl+Shift option to place all the images in a series of cascading frames, not in a grid.)

Using import options

If you've ever used a graphics application — for example, an image-editing program such as Adobe Photoshop or an illustration program such as Adobe Illustrator or CorelDraw — you're probably aware that when you save a graphics file, you have several options that control such things as file format, image size, color depth, preview quality, and so on. When you save a graphics file, the settings you specify are determined by the way in which the image will be used. For example, you could use Photoshop to save a high-resolution TIFF version of a scanned graphic for use in a slick, four-color annual report or a low-resolution GIF version of the same graphic for use on the company's Web page. Or you could use Illustrator or FreeHand to create a corporate logo that you can use in various sizes in many of your printed publications.

If you choose to specify custom import settings when you import a graphics file, the choices you make will depend on the nature of the publication. For example, if it's bound for the Web, you have no need to work with or save graphics using resolutions that exceed a computer monitor's 72 dpi. Along the same lines, if the publication will be printed, the image import settings you specify for a newspaper printed on newsprint on a SWOP (Specifications for Web Offset Publications) press are different from those you specify for a four-color magazine printed on coated paper using a sheet-fed press.

If you choose Show Import Options when you place a graphic, the options displayed in the resulting dialog boxes depend on the file format of the selected graphic. When you set options for a particular file, the options you specify remain in effect for that file format until you change them. If you don't choose Show Import Options when you place a graphic, the most recent settings for the file format of the selected graphic are used.

Import options for bitmap graphics

InDesign gives you two sets of import options for the following types of bitmap images: TIFF, GIF, JPEG, Scitex CT, BMP, and PCX. You get three options for PNG files, and a different set of three for Photoshop files. There are no import options for PICT or QuickTime movie files. Figure 25.2 shows the four possible panes for bitmap images.

Image pane

If you import a Photoshop, TIFF, or EPS file that contains an embedded clipping path, the Image pane lets you apply any embedded clipping path and/or alpha channel to the image to mask, or cut out, part of the image. (Otherwise, these options are grayed out.) Select the Apply Photoshop Clipping Path option to import the clipping path along with the image; select an alpha channel from the Alpha Channel pop-up menu to import the alpha channel along with the image.

FIGURE 25.2

FIGURE 25.2

From top to bottom: InDesign provides the Image and Color panes in the Image Import Options dialog box for most bitmap formats; PNG files have a third pane, PNG Settings; and Photoshop files also have a third pane, Layers.

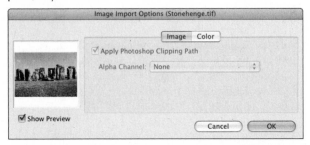

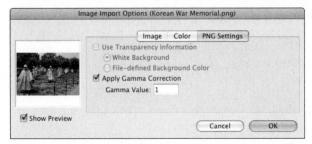

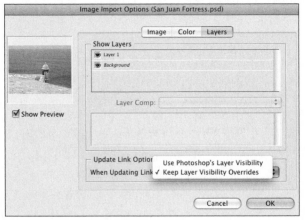

CROSS-REF   Chapter 26 covers clipping paths in more detail.

Color pane

In the Color pane, you can turn on color management for the image and control how the image is displayed.

Select the Enable Color Management option to enable color management. Using the Profile pop-up menu, choose a color-source profile that matches the color *gamut* (range) of the device (scanner, digital camera, and so on) or software used to create the file. InDesign tries to translate the colors in the file to the colors that the output device is capable of producing. (These profiles are installed in your operating system by other applications, not InDesign.)

CROSS-REF   See Chapter 27 for more information about using InDesign's color-management features.

Use the Rendering Intent pop-up menu to determine how InDesign translates the color in the selected graphics file with the gamut of the output device. If the graphic is a scanned photograph, choose Perceptual (Images). The other options — Saturation (Graphics), Relative Colorimetric, and Absolute Colorimetric — are appropriate for images that have mostly areas of solid color, such as Illustrator EPS files that have been opened in Photoshop and saved as TIFFs.

PNG Settings pane

Use this pane — available only if you place a PNG file — to use the transparency information in a PNG file, assuming it has a transparent background. You have two choices for controlling transparency handling: White Background and File-defined Background Color. The former forces the transparent portion to display as white in InDesign; the latter uses whatever background color is specified in the PNG file itself.

This pane also lets you adjust the gamma value during import — the *gamma* is a setting that describes a device's luminance, and to ensure most accurate reproduction, you want the gamma setting for the PNG file to be the same as that of your output device (a printer or monitor). It is meant to correct for the file being created on a specific type of monitor. However, to use this feature, you need to know the gamma setting for the final output device. Otherwise, leave it alone.

Layers pane

Use this pane — available only if you place a Photoshop image (or Illustrator or PDF vector file) — to select which layers you want imported into InDesign. You can then control which imported layers display in InDesign, though you cannot change their order. You'd need to go back to Photoshop and change the layer order there.

   Although you can save an image file with layers as a TIFF, InDesign does not give you the ability to manage which layers from a TIFF file import into InDesign.

Use the Layer Comp pop-up menu to select from different layer comps — if any — in the source file. A layer comp is essentially a snapshot of the Photoshop Layers panel that lets you group different layer visibility settings and save them for later use. There's also an option, in the When Updating Link pop-up menu, to control how changes to the file are handled in terms of layer management: If you choose Use Photoshop's Layer Visibility, InDesign makes all layers visible in Photoshop when you update the link to the graphic from InDesign. If you choose Keep Layer Visibility Overrides, InDesign imports only the layers chosen in this dialog box if you later update the graphic in Photoshop.

After such layered images are placed in InDesign, you can change which layers display, though you cannot change the order of layers. Note that the controls for modifying layers are pretty much the same as for importing them.

To modify which layers display, select the object with the Selection or Direct Selection tool and then choose Object ⇨ Object Layer Options. You can also Control+click or right-click the graphic and choose Graphics ⇨ Object Layer Options from the contextual menu. Either way, the Object Layer Options dialog box appears. It looks and works like the Layers pane in the Image Import Options dialog box shown in Figure 25.2.

Import options for vector file formats

If you're importing vector files, selecting the Import Options check box results in one of several dialog boxes appearing, depending on what the vector file type is. If you import older-version Illustrator or EPS files, the EPS Import Options dialog box appears; if you import PDF and newer-version Illustrator files, the Place PDF dialog box, which has two panes, appears. (Both dialog boxes are shown in Figure 25.3.) There are no import options for Windows Metafile graphics.

FIGURE 25.3

The EPS Import Options (top) and Place PDF dialog boxes (bottom). The Place PDF dialog box has two panes: General and Layers. (The Layers pane for PDF files is almost identical to the Layers pane for Photoshop files shown previously in Figure 25.2.)

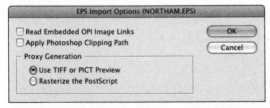

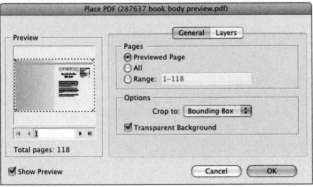

NOTE   Illustrator CS and later use PDF as their native file format, even though the filename extension is `.ai`, so InDesign detects these as PDF files and provides the PDF options during import. In earlier versions of Illustrator, the native format was actually a variant of EPS.

EPS Import Options dialog box

If you use an OPI-based proxy workflow — that is, if an OPI-based service provider supplies you with low-resolution versions of graphics files that will eventually be replaced by high-resolution files during output — select the Read Embedded OPI Image Links option if you want InDesign, rather than your service provider, to perform image replacement during output. You should also select this option if you import graphics files that contain OPI comments for other imported graphics files; for example, an EPS file that contains OPI information for an embedded TIFF graphic. Don't select this option if you don't use an OPI-based workflow or if you want your service provider to handle image replacement during output. When the Read Embedded OPI Image Links option is not selected, InDesign retains OPI comments but doesn't use them. When you print (or export) the document, the proxy image and the link information are sent.

Also use this pane to import any clipping paths embedded in images that are in the EPS file. Select the Apply Photoshop Clipping Path option to enable this.

Finally, use this pane to control how the EPS file appears on-screen in InDesign. If you select the Use TIFF or PICT Preview option, InDesign uses the low-resolution proxy image embedded in the EPS file for display on-screen and prints the graphic using the embedded high-resolution PostScript instructions. If you select the Rasterize the PostScript option, InDesign converts the PostScript file into a bitmap image during import. There's rarely a reason to rasterize an imported EPS file.

Place PDF dialog box

When you use the Place command to import a PDF file and you choose to Show Options, the Place PDF file dialog box shown in Figure 25.3 appears. In its two panes — General and Layers — you will find several controls for specifying how the file is imported.

In the General pane, you have the following options:

- In the Pages section, select Previewed Page, All, or Range to determine which pages you want to import. You can change the previewed page by clicking the arrow buttons under the preview image at left or typing a specific page number in the field below the preview image. If you want to import a range, use commas to separate pages and a hyphen to indicate range; for example, if you type **3, 5–9, 13**, pages 3, 5 through 9, and 13 are imported.

NOTE   When you place the PDF in InDesign, you get a separate loaded-graphic icon for each page, so as you place each page, a new loaded-graphic icon appears for the next page until there are no more to place. You can tell you're placing multiple pages because the loaded-graphics icon has a plus sign in it.

- In the Options section, select one of the cropping options from the Crop To pop-up menu. If you choose Bounding Box, the page's bounding box (or, if none is defined in the PDF file, a rectangle that encloses all items, including page marks) is used to build the graphics frame. Choosing Art places the area defined by the file's creator, if any, as placeable artwork. For example, the person who created the file might have designated a particular graphic as placeable artwork. Choosing Crop places the area displayed and printed by Adobe Acrobat. Choosing Trim places the graphic in an area equal to the final, trimmed piece. Choosing Bleed places the page area plus any specified bleed area. Choosing Media places an area defined by the paper size specified for the PDF document, including page marks.

  Also in the Options section, select the Transparent Background option if you want the white areas of the PDF page to be transparent. Deselect this option if you want to preserve the page's opaque white background.

Here's how you work with the controls found in the Layers pane:

- You see a list of image layers. Any that have the eye icon import into InDesign, and you can select or deselect layers by clicking the box to the right of the layer name to make the eye icon appear or disappear. You can then control which imported layers display in InDesign, although you cannot change their order (you'd need to go back to Photoshop and change the layer order there).

- Use the When Updating Link pop-up menu to control how changes to the file are handled in terms of layer management. If you choose Use PDF's Layer Visibility, InDesign makes all layers visible in Illustrator or Acrobat visible when you update the link to the graphic from InDesign. If you choose Keep Layer Visibility Overrides, InDesign imports only the layers you select in this dialog box if you later update the graphic in Photoshop.

Place InDesign Document dialog box

When you import InDesign files to use as a graphic, you have the same options as for PDF files. The Place InDesign Document dialog box is identical to the Place PDF dialog box I cover in the previous section, except, of course, for the dialog box's name.

Dealing with PDF Security

Some PDF files are protected with passwords or have printing, text editing, and other content-access functions disabled. If a PDF file is password-protected, you're prompted to type the required password; do so and click OK. Note that some PDF files have a second password, called a *permissions password*, that you also need in order to open it.

If the selected file was saved with any security restrictions (no text editing, no printing, and so on), you can't place any pages of the file into InDesign. Ask the person who produced the file for an unrestricted copy.

Using other ways to import graphics

If you want to specify custom import options for an imported graphics file, you must use the Place command. However, if you don't need this level of control, you can use one of InDesign's three other options for importing graphics:

- You can use your computer's Copy (choose File ⇨ Copy or press ⌘+C or Ctrl+C) and Paste (choose File ⇨ Paste or press ⌘+V or Ctrl+V) commands to move a graphics file between two InDesign documents or from a document created with another program into an InDesign document.

- You can drag and drop graphics file icons from your computer's desktop into InDesign documents.

- For Illustrator files, you can drag or copy and paste objects directly from Illustrator into InDesign. Depending on your Clipboard preference, these objects may be only embedded PDFs, which are not editable in InDesign.

To set your preference for copying or dragging vector objects from Illustrator into InDesign, go to the File Handling pane of the Preferences dialog box (choose InDesign ⇨ Preferences ⇨ File Handling or press ⌘+K on the Mac, or choose Edit ⇨ Preferences ⇨ File Handling or press Ctrl+K in Windows). If you want to place fully editable vector objects in InDesign, go to the Clipboard section of the Clipboard Handing pane and deselect the Prefer PDF When Pasting option. Leave it selected if you prefer to copy or drag noneditable, embedded PDFs into InDesign instead.

Placing editable vector objects can be especially useful if you need to place a vector logo graphic into a template. An editable vector object entirely contained within InDesign reduces the need to jump between graphic applications to make changes such as editing the logo's colors and vector shapes.

If you use these methods to add a graphic to an InDesign document, some of the attributes of the original graphic may not survive the trip. The operating system, the file format, and the capabilities of the originating application may all play roles in determining which attributes are preserved. If you want to be safe, use the Place command or use the method I described previously to move fully editable vector objects into InDesign.

Copy and paste

If you copy an object in an InDesign document and then paste it into a different InDesign document, the copy retains all the attributes of the original. In the case of a copied and pasted graphic, all import settings, frame modifications, and graphic modifications are retained, as is the link to the original graphics file.

When you copy and paste a graphic into an InDesign document, a link between the original graphics file and the InDesign document is not established. The graphic becomes part of the InDesign document, as though you created it using InDesign tools. A vector image, such as a pasted graphic, is editable only if you deselect Prefer PDF When Pasting in the Clipboard Handling pane of the Preferences dialog box, as described in the previous section.

Drag and drop

When an InDesign document is open, you can import a graphics file in any supported file format by clicking and dragging the file's icon into the window of the InDesign document. When you drag and drop a graphics file into a document, a link between the original graphics file and the document is established, just as it would be if you had used the Place command.

If you drag and drop an Illustrator file icon into an InDesign document window, the graphic behaves the same as it would if you had used the Place command. That is, individual elements within the graphic are not selectable or modifiable within InDesign. However, if you drag and drop Illustrator objects from an Illustrator document window into an InDesign document window, each object becomes a separate, editable InDesign object, as though you had created it in InDesign.

NOTE For Illustrator objects to be editable in InDesign, be sure that Prefer PDF When Pasting is deselected in the Clipboard Handling pane of the Preferences dialog box, as described in an earlier section.

This is a handy way of moving objects that you may want to modify between Illustrator and InDesign. For example, you can create text along a path in an Illustrator document and then drag and drop the object into an InDesign document. Each character is converted into an editable shape, which you can stroke, fill, distort, and so on, using InDesign features. However, you cannot edit text along a path after you've dragged and dropped it into InDesign. (You have to go back to Illustrator, edit the original text, drag and drop it again, and then redo all your modifications.)

Using the Copy and Paste commands to add Illustrator objects to InDesign documents is the same as dragging and dropping objects between the programs. The copied objects behave the same as objects created in InDesign when you choose Paste, and no links are established.

Summary

If you work with publishing-oriented graphics formats — EPS, PDF, Illustrator, TIFF, and Photoshop — created by mainstay programs such as Adobe Photoshop, Adobe Illustrator, CorelDraw, and Corel Photo-Paint, you likely have no difficulties importing graphics into or printing graphics from InDesign. But be sure to stick with common color models, particularly CMYK and Pantone.

And it's best to do any special effects in your graphics program; InDesign has limited abilities to manipulate graphics beyond layout-oriented functions such as resizing, cropping, flipping, slanting, and text wrap. To ease access to your graphics programs, InDesign lets you open them from within InDesign.

InDesign lets you import graphics in any of several supported graphics file formats. The preferred method for importing graphics is the Place command because it lets you customize various import settings that control how an imported graphic appears and prints. InDesign also lets you manage the visibility of layers in some imported graphics. When placing files, you can place multiple files simultaneously or one at a time, as well as draw a frame in which the placed graphic will be fitted into.

You can also import graphics into an InDesign document by dragging and dropping graphics file icons into a document window or by copying and pasting objects between InDesign documents or between documents created with other programs and InDesign documents.

If you need to use Illustrator-generated objects or graphics files in your InDesign documents, several options are available: the Place command, the Copy and Paste commands, file drag and drop, and inter-application drag and drop. When using Copy and Paste or drag and drop from Illustrator, be sure to check InDesign's File Handling preferences first to choose between creating editable vectors or embedded PDFs in your document.

Chapter 26

Fitting Graphics and Frames Together

Getting a graphic into your layout is one thing, but that's not the end of the story. At a minimum, you want to make sure the image fits in the layout.

The most common actions you'll probably take are cropping, repositioning, and resizing. *Cropping* is a fancy term for deciding what part of the picture to show by altering the dimensions of the frame holding the graphic. *Repositioning* is essentially the same as cropping, except that you move the graphic within its frame. And if you want to get really fancy, you might work with clipping paths to create "masks" around image portions or even cut the graphic into pieces. *Resizing* (also called *scaling*) changes the size of the graphic, either larger or smaller.

CROSS-REF Transformations such as resizing, flipping, rotating, and skewing that you're likely to apply to imported graphics use the same tools as for any InDesign objects, so I cover all these transformations in one place, Chapter 10. I cover other effects that you can apply to any object, including graphics, in Chapter 11.

Fitting Graphics within Their Frames

Remember, when you import a graphic using the Place dialog box (choose File ➪ Place or press ⌘+D or Ctrl+D) or by clicking and dragging a graphics file into a document window (as Chapter 25 explains), the graphic is contained in a graphics frame — either the frame that was selected when you placed the graphic or the frame that was automatically created if a frame wasn't selected. The upper-left corner of an imported graphic is automatically placed in the upper-left corner of its frame.

IN THIS CHAPTER

Cropping and positioning graphics

Working with graphics in irregular shapes

Fitting graphics into frames and vice versa

Importing, creating, and using clipping paths

NOTE   In almost every case, you select graphics with the Direct Selection tool to work with the graphic itself, rather than the frame. If you use the Selection tool, the work you do will apply to the frame. The Position tool can act on either the contents or the frame. Chapter 9 explains all three.

Resizing a graphic's frame

The easiest way to crop a graphic is to resize the frame that contains it. To resize the frame, use the Selection or Position tool to drag the frame's handles to reveal the portion of the graphic you want to print (and to conceal the portion you don't want to print). Press and hold Shift as you drag to maintain the proportions of the frame. (See Chapter 10 for details.)

Moving a graphic in its frame

You can also click a graphic with the Direct Selection tool and then drag the graphic in its frame to crop it, revealing and concealing different parts of the graphic. For example, you can crop the top and left edges of a graphic by clicking and dragging the graphic above and to the left of its original position (in the upper-left corner of the frame).

You can also crop a graphic by moving it relative to its frame using the X and Y options in the Control panel and Transform panel when the Direct Selection tool is active; this is more precise than using the mouse.

The advantage of moving the image within the frame is that when you've positioned the frame in the desired location in your layout, resizing the frame to crop the image then requires you to move the resized frame back to the desired location.

If you want to *mask out* (hide) portions of an imported graphic, you have the option of using an irregular shape as the frame, a graphic's built-in clipping path (if it has one), or a clipping path you generated in InDesign, as I cover later in this chapter.

Using an irregular frame

If you want to use an irregular shape as the frame for a graphic that's currently cropped by a rectangular frame, here's what you do:

1. **Click the Direct Selection tool (or press A if the Type tool isn't selected).**

2. **Click the graphic you want to place in a free-form shape (don't click its frame) and then choose Edit ⇨ Copy or press ⌘+C or Ctrl+C.**

3. **Click the shape (or create one if you haven't already) you want to use as a cropping frame.** It can be any kind of object except a straight line.

4. **Choose Edit ⇨ Paste Into or press Shift+⌘+V or Ctrl+Shift+V.** Figure 26.1 shows an example.

CROSS-REF   For more information about creating and modifying free-form shapes, see Chapter 27.

If you select a frame with the Direct Selection tool instead of the Selection tool, handles are displayed only at the frame corners rather than at the bounding-box corners and midpoints. When you select a frame with the Direct Selection tool, you can reshape the frame, and thus crop the graphic differently, by clicking and dragging corner points, adding and deleting points, and so on.

FIGURE 26.1

In this example, I copied and pasted the map of North America (left) into a free-form frame that reveals only Canada (right). I created the free-form frame by using the Pen tool to trace the contour of Canada.

Of course, you could also create the irregular shape first and then use the Place dialog box to place the graphic file directly into the shape. (Or choose File ➪ Place Into or press Option+⌘+V or Ctrl+Alt+V to paste a cut or copied graphic inside the shape.) Using an irregular shape to crop a graphic is similar to using a clipping path except that you create the irregular shape yourself using InDesign's object-creation tools, whereas a clipping path is either built into a graphics file or generated by InDesign, as I describe later in this chapter.

Figuring Out the Fitting Commands

If you've placed a graphic in a frame that's either larger or smaller than the graphic, you can use the Fitting commands (choose Object ➪ Fitting) to scale the graphic to fit the frame proportionately or disproportionately, or to scale the frame to fit the graphic. Another option lets you center the graphic in the frame.

You can also use the frame-fitting iconic buttons in the Control panel, shown in Figure 26.2. But note that these may not display in your Control panel; by default, InDesign shows them only if your monitor is set to a resolution whose width is 1,280 or more pixels. You can make room for them at smaller resolutions by customizing the Control panel display: Choose Customize from the panel's flyout menu and then deselect some of the Object controls to make room, as Chapter 2 explains.

FIGURE 26.2

The frame-fitting iconic buttons in the Control panel

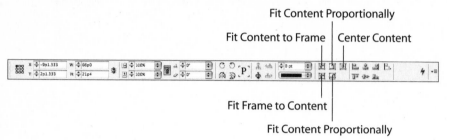

Fit Content Proportionally

Fit Content to Frame | Center Content

Fit Frame to Content

Fit Content Proportionally

Here's a description of each of the six options:

- **Fit Content to Frame:** To scale a graphic to fill the selected frame, choose Object ⇨ Fitting ⇨ Fit Content to Frame or press Option+⌘+E or Ctrl+Alt+E. If the frame is larger than the graphic, the graphic is enlarged; if the frame is smaller, the graphic is reduced. If the graphic and the frame have different proportions, the graphic's proportions are changed so that the image completely fills the frame. Note that this change in proportions can distort the graphic.

- **Fit Frame to Content:** To resize a frame so that it wraps snugly around a graphic, choose Fit Frame to Content or press Option+⌘+C or Ctrl+Alt+C. The frame is enlarged or reduced depending on the size of the graphic, and the frame's proportions change to match the proportions of the graphic.

- **Center Content:** To center a graphic in its frame, choose Center Content or press Shift+⌘+E or Ctrl+Shift+E. Neither the frame nor the graphic is scaled when you center a graphic.

- **Fit Content Proportionally:** To scale a graphic to fit in the selected frame while maintaining the graphic's current proportions (preventing distortion), choose Object ⇨ Fitting ⇨ Fit Content Proportionally or press Option+Shift+⌘+E or Ctrl+Alt+Shift+E. If the frame is larger than the graphic, the graphic is enlarged; if the frame is smaller, the graphic is reduced. If the graphic and the frame have different proportions, a portion of the frame background appears above and below or to the left and right of the graphic. If you want, you can click and drag frame edges to make the frame shorter or narrower and eliminate any portions of the background that are visible.

- **Fill Frame Proportionally:** To resize a frame to fit the selected graphic, choose Object ⇨ Fitting ⇨ Fill Frame Proportionally or press Option+Shift+⌘+C or Ctrl+Alt+Shift+C. This guarantees that no space is left between the graphic and the frame. (The Fit Frame to Content option can result in such space at the bottom and/or right sides of a graphic.)

- **Frame Fitting Options:** To control the default fitting for either the selected frame or (if no frame is selected) for newly placed graphics, use the Frame Fitting Options dialog box, shown in Figure 26.3. Here you can set the amount of crop, choose the reference point for the imported graphic (see Chapter 9), and automatically apply your choice of the Fit Content to Frame, Fit Content Proportionally, and Fill Frame Proportionally options.

NOTE If no object is selected, any settings specified in the Frame Fitting Options dialog box will be applied to all graphics placed into new empty frames from that point on. If no document is open, the settings are applied to all documents later created.

TIP InDesign offers a quick way to fit a frame to its content: Just double-click a frame handle. The handle you double-click determines how the frame is fitting: Using a corner handle fits the frame's width and height; using a left or right side handle fits the frame to the object's width; and using a top or bottom handle fits the frame to the object's height.

For frames with strokes, the fitting options align the outer edge of a graphic with the center of the stroke. A stroke will obscure a strip along the graphic's edge that is half the width of the stroke. The wider the stroke is, the more the graphic is covered up.

FIGURE 26.3

The Frame Fitting Options dialog box lets you set the default behavior for newly imported graphics.

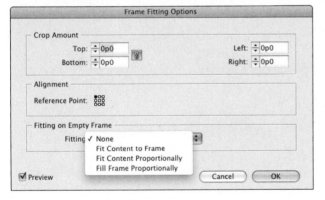

Working with Clipping Paths

A clipping path is essentially a shape that acts like a cutout mask — anything inside the shape displays and anything outside does not. It's a very handy way of displaying just the pieces of a graphic that you want to display, such as masking out extraneous background or focusing on a specific portion of a larger image. Clipping paths are also frequently used to control text wrap around graphics.

InDesign can work with clipping paths that are already part of an imported TIFF, JPEG, Photoshop EPS, or Photoshop image, as I explained earlier in this chapter, or with clipping paths you create in InDesign. And no matter the source of the clipping path, InDesign lets you modify it.

Creating Clipping Paths in Photoshop

Creating a clipping path in Photoshop is simple after you get the hang of the process. (See the *Photoshop Bible* series [Wiley Publishing] for more on creating clipping paths in Photoshop.) A path is essentially a selection, which you can create with any of the Photoshop selection tools, including tracing your own selection to hand-drawing a path. After you make the selection, here's how you make a path:

1. **Open the Paths panel by choosing Window ⇨ Paths.**

2. **Using the panel's flyout menu, choose Make Work Path.** You're asked to choose a Tolerance setting in pixels — the smaller the number, the finer the path's shape.

3. **Click OK to accept your setting.** A work path appears in the Paths panel, showing in white the area contained by the path.

4. **Convert the work path into a named path by double-clicking the work path in the panel or by choosing Save Path in the flyout menu.**

5. **Give the path a name and then click OK.**

6. **Choose Clipping Path from the flyout menu.** You're asked to choose which path to use as a clipping path (you can have multiple clipping paths in a Photoshop file); next, choose a Flatness setting. As with the Tolerance setting, the smaller the number of pixels, the finer the path's contours.

7. **Click OK.**

That's it! The tricky part is creating the selection area to begin with.

Using a graphic's own clipping path

In an ideal world, any graphics that you want to have fit in an irregular shape come with their own clipping paths. In that situation, you would first be sure to import the clipping path when you place the graphic.

Using the clipping path as a mask

To use that clipping path to mask out part of an image, you must convert the clipping path to a frame (and that frame then masks out everything that doesn't fit within it). The process is simple: Select the clipping path with the Direct Selection tool and choose Object ⇨ Clipping Path ⇨ Convert Clipping Path to Frame.

Using the clipping path as a wrap boundary

If your goal is to wrap text around the contours of the clipping path, you don't create a frame from the clipping path. Instead, you have InDesign's Text Wrap panel access that clipping path for its text wrap. Here's how:

1. Be sure to select the Show Import Options check box in the Place dialog box (choose File ➪ Place or press ⌘+D or Ctrl+D) when you import the graphic and then select the Apply Photoshop Clipping Path option in the Image Import Options dialog box.

2. Open the Text Wrap panel (choose Window ➪ Text Wrap or press Option+⌘+W or Ctrl+Alt+W), as shown in Figure 26.4.

3. Select the graphic.

4. Click the Wrap Around Object Shape button (the third one from the left) at the top of the Text Wrap panel.

5. If you want, adjust the space between the surrounding text and the obstructing shape by typing values in the Top Offset field.

6. Now select the clipping source from the Type pop-up menu in the Contour Options section of the Text Wrap panel. Choose from two relevant options:

   ▪ Alpha Channel uses the image's alpha channel, if any, to create a wrapping boundary. (An *alpha channel* is another type of clipping path and is also created in the source program such as Photoshop.)

   ▪ Photoshop Path uses the image's clipping path, if any, to create a wrapping boundary. Use the Path pop-up menu to select which path to use if your image has more than one embedded clipping path.

CROSS-REF See Chapter 12 for the details of text wraps. See Chapter 27 for details on how to edit irregular shapes such as text-wrap boundaries.

Creating a clipping path in InDesign

If you import a graphic that doesn't have its own clipping path, you have two sets of options to create a clipping path in InDesign.

The easiest is to use the Text Wrap panel as described in steps in the previous section, but in Step 6, instead choose one of the following options from the Type pop-up menu:

▪ **Detect Edges:** This option tries to determine the graphic's outside boundary by ignoring white space. You would use this for bitmapped images that have a transparent or white background.

▪ **Same as Clipping:** This option uses the clipping path for the graphic created in InDesign. You would use this when the desired clipping path can't be created through the Detect Edges option. (I cover this method of clipping-path creation shortly.)

You can further modify the clipping path by selecting the graphic with the Direct Selection tool. The text-wrap boundary appears as a blue line; you can make the boundary easier to select by setting offsets in the Text Wrap panel, which moves the boundary away from the frame edge. Now use InDesign's free-form editing tools, as covered in Chapter 27, to edit the text-wrap boundary.

FIGURE 26.4

The Text Wrap panel and its Type pop-up menu. You can see a Photoshop-generated clipping path around the North American continent.

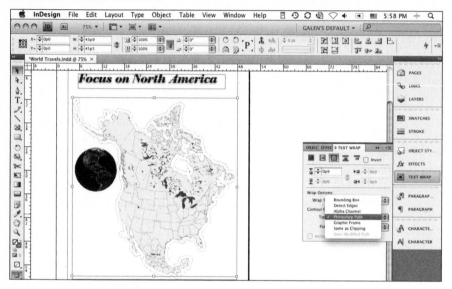

A slightly more difficult way to create a clipping path — but one that gives you more control — is to use the Clipping Path command (choose Object ➪ Clipping Path ➪ Options or press Option+Shift+⌘+K or Ctrl+Alt+Shift+K) to generate one automatically:

1. **Select the graphic to which you want to add a clipping path.** It's best to use the Direct Selection tool so that you can see the clipping path within the frame as you work.

2. **Choose Object ➪ Clipping Path ➪ Options or press Option+Shift+⌘+K or Ctrl+Alt+Shift+K.** The Clipping Path dialog box appears, as shown in Figure 26.5.

3. **To have InDesign detect the likely boundary of the image, as opposed to a white or other light background, choose Detect Edges from the Type pop-up menu.** You can use the other options to select Alpha Channel or Photoshop Path as the clipping path for graphics that have one or more of these. (InDesign can use only one alpha channel or Photoshop path as the clipping path, so use the Path pop-up menu to choose the one you want.)

4. **Type a value in the Threshold field or click and drag the field's slider to specify the value below which pixels will be placed outside the clipping path shape (that is, pixels that will become transparent).** Pixels darker than the Threshold value remain visible and thus are inside the clipping path shape. The lowest possible Threshold value (0) makes only white pixels transparent. As the value gets higher, less of the graphic remains visible. The lightest areas are removed first, then midtones, and so on. (Select the Preview check box to see the results of your changes without closing the dialog box.)

5. **Type a value in the Tolerance field.** This value determines how closely InDesign looks at variations in adjacent pixels when building a clipping path. Higher values produce a simpler, smoother path than lower values. Lower values create a more complicated, more exact path with more anchor points.

6. **If you want to enlarge or reduce the size of the clipping path produced by the Threshold and Tolerance values, type a value in the Inset Frame field.** Negative values enlarge the path; positive values shrink it. (The Inset Frame value is also applied to the path's bounding box.)

7. **Select the Invert check box to switch the transparent and visible areas of the clipping path produced by the Threshold and Tolerance values.**

8. **If you want to include light areas in the perimeter shape InDesign generates based on the Threshold and Tolerance values, select the Include Inside Edges check box.** For example, if you have a graphic of a doughnut and you want to make the hole transparent (as well as the area around the outside of the doughnut), click Include Inside Edges. If you don't click Include Inside Edges, InDesign builds a single shape (in the case of a doughnut, just the outside circle). The portion of the graphic in the shape remains visible; the rest of the graphic becomes transparent.

9. **Select the Restrict to Frame check box if you want InDesign to generate a clipping path from just the portion of the graphic visible in the graphic frame, as opposed to the entire graphic (such as if you cropped the graphic).**

10. **Select the Use High Resolution Image check box if you want InDesign to use the high-resolution information in the original file instead of using the low-resolution proxy image.** Even though using the high-resolution image takes longer, the resulting clipping path is more precise than it would be if you didn't select Use High Resolution Image.

11. **When you've finished specifying clipping path settings, click OK to close the dialog box and apply the settings to the selected graphic.**

FIGURE 26.5

The Clipping Path dialog box

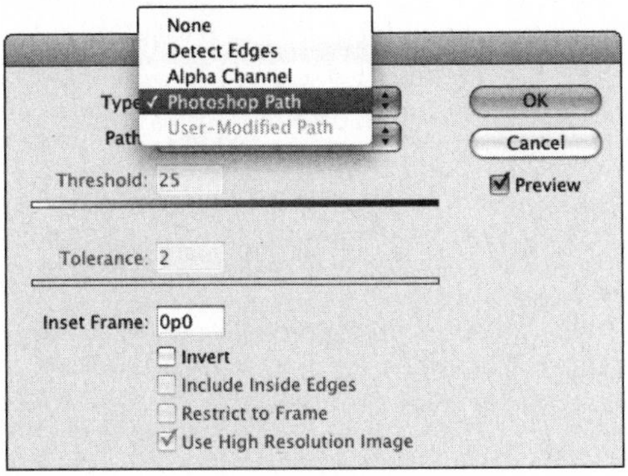

CAUTION   If you use the Clipping Path command to generate a clipping path for a graphic that has a built-in clipping path, the one that InDesign generates replaces the built-in path.

NOTE   The Clipping Path command works very well for images that have a white or light background but no clipping path. It's less useful for graphics with backgrounds that contain a broad range of intermingling values.

After you've created the clipping path, you can use it either to mask the image (by converting it to a frame) or to control text wrap — just as you can with an imported clipping path. Both are covered earlier in this chapter.

Modifying clipping paths

Whether the path was imported or created in InDesign, you can change it by choosing a different option in the Text Wrap panel — Detect Edges, Alpha Channel, Photoshop Path, or User-Modified Path — than was selected previously.

And you can edit the clipping path manually, as you can any other freeform shape, as I cover in Chapter 27.

Deleting clipping paths

Whether the clipping path was imported or created in InDesign, you can remove it by choosing None as the Type in the Clipping Path dialog box. (For an imported graphic, deleting the clipping path in InDesign does not destroy the original path in the graphic's source file.)

Summary

It's very common to need to fit a graphic to its frame or a frame to its graphic, so InDesign provides several mechanisms to do so. Likewise, it provides several mechanisms to crop a graphic so that you can control which parts of it display. Manual options include using the mouse and the Control panel. The Fitting command provides four submenu options for positioning and scaling a graphic relative to its frame.

InDesign also lets you control what part of a graphic displays and/or how text wraps around it using clipping paths, which are either imported from Photoshop files or created within InDesign.

Chapter 27

Drawing Free-Form Shapes and Curved Paths

InDesign's basic drawing tools let you create basic shapes, such as straight lines, rectangles and squares, circles and ellipses, and equilateral polygons. But what about when you need to create shapes that aren't so basic, such as amoeba or a cursive version of your first name, perhaps? That's where InDesign's Pen tool comes in. You can use the Pen tool to create any kind of line or closed shape. And you can use anything you create with the Pen tool as an independent graphic element or as a frame for text or a picture.

If you've ever used an illustration program such as Illustrator, FreeHand, or CorelDraw, or a page-layout program such as PageMaker or QuarkXPress, you may already be familiar with Bézier drawing tools. (Bézier tools are named after Pierre Bézier, a French engineer and mathematician, who developed a method of representing curved shapes on a computer in the 1970s.) If you aren't familiar with Bézier tools, you should know in advance that getting the hang of using them takes a little time and patience. Even if you're a virtuoso when drawing with a piece of charcoal or a B6 pencil, you need to practice with the Pen tool for a while before your drawing skills kick in. The good news is that when you get comfortable using the Pen tool, you can draw any shape you can imagine. (Of course, if you can't draw very well in the first place, using the Pen tool won't magically transform you into a master illustrator!) If this is new terrain for you, start simply and proceed slowly.

If you intend to use InDesign extensively as a drawing tool, you might want to purchase a drawing tablet, which can make working with the Pen tool a bit easier than using a mouse or trackball. On both Macs and PCs, you can usually hook up multiple input devices, so you can switch from tablet to mouse or trackball and back as needed.

Finding Out All about Paths

Every object you create with InDesign's object-creation tools is a path. That includes:

- Straight lines created with the Line tool
- Lines and shapes created with the Pen tool or the Pencil tool
- Basic shapes created with the Ellipse, Rectangle, and Polygon tools
- Basic frames created with the Ellipse Frame, Rectangle Frame, and Polygon Frame tools

All of InDesign's object-manipulation features are available for all paths. This includes the transformation tools, the Control panel and the Transform panel, the Stroke and Swatches panels, and the option to place a text file or graphics file either on or within the path. (You can't place text within a straight line because there is not even a partial enclosure in which to create the bounds of a text frame.)

The properties of a path

Regardless of the tool you use to create a path, you can change its appearance by modifying any of four properties that all paths share: closure, stroke, fill, and contents.

Closure

A path is either *open* or *closed*. Straight lines created with the Line tool and curved and zigzag lines created with the Pen tool are examples of open paths. Basic shapes created with the Ellipse, Rectangle, and Polygon tools and free-form shapes created with the Pen and Pencil tools are examples of closed shapes. A closed free-form shape is an uninterrupted path with no endpoints. Figure 27.1 shows the difference between open and closed paths.

FIGURE 27.1

The five paths on the left are open; the five on the right are closed. A stroke and fill have been added to show how they affect open and closed paths.

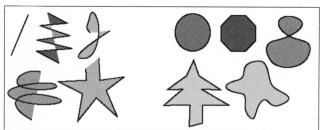

Stroke

If you want to make a path visible, you can apply a *stroke* to it, as Chapter 11 describes. (An unselected, unstroked path is not visible.) When you stroke a path, you can specify the stroke's width, color, tint, and style. Figure 27.2 shows a path before and after a stroke was added.

FIGURE 27.2

The original path (left) is selected. At right, a 2-point stroke was added to a clone of the original path.

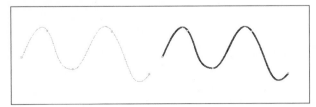

Fill

A color, color tint, or gradient applied to the background of an open path or a closed path is called a *fill*. Figure 27.3 shows some examples of fills. Chapter 7 explains how to apply them.

FIGURE 27.3

From left to right: a color fill (black), a color tint fill (50 percent black), and a gradient fill. The paths are selected and displayed in their bounding boxes.

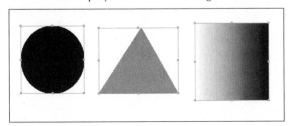

Contents

You can place a text file or a graphics file in any path (with the exception of a straight line), as Chapters 13 and 25 explain. When a path is used to hold text or a picture, the path functions as a *frame*. Although InDesign can place text in an open path, placing text and pictures in closed paths is far more common than placing them in open paths. Figure 27.4 shows several examples of pictures imported into paths.

FIGURE 27.4

Left: The same picture was imported into three different paths. (A stroke has been added to the paths to make them more visible.) Right: Text has been placed in clones of the paths at left.

The anatomy of a path

No matter how simple (a short straight line) or complicated (a free-form shape with several straight and curved edges) a path is, all paths are made up of the same components. Figures 27.5 through 27.7 show the parts that make up a path:

- A path contains one or more straight or curved *segments*, as shown in Figure 27.5.

FIGURE 27.5

Left: From left to right, for the first three paths, each path contains one more straight segment than the previous path. Right: The same three paths as at left but using curved segments.

- An anchor point is located at each end of every segment. The anchor points at the ends of a closed path are called *endpoints*. When you create a path of any kind, anchor points are automatically placed at the end of each segment. After you create a path, you can move, add, delete, and change the direction of corner points.

- There are two kinds of anchor points: *smooth points* and *corner points*. A smooth point connects two adjoining curved segments in a continuous, flowing curve. At a corner point, adjoining segments — straight or curved — meet at an angle. The corners of a rectangular path are the most common corner points. Figure 27.6 shows some examples of smooth and corner points.

FIGURE 27.6

The path on the left has only corner anchor points; the path in the center has only smooth anchor points; and the path on the right has both kinds of anchor points.

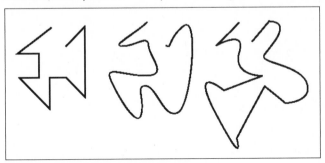

- A *direction line* runs through each anchor point and has a handle at both ends. You can control the curve that passes through an anchor point by dragging a direction line's handles. Figure 27.7 shows how you can change the shape of a path by dragging a direction line handle.

 Anchor points and direction lines do not print.

Reading about riding a bike is one thing; riding a bike is another. If you've read Chapter 8, you already know how to ride with training wheels — you can create basic shapes with the basic object-creation tools. Now that you know more about what paths are made of, you're ready to tackle more-complex shapes. You're ready to wield the Pen tool.

FIGURE 27.7

The original path on the left is cloned and then the direction handle of the right endpoint is dragged to create the path on the right.

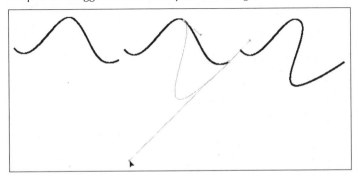

Drawing Tools

InDesign uses the same drawing tools as Adobe Illustrator and Adobe Photoshop, so if you're familiar with those, you should have no trouble using InDesign's tools. If not, it might help to get a refresher on the tools:

- **Pen tool:** This tool draws both segments and Bézier curves. It has several associated tools to add, delete, and convert corner points, which are the handles that you use to change the direction and curvature of a curve or line segment.

- **Pencil tool:** This is a free-form drawing tool that simply draws out your mouse motions. The result is a Bézier curve. A Pencil tool is great if you have a steady, accurate drawing hand; the Pen tool is better if you want to control each segment and curve as you create it.

- **Shape tools:** The shape tools create closed objects that aren't intended to hold text or graphics; they're basically shapes you can color and/or stroke. There are Rectangle, Polygon, and Ellipse versions, as described in Chapter 9.

- **Frame tools:** The frame tools are the same as the shape tools, except they're meant to create shapes that will contain text or graphics, though they can also be empty.

- **Type and Type on a Path tools:** The Type and Type on a Path tools let you add text in an object and on an object's stroke, respectively. (See Chapter 18.)

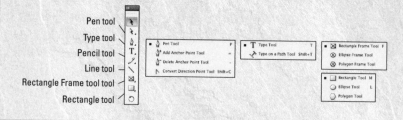

Drawing Lines with the Pen Tool

The Pen tool is very versatile. With it you can create lines (open paths) and shapes (closed paths).

Straight and zigzag lines

The simplest kind of path is a straight line (that is, an open path) with a single segment, which you can create with either the Line tool or the Pen tool. But the Pen is much mightier than the Line because it lets you draw zigzag lines with multiple straight segments, curvy lines, and lines that contain straight and curved segments. You can't draw those kinds of shapes with the Line tool, or any of the other object-creation tools, for that matter.

CROSS-REF Chapter 8 covers the Line tool.

To draw lines with straight segments:

1. **Select the Pen tool or press P if the Type tool isn't selected.**

2. **Move the Pen pointer to where you want to place one of your line's endpoints and then click and release the mouse button (make sure you don't drag before you release the mouse button).** When you click and release the mouse button while using the Pen tool, you create a corner point. A small, filled-in square indicates the anchor point, which is also an endpoint of the open shape you're creating.

3. **Move the Pen pointer to where you want to place the next anchor point and then click and release the mouse button.** When you create the second point, a straight line connects it with the first point, the first anchor point changes to a hollow square, and the second anchor point is filled in. (If you want to create a line with a single segment, you can stop drawing at this point by choosing another tool.)

4. **For each additional anchor point, move the Pen pointer and then click and release the mouse button.** If you hold down the Shift key as you click, the angles you create are limited to multiples of 45 degrees. To reposition an anchor point after you click the mouse button but before you release it, hold down the spacebar and drag.

 **If you drag before you press the spacebar, you create a smooth point and curved segments.**

5. **To complete the path, press the ⌘ key or the Ctrl key and click an empty portion of the page or choose another tool.** If you click the page, the Pen tool remains selected and you can continue creating additional paths. Figure 27.8 shows a path in various stages of being drawn.

FIGURE 27.8

As each anchor point was created (from left to right), a new, straight segment was added to the path. The finished open path is a zigzag line that contains four straight segments produced by clicking and releasing the mouse a total of five times.

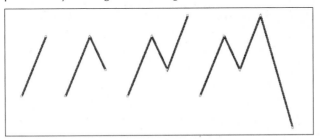

You can also complete the path by clicking the first point you created, but if you do, you create a closed path. (I discuss closed paths in the next section.)

> **TIP** As you create a path, you can move any anchor point, direction line handle, or the entire path by pressing the ⌘ or Ctrl key and then clicking and dragging whatever element you want to move.

Curved lines

If all you ever need to create are zigzag lines with corner points and straight segments, the click-and-release method in the preceding section is all you need to know. But if you want to create curvy lines, you need to take the next step up the Bézier ladder and learn to add smooth points. Creating smooth points and curved segments is much like creating corner points and straight segments — with a twist. There are two ways of connecting curved segments when drawing a path: with smooth points and with corner points. I explain both methods in the steps that follow.

Curved segments connected by smooth points

If you want to draw a continuously curvy path that contains no corner points and no straight segments, you should create only smooth points as you draw. Here's how:

1. **Select the Pen tool or press P if the Type tool isn't selected.**

2. **Move the Pen pointer to where you want to place one of your line's endpoints and then click and hold down the mouse button.** The arrowhead pointer is displayed.

3. **Drag the mouse in the direction of the next point you intend to create.** (Adobe suggests dragging about one-third of the way to the next point.) As you drag, the anchor point, its direction line, and the direction line's two handles are displayed, as shown in Figure 27.9. If you hold down the Shift key as you drag, the angle of the direction line is limited to increments of 45 degrees.

4. **Release the mouse button.**

5. **Move the Pen pointer where you want to establish the next anchor point, which ends the first segment, and then drag the mouse.** If you drag in approximately the same direction as the direction line of the previous point, you create an S-shaped curve; if you drag in the opposite direction, you create a C-shaped curve. Figure 27.9 shows both kinds of curves.

6. **When the curve between the two anchor points looks how you want it to look, release the mouse button.**

7. **Continue moving the Pen pointer, clicking and dragging, and then releasing the mouse button to establish additional smooth points and curved segments.**

8. **To complete the path, hold down the ⌘ key or the Ctrl key and click on an empty portion of the page or choose another tool.** If you click on the page, the Pen tool remains selected and you can continue creating additional paths.

You can also complete the path by clicking on the first point you created, but if you do, you create a closed path. Figure 27.9 shows a finished line that contains several curved segments.

FIGURE 27.9

Left: To create a smooth point when beginning a path, click and hold the mouse and drag in the direction of the next point. Here you see the direction line of a smooth endpoint created by clicking and dragging in the direction of the next anchor point. Center: A C-shaped curved segment and an S-shaped curved segment. Right: This line contains five anchor points — all smooth points — and four curved segments. The two segments on its left are both C-shaped curves; the two on the right are both S-shaped.

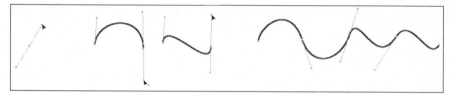

> **TIP** The two segments that form a smooth point's direction line work together as a single straight line. When you move a handle, the line acts like a teeter-totter; the opposite handle moves in the opposite direction. If you shorten one of the segments, the length of the other segment doesn't change. The angle and length of direction lines determine the shape of the segments with which they're associated.

Curved segments connected by corner points

Sometimes you may need to create a line with curvy segments that don't adjoin smoothly. Figure 27.10 shows an example of a line that's made up of several C-shaped curves that are connected with corner points. When adjoining segments — curved or straight — meet at a corner point, the transition is abrupt rather than smooth, as it is at a smooth point. To create this kind of shape, you need to be able to connect curved segments using corner points instead of smooth points. Here's how:

1. **Select the Pen tool or press P if the Type tool isn't selected.**

2. **Move the Pen pointer to where you want to place one of your line's endpoints and then click and hold down the mouse button.** The arrowhead pointer is displayed.

3. **Drag the mouse in the direction of the next point you intend to create.** As you drag, the anchor point, its direction line, and the direction line's two handles are displayed. If you hold down the Shift key as you drag, the angle of the direction line is limited to increments of 45 degrees.

4. **Move the Pen pointer to where you want to establish the next anchor point, which ends the first segment, and then press Option or Alt and click and drag the mouse.** As you drag, the anchor point's handle moves and the direction line changes from a straight line to two independent segments. The angle of the direction line segment that you create when you drag the handle determines the slope of the next segment.

5. **Release the mouse button.**

6. **Continue moving the Pen pointer and repeat Step 4 and Step 5 to create additional segments joined by corner points.**

7. **To complete the path, hold down the ⌘ key or the Ctrl key and click an empty portion of the page or choose another tool.** If you click the page, the Pen tool remains selected and you can continue creating additional paths.

Figure 27.10 shows a line with several curved segments joined by corner points.

FIGURE 27.10

Here, three corner points join four curved segments. The direction handles of the two rightmost segments are visible. The direction handles of a corner point are joined like a hinge; moving one handle doesn't affect the other handle.

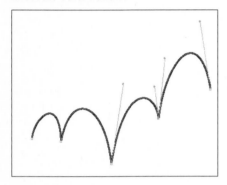

NOTE A corner point that connects two curved segments has two direction lines; a corner point that connects two straight segments has no direction lines; and a corner point that connects a straight and curved segment has one direction line. If you drag a corner point's direction line, the other direction line, if there is one, is not affected. The angle and length of direction lines determine the shape of the segments with which they're associated.

Combining straight and curved segments

By combining the techniques for drawing straight segments and curved segments, you can create lines that contain both. Figure 27.11 shows three lines made up of straight and curved segments, as well as curved segments joined by smooth points and curved segments joined by corner points.

FIGURE 27.11

Three paths with both curved and straight segments, as well as corner points and smooth points

Here's how to draw a straight segment followed by a curved segment:

1. **While drawing a path, create a straight segment by clicking and releasing the mouse button, moving the Pen pointer, and then clicking and releasing the mouse button again.**

2. **Move the Pen pointer over the last anchor point you created in Step 1.** The Convert Point icon appears. (It looks like the regular Pen icon except that a small triangle missing its base appears at the icon's lower right.)

3. **Click, drag, and then release the mouse button to create the direction line that determines the slope of the next segment.**

4. **Move the Pen pointer to where you want to establish the next anchor point and then click and drag to complete the curved segment.**

Figure 27.12 shows a step-by-step sequence of a curved segment being added to a straight segment. You can also follow a straight segment with a curved segment by simply clicking and dragging to create a smooth point. However, if you don't use the method I explain in the earlier steps, you are able to adjust the slope associated with only one of the curved segment's anchor points rather than both.

Follow these steps to draw a curved segment followed by a straight segment:

1. **While drawing a path, create a curved segment by clicking, dragging, and releasing the mouse button and then moving the Pen pointer and clicking, dragging, and releasing the mouse button again.**

2. **Move the Pen pointer over the last anchor point you created in Step 1.** The Convert Point icon appears.

3. **Click the anchor point to convert it from a smooth point to a corner point.**

4. **Move the Pen pointer to where you want to establish the next anchor point and then click and release the mouse button to complete the straight segment.**

FIGURE 27.12

At left, the steps to draw a straight segment followed by a curved segment: (1) Draw a straight segment, as shown at left. (2) Click and drag to create a smooth anchor point. (3) Move the pointer to the next desired anchor point location and then click and drag to create a curved segment. At right, the steps to draw a curved segment followed by a straight segment: (1) Draw a curved segment, as shown at left. (2) Move the pointer over the last anchor point and click that anchor point. (3) Move the pointer to the next desired anchor point location and then click and release the mouse button to create a straight segment.

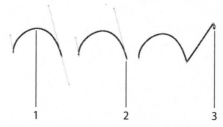

1   2   3   1   2   3

> **TIP**   When creating paths, use as few anchor points as possible. As you become more comfortable creating free-form paths, you should find yourself using fewer anchor points to create paths.

Drawing Free-Form Shapes

A closed path is an uninterrupted enclosure with no endpoints. When you apply a stroke to a closed path, there's no beginning or end. Generally, you'll create closed paths when you want to place text or pictures in free-form frames. Although you can place text or a picture in an open path, the result can look more than a little strange, especially if you add a stroke to the path. Then again, you can achieve some strange effects by using open paths as frames. If strange is your goal, go for it.

> **TIP**   For an easy way to draw free-form shapes, use the Pencil tool. It simply traces the movement of your mouse (or pen tablet) as you move it, in much the same way as a pencil works on paper. Although not as exact as the Pen tool, the Pencil tool does create Bézier curves that you can later edit.

When it comes to creating closed paths with the Pen tool, the process is exactly the same as it is for creating open paths, as explained earlier in this chapter, with one difference at the end: If you click the first endpoint you created, you create a closed path:

- To create a straight segment between the endpoint and the last anchor point you created, click and release the mouse button.

- To create a curved segment, click and drag the mouse in the direction of the last anchor point you created and then release the mouse button.

As can an open path, a closed path can contain straight and/or curved segments and smooth and/or corner points. All the techniques explained earlier in this chapter for drawing lines with curved and straight segments and smooth and corner points apply when you're drawing closed paths. Figure 27.13 shows several closed paths used as graphic shapes, text frames, and graphics frames.

FIGURE 27.13

Closed paths of various shapes

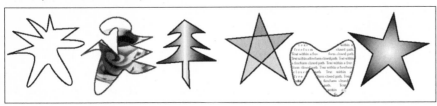

If you draw a path and it turns out to be a little (or a lot, for that matter) different from what you intended, don't worry. You can always modify it by moving, adding, deleting, and converting anchor points and by adjusting direction lines. You can also use the transformation tools, the Control panel, or the Transform panel to rotate, scale, shear, flip, and change the position of the path.

 See Chapters 9 and 10 for more information about manipulating shapes and using InDesign's transformation features.

Editing Free-form Lines and Shapes

No matter how skillful you become using InDesign's Pen and Pencil tools to create free-form paths, it's difficult to create exactly what you want on your first attempt. For example, after creating a path, you may want to add detail, smooth out a rough spot, or turn a straight segment into a curved one. No problem. InDesign lets you modify the paths you create in several ways. You can:

- Add or delete anchor points
- Move anchor points
- Change corner points to smooth points and vice versa
- Modify direction lines
- Extend an open path
- Erase parts of the path or cut paths into segments
- Change a closed path to an open path and vice versa

The path-manipulation techniques I explain in this chapter apply to all types of paths, including open and closed paths created with the Pen tool, the Pencil tool, and the object-creation tools; text and graphic frames (which are simply paths that act as containers); clipping paths created with the Clipping Path command (choose Object ➪ Clipping Path ➪ Options or press Option+Shift+⌘+K or Ctrl+Alt+Shift+K) or built into imported graphics; and text-wrap paths created with the Text Wrap panel (choose Window ➪ Text Wrap or press Option+⌘+W or Ctrl+Alt+W).

 Chapter 26 covers clipping paths and text-wrap paths, and Chapter 12 covers the general use of the Text Wrap panel.

Generally, when you want to manipulate a path, you use one of the three variations of the Pen tool, all of which are displayed in a single pop-up menu in the Tools panel (shown in the sidebar "Drawing Tools," in this chapter):

- Both the Add Anchor Point tool and the Delete Anchor Point tool let you add and delete anchor points.
- The Convert Direction Point tool lets you change smooth points to corner points and vice versa.

You can also use the Pen tool with keyboard shortcuts to perform all the functions of the Add Anchor Point, Delete Anchor Point, and Convert Direction Point tools.

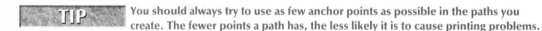

TIP If you find that you simply can't create a particular graphic effect within InDesign, you can always resort to your illustration program (assuming you have one). If you're an Adobe Illustrator user, you can easily drag and drop objects from Illustrator into InDesign documents.

Adding and deleting anchor points

If you want to add detail to an existing path, you need to add anchor points that give you more precise control over a portion of the path. Perhaps you've drawn the profile of a face and you want to add detail to the lips. Or maybe you've written your name longhand and you need to add a flourish that your original attempt lacks. In both cases, you can add smooth or corner points and then manipulate the curves associated with those points by moving them or manipulating their direction lines. (The next section explains how to move anchor points and manipulate direction lines.)

On the other hand, maybe you've created a path that's more complicated than necessary. Perhaps you drew a hand with six fingers instead of five or a camel with one too many humps. In these instances, you need to simplify the path by removing anchor points. InDesign lets you add and delete as many anchor points as you want.

TIP You should always try to use as few anchor points as possible in the paths you create. The fewer points a path has, the less likely it is to cause printing problems.

When you want to modify the shape of a path, you should begin by selecting it with the Direct Selection tool rather than the Selection tool. If you select a path with the Selection tool, the path's bounding box is displayed with eight moveable handles. In this situation, you can modify the bounding box (thereby resizing the path), but you can't modify the path itself.

To add an anchor point:

1. **Select the path by clicking it with the Direct Selection tool.** You can also select multiple paths and then modify them one at a time.

2. **Select the Pen tool, the Add Anchor Point tool, or the Delete Anchor Point tool.** You can use any of these tools to add and delete anchor points. If the Type tool is not selected, you can select the Pen tool by pressing P, the Add Anchor Point tool by pressing =, and the Delete Anchor Point tool by pressing – (hyphen).

3. **Move the Pen pointer over the selected path at the point where you want to add an anchor point.**

4. **Click and release the mouse button.** A new anchor point is created where you click. If the Delete Anchor Point tool is selected, you must hold down the ⌘ or Ctrl key to add an anchor point. If you click a straight segment between two corner points, a corner point is created. If you click a curved segment between two smooth points or between a smooth point and a corner point, a smooth point is created. You can also click, drag, and then release the mouse button if you want to adjust the direction line of the point you create. Figure 27.14 shows a before-and-after example of a path to which a smooth anchor point is added.

FIGURE 27.14

The original path (left) is modified by adding a smooth point (second from left). Dragging the smooth point (third from left) produced the final shape (right).

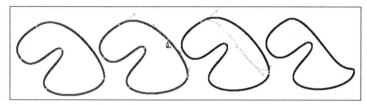

After you add an anchor point, you can hold down the ⌘ or Ctrl key or switch to the Direct Selection tool and drag it or either of its direction handles to adjust the adjoining segments.

> **TIP** Whenever you're working on a path, you can hold down the ⌘ or Ctrl key and then click and drag any element of the path — an anchor point, a direction line, or the entire path.

To delete an anchor point:

1. **Select the path by clicking it with the Direct Selection tool.** You can also select multiple paths and then modify them one at a time.

2. **Select the Pen tool, the Add Anchor Point tool, or the Delete Anchor Point tool.** You can use any of these tools to add and delete anchor points. If the Type tool is not selected, you can select the Pen tool by pressing P, the Add Anchor Point tool by pressing =, and the Delete Anchor Point tool by pressing – (hyphen) on the main keyboard or on the numeric keypad.

3. **Move the pointer over the anchor point that you want to delete and then click.** If the Add Anchor Point tool is selected, you must hold down the ⌘ or Ctrl key to delete an anchor point. Figure 27.15 shows a before-and-after example of a path from which an anchor point has been deleted.

FIGURE 27.15

The curved segment of the original path (left) is removed by deleting the smooth anchor point (center) with the Delete Anchor Point tool. The resulting path is shown on the right.

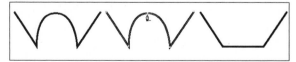

Modifying segments

As you learned earlier in this chapter, a path is made up of one or more segments, and every segment is defined by a pair of anchor points. If you want to modify a segment, you can do so by dragging either or both of its anchor points, dragging the direction handles (if present) of the anchor points, or converting either of the anchor points from smooth to corner or vice versa. For example, you could drag an anchor point on a curvy path to increase or decrease the severity of a particular bump, or you could convert a straight-edged polygon into a curvy shape by converting all its corner points to smooth points.

Moving anchor points

When you select a path with the Direct Selection tool, its anchor points are displayed as small, hollow squares. When you click and drag an anchor point, the two adjoining segments change, but the direction handles, if present, are not affected. If you hold down the Shift key as you drag an anchor point, movement is restricted to increments of 45 degrees. Figure 27.16 shows how moving an anchor point affects adjoining curved and straight segments.

FIGURE 27.16

Left group: The arc of the curve (right) is reduced by clicking and dragging the smooth anchor point at the top of the curve (center). Right group: Dragging a corner (center) point changes the two adjoining segments (right).

> **TIP** If all you need to do is resize a path — particularly a simple rectangle — rather than change its shape, you should select it with the Selection tool rather than the Direct Selection tool and then click and drag one of its bounding box handles.

Converting anchor points

If you want to change a wavy path that contains only curved segments to a zigzag path that contains only straight segments, you can do so by converting the smooth anchor points of the wavy path into corner points. Similarly, by converting corner points to smooth points, you can smooth out a path that contains straight segments. Figure 27.17 shows how straight and curved paths are affected as anchor points are converted.

FIGURE 27.17

Left group: The outer corner points of a straight-edged polygon path (left) were converted to smooth points to create the shape on the right. Right group: The zigzag path (right) was created by converting all the smooth points in the path on the left into corner points.

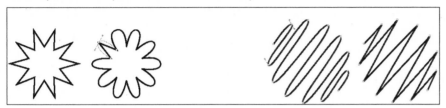

To convert an anchor point:

1. **Select the path by clicking it with the Direct Selection tool.**

2. **Choose the Convert Direction Point tool.** You can also perform the functions of this tool by holding down Option+⌘ or Ctrl+Alt when the Direct Selection tool is selected.

3. **Move the pointer over the anchor point you want to convert.** Depending on the point you want to convert, do one of the following:

   ■ To convert a corner point to a smooth point, click the corner point and then drag (direction lines are created and displayed as you drag).

   ■ To convert a smooth point to a corner point without direction lines, click and release the mouse on the smooth point.

   ■ To convert a smooth point to a corner point with independent direction lines, click and drag either of the smooth point's direction handles.

   ■ To convert a corner point without direction lines to a corner point with direction lines, click and drag the corner point to create a smooth point and then release the mouse button. Then click and drag either of the direction lines.

 **When using the Convert Direction Point tool, you can temporarily switch to the most recently used selection tool by pressing ⌘ or Ctrl.**

NEW FEATURE **InDesign CS4 adds menu options to convert paths. After selecting the path to convert, choose Object ⇨ Paths ⇨ Convert Point. There are four submenu options: Line End, Corner, Smooth, and Smooth Symmetrical.**

Manipulating direction handles

In addition to dragging and converting anchor points, you can adjust the shape of a curved segment by dragging any of the direction lines associated with the anchor points at either end of the segment. Figure 27.18 shows how moving direction lines affect a curved segment.

FIGURE 27.18

The shapes on the right in the two groups of curves were created by dragging a direction line of a smooth point (center shapes in both groups).

> **NOTE** Remember, corner points between straight segments don't have direction handles. If you want to modify the segments associated with a corner point, simply click and drag the point.

To drag a curved segment's direction handle:

1. **Use the Direct Selection tool to select the path.**
2. **Click either of the two endpoints that define the curved segment.** Handles are displayed at the ends of the two lines that make up the selected point's direction line (and the lines make up what appears to be a single, straight line). The direction lines of the two adjoining segments (if present) also appear.
3. **Click and drag any available handle.** Press Shift as you drag to constrain movement to multiples of 45 degrees. As you drag, the handle at the opposite end of the direction line moves in the opposite direction like a teeter-totter. However, if you lengthen or shorten one side of a direction line, the other side is not affected.
4. **Release the mouse button when the shape is the way you want it.**

> **NOTE** If you use the Convert Direction Point tool to click and drag a smooth point's direction-line handle, the opposite portion of the direction line remains unchanged. You can therefore adjust the segment on one side of a smooth point without affecting the segment on the other side.

Working with open and closed paths

If you've created an open path and subsequently decide that you want to extend the path at either or both ends, you can do so using the Pen tool. Along the same lines, you can use the Pen tool to connect two open paths and to close an open path. For example, if you've placed text or a graphic into an open path, you may decide that the path works better in a closed frame. And if you want to get even trickier, you can use the Scissors tool to split an open or closed path into two separate paths.

Extending an open path and connecting open paths

The steps required to extend an open path and to connect two open paths are very similar. Here's how you extend an open path:

1. **Use the Direct Selection tool to select the path you want to extend.**
2. **Move the Pen pointer over one of the path's endpoints.** When the Pen pointer is over an endpoint, a small, angled line appears below and to the right of the Pen.

3. **Click and release the mouse button.**

4. **Move the pointer to where you want to place the next anchor point.** If you want to create a corner point, click and release the mouse button. If you want to create a smooth point, click and hold the mouse button, drag the mouse and then release the mouse button.

5. **Continue adding smooth and corner points until you're done extending the path.**

6. **Finish the path by holding down ⌘ or Ctrl and clicking an empty portion of the page or choosing another tool.**

To connect two open paths, follow Steps 1 through 3 in the preceding list and then click the endpoint of another path (the other path doesn't have to be selected). The left side of Figure 27.19 shows a path before and after being extended; the right side shows an open path produced by connecting two open paths.

FIGURE 27.19

At left: The original path (left) was cloned to create the path on the right. The cloned path was then extended by clicking its right endpoint with the Pen tool and then clicking four more times to create four additional corner points. At right: Connecting the two open paths on the left with the Pen tool produced the single path on the right.

If you hold down the Shift key when you click an endpoint with the Pen tool, an endpoint for a new path is created (that is, the selected path remains unchanged). In this situation, a small *x* is displayed below and to the right of the Pen pointer. Having this endpoint is useful if you want to create two paths that touch at a particular point. For example, you could draw a path and apply a 4-point black stroke to it, and then create another path that shares an endpoint with the first path. By adding a different kind of stroke to the second path, the two paths look like a single path to which two kinds of stroke have been applied.

Closing an open path

Closing an open path is much the same as extending an open path. The only difference is that you *complete* the path — that is, you close it — by clicking the other endpoint. For example, if you slice a graphics frame into two pieces using the Scissors tool (which I explain in the next section of this chapter), two open paths are created. If you add a stroke to these open frames, a portion of the graphic edge (the nonexistent segment between the endpoints) is not stroked. If you close the path, the stroke completely encloses the graphic within. Figure 27.20 shows an open path that's been converted into a closed path.

FIGURE 27.20

The closed path on the right was created from a clone of the open path on the left.

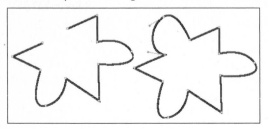

InDesign provides two quick ways to close an open path after selecting it:

- Choose Object ⇨ Paths ⇨ Close Path.
- Click the Close Path iconic button on the Pathfinder panel (which you open by choosing Window ⇨ Object & Layout ⇨ Pathfinder). Figure 27.24 later in this chapter shows the panel.

Opening a closed path

You can open a closed path in two ways after selecting that path:

- Choose Object ⇨ Paths ⇨ Open Path.
- Click the Open Path iconic button on the Pathfinder panel (Window ⇨ Object & Layout ⇨ Pathfinder).

Either way, InDesign separates the start point into a start point and endpoint, letting you move either point or the segments attached to them independently.

NOTE When you choose Objects ⇨ Paths ⇨ Open Path or click the Open Path iconic button, InDesign automatically selects the point where the path was opened, so you can immediately begin working with it (and know where it is).

Using the Scissors tool

The Scissors tool does precisely what its name suggests: It lets you slice things. Specifically, it lets you split paths — open and closed — into two pieces. There are a few things you should know about using the Scissors tool:

- It takes only one click with the Scissors tool to split an open path, but it takes two clicks to completely split a closed path.
- You can split graphics frames but you can't split text frames that contain text. If you want to split a text frame that contains text, you must first cut the text and paste it elsewhere.

- If you split a graphics frame, a copy of the graphic is placed within both frames.

- When you split a path, all stroke and fill attributes of the original path are inherited by the two offspring. After you split a path, it looks the same as before you split it until you move or modify one of the resulting paths.

To split an open path, use the Scissors tool and move the cross-hair pointer over a path then, click and release the mouse button. You can click an open portion of a segment (that is, between anchor points) or an anchor point. In both cases, two anchor points — endpoints of the two resulting paths — are created.

To split a closed path, use the Scissors tool and move the cross-hair pointer over a path and then click and release the mouse button. You can click an open portion of a segment or an anchor point. In both cases, two anchor points — endpoints of the two resulting paths — are created. Move the cross-hair pointer to a different position along the same path and then click and release the mouse button.

After you split a path, you can switch to either of the selection tools and then select, move, or modify either of the two resulting paths as you want. If you've split a closed path, you may want to close the two open paths (as I described in the previous section). The left side of Figure 27.21 shows a pair of open paths that were created using the Scissors tool on an open path. The right side of Figure 27.21 shows a closed graphics frame that's been split into two open frames.

FIGURE 27.21

Left group: The original path (left) was split into two pieces by clicking it with the Scissors tool (center). On the right, you see the two resulting paths after the one on the right has been moved. Right group: The closed path (a graphics frame) on the left was cut twice with the Scissors tool (center). On the right, one of the resulting open paths has been moved with the Selection tool.

Joining Paths

It's not uncommon to create two paths and then realize you want to join them together into one path. Doing so is easy in InDesign: Select the two paths-to-be and then choose Object ➪ Paths ➪ Join, or click the Join Paths iconic button in the Pathfinder panel (Window ➪ Objects & Layout ➪ Pathfinder), as shown in Figure 27.24, later in this chapter.

NEW FEATURE The ability to join paths is new to InDesign CS4.

Note the following about joining paths:

- Only two paths may be joined. (If you select just one path, it will be made into a closed path. If you select more than two paths, nothing will happen when you try to join them.)

- Only open paths created with the Pen and Pencil tools can be joined. Straight lines, frames, and other shapes are ignored.

- If you join a text path to a nontext path, the text will be deleted. If you join two text paths, the first text path's text will be retained and the second path's text will be deleted.

- InDesign usually creates a straight segment between the final point in the first object that was created and the first point in the next object that was created. However, if two other points are close to each other, it may join those two points instead. You will need to experiment to see what happens with your paths.

Working with Compound Paths

When more than one path is selected, you can use the Make Compound Path command (choose Object ➪ Paths ➪ Make Compound Path or press ⌘+8 or Ctrl+8) to convert the paths into a single object (still composed of separate paths). A compound path is similar to a group (choose Object ➪ Group or press Ctrl+G or ⌘+G) except that when you create a group out of several objects, each object in the group retains its original attributes, such as stroke color and width, fill color or gradient, and so on. By contrast, when you create a compound path, the attributes of the backmost path are applied to all the other paths (that is, the attributes of the backmost path replace the attributes of the other paths).

Examples of compound paths in use

Figure 27.22 shows three examples of how you can use compound paths.

FIGURE 27.22

Three examples of compound paths, from left to right: transparent areas within a path, use of a single shape or fill across multiple shapes, and complex shapes created from compound paths.

Create transparent areas within a path

By drawing a circular path in front of a graphic, you could then use the Make Compound Path command to poke a hole in the graphic and reveal the objects or the empty page behind the graphic.

As you can see in the left side of Figure 27.22, I created the graphic with the hole in it (right) by drawing a circular path (center) in front of a clone of the original graphics frame (left) and then creating a compound path from the graphics frame and the circular path. The background shape shows within the transparent hole.

Apply a single background color or graphic across several shapes

You could use the Create Outlines command (choose Type ⇨ Create Outlines or press Shift+⌘+O or Ctrl+Shift+O) to convert text characters into a compound path and then place a blend behind the path so that it extends across all characters. (I explain the Create Outlines command in Chapter 16.) Figure 27.22 shows an example of this in the center.

As you see in the center of Figure 27.22, I converted the text on the top into the editable outlines on the bottom. I then skewed the character outlines — which make up a compound path — by –30 degrees via the Shear X Angle field in the Control panel and applied a gradient fill.

Quickly create complex shapes

Some shapes are hard to draw using a mouse. For example, you could create the complex shape in Figure 27.22 by drawing each of the shaded areas as a separate, closed path. Or you could simply create a square, place four circles in front of it so that they overlap the edges of the square, and then choose Object ⇨ Paths ⇨ Make Compound Path — a process that takes only a few seconds.

That's what I did, in fact, to get the result shown in the right side of Figure 27.22. I converted the five closed paths on the left into a compound path by choosing Object ⇨ Paths ⇨ Make Compound Path to create the shape on the right. InDesign automatically applied the attributes of the original square path, which is the backmost path, to the resulting compound path. Notice that the four semicircular areas where the original shapes overlapped became holes after the shapes were converted to a compound path.

That's only the beginning of what you can do with the Make Compound Path command. Mix in a little bit of your imagination and InDesign's other path-, graphic-, and text-manipulation features, and the possibilities become endless.

Creating compound paths

You can create a compound path out of any kind of path, including open and closed paths as well as text and graphics frames. When you create a compound path, all the original paths become subpaths of the compound shape and inherit the stroke and fill settings of the path that's farthest back in the stacking order. After you create a compound path, you can modify or remove any of the subpaths.

The direction of each subpath determines whether the subpath is filled or transparent. If a particular subpath is transparent instead of filled, or vice versa, you can use the Reverse Path command (choose Object ⇨ Paths ⇨ Reverse Path) or click the Reverse Path iconic button on the Pathfinder panel (choose Window ⇨ Objects & Layout ⇨ Pathfinder) to switch the behavior of a subpath. (Figure 27.24, which appears later in this chapter, shows the Pathfinder panel.)

If the results of choosing Object ➪ Paths ➪ Make Compound Path are not what you expected or want, you can undo the operation (choose Edit ➪ Undo or press ⌘+Z or Ctrl+Z). Paths often don't combine as expected because of how they are stacked; typically, an intervening object affects how InDesign combines the paths. To get a different result, try changing the stacking order and then choose Object ➪ Paths ➪ Make Compound Path again.

To change an object's stacking order (to determine which path's attributes are used for the compound path), choose Object ➪ Arrange ➪ Send Backward or press ⌘+[or Ctrl+[, or choose Object ➪ Arrange ➪ Bring Forward or press ⌘+] or Ctrl+]. (Chapter 12 explains stacking order in more detail.)

If frames that contain text and/or graphics are selected when you choose Make Compound Path, the resulting compound path retains the content of the frame that's closest to the bottom of the stacking order. If the bottommost frame doesn't have any content, the content — text or graphic — of the next highest nonempty frame is retained in the compound path. The content of all frames above the frame whose content is retained is removed.

Editing compound paths

After you create a compound path, you can change the shape of any of the subpaths by clicking one with the Direct Selection tool and then clicking and dragging any of its anchor points or direction handles. The Pen, Add Anchor Point, Delete Anchor Point, and Convert Direction Point tools work the same for subpaths as they do for other paths, which means that you can reshape them however you want.

The Stroke panel (choose Window ➪ Stroke or press ⌘+F10 or Ctrl+F10), Swatches panel (choose Window ➪ Swatches or press F5), and Color panel (choose Window ➪ Color or press F6) — as well as the transformation tools, the Control panel (choose Window ➪ Control or press Option+⌘+6 or Ctrl+Alt+6), and the Transform panel (choose Window ➪ Object & Layout ➪ Transform) — also let you change the appearance of a compound path. When you change the appearance of a compound path, the changes are applied uniformly to all subpaths.

Moving a subpath is a little tricky because you can't drag just that subpath. If you try, all the connected subpaths move. If you want to move an entire subpath, you must move each of the subpath's anchor points individually. In this case, it's probably easier to release the compound path, as I describe next, move the path as needed, and then re-create the compound path by choosing Object ➪ Paths ➪ Make Compound Path or pressing ⌘+8 or Ctrl+8.

If you want to delete a subpath, you must use the Delete Anchor Point tool to delete all its anchor points. If you delete an anchor point of a closed subpath, it becomes an open subpath.

NOTE If the Selection or Position tool is active, you can't delete anchor points using the Cut command (choose Edit ➪ Cut or press ⌘+X or Ctrl+X), the Clear command (choose Edit ➪ Clear or press Delete or Backspace), or the Del or Delete key. (Note that the Del key is labeled Delete→ on newer Mac keyboards.) All these keyboard commands remove the entire path. To work on those individual points, be sure the Direct Selection tool is active.

Changing a path's direction

When you create a path, it has a built-in direction — clockwise or counterclockwise — that is generally not noticeable but affects a compound path. Generally, you can't determine the direction of a path by looking at it. However, you can tell whether paths' directions differ by how subpaths in a compound path interact:

■ If a subpath in a compound path has the same direction as the backmost path, the area within the subpath is transparent.

■ Conversely, if a subpath's direction is different than the backmost path, the area within the subpath will be filled.

If a subpath is filled in and you want it to be transparent, or vice versa, click the compound path with the Direct Selection tool and then click the compound path whose direction you want to change and choose Object ➪ Paths ➪ Release Compound Path or press Option+Shift+⌘+8 or Ctrl+Alt+Shift+8 to separate the subpaths. Figure 27.23 shows how changing the direction of a subpath changes it from filled to transparent.

FIGURE 27.23

The gray square and circle on the left have been combined into a compound path, but the direction of the circular subpath causes it to be filled in instead of transparent. Changing the subpath's direction produced the results on the right: a transparent hole in the square shape.

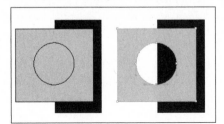

Splitting a compound path

If you decide you want to deconstruct a compound path, you can do so by clicking anywhere within the compound path and then choosing Object ➪ Paths ➪ Release Compound Path or pressing Option+Shift+⌘+8 or Ctrl+Alt+Shift+8. The resulting paths retain the attributes of the compound path.

 The Release command is not available if the selected compound path contains text or if it's nested within a frame.

Using the Pathfinder

Sometimes, you want to combine multiple paths. You can join them, as I describe earlier, or you can use the Pathfinder panel or menu options, as you prefer:

- To use the Pathfinder panel and its iconic buttons, choose Window ⇨ Object & Layout ⇨ Pathfinder.
- To use the menu options, choose Object ⇨ Pathfinder and then choose the desired five options from the submenu: Add, Subtract, Intersect, Exclude Overlap, and Minus Back.

Figure 27.24 shows the Pathfinder panel and Figure 27.25 shows how each of the five options affects a group of closed paths (shapes).

NEW FEATURE   **The Pathfinder adds the Join Path iconic button and has rearranged the other buttons for better separation among the path, Pathfinder, and shape-conversion functions.**

Here's what the five Pathfinder options do:

- **Add:** This option adds all objects' shapes together.
- **Subtract:** This option subtracts all objects from the bottommost object in the stack.
- **Intersect:** This option creates an object where objects overlap. This works only on closed paths.
- **Exclude Overlap:** This option removes overlapping paths and keeps the nonoverlapping paths of all objects.
- **Minus Back:** This option subtracts all objects from the top object in the stack.

FIGURE 27.24

The Pathfinder panel has five iconic buttons for pathfinding tasks, nine for shape conversion, and four for joining, opening, closing, and reversing paths.

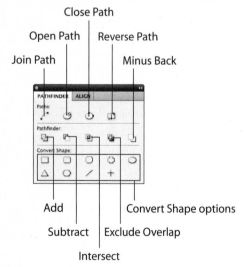

FIGURE 27.25

Three closed paths (shapes) with the five Pathfinder options applied to them. From left to right: the two original paths and the same paths after applying after applying Add, Subtract, Intersect, Exclude Overlap, and Minus Back options.

Using Other Path Effects

InDesign provides several other functions to manipulate paths: the Convert Shape menu options, the Smooth tool, the Erase tool, and the Corner Options dialog box.

The Convert Shape options

While you can edit a shape with the Bézier tools I describe earlier in this chapter, it can be a lot of work for what should be a simple operation. InDesign gives you two easy ways to convert an object's shape:

- Choose Object ➪ Convert Shape and then choose one of the submenu options: Rectangle, Rounded Rectangle, Beveled Rectangle, Inverse Rounded Rectangle, Ellipse, Triangle, Polygon, Line, or Orthogonal Line.

- Click the iconic button in the Convert Shape section of the Pathfinder panel that corresponds to the desired Convert Shape submenu option. Choose Window ➪ Object & Layout ➪ Pathfinder to open the panel. (See Figure 27.25 to see the Pathfinder panel and its shape-conversion iconic buttons.)

The Smooth tool

Available via the Pencil tool's pop-out menu is the Smooth tool, as shown in Figure 27.26. Although it's a bit tricky to use, its concept is simple: It smoothes out corner points and the shapes of curved segments.

To use it, select the Smooth tool and then move the pointer back and forth over a path (open or closed) that you want to smooth. If the path has multiple anchor points, it moves them to smooth out the curve, smoothing it more as you move the tool more. If the path is a corner such as for a frame, repeated movement of the Smooth tool converts the angular corner into a rounded corner.

FIGURE 27.26

The Smooth tool and Erase tool are available via the Pencil tool's pop-out menu in the Tools panel.

The Erase tool

Just as it has tools to create paths, InDesign has a tool to delete them: the Erase tool, which is accessible via the Pencil tool's pop-out menu.

To erase straight lines, first select the path to work with using the Selection tool. Then switch to the Erase tool and drag it alongside the path segment to cut — making sure not to cross the path — and then release the mouse. The segment disappears.

But for shapes, the tool takes some experimenting with. After selecting the shape with the Selection tool, switch to the Erase tool and then draw a path through the shape to erase part of it. The tool typically removes anchor points away from the direction of the mouse movement, causing part of the shape to disappear. Unfortunately, it's hard to predict what will be erased, so be patient and use the Undo command (choose Edit➪Undo or press ⌘+Z or Ctrl+Z) whenever the result is not what you want. Figure 27.27 shows two examples.

FIGURE 27.27

The Erase tool deletes path segments (at right) for the two originals (at left) in this composite image.

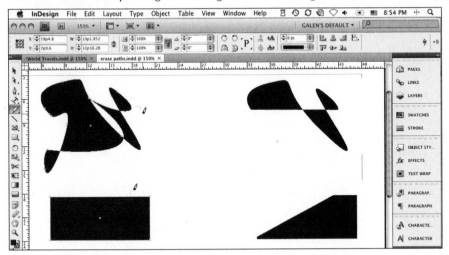

The Corner Options dialog box

When a path is selected, the Corner Options dialog box (choose Object ➪ Corner Options) lets you apply any of several graphical embellishments to its corner points (if the path has any corner points). Generally, corner options work best with rectangular shapes, but they can also produce interesting results when you apply them to free-form shapes and open paths. Figure 27.28 shows examples of corner options applied to a closed path and two open paths.

CROSS-REF Chapter 11 shows all five corner options as applied to closed paths (shapes), as well as explains how to use the Corner Options dialog box.

FIGURE 27.28

The effects of corner options on one closed path and two open paths. Left group: The original paths. Right group: The modified paths.

Summary

If you need to create free-form paths — zigzag or curvy lines or complex closed shapes — you must use the Pen tool. All paths are made up of one or more segments, which begin and end in anchor points. Direction lines control the behavior or anchor points, which in turn control the transition between adjoining segments. When you create an open or a closed path using the Pen tool, you have the option of creating straight segments or curved segments, and corner points or smooth points.

When it comes to drawing with the Pen or Pencil tool, close is plenty good enough. That's because InDesign lets you modify paths in many ways — by moving, adding, and deleting anchor points; by switching smooth points to corner points and vice versa; and by clicking and dragging direction lines. You also have the option to extend either or both ends of an open path and to close open paths.

If a path requires more drastic surgery, you can use the Scissors tool, which lets you split any kind of path into two pieces. And you can use the join capability to join two paths together, though this works only with paths drawn with the Pencil and Pen tools and can join just two such paths at a time.

Because InDesign is primarily a page-layout program, it doesn't contain the breadth of illustration-specific features that you would find in a dedicated vector-based drawing program. Although you may decide that you need a dedicated illustration program to handle your industrial-strength drawing tasks, InDesign does have several features for creating complex shapes.

For example, the Make Compound Path command lets you combine several paths into a single object. If you want to add a graphic flourish to the corners of a path, you can use the Corner Options dialog box to apply any of several built-in corner styles and specify the size of the corner.

Part VII

Output Fundamentals

Chapter 28

Preparing for Color Prepress

Since their invention in the mid-1980s, desktop-publishing programs have broadened their features to cover more and more color publishing needs. Many of the color-oriented features have caused consternation among professional color separators and printers who have seen amateurs make a tough job worse or ruin an acceptable piece of work. This situation is familiar to anyone in desktop publishing in the early years when the typographic profession looked on in horror at amateurs publishing documents without understanding tracking, hyphenation, and many other fundamental areas.

Some programs have added more and more high-end color prepress features. InDesign is one of those and offers the following: two types of trapping engines; the ability to control trapping of individual objects and pages; the ability to apply color models to imported pictures to help the printer adjust the output to match the original picture's color intent; and support for composite workflow, which creates files that have a version for output on a proofing printer such as a color inkjet and a version for output on an imagesetter as film negatives or directly to plate.

The perfect scenario for InDesign color output is that you're using all Adobe software in their latest versions: Photoshop CS4 (11.0), Illustrator CS4 (14.0), and a PostScript Level 3 output device or PDF/X export file. But most people won't have that perfect scenario, especially the PostScript Level 3 part, because it's fairly new and the output devices that commercial printers use are expensive and not replaced often. And although companies such as Adobe hope that users upgrade all their software every two years when the new releases come, the reality is that people tend to upgrade the tools they use the most, letting the others slide. So, you might well use Photoshop CS4 and InDesign CS4 but Illustrator CS2 and Acrobat Professional 8.

Then there's the fact that not everyone uses Illustrator or Photoshop: Both CorelDraw and ACD Canvas have established a toehold among Windows-based artists. Photoshop has less competition, though there are dedicated users of Corel Photo-Paint and Corel PaintShop Pro (again, in Windows — the Mac is an Adobe-owned company town when it comes to graphics software).

Having said that, I also assure you that you don't need to panic if you're not using cutting-edge equipment and software. After years of user education and efforts by software developers like Adobe to build in some of the more basic color-handling assumptions into their programs, most desktop publishers now produce decent color output by simply using the default settings, perhaps augmented by a little tweaking in Photoshop or an illustration program. To really use the color-management and trapping tools in InDesign effectively, you should understand color printing. But if you don't, you can be assured that the default settings in InDesign will produce decent-quality color output.

CROSS-REF   The illustrations and figures in this chapter are in black and white. You need to look at your color monitor to see the effects of what I describe here, or download the image files from the companion Web site (www.InDesignCentral.com). Also take a look at the full-color examples in this book's special eight-page insert, "Color Techniques."

Managing Color Management

InDesign comes with several color management system (CMS) options. A CMS helps you ensure accurate printing of your colors, both those in imported images and those defined in InDesign. What a CMS does is track the colors in the source image, the colors your monitor can display, and the colors your printer can print. If the monitor or printer does not support a color in your document, the CMS alters (recalibrates) the color to its closest possible equivalent.

Don't confuse InDesign's CMS capabilities with color *matching*. It is impossible to match colors produced in an illustration or paint program, or through a scanner, with what a printer or other output device can produce. The underlying differences in color models (which actually determine how a color is defined) and the physics of the media (screen phosphors that emit light versus different types of papers with different types of inks that reflect light) make color matching impossible. But a calibration tool such as a CMS can *minimize* differences.

You can set the CMS settings in InDesign by choosing Edit ➪ Color Settings (there is no keyboard shortcut unless you assign one yourself; I explain how to do this in Chapter 3) to get the dialog box shown in Figure 28.1. (I get to these options a bit later in this chapter.)

If you're creating colors in a program and importing those colors into InDesign, it's important to calibrate them in the same way, or at least as closely as the different programs will allow. Other programs may have similar settings for calibrating their display against your type of monitor. The print-oriented applications in Adobe's Creative Suite 4 (CS4) have the same dialog box that appears in Figure 28.1:

- **Bridge CS4:** Choose Edit ⇨ Creative Suite Color Settings or press Shift+⌘+K or Ctrl+Shift+K.

- **Acrobat Professional 9:** Choose Acrobat ⇨ Preferences or press ⌘+K on the Mac; choose Edit ⇨ Preferences or press Ctrl+K in Windows and then go to the Color Management pane. Note that this pane's appearance differs from the appearance of other CS4 applications' Color Settings dialog boxes.

- **Illustrator CS4:** Choose Edit ⇨ Color Settings or press Shift+⌘+K or Ctrl+Shift+K.

- **Photoshop CS4:** Choose Edit ⇨ Color Settings or press Shift+⌘+K or Ctrl+Shift+K.

Note that there are no CMS controls for the Web-oriented Adobe Device Manager, Dreamweaver, Fireworks, or Flash Professional applications.

If you use Adobe Creative Suite 4, you can ensure that all CS4 programs use the same CMS, ensuring color consistency for elements that move among Photoshop, Illustrator, Acrobat, and InDesign. To select the CMS, open the Adobe Bridge CS4 application and choose Edit ⇨ Creative Suite Color Settings and then select the desired CMS settings and click Apply. I recommend that you first select the Show Expanded List of Color Settings Files option before you click Apply. Figure 28.1 shows the dialog box.

Note that if individual CS4 applications' color settings differ from the CS4-wide settings, you see a note to that effect at the top of the affected applications' Color Settings dialog box. Similarly, Bridge's Suite Color Settings dialog box will alert you (as shown in Figure 28.1) if CS4 applications use different CMS settings — and it lets you force the same setting on all of them.

FIGURE 28.1

Left: InDesign's Color Settings dialog box lets you set application color defaults. Right: Set a consistent color management profile for all Creative Suite 4 programs using Adobe Bridge.

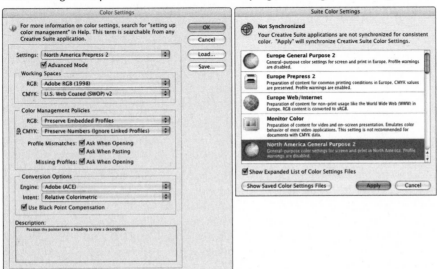

TIP If you use a mix of CS4, CS3, and CS2 applications, set the same color settings in Bridge CS4, Bridge CS3, and Bridge CS2 so that all your applications have the same defaults. The CS2 and CS3 applications have the same color setting options (and user interface) as CS4 applications, making this easy to do.

Setting up your system

To achieve the best reproduction of printed colors on-screen, you need a closely controlled environment for your computer. Most people don't bother, relying instead on their brain's ability to mentally substitute the print color for what they see on-screen after they've had experience seeing what happens in actual printed documents. But the more you do to control the color viewing environment, the closer the match between what you see on-screen and what you see on the page.

These tips on setting up your system are in order from simplest to most complex:

- **Dim the lights.** Most people turn the brightness of their monitors too high, which distorts colors by overdoing the blues and underdelivering on the reds. Adjust the brightness level of the monitor to between 60 and 75 percent maximum. To make sure you can still see the screen, lower the amount of light in your workspace by using lower-wattage bulbs, turning off overhead lighting right above your monitor, and/or using translucent shades in nearby windows.

- **Change the color temperature of your monitor to 7,200 degrees on the Kelvin scale.** Most monitors have on-screen controls to do so.

- **If your monitor has a color profile, use it.** Where you manage profiles varies based on your operating system (note that some monitors or video cards come with their own color-setup software):

  - On the Mac, the Displays system preference has an option in its Color pane for setting color to a profile (stored in the `System:Library:ColorSync:Profiles` folder), or you can use the Color pane's Calibrate button to alter a profile based on your monitor's actual display.

  - In Windows XP, use the Display control panel; the Settings pane has an option called Advanced that will open a dialog box that has a Color Management pane. The profiles are stored in the `Windows\System32\Spool\Drivers\Color` folder. (Note that the `Windows` folder may have a different name on your computer, such as `WinXP`.)

  - In Windows Vista, use the Color Settings control panel and click the Add button in the Devices or All Profiles panes to add profiles. Change profiles in the Advanced pane. The profiles are stored in the `Windows\System32\Spool\Drivers` folder.

- **Use a calibration tool.** Professional tools such as X-Rite's $518 i1Display colorimeter and EZcolor software bundle, as well as lower-end tools such as X-Rite's $90 Pantone Huey colorimeter, calibrate your monitor and create a color profile specifically for it. Note that color calibration software without a hardware calibrator device (a colorimeter) is worthless; without being able to measure what colors actually come from your monitor, there's no way the software can meaningfully adjust the colors in your display. Also note that monitors vary their color display over their lifetime (they get dimmer), so you should recalibrate every six months. For most users, the variances in monitor brightness, color balance, and contrast — coupled with the varying types of lighting used in their workspace — mean that true calibration is impossible for images created on-screen and displayed on-screen. Still, using the calibration feature makes the on-screen color closer to what prints, even if it's not an exact match.

■ **Work in a color-controlled room.** In such a room, the lighting is at 5,000 degrees Kelvin, so the light reflecting off your color proofs matches that of a professional prepress operation. Monitors should also be set with a white point of D65 (something done with calibration hardware and software). Also try to buy monitors with a neutral, light-gray shade — or paint them that way — so that your brain doesn't darken what you see on-screen to compensate for the off-white monitor frame right next to the screen image. Similarly, all furnishings should be neutral, preferably a light gray. Avoid having anything with a strong color in the room — even clothes.

NOTE There's long been a standard (the latest version of which is called ISO 3664) that has set 5,000 degrees Kelvin as the industry standard for proofing color printing. Basically, 5,000 degrees is filtered daylight in which the red, green, and blue components are equal. The International Prepress Association (`www.ipa.org`) has a lot of standards information and resources related to color accuracy.

Adjusting the on-screen display

There are several factors that control how InDesign's CMS works in practice, some related to the operating system's settings and some to the settings in InDesign's Color Settings dialog box.

Setting monitor bit depth

To have color calibration in effect for a monitor, you must be displaying thousands of colors (16-bit color depth) or more colors (or a higher color depth, such as 24-bit). The process depends on your operating system:

■ On the Mac, use the Displays system preference to change your monitor's bit depth.

■ In Windows XP, use the Settings pane of the Display control panel.

■ In Windows Vista, use the Display Settings control panel (which you typically access from the Personalization control panel).

Adjusting InDesign's color display settings

The Color Settings dialog box (choose Edit ⇨ Color Settings) in InDesign is where you control how InDesign manages color display on-screen.

Select the monitor or color space in the RGB pop-up menu in the Working Spaces section of the Color Settings dialog box (refer to Figure 28.1). The monitor or color space that you select tells InDesign how to display imported images and colors defined within InDesign.

Defining Color Models

Whether you define colors in InDesign or in your illustration or paint program, the method you use to define them is critical to ensuring the best possible output. Defining all colors in the same model as the target output device is best. Use the following guidelines:

- If your printer is RGB (this is rare) or if you plan on publishing HTML, Flash, or PDF documents (that you don't expect to be printed), use the RGB model to define colors.

- If your printer is CMYK (such as an offset printer or most inkjets), use CMYK to define colors. However, InDesign is so good at converting RGB-based images — which is what monitors display best — to CMYK that many designers don't bother to define images they create as CMYK.

- If you're using Pantone colors for traditional offset printing, pick one of the Pantone solid models if your printer is using Pantone inks. Pick the Pantone Process Coated model if your printer is using inks from companies other than Pantone.

- If you're using Pantone colors for traditional offset printing, pick the Pantone Process Coated model if you will color-separate those colors into CMYK.

- Trumatch and Focoltone colors were designed to reproduce accurately whether they output as spot colors or are color-separated into CMYK. Other models (such as Toyo, ANPA, and DIC) may or may not separate accurately for all colors, so check with your printer or the ink manufacturer.

- If you're using any Pantone, Focoltone, Trumatch, Toyo, ANPA, or DIC color and outputting to a desktop color printer (whether RGB or CMYK), watch to ensure that the color definition doesn't lie outside the printer's gamut, as I explain in the next section.

- Never rely on the screen display to gauge any non-RGB color. Even with the InDesign CMS's monitor calibration, RGB monitors simply cannot match most non-RGB colors. Use the on-screen colors only as a guide, and rely instead on a color swatchbook from your printer or the color ink's manufacturer.

- InDesign's CMS does *not* calibrate color in EPS or PDF files. If you use EPS, I strongly recommend that you use the DCS (pre-separated CMYK) variant. If you use PDF files, embed the correct color profile in the application from which you create the PDF file or use Adobe Acrobat Distiller's options to set color profiles.

The first five options — Adobe RGB (1998), Apple RGB, ColorMatch RGB, ProPhoto RGB, and sRGB IEC61966-2.1 — are all neutral color spaces, meaning that they aren't adjusted for specific monitors. Adobe programs typically save their images with the sRGB (standard RGB) profile, which works well if you define colors based on swatches and use exact RGB settings or existing swatches.

The other options are monitor-specific profiles, which make sense to use if you choose your colors based on what you see on-screen. Which ones you get depend on what profiles are installed on your computer by the operating system and/or the software that came with your monitor.

The rest of the Color Settings dialog box's options affect how InDesign manages color when printing your document.

Adjusting color output settings

Setting how colors are displayed on-screen is just part of what you need to do to manage color in InDesign. You also have to tell InDesign how to handle colors during printing, which you do in a few locations. Most of the controls are in the Color Settings dialog box, though a few are in the Preferences dialog box.

Setting color management policies

The Color Management Policies section of the Color Settings dialog box (choose Edit ⇨ Color Settings) is where you tell InDesign how to handle color calibration when printing.

But before you set these policies, you need to tell InDesign what your target printer or imagesetter is so that it knows what colors to aim for in its calibration. You do this in the CMYK pop-up menu of the dialog box's Working Spaces section.

Now you set how imported images' colors are managed in the Color Management Policies section of the dialog box. The RGB and CMYK pop-up menus let you manage how imported RGB and CMYK images are handled within InDesign.

- For the RGB pop-up menu, the default option is Preserve Embedded Profiles, which is the best option if your graphics sources have already had color profiles applied intentionally (such as in Illustrator or Photoshop) to help calibrate the output. Your other options are Off (no color management) and Convert to Working Space (which applies the setting in the Working Spaces section's RGB pop-up menu to all imported graphics, overriding their profiles).

- For the CMYK pop-up menu, the default option is Preserve CMYK Color Numbers, which ensures the actual CMYK values are preserved instead of any color profiles that may be applied. Your other options are Off, Convert to Working Space, and Preserve Embedded Profiles, which work for CMYK files the same as they do for RGB files in the RGB pop-up menu.

If your pictures are not usually color-managed at the source, it's best to override the embedded profiles for these two pop-up menus and choose either Convert to Working Space, which uses the color profiles selected in the Working Spaces section of the dialog box, or Off, which strips out any color profiles.

The Color Management Policies section also has options for when to notify you of profile mismatches (Ask When Opening and Ask When Pasting) and one to alert you to imported graphics have no profile applied (Ask When Opening). If you are color-managing your documents, you should select all three check boxes. There is one exception to this advice: If you choose Convert to Working Space in the RGB and CMYK pop-up menus, you can deselect Ask When Opening for Missing Profiles because you won't be using any embedded profiles from the original graphic.

Understanding Profiles

The mechanism that a color management system (CMS) uses to do its calibration is the profile that contains the information on color models and ranges supported by a particular creator (such as an illustration program or scanner), display, and printer. InDesign includes dozens of such predefined profiles.

A CMS uses a device-independent color space to match these profiles against each other. A color space is a mathematical way of describing the relationships among colors. By using a device-independent color model (the CIE XYZ standard defined by the Commission Internationale de l'Éclairage, the International Commission on Illumination), a CMS can compare gamuts from other device-dependent models (such as RGB and the others). What this means is that a CMS can examine the colors in your imported images and defined colors, compare them against the capabilities of your monitor and printer, and adjust the colors for the closest possible display and printing.

Adjusting bitmap images' color

Use the Conversion Options section to control the display and printing of bitmapped images. (Make sure the Advanced Mode check box is selected near the top of the Color Settings dialog box to display this section.) InDesign provides these controls for bitmap images to essentially compensate for the fact that when photos are scanned or images saved, the color pixels may not accurately replicate the creator's intent. For example, a PowerPoint slide that has solid color areas may end up with slight variations in color among pixels — or perhaps with unexpectedly muted colors — when copied into Photoshop.

The first setting — the Engine pop-up menu — controls which adjustment engine to use: Adobe's or the one that comes with your operating system. Your choices are Adobe (ACE) and Apple CMM on the Mac, and Adobe (ACE) and Microsoft ICM in Windows. If you work in a cross-platform environment, choose Adobe (ACE); if you work in a Mac-only or Windows-only environment, pick whatever you prefer based on output tests you conduct with your service bureau.

The Intent pop-up menu is where you specify how you want your bitmap images' color to be adjusted. There are four options in the Intent pop-up menu:

- **Perceptual:** This selection tries to balance the colors in an image when the adjustment engine translates from the original color range to the output device's color range under the assumption that it's a photograph and therefore needs to look natural. This is appropriate for photographs.

- **Saturation:** This selection tries to create vivid colors when the adjustment engine translates a graphic from the original color range to the output device's color range — even if doing so means that some colors are printed inaccurately. This is appropriate for charts and other slide-like graphics whose colors are intended for impact rather than naturalness.

- **Relative Colorimetric:** This selection shifts all the colors to compensate for the white point of the monitor as set in the operating system's display profile (essentially, adjusting the brightness of the output to compensate for any dimness or excess brightness in the monitor). It makes no other adjustments to the colors during output.

- **Absolute Colorimetric:** This selection makes no adjustments to the colors during output. So it allows, for example, an image that uses two similar colors to end up being output as the same color because of the printer's limited color range.

Depending on what kinds of documents you produce, you likely want Perceptual or Saturation as your setting.

Adjusting blackness

You might think that black is black is black, but that's not true. So InDesign lets you control how black is treated during output as well.

In an RGB bitmap image, for example, black is actually created by mixing red, green, and blue, so it's often really a very dark gray. The Conversion Options section of the Color Settings dialog box has the Black Point Compensation check box to look for those dark grays and convert them to true black. Select this option (its default setting) to adjust the color range for maximum range, which permits truer colors in most cases and a more natural look with converted photographs. You should leave this option selected unless you know that your source image has a small range (such as being mostly midtones), in which case black-point compensation can distort shadows and subtle colors in an effect similar to a moiré pattern.

InDesign also has controls for how black is treated in all elements of your layout, not just bitmap images. They reside in the Appearance of Black pane of the Preferences dialog box (choose InDesign ⇨ Preferences ⇨ Appearance of Black or press ⌘+K on the Mac, or choose Edit ⇨ Preferences ⇨ Appearance of Black or press Ctrl+K in Windows), which is shown in Figure 28.2. These controls affect how the [Black] swatch is treated during output, both for objects you create in InDesign and for those imported files (such as Illustrator, EPS, and PDF files) that have a black color swatch applied to their elements.

The Appearance of Black pane lets you control both the on-screen display of black and the output of black. Both the On Screen and Printing/Exporting pop-up menus offer the same two options:

- **Display (or Output) All Blacks Accurately:** This does exactly what it says, which can lead to weaker-looking blacks in documents that are otherwise rich in color.
- **Display (or Output) All Blacks as Rich Black:** This boosts the black output for better clarity, essentially by adding some magenta ink to make it appear darker. This helps black colors not look flat when surrounded by other rich colors.

By default, InDesign sets the On Screen pop-up menu to Display All Blacks as Rich Black and the Printing/Exporting pop-up menu to Output All Blacks as Rich Black.

I'm not sure you should stick with the Output All Blacks as Rich Black setting for output because you no longer get just black when you print. You can always use the [Registration] color swatch to get rich black (also known as *superblack*) and thus use that color specifically when you want to, rather than have all blacks automatically changed. Although rich black helps blacks stand out when they're surrounded by other saturated colors, it can lead to overinking and bleedthrough in documents on thinner paper. You should experiment with your printing press and paper to see what works best for you.

FIGURE 28.2

The Appearance of Black pane in the Preferences dialog box

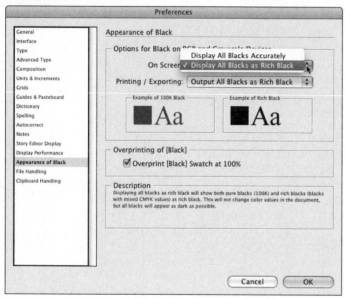

Applying profiles to images

You can apply the desired profiles for individual images when you import them. Select Show Import Options when you place a graphic into InDesign in the Place dialog box (choose File ➡ Place or press ⌘+D or Ctrl+D). In the resulting Image Import Options dialog box, go to the Color pane and select the appropriate profile from the Profile menu, as well as the appropriate rendering intent from the Intent pop-up menu. Figure 28.3 shows the Image Import Options dialog box.

You can apply or change the profile to a placed image at any time by selecting it and choosing Object ➡ Image Color Settings. Doing so opens the Image Color Settings dialog box, also shown in Figure 28.3, in which you set a new profile and/or rendering intent. (You can also choose Graphics ➡ Image Color Settings from the contextual menu to open the Image Color Settings dialog box.)

When you open a document, InDesign checks all the images imported into that document to see if they have a color-management profile embedded or applied. Based on the settings defined in the Color Settings dialog box (choose Edit ➡ Color Settings), described earlier in this chapter, it may apply default profiles to them, do nothing, or ask you what to do. If there is no embedded color profile in the document and if the Ask When Opening check box is selected in the Color Settings dialog box, the Missing Profile dialog box appears when you open the document. When opening a document, you might get two such dialog boxes, one for RGB profile and/or one for CMYK profile, depending on what's embedded (if anything) in the documents' images.

FIGURE 28.3

Left: You can apply color profiles when importing pictures through the Image Import Options dialog box. Right: Using the Image Color Settings dialog box, you can apply color profiles to an object after it's placed in your document.

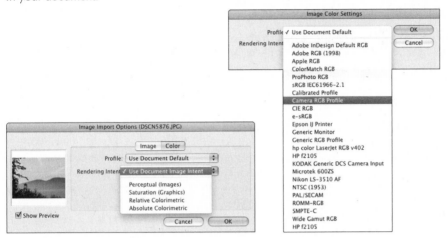

Your choices are as follows:

- **Leave as Is (Use Current Working Space):** This option uses the document's default profile to the image, as specified in the Color Settings dialog box, but does not embed that profile in the image.

- **Assign Current Working Space:** This option applied the document's default profile to the image, embedding that profile in the image so that even if the document's default profile changes later, the image's profile does not.

- **Assign Profile:** This option lets you choose the desired profile to be applied to and embedded in this image from the pop-up menu at the right. Use this when you have a specific reason not to use the document's default profile.

Whichever method you use to apply profiles, only profiles appropriate for the image type appear in these pop-up menus. For example, only CMYK profiles (generally, these are output devices) appear for a CMYK TIFF file, even though the image may have been scanned using an RGB scanner and later converted to CMYK with Photoshop. This limitation exists because InDesign assumes that the image is designed for output to that specific printer and, thus, calibrates it with that target in mind. For RGB files, InDesign lets you apply monitor-oriented profiles and scanner-oriented profiles.

Changing document color settings

If you put together a document with specific color settings, as described earlier, but then decide you want to apply a new profile across your graphics or replace a specific profile globally in your document, you can. There are two options for setting color profiles:

- Choose Edit ⇨ Assign Profiles to replace the color management settings globally, as shown in Figure 28.4. This action sets the target color settings for output. You can set the RGB profile and CMYK profiles separately, as well as set the color intent for solid colors, bitmap images, and gradient blends using the Solid Color Intent, Default Image Intent, and After-Blending Intent pop-up menus.

- Change the document's working color workspace by choosing Edit ⇨ Convert to Profile, which opens the Convert to Profile dialog box, also shown in Figure 28.4. It also lets you change the CMS engine, rendering intent, and black-point compensation settings. This action does not change your output color settings but instead changes the source profiles assigned to the images so you can test different color settings in onscreen preview mode (choose View ⇨ Proof Colors).

There's real overlap in these two dialog boxes' controls, even though they are applied to different aspects of your document's color profiles and thus have some differences. Using the Assign Profiles dialog box to replace the document profile does the same as the Convert to Profile dialog box when it comes to replacing the profiles. The only difference is that the Assign Profiles dialog box can also remove profiles from the document. Both dialog boxes let you change the rendering intents for colors, though the Assign Profiles dialog box gives you several levels of control not available in the Convert to Profile dialog box. But the Convert to Profile dialog box lets you change the black-point compensation and the CMS engine.

A related set of controls resides in the Profile or Policy Mismatch dialog box, which appears as you open a document if InDesign detects a mismatch between a document's color settings and those specified in InDesign's Color Settings dialog box. You can leave the document as is or assign a new profile to the document (using the Assign Profile pop-up menu) and, independently, choose whether to override the profiles applied to the document's images using the Placed Content pop-up menu. Figure 28.5 shows the dialog box.

FIGURE 28.4

InDesign provides two dialog boxes — Assign Profiles (left) and Convert to Profile (right) — to change color-management preferences throughout a document.

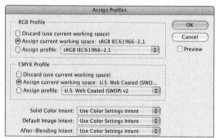 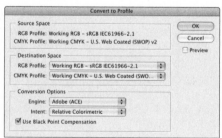

If InDesign detects a mismatch between a document's color settings and those specified in InDesign's Color Settings dialog box, it displays the Profile or Policy Mismatch dialog box when you open that document.

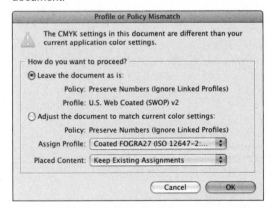

Managing color during output

When you're ready to output your document to a printer or other device, you set the profile and rendering intent for that destination device in the Color Management pane of the Print dialog box (choose File ⇨ Print or press ⌘+P or Ctrl+P), which has a Print Space section with a Profile pop-up menu and an Intent pop-up menu. Here you select the appropriate options for your output device.

 **Chapter 30 covers printing in more detail.**

Saving color-management preferences

You can save and use color-management settings in other documents. The process is simple: Click Save in the Color Settings dialog box to save the current dialog box's settings to a file. If you want to use that saved color-settings information in another document, open that document, click Load in the Color Settings dialog box, and then browse for and select the color-settings file. That's it! This is a handy way to ensure consistency in a workgroup.

Proofing on-screen

Although nothing is as accurate as the final printed document — not even the printed proofs such as Matchprints that many service bureaus can provide — it can be useful to do an on-screen "soft proof" of your document before printing, especially if you are using new color settings or a new printer. InDesign lets you do such on-screen proofing.

First, specify your proofing setup by choosing View ➪ Proof Setup and choose the appropriate color space — the document and working spaces as defined in the Color Settings dialog box — or create a custom space by choosing Custom. Figure 28.6 shows the Customize Proof Condition dialog box that results.

With the desired proofing setup enabled, turn on proofing by ensuring that a check mark appears to the left of View ➪ Proof Colors; if not, choose this menu option. If you want to also see how overprinting colors will appear, be sure that a check mark appears to the left of View ➪ Overprint Preview; if not, choose this menu option or press Option+Shift+⌘+Y or Ctrl+Alt+Shift+Y. Now you can go from page to page and get an approximation of how your pages' colors will appear when printed.

FIGURE 28.6

InDesign has two tools to help you proof your document onscreen before printing: the Customize Proof Condition dialog box (left) and the Separations Preview panel and its flyout menu (right).

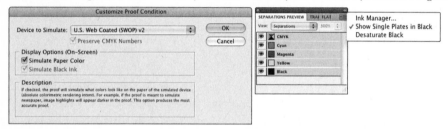

InDesign provides two other preview options. One is the Flattener Preview panel, which lets you see how transparency appears, as I cover in Chapter 29. The other is the Separations Preview panel (choose Window ➪ Output ➪ Separations Preview or press Shift+F6), which lets you turn on and off the display of specific color plates. Figure 28.6 shows the panel and its flyout menu. Choose Separations in the unnamed pop-up menu at upper left and then click the square to the left of each color plate to toggle the display on and off; if an eye icon appears, the plate is displayed. Then go from page to page to check the plates of interest to you.

The Separations Preview panel also lets you view the Ink Limit (choose Ink Limit from the pop-up menu at the upper right and then the limit value in the unnamed pop-up menu at the upper right. InDesign will display in red any part of an object that exceeds that value. Again, go from page to page to see whether any overinking is displayed.

The panel's flyout menu has several options. Select the Show Single Plates in Black option to display individual plates in black rather than in their actual color. (This is helpful when displaying light colors such as yellow; it improves on-screen clarity.) Select the Desaturate Black option to better differentiate regular black from rich blacks such as [Registration]. The Ink Manager menu option opens the Ink Manager dialog box that Chapter 30 covers.

Working with Color Traps

Color trapping controls how colors overlap and abut when printed. InDesign offers moderate controls over trapping, enough to set the basics document-wide without getting into the expertise level of a commercial printer. It's also a feature that novice users can abuse terribly, which is one reason InDesign hides these options. If you don't know much about trapping, leave the features of the program at the default settings. Before you use InDesign trapping tools, study some books on color publishing, talk to your printer, and experiment with test files that you don't want to publish. If you're experienced with color trapping — or after you become experienced — you should find InDesign trapping tools easy to use.

You still want to use the trapping tools within the illustration product with which you create your EPS and PDF graphics because these tools help you to finely control the settings for each image's specific needs. Also, if you're using a service bureau that does high-resolution scanning for you and strips these files into your layout before output, check to make sure that the bureau is not also handling trapping for you with a Scitex or other high-end system. If it is, make sure you ask whether and when you should be doing trapping yourself.

If you print to a color laser, dye-sublimation, inkjet, or thermal wax printer, don't worry about trapping. You're not getting the kind of output resolution at which this level of image fine-tuning is relevant. But if you output to an imagesetter (particularly if you output to negatives) for eventual printing on a Web-offset press or other printing press, read on.

Understanding trap methods

So what is trapping, anyway? Trapping adjusts the boundaries of colored objects to prevent gaps between abutting colors. Gaps can occur because of misalignment of the negatives, plates, or printing press — all of which are impossible to avoid.

Colors are trapped by processes known as *choking* and *spreading*. Both make an object slightly larger — usually a fraction of a point — so that it overprints the abutting object slightly. The process is called choking when one object surrounds a second object and the first object is enlarged to overlap the second. The process is known as spreading when you enlarge the surrounded object so that it leaks (bleeds) into the surrounding object.

The difference between choking and spreading is the relative position of the two objects. Think of choking as making the hole for the inside object smaller (which in effect makes the object on the outside larger), and think of spreading as making the object in the hole larger.

TIP **The object made larger depends on the image, but you generally bleed the color of a lighter object into a darker one. If you did the opposite, you'd make darker objects seem ungainly larger. Thus, choke a dark object inside a light one, and spread a light object inside a dark one. If the objects are adjacent, spread the light object.**

Figure 28.7 shows the three types of trapping techniques. Spreading (left) makes the interior object's color bleed out; choking (second) makes the outside color bleed in, in effect making the area of the choked element smaller. The black lines show the size of the interior object; as you can see in the second image from the left, when you choke a darker object into a lighter one, the effect is to change its size (here, the interior object gets smaller). At the far right is an untrapped image whose negatives shifted slightly during printing, causing a gap.

InDesign supports a third type of trapping technique: *centering*, which both chokes and spreads, splitting the difference between the two objects. This makes traps look nicer (see the third object from the left in Figure 28.7), especially between light and dark colors where regular choking and spreading can encroach on the light object.

Finally, InDesign offers a fourth trapping method, *neutral density,* that adjusts the trap as color hues and tints shift to minimize the possibility of darker lines where colors trap. But this can be dangerous; for a bitmap image, the neutral density method will most likely create an uneven edge as the trapping changes from pixel to pixel.

FIGURE 28.7

Three kinds of traps, from left to right: spreading, choking, and centering, with an untrapped image at the far right that was misregistered during printing.

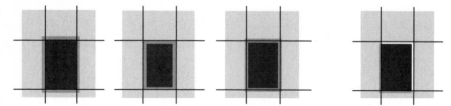

Specifying knockout and overprinting

In practice, trapping also involves controlling whether colors *knock out* or *overprint*. The default is to knock out — cut out — any overlap when one element is placed on top of another. If, for example, you place two rectangles on top of each other, they print like the two rectangles on the right side of Figure 28.8. If you set the darker rectangle in this figure to overprint, the rectangles print as shown on the left side of the figure. Setting colors to overprint results in mixed colors, as shown on the left, and setting colors to knock out results in discrete colors, as shown on the right.

In InDesign, you use the Attributes panel (choose Window ➪ Attributes) for individual objects — text, frames, shapes, and lines — to pick from the panel's three trapping options: Overprint Fill, Overprint Stroke, and Overprint Gap. Having three options means you can separately control which parts of an object overprint or knock out. When these options are deselected (the default), InDesign knocks out the objects. When these options are selected, InDesign overprints them.

CROSS-REF The Attributes panel's Nonprinting option has nothing to do with trapping. Instead, it controls whether a specific object prints at all, as I explain in Chapter 9.

Most objects don't have all three trap-related settings available because not all objects have fills, gaps, and strokes, but all objects have Nonprinting available, which prevents the object from printing. All three options are normally deselected because you usually want objects' fills, gaps, and strokes to knock out. Figure 28.9 shows the panel.

FIGURE 28.8

The two kinds of untrapped options: overprint (left) and knockout

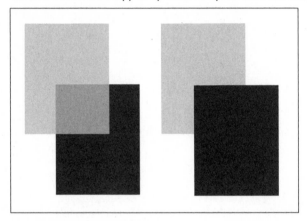

FIGURE 28.9

The Attributes panel lets you set whether objects' fills, strokes, and gaps overprint or knock out (the default, or deselected, status).

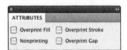

Specifying trapping presets

In InDesign, document-wide trapping settings are handled as part of the printing process (see Chapter 30). But you specify them the same way as you do colors or other document attributes, through a panel. In this case, you use the Trap Presets panel (choose Window ⇔ Output ⇔ Trap Presets) that is shown in Figure 28.10. Choose New Preset from the panel's flyout menu to create a new preset, or select an existing preset and choose Preset Options to modify it. (Figure 28.10 also shows the New Trap Preset dialog box.) You can also delete and duplicate trap presets from the flyout menu, as well as import them from other documents (through the Load Trap Presets option).

NOTE Consult your service bureau or commercial printer before changing the default settings. The people there will know what setting you should use based on the paper, inks, printing press, and image types you're using.

FIGURE 28.10

The Trap Presets panel (left) and the New Trap Preset dialog box (right)

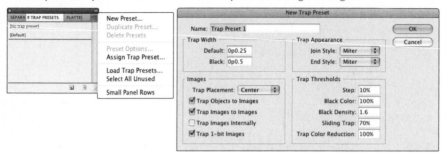

Here are the settings you can change when creating or modifying a trap preset:

- **Name:** Type a name for the trap style in the Name field. Make sure it's a meaningful name, such as Choke, rather than New Preset 1, so that in the future you'll know what it's for.

- **Trap Width:** Set your *trap width* (the amount of overlap you want between adjacent colors). The default is 0.25 point, a common setting. The Default field is for all colors except black and white. You set the trap width separately for black, using the Black field; this value is usually one and a half to two times as much as the regular trap settings because it controls how colors spread into black objects. The value is higher because you have more leeway with black — spreading a color into it doesn't change it from being black, whereas, for example, spreading yellow into blue makes a green, so you want to minimize that spreading.

- **Trap Appearance:** You can choose the type of joins and ends for traps, just as you do for strokes, with options of Miter, Round, and Bevel for both Join Style and End Style. In almost every case, you want to select Miter because this keeps the trap confined to the abutting images. If you choose another option, the choke or spread extends past the trapped objects a tad. If you think of the boundary of the trap as a line, then choosing Bevel or Round extends that line slightly past the objects. If the objects have white or a light color on either side, readers might notice that slight extension.

- **Images:** InDesign lets you use several options to control how trapping is applied: Trap Placement plus four picture-specific settings, Trap Objects to Images, Trap Images to Images, Trap Images Internally, and Trap 1-bit Images.

□ **Image Trap Placement:** This option determines how to handle trapping between an image and an abutting solid color. Your choices are Center, in which the trap straddles the edge between the image and the abutting color object; Choke, in which the abutting color object overprints the image by the Trap Width amount; Spread, in which the image overprints the abutting color object by the Trap Width amount; Neutral Density, which was defined earlier; and Normal, in which each pixel is trapped in the image individually and thus can result in an uneven edge between the image and the abutting object.

□ **Trap Objects to Images:** This turns on trapping for images and any abutting objects such as text or graphics created in InDesign.

□ **Trap Images to Images:** This turns on trapping for images and any abutting images.

□ **Trap Images Internally:** This actually traps colors within the bitmap image. Use this only for high-contrast bitmaps, such as cartoons and computer screen shots, where the color has fewer gradations and more broad, consistent swaths.

□ **Trap 1-bit Images:** This traps black-and-white bitmaps to any abutting objects (including those underneath). This prevents the appearance of white ghost areas around black portions if there is any misregistration when printing.

■ **Trap Thresholds:** These guide InDesign in how to apply your trapping settings:

□ **Step:** This threshold value gives InDesign the color-difference threshold before trapping is implemented. The default is 10 percent, a value that traps most objects. A higher value traps fewer objects. The way this works is that the value represents the difference in color variance between adjacent objects, and you're telling InDesign not to worry about colors that are within the percentage difference. This is usually a low setting because it means you don't care whether there are traps between similar colors because the human eye notices misregistration less between them, because they are, in fact, similar. In most cases, keep this value between 8 percent and 20 percent.

□ **Black Color:** This defines at what point InDesign should treat a dark gray as black for the trap width in Black Width. For coarse paper, which usually absorbs more ink, dark tints and grays often end up looking like a solid color — 85 percent black appears as 100 percent black. Use Black Color Limit in such cases so that an 85 percent black object traps as it if were a 100 percent black object.

□ **Black Density:** This is similar to Black Color Limit, except that it treats dark colors as black (like navy blue), based on their ink density. You can type a value of 0 to 10, with 1.6 being the default (0 is full black; 10 is white).

□ **Sliding Trap:** This adjusts the way a choke or spread works. The normal value is 70 percent. When the difference in ink density (a good measure of color saturation) is 70 percent or more, this tells InDesign not to move the darker color so much into the lighter color. The greater the contrast between two colors, the more the lighter object is distorted as the darker color encroaches on it. At 0 percent, all traps are adjusted to the centerline between the two objects; at 100 percent, the choke or spread is done at the full trap width.

■ **Trap Color Reduction:** This controls overinking that some traps can create. The default is 100 percent, which means that the overlapping colors in a trap are produced at 100 percent, which in some cases can cause the trap to be darker than the two colors being trapped, due to the colors mixing. Choosing a lower value in Trap Color Reduction lightens the overlapping colors to reduce this darkening. A value of 0 percent keeps the overlap no darker than the darker of the two colors being trapped.

Applying trapping to pages

After you create trapping presets, you apply them. To do so, choose the Assign Trap Presets option in the Trap Presets panel's flyout menu. Figure 28.11 shows the dialog box.

 The [Default] preset, which you can modify, is applied to all pages by default.

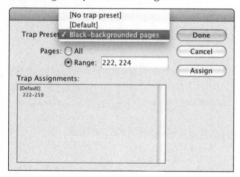

FIGURE 28.11

The Assign Trap Presets dialog box

The process is simple: Choose the desired trap preset from the Trap Preset pop-up menu and then select the pages to which the preset will be applied. Make your selection in the Pages section (select All or Range; if you select Range, type the page numbers in the Range field). Click Assign to complete the application of the trap preset to the selected pages. You can set multiple presets in a document to different page ranges, so if you want, select another trap preset and assign it to the desired pages. InDesign will show you which pages have which trap presets applied at the bottom of the dialog box. When you're finished, click Done.

 If your document uses sections, you can type page numbers in the Range field using the section numbering style (such as A–2, D–3, F–5–F–10) or by using absolute page numbers (+1, +5, +10–+15).

Summary

Although it's often impossible to precisely match colors from an electronic image when printing, InDesign can help make the color fidelity as high as possible through its support of color profiles and color management. It can also help make what you see on-screen and print on proofing devices look close to the final output, which helps you better gauge your actual colors.

If you use a compatible output device, InDesign also lets you control how adjacent colors print in a process known as *trapping*, which minimizes the chances of gaps appearing between colored objects. Fortunately, most users don't need to worry about fine-tuning trapping settings because InDesign's default settings handle most objects well.

Chapter 29

Preparing for Printing

After your document is created and all elements are perfectly in place, with the right colors, frame strokes, kerning, and so on, it's time to make tangible all that work you've done on-screen. You're ready to print the document.

Well, not quite. You may in fact be ready to just print your document, but if your document is at all complex or will be output at a service bureau or through your company's creative services group or print shop, you should take a few minutes and dot your *i*'s and cross your *t*'s. Little things can go wrong as you or your team work on a document — a font might deactivate, a picture might move or be renamed, or a new output device might be acquired.

That's where InDesign's preflighting and packaging capabilities come into play. The preflighting capability checks your document to make sure that all elements are available and meet your production requirements, while the packaging capability copies all required elements — from fonts to graphics — to a folder so that you can give your service bureau all the pieces it needs to print your document accurately.

Making Initial Preparations

Before you can do anything, you need to make sure your system is set up with the right printer driver and printer description files because without these, your output is not likely to match your needs or expectations. It's important to set these up before you do any preflighting because preflighting checks your document against the printer settings you have active (such as color separations), and you can't have selected printer settings until the printer is set up.

 The Mac and Windows platforms handle printing differently, so in this chapter, I've divided all system-specific printing information, such as the coverage of drivers, into platform-specific sections.

Setting up Macintosh printers

Although you choose the printer type in the Setup pane of the InDesign Print dialog box, you still need to set up the printer on your Mac before you can use it.

In some cases, Mac OS X sets up the printer for you. In other cases, you may need to run an installation program that comes with the printer; sometimes, you need to run this software before you connect the printer to the Mac. Your printer documentation will explain the correct steps.

To see whether your printer is actually installed correctly, as well as to change its settings, you use the Print & Fax system preference by choosing ⌘ ⇨ System Preferences ⇨ Print & Fax and then clicking Set Up Printers in the resulting Print & Fax system preference. The Printing pane should display by default (if not, go to it) and list any installed printers.

If you see the printer to which you want to print in the Print & Fax system preference, you've already installed your printer. Otherwise, make sure the printer you want to set up is connected to your Mac (directly or through the network) and turned on. (If you use a network printer, make sure the right network protocols, such as IP and AppleTalk, are turned on through the Network pane in the System Preferences dialog box, which you access by choosing ⌘ ⇨ System Preferences.) Then click the + iconic button below the printer list. What appears next depends on the version of the Mac OS you have:

- In Mac OS X 10.5 (Leopard), an unnamed dialog box displays.
- In Mac OS X 10.4 (Tiger), the Print Browser dialog box displays.

Both dialog boxes let you locate the printer, whether it's directly attached or available via the network. Select the desired printer and be sure the correct driver is selected in the Print Using pop-up menu. Click Add so that the printer displays in your applications' Print dialog boxes.

Figure 29.1 shows the dialog boxes for adding a printer.

NOTE You may need to install a PostScript Printer Description (PPD) file that contains specific details on your printer; this file should come on a disk or CD with your printer and is often installed with the printer's setup program. Otherwise, download it from the printer manufacturer's Web site. These files should reside in the PPD's folder in the Mac's System:Library:Printers folder. Note that Mac OS X preinstalls some PPDs for you, particularly those for Apple-branded printers and some Hewlett-Packard printers.

FIGURE 29.1

Top: Mac OS X 10.5 (Leopard)'s Print & Fax system preference and its unnamed dialog box show which printers are available and let you add and configure them. Bottom: Mac OS X 10.4 (Tiger) has essentially the same interface but names the dialog box Print Browser.

If you're installing a printer not connected to your computer or network, such as the imagesetter used by your service bureau, you need to install the PPD files so that InDesign knows what its settings are. Installing the printer software isn't necessary.

Mac OS X supports multiple printers, but it also lets you define the default printer — the one used unless you change it through a button or pop-up menu in an application's Print dialog box. (InDesign uses a pop-up menu called Printer to change the printer from the default setting; see Figure 29.2.) In the Print & Fax dialog box, double-click the printer you want to be the default, which opens a job status dialog box for that printer. Choose Printer ⇨ Make Default or press ⌘+D (refer to Figure 29.1) and then close the job status dialog box. In the Print & Fax dialog box, the name of the default printer is displayed in bold in the printer list.

FIGURE 29.2

The job status dialog box for a specific printer lets you set that printer as the default printer for all applications.

Setting up Windows printers

The process for setting up printers varies based on the version of Windows you have.

Windows XP

In some cases, Windows XP sets up the printer for you. In other cases, you may need to run an installation program that comes with the printer; sometimes, you need to run this software before you connect the printer to the PC. Your printer documentation will explain the correct steps.

To see whether your printer is actually installed correctly, as well as to change its settings, you use Windows XP's built-in Printers control panel. The process to open this control panel depends on what version of Windows XP you have installed (Home or Professional) and whether you are running it in the Classic interface. Most people will use one of the following menu sequences to start the printer-installation process:

- Choose Start ⇨ Settings ⇨ Printers and Faxes
- Choose Start ⇨ Control Panel ⇨ Printers and Other Hardware

Either way, you get a window with a list of existing printers and an icon labeled Add New Printer. Double-click the printer that you want to set up or double-click Add New Printer. (You likely need either a disk that came with the printer or the Windows CD-ROM if you add a new printer because Windows needs information specific to that printer).

NOTE If you're setting up a printer connected through the network, you usually should select the Local Printer option during installation. The Network Printer option is for printers connected to a print server, as opposed to printers connected to a hub or router. (A print server is a special kind of router, but it's typically used only for printers that don't have networking built in, such as many inkjet printers.) In some cases, even if your printer uses a print server, you'll still install the printer as a local printer and then create a virtual port that maps to a network address (Hewlett-Packard uses this approach, for example).

If you're installing a printer not connected to your computer or network, such as the imagesetter used by your service bureau, you need to install the PPD files so that InDesign knows what its settings are. You don't need to install the printer software.

When you open an existing printer, the dialog box shown in Figure 29.3 appears when you choose Printer ⇨ Properties. One pane matters greatly: The Device Settings pane. Here you specify all the device settings, from paper trays to memory to how fonts are handled. (Note that some printers — such as Epson inkjet printers — do not have this pane, and that's because they come with their own configuration software that handles these controls.)

For PostScript-compatible printers — the typical type of printer in a professional publishing environment — this pane has several key options:

- **Font Substitution Table:** This option opens a list of available fonts and lets you select how any TrueType fonts are translated to PostScript. The best (and default) setting is to have the printer translate TrueType fonts such as Arial to PostScript fonts such as Helvetica. (The Windows standards of Arial, Times New Roman, Courier New, and Symbol are set by default to translate to the PostScript fonts Helvetica, Times, Courier, and Symbol. PostScript fonts are set by default to Don't Substitute.)

- **Add Euro Currency Symbol to PostScript Fonts:** Be sure to select this option in this pane so that the euro symbol (€) is available in all output.

NOTE You may need to install a PostScript Printer Description (PPD) file that contains specific details on your printer; this file should come on a disk or CD with your printer and is often installed with the printer's setup program. Otherwise, download it from the printer manufacturer's Web site. (Windows places PPD files in the `Windows\System32\spool\ drivers\w32x86` folder; note that the first folder may be named WinNT or WinXP instead of Windows.)

To set a printer as the default printer, right-click the printer in the Printers window (Start ⇨ Settings ⇨ Printers and Faxes) and select Set Default Printer from the contextual menu that appears. (Some Windows XP users will need to choose Start ⇨ Control Panel ⇨ Printers and Other Hardware.)

FIGURE 29.3

The Device Settings pane in Windows XP's setup for PostScript devices is the key pane in the Properties dialog box for a Windows printer. (Not all panes appear for all printers; whether a pane appears depends on the printer type chosen and the network protocols installed.)

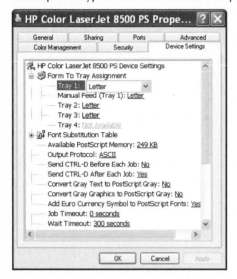

Windows Vista

The newest version of Windows, Vista, has a different interface for adding a printer, although the underlying process is the same as in previous versions.

Vista automatically adds USB printers that are powered on. For other printers, follow this process:

First, choose Start ➪ Control Panel and then click the Printer link in the Hardware and Sound section. (Or choose Start ➪ Control Panel, select Classic view from the left side of the dialog box, and double-click the Printers icon in the pane at the right.)

You get a window with a list of existing printers. Double-click the printer that you want to set up or click the Add a Printer button at the top of the pane (you likely need either a disk that came with the printer or the Windows CD-ROM if you add a new printer because Windows needs information specific to that printer).

If you're adding a printer connected through the network, you usually select the Add a Local Printer option during installation. The Add a Network, Wireless, or Bluetooth Printer option is for printers connected to a print server, as opposed to printers connected to a hub or router. (A print server is a special kind of router, but it's typically used only for printers that don't have networking built in, such as many inkjet printers.) In some cases, even if your printer uses a print server, you still install the printer as a local printer and then create a virtual port that maps to a network address. (Hewlett-Packard uses this approach.)

If you're adding a printer not connected to your computer or network, such as the imagesetter used by your service bureau, you need to install the PPD (PostScript Printer Description) file so that InDesign knows what its settings are. (You don't need to install the printer software.) This file should come on a disk or CD with your printer and is often installed with the printer's setup program. Otherwise, download it from the printer manufacturer's Web site. (Windows places PPD files in the `Windows\System32\spool\drivers\w32x86` folder.)

To configure a printer after it has been added, select it from the printer list and then click the Select Printing Preferences button at the top of the pane shown in Figure 29.4. The one pane you most need to pay attention to is the Advanced Options pane, which is where you specify all the device settings, from paper trays to memory to how fonts are handled. (Note that some printers — such as Epson inkjet printers — will not have this pane; they come with their own configuration software that handles these controls.) You access this pane by clicking the Advanced button in the Layout pane of the Printing Preferences dialog box.

Another way to configure a printer is to double-click its icon in the pane to open the printer queue. Choose Printer ➪ Properties and go to the Device Settings pane, which is nearly identical to the Windows XP setup pane of the same name (see previous section).

FIGURE 29.4

The Advanced Options pane in Windows Vista's setup for PostScript devices is the key pane in the Properties dialog box for a Windows printer. (Not all panes appear for all printers, depending on the printer type chosen and the network protocols installed.)

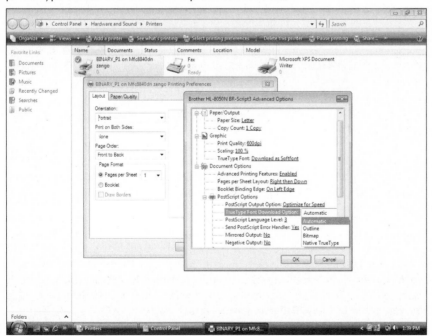

For PostScript printers — the typical type of printer in a professional publishing environment — this pane contains several key options in the PostScript Options section.

One option, TrueType Font Download Option, has a pop-up menu that lets you choose how TrueType fonts are handled. The default setting of Automatic should work in most cases, but if you are outputting to an imagesetter, check with your service bureau as to whether it would prefer Outline instead (or, more rarely, Native TrueType).

The other PostScript Options settings should not be changed unless your service bureau requests it. Note that InDesign provides the three key controls in its own Print dialog box matching what you can do here: PostScript Language Level (the PostScript pop-up menu in the Print dialog box's Graphics pane), Mirrored Output (the Flip pop-up menu in the Output pane, and Negative Output (the Negative check box in the Output pane).

Preflighting Your Document

The preflighting capability that's part of InDesign examines your document for any issues of concern and gives you a report on what may need to be fixed.

You might wonder why you need a preflight tool to check for things such as missing fonts and images, considering that InDesign lists any missing fonts and graphics when you open a document. The answer is that sometimes fonts and graphics files are moved after you open a file, in which case you don't get the alerts from InDesign. This is more likely to happen if you work with files and fonts on a network drive, rather than with local fonts and graphics. Preflighting also checks for other problematic issues, such as the use of RGB files and TrueType fonts.

NEW FEATURE   **InDesign CS4 has significantly revamped how preflighting works, which has changed all the dialog boxes and most related settings compared to previous versions of InDesign.**

InDesign CS4's preflighting function checks your document as you work, keeping a running tally of issues at the bottom left of your document window, as Figure 29.5 shows. It also lets you decide what issues to look for as you work in the Preflighting panel.

NOTE   **If you're working with the InDesign book feature (see Chapter 24), you can preflight the book's chapters from an open book's panel by using the Preflight Book option in its flyout menu. (If one or more documents in the book are selected in the panel, the menu option changes to Preflight Selected Documents.) The options are the same as for preflighting individual documents.**

You can turn preflighting on or off using either of these methods:

- In the Preflight pop-up menu at the bottom of the document window, choose Preflight Document to toggle between off and on. If the menu option is selected, preflighting is turned on (the default setting). You can also toggle off and on Enable Preflight for All Documents, which sets the default action for all documents.

■ In the Preflight panel (choose File ↪ Preflight or press Shift+Option+⌘+F or Ctrl+Alt+Shift+F), select the On option to turn preflighting on, and disable it to turn preflighting off. The flyout menu has the Enable Preflight for All Documents option, as Figure 29.6 shows.

At the bottom of the Preflight panel, you can select specific pages to check (select the Pages radio button and then enter the desired page range) or use the default setting of All.

In the Preflight panel's flyout menu, use the Save Report option to create a text file that lists all the errors reported for the current document. You can also control how many rows of error messages will display per error class (the all-capitalized labels in the Preflight panel's Error pane) using the Limit Number of Rows per Error option.

FIGURE 29.5

The preflight alert at the bottom of a document, as well as its menu options

FIGURE 29.6

The Preflight panel and its flyout menu

Embed Profile

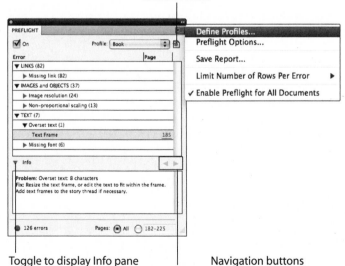

Toggle to display Info pane

Navigation buttons
(when there are multiple errors per category)

Telling InDesign what to look for

InDesign has its default set of issues to look for when preflighting. But you can set up your own options based on your specific needs. The process is easy, although you will likely need to consult with your production manager or service bureau to determine what settings you want to enable in your profile — these are typically expert decisions.

Even if the choices require expertise to make (consult your production manager or service bureau), the process for setting up your preflight options is easy:

1. **In the Preflight pop-up menu at the bottom of the document window or in the Preflight panel's flyout menu, choose Define Profiles to open the Preflight Profiles dialog box.** (To open the Preflight panel, choose File ⇨ Preflight or Window ⇨ Output ⇨ Preflight or press Shift+Option+⌘+F or Ctrl+Alt+Shift+F.)

2. **In the Preflight Profiles dialog box, shown in Figure 29.7, click the + (plus) iconic button to add a new profile.** (Use the – [minus] iconic button to delete a selected profile.)

3. **Give your new profile a name and go through the options and select the ones you want InDesign to preflight for as you work.** If you see a right-pointing triangle to the left of an option, that means there are suboptions you can select from; click the triangle (it will then point down) to get those suboptions. (Click it again to "collapse" the suboptions so that they're not in view.)

4. **Click Save when done.**

5. **Use the + (plus) and – (minus) iconic buttons at the left to add more profiles or remove existing profiles.**

6. **Click OK when done to exit the Preflight Profiles dialog box.**

7. **In the Preflight panel, choose the desired profile for the current document by the Profile pop-up menu.** If a profile name in the menu is followed by *(working)*, that profile is set as the default profile in the Preflight Options dialog box.

You can fine-tune how InDesign CS4 preflights your document and how it handles the default profile (called a working profile). Open the dialog box by choosing Preflight Options from the Preflight panel's flyout menu. Choose the desired working profile in the Working Profile pop-up menu. To make this working profile be used in all new documents, select the Embed Working Profile in New Documents option. You can also tell InDesign whether to apply that working profile to documents that have a different embedded profile by choosing Use Working Profile in the When Opening Documents section, or have it follow the embedded profile instead by choosing Use Embedded Profile (the default option).

In the dialog box's Include section, you can also tell InDesign how to handle invisible and non-printing layers, pasteboard objects, and nonprinting objects during preflighting.

The Preflight Profiles dialog box (left) and the Profile Options dialog box (right)

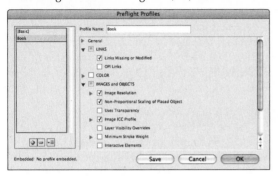

Fixing preflight problems

The Preflight panel shows the details on the problems it has found. Just go to the Error pane and click any error identified to see the details. If you see a right-pointing triangle to the left of an error, click it to see more details, as Figure 29.7 shows. When you get to the specific detail, you'll see a hyperlink at right to the page that has the issue, so you can quickly go there.

 **TIP** You can also get a detailed explanation of the issue by clicking the right-pointing arrow icon in the Info pane below the Error pane.

Next, make whatever adjustments are necessary to your layout. InDesign will update the preflight errors status as you do.

Creating a Document Package

If you've ever had the experience of giving a page-layout document to a service bureau, only to be called several hours later by the person who is outputting your document because some of the files necessary to output it are missing, you'll love the packaging capability in InDesign.

This capability, which you access by choosing File ⇨ Package or pressing Option+Shift+⌘+P or Ctrl+Alt+Shift+P, copies into a folder all the font, color-output, and graphics files necessary to output your document. It also generates a report that contains all the information about your document that a service bureau is ever likely to need, including the document's fonts, dimensions, and trapping information. You can also create an instructions file that has your contact information and any particulars you want to say about the document.

Final preflighting before you package

Whether or not you use the Preflight panel or have preflighting turned on, as described in the previous section, the first thing InDesign does when you tell it to package a document is to run a basic preflight check. This packaging action's preflight check is based not on whatever settings you used in the Preflight panel (described in the previous section) but on InDesign's own list of what to check for. Think of it as a last-minute check for essential issues. You should look through any issues identified in the six preflight-oriented six panes before clicking the Package button to have InDesign actually assemble the documents for you.

Here's a walk-through of what the six preflight-oriented panes in the Package dialog box do:

- **Summary:** This pane (shown in Figure 29.8) shows you a summary of alerts. If your document has layers, you can select or deselect the Show Data for Hidden and Non-printing Layers option. If this option is selected, layers that don't print are analyzed for font, image, and other issues. Select this option only if the person receiving your document plans to print hidden layers. For example, in a French-and-English document, you may have hidden the French layer for proofing but still want it checked because the service bureau is instructed to print the document twice — once with the English layer on and the French layer off, and once with the English layer off and the French layer on.

- **Fonts:** This pane (shown in Figure 29.9) shows the type of each font (Type 1 PostScript, OpenType, or TrueType) so that you can spot any TrueType fonts in use before the document goes to your service bureau. (TrueType fonts usually don't print easily on imagesetters, so use a program such as FontLab Studio Pro or FontLab Fontographer to translate them to PostScript instead.) The pane also shows any bitmap fonts, which you should replace if possible with another type because bitmap fonts usually print poorly. (Fortunately, bitmap fonts are fairly rare.) And finally, the pane shows whether any fonts are missing from your system. You can search for specific fonts in the document by clicking Find Font.

  You can also limit the list of fonts to those with problems by selecting the Show Problems Only option.

- **Links and Images:** This pane (shown in Figure 29.10) shows whether any graphics files are missing or the original image has been modified since you placed it in your layout. Click Relink to correct any such bad links one at a time, or click Repair All to have InDesign prompt you in turn for each missing or modified file. The pane also shows whether a color profile is embedded in your graphics in case files that should have them don't or in case a file that should not have an embedded profile has one. It also alerts you if you use RGB images; although such images will print or color-separate, InDesign provides the warning because it's usually better to convert RGB images to CMYK in an image editor or illustration program so that you can control the final appearance, rather than rely on InDesign or the output device to do the translation.

  You can also limit the list of linked files to those with problems by selecting the Show Problems Only option.

FIGURE 29.8

The Summary pane of the Package dialog box

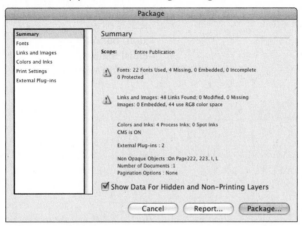

FIGURE 29.9

The Fonts pane of the Package dialog box

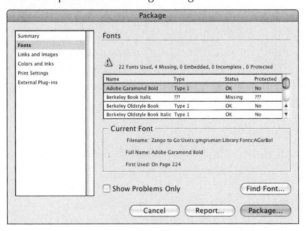

- **Colors and Inks:** This pane (shown in Figure 29.11) shows the inks used in the output, as well as their print settings. (If you are printing color separations, these correspond to the color plates that will eventually be used to print the document on a printing press.) You can't modify anything here; it's simply for informational purposes.

- **Print Settings:** This pane (shown in Figure 29.12) shows how the document is configured to print in the Print dialog box. That's why it's important to configure the output settings, as described earlier, before preflighting your document.
- **External Plug-ins:** This pane shows any plug-in programs required to output the file. Some third-party plug-ins make changes to the InDesign document that require the same plug-in to be installed at each computer that opens the file. This dialog box alerts you if you have such a dependency.

FIGURE 29.10

The Links and Images pane of the Package dialog box

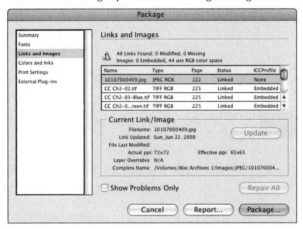

FIGURE 29.11

The Colors and Inks pane of the Package dialog box

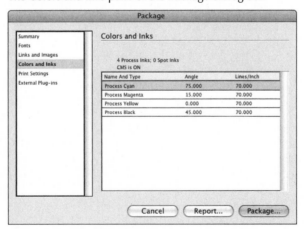

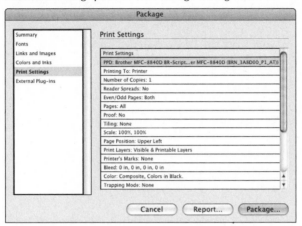

FIGURE 29.12

The Print Settings pane of the Package dialog box

You can create a report of the preflight information by clicking Report in any pane of the Package dialog box. It generates a text file containing the information from the Package dialog box's panes, which you can give to your service bureau to check its settings and files against.

Putting the package together

After you review the preflight information, click the Package button to gather all related fonts and files into one folder for delivery to a service bureau or other outside printing agency. (Click Cancel to exit the Package dialog box and go back to your document.)

If you did not save the document before initiating the package function, InDesign will ask you to save the document or cancel the packaging.

Next, the Printing Instructions dialog box, shown in Figure 29.13, displays. You can change the default filename from `Instructions.txt` to something more suitable, such as the name of your print job.

CAUTION If you don't want to create an instructions form, don't click Cancel — that cancels the entire package operation. Just click Continue, leaving the form blank. Similarly, you must click Save at the request to save the document; clicking Cancel stops the package operation as well.

The next step is to create or select the package folder. You do this in the dialog box that follows the Printing Instructions form, which on the Mac is called Create Package Folder and in Windows is called Package Publication. Figure 29.14 shows the Mac version, which except for the name at the top is the same as the Windows version.

The Printing Instructions dialog box

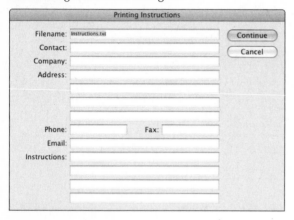

The Create Package Folder dialog box for Mac InDesign (in Windows InDesign, it's called the Package Publication dialog box)

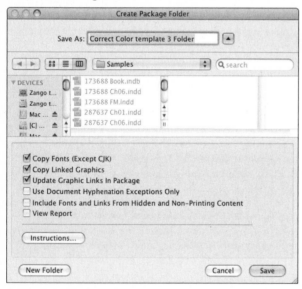

In the dialog box, you can select what is copied: the fonts, color-output profiles, and *linked graphics* (graphics pasted into an InDesign document rather than imported are automatically included). You can also have InDesign update the graphics links for those graphic files that were modified or moved; if this option is not selected, any missing or modified graphics files will not be copied with the document.

You can tell InDesign to include fonts and links from hidden layers (which you would do only if you want the service bureau to print those hidden layers or if you were giving the document's files to a colleague to do further work).

You also can specify whether the document should use only the hyphenation exceptions defined within it. This often makes sense because it ensures that the printer's hyphenation dictionary — which may differ from yours — doesn't cause text to flow differently.

CROSS-REF See Chapter 15 for more details on these dictionaries. The next section of this chapter explains which files you should send to others using your documents.

You can also modify the instructions text file by clicking Instructions.

Finally, you can choose to view the report after the package is created. On the Mac, InDesign launches TextEdit and displays the report file; on Windows, it launches Notepad and displays the report file.

Click Save (on the Mac) or Package (in Windows) when everything is ready to go. Your document is placed in the folder you specify, as is the instructions file (the report). Within that folder, InDesign creates a subfolder called Fonts that includes the fonts, a subfolder called Links that has the graphics files, and a subfolder called Output Profiles that has the color output profiles.

TIP When you package a document, any source files for objects on the pasteboard are not gathered. If you want such files included, increase the document's slug size (see Chapter 4) to encompass all the objects whose source files you want gathered in the package.

I strongly recommend using the packaging capability. It ensures that your service bureau has all the necessary files and information to output your document correctly.

Dealing with Service Bureaus

Service bureaus are great: Their staffs keep and maintain all the equipment, know the ins and outs of both your software and your printing press requirements, and turn jobs around quickly, at least most of the time. Working with a service bureau involves commitment and communication between both parties. It needs your business; you need its expertise and equipment.

To ensure that you get what you want (fast, accurate service) and that the service bureau gets what it wants (no-hassle clients and printing jobs), make sure that you both understand your standards and needs. Keep in mind that the service bureau has many customers, all of whom do things differently. Service bureaus likewise must not impose unreasonable requirements just for the sake of consistency, because customers can have good reasons for doing things differently.

Paying attention to a few basic issues can help you establish a productive relationship with your service bureau.

NOTE When I say *service bureau*, I include your company's production or prepress department and your commercial printer, not just an outside prepress production firm — the people who actually convert your files into the final product.

Sending documents versus output files

Because InDesign has the packaging capability, should you give the service bureau your actual InDesign documents or should you send a PostScript or PDF output file?

CROSS-REF   Chapter 31 shows you how to create output files.

Often, your service bureau will have its requirements and preferences as to what kinds of output files it wants and when it wants output files rather than native InDesign files. You usually should provide what the service bureau wants, but there are times that your goals or concerns will override the service bureau's. Among the issues that play into deciding what files to provide are the following:

- A document file, even if the graphics files are copied with it, takes less space than an output file created from your document, which means fewer disks or cartridges to sort through and less time copying files from your media to the service bureau's (or transferring them over an FTP connection).

- A document file can be changed accidentally, resulting in incorrect output. For example, a color might be changed accidentally when the service bureau checks your color definitions to make sure that spot colors are translated to process colors. Or document preferences might be lost, resulting in text reflow.

- The service bureau cannot always edit an output file. So it may not be able to come to your rescue if you make a mistake such as forgetting to print registration marks when creating the output file or specifying landscape printing mode for a portrait document.

Basically, the question is: Where should the control ultimately be — with you or the service bureau? Only you can answer that question. But in either case, you can do two things to help prevent miscommunication: Provide the report file to the service bureau, and provide a proof copy of your document. The service bureau uses these tools to see if its output matches your expectations, regardless of whether you provide a document file or output file.

Determining output settings

A common area of miscommunication among designers, service bureaus, and printers is determining who sets controls over line screens, registration marks, and other output controls. (In some cases, when the company taking care of the printing is doing the film/plate output, it acts as both the service bureau and printer.) Whoever has the expertise to make the right choices should handle these options. And it should be clear to all parties who is responsible for what aspect of output controls — you don't want to use conflicting settings or accidentally override the desired settings:

- Assuming you're sending InDesign documents to the service bureau or printer, for output controls such as line screens and angles, the layout artist should determine these settings and specify them on the proof copy provided to the service bureau. That way the service bureau or printer can use its own PPD files rather than take the chance you have incorrect or outdated ones.

- If the publication has established production standards for special effects or special printing needs or if the job is unusual, I recommend that the layout artist determine the settings for such general printing controls as the registration marks and the printer resolution.

CROSS-REF InDesign print-control setup is described in Chapter 30.

- For issues related to the service bureau's and/or printer's internal needs and standards, such as how much gap to have between pages and what trapping settings should be, I recommend that the service bureau and/or printer determine its own settings. If you're sending the service bureau or printer output files instead of InDesign documents, you'll have to type these settings in the Print dialog box before creating the file, so be sure to coordinate these issues with the service bureau and/or printer in advance.

- Coordinate issues related to the printing press (such as which side of the negative the emulsion should be on) with the printer and service bureau. Let the service bureau or printer determine this data unless you send output files.

In all cases, determine who is responsible for every aspect of output controls to ensure that someone does not specify a setting outside his or her area of responsibility without first checking with the other parties.

Smart service bureaus and printers do know how to edit an output file to change some settings, such as dpi and line screen, that are encoded in those files, but don't count on them doing that work for you except in emergencies. And then they should let you know what they did and why. And remember: Not all output files can be edited (such as EPS and PostScript files created as binary files), or they can be edited only in a limited way (such as PDF files).

The preceding issues often take the form of a conversation among the printer, the service bureau, and the designer. This conversation should touch on the topics of traps, ink spread, registration, and so forth. Relying on only the service bureau to get all the details correct without that three-way conversation can result in a less-than-optimal final printed product. Also, including the printer (and service bureau) earlier in the design phase of complex jobs can help avoid printing and production issues. All three parties bring an area of expertise to the job and so can educate each other a little about the goals of the piece. A designer with some production skills who knows the limitations of output and a given press can avoid excessive costs and poor output.

Ensuring correct bleeds

When you create an image that bleeds, it must actually print beyond the crop marks. There must be enough of the bleeding image that if the paper moves slightly in the press, the image still bleeds. (Most printers expect 1/8 inch, or 9 points, of *trim* area for a bleed.) In most cases, the document page is smaller than both the page size (specified in InDesign through the File ⇨ Document Setup menu option) and the paper size so that the margin between pages is sufficient to allow for a bleed. If your document page is the same size as your paper size, the paper size limits how much of your bleed actually prints: Any part of the bleed that extends beyond the paper size specified is cut off. (This problem derives from the way PostScript controls printing; it has nothing to do with InDesign.)

This paper-size limit applies even if you set bleed and slug space in the Document Setup dialog box. These tell the printer how much of the material outside the page boundaries to output, so they're not cropped out automatically. But the paper, film negatives, or plates to which they are output must still be large enough to physically accommodate them.

Make sure that your service bureau knows that you're using bleeds and whether you've specified a special paper or page size, because that may be a factor in the way the operator outputs your job.

Sending oversized pages

If you use a paper size larger than U.S. letter size ($8\frac{1}{2} \times 11$ inches), tell the service bureau in advance because the paper size might affect how the operator sends your job to the imagesetter. Many service bureaus use a utility program that automatically rotates pages to save film because pages rotated 90 degrees still fit along the width of typesetting paper and film rolls. But if you specify a larger paper size to make room for bleeds or because your document will be printed at tabloid size, this rotation might cause the tops and/or bottoms of your document pages to be cut off.

I've worked with service bureaus that forgot that they loaded this page-rotation utility, so the operator didn't think to unload it for my oversized pages. It took a while to figure out what was going on because my publication's layout staff was certain that it wasn't doing the rotation (the service bureau assumed my publication's staff had), and the service bureau had forgotten that it was using the rotation utility.

Setting up Booklets

One of the trickiest types of documents to print is a folded booklet, because you can't simply print the pages in sequence and have them end up on the right location on the final sheets of paper. When you fold them, the page order is rearranged because of the folding, especially in two-sided documents.

The tried-and-true approach is to use a booklet template that essentially provides a map of where pages should be — so when they are printed and folded, they end up in the right place — and then arrange your pages in that order via the Pages panel. Figure 29.15 shows the natural order (1–8) that you typically think a booklet has, as well as the actual page order (8,1; 2,7; 6,3; and 4,5) that it must be printed as, so after it is folded and stapled it appears to the reader in the sequence of 1 through 8.

There is an easier way: the Print Booklet dialog box (File ⇨ Print Booklet). Here, you arrange your pages in the Pages panel in sequential order (1–8, in this case) and let the InDesign software figure out how to rearrange them for printing. Much easier! Figure 29.16 shows the Print Booklet dialog box's Setup pane.

FIGURE 29.15

Left: The logical order of pages for a folded, saddle-stitched booklet. Right: The order pages must be moved to so that they print in the right sequence to be folded.

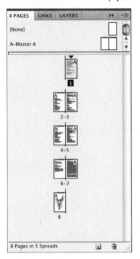
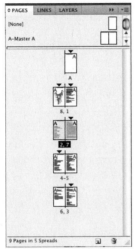

FIGURE 29.16

The Setup pane of the Print Booklet dialog box

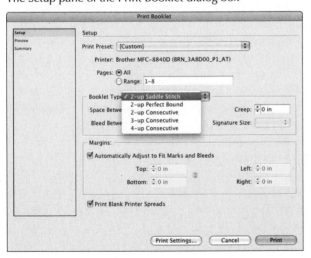

Here are the key controls:

- **Booklet Type:** This pop-up menu is the key control. Here, you choose the type of booklet, which tells InDesign how to arrange the pages when printing so that they are in the right sequence after folding. Your options are as follows:
  - **2-up Saddle Stitch:** A folded sheet that contains two pages on each side, with the staples in the centerfold, between the pages. This is used in newsletters, smaller magazines, and many office documents.
  - **2-up Perfect Bound:** A folded sheet that contains two pages on each side, where the pages are stacked and folded, and then cut and held together with a glued backing or spine-based binding. This is typically used in books, larger magazines, and catalogs (because the square binding holds more pages than saddle-stitching does).
  - **2-up Consecutive:** A sheet that contains two pages on one side, with each page then cut and bound. This is essentially normal printing except that it uses a two-page sheet to print two pages at a time rather than a separate sheet for each page.
  - **3-up Consecutive:** This option is like 2-up Consecutive, except there are three pages on a sheet.
  - **4-up Consecutive:** This option is like 2-up Consecutive, except there are four pages on a sheet.
- **Space Between Pages:** (This option is not available for 2-up Saddle Stitch.) It lets you adjust the relative spacing among pages and objects, typically to provide additional white space around the folds.
- **Bleed Between Pages:** (This option is available for 2-up Perfect Bound only.) As with Space Between Pages, it lets you adjust the relative spacing among pages and objects, typically to provide additional white space around the folds.
- **Creep:** (This option is not available for the Consecutive options.) Creep shifts pages' contents away from the spine in increasing amounts as pages fall from the center of the booklet to the outside of it. Because outside pages have to fold over many inside pages, their content can end up obscured in the inside margins — their gutter is eaten up by folding over those other pages. Creep corrects this problem.
- **Signature Size:** (This option is available only for 2-up Perfect Bound.) Signature Size specifies how many pages are printed on each side of a sheet: 4, 8, 16, or 32.
- **Automatically Adjust to Fit Marks and Bleeds:** This option ensures that crop marks, bleeds, and other content that appears outside the page boundary is properly handled for the chosen booklet type. If the option is not selected, you can manually adjust these settings using the Top, Bottom, Left, and Right fields.

When using these features, consult with your commercial printer or service provider for the appropriate settings. If you are printing the documents yourself, do a test run and then fold, cut, and/or staple the sample document to make sure it works as expected before printing out lots of copies. The Preview pane, shown in Figure 29.17, helps to show the results of your choices, but doing a dry run is always the safest option.

When you're happy with your settings, choose Print to get the standard Print dialog box (covered in Chapter 30). You can also choose Print Settings to set up printer-specific controls (also covered in Chapter 30).

FIGURE 29.17

The Preview pane of the Print Booklet dialog box

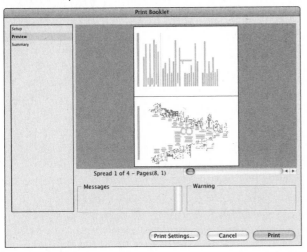

Summary

After you install the printer drivers for the various printers you'll use — both those on-site for proofing and those at a service provider or prepress house — you should turn your attention to setting global printing defaults, the ones that affect all printing jobs, such as the use of paper trays and the handling of TrueType fonts.

InDesign can check your document as you work on it for violations of production requirements and standards that you specify in the Preflight panel.

You also can create a print package — which collects all graphics, fonts, and a copy of the document file — to send to your service bureau or other output service. As part of that package operation, InDesign checks your document for possible output problems using a second set of preflight tools.

Use the Print Booklets dialog box to have InDesign arrange pages correctly for n-up printing, such as saddle-stitched and perfect-bound documents in which several pages are printed on a single sheet of paper and then folded into the final configuration.

Understanding Imposition

Layout artists may work on single pages or spreads, but printing presses rarely do. Sure, for short-run jobs, your printer may actually work with one page at a time, but typically, it works with forms, also called *signatures*. (In today's electronic age, the term *n-up printing* is now widely used to describe printing as signatures.)

Forms are groups of pages aligned so that when they are folded, cut, and trimmed they end up in proper numerical sequence. This act of arranging pages on a form is called *imposition*.

One popular printing method takes a huge sheet that encompasses anywhere from four to 64 pages, folds it, cuts it into pages, and trims the pages. This results in a stack of pages in the right order — a process known as *perfect binding*. This technique is used for square-backed publications such as books, many magazines, and many catalogs.

The other popular printing method also uses forms, but alignment is completed in a different way. Here, the form is broken into two-page spreads that are cut and trimmed, and then stacked separately. A page from each stack is added to a pile, and the pile is then folded to create the right page sequence — this is called a *booklet*. These folded spreads are stapled in the center in a process known as *saddle stitching*. Many magazines and catalogs use this approach.

Both approaches usually use large sheets of paper, called a *web*, which is why such commercial printing is known as SWOP, or Specifications for Web Offset Publications. (*Offset* refers to the way the ink is delivered to the page, with the ink offset to an intermediate roller between the color plate and the paper. This ensures that just the right amount of ink is placed on each sheet, sort of how an ink stamp works.)

Understanding how forms are configured will show you why what InDesign calls a *reader's spread* — the two adjacent pages that a reader sees when reading (and that a layout artist sees when designing on-screen) — is usually not how you want to output pages for use at a commercial printer. Printing reader's spreads makes more sense if you are, for example, wanting to show a client a mockup of the document, so you print spreads together on large paper (such as printing two 81/2-x-11-inch pages on an 11-x-17-inch sheet of paper).The figure shows how a perfect-bound publication form is numbered, as well as a saddle-stitched form. Note that a form can have a number of pages other than 16 but must be in multiples of 4 pages.

16-Page Perfect-Binding Form

Front   *Back*

| ↑ | 4 | 13 | 16 | 1 | | 2 | 15 | 14 | 3 | ↑ |

| ↓ | 5 | 12 | 9 | 8 | | 7 | 10 | 11 | 6 | ↓ |

16-Page Saddle-Stitched Form

Front   *Back*

Sheet 1   Sheet 2   Sheet 1   Sheet 2

16	1	14	3	4	13	2	15
7	10	5	12	11	6	9	8

Sheet 3   Sheet 4   Sheet 3   Sheet 4

To figure out the page sequence for a perfect-bound form, take a sheet of paper, and fold it in half as often as needed to create the number of pages on the form. You now have a booklet. Number the pages (front and back) with a pencil, and then unfold the paper to see how the form is put together. The front sides are one form, and the back sides are another.

To figure out the page sequence for a saddle-stitched form, you can take a sheet of paper for each spread, stack them, fold them once, and then number the pages (front and back) with a pencil, and then separate the sheets to see how the form is put together. The front sides are one form, and the back sides are another. Another way to do it is to realize that the bottom sheet contains page 1 and the final page on the back, and page 2 and the next-to-final page on the front. The sheet on top will have pages 3 and FP–2 (where FP is the final page number) on the front and pages 4 and FP–3 on the back, and so on until the middle sheet.

Chapter 30

Printing Documents

Your document is done. Your printers and printer options are set up, and you've preflighted your document, as described in Chapter 29. You're ready to see all that effort become reality by printing a proof copy or an actual version on a high-resolution imagesetter or printer.

The good news is that your hard work is over. Printing from InDesign is straightforward after everything has been set up. Just choose File ⇨ Print or press ⌘+P or Ctrl+P to go to the Print dialog box.

If you're working with the InDesign book feature (see Chapter 24), you can print the book's chapters from an open book's panel using the Print Book option from its flyout menu. (If one or more documents in the book are selected in the panel, the menu option changes to Print Selected Documents.) The setup options are the same as those for printing individual documents described in this chapter.

If you want to print booklets and have InDesign figure out the right printing order for their pages, use the File ⇨ Print Booklet menu option that Chapter 29 describes. After you tell InDesign what kind of booklet you want so that it can figure out the right page arrangement, you get the same printing options as described in this chapter.

And if you want to print to file, such as to create an EPS, PostScript, or PDF output file for use by a service bureau, set up the print options as described in this chapter and then use the output techniques that Chapter 31 covers.

Selecting InDesign Printing Options

The Print dialog box has eight panes as well as several options common to all the panes. Change any options and choose Print, and InDesign sends your document to the printer. Figure 30.1 shows the dialog box.

Common options

The common options available in the dialog box, no matter what pane is selected, are as follows:

- **Print Preset pop-up menu:** This pop-up menu lets you choose a previously defined set of printer settings. (See the sidebar "Using Printer Presets.")

- **Printer pop-up menu:** This pop-up menu lets you select the printer to use.

- **PPD pop-up menu:** This pop-up menu lets you select a PostScript Printer Description (PPD), which is a file that contains configuration and feature information specific to a brand and model of printer. PPD files are usually installed into your operating system using software that comes from your printer manufacturer, often as part of the printer installation process (see Chapter 29). If it finds no compatible PPDs, InDesign uses generic options. If it finds just one compatible PPD, it uses that one automatically; otherwise, it lets you select a PPD.

FIGURE 30.1

The General pane of the Print dialog box

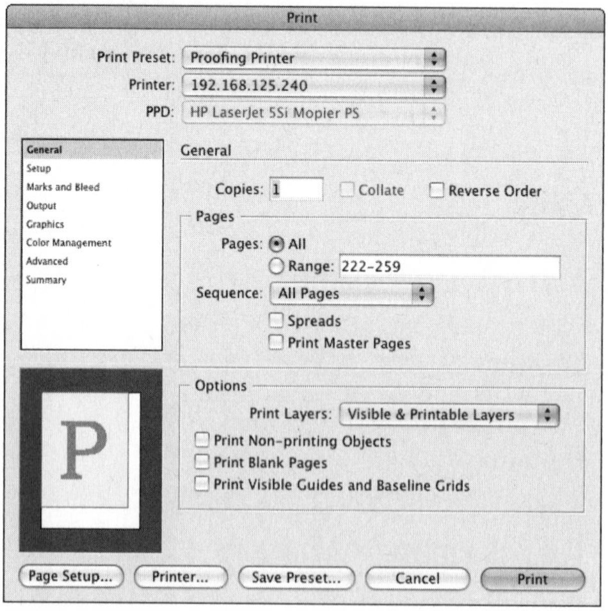

- **Setup button (Windows); Page Setup and Printer buttons (Mac):** These buttons give you access to printer-specific controls. Figures 30.2 and 30.3 show the resulting dialog boxes. You use these dialog boxes to specify options such as printing to file, paper sources, and printer resolution. Note that if you add a printer, you may need to quit InDesign and restart it for it to see the new printer.

PLATFORM DIFFERENCES Windows and Mac OS X provide access to printer controls in different ways. In Windows, the Setup button gives you access to these, whereas on the Mac you use both the Page Setup and Printer buttons to access these controls.

- **Save Preset button:** This lets you save Printer dialog box settings as a preset. (See the sidebar "Using Printer Presets.")

- **Cancel button:** Clicking this button closes the Print dialog box without printing. Use this if you've clicked Save Preset but don't want to print, as well as when you have any reason not to print.

FIGURE 30.2

Mac OS X's Page Setup dialog box (left) and Print dialog box (right)

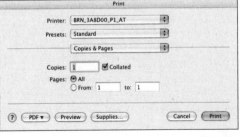

FIGURE 30.3

Windows XP's Print dialog box (left) and Windows Vista's Print dialog box (right)

■ **Print button:** Clicking this button prints the document based on the current settings.

■ **Page preview subpane:** This subpane at lower left shows the current settings graphically. The page is indicated by the blue rectangle, and the direction of the large *P* indicates the printing orientation — in Figure 30.1, shown previously, it's an unrotated portrait. The figure's subpane shows that the paper is the same size as the page. (If the page were larger than the paper, the overflow would be highlighted in light gray.) This preview changes as you adjust settings in the dialog box.

The General pane

The Print dialog box's General pane (refer to Figure 30.1) contains the basic settings for your print job:

■ **Copies:** This text field is where you tell InDesign how many copies of the document you want to print. You can also select the Collate option to have InDesign print the pages in sequence. This is useful when you're printing multiple copies, so you get, for example, pages 1 through 16 printed in sequence and then printed again in sequence if you're making two copies. Otherwise, InDesign prints two copies of page 1, two copies of page 2, and so on, forcing you to manually collate them. If you select the Reverse Order option, InDesign prints from the last page to the first page, which is meant for printers that stack pages face up rather than the usual face down.

■ **Pages:** These options let you choose to print all pages or a range of pages, in which case you type a range in the Range field. When specifying a range of pages, you can type non-consecutive ranges, such as **1–4, 7, 10–13, 15, 18, 20**.

If you want to print from a specific page to the end of the document, just type the hyphen after the initial page number, such as **4–**. InDesign figures out what the last page is. Similarly, to start from the first page and end on a specified page, just start with the hyphen, as in **–11**.

InDesign lets you type absolute page numbers in the Range field. For example, typing **+6–+12** would print the document's sixth through twelfth pages, no matter what their page numbers are.

■ **Sequence:** The pop-up menu lets you choose from All Pages, Odd Pages Only, and Even Pages Only.

■ **Spreads:** Selecting this option prints facing pages on the same sheet of paper; this is handy when you're showing clients comps, but make sure you have a printer that can handle that large paper size or that you scale the output down to fit (through the Setup pane, covered in the next section).

CAUTION You may not want to use the Spreads option when outputting to an imagesetter if you have bleeds because there will be no bleed between the spreads. If you use traditional *perfect-binding* (square spines) or *saddle-stitching* (stapled spines) printing methods, in which facing pages are not printed contiguously (see the material about booklets in Chapter 29), do not use this option.

- **Print Master Pages:** Select this option if you want to print your master pages. This is handy for making reference copies available to page designers.

- **Options section:** This section contains three options that are self-explanatory: Print Non-Printing Objects, Print Blank Pages, and Print Visible Guides and Baseline Grids. Print Blank Pages is usually used for collation, such as when blank pages divide sections of a manual. The other two are used typically by page designers to display hidden designer notes or wrap objects, as well as to ensure that objects really do align to the standard grids.

  The Print Layers pop-up menu in the Options section gives you additional control over how layers marked as nonprinting print. It used to be that if you marked a layer as nonprinting, you would have to leave the Print dialog box to open the Layers panel to make it printable. Now, you can skip that step and override layers' nonprinting status using this pop-up menu. The default option, Visible & Printable Layers, honors your layers' printing status. Visible Layers prints all visible layers, including those marked as nonprinting. All Layers prints both visible and hidden layers, including those marked as nonprinting. (See Chapter 6 for more on layers.)

The Setup pane

The Setup pane, shown in Figure 30.4, is where you tell InDesign how to work with the paper (or other media, such as film negatives) to which you're printing. The options are straightforward.

Using Printer Presets

InDesign lets you save printer settings as presets, so you can easily — and consistently — use them over and over. There are two ways to create them:

- In the Print dialog box, after setting up the various panes' options to the desired state, click the Save Preset button. This saves all the current settings into a preset whose name you specify in a dialog box that then appears.

- When you're not working in the Print dialog box, choose File ➪ Print Presets ➪ Define, or edit an existing preset by choosing File ➪ Print Presets ➪ *preset name*. When you click New or Edit in the resulting dialog box, a dialog box identical to the Print dialog box appears, except that the Print button becomes the OK button.

To apply a print preset when printing, choose it from the Print dialog box's Print Preset pop-up menu.

Note that if you have selected a print preset and then you change settings in the Print dialog box, InDesign changes the name of the current preset in the Print Preset pop-up menu to [Custom] to remind you that the settings have changed and are not saved. Click Save Preset to save these changes; a dialog box appears in which you can use the existing preset name to update it with the new settings or specify a new name to save the changed settings as a new preset.

Paper size and orientation

In the Paper Size section, choose the paper size using the Paper Size pop-up menu. You can also select the page orientation in the Orientation section by clicking any of the four iconic buttons that rotate the image as follows from left to right: 0 degrees (standard portrait), −90 degrees, 180 degrees, and 90 degrees (standard landscape).

The Setup pane of the Print dialog box

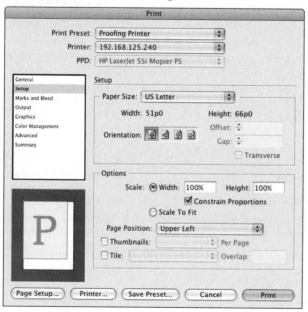

Choosing some printer models lets you choose the Custom option in the Paper Size pop-up menu, in which case you type the dimensions in the Width and Height fields, as well as position the output through the Offset and Gap fields. The latter two options are usually used when printing to a roll, such as in an imagesetter using photo paper (called *RC paper*, a resin-coated paper that keeps details extremely sharp), so that you can make sure there is space between the left edge of the roll and the page boundary (the offset) as well as between pages (the gap). Most printers can't print right to the edge, thus the Offset setting; you also want to have a gap between pages for crop and registration marks, as well as room to physically cut the pages.

The Transverse option, if selected, rotates the output 90 degrees. This is done mainly for imagesetters whose paper and film negatives are usually about 12 inches wide. At that width, it's cheaper for the service bureau to rotate the pages 90 degrees in most cases (because most publications are usually no taller than 11 inches), packing more pages onto the RC paper or film.

Potential Challenges for Page Positioning

Which Page Position option — Upper Left, Center Horizontally, Center Vertically, and Centered — you choose in the Print dialog box's Setup pane depends on what you are printing to. As a rule of thumb, use Centered for printing to paper. Use one of the other three choices for imagesetters. Talk to your service bureau to find out which one is best.

Here's the potential problem: On a proofing devices such as an inkjet, thermal wax, or laser printer, the Upper Left, Center Horizontally, and Center Vertically options run the risk of putting part of the page outside the printer's imaging margin (a space of a pica or so from the paper edge in which the printer cannot print). That's why it's best to use the Page Position setting of Centered when printing to paper. This option also makes room available on all sides where possible for crop marks and bleeds.

But when you print to an imagesetter or platesetter, Centered may not be the best option. That's because your service bureau or commercial printer may not want the pages centered because it may be spacing them or rotating them to minimize waste of paper or film negatives. Imagesetters output to rolls of paper or film, so the service bureau or commercial printer has some control over the page's size. Always check first.

CAUTION Many service bureaus use a utility program that automatically rotates pages to save film, so check with your service bureau to make sure that selecting the Transverse option won't conflict with any rotation it might do. Also, if you specify a larger paper size to make room for bleeds or because your document will be printed at tabloid size, this rotation might cause the tops and/or bottoms of your document pages to be cut off. The basic rule: Discuss all output settings with your service bureau or prepress department first.

Scaling, positioning, and tiling options

The Setup pane also lets you set scaling, positioning, and tiling settings in the Options section.

The Scale settings are straightforward. You can choose separate Width and Height scaling settings to reduce or enlarge the page image. If the Constrain Proportions option is selected, then a change in the Width field is applied to the Height field, and vice versa. To make a page fit the paper size, select the Scale to Fit option. InDesign will then display the actual percentage it will use. Note that Scale to Fit takes into account bleeds and crop marks, so even if the document page size is the same as the output device's paper size, Scale to Fit reduces it to make room for those elements.

The Page Position pop-up menu lets you choose how the page image is positioned on the paper to which you're printing. The default position is Centered, which centers the page image vertically and horizontally. You can also choose Center Horizontally, which aligns the top of the page image to the top of the paper and centers the page horizontally; Center Vertically, which aligns the left side of the page image to the left side of the paper and centers the page vertically; and Upper Left, which places the page image's upper-left corner at the paper's upper-left corner.

A very nice option is InDesign's Thumbnails check box and its adjoining pop-up menu. Here, you can have InDesign print *thumbnails* — miniature versions of pages, several to a sheet — for use in presenting comps, seeing whole articles at a glance, and so on. If you select the Thumbnails option, you then show many thumbnails you want per page from the adjoining pop-up menu. Its menu options are 1×2, 2×2, 3×3, 4×4, 5×5, 6×6, and 7×7. InDesign sizes the pages based on what it takes to make them fit at the number of thumbnails chosen per page, the page size, and the paper size.

Use the Tile options to print oversized documents. If Tile is selected, InDesign breaks the document into separate pages called *tiles* that you later can assemble together. To turn on tiling, select the Tile check box and then choose the appropriate option from the adjoining pop-up menu:

- **Manual:** This lets you specify the tiles yourself. To specify a tile, you change the zero point (also called the origin) on the document ruler, and that becomes the upper-left corner of the current tile. To print multiple tiles this way, you need to adjust the zero point and print, adjust the zero point to the next location and print, and so on, until you're done.

CROSS-REF   Chapter 2 covers the zero point in more detail.

- **Auto:** This lets InDesign figure out where to divide the pages into tiles. You can change the default amount of overlap between tiles of 1.5 inches using the Overlap field. The overlap lets you easily align tiles by having enough overlap for you to see where each should be placed relative to the others.

- **Auto Justified:** This is similar to Auto except that it makes each tile the same size, adjusting the overlap if needed to do that. The Auto option, by contrast, simply starts at the origin point and then does as much of the page as will fit in the tile, which means the last tile may be a different width than the others. You can see the difference between the two by watching how the page preview window at left changes as you select each option.

The Marks and Bleeds pane

The Marks and Bleed pane, shown in Figure 30.5, lets you specify which printer marks are output with your pages, as well as areas to reserve for items that bleed off the page. The printer's marks are set in the Marks section and the bleeds are set in the Bleed and Slug section.

Printer's marks

In most cases, you'd select the All Printer's Marks option and have all print on each sheet or negative. But you can select which marks you want to print. Here's what each option means:

- **Crop Marks:** These are lines at the corners of the page that tell a commercial printer where the page boundaries are, and thus to where the paper is trimmed.

- **Bleed Marks:** These add a very thin box around your page that shows the bleed area — where you expect items to print into, even though they're past the page boundary. (A *bleed* is an object that you want to cut at the page boundary; the object needs to overshoot that boundary in case, during printing, the page is not trimmed exactly where it should be. Normally, 0p9 (9 points), or 0.125 inches, is sufficient area for a bleed. You set the bleed area in the Marks and Bleeds pane, which I cover in the next section.

FIGURE 30.5

FIGURE 30.5

The Marks and Bleed pane of the Print dialog box

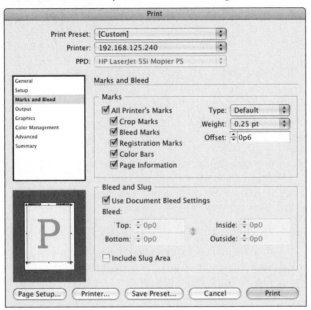

- **Registration Marks:** These are the cross-hair symbols used to ensure that the color negatives are properly aligned on top of each other when combined to create a color proof and to make sure that the colors are not misregistered on the final pages when they are lined up on a printing press.

- **Color Bars:** These print the CMYK colors and tints so that a commercial printer can quickly check during printing whether ink is under- or oversaturated — the shades could be too light or dark. The CMYK colors also help a commercial printer know which color a particular negative is for (after all, negatives are produced using transparent film with black images).

- **Page Information:** This lists the filename and page number.

If a printer has options for printer's marks, they display in the Type pop-up menu, but most simply have one option: Default. You can also adjust the thickness of the printer's marks using the Weight pop-up menu settings of 0.125, 0.25, and 0.5 points; the default is 0.25 points (a hairline rule). You can also control the offset of crop marks from the page corners by adjusting the Offset value; the default of 0.833 inches (6 points) usually suffices. For all of these, check with your service bureau.

Because printer's marks print outside the page, your paper size may not be large enough to print the printer's marks. For example, if your page is 8 1/2 × 11 inches and your paper is the same size, no room is available for the printer's marks. (The page preview subpane on the left of the Print dialog box will show you whether printer's marks fall outside the page's boundaries.) Be sure that your paper size is at least 1 inch wider and taller than your page size if you use printer's marks.

NOTE   When InDesign outputs PDF files, it is smart enough to automatically increase the paper size to add room for the printer's marks.

Bleeds and slugs

The Bleed and Slug area of the Marks and Bleed pane controls how materials print past the page boundary.

A bleed is used when you want a picture, color, or text to go right to the edge of the paper. Because slight variation on positioning occurs when you print because the paper moves mechanically through rollers and might move slightly during transit, publishers have any to-the-edge materials actually print beyond the edge so that there are never any gaps. It's essentially a safety margin. A normal bleed margin would be 0p9 (¹/₈ inch), though you can make it larger if you want.

TIP   You can control whether all bleed margins are changed if any of them is changed by clicking the Make All Settings the Same iconic button: If the chain icon is broken, each can be adjusted separately; if the chain icon is unbroken, changing one causes the others to change automatically. Click the button to toggle between the two behaviors.

A *slug* is an area beyond the bleed area in which you want printer's marks to appear. The reader never sees this, but the staff at the service bureau or commercial printer does, and it helps them make sure they have the right pages, colors, and so on. As is the bleed, the slug area is trimmed off when the pages are bound into a magazine, a newspaper, or whatever. (The word *slug* is an old newspaper term for this identifying information, based on the lead slug once used for this purpose on old printing presses.) The purpose is to ensure that enough room exists for all the printer's marks to appear between the bleed area and the edges of the page. Otherwise, InDesign will do the best it can.

It's best to define your bleed and slug areas in your document itself when you create the document in the New Document dialog box (choose File ➪ New ➪ Document or press ⌘+N or Ctrl+N), as covered in Chapter 4. You can also use the Document Setup dialog box (choose File ➪ Document Setup or press Option+⌘+P or Ctrl+Alt+P). The two dialog boxes have the same options; if they don't show the Bleed and Slug section, click More Options to see them.

But if you didn't define your bleeds previously, you can do so in the Print dialog box's Marks and Bleed pane. You can also override those document settings here. To use the document settings, select the Use Document Bleed Settings option. Otherwise, type in a bleed area using the Top, Bottom, Inside, and Outside fields. (The Inside and Outside fields are labeled Left and Right, respectively, in a document composed of single pages rather than facing pages.)

If you want the bleed area to be the same on all four sides, click the broken-chain button to the right of the Top field; it becomes a solid chain, indicating that all four fields have the same value if any is modified. Any bleed area is indicated in red in the page preview subpane at the bottom left.

If you want to set the slug area, select the Include Slug Area option. InDesign reserves any slug area defined in the New Document or Document Setup dialog box. You cannot set up the slug area in the Print dialog box.

The Output pane

The next pane is the Output pane, which controls the processing of colors and inks on imagesetters, platesetters, and commercial printing equipment. You definitely want to check these settings with your service bureau. For proof printing, such as to a laser printer or inkjet printer, the only option that you need to worry about is the Color pop-up menu, shown in Figure 30.6.

 These options should be specified in coordination with your service bureau and commercial printer — they can really mess up your printing if they're set incorrectly.

FIGURE 30.6

The Output pane of the Print dialog box

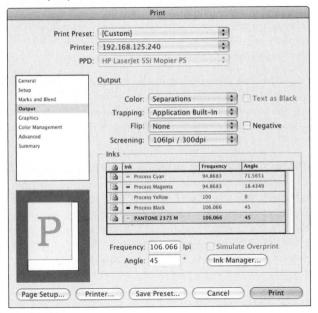

Here's what the options do:

- **Color:** Use this pop-up menu to choose how you want the document to print. Your options are Composite Leave Unchanged, Composite Gray, Composite RGB, Composite CMYK, Separations, and In-RIP Separations. (*RIP* stands for raster-image processor, the device in a printer or imagesetter that converts lines, curves, colors, and pictures into the tiny dots that make up printed output.)

  The Composite menu options are meant for proofing devices such as inkjets and laser printers. Most such printers are black-and-white or CMYK, so you usually choose Composite Gray or Composite CMYK. Choose Composite RGB for documents output to

PDF format for display on screen. Composite Leave Unchanged is meant for proofing printers that support specialty ink swatches such as Pantone; very few do. (If your document uses colors such as Pantone colors, you typically pick Composite CMYK, and your printer approximates the Pantone colors. Choose Composite Leave Unchanged only if your proofing printer has actual Pantone inks.)

Choose Separations if you're printing to an imagesetter to create film negatives or to a platesetter to create color plates. If your output device supports in-RIP separations — in which the device creates the separate color plates rather than having InDesign do it — choose In-RIP Separations. (Note that only a few printers' PPDs support this option.)

- **Text as Black:** If you select this check box, text appears in pure black, rather than being converted to gray or printed in a color (even if you apply a color to the text). This can make text more readable in a proof copy.

- **Trapping:** Use this pop-up menu to select how color trapping is handled. (It is grayed out if Separations or In-RIP Separations are not selected in the Color pop-up menu.) The choices are Off, Application Built-In (meaning, as set in InDesign), and Adobe In-RIP (available only for printers that support Adobe's in-RIP separations technology).

> **NOTE**   At this point, the publishing world has not standardized on PostScript Level 3 printing language or default trapping and color technologies. Therefore, you'll likely choose the standard Separations option that uses whatever settings you created in InDesign, or you'll choose the Off option and let your service bureau manage trapping directly. Check with your service bureau.

- **Flip:** Use this pop-up menu and the associated Negative option to determine how the file prints to film negatives or plates. Service bureaus and commercial printers have different requirements based on the technology they use. They tend to use language such as *right reading, emulsion side up*, which can be hard to translate to InDesign's Flip settings. Type on the page is *right reading* when the photosensitive layer is facing you and you can read the text. Horizontally flipping the page makes it *wrong reading* (type is readable when the photosensitive layer is facing away from you). Check with your service bureau as to whether and how you should flip the output. Pages printed on film are often printed using the Horizontal & Vertical option in the Flip pop-up menu.

- **Negative:** Selecting this check box creates a photographic negative of the page, which some commercial printers may request. This option is available only if Composite Gray, Separations, or In-RIP Separations is chosen in the Color pop-up menu.

- **Screening:** This pop-up menu works differently depending on whether you choose Composite Gray or one of the separations options in the Color pop-up menu:
  - If you choose Composite Gray in the Color pop-up menu, your Screen pop-up menu choices are Default and Custom. If you choose Custom, you can specify the preferred line screen frequency and angle at the bottom of the pane using the Frequency and Angle fields. (See the sidebar "What lpi and dpi mean" for details on line screens, and the section "Adjusting screen angles," later in this chapter, for more details on screen angles.)

■ If you choose Separations or In-RIP Separations in the Color pop-up menu, you get a series of options that vary based on the selected printer and PPD. But all show an lpi setting and a dpi setting. (See the sidebar on lpi and dpi in this chapter for more about these.) And the Frequency and Angle fields at the bottom of the pane display very precise angles optimized for the selected output device based on the chosen lpi/dpi settings. Although you can change the Frequency and Angle fields, you shouldn't.

The Inks section of the pane lets you see the frequency and angle settings for selected colors; you change a specific color plate's settings by first selecting the color and then altering the Frequency and Angle fields. You can also disable output of specific color plates by clicking the printer icons to the left of the colors — a red line is drawn through the icon for disabled plates — as well as control color plate output by clicking Ink Manager, which I cover later in this chapter.

Selecting the Simulate Overprint check box at the bottom of the Output pane lets InDesign overprint colors for printers that normally don't support this feature. (You would set an object to overprint another by selecting one of the Overprint options in the Attributes panel, as Chapter 28 explains.) This option is available only if the Color pop-up menu is set to Composite Gray, Composite CMYK, or Composite RGB.

The Graphics pane

The Graphics pane, shown in Figure 30.7, controls how graphics are printed and how fonts are downloaded. The options here are meant for professional printing, such as when you send your files to imagesetters, meaning that you're working with a service bureau or in-house printing department.

FIGURE 30.7

The Graphics pane of the Print dialog box

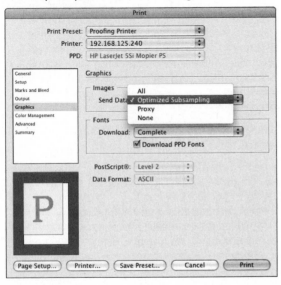

What lpi and dpi Mean

The smallest dots on the physical output — paper, film, or press plate — are measured as dots per inch (dpi) and have a fixed size determined by the output device: a laser printer, imagesetter, or digital platemaker. An output device typically supports 600 to 3600 dpi, dots that are too small to reproduce on an offset press. To create a continuous-tone image that can be reproduced with ink on a press, these fixed-size dots are combined to form much larger, variable-sized dots called a *line screen*, measured as lines per inch (lpi). An image's line screen typically ranges from 80 lpi for a photo on newsprint to 250 lpi for high-end color art prints on coated paper.

Lines per inch specifies, in essence, the grid through which an image is filtered, not the size of the spots that make it up. Thus, a 100-lpi image with variably sized dots will appear finer than a 100-dpi image. The figure shows an example, with a fixed-dot arrow at left and a variably sized–dot arrow at right.

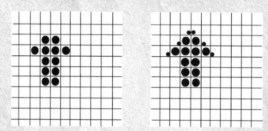

The output device's dpi capabilities thus have a bearing on the lpi capabilities, and lpi is typically how a production person thinks of the desired output quality. A 300-dpi laser printer can achieve about 60-lpi resolution; a 1270-dpi imagesetter can achieve about 120-lpi resolution; a 2540-dpi imagesetter about 200-lpi resolution. Resolutions of less than 100 lpi are considered coarse, and resolutions of more than 120 lpi are considered fine.

But there's more to choosing an lpi setting than knowing your output device's top resolution. An often-overlooked issue is the type of paper the material is printed on. Smoother paper (such as *glossy-coated* or *super-calendared*) can handle finer halftone spots because the paper's coating (also called its *finish*) minimizes ink bleeding. Standard office paper, such as that used in photocopiers and laser printers, is rougher and has some bleed that is usually noticeable only if you write on it with markers. Newsprint is very rough and has a heavy bleed. Typically, newspaper images are printed at 85 to 90 lpi; newsletter images on standard office paper print at 100 to 110 lpi; magazine images print at 120 to 150 lpi; calendars and coffee-table art books print at 150 to 200 lpi.

Other factors affecting lpi include the type of printing press and the type of ink used. Your printer representative should advise you on preferred settings.

If you output your document from your computer directly to film negatives (rather than to photographic paper that is then shot to create negatives), inform your printer representative. Outputting to negatives allows a higher lpi than outputting to paper because negatives created photographically cannot accurately reproduce the fine resolution that negatives that output directly on an imagesetter have. (If, for example, you output to 120 lpi on paper and then create a photographic negative, even the slightest change in the camera's focus makes the fine dots blurry. Outputting straight to negatives avoids this problem.) Printer representatives often assume that you're outputting to paper and base their advised lpi settings on this assumption.

Your first option is the Send Data pop-up menu in the Images section. It has four options: All, Optimized Subsampling, Proxy (a low-resolution, 72-dpi version), and None. The Optimized Subsampling and Proxy options are meant to increase the speed of proof prints, with Proxy being the fastest. The None option is handy for quick proofs meant to focus on the layout and the text.

The Fonts options require that you understand how your output device is configured to handle fonts. Be sure to ask your service bureau what options it prefers. Here are the options available:

- **Download:** This pop-up menu specifies how fonts are downloaded to the printer, something you may need to do if the printer doesn't have its own store of fonts for use in printing text correctly. There are three choices:
  - **Subset:** Normally, when printing to a local printer, choose the Subset option, which sends font data to the printer as fonts are used. This means that if you use just one character of a font on a page, only that character is sent for that page, and if more characters are used on later pages, they are sent at that time. This is an efficient way to send font data to printers that don't have a lot of memory or hard drive space to store complete font information for many typefaces.
  - **Complete:** If you're printing to a device that has a lot of font memory — or if your document has many pages and uses a font in bits and pieces throughout — choose this option from the Download pop-up menu. This option sends the entire font to the printer's memory, where it resides for the entire print job. In cases such as those described, this approach is more efficient than the standard Subset method.
  - **None:** Choose this option from the Download pop-up menu if you're certain all the fonts you use reside in the printer's memory or on a hard drive attached to the printer. Many service bureaus load all the fonts for a job into the printer memory and then print the job. They then clear out the printer memory for the next job and load just the fonts that job needs. This method is efficient when a service bureau has lots of clients who use all sorts of fonts. Alternatively, some service bureaus attach a hard drive loaded with fonts to their imagesetters, saving the font-loading time for them and for InDesign.
- **Download PPD Fonts:** If this check box is selected, InDesign downloads any fonts specified as resident in the printer's PPD file. Normally, PPD files include lists of fonts that should reside in printer memory and thus don't need to be downloaded with each print job. Selecting this option overrides this behavior and instead downloads those fonts from your computer even if they should reside in the printer's memory. You rarely need to select this option; it's more of a safety when creating output files for printing by someone else.

Finally, you can specify what PostScript language is used and how PostScript data is transmitted. Although you set these up in the Mac OS X and Windows printer settings (refer to Figures 30.2 and 30.3), InDesign gives you the opportunity to override any defaults here, which can be handy when creating output files for printing elsewhere:

- From the PostScript pop-up menu, you can choose Level 2 or Level 3; choose whichever the output device supports. (Most still use Level 2.)

- The Data Format pop-up menu is grayed out unless you chose PostScript File in the Printer pop-up menu; your choices are ASCII and Binary. If you choose ASCII, the PostScript file is more likely to be editable in programs such as Adobe Illustrator but the file will be larger. Ask your service bureau which it prefers.

The Color Management pane

The Color Management pane, shown in Figure 30.8, is where you manage color output (apply color calibration). The options are straightforward.

CROSS-REF Chapter 28 covers the techniques for and issues of applying color profiles and other color management settings that the profiles in the Color Management pane use.

- **Document or Proof:** In the Print section, select one of these options based on whether you want to use the document's profile or a different profile for proofing. The Proof option is available only if you choose an output device such as an imagesetter, for which you might make a proof locally using an inkjet or other printer and then use the imagesetter's color profile (as explained in Chapter 29) when producing your final output. (Using the Proof option ensures that InDesign simulates on your proofing printer how the document's colors will appear when printed on the final output device, such as an imagesetter. Using the Document option tells InDesign not to factor in how the final output device will alter the color during printing but instead to simulate what you see on screen instead.)

- **Color Handling:** In the Options section, use this pop-up menu to choose between Let InDesign Determine Colors and PostScript Printer Determines Color. The first option uses the color-management options set in InDesign, whereas the second lets the PostScript output device choose the color-management approach. This latter option is not available unless you have chosen a color PostScript printer as the destination. (If you choose Composite Leave Unchanged in the Output pane's Color pop-up menu, you have the No Color Management option in the Color Handling pop-up menu.)

- **Printer Profile:** Use this pop-up menu to select the color profile of the device to which the document will ultimately be printed, for handling color management at output. This is by default the same as the color profile selected in the Color Settings dialog box, which I cover in Chapter 28. But you can override that default here, such as when you are using a different printer temporarily.

Depending on which Color Handling and Printing Profile options you select, you may be able to use one or both of the following options:

- **Preserve CMYK Numbers:** When selected, this option prevents the color management options from overriding the CMYK values in noncolor-calibrated imported graphics.

- **Simulate Paper Color:** If you choose Proof of a Printing Condition as the Color Handling Method, selecting this check box makes InDesign simulate the typical color of the paper you've chosen for proofing (through View ➪ Proof Setup; see Chapter 28).

FIGURE 30.8

The Color Management pane of the Print dialog box

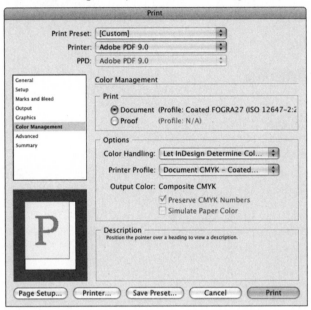

The Advanced pane

The options in the Advanced pane, shown in Figure 30.9, control printing of files as bitmaps, manage graphics file substitutions in an Open Prepress Interface (OPI) workflow, and set transparency flattening, which manages how transparent and semitransparent objects are handled during output.

Bitmap printing

For certain printers — mainly inkjet printers — InDesign lets you control the output resolution when you are printing the file as grayscale (by choosing Composite Gray in the Output pane's Color pop-up menu). To do so, select the Print as Bitmap check box in the Advanced pane and select the desired dpi value from the pop-up menu at the right.

Note that this feature is available only if you choose a compatible printer in the Printer pop-up menu *and* set the output to Composite Gray.

OPI settings

If graphics files exist in high-resolution versions at your service bureau — typically, this occurs when the bureau scans in photographs at very high resolutions and sends you a lower-resolution version for layout placement — select the OPI Image Replacement option. This ensures that InDesign uses the high-resolution scans instead of the low-resolution layout versions.

The Omit for OPI section provides three additional related graphics file-handling options. You can have InDesign *not* send EPS, PDF, and bitmap images (such as TIFF files) by selecting the appropriate options. You would do so either to speed printing of proof copies or when the service bureau has such files in higher-resolution or color-corrected versions and will substitute its graphics for yours. InDesign keeps any OPI links, so the graphics at the service bureau will relink to your document during output.

Transparency flattening

There are just two options in the Transparency Flattener section:

- **Preset:** This pop-up menu lets you choose a transparency preset (a saved set of options). At the least, InDesign provides the three default transparency-flattening options: [Low Resolution], [Medium Resolution], and [High Resolution].

- **Ignore Spread Overrides:** If this check box is selected, any transparency settings you manually applied to document spreads are ignored and the selected preset is used instead for the entire document.

CROSS-REF Transparency settings and presets are covered later in this chapter.

FIGURE 30.9

The Advanced pane of the Print dialog box

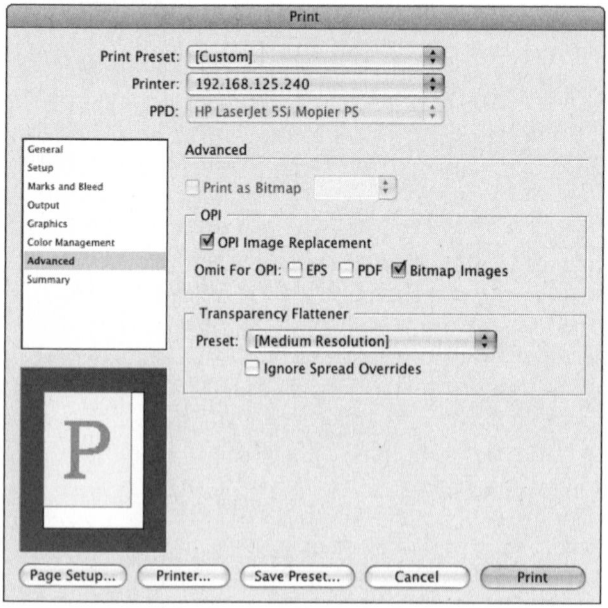

The Summary pane

The final Print dialog box pane is the Summary pane. It simply lists your settings all in one place for easy review. The only option — Save Summary — saves the settings to a file that you can include with your files when you deliver them to a service bureau or distribute them to other staff members; this way, everyone knows the preferred settings.

Working with Spot Colors and Separations

When you print color separations, InDesign gives you expected control over how colors separate — which are converted to CMYK and which are printed on their own plates. But it goes much further, letting you control much of how those plates print, such as the order that plates print in and the angle of each color's line screens.

Managing color and ink output

Accidentally using spot colors such as red and Pantone 2375M (say, for graphics and text frames) in a document that contains four-color TIFF and EPS files is very easy. The result is that InDesign outputs as many as six plates: one each for the four process colors, plus one for red and one for Pantone 2375M, rather than convert red and Pantone 2375M into CMYK mixes and thus output just the four CMK plates. But, you can avoid these kinds of mistakes.

That's exactly where the Ink Manager dialog box comes in. Accessed by clicking Ink Manager in the Output pane, this dialog box gives you finer control over how color negatives output. Figure 30.10 shows the dialog box.

If any colors should have been converted to process color but weren't, you have three choices:

- **Click the spot-color iconic button:** You can override the spot color in the Ink Manager dialog box by clicking this iconic button (a circle) to the left of the color's name. That converts it to a process color and causes the iconic button to change to a four-color box that indicates a process color. (Clicking the four-color-box iconic button converts a process color back to a spot color, as well as changes the iconic button back to a circle.) This is the way to go for a quick fix.

- **Make it a process color instead:** Do this by closing the Ink Manager and Print dialog boxes and editing the color that was incorrectly set as a spot color in the Swatches panel (choose Window ➪ Swatches or press F5), as covered in Chapter 7. This ensures that the color is permanently changed to a process color for future print jobs.

- **Convert all spot colors to CMYK process equivalents:** Do this by selecting the All Spots to Process check box. This is the easiest method to make sure you don't accidentally print spot-color plates for a CMYK-only document. (You can also use the All Spots Process option to quickly convert all spot colors to process, and then convert back to spot colors just those colors you really do want on their own plates.)

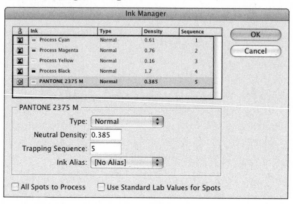

FIGURE 30.10

The Ink Manager dialog box

The other Ink Manager options are for experts and should be changed only in consultation with your service bureau and commercial printer:

■ **You can change the ink type in the Type pop-up menu.** Most inks — including the process inks — should be left at Normal. Use Transparent for varnishes and other finishes that let color through — you don't want InDesign to trap to such colors. If it did, no color would print under the varnish or finish. (A varnish is often used to highlight part of a page, such as making the text reflective in contrast to the rest of the page.) Use Opaque for metallics, pastels, and other thick colors; this setting lets adjacent colors trap to the edge of opaque objects, but it prevents trapping of underlying colors (because they will be totally covered over). Finally, use Opaque Ignore for inks that don't trap well with any other color — your service bureau or commercial printer tells you when you need to do this.

■ **You can change the neutral density for each ink.** This tells InDesign how to handle the trapping of differently saturated inks. For example, a dark color (highly saturated) needs to be trapped more conservatively against a light color to prevent excess intrusion. In coordination with your commercial printer, you might want to override the default neutral density settings if you find that the defaults don't properly handle some trapping combinations. It's possible that your commercial printer is using a different brand of ink than is assumed in the settings, for example, and that could require a density adjustment.

■ **Arrange the order in which color negatives print.** Sometimes commercial printers permit you to do this. It affects the trapping, because InDesign presumes that the colors are printed in the standard order — cyan, then magenta, then yellow, then black, then any spot colors — and factors that into its trapping adjustments. In some cases, changing the printing order improves a publication's color balance, because it happens to favor a range of tones that the standard order might not treat properly. For example, if there's a lot of black in the background, you might want to print black first. Other colors overprint it, giving it a warmer feel than if black is printed on top of the other colors as it is normally. To change the order of output used by InDesign's trapping calculations, select a color, and change its ink sequence number in the Trapping Sequence field; all other colors' sequences are automatically adjusted.

■ **Apply a process color's settings to a spot color.** You can use the Ink Alias pop-up menu to do this, but I don't recommend you do this very often, as it makes the spot color print each dot over the dots of the selected process color, rather than be offset slightly so the color remains visible. You set an ink alias only if you are using a spot color in place of a standard process color — such as substituting a yolk color for standard yellow to create a special effect. In this case, the yolk color overprints the yellow color, replacing the yellow where both colors have been used.

■ **Force one plate to be used for several versions of the same color.** Another case for using the Ink Alias feature is when your document has several color swatches that should be the same color. (Perhaps PDF files you placed used different names for the same color, such as PMS 2375M and Pantone 2375M, so these multiple swatch names were all added to your document.) Ink Alias lets you have all these "colors" print on the same plate.

■ **Force InDesign to substitute the basic CMYK process colors for the similar colors defined by the Pantone and HKS spot-color models.** Do this by selecting the Use Standard Lab Values for Spots option. In most cases, the substitute colors are almost identical, so no one will notice, but check with your printer first, because the type of paper you use or other factors may cause a different output than expected.

CROSS-REF Chapter 9 covers how to create color swatches, how to specify which are to print as spot colors and which are to be converted to process colors, and how to use the various color models and ink libraries. Chapter 28 explains how to preview color separations on-screen.

Adjusting screen angles

When you print using color plates, each plate — cyan, magenta, yellow, and black, or any spot colors — is rotated slightly so that its dots don't overprint the dots of other plates. This ensures that each color is visible on the paper and this is visible to the eye, which then blends them into various colors, simulating natural color. These rotations called *screening angles* determine how the dots comprising each of the four process colors are aligned so that they don't overprint each other. Normally, you'd probably never worry about the screening angles for your color plates. After all, the service bureau makes those decisions, right? Maybe.

If you have your own imagesetter, or even if you're just using a proofing device, you should know how to change screen angles for the best output. If you're working with spot colors that have shades applied to them, you'll want to know what the screen angles are so that you can determine how to set the screening angles for those spot colors.

The rule of thumb is that dark colors should be at least 30 degrees apart, whereas lighter colors (for example, yellow) should be at least 15 degrees apart from other colors. That rule of thumb translates into a 15-degree angle for cyan, a 75-degree angle for magenta, no angle (0 degrees) for yellow, and a 45-degree angle for black.

But those defaults sometimes result in *moiré patterns*, which are distortions in the image's light and dark areas caused when the dots making up the colors don't arrange themselves evenly. With traditional color-separation technology, a service bureau has to adjust the angles manually to avoid such moirés — an expensive and time-consuming process. With the advent of computer technology, modern output devices, such as imagesetters, can calculate angles based on the output's lpi settings to avoid most moiré patterns. (Each image's balance of colors can cause a different moiré, which is why there is no magic formula.) Every major imagesetter vendor uses its own proprietary algorithm to make these calculations.

InDesign automatically uses the printer's PPD values to calculate the recommended halftoning, lpi, and frequency settings shown in the Output pane of the Print dialog box. But for spot colors, it's basically a guess as to what screening angle a color should get. The traditional default is to give it the same angle as yellow, because if a spot color's dots overprint yellow dots, the effect is less noticeable than if it overprinted, say, black dots. But if you have multiple spot colors, that approach doesn't work. In that case, choose a screening angle for the color whose hue is closest to the spot colors. Fortunately, InDesign calculates a recommended angle for you, so you don't have to make any guesses. As always, don't forget to consult your service bureau or printing manager.

Working with Transparency

InDesign lets you import objects with transparent portions, as well as create transparent objects using the Effects panel (see Chapter 11). Using features such as the Drop Shadow and Feather options in the Effects dialog box also might create transparency. But working with transparency can create unintended side effects in how overlapping objects actually appear when printed or viewed on-screen in a PDF file. To address that, InDesign gives you the ability to control transparency on selected objects and groups, as well as control how transparency is handled during output.

Using transparency the ideal way

The use of transparency can result in very cool effects in your layout, but it can also cause major problems when you print because transparency requires very complex calculations for the imagesetter to handle, calculations that can be tripped up by how source files and other settings are applied.

So it's important to apply transparency wisely. Follow these techniques to get the best results when you print:

- All objects containing text should be stacked above any object with transparency effects. The flattening process can distort type unpleasantly when objects with effects are arranged above type objects. Obviously, arranging objects in this way is not always possible, but the difference in quality makes it worth the time to fix this when it is possible to do so.

- Similarly, keep transparent objects on their own layers when possible.

- Be sure to set the document's transparency blend space to match the type of output: RGB (for on-screen output such as PDF files) and CMYK (for printed documents). Do so by choosing either Edit ⇨ Transparency Blend Space ⇨ Document CMYK or Edit ⇨ Transparency Blend Space ⇨ Document RGB.

- Don't mix RGB and CMYK objects in the same layout if you use transparency; convert your source images to the same color model in their originating programs, such as Adobe Illustrator and Photoshop. Convert spot colors to CMYK in those programs as well, except, of course, for those that print on their own plates.

- Be careful when using Color, Saturation, Luminosity, and Difference blending modes with spot colors or gradients — they may not print correctly, so you may need a design alternative if such output problems occur.

- If your source files have transparency, neither flatten them in the program that created them nor save them in formats that flatten them. That means you should keep files with transparency in these formats: PDF 1.4 or later, Illustrator 10 or later, and Photoshop 6 and later. Note that Illustrator Encapsulated PostScript (EPS) files keep their transparent areas separate when worked on in Illustrator but not when used by separate programs, so don't use the Illustrator EPS format for transparent objects if you can avoid it.

Flattening transparency during output

The more objects you have overlapping each other with transparency settings applied, the more complex the output calculations are to print those effects. This can prevent a document from printing because it can overwhelm the printer or other output device. That's why many commercial printers and prepress houses dread transparency.

Adobe PostScript Levels 1 and 2, EPS, and Adobe PDF 1.3 do not support Adobe's transparency technology in its native state. Therefore, transparency information must be flattened for export to EPS or Adobe PDF 1.3 format, or for printing to PostScript desktop printers, PostScript Level 2 raster-image processors (RIPs), and some PostScript 3 RIPs. (Although newer Adobe applications and the PDF 1.4 format do support transparency, many service bureaus and commercial printers use older imagesetters that do not, because their high cost requires they be used for many years so that they can recoup its investment.)

Ideally, your service bureau or commercial printer handles the flattening of your files, so it can optimize the results for its equipment. If you send the service bureau native Creative Suite files or PDF 1.4 or later output, the bureau's staff should be able to work with the native transparency and do the flattening. Otherwise, it has to live with the flattening results you create, so be sure to test files to identify any issues early.

When InDesign flattens transparency, it converts the overlapping elements in a stack of transparent objects to a single, flat layer of distinct opaque graphics during output, creating a mosaic of pieces that produce the intended effect.

Creating flattener presets

InDesign comes with three transparency flattening settings — [Low Resolution], [Medium Resolution], and [High Resolution] — which you can edit in the Transparency Flattener Presets dialog box. To open this dialog box, shown in Figure 30.11, choose Edit ⇨ Transparency Flattener Presets. The dialog box shows the settings for each preset as you select them. Use this dialog box to create, modify, delete, export (Save), and import (Load) presets. (You cannot modify or delete the three default presets.)

> **NOTE**   InDesign uses pixels per inch, or ppi, rather than dpi in the Transparency Flattener Preset Options dialog box. They're equivalent measurements for computer-generated images. InDesign uses ppi for transparency because it's working with the pixels of your images rather than with the dots output by your printer.

FIGURE 30.11

The Transparency Flattener Presets dialog box (left) and the Transparency Flattener Preset Options dialog box (right)

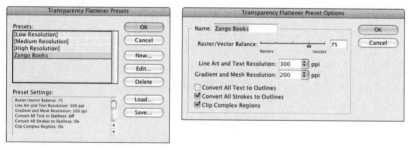

Figure 30.11 also shows the Transparency Flattener Preset Options dialog box, which appears when you create or modify a preset. There's a lot of trial and error in developing transparency flattener presets because the complexity of your documents and the capacity of your output devices will vary widely. But here are some guidelines:

- The most accurate transparency blends are achieved with a Raster/Vector Balance set to 100, which means you should use all vectors rather than convert blends to bitmap images. The [Low Resolution] preset is set at 75, which means that three-quarters of the blends are vectors and one-quarter is converted to bitmaps. The other options have higher vector proportions.

- Flattener resolution should be set to a value that corresponds with your output device's dpi. For Line Art and Text Resolution, 600 ppi or higher is fine, while 150 ppi is fine for gradients and meshes (overlapping transparencies). But the higher the output resolution of your output device, the higher you will make these values.

- If you apply transparency to objects that overprint or underprint text, you likely will select the Convert All Text to Outlines option; otherwise, InDesign may make the text that interacts with transparent objects thicker than text that doesn't.

- Convert Strokes to Outlines has the same effect on lines and strokes for InDesign objects that overlap or underlap objects with transparency.

- The Clip Complex Regions options apply only if the Raster/Vector Balance is less than 100. It corrects for a phenomenon called *stitching,* in which a transparent area has both vectors and bitmaps that create a blocky feel. This option isolates those areas and forces them to be all-vector.

Applying flattener presets

You can apply transparency flattener presets directly to a spread when working on a layout by selecting a spread in the Pages panel (choose Window⇨Pages or press ⌘+F12 or Ctrl+F12) and then choosing Spread Flattening⇨Custom from the flyout menu. You get the Custom Spread Flattener Settings dialog box, which (other than its name) is identical to the Transparency Flattener Presets dialog box shown in Figure 30.11, except that any settings created in the Custom Spread Flattener Settings dialog box are applied only to the selected spread and are not saved as a preset for use elsewhere.

You can also apply transparency presets globally to your document — overriding any spread settings — in the Advanced pane of the Print dialog box as I describe earlier in this chapter.

Previewing flattener settings

InDesign lets you preview flattening settings; to do so, you use the Flattener Preview panel. Shown in Figure 30.12, this panel lets you preview transparent objects and their flattening. To open the panel, choose Window⇨Output⇨Flattener Preview.

In the panel, you can select what to preview in the Highlight pop-up menu. Your options are None, Rasterized Complex Regions, Transparent Objects, Affected Objects, Affected Graphics, Outlined Strokes, Outlined Text, Raster-Fill Text and Strokes, and All Rasterized Regions. (Note that the rasterized options display overlapping transparent objects that InDesign needs to convert to bitmaps during flattening — not simply any bitmap images in your document.) Choose the area you're concerned may not output at sufficient quality.

FIGURE 30.12

The Flattener Preview panel and its flyout menu (left) and the Highlight pop-up menu's options in that panel (right)

 If you select the Auto Refresh Highlight check box, InDesign updates the preview if you change any settings; if not, you can update the preview by clicking Refresh.

You can also check the flattening results of different presets — just choose a preset from the Preset pop-up menu. Likewise, you can see what would happen to a spread that has a custom flattening applied if you were to override those custom settings — just select the Ignore Spread Overrides check box.

If you like how the flattening looks, you can preapply them to the Print dialog box by clicking Apply Settings to Print.

Summary

In InDesign, you have many options from which to choose to control exactly how your document prints. The right options depend on the document's contents and the output device you're using.

Be sure to define your colors as process colors unless you want them to print on their own plates. Although InDesign lets you convert all colors to process colors when you print, there are times when you want some colors to print on their own plate (these are called *spot colors*) and others to be converted to process, and the only way to make that happen is to define colors as process or as spot in the first place.

InDesign's transparency options let you control how overlapping objects print, as well as how those overlapping areas are handled during output to ensure both quality reproduction and speedy processing.

Chapter 31

Creating Prepress Files

I n this electronic age, there are many reasons not to print a document, at least not directly. You may want to deliver the document to readers in an electronic format, such as in HTML or as an Adobe PDF. Or you may want to generate a prepress file that your service bureau can output for you at an imagesetter — one you may send over a network, through the Internet, on a high-capacity disk, or even as an electronic-mail attachment to a device that could be down the hall or in another state.

Selecting the Best Prepress File Option

InDesign has several options for creating prepress files:

- You can export to two variants of the PostScript printing language: Adobe Portable Document Format (PDF) or Encapsulated PostScript (EPS). Service bureaus typically prefer files exported this way — particularly in the form of PDF files.

- You can print to file using all the settings described in Chapter 30 — creating a PostScript output file — rather than output directly to a printer, creating a file tuned specifically to the printer driver that you selected. These output files can cause problems at a service bureau, so you're less likely to use this approach.

CROSS-REF InDesign can also export both individual objects and document pages as JPEG graphics files. Chapter 4 explains how to do this.

IN THIS CHAPTER

Evaluating prepress output options

Creating Portable Document Format files

Creating Encapsulated PostScript files

Creating output files

 Throughout this chapter, when I say "service bureau," I include commercial print-ers and internal printing departments.

The export option you pick has several advantages and consequences; here's a look at each choice separately.

Exporting to PDF

This option creates a file that can be linked to from a Web page, whether on the Internet or on a corporate intranet. It can also be accessed from a CD or other disk medium, as long as the recipi-ent has the free Adobe Reader program (available for download from www.adobe.com/acrobat). Finally, a service bureau can use a PDF file as the master file from which to print your documents.

This file can include some or all of the fonts, or expect the ultimate output device to have them. You also have control over the resolution of the graphics, which lets you, for example, create a high-resolution file for output on an imagesetter or a low-resolution version for display on the Web.

The PDF file won't have information on the specific printer, so a service bureau could use it on any available output devices. But not all service bureaus are geared to print from PDF files; although this is an increasingly popular option, it is by no means ubiquitous. To print a PDF file directly, the output device must be a PostScript 3 device; otherwise, the service bureau must open the PDF file in Adobe Acrobat or in a high-end PDF-oriented workflow publishing system to then print the file to the output device.

Exporting to EPS

This option creates files that can be sent to many output devices or edited by a PostScript-savvy graphics program such as Illustrator or CorelDraw. With InDesign, you can add a margin for bleeds, but you can't include printer's marks.

Most service bureaus can print directly from EPS files. But note that each page or spread in your InDesign document is exported as a separate EPS file, so a service bureau may prefer a prepress-oriented PostScript file or a PDF file that combines all pages into one file, which simplifies its out-put effort.

The lack of printer's marks might also bother your commercial printer because it needs them to properly combine film negatives. But some high-end workflow systems can add printer's marks and integrate high-resolution and color-corrected images — so EPS can remain a solid output option, provided that your service bureau has these capabilities.

TIP   If you're creating PDF files, it's best to export just the page or spread you want to use; otherwise, the file contains the data for all other pages, possibly and unneces-sarily making its size unwieldy. (When exporting to EPS, a separate file is created for each page or spread, so this is not an issue.)

Using Prepress Files in Your Layout

Exported PDF or EPS files can be imported back into InDesign (or other programs, including QuarkXPress, Microsoft Publisher, Apple Pages, Adobe Illustrator, CorelDraw, Adobe Photoshop, ACD Canvas, and Corel Photo-Paint) as graphics. This is handy if you want, for example, to run a small version of the cover on your contents page to give the artist credit, or if you want to show a page from a previous issue in a letters section where readers are commenting on a story. (Chapter 25 explains how to import these files into InDesign.)

Printing to EPS or PostScript files

If you know exactly what device your service bureau will use to output your document, and you know all the settings, you can create an EPS or PostScript output file. All your printer settings from the Print dialog box are embedded in that file, making it print reliably only on the target printer.

NOTE Remember to work with your service bureau to understand what its needs and expectations are. Although some output files are fully or partially editable, it's usually not easy to know what might be incorrect in a document until you reach the expensive step of actually printing pages or negatives.

Creating PDF Files

Typically, you want to directly export your InDesign files as PDF files rather than create a PostScript file and translate to PDF using the separate Adobe Acrobat Distiller product. First, I show how to export and then I explain how to print to PDF on those occasions when that's the better option.

Exporting PDF files

An easy way to create a PDF file from InDesign is to export it by choosing File ➪ Export or pressing ⌘+E or Ctrl+E. The Export dialog box appears, which, like any standard Save dialog box, lets you name the file and determine what drive and folder it is to be saved in. The key control in the Export dialog box is the Formats pop-up menu, where you choose the format (in this case, Adobe PDF).

The fastest way to create a PDF file is to choose File ➪ PDF Export Presets and then select a preset from the submenu. There are seven presets optimized for different output needs. You can also add your own, as I explain a bit later in this chapter. When you select a preset from the submenu, you then see the Export dialog box. Choosing a preset defaults the Formats pop-up menu to Adobe PDF and preconfigures the PDF export settings covered in the following sections.

TIP   If you're working with the InDesign book feature (see Chapter 24), you can export the book's chapters to PDF files from an open book's panel. The setup options are the same as they are for exporting individual documents.

After you've selected Adobe PDF in the Export dialog box's Formats pop-up menu and given the file a name and location, click Save to get the Export Adobe PDF dialog box shown in Figure 31.1. The dialog box has seven panes; General is the one displayed when you open the dialog box.

Common options

There are several common options that are accessible from all seven panes:

- **Adobe PDF Preset pop-up menu:** This pop-up menu lets you select from both predefined sets of PDF-export settings (similar to the printer presets covered in Chapter 30), as well as any presets you may have created. (I describe these presets later in this chapter.)

- **Standard pop-up menu:** This pop-up menu lets you choose which PDF interchange (PDF/X) format to use. For prepress workflow, you might choose one of the PDF/X-1a, PDF/X-3, or PDF/X-4 options in the Standard pop-up menu (the four-digit numbers at the end of the option names refer to the year that any revisions to the standard were added). PDF/X is a standard version of PDF, sanctioned by the International Organization for Standardization (ISO), meant to ensure consistent reproduction across a range of equipment. Irrelevant for on-screen viewing, PDF/X should be used if your service bureau is using compatible equipment. Otherwise, leave this pop-up menu at the default setting of None.

- **Compatibility pop-up menu:** This pop-up menu lets you choose which PDF file version to save the file as. Your options are Acrobat 4 (PDF 1.3), Acrobat 5 (PDF 1.4), Acrobat 6 (PDF 1.5), Acrobat 7 (PDF 1.6), and Acrobat 8 (PDF 1.7). (Acrobat 9 (PDF 1.7).) Theoretically, choosing Acrobat 4 (PDF 1.3) is the best option for documents that will be distributed on CD or over the Web because it ensures that the largest number of people will be able to view the file. But it also limits the ability to use some features, particularly those that protect the document from unauthorized usage, such as copying its contents. For general-purpose distribution, I recommend that you choose Acrobat 6 (PDF 1.5) because that version is a half decade old, so practically any active computer user has that or a more recent version of Acrobat Reader. If you're sending the PDF file to a service bureau, use the version of Acrobat it uses because later versions of Acrobat support more features, especially for commercial printing. (PDF formats 1.5 and later, for example, support native transparency.)

- **Save Preset button:** Click this to save any settings made in the Export Adobe PDF dialog box as a new preset. (You can also define new PDF presets by choosing File ➪ PDF Export Presets.)

- **Cancel button:** Click this to cancel PDF export.

- **Export button:** Click this to create the PDF file based on the settings selected in the various panes.

The General pane

Use the General pane to determine what is exported. The pane has four sections: Description, Pages, Options, and Include.

In the Description field, type in the description text that you want to appear in the PDF file when it's opened in Adobe Acrobat. The description appears in the Description pane of Acrobat's Document Properties dialog box (choose File➪Document Properties or press ⌘+D or Ctrl+D).

In the Pages section, you can set the following options:

- **All and Range:** Select All to print all pages or select Range to print a range. If you select Range, you type the desired page range in the Range field. When specifying a range of pages, you can type nonconsecutive ranges, such as **1–4, 7, 10–13, 15, 18, 20**. If you want to print from a specific page to the end of the document, just type the hyphen after the initial page number, such as **4–**. InDesign figures out what the last page is. Similarly, to start from the first page to a specified page, just start with the hyphen, as in **–11**. InDesign also lets you type absolute page numbers in the Range field. For example, typing **+6–+12** prints the document's sixth through twelfth pages, no matter what their page numbers are.

- **Spreads:** When this option is selected, the document prints facing pages on the same sheet of paper, which is handy when showing clients comps, but make sure you have a printer that can handle that large paper size.

> **TIP** You may not want to use the Spreads option when outputting a PDF file for eventual printing on an imagesetter if you have bleeds, because there will be no bleed between the spreads. If you use traditional *perfect-binding* (square spines) or *saddle-stitching* (stapled spines) printing methods in which facing pages are not printed contiguously, do not use this option.

In the Options section, you can select the following options:

- **Embed Page Thumbnails:** Select this option if you're creating a PDF file to be viewed on-screen — these thumbnails help people using the Adobe Reader program navigate your document more easily. But if the PDF files are being sent to a service bureau or commercial printer for printing, you don't need to generate the thumbnails.

- **Optimize for Fast Web View:** Always select this option; it minimizes file size without compromising the output.

- **Create Tagged PDF:** Select this option to embed XML tag information into the PDF file. This is useful for XML-based workflows and Adobe eBooks.

- **View PDF after Exporting:** Select this option if you want to see the results of the PDF export as soon as the export is complete. Typically, however, you should not select this option because you likely have other things you want to do before launching Adobe Reader (or the full Adobe Acrobat program, if you own it) to proof your files.

- **Create Acrobat Layers:** If you selected Acrobat 6 (PDF 1.5) or later in the Compatibility pop-up menu, you can select this option, which outputs any InDesign layers to separate layers in Acrobat. (Acrobat 6 was the first version of Acrobat to support layers.) If you choose a different Compatibility option, Create Acrobat Layers is grayed out.

- **Export Layers:** This pop-up menu gives you additional control over how layers marked as nonprinting are exported to the PDF file. It used to be that if you marked a layer as nonprinting, you would have to leave the Export Adobe PDF dialog box to open the Layers panel to make it exportable. Now, you can skip that step and override layers' non-printing status using this pop-up menu. The default option, Visible & Printable Layers, honors your layers' printing status. Visible Layers exports all visible layers, including those marked as nonprinting. All Layers exports both visible and hidden layers, including those marked as nonprinting. (See Chapter 5 for more on layers.)

FIGURE 31.1

The General pane of the Export Adobe PDF dialog box

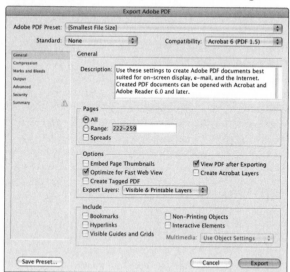

736

In the Include section, you can select the following options:

- **Bookmarks:** This takes InDesign table-of-contents (TOC) information and preserves it as bookmarks in the exported PDF file.

- **Hyperlinks:** This preserves any hyperlinks added in InDesign. Otherwise, the hyperlinks are converted to standard text. (Chapter 32 explains how to create hyperlinks in InDesign.)

- **Visible Guides and Grids:** This includes the on-screen guides and grids in the output version — an option you'd use only when creating PDF files meant to be used as designer examples, not for readers or for prepress.

- **Non-Printing Objects:** This includes any objects marked as Nonprinting through the Attributes pane (choose Window ➪ Attributes), as Chapter 9 explains.

- **Interactive Elements:** This preserves interactive objects such as buttons rather than converting them to static graphics.

- **Multimedia:** This pop-up menu lets you control how embedded sound and video are handled. This option is available only if you choose Acrobat 6 (PDF 1.5) or later in the Compatibility pop-up menu and select the Interactive Elements check box. The options are Use Object Settings, Link All, or Embed All. In InDesign, you can embed a sound or movie file, or link to one. This option lets you override the individual settings and make all such objects embedded or linked.

 **Chapter 32 covers interactive documents, including the use of buttons and multimedia elements.**

The Compression pane

All the options in this pane, shown in Figure 31.2, compress your document's graphics. For documents you're intending to print professionally, make sure that for Color, Grayscale, and Monochrome image types, the No Sampling Change option is selected (Figure 31.2 shows the option set to Bicubic Downsampling To) and that Compression is set to None. You don't want to do anything that affects the resolution or quality of your bitmap images if you're outputting to a high-resolution device.

But it's fine to select the Crop Image Data to Frames option because this discards portions of pictures not visible on-screen, reducing file size and reducing processing time during output (imagesetters and other devices usually have to process the entire image, even if only part of it is actually printed).

It's also fine to select the Compress Text and Line Art option. It compresses vector graphics (both imported and those created in InDesign) as well as text, but does so without affecting output quality.

The compression settings are more appropriate for documents meant to be viewed online, as I explain in the sidebar "Settings for On-Screen Usage," later in this chapter. You usually leave the image downsampling at 150 pixels per inch (ppi) for color and grayscale images and at 300 ppi for black-and-white images. Even though a computer monitor's resolution is 72 ppi, you want enough resolution so that when a reader zooms in, the images are still clear. A good rule of thumb for documents to be printed is that the downsampling or subsampling ppi for color and grayscale images should be at least double the printer's lpi. (I explain downsampling and subsampling in the sidebar "Understanding Compression Methods," later in this chapter.)

FIGURE 31.2

The Compression pane of the Export Adobe PDF dialog box

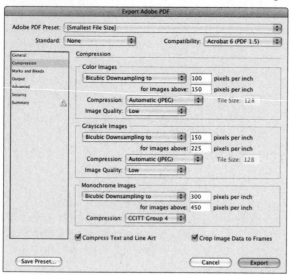

For the Image Quality setting for images, Medium quality is fine for on-screen documents, but not for documents you intend to let readers print or that will be output at a service bureau. A rule of thumb is to choose High if the documents will be printed on an inkjet or laser printer, and Maximum if they will be printed at an imagesetter or other high-end output device.

Note that JPEG compression is *lossy*, meaning that it discards data to save space. That's why its Image Quality settings are characterized with subjective terms such as Low, Medium, and High. Zip compression is lossless, so no image detail data is discarded. Instead, you limit the color depth by choosing between 4-bit (16 colors) and 8-bit (256 colors).

When Compatibility is set to Acrobat 6 or later (format version 1.5 or later) and Compression is set to Automatic (JPEG 2000), a Tile Size field is available and determines the size of the tiles for progressive display. (For all other options, the tile size is automatically set, and restricted to, 128 pixels.) For large images, this option shows subsequent pieces, or tiles, of the image, until the full image has been displayed, so the reader has a visual indication that the page is in fact loading. You can change the size of the tile from the default of 256 pixels.

TIP You can control whether all bleed margins are changed if any of them is changed by clicking the Make All Settings the Same iconic button: If the chain icon is broken, each can be adjusted separately; if the chain icon is unbroken, changing one changes the others automatically.

Understanding Compression Methods

The act of choosing a compression method for the color, grayscale, and monochrome images in a PDF is simple — you just pick something from a menu in the Compression pane of the Export Adobe PDF dialog box. The challenge is in knowing what to pick. Take a look at the type of images for which the compression methods work best (see the following list), and then choose the one that represents the bulk of the images in your layout.

- Zip compression is appropriate for black-and-white or color images with repeating patterns (usually screen shots or simple images created in paint programs).

- JPEG compression works well for continuous-tone photographs in grayscale or color. JPEG results in smaller files than Zip compression because it throws out some image data, possibly reducing image accuracy.

- CCITT compression works for black-and-white images or 1-bit images. Group 4 works well for most monochrome images, while Group 3 is good for PDFs that will be faxed electronically.

Downsampling and subsampling accomplish similar goals but use different mathematic techniques to do so. When you reduce the dpi, you're essentially throwing away image data to make it smaller — for example, replacing a 100-x-100-pixel image with a 25-x-25-pixel version reduces the file size to 1/16th of its original size. Downsampling averages adjacent pixels' colors and replaces the cluster of adjacent pixels with one averaged pixel as it reduces the image size. (There are two methods for downsampling: bicubic and average. Bicubic usually, but not always, results in a truer image. Average downsampling tends to work better in nonphotographic images, with less minute detail.) Subsampling does no averaging; it simply throws away pixels in between the ones it retains. Downsampling looks better for photographic images with lots of detail and color; subsampling looks better for images with clear color differences and few intricate details.

For prepress purposes, the resolution should be one and a half to two times the line screen ruling used to print the file. For on-screen purposes, keep in mind that higher resolutions are better when users need to increase the view scale in the PDF (for example, if they need to see detail in a map). In the Acrobat support section of www.adobe.com, you can find more details about specific image resolutions that work well with printer resolutions.

The Marks and Bleeds pane

Use the Marks and Bleeds pane, shown in Figure 31.3, to set the page bleed and printer's marks.

You typically set printer's marks only for files meant to be output on an imagesetter or other prepress device. Typically, you should select All Page Marks. Your Offset amount should be the same as or more than the bleed amount — if your Offset is less than the bleed, the marks could appear in your page's margins.

FIGURE 31.3

The Marks and Bleeds pane of the Export Adobe PDF dialog box

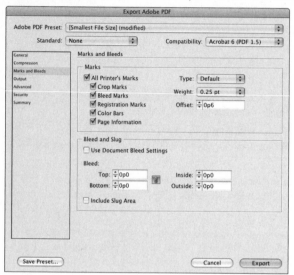

If you have elements bleeding off the page, you want a Bleed setting of at least 0p9 (⅛ inch). That setting builds in enough forgiveness so that when the pages are folded and trimmed, any elements that bleed off the page actually do so even if there's a slip in the page alignment.

If you specified a slug area (which specifies space for the printing of printer's marks) in the New Document (choose File ⇨ New ⇨ Document or press ⌘+N or Ctrl+N) or Document Setup (choose File ⇨ Document Setup or press Option+⌘+P or Ctrl+Alt+P) dialog boxes, select the Include Slug Area option to reserve that space in your PDF file.

Likewise, if you specified bleed settings in the New Document or Document Setup dialog boxes, you can have InDesign use those settings by selecting the Use Document Bleed Settings option.

CROSS-REF These marks, bleed, and slug options are the same as they are for direct printing and are covered in detail in Chapter 30.

The Output pane

The Output pane, shown in Figure 31.4, has two sections — Color and PDF/X — where you control color calibration.

In the Color section, you have the following options:

- **Color Conversion:** This pop-up menu lets you choose from among No Color Conversion, which keeps the colors in whatever model in which they were defined; Convert to Destination, which converts them to the printer's color space (typically CMYK); and Repurpose, which converts only colors in objects that have color profiles assigned to them.

FIGURE 31.4

The Output pane of the Export Adobe PDF dialog box

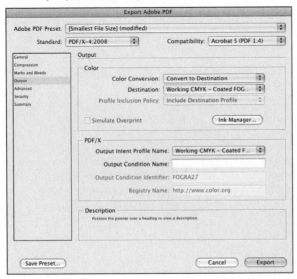

- **Destination:** This pop-up menu lets you choose the target output device.
- **Profile Inclusion Policy:** This pop-up menu lets you embed the color profile for the destination device in the PDF file or exclude it. You can choose from Don't Include Profiles, Include All Profiles, Include Tagged Source Profiles, and Include All RGB and Tagged Source CMYK Profiles. (A tagged profile is one that is set in InDesign, as opposed to an object imported with no profile. In other words, any images without profiles do not get the default profile assigned to them.)
- **Simulate Overprint:** Select this check box if you're exporting to Acrobat 4 (PDF 1.3) format and have objects overprinting each other (through the Attributes panel). This option is grayed out if you're exporting to Acrobat 5 or later format, because these formats support actual overprinting.
- **Ink Manager:** Click this button to change which color plates print, adjust ink density, and alter trapping sequence. (See Chapter 30 for more on this option, which is also offered when printing.)

In the PDF/X section, you have the following options:

- **Output Intent Profile Name:** If you're exporting with PDF/X compatibility, you can choose which output device or standard to be compatible with through this pop-up menu in the PDF/X section. (Note that whatever you choose here changes the Destination pop-up menu's setting as well.)

- **Output Condition, Output Condition Identifier, and Registry Name:** Depending on the output device or standard you select, you may be able to add device-specific comments in the Output Condition, Output Condition Identifier, and/or Registry Name fields; consult with your service bureau.

CROSS-REF See Chapter 28 for more on color matching, rendering intent, and color trapping settings. See Chapter 30 for more on working with color plates, the Ink Manager, and ink density.

The Advanced pane

Use the Advanced pane, shown in Figure 31.5, to manage font embedding, Open Prepress Interface (OPI) image substitution, and transparency flattening.

The Fonts section lets you control which fonts are included in the PDF file. Including fonts increases the file size but ensures that the document displays or prints correctly, regardless of whether the recipient has the same fonts the document uses. The Subset Fonts When Percent of Characters Used Is Less Than field tells InDesign how to embed fonts in the exported PDF file. The default value of 100% tells it to include the entire font for each typeface used. This is the best option because it ensures that if your service bureau needs to edit the file later, the file will include all font information. If you choose a lower value and the service bureau changes some text, some characters used in the editing may not be in the file.

The value is a threshold, telling InDesign that if the file uses less than that percentage of the font's characters, to embed just the characters used; or, if the file uses more than that percentage, to embed them all. If your document uses many fonts but just a few characters in each, you might want to pick a value such as 35% because you're less likely to have typos in such documents (they tend to be ads and posters that are heavily proofed beforehand).

You can use a lower threshold for documents to be viewed solely on-screen because you don't expect readers to edit the files. In fact, you may lock the file to prevent such modification.

NOTE Some fonts can be locked, preventing their inclusion in PDF files. To avoid that problem, simply don't use them.

In the OPI section, use the three options in the Omit for OPI section to strip out EPS, PDF, and/or bitmap images — you would use this only if you had high-resolution or color-corrected versions of these files at a service bureau and wanted the bureau to substitute those files for the lower-resolution placeholder files you used during layout.

In the Transparency Flattener section, if you are exporting to Acrobat 4 (PDF 1.3) format, you can select a transparency preset as well as override any transparency settings applied to individual spreads. Transparency flattening reduces the complexity of documents that have lots of transparent and semitransparent objects overlapping each other, which can dramatically increase output time and even prevent printing. If you are exporting to later versions of Acrobat, InDesign's flattening settings are passed on unchanged.

CROSS-REF See Chapter 30 for more on OPI and transparency flattening.

Finally, the Create JDF File Using Acrobat option essentially passes on the instructions for the PDF creation onto Adobe Acrobat Professional 7 or later (which must be installed on your system) and has it actually implement them. This gives the service bureau (or whoever is producing the final file) the job instructions separate from the underlying data, so the instructions can be changed as needed. Otherwise, the PDF file produced in InDesign cannot be changed unless you regenerate it in InDesign. Note that job definition files (JDFs) work only with the versions 7 or later of Acrobat Professional software, so this option is useless for organizations using earlier versions of Acrobat Pro.

The Security pane

The Security pane, shown in Figure 31.6, has no relevance to documents intended to be output at a service bureau or commercial printer, so make sure the Require a Password to Open the Document and the Use a Password to Restrict Printing, Editing, and Other Tasks options are not selected in that case.

FIGURE 31.5

The Advanced pane of the Export Adobe PDF dialog box

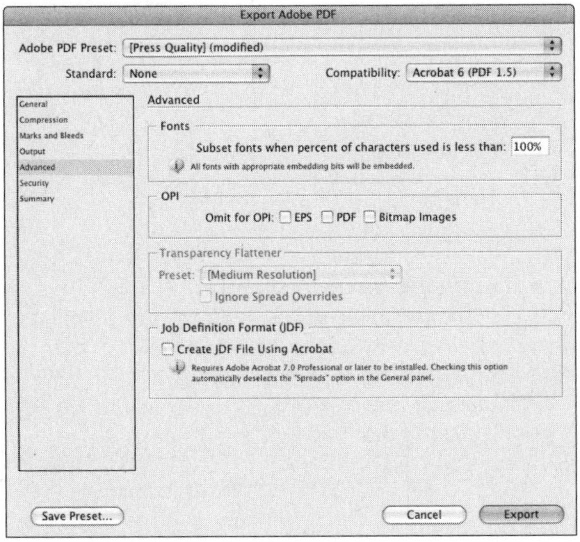

These settings are useful if you're publishing the document electronically, because they control who can access the document and what those users can do with the document when it's open. Here's how the settings work:

- **Encryption Level:** This section's options depend on the option set in the Compatibility pop-up menu; Acrobat 5 (PDF 1.4) or higher use High (128-Bit RC4) encryption, while earlier versions use 40-bit RC4.

- **Document Open Password:** In this section of the Security pane, you can require a password to open the exported PDF file by selecting this option and typing a password in the associated text field. If no password is typed here, you're forced to type one in a dialog box that appears later. To access protected content, recipients must use the Security pane in Acrobat (choose File ⇨ Document Properties or press ⌘+D or Ctrl+D).

FIGURE 31.6

The Security pane of the Export Adobe PDF dialog box

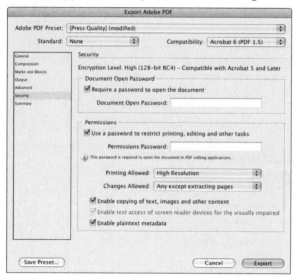

- **Use a Password to Restrict Printing, Editing, and Other Tasks:** You can restrict recipients' actions by selecting this option and then specifying permissible actions by using the Printing Allowed and Changes Allowed pop-up menus, as well as selecting from among the options that follow. You can also require a password to allow editing of the file in another application.

  - **Printing Allowed:** You can choose None, Low-Resolution (150 dpi), and High Resolution.

  - **Changes Allowed:** You can choose None; Inserting, Deleting, and Rotating Pages; Filling in Form Fields and Signing; Commenting, Filling in Forms Fields, and Signing; and Any Except Extract Pages. (*Signing* means using digital signatures to verify sender and recipient identities.)

■ **Enable Copying of Text, Images, and Other Content:** If it's okay for recipients to use the PDF file's objects, select this check box.

■ **Enable Text Access of Screen Reader Devices for the Visually Impaired:** If you want the file to be accessible to visually impaired recipients that read text aloud, select this check box. Note that this option is visible only if you are exporting to Acrobat 5 (PDF 1.4) or later.

■ **Enable Plaintext Metadata:** For documents with *metadata* — authoring information associated with XML documents and Web pages — you can make that metadata visible to Web-based search engines and similar applications by selecting this check box. Note that this option is visible only if you are exporting to Acrobat 6 (PDF 1.5) or later.

Settings for On-Screen Usage

If your output is destined for use on a monitor — such as from CD, on the Web, or in a corporate intranet — the settings you choose differ from the print-oriented ones described in the "Exporting PDF files" section. Here's what you need to do:

■ In the PDF Options pane, change the Color pop-up menu to RGB, change the Images pop-up menu to Low Resolution, and select the Generate Thumbnails option. These settings optimize the color and file size for on-screen display.

■ In the Compression pane, choose Downsample to or Subsample to in all three image types' sections. The dpi value should be either 72 (if you intend for people to view the images on-screen only) or 300 or 600 (if you expect people to print the documents to a local inkjet or laser printer — pick the dpi value that best matches most users' printers' capabilities). For the Compression pop-up menus, choose Automatic for the color and grayscale bitmaps, and CCITT Group 3 (the standard method for fax compression) for black-and-white bitmaps. Set Image Quality to Maximum for color and grayscale bitmaps. Finally, select the Compress Text and Line Art check box.

■ In the Marks and Bleeds pane, make sure no printer's marks are selected. Select Reader's Spreads if your facing pages are designed as one visual unit.

■ In the Security pane, select User Security features and the options for which you want to add security. Use the Printing and Copying Text and Graphics options to prevent readers from copying and pasting your content, or to prevent printing; this is particularly aimed at Web-based readers or publicly distributed documents. The Changing the Document and Adding or Changing Notes and Form Fields options are meant for internally distributed documents, when you don't want a recipient who has the Acrobat program to modify the PDF file and then pass it on to someone else who might not realize it was altered. Similarly, you typically would use the passwords only for documents distributed internally, when you don't want all employees to have access to all documents. For Web-based documents, the presumption is that a page and its content are meant for public consumption unless the whole page has a password required, so these settings are usually irrelevant.

The Summary pane

The final Export Adobe PDF dialog box pane is the Summary pane. It simply lists your settings all in one place for easy review. The only option — Save Summary — saves the settings to a file so that you can include it with your files when delivering them to a service bureau, or for distribution to other staff members so that they know the preferred settings.

Using Distiller job options

In addition to setting up PDF export presets as I describe in the last section, InDesign lets you import such settings from Acrobat Distiller job-options files. You can load such job-option files by clicking Load in the Adobe PDF Presets dialog box (choose File ➪ PDF Export Presets ➪ Define) or simply by opening them in the Open a File dialog box (choose File ➪ Open or press ⌘+O or Ctrl+O).

You can also create and edit these job-option files in this dialog box for sharing with Acrobat Distiller 7 or later, as well as with users of other Creative Suite 2 or later; click Save to save them for use by others. Figure 31.7 shows the dialog box.

FIGURE 31.7

The Adobe PDF Presets dialog box. When creating or editing these PDF presets, you get the same options described in the previous section for the Export PDF dialog box.

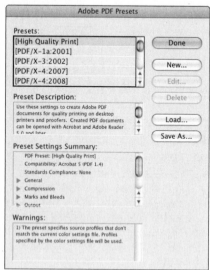

Printing to PDF files

Sometimes, you may want to create a PDF file when printing, such as to save printer-specific options in the file. Note that using this method, you need the $449 Adobe Acrobat Professional software to create a PDF file for prepress output, or the $299 Acrobat Standard for documents meant for display on-screen and printing on inkjet, laser, and other medium-resolution printers. You can also use the new $699 Acrobat Professional Extended, which is designed for high-end, multiple-format document environments. All three include the Acrobat Distiller program that creates PDF files. (The free Adobe Reader is only for viewing PDF files and, in version 7 and later, for making comments viewable only by other version 7 or later users.)

CAUTION Mac OS X can create PDF files without your having to buy Acrobat: Choose the PDF button in the Mac OS X's Print dialog box (get there by clicking Printer in InDesign's Print dialog box) to have the Mac OS create a generic-quality PDF file. But that file may not be print quality, and you will not be able to set specific printer options as you can using the steps in this section.

Set up your Print dialog box settings as described in Chapter 30, but don't click Print. Instead, follow these steps:

1. **Whether you use a Macintosh or a Windows PC, open the Acrobat Distiller program.** In Acrobat Distiller 4 and 5, choose Settings ➪ Job Options to set the output options. In Acrobat Distiller 6 and later, choose a setting from the Default Settings pop-up menu in the Acrobat Distiller dialog box. Then go back to the InDesign Print dialog box.

2. **The process to actually print the file depends on your operating system:**
   - In Mac OS X 10.4 (Tiger) and 10.5 (Leopard), click the Printer button, choose the Output Options menu item from the pop-up menu in the resulting dialog box, select the Save as File option, choose the file format (PDF) from the Format pop-up menu, and click Save. The Save to File dialog box appears.
   - In Windows XP and Vista, select Acrobat Distiller from the Printer pop-up menu and click Print. In a few seconds, a new window appears, asking for a filename and file location.

3. **Choose the filename and location and then click Save to save the file.**

You can also create PDF files by exporting to an EPS or a PostScript file and then using the Acrobat Distiller program to convert the file to PDF. You don't need to do this if you have InDesign unless you happen to have EPS or PostScript files that you've previously generated and would rather convert to PDF through Distiller than find the InDesign originals and export PDFs from InDesign. You can, of course, use Distiller to create PDFs from any PostScript or EPS file, no matter what program created it.

Exporting EPS Files

To create an EPS file from InDesign, choose File ⇨ Export or press ⌘+E or Ctrl+E. The Export dialog box appears, which, as is true of any standard Save dialog box, lets you name the file and determine on what drive and in what folder the file is to be saved in. The key control in the Export dialog box is the Formats pop-up menu, where you choose the format (EPS, in this case).

After you've selected EPS in the Export dialog box's Formats pop-up menu (Mac) or Save as Type pop-up menu (Windows) and given the file a name and location, click Save to get the Export EPS dialog box, shown in Figure 31.8. The dialog box has two panes; the General pane is displayed when you open the dialog box.

The General pane

Most export options are in the General pane.

FIGURE 31.8

The General pane of the Export EPS dialog box (left) and the Advanced pane (right)

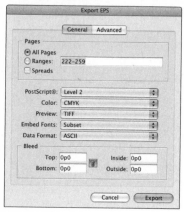
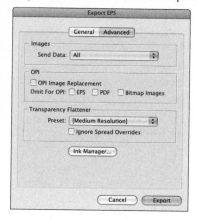

In the Pages section, you can set the following options:

- **All Pages:** Select this option to print all pages in a document.
- **Ranges:** Select this option when specifying a range of pages that you want to print. You can type nonconsecutive ranges, such as **1–4, 7, 10–13, 15, 18, 20**. If you want to print from a specific page to the end of the document, just type the hyphen after the initial page number, such as **4–**. InDesign figures out what the last page is. Similarly, to start

from the first page to a specified page, just start with the hyphen, as in –11. InDesign lets you type absolute page numbers in the Range field. For example, typing +6–+12 prints the document's sixth through twelfth pages, no matter what their page numbers are.

- **Spreads:** Select this option to print facing pages on the same sheet of paper — handy when showing clients comps, but make sure you have a printer that can handle that large paper size.

TIP You may not want to use the Spreads option when outputting an EPS file for eventual printing on an imagesetter if you have bleeds because there will be no bleed between the spreads. If you use traditional *perfect-binding* (square spines) or *saddle-stitching* (stapled spines) printing methods in which facing pages are not printed contiguously, do not use this option.

The unnamed, middle section of the pane controls the handling of fundamental elements: PostScript version, graphics, and fonts. Here are the options:

- **PostScript:** Use this pop-up menu to choose the version of the PostScript language to use in creating the EPS file: The Level 2 option works on a PostScript Level 2 or later printer (the majority in professional environments), whereas Level 3 works only on the newer PostScript 3 devices, which can include built-in color calibration, color separation, and trapping. Be sure to ask whoever is outputting your files which version to use.

- **Color:** Use this pop-up menu to determine what happens to colors. Your options are CMYK (for commercial printing), RGB (for online display), Gray (for black-and-white printing), or PostScript Color Management (which lets the output device figure out what to do with the colors based on the PostScript settings in the EPS file). For commercial printing, choose either CMYK or PostScript Color Management, depending on your service bureau's recommendations and the capabilities of its output devices. If your file uses spot colors, you want to use PostScript Color Management so that they aren't converted to process colors, but the service bureau will need to have a printer that can handle that format.

- **Preview:** This pop-up menu lets you choose the format for the EPS file's on-screen preview, which is what you see on-screen when you place an EPS file in a program such as InDesign, Adobe Illustrator, or QuarkXPress. Your options are None, TIFF, and — on the Mac only — PICT. TIFF is a safe option if you use recent versions of image editing, desktop publishing, and illustration programs. (You may need to select PICT to see the preview in older Mac programs.)

- **Embed Fonts:** Use this pop-up menu to determine whether all fonts, no fonts, or just the characters used are embedded into the documents; the corresponding menu options are Complete, None, and Subset. Complete is the best option because it ensures that if your service bureau needs to edit the file later, the file includes all font information. If you choose Subset and the service bureau changes some text when editing the EPS file (such as to fix a typo), some characters used in the editing may not be in the file. Use None only if the service bureau has all the fonts you use and knows to load them into the printer before outputting this file.

- **Data Format:** Use this pop-up menu to select ASCII or Binary. The ASCII option creates a larger file but can be edited by someone who understands the PostScript language; the Binary option creates a smaller file that is not editable. The one you choose depends on whether you want or expect your service bureau or commercial printer to try to fix any problems in your file encountered during output. Be sure to talk to those people up front so that you and they agree on whether such efforts should be made.

In the Bleed section, you can set the bleed area for the Top, Bottom, Left, and Right sides of the page. If you have elements bleeding off the page, you want a bleed setting of at least 0p9 (⅛ inch); that setting builds in enough forgiveness so that, when the pages are folded and trimmed, any elements that bleed off the page will in fact do so, even if there's a slip in the page alignment.

> **TIP** You can control whether all bleed margins are changed if any of them is changed by clicking the Make All Settings the Same iconic button. If the chain icon is broken, each can be adjusted separately; if the chain icon is unbroken, changing one changes the others automatically.

The Export EPS option does not let you use any bleed settings you may have set in the New Document (choose File ➪ New ➪ Document or press ⌘+N or Ctrl+N) or Document Setup (choose File ➪ Document Setup or press Option+⌘+P or Ctrl+Alt+P) dialog boxes. That's odd, because the Export PDF (choose File ➪ Export or press ⌘+E or Ctrl+E) and Print (choose File ➪ Print or press ⌘+P or Ctrl+P) dialog boxes *do* let you use those document settings.

The Advanced pane

The Advanced pane contains specialty settings affecting image substitution, transparency flattening, and color plates. Figure 31.8, shown previously, shows the pane.

The options are as follows:

- **Send Data:** In the Images section's Send Data pop-up menu, you can select either All or Proxy. Use the All option (the default) for all documents that will be printed, even if you're publishing the file electronically (on a CD or through the Web). Use Proxy (which sends a low-resolution, on-screen preview version of the document's images) only for documents that are viewed on-screen and not printed (or when you don't care that the printouts have low-quality graphics).

> **CROSS-REF** See Chapter 30 for more on OPI and transparency flattening, as well as overprint simulation and the Ink Manager.

- **OPI Image Replacement:** In the OPI section, select the OPI Image Replacement option if you're using Open Prepress Interface (OPI) image substitution, in which the high-resolution files are stored elsewhere and the layout uses for-position-only versions to save drive space and save screen redraw time. You can also use the three options in the Omit for OPI section to specify which images should be stripped out: EPS, PDF, and/or Bitmap Images. You would use this only if you have high-resolution or color-corrected versions of these files at a service bureau and want it to substitute those files for the lower-resolution placeholder files you used during layout. By omitting these graphics files from the EPS file, you make the EPS file much smaller.

■ **Preset:** In the Transparency Flattener section, you can select a transparency preset as well as override any transparency settings applied to individual spreads. Transparency flattening reduces the complexity of documents that have lots of transparent and semitransparent objects overlapping each other, which can dramatically increase output time and even prevent printing. Select the Ignore Spread Overrides option to tell InDesign to ignore any transparency flattener overrides you may have made to specific spreads in the Pages panel (choose Window ➪ Pages or press ⌘+F12 or Ctrl+F12).

■ **Ink Manager:** At the bottom of the pane, click Ink Manager to change which color plates print, adjust ink density, and alter trapping sequence.

Creating Output Files

Service bureaus generally don't want to receive an output file because they have little or no control over it, and mistakes you make could harm the output quality or even prevent printing. But sometimes this option is what the service bureau wants, based on its equipment and expertise.

CAUTION Do not send an output file to your service bureau unless the service bureau requests it and also provides the PostScript Printer Description (PPD) file and output instructions. (Chapter 29 covers PPD files in detail.)

To create an output file, you have two options. The simplest is to choose PostScript File from the Printer pop-up menu in the Print dialog box, as well as the appropriate PostScript Printer Description using the PPD pop-up menu (this should be the PPD for the ultimate output device). Then set the various options in the Print dialog's panes and click Save when done (the Print button becomes Save when you choose PostScript File in the Printer pop-up menu).

The other method is to print to file. *After* setting all the appropriate attributes in the Print dialog box (choose File ➪ Print or press ⌘+P or Ctrl+P), do the following, as appropriate for your platform:

■ In Mac OS X 10.4 (Tiger) and 10.5 (Leopard), click Printer, choose the Output Options menu item from the unnamed (third) pop-up menu in the Mac OS X's Print dialog box that appears, select the Save as File Option, choose the file format (PostScript, in this case) from the Format pop-up menu, and click Save. (You'll then be returned to InDesign's Print dialog box.) Note that not all printers have the Output Options menu item, so you may need to choose the PDF button instead in the Mac OS's Print dialog box to get a generic-quality PDF file.

■ In Windows XP and Vista, click Setup and then select the Print to File check box in the Windows's Print dialog box. Next, click Print. (You'll then be returned to InDesign's Print dialog box.)

Summary

In many cases, you want to generate an output file that ensures that your service bureau prints your document exactly as you want it, with no chance to accidentally make a change to your InDesign document. In most cases, the service bureau's equipment dictates the format of these output files: EPS, PDF, or PostScript. Each option has pros and cons, and varying levels of controls, so be sure to use the option that gives you the most control and works with your service bureau's equipment.

Part VIII

Electronic Publishing Techniques

Chapter 32

Creating Web, Interactive PDF, and Flash Documents

In most respects, a document is a document is a document. But in today's electronic world, documents have evolved to include more than the text and graphics that have comprised documents for centuries. Not only can you print documents the traditional way, but also you can deliver them electronically as Adobe Portable Document Format (PDF) files, as files in the Web's XHTML format, as Flash presentations, and as Adobe eBook "digital edition" files. And that electronic delivery format permits a degree of interactivity never possible in printed documents, including hyperlinks, automated page actions, and the use of audio and video objects.

You create interactive documents — also called "rich media" documents and multimedia documents — just as you create print documents. InDesign's interactive functions work with those traditional capabilities — there's no special "interactive" mode to work under.

InDesign's ability to export in these various "rich media" formats does raise some key questions as you create your multimedia documents. Theoretically, you could design a document to support all of these formats, but the reality is that not all functions work in all media: The fancy page-transition effects, for example, display only in Flash and full-screen-view PDF files, whereas support for audio and video formats varies widely across the supported multimedia formats. So, it's more likely you will have one or two formats in mind as you create a document, and you'll use just the capabilities available in them.

Regardless of what specific multimedia files you intend to create, the building blocks are common across most of them. For example, most of the supported multimedia formats can take advantage of hyperlinks as well as some button capabilities. Button-based page actions work in interactive PDF, eBook, and Flash files. This chapter goes through the building-block functions first — hyperlinks, bookmarks, buttons and page actions, and audio and video file usage. Then I explain the issues in exporting to each of the supported file formats (XHTML, Flash, interactive PDF, and eBook).

Using Hyperlinks

The most common attribute you add to a print document to make it more useful when it's distributed electronically is hyperlinks. Web pages, Flash files, PDF files, and eBook files can include at least some of these hot spots that, when clicked, direct a browser to open a new file or page.

InDesign uses its Hyperlinks panel (choose Window ➪ Interactive ➪ Hyperlinks) to add, edit, and delete hyperlinks. In a sense, a hyperlink is a character attribute — it's applied to selected text. But it can also be applied to other objects, such as lines, imported graphics, and frames, although hyperlinks on such other objects aren't always supported in exported files. Figure 32.1 shows the Hyperlinks panel and its flyout menu.

FIGURE 32.1

The Hyperlinks panel and its flyout menu

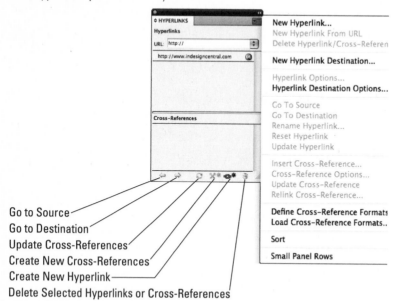

Go to Source
Go to Destination
Update Cross-References
Create New Cross-References
Create New Hyperlink
Delete Selected Hyperlinks or Cross-References

Creating hyperlinks

Although the process of creating a hyperlink is straightforward, InDesign's terminology can make it getting started confusing. That's because InDesign has three types of hyperlinks: hyperlink destinations, hyperlink sources, and cross-references. They're not wholly separate entities — a hyperlink source can point to a hyperlink destination or define its own destination, for example — so knowing when to use each is often a hit-or-miss exercise. Here are some basic guidelines:

- Use hyperlink destinations to create links before you need them. They let you specify pages and text anchors in the current document, as well as Web addresses, that can be applied to specific text or frames later. You might use this type of hyperlink if you have a standard selection of addresses you want available to the person creating a document.

- Use hyperlink sources to create links

- Use cross-references to create links from a selected frame or text to text anchors or specific paragraphs in the current or other documents.

Creating hyperlink destinations

You create a hyperlink destination by choosing New Hyperlink Destination from the Hyperlinks panel's flyout menu. Figure 32.2 shows the New Hyperlink Destination dialog box that appears.

1. Give the destination a name in the Name field.

2. **Choose from one of the three options in the Type menu:**

   - **Page:** This option lets you specify a specific page in a selected document. If you select this option, InDesign provides a Page field in which you specify the page number to open in the selected document, as well as the Zoom Setting pop-up menu, which lets you select how the page is displayed. (Options are Fixed, meaning at the default size in Adobe Reader; Fit View; Fit in Window; Fit Width; Fit Height; Fit Visible; and Inherit Zoom, which uses the current zoom setting in Adobe Reader.)

   - **Text Anchor:** This option lets you specify a specific piece of text in the selected document. This would be the selected text.

   - **URL:** This is a Web page address (the official name is Uniform Resource Locator), as shown in the New Hyperlink dialog box in Figure 32.2. If you select this option, InDesign displays the URL field in which you type the Web address.

3. **Click OK to save the hyperlink destination.** Note that the Hyperlinks panel will not usually show the added hyperlinks' destinations, but they have in fact been saved. You can access them when creating new hyperlink sources, as described in the next section.

NEW FEATURE In some cases, the Hyperlinks panel *can* show the added hyperlink destinations. For example, if you select some text, the URL pop-up menu will display all the saved hyperlink destinations. You can then choose one from the list to turn your selected text into a hyperlink that points to that destination.

FIGURE 32.2

The New Hyperlink Destination dialog box's three variants, selected via the Type pop-up menu, are (from top to bottom) Page, Text Anchor, and URL.

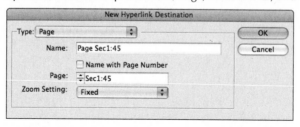

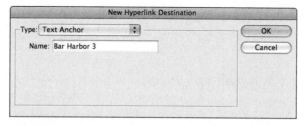

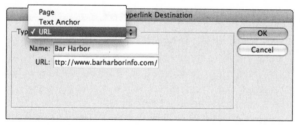

You may have noticed that hyperlink destinations are limited to URLs and to pages and text anchors in the current document. But what if you want to link to other documents' elements? That's where a separate facility comes in: the New Hyperlink dialog box, which you open from the Hyperlinks panel's flyout menu by choosing New Hyperlink.

To distinguish them from hyperlink destinations, I call these hyperlinks *hyperlink sources*. There are two key differences between hyperlink sources and hyperlink destinations to understand up front:

- Before you create hyperlink sources, you must first select a frame or piece of text in your current document. This selection will be what the user clicks to open whatever you are linking to. By contrast, nothing needs to be selected for you to create a hyperlink destination; these are link destinations you create for possible use later, much as you can create paragraph styles for a document but are not required to use them.

- When you create a hyperlink source, you are actually creating a destination that you're tying to a source (the selection) in your document. So you are defining both the source and the destination at the same time. Note that the destination could be a hyperlink destination you created using the New Hyperlinks Destination dialog box.

NEW FEATURE A quick way to add a URL-based hyperlink source is simply to enter that URL in the URL field of the Hyperlinks panel and then press Return or Enter. This new InDesign CS4 feature supplements another easy way from previous versions of InDesign to add a URL hyperlink source: If your text has a URL in it, just highlight that URL with the Type tool and choose New Hyperlink from URL from the Hyperlinks panel's flyout menu.

Also new: If you don't want to retype a previously entered URL, just pick it from the pop-up menu. Any previously entered hyperlink destinations that are URLs will appear.

Creating hyperlink sources

Whether or not you created hyperlink destinations, you can create hyperlink sources to make frames or text selections clickable links to other pages, documents, or Web addresses. To create a hyperlink source:

1. **Select the text or object that you want to be a hyperlink's source, and then choose New Hyperlink from the Hyperlinks panel's flyout menu.** Doing so opens the New Hyperlink dialog box, as shown in Figure 32.3.

FIGURE 32.3

The New Hyperlink dialog box

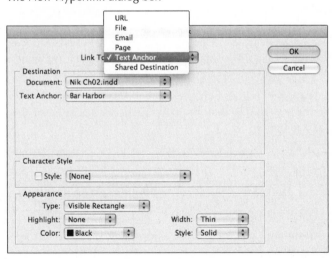

2. **Use the Link To pop-up menu to determine what you're hyperlinking to.** You have the same three options as in the New Hyperlink Destination dialog box's Type menu — Page, Text Anchor, and URL — except that you can choose to link to the Page and Text Anchor

items not only in your current document but also in any other InDesign document by using the Document pop-up menu that appears if you choose either option. The New Hyperlink dialog box's Link To pop-up menu also has three new options that are not available in the New Hyperlink Destination dialog box's Type pop-up menu; these options are as follows:

- Email lets you enter an e-mail address as well as a default subject for that e-mail, if you like.

- File lets you point to any file and make that into a link; of course, any file you link to this way needs to be something your reader has the software to open.

- Shared Destination lets you select an InDesign document, including the current one, and then select from any destinations of any type defined in it — including any hyperlink destinations previously created in the document.

Note that with the URL, Email, and File options, you can select the Shared Destination check box, which makes the new hyperlink visible as a hyperlink destination when working in other documents. To get these shared hyperlink destinations, you or other InDesign users choose the Shared Destination option in the Linked To pop-up menu and choose a document with the shared hyperlink destinations as the File source when creating hyperlink sources. Selecting the Shared Destination check box also makes the new hyperlink source available to you as a hyperlink destination within the current document.

NOTE When creating links to elements in other documents, it's key to remember that InDesign will link not to the other InDesign document but rather to the PDF file it expects you to create from that other document. That PDF version of the document must use the same filename, except for the filename extension. For example, if you link to `ITWForm.indd`, the link is actually to `ITWForm.pdf`. The link will also assume that the other PDF file is in the same location (Web address or file folder) as the current document. I suggest that you put all related InDesign files that contain such links among each other into a book (see Chapter 24) and then export the entire book to a PDF file; that way, all the links will work within the exported PDF.

3. **In the Character Style section, you can tell InDesign to apply a specific character style to the hyperlinked text.** Just select the check box and then choose a character style from the pop-up menu.

NOTE The Character Style section's settings are sticky, meaning they remain active each time you create a new hyperlink source. That's convenient if you want the same character style applied to each; select the character style for the first one and then create the rest without worrying about these settings. But it's not convenient if you forget that the setting is sticky and thus apply character styles to all your hyperlinks without realizing it.

4. **In the Appearance section, you can control how the hyperlink appears on-screen:**

- Use the Type pop-up menu to choose Invisible Rectangle or Visible Rectangle. The Invisible Rectangle option gives no visual indication that the text contains a hyperlink, except that the mouse pointer becomes a hand icon when the reader maneuvers through the document. (You would typically pick this option when you've used blue underline as a character attribute for the hyperlink text to mirror the standard Web way of indicating a hyperlink.) The Visible Rectangle option puts a box around the text using the four settings I describe next (they are grayed out if Invisible Rectangle is selected).

- The Highlight pop-up menu lets you choose how the source text or frame is highlighted: None, Invert (reverses the foreground and background colors), Outline (places a line around the source), and Inset (places a line around the source, but inside any frame stroke; for text, it's the same as Outline.

- The Color pop-up menu displays Web-safe colors, as well as any colors you defined in the document.

- The Width pop-up menu lets you choose the thickness of the line used in the Outline and Inset options from the Highlight pop-up menu. The choices are Thin, Medium, and Thick.

- The Style pop-up menu lets you choose the type of line; the choices are Solid or Dashed.

5. **When you're done defining the hyperlink source, click OK.** The hyperlink source will appear in the Hyperlinks panel's list (its name will be the same as the text you selected when creating the hyperlink source in Step 1), followed by an icon that indicates its type: a globe for URLs, e-mail addresses, and external files; a blank page for page links; a page with arrow for pages that have a fit-to view applied; and a ship's anchor for a text anchor.

NEW FEATURE In InDesign CS4, The New Hyperlink dialog box adds three new types of hyperlinks — Email, File, and Shared Destination — and lets you apply character styles to the hyperlink sources. (Well, they *did* exist in previous versions, but not as explicit options in the New Hyperlink dialog box, so many users assumed they didn't exist.)

Gone is the ability to name the hyperlink source, as is the All Types option in the Type pop-up menu (which has moved and been renamed as Link To). But you can rename the hyperlink source by choosing Rename Hyperlink from the Hyperlinks panel's flyout menu.

After your hyperlink sources are defined, you can easily apply them by selecting text and clicking an existing hyperlink source from the Hyperlinks panel. You can also jump to the source or destination by selecting the desired hyperlink in the Hyperlinks panel and choosing either Go to Source or Go to Destination from the flyout menu, or by clicking the Go to Hyperlink Source or Go to Hyperlink Destination iconic buttons at the bottom of the panel. These make a handy way to verify that the hyperlinks are correct.

 **TIP** If you hover the mouse over a hyperlink source in the Hyperlinks panel, InDesign displays a Tool Tip that shows the URL or destination associated with the source.

Creating cross-reference hyperlinks

InDesign's new capability of creating cross-references to text based on text anchors and paragraph styles applied can also be used to create hyperlinks to such cross-references.

Essentially, a cross-reference is a special type of hyperlink source. In the context of hyperlinks, you create them the same way, knowing that the cross-references will become hyperlinks to a PDF file if you export the document using the cross-references to interactive PDF, Flash, or Web formats.

Note that the Go to Source and Go to Destination flyout menu options for hyperlink sources also work for cross-references, as do the Go to Hyperlink Source or Go to Hyperlink Destination iconic buttons at the bottom of the Hyperlinks panel.

CROSS-REF   Chapter 22 explains how to create, modify, and format cross-references.

Importing hyperlinks

When you place text that includes embedded hyperlinks (such as in RTF and Word files), InDesign imports its hyperlinks as well. In the Hyperlinks panel, these imported hyperlinks will appear in the list of hyperlink sources. They will be named Hyperlink 1, Hyperlink 2, and so on, or they will be named based on the actual embedded URL (such as `http://www.indesign central.com` or `http://www.wiley.com`) — it depends on how InDesign reads the links during import. Their destinations (the URLs) will be available as hyperlink destinations in the InDesign document.

Modifying and deleting hyperlinks

It's easy to modify hyperlinks. The process is similar no matter what type of hyperlink you want to modify or delete.

Hyperlink destinations

For hyperlink destinations, select *any* hyperlink source in the Hyperlinks panel, choose Hyperlink Destination Options from the flyout menu to open the Hyperlink Destination Options dialog box, and then select the desired hyperlink destination from the Destination pop-up menu. The Hyperlink Destination Options dialog box's options are the same as the New Hyperlink Destination dialog box (refer to Figure 32.2). Click Edit to modify the hyperlink destination. Click Delete to delete the selected hyperlink destination, or click Delete All to delete all hyperlink destinations in the document. Click OK when you're done.

NEW FEATURE   In InDesign CS4, you can easily change a URL destination — if it is a URL — by selecting its hyperlink source in the Hyperlinks panel and changing the URL in the URL field at the top of the panel.

Hyperlink sources

For hyperlink sources, select the hyperlink source in the Hyperlinks panel and then choose Hyperlink Options from the Hyperlinks panel's flyout menu to open the Hyperlink Options dialog box, which has the same options as the New Hyperlinks dialog box, shown in Figure 32.3, to modify the source. Click OK when done.

You can change the source text or frame by selecting it, then clicking the hyperlink name in the Hyperlinks panel, and finally choosing Reset Hyperlink from the panel's flyout menu. To change the target for a hyperlink to an InDesign document, choose Update Hyperlink from the flyout menu (press and hold Option or Alt to select a file that is not open).

To delete a hypertext source, select it in the Hyperlinks panel and then choose Delete Hyperlink/Cross-Reference from the flyout menu or click the Delete Selected Hyperlinks or Cross-References iconic button at the bottom of the Hyperlinks panel.

To rename a hyperlink source, choose it in the Hyperlinks panel's list and then choose Rename Hyperlink from the flyout menu. A dialog box will appear in which you can rename it. The most common reasons to rename hyperlink sources are when imported hyperlinks have unintuitive names such as Hyperlink 1 and when you created a hyperlink from a long URL that is hard to read in the hyperlinks list. In both cases, you typically want to rename the hyperlinks to a friendlier and/or more memorable name.

NEW FEATURE The Rename Hyperlink menu option is new to InDesign CS4. Before, you had to choose the Hyperlink Options menu option and change the name in the Hyperlink Options dialog box. Note that to rename hyperlink destinations, you still must use the Hyperlink Destination Options dialog box, accessed via the Hyperlink Destination Options menu item in the Hyperlinks panel's flyout menu.

Cross-reference hyperlinks

For cross-reference hyperlinks, select the cross-reference in the Hyperlinks panel and then choose Cross-Reference Options from the Hyperlinks panel's flyout menu to open the Cross-Reference Options dialog box, which Chapter 22 covers, to modify the source. Click OK when done.

You can *update* the cross-reference destination referred to in a document's source text or frame by selecting it, clicking the cross-reference name in the Hyperlinks panel, and then choosing Relink Cross-Reference from the panel's flyout menu. This is particularly useful when InDesign can't find a cross-reference destination in another chapter. For example, if a cross-reference in Chapter 1 is made to text in Chapter 2, and Chapter 2 is later renamed Chapter 3, you would use the Relink Cross-Reference option while working in Chapter 1 to select Chapter 3 as the new destination, and InDesign would update all the Chapter 2 destinations in Chapter 1 to be Chapter 3 destinations.

To *change* the target for a hyperlink to an InDesign document (perhaps you've changed your mind as to what to cross-reference), choose Update Cross-Reference from the flyout menu. (Press and hold Option or Alt to select a file that is not open.) For example, if you make a cross-reference to the heading "New York" and later change that heading to "New York State," you can click the Update Cross-Reference button or choose the Update Cross-Reference option in the flyout menu to update all the cross-reference's source text.

To delete a cross-reference, select it in the Hyperlinks panel and then choose Delete Hyperlink/Cross-Reference from the flyout menu or click the Delete Selected Hyperlinks or Cross-References iconic button at the bottom of the Hyperlinks panel.

What works where

When using hyperlinks, keep the following usage limits in mind for your intended output format:

- PDF files: All hyperlinks are retained except those that specify a specific page in an external document. However, those hyperlinks to pages *are* retained if you put all the documents involved in a book (see Chapter 24) and export the entire book to PDF.

- eBook files: No hyperlinks are retained for frames. For hyperlinks applied to text selections, hyperlinks to files, to anchored text in the current document, to Web addresses, and to e-mail addresses are retained. Hyperlinks to anchors in other documents are retained *only* if you put all the documents involved in a book (see Chapter 24) and export the entire book to eBook format.

- Flash files: When you export to the SWF presentation Flash format, all hyperlinks are retained except those that specify a specific page in an external document and those to an e-mail address. Also, any hyperlinks that appear in or over objects that have transparency applied will not be retained. When you export to the XFL Flash exchange format so that you can further work on the layout in Flash Professional, *no* hyperlinks are retained.

- Web pages: Hyperlinks that point to URLs, e-mail addresses, files, or text anchors within the current document are retained. Text anchor links in the document (including bookmarks) are also retained. Hyperlinks from objects and images are not retained, and hyperlinks to any location, including text anchors, *outside* the document are not retained.

Creating Bookmarks

Bookmarks are an indexing mechanism used in Adobe PDF files. They typically act like tables of contents, letting you view the organization of a document through a set of clickable headings. Figure 32.4 shows an example file viewed in Adobe Acrobat Professional.

InDesign has two ways to create bookmark entries. One is simply to create a table of contents using the standard InDesign table-of-contents tool. (Be sure that the Create PDF Bookmarks option is selected in the Table of Contents dialog box.) The other is to specify bookmarks to specific pages, objects, and/or text using the Bookmarks panel. Figure 32.5 shows the Bookmarks panel (choose Window ➪ Interactive ➪ Bookmarks) and its flyout menu.

> **NOTE** The Bookmarks panel will include any TOC entries in your document if Create PDF Bookmarks option was selected in the Table of Contents dialog box. Chapter 23 covers the table of contents feature.

Using the Bookmarks panel

To create your own bookmark entries — either instead of or in addition to having InDesign use the table of contents — select what you want the bookmark to refer to (what will appear on-screen in the PDF file when a user clicks the bookmark in Acrobat or Adobe Reader). This can be a text selection or an object (frame or line); if nothing is selected, the bookmark is to the current page. Then choose New Bookmark from the Bookmarks panel's flyout menu, or click the Add Bookmarks iconic button — the page icon — at the bottom of the panel. After you create the bookmark, use the Rename Bookmark menu option to give it a meaningful name; this is the name that appears in the Bookmarks pane in Acrobat or Adobe Reader.

FIGURE 32.4

An example PDF document with bookmarks (at left)

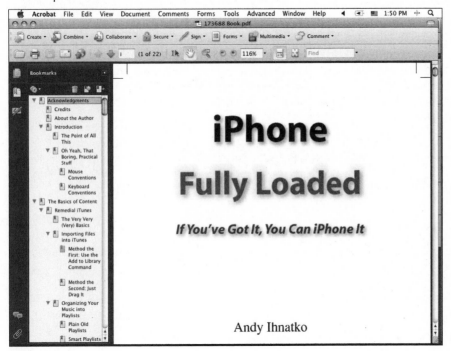

FIGURE 32.5

The Bookmarks panel and its flyout menu

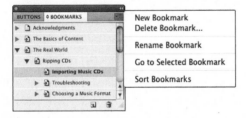

If you want a bookmark to be a subentry of another bookmark — the equivalent to a second-level or third-level headline in a table of contents — make sure that, before you create the bookmark, you select a bookmark in the Bookmarks panel. Any new bookmark is made a child of the selected bookmark.

The other Bookmarks panel flyout menu options are straightforward:

- Choose Delete Bookmark to delete any bookmarks selected in the panel. (You can also click the Delete Bookmarks iconic button — the trash can icon — at the bottom of the panel.)
- Choose Go to Selected Bookmark to jump to that page in your InDesign document. An easier way is to simply double-click the bookmark entry in the pane.
- Choose Sort Benchmarks to sort benchmark subentries — this alphabetizes second-level, third-level, and other page-based subentries, and it sorts in order of appearance on the page any text- and/or object-based entries. It does not sort the top-level bookmarks, which appear in sequential order from the beginning of the document.

However you create your bookmarks, InDesign places them into your PDF file during PDF export — if you tell it to. Here's how: Make sure the Bookmarks check box is selected in the General pane's Include section in the PDF Export dialog box. (Choose File ➪ Export or press ⌘+E or Ctrl+E; then, choose Adobe PDF in the Format [Mac] or Save as Type [Windows] pop-up menu to get that dialog box. Chapter 31 covers PDF export options in detail.)

What works where

When using bookmarks, keep the following usage limits in mind for your intended output format:

- **PDF files:** All bookmarks are retained.
- **eBook files:** No bookmarks added through the Bookmarks panel are retained, though you can have InDesign export bookmarks into the eBook file from the document's TOC.
- **Flash files:** No bookmarks are retained.
- **Web pages:** Bookmarked are converted into text anchors (<a name> HTML tags).

Creating Buttons and Page Actions

One underused feature of the PDF format is the ability to set page actions. Most people simply create PDF files that are on-screen versions of the print document — static representations — but PDF files can include forms, buttons, and other interactive elements. One reason for the underuse of page actions is that few tools let you create the placeholder items for them, and adding them in Acrobat Standard or Acrobat Professional is awkward; they really work best when they're created in the program that creates the whole document. InDesign addresses this reality with its support for interactive features.

NEW FEATURE These buttons and page actions also work in Flash files, which InDesign CS4 now lets you create. In fact, there is a special type of page action called a page transition that works only in Flash files and in PDF files when viewed in full-screen mode in Adobe Reader or Acrobat.

Creating buttons

In InDesign, you use the Buttons panel to create buttons and other objects that have actions associated with them.

NEW FEATURE The Buttons panel replaces the States panel and Button tool from previous versions of InDesign and adds a few new states to match what Web browsers can support.

Also, InDesign CS4 no longer has a Button tool to create buttons; instead, you simply convert any selected item — not just frames, as in past versions of InDesign — into a button.

The first thing you do is draw your button using any InDesign frame, shape, line, or path tools. Even a text frame can be a button, though a text selection cannot. (Don't let the term "button" fool you: You're not limited to something that looks like a traditional button.) Select the object and choose Object ➪ Interactive ➪ Convert to Button to turn the object into a button. The Buttons panel will then appear. Or select the object and click the new Convert to Button iconic button (the rectangular outline) at the bottom of the Buttons panel.

Be sure to add a name for the button in the Name field of the Buttons panel; InDesign will put in a default name such as Button 1, but that kind of generic name is hardly going to help you remember what that button is if you need to work on it later.

NEW FEATURE InDesign CS4 comes with a library of buttons you can use rather than have to create your own. Just choose Sample Buttons from the Buttons panel's flyout menu to open the Sample Buttons library file. (Choose Window ➪ Interactive ➪ Buttons to open the panel.) Then just drag the desired buttons from that library to your layout. Close the library when done. (Chapter 6 covers libraries in detail.)

Figure 32.6 shows the Buttons panel and its flyout menu, as well as a button created from a graphic. Note the button icon at the lower right of the graphic frame; InDesign places this non-printing indicator automatically so that you know what objects are buttons.

FIGURE 32.6

Top: A sample button created from a graphics frame, the Buttons panel, and its flyout menu. The button is in its default [Normal] state. Bottom left: The same button and the Button panel in its [Rollover] state, where I added a glow to the object so that the user could more easily tell this is a button. Bottom right: The same button and the Button panel in its [Click] State, where I added a fill to indicate that the click was successful.

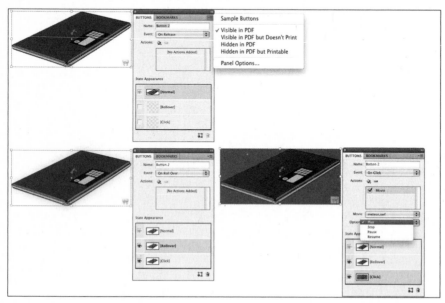

Creating states

Buttons work by invoking different states, or appearances, based on what the user is doing with them. Each button has three possible state appearances: [Normal], [Rollover], and [Click]:

- The [Normal] state is added automatically when you create a button — it's how the button appears when the user's mouse is not over it or hasn't clicked it. In other words, it's what shows when the user has done nothing other than display the page.

- The [Rollover] state determines what happens when a user passes the mouse over the button. Typically, you want a visual change to occur so that the user realizes that the object is in fact a button.

- The [Click] state determines what happens when a user clicks the button. Here, you would typically have a visual indication that the button was in fact clicked.

To determine the button appearance for any state, simply select that state in the Buttons panel and then make your modifications using InDesign's standard tools. For example, for the [Rollover] state in Figure 32.6, I used the Effects panel to add an outer glow, and for the [Click] state, I added a red fill. You could do much more than that, such as change a frame's contents, shape, and as many other attributes as desired.

NEW FEATURE InDesign CS4 has no controls in the Buttons panel for placing content into states, controls that the previous versions' States panel used. So the Buttons panel's flyout menu and iconic buttons related to content states are gone in InDesign CS4. Instead, you simply use InDesign's standard methods (such as choosing File ⇨ Place or pressing ⌘+D or Ctrl+D, or choosing Edit ⇨ Paste Into or pressing Option+⌘+V or Ctrl+Alt+V) to place content into the buttons.

Setting actions

There are six types of mouse-related conditions you can use as triggers for button actions. Even though at first they may seem related, these actions have nothing directly to do with states; you can have only one state yet have all six triggers invoke actions.

NEW FEATURE InDesign CS4 radically changes the user interface for associating actions to mouse-related conditions, making it easily accessible through the Event pop-up menu rather than be an option in the hard-to-find Button Options dialog box. But the capabilities are the same, with the sole addition of the ability to specify a specific page to send the user to (something that works only in exported Flash files).

You associate actions to these triggers in the Event pop-up menu. (If no action is associated to a trigger, that trigger is inactive.) The triggers in the Event pop-up menu are as follows:

- **On Release:** Here, you can set what actions occur when a user releases the mouse after clicking the button. Typically, you want the button to do nothing in this case; if so, you simply set no action.

- **On Click:** Here, you can set what actions occur when a user clicks the button.

- **On Roll Over:** Here, you can set what actions occur when a user's mouse moves within the button's boundaries.

- **On Roll Off:** Here, you can set what actions occur when a user's mouse moves past the button's boundaries. Typically, you want the button to do nothing in this case; if so, you simply set no action.

- **On Blur:** Here, you can set what actions occur when a user clicks another button or form element.

- **On Focus:** Here, you can set what actions occur when a user clicks this button after having clicked another button or form element.

Each event trigger can have one or more actions assigned to it. Click the + iconic button below the Event pop-up menu to add an action, and add as many actions as you want to be triggered by the mouse event shown in the Event pop-up menu. (Use the – iconic button to remove a selected action.) You can reorder actions by dragging them within the list.

When you click the + button, the Buttons panel displays the Actions pop-up menu. Choose the desired action for the current event and then specify any related settings (such as page number or movie file to play) appropriate for the selected action in the pop-up menus and fields that appear below the actions list. As an example, Figure 32.6's bottom-right Buttons panel shows a Movie action applied to an On Click event, as well as the specific controls related to that action.

The options in the Actions pop-up menu are Close, Exit, Go to Anchor, Go to First Page, Go to Next Page, Go to Last Page, Go to Next View, Go to Page (SWF Only), Go to Previous Page, Go to Previous View, Go to URL, Movie, Open File, Show/Hide Buttons, Sound, and View Zoom. (Go to Page works only in exported Flash files, and View Zoom lets you change the page magnification.)

By combining state appearances, events, and actions, you can create a truly interactive document for export to PDF or Flash formats.

What works where

When using buttons and page actions, keep the following usage limits in mind for your intended output format:

- **PDF files:** All states are retained, as are all the page actions except Go to Page (SWF Only).

- **eBook files:** No buttons or states are retained.

- **Flash files:** All states are retained, but only the Go to Anchor, Go to First Page, Go to Next Page, Go to Last Page, Go to Page (SWF Only), Go to Previous Page, Go to URL, and Show/Hide Buttons actions are retained.

- **Web pages:** No buttons or states are retained.

Embedding Movies and Sound

In Design lets you place a movie or sound file in your InDesign document, to allow playback in some multimedia files. (After you've placed the file, you can size it like any other placed graphic: You're essentially sizing the window in which the movie or sound plays.)

InDesign has several limits in what kind of movie and audio files it can import, as well as how those files can be used in exported files:

- InDesign can place only QuickTime (.mov files) and Microsoft AVI movies, so be sure your movies are in one of those formats. These movies can be used only in exported PDF files.

- InDesign also supports Adobe Flash presentations (SWF files), though it can export those presentations only to PDF files compatible with Acrobat 6 and later or for use in HTML pages and eBooks.

- For sounds, InDesign supports just the Apple AIFF and Microsoft WAV formats and can export them only to PDF files.

The Movie Options dialog box

To control how a movie behaves and what control the reader has, choose Object ➪ Interactive ➪ Movie Options, as seen in Figure 32.7.

FIGURE 32.7

The Movie Options dialog box

> **TIP** A faster way to set movie and sound settings is to double-click the frame containing the movie or sound; the Movie Options dialog box or Sound Options dialog box appears, as appropriate.

The options in the Movie Options dialog box are straightforward:

- In the Source section, select whether the movie file is copied into your document or simply linked to a URL on the Web or on a CD. If you're embedding the movie file and plan to export the InDesign document as a PDF file that won't be used on a computer with Internet access, be sure to select the Embed Movie in PDF option so that everything the user needs is in the PDF file.

- In the Options section, you can change the Poster — the on-screen image inside the frame containing the movie. The default, Default Poster, lets Acrobat choose what displays (usually, it's the first frame of the move). You can also select None (for a blank frame), Standard (for the Adobe logo), Choose Image as Poster (in which case you select an image using the Browse button, such as perhaps the QuickTime logo), or Frame from Movie (to select a specific frame from the movie; not all movies will let you select this option).

■ You also set the Mode — Play Once Then Stop, Play Once Stay Open, and Repeat Play — to determine the movie's playback action. Note that the Play Once Stay Open option lets the user choose to play the movie again.

■ The Play on Page Turn option, if selected, plays the movie when a reader moves to the page containing it (as opposed to going directly to the page through a hyperlink).

■ The Show Controller During Play option displays the QuickTime movie controller to adjust sound volume; pause and resume play; and rewind and fast-forward the movie.

■ The Floating Window option puts the movie in a window that the reader can move. If selected, the dialog box also makes two pop-up menus accessible: Size, which determines the size of the window relative to the movie frame size, and Position, which places the floating window on the page.

Fancy Page Transitions

A new feature in InDesign CS4 is support for page transitions, the kind of effects you typically see in PowerPoint slide shows. You add such transitions in one of four ways:

■ Choose Page Transitions ⇨ Choose from the Pages panel's flyout menu (choose Windows ⇨ Pages or press ⌘+F12 or Ctrl+F12)

■ Choose Layout ⇨ Page Transitions ⇨ Choose

■ Choose Choose from the Page Transitions panel's flyout menu (choose Window ⇨ Interactive ⇨ Page Transitions)

■ Choose an option from the Page Transitions panel's Transitions pop-up menu

For the first three methods, you get the Page Transition dialog box shown in the figure below. If you use the Transitions pop-up menu, you don't get that visual selection when choosing an option. But after you choose a page transition, a thumbnail preview appears in the Page Transition dialog box; if you hover your mouse on that thumbnail, InDesign will animate it so that you can see the effect in action.

Select the transition you want to apply. Unless you select the Apply to All Spreads check box, these page transitions are applied to just the selected pages. The

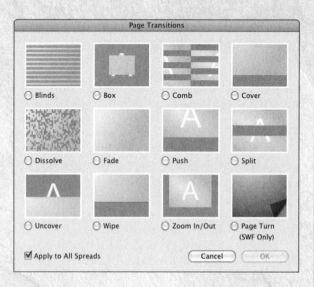

The Sound Options dialog box

The options in the Sound Options dialog box (shown in Figure 32.8) are also straightforward:

- You can change the sound by clicking Choose to the right of the filename and then selecting a new sound.

- Using the Poster pop-up menu, you can change the placeholder image that appears on the page where you place the sound. Your options are None to have no placeholder image, Standard to have the Adobe logo, and Choose Image as Poster to use an image of your own choice (click Choose to the right of the Poster pop-up menu to select the image file).

- If selected, the Play on Page Turn option automatically plays the sound when someone moves to this page in the exported PDF file.

Pages panel will show a double-page icon to the lower right of the spreads that have transitions applied, as you can see in the figure below. You can edit these effects in the Page Transitions panel, such as by setting the transitions speed and direction, as also shown below. In addition to editing the Page Transitions panel directly, you can also get to it by choosing Layout ⇨ Page Transitions ⇨ Edit or by choosing Page Transitions ⇨ Edit from the Pages panel's flyout menu.

If you applied a page transition to just selected pages but then decide you want to apply a page transition to all spreads, just go to one of the pages that has the page transition applied, or select that page in the Pages panel and then choose Apply to All Spreads in the Page Transitions panel's flyout menu or click the Apply to All Spreads iconic button at the bottom of the panel. To change selected pages' transitions, simply choose a new one using the Choose menus described earlier or choose a new transition from the Page Transitions panel.

Note that you can remove all page transitions by choosing Page Transitions ⇨ Clear All from the Pages panels' flyout menu, choose Layout ⇨ Page Transitions ⇨ Clear All, or choose Clear All from the Page Transitions dialog box's flyout menu.

Also note that these page transitions display only in PDF and Flash SWF files. And one page transition — Page Turn — works only in Flash files. Furthermore, to see the page transitions, you need to run Adobe Reader or Adobe Acrobat in full-screen mode (for PDF files) or use Flash Player 10 (for SWF files).

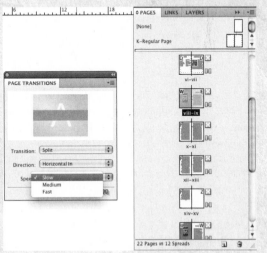

FIGURE 32.8

The Sound Options dialog box

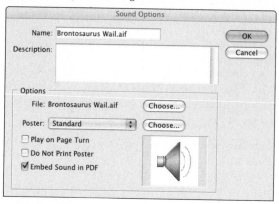

- If selected, the Do Not Print Poster option hides the poster icon when someone prints the PDF page containing the sound.

- If selected, the Embed Sound in PDF option ensures that the PDF file exported from the InDesign document includes the sound file.

What works where

When using movies and sounds, keep the following usage limits in mind for your intended output format:

- **PDF files:** All movies and sounds are retained and can be played. Flash SWF files are supported only if you export Acrobat 6 (PDF 1.5) format or newer.

- **eBook files:** Only SWF files are retained.

- **Flash files:** No movies or sounds are retained, though the poster graphics are retained as static images.

- **Web pages:** Only SWF files are retained.

CAUTION Note that Adobe Reader and Acrobat often cannot play Flash SWF files in PDF files exported from InDesign. Such incompatible files are typically SWFs that include interactivity, JavaScripts, or other such nonmovie elements.

Exporting to the Web

InDesign lets you export your layouts to the XHTML format that Web pages are based on. (XHTML is the standardized version of the Hypertext Markup Language, or HTML, format that Web pages use.)

The intent of InDesign's Web-export feature is not to create Web-ready pages but to take the supported elements in a document and put them into an XHTML file that you can then work on in Web-page-editing programs such as Adobe Dreamweaver. Adobe's thinking is that the Web is so different from the print medium that you're going to rethink the layout of any print document anyhow when creating a Web page based on it. What that means in practice is that your text and images are exported, but no objects such as lines and frames created in InDesign are exported.

To export selected objects or the entire layout to XHTML format, simply choose File ⇨ Export for Dreamweaver. (Despite the name, your files are not limited to use by Adobe's Dreamweaver software.) If you want to export just specific items on a page, select them with one of the selection tools before choosing this menu option.

NEW FEATURE   The menu option for exporting to XHTML format has changed in InDesign CS4. It had been File ⇨ Cross-Media Export ⇨ XHTML/Dreamweaver in the previous version.

The Save As dialog box opens, where you choose the disk and folder to store the exported Web page, as well as the page's filename. After you click Save, the XHTML Export Options dialog box opens, in which you specify how InDesign converts the layout to the Web format.

The following sections describe the options in that dialog box's three panes, although you want to be sure to consult with your Web master on preferred settings if you're new to working on a specific Web site's pages.

General pane

In the General pane, you choose whether to export the currently selected objects or the entire document by selecting the Selection or Document option. Note that Selection is available only if you had selected one or more objects in your layout before starting the file export.

The other major option in this pane is a set of controls for bulleted and numbered lists formatted using InDesign's bullet and numbering capabilities. The Bullets pop-up menu has two options:

- Map to Unordered Lists, which converts bulleted lists into the Web's bulleted lists (the `<ul>` type for HTML-savvy readers).
- Convert to Text, which treats the bulleted lists as regular paragraphs, inserting a hard-coded bullet character before each one.

The Numbers pop-up menu has three options:

- Map to Ordered Lists, which converts numbered lists into the Web's numbered lists (the `<ol>` type).
- Map to Static Ordered Lists, which converts numbered lists into the Web's numbered lists (the `<ol>` type, with each item's `<li>` tag specifying the specific number — such as `<li value="1">` — so if the list items are reordered, the numbering does not change automatically).
- Convert to Text, which treats the numbered lists as regular paragraphs, inserting the numerals as regular characters at the beginning of each one.

Images pane

In the Images pane, you choose how your images are converted to the Web's GIF and JPEG formats, selecting options such as image quality and color palette:

- **Copy Images:** Use this pop-up menu to determine how the InDesign document's images are converted when copied to the folder you are saving your XHTML pages to. Your options are Original, which leaves them untouched (meaning that they won't be converted into Web-compatible formats); Optimized, which converts them to the Web format specified in the Image Conversion pop-up menu; and Link to Server Path, which does not copy the file but instead inserts an image link <img src>) to the current location.

- **Formatted:** Select this check box to export the images to reflect any modifications made to them in InDesign, such as cropping, transparency, or scaling. Otherwise, the "raw" source files are exported (under the assumption that you will manipulate them further in a Web editor or image editor).

- **Image Conversion:** Use this pop-up menu to specify which format images are converted to GIF, JPEG, or Automatic (which selects the best format on a case-by-case basis).

- **GIF Options:** Use the Palette pop-up menu to choose the color palette for the image: Adaptive (No Dither), Web, System (Win), or System (Mac). For Web display, the first two are best; use the other two for pages meant to be displayed on a specific platform, such as pages available only on an internal company Web site. Select the Interlace check box to speed up the initial screen display of the images while the page is loading, but note that this can slow down overall page loading, so you should use it only with very large images.

- **JPEG Options:** Use the Image Quality pop-up menu to select the image quality and thus the amount of compression (greater compression means lower quality): Low, Medium, High, or Maximum. Use the Format Method pop-up menu to control how the image displays as it loads on the Web page: Baseline (all at one time) or Progressive. Note that choosing Progressive can slow down overall page loading, so you should use it only with very large images.

Advanced pane

In the Advanced pane, you set how text formatting is converted to the Web's version of styles, called *cascading style sheets*, or *CSS*. The CSS options are the following:

- **Empty CSS Declarations:** This creates a CSS style list within the document but leaves the formatting unspecified so that your Web designer can specify the actual style specifications using a Web editor. Text that had styles applied have the styles indicated using <p class> tags for paragraph styles and <span class> tags for character styles.

- **No CSS:** This ignores style information in the InDesign file, thus placing just simple `<p>` tags at each paragraph and stripping out any `<span>` tags. Essentially, you get unformatted text.

- **External CSS:** This option adds a `<link href="name" rel="stylesheet" type="text/css">` tag in the `<head>` section of the exported file, using the style name specified in the field below the External CSS radio button. (Don't forge the `.css` filename extension!) This means that after someone creates the specified CSS style file, the document will know what formatting to apply to the text. (Text that had styles applied have the styles indicated using `<p class>` tags for paragraph styles and `<span class>` tags for character styles.) External CSS style files ensure consistency across multiple Web pages, all of which can call on the same style file. But note that InDesign does not create a style file for you based on your InDesign document's formatting — all style definitions must be done in your Web editing software.

The Advanced pane also lets you specify whether InDesign inserts a `<script type="text/javascript" src="name.js"></script>` tag in the `<head>` section of the exported file, using the script name specified in the field below the Link to External JavaScript check box, which must be selected for this to work. (Don't forget the `.js` filename extension!) You must create your JavaScript elsewhere.

Working with exported files

After you've adjusted the XHTML Export Options dialog box's settings as desired, click Export to create the XHTML file.

The export process is simple, so it's easy to forget that converting print layouts to the Web's format is rarely a "point and shoot" activity. Expect your Web designer to do major work on those exported pages in his or her Web editing program, to optimize them for the Web environment. That's no reflection on you or InDesign, just the reality of working in different media. Figure 32.9 shows a fairly simple InDesign document; Figure 32.10 shows how it appears when exported to XHTML format and opened in Dreamweaver.

Essentially, InDesign is concerned with exporting the text so that the various stories are kept together, the style names are retained (unless you say they shouldn't be), and the images are converted to Web format (unless you say they shouldn't be). InDesign makes no attempt to preserve the layout; multiple pages are all poured into the one HTML file. Instead, InDesign places each story and each graphic one after the other. Your Web designer then needs to do the layout and formatting work.

It's almost as though you gave the Web designer the original source files for your layout and suggested that she start from scratch with those. The difference is that by exporting these files from InDesign, you can be sure that all text changes made in the layout are passed on to the Web designer and that all the graphics are Web ready.

FIGURE 32.9

The original InDesign layout

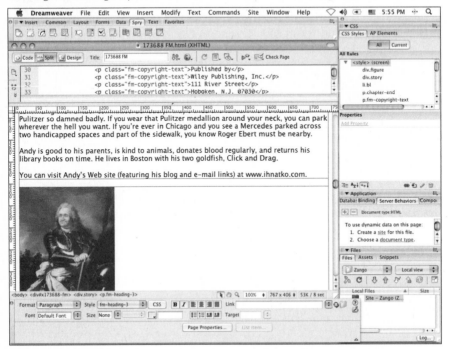

Exporting to Flash Files

InDesign CS4 lets you export documents, or specific pages, as Flash files. When you choose File ⇨ Export or press ⌘+E or Ctrl+E, you get a dialog box, where among the various Format pop-up menu (Mac) or Save as Type pop-up menu (Windows) options are two Flash options: Adobe Flash presentation file (SWF) and Adobe Flash CS4 Pro exchange file (XFL).

- A **SWF file** is a ready-to-play presentation file that can contain animations, video, or, in the case of those generated from InDesign, some page actions; you can't edit a SWF file. SWF files are playable by the Adobe Flash Player, either on a computer or via a Web browser. There's not a lot of reason to use this option except to create slideshows based on your layouts (so that you don't have to re-create them in PowerPoint or Keynote presentations). Even then, you're just as likely to export the presentations as PDF files. One possible reason to create SWF versions of your layout is for use as a Web-based magazine, because the Flash player plays within Web pages, whereas PDF files when clicked on a Web page typically open a separate reader application.

- An **XFL file** is one that Adobe Flash Professional CS4 (but not earlier versions) can open for further work, and is the option you should pick if the InDesign-exported file is meant to be the starting point for your Flash project. In the exported XFL file, all the InDesign layout objects are maintained as individual Flash objects, so you can work with each one. Likewise, all the text is editable. That makes it easy, for example, to animate parts of an InDesign layout in Flash Pro. When done, you can export the Flash project as a presentation (SWF) or video (FLV) file from Flash Pro for use on the Web or other environments.

Either way, if you're not a Flash expert, consult with your Flash project manager on what settings are appropriate for your files' intended usage.

NEW FEATURE The ability to export to Flash file formats is new to InDesign CS4.

CAUTION It's possible that a Flash SWF file that you create in InDesign will not play if embedded in a PDF file (whether you add the SWF file directly to a PDF file in Acrobat Pro or you place the SWF file into an InDesign document and then export it to a PDF file). Using the interactive features in the SWF file — such as the buttons and page actions you can set in InDesign — is what makes the files unplayable in PDF files.

The Export SWF dialog box

If you choose to export a SWF file, the Export SWF dialog box appears with the following options:

- **Size (pixels):** The three radio button options here let you determine how to size the exported Flash file. Your choices are as follows: Scale, which lets you then set a percentage of reduction or enlargement; Fit To, whose pop-up menu lets you select from eight standard Web screen sizes; and Width Height, where you enter the specific width and height in pixels. For the last option, note that the dimensions are kept proportional, so if you change one of these settings, the other is recalculated automatically.

- **Pages: The several options here control mainly how pages are exported:**

  - You choose which pages by selecting either the All radio button or the Range radio button (in which case, you can also enter the desired page range in the adjacent field).

  - Select the Spreads check box to export the pages as spreads rather than break up any existing spreads into separate pages.

  - Select the Rasterize Pages check box to convert the contents of each page to one big bitmap. This can be helpful for display on older browsers or if you don't want someone to be able to copy text from the SWF.

  - Select the Generate HTML File check box to create a Web page that contains the SWF file. You might do this if you plan on building a Web page around the SWF file generated, as a convenience.

  - Select View SWF after Exporting to launch the Flash Player (either directly or via a browser, whichever your computer decides based on how the player in installed) after the SWF file is created so that you can see how it looks.

- **Text:** this pop-up menu has three options that control how text in the InDesign document is handled during export: converted to Flash-format text, converted to vector illustrations, or converted to bitmaps.

- **Interactivity:** The four check boxes let you determine which interactive features are retained (select the desired boxes to retain them): buttons, hyperlinks, page transitions, and interactive page curls. (The sidebar "Fancy Page Transitions" explains how to set page transitions.)

- **Graphics handling:** The final three pop-up menus each handles a quality aspect to the exported images in the Flash file:

  - The Image Compression pop-up menu lets you choose standard JPEG compression, lossless compression (no compression, and Auto (which lets InDesign decide based on its analysis of each image).

  - The JPEG Quality pop-up menu lets you decide the level of compression used. The higher the quality, the larger the file size.

  - The Curve Quality pop-up menu lets you decide how InDesign handles curves in vector graphics, text converted to vector graphics, and shapes created in InDesign during export to Flash. The higher the quality, the larger the file size.

The Export Adobe CS4 Flash Professional (XFL) dialog box

If you choose to export an XFL file, the Export Adobe CS4 Flash Professional (XFL) dialog box appears with the following options:

- **Size (pixels):** The three radio-button options here let you determine how to size the exported Flash file. Your choices are Scale, which lets you then set a percentage of reduction or enlargement; Fit To, whose pop-up menu lets you select from eight standard Web screen sizes; and Width Height, where you enter the specific width and height in pixels. For the last option, note that the dimensions are kept proportional, so if you change one of these settings, the other is recalculated automatically.

- **Pages: The several options here control mainly how pages are exported:**

  - You choose which pages to export by selecting either the All radio button or the Range radio button (in which case, you can also enter the desired page range in the adjacent field).

  - Select the Spreads check box to export the pages as spreads rather than break up any existing spreads into separate pages.

  - Select the Rasterize Pages check box to convert the contents of each page to one big bitmap. This can be helpful for display on older browsers or if you don't want someone to be able to copy text from the SWF.

  - Select the Flatten Transparency check box to simplify transparent objects in the layout by converting them to opaque pixels. This will not make transparent objects solid, but it will change how they are made to appear transparent so that they take fewer resources from a Web browser or the Flashy player.

- **Text:** This pop-up menu has three options that control how text in the InDesign document is handled during export: converted to Flash-format text, converted to vector illustrations, or converted to bitmaps.

Exporting to Interactive PDFs and eBooks

PDF files are the most versatile file format that Adobe has created because they support both print and interactive features in one file. Because of the ubiquity of the Adobe Reader, they also have become a de facto standard way to distribute multimedia information on computers and via the Web.

eBooks, also called Digital Edition files, are loosely based on the PDF format. Adobe created eBooks as a limited variation of PDFs for use in electronic book readers, as well as for distribution via a separate reader application. eBook files are meant to be used like traditional book pages, so they strip out most interactivity.

Considerations for exporting interactive PDFs

Most of what you need to do to export interactive PDF files is the same as for regular print documents. The biggest difference is that there are several options in the Export Adobe PDF dialog box specific to interactive documents that you should use.

CROSS-REF Chapter 31 covers how to export InDesign documents to PDF files for print usage.

To start your export, choose File ⇨ Export or press ⌘+E or Ctrl+E and then choose Adobe PDF in the Format pop-up menu (Mac) or Save as Type pop-up menu (Windows). The Export Adobe PDF dialog box then appears. The controls over the interactivity features are all in the General pane's Include section. The following interactivity options are available in that section:

- **Bookmarks:** This option takes InDesign table-of-contents (TOC) information and preserves it as bookmarks in the exported PDF file. (See Chapter 23 for details on TOCs.)

- **Hyperlinks:** This choice preserves hyperlinks added in InDesign. Otherwise, the hyperlinks are converted to standard text in the PDF file. (The first part of this chapter explains how to create hyperlinks in InDesign.)

- **Interactive Elements:** This option preserves interactive objects — meaning buttons and their page actions — rather than convert them to static graphics.

- **Multimedia:** This pop-up menu lets you control how embedded sound and video are handled. This option is available only if you choose Acrobat 6 (PDF 1.5) or later in the Compatibility pop-up menu. The options are Use Object Settings (which uses the settings for each movie in the Movie Options dialog box, covered earlier in this chapter), Link All, or Embed All. (The last two options override the settings in the Movie Options dialog box).

CAUTION If you include Flash SWF files in your exported PDF, note that they will likely not play if they include interactive features such as JavaScripts, buttons, and page actions.

Considerations for exporting eBooks

You export InDesign files to the eBooks format by choosing File ⇨ Export for Digital Editions. Choose a filename (the filename extension is automatically set to .epub) and location in the Save As dialog box that appears and then click Save. The Digital Editions Export Options dialog box appears, where you specify how formatting and graphics are handled. The dialog box has three panes: General, Images, and Content. Their options are similar to those for exporting XHTML pages, as covered earlier in this chapter.

After you've set the various options in these three panes, click Export to create the eBook file.

 **InDesign CS4 changes the menu sequence to export files to eBooks format. It is no longer File ⇨ Cross-Media ⇨ XHTML/Digital Editions, as in the previous version.**

The Digital Editions Export Options dialog box has changed slightly to make some options clearer. The ability to embed fonts is also new.

General pane

The General pane is where you determine how text formatting is handled during export:

- In the eBook section, select the Include Metadata check box to include information about the document (set in the File Info dialog box, which you access by choosing File ⇨ File Info or pressing Option+Shift+⌘+I or Ctrl+Alt+Shift+I). This metadata can be helpful for search engines and other Web tools. You can also add publisher information in the Add Publisher Entry field.

- In the Base for CSS Styles section, you have three options:
  - The Local Formatting radio buttons uses no cascading style sheet; instead, it applies all formatting as local formats. Doing so makes it hard to change the text formatting quickly and consistently in an eBook-editing application.
  - The Defined Styles radio button tells InDesign to create a CSS file using the style definitions in the InDesign file.
  - The Style Names Only radio button tells InDesign not to export its style definitions into the eBook file, but instead just indicate the styles in the text as they are used. You would do this when you already have a CSS file created elsewhere whose formatting you want the exported document to use instead. (Of course, the names of the styles in that existing CSS file must match the style names in InDesign for the styles to be applied properly.)

- The Bullets and Numbers section has two options for how bulleted lists and numbered lists are handled during export.
  - The Bullets pop-up menu has two options: Map to Unordered Lists, which converts bulleted lists into the Web's bulleted lists (the <ul> type for HTML-savvy readers), and Convert to Text, which treats the bulleted lists as regular paragraphs, inserting a hard-coded bullet character before each one.

- The Numbers pop-up menu has three options: Map to Ordered Lists, which converts numbered lists into the Web's numbered lists (the <ol> type); Map to Static Ordered Lists, which converts numbered lists into the Web's numbered lists (the <ol> type, with each item's <li> tag specifying the specific number — such as <li value="1"> — so if the list items are reordered, the numbering does not change automatically); and Convert to Text, which treats the numbered lists as regular paragraphs, inserting the numerals as regular characters at the beginning of each one.

- If selected, the Include Embeddable Fonts check box copies into the eBook any fonts that allow themselves to be embedded. This embedding ensures accurate display of the text.

- If selected, the View eBook after Exporting check box opens an eBook editor or eBook-compatible browser (if you have one) to display the exported file so that you can make sure it looks as you expected.

Images pane

In the Images pane, you choose how your images are converted to the Web's GIF and JPEG formats, selecting options such as image quality and color palette:

- **Copy Images:** Use this pop-up menu to determine how the InDesign document's images are converted when copied to the folder you are saving your XHTML pages to. Your options are Original, which leaves them untouched (meaning that they won't be converted into Web-compatible formats); Optimized, which converts them to the Web format specified in the Image Conversion pop-up menu; and Link to Server Path, which does not copy the file but instead inserts an image link <IMG SRC>) to the current location.

- **Formatted:** Select this check box to export the images to reflect any modifications made to them in InDesign, such as cropping, transparency, or scaling. Otherwise, the "raw" source files are exported (under the assumption that you will manipulate them further in a Web editor or image editor).

- **Image Conversion:** Use this pop-up menu to specify which format images are converted to GIF, JPEG, or Automatic (which selects the best format on a case-by-case basis).

- **GIF Options:** Use the Palette pop-up menu to choose the color palette for the image: Adaptive (No Dither), Web, System (Win), or System (Mac). For Web display, the first two are best; use the other two for pages meant to be displayed on a specific platform, such as pages available only on an internal company Web site. Select the Interlace check box to speed up the initial screen display of the images while the page is loading, but note that this can slow down overall page loading, so you should use it only with very large images.

- **JPEG Options:** Use the Image Quality pop-up menu to select the image quality and thus the amount of compression (greater compression means lower quality): Low, Medium, High, or Maximum. Use the Format Method pop-up menu to control how the image displays as it loads on the Web page: Baseline (all at one time) or Progressive. Note that choosing Progressive can slow down overall page loading, so you should use it only with very large images.

Contents pane

In the Contents pane, you select the eBooks file type you want to save in, as well as specify how tables of contents are handled:

■ In the Format for EPUB Content section, you choose the desired variation of the eBook format to export to: XHTML or DTBook. The choice depends on the reader you intend people to use. Note that XHTML does a slightly better job of preserving interactive features.

■ In the Table of Contents section, you can select the Include InDesign TOC Entries check box to have a TOC created in the eBook based on the TOC created in InDesign (see Chapter 23), as well as specify the TOC style to use for the generated TOC. Another option, available only if Include InDesign TOC Entries is selected, is Suppress Automatic Entries for Documents. If selected, this option uses only the InDesign TOC entries, stripping out additional TOC entries that would otherwise be created by the eBooks export.

Summary

InDesign lets you create hyperlinks and anchors within your documents — to Web addresses, pages, files, and text in your InDesign document, and to pages and text in other InDesign documents — that are then clickable from a PDF file created from your InDesign file.

You can also create buttons that have associated actions — such as opening a movie file, closing a page, changing the zoom level, or moving to a new page — when exported as a PDF or eBook file. InDesign also lets you import movie and sound files that likewise play in exported PDF and eBook files, as well as Flash animations for export to PDF, eBook, or XHTML files. Bookmarks, both those taken from InDesign TOCs and those manually added, can be exported for use in PDF files as well.

InDesign can export layouts or selected objects to the Web's XHTML format, converting graphics to Web-compatible versions and indicating style usage in text. But these exported files make no attempt to replicate the layout. Instead, InDesign ensures that the Web designer has the latest versions of all the document's contents in a format that the designer can work on directly using a Web editor such as Adobe Dreamweaver.

InDesign can also export entire layouts to the Flash SWF format, keeping some of the interactive features in these files. A related option is the ability to export Flash project files for further work in Adobe Flash CS4 Professional.

Chapter 33

Working with XML

O ne of the most complex features in InDesign is its set of Extensible Markup Language (XML) features. XML is a structured language that essentially treats document components as data, so you can manage them through a database. The XML tools in InDesign let you treat InDesign documents as sources for XML databases, which are then linked into Web pages, PDF files, CD-ROMs, and so forth. They also let you create InDesign templates into which you flow data from XML files, all formatted and in the proper frames.

The key to XML is the fact that it's extensible. You create the tags, or labels, for various kinds of content (these are called *document type declarations,* or DTDs) based on what makes sense for your content. Then you specify what happens to each of the types of labeled content in terms of what's published, how it's presented, and so forth. Compare that to the more rigid HTML and PDF systems, where there are only certain tags available that cannot be changed, and the presentation is fixed based on the label chosen.

XML code is similar to HTML in the sense that there are tags surrounded by angle brackets (< and >) and that commands and labels are turned on and off (such as `<standardHeader>` at the beginning of a header item and `</standardHeader>` at the end of it). Comments begin with `<!--` and end with >, whereas custom commands and declarations (called *processing instructions*) begin with `<?` and end with `?>`. You don't have to understand this level of detail — just keep in mind that there are different codes to look for in examining XML code, if the need arises.

IN THIS CHAPTER

Understanding XML

Creating XML tags in InDesign

Importing XML tags into InDesign

Exporting InDesign documents for use in XML documents

Exporting to IDML format

> **NOTE** The use of XML will likely involve assistance from a Web master, content engineer, or other programming-savvy person. Page designers might also want to read *Beginning XML*, 4th Edition, or *Professional XML* (both from Wiley Publishing), depending on their level of experience. *Adobe InDesign CS4 Bible* limits itself to an overview of InDesign XML functions and is no substitute for a thorough understanding of XML.

Importing and Creating XML Tags

Chances are that most of the time, you export InDesign documents for use in XML databases, such as converting a publication's articles into a structured format used by a Web site's content management system. To export content properly, you need to apply tags to it. In InDesign, you can do that directly or have InDesign translate style tags into XML tags. You'll use both methods, because some content (such as images) won't have style tags associated with it but will need XML tags for proper processing in an XML database.

Those tags come from two sources: They're imported from a file provided by the Web site's content engineer, or they're created in InDesign by the page designer. Most of the time, you should use tags created by the content engineer, because that engineer is creating a standard set of tags for multiple page designers (both print- and Web-based). You might create your own tags when helping develop the initial tags in concert with that content engineer — or if you also are the content engineer, as well as page designer.

Importing tags

There are two places where you import tags: the Tags panel (choose Window ⇨ Tags) and the Import XML dialog box (choose File ⇨ Import XML). In the Tags panel, shown in Figure 33.1, you use the Load Tags option in the panel's flyout menu to import tags from an XML file or an InDesign document that has tags defined in it. All tags are imported when you choose Load Tags.

FIGURE 33.1

The Tags panel and its flyout menu

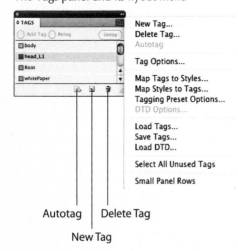

The other way to import XML tags is to choose File ➪ Import XML, which imports not only XML tags but also XML content from an XML file. This process works two ways, depending on how your document is set up:

- If your document has no content, importing an XML file adds the XML tags to the Tags panel and into the document's Structure panel. It also adds the content to the Structure panel, where you can click and drag it into InDesign frames in your layout. (The Structure panel is covered later in this chapter.)

- If your document has content, importing an XML file brings in the content to your document and places it in frames in your document that have the same tags already applied. This is a way to automatically populate a layout in InDesign.

CAUTION The order of the tags in the XML file's tags definitions is important. If the XML file has three tags — defined in the order of Body, Head, and Caption — but the Structure pane in InDesign lists them in the order Head, Body, and Caption, InDesign imports only Body and Caption content. That's because it imports Body first and then looks for the first occurrence of the Body tag in the InDesign file. It then begins matching style tags at that point. Because Head is listed in InDesign before Body, Head is ignored. (All the tags are in the Structure pane, so you can manually place the imported Head content.)

When importing XML documents, you can control some of the import operations by ensuring that Show XML Import Options is selected in the Import XML dialog box. When you choose an XML document and then click Open, a dialog box opens with the following import options:

- **Mode:** This pop-up menu gives you the options of merging the content into your InDesign document or appending it. Merge Content is the default and will match up content by tags during the import, overwriting content based on other options chosen in this dialog box. The other is Append Content, which simply adds the imported XML data after the current data, duplicating any similar hierarchies and same-named data. (The Import XML dialog box also offers these options via the Append Content and Merge Content radio buttons.)

- **Create Link:** If this check box is selected, InDesign adds a link to the XML file in the Links panel (see Chapter 12).

- **Apply XSLT:** If this check box is selected, InDesign imports the XSLT style sheet either from the XML file or from a separate file; you specify which by using the pop-up menu to its right. XSLT is the Extensible Stylesheet Language Transformation, a method for translating XML files from one structure (schema) to another, to enable movement of data across different XML databases. Think of it as a set of styles for the XML file's data structure.

- **Clone Repeating Text Elements:** If this check box is selected, the styles in the current InDesign document are preserved when importing content in the XML file that uses the same element names. In other words, it applies existing styles to new elements that use the same tags as existing elements.

- **Only Import Elements That Match Existing Structure:** If this check box is selected, elements in the imported file that vary from or are not defined by the existing InDesign document are stripped out.

- **Import Text Elements into Tables if Tags Match:** If this check box is selected, any text tagged in XML with the same tags as specified for cell contents in InDesign tables is imported into InDesign. Essentially, this lets users match XML data to specific table cells.

- **Do Not Import Contents of Whitespace-Only Elements:** If this check box is selected, elements that consist of nothing but spaces are ignored, so these blank elements do not overwrite same-name elements in InDesign. It also eliminates extraneous spaces where one will do, such as in documents that have two spaces at the end of each sentence.

- **Delete Elements, Frames, and Content That Do Not Match Imported XML:** If this check box is selected, any elements and items in the InDesign document that are not defined in the XML document are removed. In other words, this makes the imported XML document overwrite the InDesign document.

- **Import CALS Tables as InDesign Tables:** If this check box is selected, InDesign converts tables specified via the CALS standard to InDesign tables. CALS is essentially an extension to XML developed by the U.S. Defense Department's Continuous Acquisition and Life-Cycle Support project to specify table formatting in XML and SGML (another way of representing complex documents in database-oriented publishing systems).

The Import XML dialog box also has three other options you should note:

- **Import into Selected Element:** If this check box is selected, InDesign brings the imported XML data into the currently selected object (typically a frame) rather than into a new frame.

- **Merge Content:** If this check box is selected, InDesign merges the XML file into the existing XML data, flowing into the same structure, overriding same-named data and adding new data. (This control is also available in the XML Import Options dialog box.)

- **Append Content:** If this check box is selected, InDesign simply adds the imported XML data after the current data, duplicating any similar hierarchies and same-named data. (This control is also available in the XML Import Options dialog box.)

Creating tags

You also create XML tags in the Tags panel using the New Tag flyout menu. A tag simply consists of the tag name and the tag color; its formatting is defined in the XML database or in a DTD file.

Note that a DTD may define several types of content that have their own subcontent types and rules. These are called *branches*. For example, there could be an AuthorInformation branch and a CustomerList branch that both contain tags named Name. You need to know which branch that text tagged Name should go into, because XML won't know the context.

Mapping tags and styles

In the Tags panel's flyout menu, you can also map style tags to XML tags and vice versa using the Map Tags to Styles menu option and the Map Styles to Tags menu option, respectively. (They're also available in the Structure panel's flyout menu.) Figure 33.2 shows the Map Styles to Tags dialog box; the Map Tags to Styles dialog box is nearly identical, except the two columns are switched. Here's what they do:

FIGURE 33.2

The Map Styles to Tags dialog box

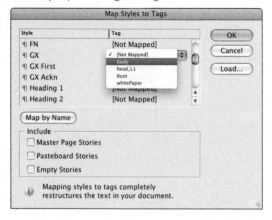

- Map Tags to Styles tells InDesign what XML tag to substitute for a specified character or paragraph style during XML export. The text retains its original InDesign style tags.

- Map Styles to Tags tells InDesign to immediately replace the specified styles with the XML tags. You see colored brackets around each string of text (paragraphs for paragraph styles and text selections for character styles) to indicate the text has an XML tag applied to it. The color corresponds to the tag color in the Tags panel. (You can change tag colors, as well as the tag name, using the Tag Options menu in the panel's flyout menu or simply by double-clicking the tag name in the panel.)

NOTE InDesign checks to make sure that you include valid XML tag names according to XML standards. If you include a space or an illegal character in the tag name, an alert message appears when you click OK.

Applying Tags

It's easy to apply tags to text: Simply select the text and click the tag name in the Tags panel. If you want to replace the tag for selected text, be sure to select the Retag option in the Tags panel; otherwise, the original tag remains *and* the new tag is applied. Unless they're style tags, multiple XML tags can be applied to the same object or text. If you choose View➪Structure➪View Tag Markers, tagged text displays brackets around it in the color of the tag in the Tags panel. Similarly, if you choose View➪Structure➪Show Tagged Frames, tagged frames and lines also show a color indicator.

You can remove a tag by selecting the tagged text or object and then clicking the Untag button in the Tags panel.

It gets slightly more complex if you're using the Structure panel — which appears automatically to the left of the document window after you import XML data — to place tagged content imported from an XML file into InDesign objects. Figure 32.3 shows the Structure panel. (You show this panel by choosing View➪Structure➪Show Structure or pressing Option+⌘+1 or Ctrl+Alt+1 — note that the shortcuts use the numeral 1. To hide it, use the same keyboard shortcuts or choose View➪Structure➪Hide Structure.)

The panel shows the document's tagged content as well as the tags associated with it. The content appears in a hierarchy, reflecting any nesting in the tags (similar to how a character style can be thought of as a subset of a paragraph tag, because it applies to a component of a paragraph).

To apply XML content to a frame, simply click and drag the appropriate content (indicated with the Text Content icon) onto a frame. As you apply tags from the Tags panel to selected objects, you'll see icons for text and objects appear along with the name of the applied tags.

You can reorder the tags in the Structure panel to reflect the hierarchy of elements. Do this in coordination with your content engineer because the hierarchy in the InDesign file needs to match the hierarchy expectations in the XML database or content system.

Taking Advantage of Other XML Options

For the more XML-savvy, InDesign offers several controls in the Structure panel and its flyout menu, shown in Figure 33.3.

In the panel, you have these options:

- **Validate Structure:** This iconic button checks the current XML structure in the Structure pane and compares it against the DTD file imported with the XML data or imported later using the Import DTD option in the pane's flyout menu. There's a copy of the Validate Structure iconic button at the bottom of the pane, along with the View Errors List iconic button that shows any errors found.

- **Add an Attribute:** This iconic button lets you add an XML attribute, which is essentially a comment such as the revision date. It has no effect on the flow of information or the appearance or role of an element.

- **Add an Element:** This iconic button lets you add an XML element, which is a tag applied to text or an object.

- **Remove Selected Elements:** This iconic button removes any selected elements.

In the flyout menu, you have these options:

- The New Element, New Parent Element, New Attribute, New Comment, and New Processing Instruction menu items let you add those items.

- Delete deletes items.

- Edit edits items.

- Untag Element removes an elements XML tag.

- Go to Item lets you quickly move to the item with the selected tag.

- Validate from Root Element verifies the structure starting at the *root* (topmost) object against the DTD information.

- Validate from Selected Element starts the validation at the selected item.

- View List of Errors shows a dialog box with any validation errors found.

- Load DTD imports a document type declaration file, which defines the "role" of tags (such as indicating that the Head tag begins a section of a story).

- Delete DTD removes the DTD file from the InDesign document but leaves the structure untouched.

- DTD Options opens a dialog box in which you specify a specific element to validate the DTD from.

- View DTD shows a dialog box with the actual DTD information (similar to a code preview in an HTML editor).

- Import XML and Export XML duplicate the options in the File menu to import and export XML files.

- The Hide Attributes, Hide Comments, and Hide Processing Instructions menu options remove these noncontent markers from view in the Structure pane so that you can concentrate on just the elements.

- Show/Hide Text Snippets shows or hides the first few words of text for each Text Content icon in the pane. Seeing these snippets is very helpful in knowing what each element actually contains.

- Add Untagged Items adds to the Structure pane all objects in the InDesign document that aren't already tagged with an XML tag. This helps ensure that you don't miss any object when reviewing the document structure.

- The Map Tags to Styles and Map Styles to Tags menu options match InDesign styles to XML tags, as I cover earlier in this chapter.

- Tagging Preset Options lets you specify the default mapping of tags to specific kinds of content: text frames, tables, and table cells. By choosing tags for each of these, you can specify globally how specific types of tagged content are assigned within InDesign.

FIGURE 33.3

At left: the Structure panel and its flyout menu. At right: The panel after validation, showing additional controls that appear if errors are found.

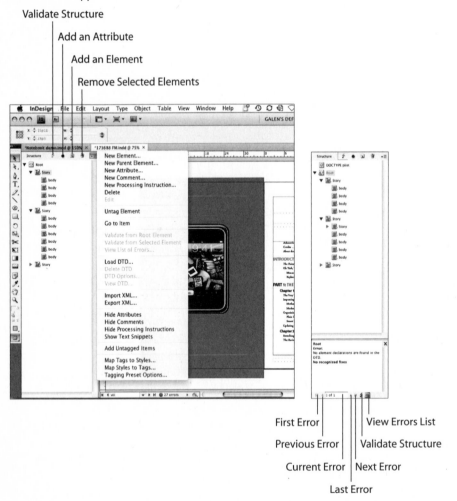

Exporting XML Files

When the InDesign document has the proper elements properly tagged to the document's content, you're ready to export it to an XML file for use by a Web site's content-management system or other XML database. Choose File ⇨ Export or press ⌘+E or Ctrl+E to open the Export dialog box. In this dialog box, give the XML file a name in the Save As field (InDesign automatically adds the filename extension .xml), select a folder in which to place the file, and — most important — choose XML from the Format pop-up menu (Mac) or Save as Type (Windows) pop-up menu. Then click Save.

The Export XML dialog box appears. It opens with the General pane. This pane is simple:

- **Include DTD Declaration:** Select this check box to include the DTD information in the exported file. Otherwise, the XML database will need to import the DTD file separately.

- **View XML Using:** Select this check box and select a Web browser or Web-supporting application in the adjacent pop-up menu to preview the XML file in that browser or program.

- **Export from Selected Element:** If an element is selected in the Structure pane, the Export from Selected Element check box will be available; if it's selected, it exports the XML file only from that element on.

- **Export Untagged Tables as CALS XML:** To convert InDesign tables not tagged with XML attributes to the CALS XML format, select this check box.

- **Remap Break, Whitespace, and Special Characters:** To convert special characters to their XML codes, select this check box.

- **Apply XSLT:** If this check box is selected, InDesign applies the XSLT style sheet either from the XML file or from a separate file; you specify which by using the pop-up menu to its right.

- **Encoding:** Use this pop-up menu to choose the text encoding mechanism — a way of representing international characters across different computer systems. Your content engineer or Web master will tell you whether to select UTF-8, UTF-16, or Shift-JIS.

In the Graphics pane, you tell InDesign how to handle the output of any tagged pictures. Your options are as follows:

- **Image Options section:** Here, you indicate which images to copy to the Images subfolder that InDesign creates. Your choices are Original Images, Optimized Original Images, and Optimized Formatted Images. You can select any or all of these. The optimized images are converted to GIF or JPEG for use on the Web unless you specify GIF or JPEG in the Image Conversion pop-up menu rather than leave the default setting of Automatic; the formatted images crop the images to reduce file size.

- **GIF Options section:** Here, you choose the color palette in the Palette pop-up menu, with choices of Adaptive (No Dither), Web, System (Mac), and System (Win). Ask your Web master what to use; usually, you select Adaptive (No Dither). For very large images, interlacing can make on-screen display over the Web seem faster (by building the image line by line rather than waiting until the whole image has been transferred to the browser before anything is displayed); if you want to have such interlaced display of GIF files, select the Interlace option.

- **JPEG Options section:** Here, you have options similar to those for GIF files. In the Image Quality pop-up menu, choose the desired image quality (Low, Medium, High, and Maximum). In the Format Method, choose Progressive to have the file displayed progressively (similar to the interlace option for GIF files) or Baseline to display it all at one time. Unless your images are very large, keep the default Baseline.

When you export an XML file with graphics, InDesign automatically embeds XMP media management properties with the graphics' tags. You can view those properties by choosing File ➪ File Info or pressing Option+Shift+⌘+I or Ctrl+Alt+Shift+I and then choosing the Advanced pane. This information may be of interest to your content engineer but has no real meaning for the page designer. However, the content engineer may want to fill out the information in the File Info dialog box's other panes — Description and Origin — into which you can add comments, creator information and contact details, copyright information, credit and source information, keywords, and copyright URLs.

Exporting to IDML

Another way to export to XML format is by using the new InDesign Markup Language (IDML) format. IDML is based on XML, so developers can work on InDesign layouts without needing InDesign. Note that IDML is not exactly XML, so only IDML-aware programs can use the IDML format; these are typically special apps or plug-ins to XML-aware apps that are meant to work specifically with InDesign files. For example, a company might add IDML capabilities to a catalog publishing system so that it can generate InDesign files directly from its catalog databases.

NEW FEATURE   The InDesign Markup Language (IDML) format is new to InDesign CS4.

By using XML as the IDML file format's basis, all of InDesign's capabilities and content attributes are available to developers for, for example, layout automation, database publishing, and content management system applications. This supplements InDesign's existing ability to expose all its internal XML capabilities via scripting, so other XML- and script-aware apps can work with InDesign directly. Note that none of this will affect the designer using InDesign in terms of using InDesign itself.

You export an InDesign layout to IDML format by choosing InDesign Markup (IDML) as the file type in the Export dialog box (choose File ➪ Export or press ⌘+E or Ctrl+E). There are no options; InDesign just creates the IDML file when you click Save.

Summary

InDesign lets you tag content within documents with XML tags, so you can transfer that content to an XML database or Web content engine from which it can be used in a variety of media, formatted as appropriate for each. You can also import XML content into InDesign, automatically placing content into the appropriate frames if you've created an appropriate template and tagged it with the right XML tags. But InDesign's XML tools are only the beginning — you need an XML database and content-creation and content-presentation tools to use the XML data derived from InDesign documents.

For organizations creating complex content creation and management workflows using XML, InDesign exposes all of its functionality as XML rules that can be scripted, essentially letting you flexibly control the creation of InDesign files based on XML programming and XML data attributes. It also has the new InDesign Markup Language (IDML) file format that is based on XML, so developers can create and work with InDesign-compatible files in their own apps, using XML as the standard description for any elements they work with across apps.

Part IX

Workgroup Publishing Techniques

Chapter 34

Working with Others

Publishing is rarely a one-person enterprise. Chances are that the creators of your text and graphics are not the same people who do your layout. And in many environments, the chances are high that many people are involved in layout and production.

By its very nature, publishing is a group activity, so publishing programs must support workgroups. Yet a Mac or a PC is a *personal* computer, so it's easy to work on a Mac or PC without worrying about how your setup and work style might affect others. InDesign lets you create your own balance between the individual and the workgroup.

The key to working effectively in a workgroup environment is to establish standards and make sure they're easy to stick to. A basic way to accomplish this task is to place all common elements in one place so that people always know where to get the standard elements. This practice also makes it easy to maintain (add, modify, and delete) these elements over time, which is essential because no environment is static. How you do this depends on your computing environment:

■ If you don't use a network, keep a master set of disks and copy elements from the master set in a folder with the same name on each person's computer. Update these folders every time a standard element changes on the master disk.

■ If you do use a network, keep a master set of disks (networks do go down, so you'll want your files accessible when that happens) and create a folder for your standard elements on a network drive accessible to all users. Update this folder whenever a standard element changes on the master disk.

IN THIS CHAPTER

Sharing common elements with multiple users

Sharing document and general preferences with other documents

Transferring files safely between Mac and Windows versions of InDesign

Working with other CS4 applications

Sharing Elements with Other Users

Some standard elements can be accessed easily from a common folder because InDesign can import certain elements that are stored outside InDesign documents. These elements include graphics files, libraries, keyboard shortcut sets, and spelling dictionaries.

Other elements reside within documents and templates and cannot be saved in separate files. These elements include styles and master pages. But styles can be exported or imported from one document to another.

CAUTION In several cases, multiple users can share the same preferences or other file using the Mac's alias feature or the Windows shortcut feature. (I note these where I cover specific features that permit this.) But keep in mind that, as with all over-the-network alias/shortcut solutions, there are some risks. For example, it is easier to corrupt the file. Also, the network and the host machine must be available at all times. Finally, if two users save changes to the file at the same time, only one user's changes will get through.

Where InDesign stores what

InDesign stores its building-block files, such as presets and preferences, in several locations.

Many of these files are stored in the folder containing the InDesign application:

- The `Presets` folder contains subfolders for several kinds of preference-related elements: Autocorrect, Button Library, Default, Find-Change Queries, InDesign Shortcut Sets, Images, InDesign Workspaces, Page Sizes, Page Transitions, StartPage, and Swatch Libraries.

- Scripts available to all users of the computer are stored in the `Scripts` folder. This folder can contain a subfolder named `Version 5.0 Scripts` (just create it yourself if it doesn't exist), in which you can place InDesign CS3 scripts and ensure that they run in InDesign CS4.

- Plug-ins — both those that come with InDesign and those you buy from other companies — are stored in the `Plug-ins` folder, often in subfolders within it.

- The spelling and hyphenation exception dictionaries that come with InDesign are stored in the `Dictionaries` subfolder within the `Plug-ins` folder.

NEW FEATURE In the `Presets` folder, the `Button Library` and `Page Transitions` subfolders are new to InDesign CS4, providing a location for the presets for these new features. Other new subfolders are `Default`, `Images`, and `StartPage`, which contain items that are used by the InDesign application (and should not be modified). Also, the `New Doc Sizes.txt` file, which contains paper size definitions and used to be in the `Presets` folder along with the subfolders, has been moved in InDesign CS4 to the `Page Sizes` subfolder.

Other files are stored with individual users' application preferences, so if users share a computer (switching from one user environment to another by logging in and out using the Windows or Mac OS X multiple-user feature), they can have different setups, even if they both use InDesign. To manage these different user environments, Mac OS X and Windows place many preference and related files in hard-to-find locations so that users don't accidentally change them:

- On the Mac, the path is `Users:user name:Library:Preferences:Adobe InDesign:Version 6.0`.

- In Windows XP, the path is `Documents and Settings\user name\Application Data\Adobe\InDesign\Version 6.0`.

- In Windows Vista, the path is `Users\user name\AppData\Local\Adobe\ InDesign\Version 6.0`.

Inside the `Version 6.0` folder, the following presets and other preference files are stored as follows:

- The InDesign preferences file (called `InDesign Defaults`).

- User-created autocorrections are stored in the `Autocorrect` folder.

- User-created spelling and hyphenation exception dictionaries are stored in the `Dictionaries` folder's `Proximity` subfolder.

- User-created find/change queries are stored in the `Find-Change Queries` folder.

- User-created glyph sets are stored in the `Glyph Sets` folder.

- User-created keyboard shortcuts are stored in the `InDesign Shortcut Sets` folder.

- User-created menu sets are stored in the `Menu Sets` folder.

- User-created workspaces are stored in the `Workspaces` folder.

- Scripts can be stored in the `Scripts` folder; store the scripts you want available to all users in the `Presets` folder in the application folder.

Unhiding the Windows Application Data Folder

The `Application Data` folder in Windows is hidden by default.

To see it in Windows XP, open any folder in Windows and then choose Tools ➪ Folder Options to open the Folder Options dialog box. Go to the View pane and select the Show Hidden Files and Folders option. Click OK.

To see it in Windows Vista, choose Start ➪ Computer and then choose Organize ➪ Folder and Search Options in the dialog box that appears. Go to the View pane and select the Show Hidden Files and Folders option. Click OK.

Trap presets, print presets, PDF export presets, transparency flattener presets, and stroke styles are *not* stored in files you can access — *unless* you explicitly store them using the Save commands in their dialog boxes or panels' flyout menus. Other presets and styles — such as text variables, and bulleted and numbered lists — are stored in the InDesign preference file (if no document was open when they were created) or in a specific document (if one was open when they were created).

> **NOTE** InDesign should not be open or running when you copy any of these building-block folders into the folders it uses. It sees only new files the next time you open the application.

Preference files

When no document is open and you change the preferences, add swatches and styles, modify tool settings (such as change the number of sides on the Polygon or Polygon Frame tool by double-clicking it), and modify the default settings of some panels and dialog boxes (such as Text Wrap and Text Frame Options), these changes are saved in the InDesign Defaults file.

Color definitions

Wanting to keep color, tint, and gradient definitions consistent across documents isn't unusual. This consistency helps you ensure, for example, that corporate identity colors, if you have them, are used instead of someone's approximations.

You can import swatches created in other documents (and templates) by having both documents open and then clicking and dragging the swatch from the source document's Swatches panel (choose Window ⇨ Swatches or press F5) to anywhere in the other document's window. By creating a file that contains nothing but swatches, you can, in effect, create a color library for users.

Using a Common Settings Files

You can use the Mac's alias feature or the Windows shortcut feature to use an InDesign settings file stored in a folder other than the one in which InDesign resides. On a network, being able to use this technique means that everyone can share the same InDesign settings files, such as the InDesign Defaults file, keyboard shortcuts sets, spelling and hyphenation dictionaries, libraries, and swatch libraries. Note that if you're sharing these files across platforms, you need to create a Windows shortcut from Windows to these files as well as a Mac alias from the Mac.

But note that the InDesign Defaults file *cannot* be shared across platforms, so if you want to have a master copy on a network server for shared use, you'll need to maintain two masters — one for Mac and one for Windows. Because the files have the same name on both platforms (there is no filename extension for this file in Windows), you'll need to store them in separate directories or add something to the name such as "Mac" and "Windows." If you do change the name, note that the alias and shortcut on each user's system must simply be named InDesign Defaults.

You can't add swatches to a library, but any swatch used in a library element is copied to a document along with that element. So you could use a library that has a series of rectangles, each with a different swatch applied, as another way of creating a color library.

InDesign also lets you share swatch libraries, even across platforms. (Just be sure the Adobe Swatch Exchange [also called ColorBook] swatch library file has the filename extension .ase if you're transferring a swatch library from the Mac to Windows.)

CROSS-REF See Chapter 7 for more on creating swatches.

PLATFORM DIFFERENCES On the Mac, color profiles are stored in the path Users:user name:Library: ColorSync:Profiles. In Windows XP, they're stored in the Windows\ System32\Spool\Drivers\Color folder. In Windows Vista, they're stored in Windows\ System32\Spool\Drivers.

Paragraph, character, table, cell, and object styles

The various style panels — Character Styles, Paragraph Styles, Table Styles, Cell Styles, and Object Styles — include an option in the flyout menu to import styles from other InDesign documents and templates. In the Character Styles and Paragraph Styles panels, you'll see flyout menu options to import (load) just character styles or just paragraph styles, respectively, or both types of styles. Similarly, in the Table Styles and Cell Styles panels, you'll see flyout menu options to import just table styles or just cell styles, respectively, or both types of styles. The Object Styles panel's flyout menu simply has the Load Object Styles flyout menu option.

Note that the Load dialog boxes accessed through the various styles panels' flyout menus let you select which styles to load, as well as let you decide how to handle the import of styles that have the same names in the two documents.

TIP By importing styles with no document open, you copy all new styles into your global defaults (those stored in the InDesign Defaults file that I cover earlier in this chapter). This technique is a handy way of bringing new styles into your default settings without affecting existing styles.

CROSS-REF See Chapter 19 for more on paragraph and character styles, Chapter 21 for more on table and cell styles, and Chapter 12 for more on object styles.

Spelling dictionaries

InDesign saves any spelling or hyphenation exceptions you add by choosing Edit ➪ Dictionary, or when you're spell-checking by choosing Edit ➪ Check Spelling or pressing ⌘+I or Ctrl+I. You can copy these exception dictionaries from one computer to another (regardless of platform), or you can use an alias or shortcut from each computer to a central location on a server.

On both Mac and Windows, hyphenation exception files have the filename extension `.not`, and the spelling exception dictionaries have the extension `.udc`. The files will have the same name as the language dictionaries (but different filename extensions) to which they are associated, such as `FREN.not` for French hyphenation exceptions and `USA.udc` for U.S. English spelling exceptions.

CROSS-REF   See Chapter 15 for more on hyphenation and spelling dictionaries.

Graphics and text files

Perhaps the most obvious elements to standardize are the *source elements* — the text and graphics that you use in your documents — especially if you have common elements, such as logos that are used in multiple documents.

The simplest method of ensuring that the latest versions of these common elements are used is to keep them all in a standard folder (either on each computer or on a network drive). This method works well when you first use a text or graphic element, but it does not ensure that these elements are updated in InDesign documents if the elements are changed after being imported.

For text and graphics files, using InDesign's links feature — when you keep common elements in a common location — can ensure consistency across documents. You can also use libraries and snippets to store commonly used graphics and text blocks (including any formatting for the text and its frame).

CROSS-REF   See Chapter 12 for more on managing file links.

You can also share stroke styles if you save them from the Strokes Styles dialog box (open the Stroke panel by choosing Window➪Stroke or pressing ⌘+F10 or Ctrl+F10, and then choose Stroke Styles from the flyout menu). Click Save to save the selected style; click Load to import a stroke style file (which has the filename extension `.lnst`).

CROSS-REF   Chapter 11 covers strokes in more detail.

Libraries

InDesign libraries are a great aid for keeping documents consistent. Because libraries are stored in their own files, common libraries can be put in common folders. You can even access them across the network. If you want, you can keep an alias to a library elsewhere on the network on your computer's local drive.

For many people, libraries offer more flexibility than just links to graphics files because all attributes applied to graphics and their graphics frames are also stored in the library.

Libraries can be shared across platforms, and although Windows InDesign libraries have the filename extension `.indl`, that extension is not required for Windows InDesign to open and use Mac libraries.

CROSS-REF See Chapter 6 for more information on libraries.

Snippets

You can also share elements through snippets, which contain InDesign objects. Snippet files have the filename extension `.idms` and can be placed in an InDesign document as can any graphic or text. They retain all their attributes, much as libraries do, except that each snippet is stored in its own file. In contrast to library items, snippets retain their object coordinates, which can create some minor issues when you place a snippet made from a larger document into a second, smaller document. The objects don't fall off the pasteboard, but it may take some effort to find them.

NEW FEATURE The filename extension for InDesign CS4 snippets has changed to `.idms`. Snippets created in previous versions have the filename extension `.inds` (and can still be used in InDesign CS4).

CROSS-REF See Chapter 9 for more information on snippets.

Templates

In the course of creating documents, you're likely to evolve templates that you want to use over and over. InDesign can save a document as a template. The only difference between a template and a document is that a template forces you to use Save As rather than Save in the File menu so that you don't overwrite the template but instead create new documents based on it.

Although the optimum approach is to design a template before creating actual documents, the truth is that no one can foresee all possibilities. Even if you create a template (and you should) with styles, swatches, and master pages intended for use in all new documents, you can expect to modify your template because working on real documents brings up the need for modifications and additions.

Whether or not you use templates, you still need to transfer basic layout elements such as styles and master pages from one document to another, as I describe earlier in this chapter.

Templates can be shared across platforms, and although Windows InDesign templates have the filename extension `.indt`, that extension is not required for Windows InDesign to open and use Mac templates. (I still recommend that you always use the filename extensions, so the correct icons appear in your folders.)

CROSS-REF See Chapter 4 for more on templates.

Output settings

Several output-related settings — print presets, transparency flattener presets, and PDF export presets (also called *job-option files*) — can be shared by saving them to files and then loading them into other users' copies of InDesign. Print presets have the filename extension `.prst`; transparency flattener presets, `.flst`; and PDF export presets, `.joboptions`.

Another output-related setting — trap presets — is stored within InDesign documents and can be opened using the Load command from the Trap Presets panel's flyout menu. (Access this panel by choosing Window ⇨ Output ⇨ Trap Presets.)

CROSS-REF   See Chapter 30 for more on print, transparency, and flattener presets. See Chapter 31 for more on PDF export presets. See Chapter 28 for more on trap presets.

Master pages

You can import master pages from one document to another by using the Load Master Pages flyout menu option in the Pages panel (choose Window ⇨ Pages or press ⌘+F12 or Ctrl+F12). In the resulting dialog box, select the InDesign document whose master pages you want to import.

CROSS-REF   See Chapter 6 for more on master pages.

InDesign documents

An easy way to share InDesign documents with others is to use the Package feature (choose File ⇨ Package or press Option+Shift+⌘+P or Ctrl+Alt+Shift+P), which copies all files needed to one folder. This lets you place a complete package for others to work on in one location, whether on a network folder or on a removable medium such as a CD-RW.

CROSS-REF   Chapter 29 covers the package feature.

Document presets and the `New Doc Sizes.txt` paper-size file can be shared as well. You can save and load document presets (filename extension `.dcst`) using the Document Presets dialog box. To share paper size definitions, copy the `New Doc Sizes.txt` file from the `Page Sizes` subfolder in the InDesign application folder's `Presets` subfolder on the computer containing the desired definitions to the same folder on other computers' InDesign applications folders.

CROSS-REF   Chapter 4 covers document presets and paper size definitions.

If you're working on a network, the Version Cue file-version management software that comes with Adobe Creative Suite 4 applications, including InDesign CS4, can also help. It lets you create shared folders across the network that you save your files to when you're ready for others to work on them. Version Cue also retains earlier versions, so there is a history of changes that you can use to undo design directions that don't work out. A related tool is the InCopy CS4 software that Adobe sells separately; this software lets development editors and copy editors work on an InDesign document's text while the designer is working on the layout.

CROSS-REF
Version Cue is covered in Appendix C; Chapter 35 provides an introduction to InCopy.

Interface preferences

You can share three types of interface settings as files: customized menus (filename extension `.inms`), custom keyboard shortcuts (`.indk`), and custom workspaces (`.xml`). They are available only to a specific user or to all users of a computer, depending on where you copy them to, as I describe earlier in this chapter.

CROSS-REF
These interface preference settings are covered in Chapter 3.

Mixing Mac and Windows Environments

As a cross-platform application, InDesign appeals strongly to all sorts of users who find that they must deal with "the other side." This includes corporate users whose various divisions have standardized on different platforms, service bureaus whose clients use different computers, and independent publishers or layout artists who deal with a range of clients.

InDesign differences

InDesign can read document files from either platform. However, the Windows version may not recognize a Mac-generated file as an InDesign file unless you do one of two things:

- **Add a filename extension:** Add `.indd` for documents or `.indt` for templates to the Mac-generated file's name. InDesign adds an extension automatically, so unless a user removed the filename extension, most files will have it. If the filename extension is missing, be sure to choose All Documents from the Enable pop-up menu (Mac) or Files of Type pop-up menu (Windows) in the Open a File dialog box. Table 34.1 lists the common filename extensions for the files InDesign typically works with.

- **Select the All Files option:** Choose this in the Enable pop-up menu (Mac) or File of Type pop-up menu (Windows) in the Open a File dialog box (choose File ⇨ Open or Ctrl+O) for cases when the document does not have its identifying filename extension.

On the Mac, you may not be able to double-click a PC-generated InDesign document (this is usually true when you see a PC icon rather than the InDesign icon for the file). When you can't open a document by double-clicking it, you'll need to open it from the InDesign Open a File dialog box (choose File ⇨ Open or press ⌘+O).

TABLE 34.1

Filename Extensions

File	Filename Extension
InDesign Files	
Document	`.indd`
Interchange	`.inx`
Template	`.indt`
Library	`.indl`
Snippet	`.idml` (CS4), `.inds` (previous)
ColorBook swatches	`.ase`
Hyphenation exception dictionaries	`.not`
Spelling exception dictionaries	`.udc`
Stroke styles	`.lnst`
Document presets	`.dcst`
Print presets	`.prst`
Transparency flattener presets	`.flst`
PDF export presets	`.joboptions`
Customized menus	`.inms`
Customized keyboard shortcuts	`.indk`
Customized workspaces	`.xml`
InCopy Files	
Document	`.icml` (CS4), `.incd` (previous)
Interchange	`.incx`
Assignment	`.icma` (CS4), `.inca` (previous)
Package	`.icap` (CS4), `.incp` (previous)
Other Files	
JavaScript	`.js`, `.jsx`
Data type description	`.dtd`
XML	`.xml`
XSLT	`.xlst`
GIF	`.gif`
JPEG	`.jpg`, `.jpeg`
Photoshop	`.psd`

File	Filename Extension
Other Files	
TIFF	`.tif`, `.tiff`
EPS	`.eps`
Illustrator	`.ai`
PDF	`.pdf`
Flash presentation	`.swf`
Flash CS4 project interchange	`.xfl`
Flash project	`.fla`
ASCII text (text-only)	`.txt`
Rich Text Format	`.rtf`
Word	`.doc` (pre-2007), `.docx` (2007-08)
Excel	`.xls` (pre-2007), `.xlsx` (2007-08)

Which elements transfer

The following elements may be transferred across platforms, with any limits noted:

- **Color, tint, and gradient swatches:** These are retained and may also be imported across platforms, both directly from other documents and by loading individual swatch files. For Adobe Swatch Exchange (ColorBook) swatch libraries copied from the Mac to Windows, be sure to add the filename extension `.ase` if it's not already there.

- **Color profile files:** Although these cannot be exchanged across the two platforms, both the Mac and Windows InDesign versions retain color-profile information from the other platform's files. And if both platforms have color profiles for the same device (monitor, scanner, printer, and so on), InDesign applies the correct color profiles. If a color profile is not available on the new platform, you can apply a new profile or ignore the issue. (If you ignore this issue, the correct profile will be in place when you bring the document back to the original platform.) If you print with a missing profile, InDesign substitutes the default profile based on the type of color model used (RGB or CMYK).

- **Paragraph, character, table, cell, and object styles; master pages; and trap presets:** These are retained and you may also import them from other documents across platforms.

- **Stroke styles, print presets, document presets, Adobe PDF export presets, and transparency flattener presets:** These are retained and you may also import them across platforms after saving them to their own files.

- **Hyphenation and spelling exceptions:** These are retained. The files use a filename extension on both the Mac and in Windows: `.not` for hyphenation additions, `.udc` for spelling additions.

- **Document preferences:** These are retained, but the `InDesign Defaults` file cannot be shared across platforms.

- **Plug-ins:** These files are not interchangeable across platforms. Plug-ins must be present on both platforms if you move documents that use the features of specific plug-ins. You'll need versions specific to each platform because these are essentially miniprograms that must be written to work on the Mac or Windows.

Which elements don't transfer

Adobe has removed most barriers between Mac and Windows in InDesign. Only the following elements cannot be moved across platforms:

- Shortcut sets

- Color profiles

- The `InDesign Defaults` preferences file

- AppleScripts and VBScripts (but you can share JavaScripts)

Working with Multiple Versions of InDesign

Many designers have more than one version of InDesign installed on their computer so that they can work with multiple clients' files in the same version of the software that the client uses, to ensure file compatibility and to prevent the use of features from a new version in the files of a client who has an older version.

When working with multiple copies of InDesign, double-clicking a filename from a folder launches the most recent version of InDesign installed, which may not be the one you want. So you typically have to launch the desired version of InDesign first and then open the file from within it.

On the Mac, there's a wrinkle. When you double-click a file with no filename extension, the Mac OS looks for a pair of attributes embedded in the file itself, called the *file type* and *file creator*, that pre-X versions of the Mac OS used instead of filename extensions. If it finds them, it launches the associated program. (But if the file has a filename extension, Mac OS X doesn't bother looking at the file type and creator.)

The file type and creator tell the Mac OS which version of the program to launch, so you can remove the filename extension for a file and then double-click it to have the proper version of InDesign launch and open the file for you. (There is no way to do this double-click trick in Windows.) Note that this trick won't always work, and that removing the filename extension also removes the InDesign logo from the file icon. If you use this trick, be sure to put the filename extension back (so that the InDesign logo reappears) when you're done with the file.

Platform differences

There are also some general differences between Windows and Mac themselves that will add a few bumps along the road to cross-platform exchange.

Filenames

The most noticeable difference between Windows and Mac is the file-naming convention, and that difference is no longer so great since the advent of Mac OS X a decade ago. To be cross-platform compatible, restrict your filenames to 250 characters (including the filename extension), always use a filename extension, and do not use any of the following characters as part of the filename: : / | . * " < > ? / \. These restrictions conform to the Mac OS X standards, but Windows users will need to make a couple of compromises:

- You can't use the full Windows filename size of 255 characters.
- You can't use the : / | . * " < > ? / \ characters in your filenames even though Windows supports all of them but : .

Although the Mac OS X supports filenames as long as 250 characters, you may have trouble copying Windows files to the Mac if the Windows filenames exceed 31 characters and you use the AppleTalk networking protocol to connect your Macs and PCs. That's because of limits in some of the software to make these cross-platform connections, which enforce pre–Mac OS X filename conventions on all files. It's easy enough to test whether your software is limiting you to 31 characters: Just transfer a file and see whether either the software shortens the name or refuses to transfer the file. In either case, it's time to upgrade your networking software or switch to a protocol such as IP.

Displaying Filename Extensions

Windows and Mac OS X use filename extensions to identify the file type. But they're typically not displayed to the user. Here's how to make filename extensions visible:

- In Mac OS X 10.4 (Tiger) and 10.5 (Leopard), choose Finder ➪ Preferences. (You have to be using the Finder, not be in an application, to see the Finder menu.) In the Preferences dialog box that appears, go to the Advanced pane, select the Show All File Extensions check box, and close the dialog box.

- In Windows XP, open any folder and then choose Tools ➪ Folder Options. (You have to have a disk or folder open to have the View menu.) In the Folder Options dialog box that appears, go to the View pane. Deselect the Hide Extensions for Known File Types check box and then click OK.

- In Windows Vista, choose Start ➪ Computer and then choose Organize ➪ Folder and Search Options in the dialog box that appears. Go to the View pane, select the Show Hidden Files and Folders check box, and then click OK.

CAUTION If you rename your files in Windows or on the Mac OS X, either before transferring or while transferring them, you'll confuse InDesign. That's because InDesign's internal pointers to files such as graphics and swatch libraries retain the original name, so it keeps looking for those names. So it's best to make sure your filenames meet the cross-platform requirements before using them in InDesign.

Font differences

Although the major typeface vendors such as Adobe Systems, Linotype, and Agfa offer their typefaces for both Windows and Mac users, these typefaces are not always the same on both platforms. Cross-platform differences are especially common among typefaces created a few years ago, when multiplatform compatibility was not a goal for most users or vendors.

Differences occur in three areas:

- **Internal font name:** The name used by the printer and type scalers (such as Extensis Suitcase, Insider Software FontAgent Pro, and Adobe Type Manager) is not quite the same for the Mac and Windows version of a typeface. This discrepancy results in an alert box listing the fonts used in the document that are not on your computer. The solution is to use the Find Font dialog box or the Find/Replace dialog box (both covered in Chapter 15) to replace all instances of the unrecognized font name with the correct one for the current platform.

- **Tracking, kerning, and character width:** These may vary between the two platforms, even if typefaces use the same internal names, and could result in text reflow. The solution is to check the ends of all your stories to make sure text did not get shorter or longer.

- **Symbols:** Even when created by the same vendors, the character maps for each font file differ across platforms because Windows and the Mac use different character maps. This problem is complicated by the fact that some vendors didn't stick to the standard character maps for any platform or didn't implement all symbols in all their typefaces. The solution is to proofread your documents, note the symbols that are incorrect, and then use the Find/Change dialog box to replace them with the correct symbol. (Highlight the incorrect symbol and use the copy and paste commands to put it in the Text field of the Find/Change dialog box rather than try to figure out the right keypad code in Windows or the right keyboard shortcut on the Mac.) If you use OpenType fonts, you find far fewer issues with symbol translation than with PostScript Type 1 and TrueType fonts.

To minimize font problems, use a program such as FontLab Fontographer or Studio Pro to translate your TrueType and PostScript files from Mac to Windows format or vice versa. This ensures that the internal font names, width information, and symbols are the same on both platforms. The companion Web site (`www.InDesignCentral.com`) includes links to these and other utilities.

CROSS-REF See Chapter 20 for more information on using special characters.

Transfer methods

Moving files between Macs and Windows PCs is easier now than ever before, thanks to the built-in support of Windows formats and networking in Mac OS X, the use of TCP/IP networking by both the Mac and Windows, and a selection of products on both platforms that let each machine read the other's disks (floppies, removable disks like CD-Rs, and even hard drives). This book's companion Web site www.InDesignCentral.com lists such tools.

Working with Other Creative Suite Applications

One of the strengths of InDesign is that it is part of the Adobe Creative Suite, making it easy to work with graphics sources and other files directly in the environment used to create them. The integration is especially tight among InDesign, Photoshop, and Illustrator. You'll also see similar user interfaces and controls across the applications, letting you apply your skills in more than one context.

Working with graphics and colors

At the most basic level, InDesign can place Photoshop and Illustrator files directly, so there's no need to use an intermediate format such as TIFF or EPS. You can import the files using the Place dialog box, drag them (or pieces of them) directly into InDesign, or copy and paste them (or pieces of them). InDesign preserves any formatting such as layers and color swatches.

You can edit placed graphics files (not copied or dragged files) by choosing Edit Original from the contextual menu or from the Links panel's flyout menu. If the file has layers, you can manage those layers using Object Layers Options from the contextual menu or from the Object menu. You can also work with clipping paths and alpha channels in Photoshop files, because InDesign preserves them. If you drag or copy and paste graphics (but not place) from Illustrator, you can edit them directly in InDesign.

You can use the same color swatch libraries in InDesign, Photoshop, and Illustrator. These Adobe Swatch Exchange (ColorBook) files have the filename extension .ase, and you can save and load them using the Swatches panel in InDesign, Photoshop, and Illustrator. (Be sure to use the Save Swatches for Exchange flyout menu options in Photoshop and Illustrator, and the Save Swatches flyout menu option in InDesign, to save these swatches, and the Load Swatches flyout menu item to import them in all three programs.)

CROSS-REF Part VI covers how to import and work with graphics files. Chapter 7 covers the process of creating colors and opening color libraries.

Working with Web content

You can export entire InDesign layouts or just selected objects in those layouts for use in Adobe Dreamweaver, as Chapter 32 explains. InDesign creates XHTML files containing your text and basic formatting such as indicating paragraphs, styles used, and story boundaries, as well as converts any graphics to JPEG or GIF formats automatically. You can also simply export individual objects to JPEG format, as Chapter 4 explains.

Dreamweaver's support of InDesign content via copy and paste is limited: You can copy only text selections, not frames, and you cannot copy images into Dreamweaver from InDesign.

> **TIP** In Dreamweaver, choose Edit ⬧ Paste Special or press Shift+⌘+V or Ctrl+Shift+V to get some control over how pasted text is handled, such as how the text's line breaks and how structured text such as lists and tables are handled.

Working with Adobe Flash Professional

InDesign CS4 can export documents to your choice of the playable Flash SWF format (`.swf`) or the new Flash Professional CS4 project interchange format (`.xfl`), which lets you do further work on the exported InDesign document in Flash CS4 Pro (but not in previous versions).

As with exporting HTML documents for Web-editing applications, this is a one-way workflow, where you do some basic work in InDesign and then export for refinement and finalization in Flash CS4 Pro. There is no ability to do further refinement in InDesign on the exported Flash file.

> **NEW FEATURE** The ability to export to Flash formats is new to InDesign CS4. Chapter 32 covers creating interactive documents and then exporting them to Flash format.

Working with Adobe Bridge

The Adobe Bridge application is meant to be a central command point for your Creative Suite documents and their component files, such as graphics and swatch libraries. You don't have to use Bridge — the standard Windows and Mac folder systems work perfectly well — but it does give you more context about your files, should you need it, as well as let you control some aspects of the Creative Suite's functionality.

File context

Figure 34.1 shows the Bridge's default (Essentials) view of a folder containing a bunch of InDesign files. Note the previews of individual files, which help you know you're selecting the ones you want. And note the Filter panel at the left-hand side of the Bridge window; you can quickly use this to find files that match specific file types, creation dates, and modification dates, as well as control whether the files are sorted by name, document kind, creation date, dimensions, or any of seven other attributes.

Bridge CS4 provides several views, called workspaces, of files. You switch to them using the labels at top such as Filmstrip, Metadata, and Output. You can access and manage other workspaces by clicking the pop-up menu to the right of Output. There is also a series of quick-access iconic pop-up menus to the left of the workspace labels for various file, sorting, and related functions.

Also note the Metadata panel at the right-hand side; this panel can include all sorts of information (metadata) about the file, such as the creator of it, that helps other members of a project get the right context so that they know how and when to use the file. For example, the figure shows which fonts the selected layout uses, so you know which ones you'll need to work on it.

Some metadata information, such as creation date and fonts used, is automatically included in the files saved by Creative Suite applications. You can also modify and add metadata to a file within applications such as InDesign by choosing File⇨ File Info or pressing Option+Shift+⌘+I or Ctrl+Alt+Shift+I.

You can add or modify this information later from Bridge by selecting a file in Bridge and choosing File⇨ File Info — or by right-clicking it or Control+clicking the filename in Bridge and choosing File Info from the contextual menu. Note that the File Info dialog box is the same in Bridge as it is in InDesign.

FIGURE 34.1

The default Bridge folder view

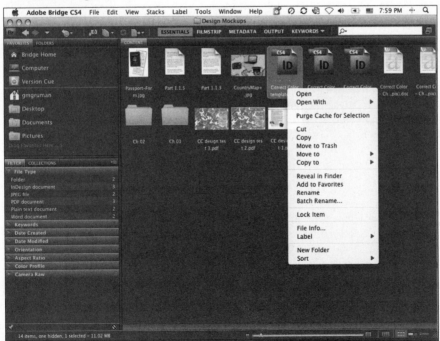

In the Preferences dialog box's Metadata pane (choose Bridge CS4➪Preferences on the Mac or Edit ➪Preferences in Windows), you can set which metadata properties you want to be displayed for all files by selecting the desired check boxes.

Bridge interface

The Preferences dialog box (choose Bridge CS4➪Preferences on the Mac or Edit ➪Preferences in Windows) lets you control Bridge's user interface. Available controls include setting the color scheme and which folders display in the Favorites pane using the General pane, how thumbnail previews are generated using the Thumbnails pane, which applications are launched by double-clicking specific types of files using the File Type Associations pane, and how color management and language display are handled in Bridge using the Advanced pane.

Suite functionality

Bridge lets you set the default color management settings for all Creative Suite applications, to ensure consistent color representation as files move from one application to another. Choose Edit ➪Creative Suite Color Settings, or press Shift+⌘+K or Ctrl+Shift+K, to open the Suite Color Settings dialog box and choose the desired color settings.

You can also use Bridge to set up Version Cue projects as well as check out files, promote versions over each other, and otherwise manage the files. The functionality here is the same as in individual Creative Suite applications, except that you can work on multiple types of project files from one location. Choose Tools➪Version Cue to access these functions.

CROSS-REF Chapter 28 covers color management in detail. Appendix C covers Version Cue management in detail.

NEW FEATURE Bridge CS4 removes from its Tools menu the Contact Sheet utility available in previous versions that created an InDesign file in which thumbnails of selected images were placed in rows, appearing as if they were images in physical filmstrips. The Tools menu retains utilities for Photoshop, Illustrator, and Fireworks.

Summary

When working with other users, you can share preferences by copying or making aliases to just one InDesign Defaults file, ensuring that all users have the same preferences. But the InDesign Defaults file is not cross-platform compatible, so Windows users cannot use a Mac user's file or vice versa.

Except for shortcut sets, color profiles, the InDesign Defaults preferences file, plug-ins, AppleScripts, and VBScripts, cross-platform users can share InDesign support documents. Otherwise, sharing files between PC and Mac users is very simple, thanks to a variety of disk- and network-based utilities now available for both platforms.

InDesign works well with several other Adobe Creative Suite 4 applications, including Photoshop and Illustrator. You can export Flash CS4 project files that let you begin an interactive document in InDesign and finish it in Flash CS4 Pro. There is also some direct copy-and-paste support from InDesign to Dreamweaver.

The Bridge application is meant to act as a central hub and repository for all Creative Suite 4 applications, providing a unified location to store project files and to get information on files, such as creation date and fonts used. You can also set Creative Suite–wide color settings and manage Version Cue projects involving files from multiple programs.

Chapter 35

Workgroup Editing with InCopy

P
ublishing is almost always a workgroup activity involving writers, editors, copy editors, layout artists, and production editors. Even when a
person has multiple roles, most publications still involve multiple
people. And that means that files go back and forth as edits are made, layouts are created, and text and other elements are adjusted to fit the available
space. Just as its rival QuarkXPress has the CopyDesk companion product,
InDesign has a companion product (called InCopy) to facilitate this constant
"paper shuffling." InCopy is not as powerful as InDesign — it's not a layout
tool — but it does let copy editors, editors, and other wordsmiths work on
InDesign layouts to make sure headlines fit, stories fit, and captions can be
written in context without needing a full copy of InDesign.

InCopy works best in a networked environment, where everyone shares files
from a common folder (using Adobe's Version Cue or not, as you prefer).
That way, a copy editor can work on a layout without worrying that the
designer might be working on a local copy at the same time, for example.

InCopy is both a separate program that runs by itself for text-editing stories
in an InDesign layout and a plug-in that works within InDesign to provide
shared editing capabilities.

Setting up Workgroup Assignments

InDesign comes ready out of the box to work with InCopy, in the form of the Assignments panel (choose Window➪Assignments), which contains the various menu options available by choosing the Edit➪InCopy, and the File➪User menu commands.

Identifying the user

The first thing you should do if you plan to use the InCopy features within InDesign is to set up your username so that InCopy can track every change you make. Choose File➪User to open the User dialog box. Enter a name for yourself and choose your preferred color from the Color pop-up menu. (InDesign and InCopy use the same colors to help you quickly identify who made specific changes.) Then click OK.

Preparing story files for InCopy

Before an InCopy user can work on a layout, an InDesign user has to InCopy-enable that layout. There are two ways to do that: use the Assignments panel or export individual stories as InCopy files.

You should use the Assignments panel as the primary mechanism because it gathers all files into one convenient group — an assignment — that is associated to this layout. You can create multiple assignments for the layout, grouping stories based on who should work on them or whatever division makes sense for your workflow.

Exporting InCopy files directly makes more sense when you want to share a specific story with an InCopy user, rather than have that user work on stories within the InDesign layout file itself (where inadvertent damage could be caused to other parts of the layout). It's essentially the same concept as sending an RTF file for an editor to work on in Word, except that an InCopy story retains all the InDesign text formatting so that it can more easily be brought back into the layout.

But if you export stories this way, they're still available in the Assignments panel, so it's not a completely either/or approach between using the Assignments panel to create assignments versus exporting InCopy files. I prefer starting with the Assignments panel because I find it a simpler way to work.

Either way, an InCopy user can open an assignment and work on the text within a replica of the layout, to understand the relationships among stories and space constraints, for example. Yet that InCopy user cannot modify the layout or graphics, so designers don't have to worry about unexpected or accidental changes.

Creating story assignments

To create a new assignment, choose New Assignment from the Assignment panel's flyout menu. You see the New Assignment dialog box (refer to Figure 35.1) in which you name the assignment, enter who the text is assigned to and what color icon is associated with the assignment, establish a default location for all InCopy stories associated with that assignment, choose whether to make the files compatible with InCopy CS4 or InCopy CS3, and determine which layout frames (and thus stories) are available to the InCopy user working on the assignment.

The ability to choose whether to make InCopy assignments compatible with the current or previous version is new to InDesign CS4. Note that the various InCopy filename extensions differ based on the file version. In InCopy CS4, documents have the filename extension .icml, whereas in CS3 they have .incd. Assignments' filename extensions are .icma (CS4) and .inca (CS3), and packages' extensions are .icap (CS4) and .incp (CS3).

The four options related to layout frames are important to understand. The three radio buttons in the Include section do the following:

- **Placeholder Frames:** The InCopy user sees just the layout "hole" containing the assigned stories' text; this provides the least visual context but keeps the file small.

- **Assigned Spreads:** The InCopy user sees all spreads on which the story in the assignment exists. Other spreads are excluded, helping keep the file size manageable. All objects on those spreads, except for those containing stories in the assignment, are locked so that the InCopy user cannot modify them. (This applies to text frames, not just graphics, lines, and so forth.)

- **All Spreads:** The InCopy user sees the entire layout, providing the maximum content and the largest file size. But all objects other than those text frames containing stories in the assignment are locked.

There's a fourth option, the Linked Image Files When Packaging check box. When selected, this option provides links to the source images, for maximum display quality. (The InCopy user will have to have access to those files, such as by using the same server or working in a Version Cue environment.) If this option is not selected, the InCopy user gets only a low-resolution preview; typically, you deselect this option when the InCopy user will not have access to the graphics files and so having a low-resolution preview is better than having no preview at all.

When you create an assignment, InDesign creates an assignment file (with filename extension of .inca) that contains all the relationships of the stories to the layout and to each other.

You can modify an assignment's settings by choosing Assignment Options from the flyout menu. The Assignment Options dialog box is identical to the New Assignments dialog box.

In addition to setting the default location for an assignment, you can also change an assignment file's location by selecting the assignment and choosing Change Assignment Location in the flyout menu. In the Select the New Location dialog box, choose a new folder and/or drive for the file and then click Save. This is useful when working in a networked environment so that you can place the assignment file in the appropriate server folder for the current workflow stage.

To quickly see where an assignment file is, select it in the Assignments panel and choose Reveal in Finder (Mac) or Reveal in Explorer (Windows) from the flyout menu to open the folder on your computer. Or choose Reveal in Bridge to open the Bridge program and have it open the folder for you.

FIGURE 35.1

The New Assignment dialog box (left) and the Assignments panel and flyout menu (right)

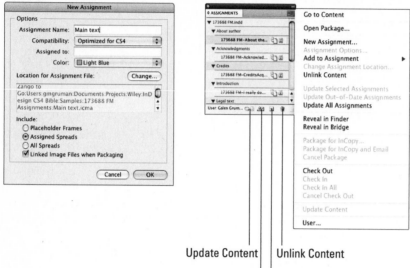

Update Content   Unlink Content

Check In/Out Selection New Assignment

Adding stories to assignments

An assignment by itself is an empty shell. It is useful only when it contains stories. To add a story to an assignment, select it (its frame or any of its text) and then choose Add to Assignment from the Assignments panel's flyout menu. (If you want to create a new assignment at the same time, just choose Add to Assignment ⇨ New from the flyout menu.) You can also add a story by selecting anywhere in its text frame and choosing Edit ⇨ InCopy ⇨ Add Selection. Figure 35.1 shows the Assignments panel with some stories in it.

 You can just add a story to an assignment by dragging its frame into the Assignments panel using any of the selection tools.

To change a story's assignment, just move the story from its current location in the Assignments panel list into the assignment in the list you want it to be part of. Or select the story in the Assignments panel and then choose Add to Assignment from the flyout menu, which moves it to the newly chosen assignment.

A story can have multiple assignments, to help you organize access to the constituent files based on whatever criteria you have. For example, you might create an assignment called Headlines and place the text of all headline-containing frames into that assignment to make them available as a group for use by a headline writer.

Exporting InCopy story files

The other way to add stories to an assignment is to export the stories from InDesign to separate InCopy story files. (InCopy story files have a filename extension of .icml.)

To export stories, choose Edit ⇨ InCopy ⇨ Export. A dialog box appears that lets you choose what to export: the selection, layer, all stories, all graphics, or all graphics and stories. (A story is all text in a text frame or path and any frames and/or paths linked to it.) After navigating to the folder where you want to store the InCopy file, click Export and then click OK. (If you have not provided a username already, you must do so.)

But be careful when exporting all stories. This option likely won't act as you expect. That's because by *story*, InDesign means any text in any text frame. So, if your headlines are in separate frames and not linked to their body copy frames, the headlines will each be a separate story. Ditto for any captions or text in figures. This can create dozens of files in your project folder. So it's usually better not to choose Export All Stories and instead export each story individually that you want to be editable.

NOTE The reason that InCopy exports all these separate story files is so that multiple users can work on the same layout, but on different stories, at the same time. An assignment provides the same benefit without having so many files.

All the exported stories are automatically added to an assignment called Unassigned InCopy Content. You can, of course, then move them into other assignments, as I describe in the previous section.

Packaging assignments

Tools such as InCopy make a lot of sense when you're working in a network-connected workgroup. But what if one of the project members, such a freelance copy editor or a traveling editor, is offsite? You can collect all the relevant files for these project members and package them into one file that you can send via e-mail (or disk).

To do so, select the assignments you want to package in the Assignments panel and choose Package for InCopy from the flyout menu. (You can also choose Package for InCopy and Email, which packages the files and then launches your e-mail program.) InDesign will create the InCopy package file (with the filename extension .icap).

The recipient would choose Open Package from the flyout menu in InCopy's Assignments panel to open the file, and would then choose Package for InDesign to send you back all the files in one package.

Editing and manipulating assigned stories

When text is assigned, it is automatically checked in, making it unavailable for editing in the layout. To edit the text, you need to *check out* the story, making it available to you but to no one else. To do so, click the frame containing the story you want to edit and then choose Edit ⇨ InCopy ⇨ Check Out or press ⌘+F9 or Ctrl+F9. To ensure that your changes are saved, I recommend that you choose Edit ⇨ InCopy ⇨ Save Content periodically as you work.

 A quick way to check out a story is to begin editing its text. InDesign will ask whether you want to check out the story. Click Yes, and the story is checked out to you.

When you're done, choose either Edit ⇨ InCopy ⇨ Check In or press Shift+⌘+F9 or Ctrl+Shift+F9, or choose Edit ⇨ InCopy ⇨ Check In All or press Option+Shift+⌘+F9 or Ctrl+Alt+Shift+F9 to return the stories so that others can use them. (Or choose Edit ⇨ InCopy ⇨ Cancel Check Out to undo all your changes and leave the story unchanged.)

You can keep doing design work on the frames associated to an assignment — such as resizing frames, adding graphics, and even changing the text's color — regardless of whether a story's text is checked in or out.

When you are working on a story, InDesign displays an icon indicating its status at the top of its text frame, as well as in the Assignments panel. These icons are shown here in the margin.

 ■ Checked Out: You have selected this story and thus can edit it; no one else can edit it as long as it retains this status.

 ■ Available: No one is editing this story, so it is available for anyone to edit.

 ■ Checked Out Elsewhere: Another user is editing this story, so no one else can edit it until it's checked back in.

 ■ Out of Date: The story has been edited but what displays in the InDesign file is not the most current version. Choose Update Out-of-Date Assignments from the Assignments panel's flyout menu to update the story.

If someone else is working on a story, you can have InDesign apply the current design changes to the layout on your screen by choosing Edit ⇨ InCopy ⇨ Update Story or pressing Control+⌘+F5 or Ctrl+F5.

Using the Stand-Alone InCopy Program

The separately purchased InCopy application looks and works very much like the InDesign Story Editor. You can also find a bevy of familiar panels — Notes, Scripts, Swatches, Tags, Tools, and the various text-editing panels — in the Window menu. You'll also find the standard Edit and Type menu options to change text attributes and do a spelling check. Plus, you find many of the standard InDesign preferences panes in the Preferences dialog box.

NEW FEATURE InCopy CS4 lets you save workspaces with your preferred panels and menus, just as InDesign CS4 does. (See Chapter 2.) That also means that not all menu options may display, depending on your current workspace's settings. To see all your menu options, be sure to choose Window ⇨ Workspace ⇨ Show Full Menus.

NOTE Just as in InDesign, you must set a username when working in InCopy so that the program can track who has made what change. The User dialog box (choose File ⇨ User) is the same as the one I cover earlier in this chapter for InDesign.

What's different? Plenty.

Story views

First, there are three panes in which to view the story:

- The Story pane (choose View ⇨ Story View or press Option+⌘+G or Ctrl+Alt+G) is the plainest view, essentially the same as the InDesign Story Editor. Here, you work on text as though you were in a word processor, with applied styles shown at left. The left side of Figure 35.2 shows this view.

- The Layout pane (choose View ⇨ Layout View or press ⌘+L or Ctrl+L) shows the story as it appears in InDesign. The middle of Figure 35.2 shows this view.

- The Galley pane (choose View ⇨ Galley View or press ⌘+G or Ctrl+G) is like the Story pane except that each line breaks as it does in InDesign, so you can see where lines end and whether the last lines in paragraphs have room for more text or whether small text deletions could easily eliminate a short last line during copyfitting.

TIP You can quickly switch views by clicking the Galley, Story, and Layout tabs in the main story window.

NOTE Note that the Story and Galley panes, as well as the Assignments panel, will show all InCopy stories associated with an InDesign file; InCopy adds them all automatically if you open any of them. In any of these panes, you can display and hide stories by clicking the triangles to the left of the story name.

Story checkout, check-in, and saving

You can edit both individual InCopy story files (`.icml` for CS4 and `.incd` for CS3) and InCopy assignment files (`.icap` for CS4 and `.inca` for CS3) in InCopy. An assignment may contain multiple stories.

When you open an InCopy Interchange file (`.incx`) — the format used to share stories with InCopy CS3 — or an InCopy assignment file in InCopy, you need to check stories out to edit them and check them in to make them available to others, as I describe doing for InDesign in the previous section. To check out stories, go to the story in any of the panes and then choose

File⇨Check Out or press ⌘+F9 or Ctrl+F9. You check the story you are working on back in by choosing File⇨Check In or pressing Shift+⌘+F9 or Ctrl+Shift+F9.

You check back in all stories by choosing File⇨Check In All or pressing Option+Shift+⌘+F9 or Ctrl+Alt+Shift+F9. The Assignments panel (choose Window⇨Assignments or press Option+⌘+F10 or Ctrl+Alt+F10) shows which stories are already checked out.

You can also choose File⇨Cancel Checkout to make a story available to others without saving any changes you made. Choose File⇨Revert Story instead to undo changes you made since the last save but keep the story checked out for your use.

FIGURE 35.2

Adobe InCopy CS4, with a layout viewed in the Story pane

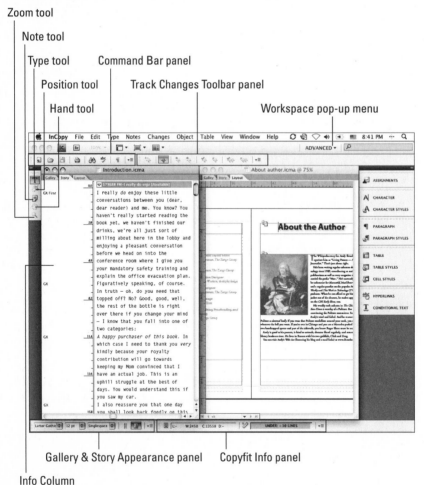

Zoom tool

Note tool

Type tool

Position tool

Hand tool

Command Bar panel

Track Changes Toolbar panel

Workspace pop-up menu

Gallery & Story Appearance panel

Copyfit Info panel

Info Column

To save a story, you have four options in the File menu:

- Choose Save Content or press ⌘+S or Ctrl+S to save the current story.

- Choose Save Content As or press Shift+⌘+S or Ctrl+Shift+S to save the current story with a new name or in a new location. You have to import such a story into the InDesign layout.

- Choose Save Content Copy or press Option+⌘+S or Ctrl+Alt+S to save a copy of the current story, such as for archiving story versions.

- Choose Save All Content or press Option+Shift+⌘+S or Ctrl+Alt+Shift+S to save all stories. This option helps ensure that all changes are made to the InDesign document, no matter what stories the changes occurred in.

Revisions tracking

InCopy can track who made what changes to InDesign files — including changes made by the designer in the InDesign layout itself, not just changes made by InCopy users. To turn on such revisions tracking, choose Changes ➪ Track Changes in Current Story or press ⌘+Y or Ctrl+Y. If multiple stories are open (such as when you are working with an InCopy assignment), you can choose Changes ➪ Enable Tracking in All Stories.

NOTE InCopy can also show you revisions from your original Microsoft Word file (if you used its changes-tracking feature) — but only if you selected the Track Changes option in the Import Options dialog box when you first placed the text file, as explained in Chapter 13.

NEW FEATURE InCopy CS4 now can display tracked changes in tables.

When reviewing changes, you can move from change to change by choosing Changes ➪ Next Change or pressing ⌘+↓ or Ctrl+↓. You can move backward by choosing Changes ➪ Previous Change or by pressing ⌘+↑ or Ctrl+↑. You can accept individual changes by choosing Changes ➪ Accept Change or pressing Shift+⌘+O or Ctrl+Shift+O, and you can accept all changes by choosing Changes ➪ Accept All Changes or pressing Option+Shift+⌘+O or Ctrl+Alt+Shift+O.

Likewise, you can reject changes individually by choosing Changes ➪ Reject Change or pressing Shift+⌘+; (semicolon) or Ctrl+Shift+; (semicolon). Or you can reject changes globally by choosing Changes ➪ Reject All Changes or pressing Option+Shift+⌘+; (semicolon) or Ctrl+Alt+Shift+; (semicolon).

You can also use the Track Changes Toolbar panel to move among revisions and accept or reject changes. The iconic panel offers the following buttons from left to right: Track Changes in Current Story, Show/Hide Changes, Previous Change, Next Change, Accept Change, Reject Change, Accept All Changes, and Reject All Changes.

When reviewing changes, you can get information on who made the change and when by having the Change Info panel open (choose Window ➪ Change Info or press Shift+⌘+F3 or Ctrl+Shift+F3).

For text added by InCopy users, InCopy highlights the text in the Story and Galley views using each editor's color (specified via File ⇨ User). This highlighting is easier than using the Change Info panel because it doesn't require you to highlight the text to see who made the change. But note that you must use the Change Info panel to see who deleted text; such text is not color-coded based on user in the Story and Galley views. And you must also use it to see information on who added text for revisions imported from Word; these are not color-coded for easy identification in the Story and Galley views.

 You can hide changes as you make them by choosing View ⇨ Hide Changes or pressing ⌘+7 or Ctrl+7. To review changes, you need to make changes visible.

Special features

The editing and formatting features are almost the same as in InDesign, so this chapter does not cover them. Likewise, the notes features are the same as those I describe in Chapter 15. But there are some specific InCopy features you should know about:

- You can transpose two letters by inserting the text-insertion pointer between them and choosing Edit ⇨ Transpose or pressing Option+⌘+4 or Ctrl+Alt+4.

- You can create text macros in the Text Macros panel (choose Window ⇨ Text Macros or press Shift+⌘+F10 or Ctrl+Shift+F10). You add a macro by choosing New Macro from its flyout menu or by pressing Option+⌘+F8 or Ctrl+Alt+F8.

- You can look up a word in an electronic thesaurus to find better alternatives. Choose Window ⇨ Thesaurus or press Option+⌘+F7 or Ctrl+Alt+F7 to open the panel. If a word is selected, click the Load Word iconic button (the eyedropper icon) from the bottom of the panel to add it. Click the Lookup Word iconic button (the magnifying-glass icon) to look up alternatives. If you want one of the alternatives, select it and then click the Change Word iconic button (the dual-curved-arrows icon).

- The Command Bar panel (choose Window ⇨ Command Bar or press Shift+⌘+F2 or Ctrl+Shift+F2) provides iconic button access for, from left to right, New Document, Open Document, Save, Print, Find, Check Spelling, and Show/Hide Hidden Characters.

- The Galley & Story Appearance panel likewise provides Font, Size, and Text Preview Spacing pop-up menus to change the Story and Galley panes' text display, plus iconic buttons to Show/Hide Line Numbers and Show/Hide Paragraph Styles. You can also change these settings, plus the text cursor display, through the Galley & Story Display pane in the Preferences dialog box (choose InCopy ⇨ Preferences or press ⌘+K on the Mac, or choose Edit ⇨ Preferences or press ⌘+K in Windows). The pane is identical to the Story Editor preferences pane covered in Chapter 15. The show/hide options in the Galley & Story Appearance pane are also available in the View menu.

- The Copyfit Info panel shows how many lines a story is over what fits in its text frames and/or paths, using the bar at its far right. As you delete text, the progress bar gets smaller and smaller until there is no runover. The panel also tracks the number of lines, words, characters, and column depth. The Update Copyfit Progress Info iconic button (the ruler icon) checks the current InDesign layout to see whether changes to the layout have solved or created copyfitting problems, in which text overflows its text frames. The panel also has the Update Story Info iconic button (the downward arrow) at the far left that updates the Change Info panel (choose File ⇨ Change Info or press Shift+⌘+F3 or Ctrl+Shift+F3) with the name of the current reviser.

These last three panels, as well as the Track Changes Toolbar panel, are shown in Figure 35.2.

CROSS-REF The Quick Apply panel, which Chapter 2 covers, provides quick access via the keyboard to styles and other formatting controls. Given that InCopy users tend to do a lot of work via the keyboard, this panel can be a very handy tool for fast formatting.

Summary

InDesign comes out of the box with the tools needed to prepare stories for editing in a workgroup environment. The Assignments panel contains most of the tools you'll use to make stories available to others.

The separately purchased InCopy lets copy editors and other people who need access just to the layout's text revise that text (such as for copyfitting and headline writing) without needing the full InDesign program. By having such users work on text via InCopy, designers can also ensure that the layouts themselves are unchanged by nondesigners.

Part X

Extending InDesign

Chapter 36

Using Plug-Ins

From the very get-go, the InDesign team engineered the software to be extensible — meaning you can extend its capabilities by adding more software. To do this, you use plug-ins, which are small software modules often developed by third parties. If you're a Photoshop user, you might be familiar with plug-ins such as Alien Skin's Eye Candy; or if you're a QuarkXPress user, you're probably familiar with the concept of add-on software through XTensions. Even if you're new to publishing, you may have purchased add-on software for your operating system, such as a custom screen saver or virus-protection software.

Extensible programs solve the one-size-fits-all nature of most software, letting you customize your tools to your workflow. If InDesign doesn't meet a need of yours — such as indexing, table editing, or imposition — you can look for a plug-in that does.

IN THIS CHAPTER

Using the default plug-ins

Purchasing special-purpose plug-ins

How plug-ins work within InDesign

Managing plug-ins

Using the Default Plug-Ins

Many core features in InDesign are actually implemented through plug-ins. When you launch the application, you may notice the words *Caching plug-ins* on the InDesign startup screen; this is when the plug-ins load. Structuring the software this way lets Adobe update or modify a finite area of the software and then distribute a new plug-in, instead of updating and distributing the entire application. Go to the Adobe Web site (www.adobe.com) periodically to look for both fixes and new plug-ins. There's also a directory of plug-ins at this book's companion Web site (www.InDesignCentral.com).

The default plug-ins are stored in a folder called `Plug-Ins` inside your `InDesign` application folder. If you open the `Plug-Ins` folder, you'll notice the plug-ins have been consolidated into special-purpose folders such as `Filters` and `Text`. You should leave the default plug-ins alone, for the most part.

Purchasing Special-Purpose Plug-Ins

With the backing of a software and publishing giant like Adobe, InDesign has enticed a variety of proven developers to create special-purpose plug-ins.

Many plug-in developers provide a free evaluation copy so that you can try before you buy. This is important because you can figure out whether the plug-in really solves your problem, whether everyone in your workgroup needs it, and whether your service bureau needs it as well.

 To quickly find available InDesign plug-ins, go to the Plug-Ins page of this book's companion Web site (`www.InDesignCentral.com`).

Understanding How Plug-Ins Work within InDesign

To use a new plug-in, the first thing you need to do is install it. Many plug-ins include their own installers that search out your copy of InDesign and plant themselves in the `Plug-Ins` folder. If a plug-in doesn't include an installer or installation instructions, try clicking and dragging it into the `Plug-Ins` folder. When a plug-in is in the correct location, you need to restart InDesign so that the plug-in is recognized and its code is loaded. You cannot install a new plug-in while InDesign is running; you should always quit the application before changing anything in the Plug-Ins folder and then restarting.

If a plug-in cannot load with InDesign, an alert appears while the application is starting up. Usually, loading errors result from incompatible versions of InDesign and the plug-in. Check the plug-in's `ReadMe` file or contact the developer for assistance. To remove a plug-in, simply click and drag it out of the subfolder of the `Plug-Ins` folder and store it someplace else. (You might create a folder called `Disabled Plug-Ins` in which to store plug-ins that you're not using. Just be sure it's not stored in the `Plug-Ins` folder!)

Plug-ins are designed for specific platforms (Mac or Windows) as well as for specific versions of InDesign (1, 1.5, 2, CS, CS2, CS3, or CS4), so you need to get new versions of your plug-ins if you change platforms or upgrade to a new version of InDesign.

When a plug-in is loaded with InDesign, new controls appear in the interface. You might see entire menus, menu commands, dialog boxes, panels, and tools added to the application by a plug-in. No matter the combination of interface elements, when you're using the features of a plug-in, it should look and feel as though you're using InDesign. Some plug-ins meet this criterion; others do not.

For example, the History plug-in from FTP Tools adds a History panel that works like the one familiar to Photoshop users to display every change made to a document and provide an easy way to undo specific changes, while leaving the others alone. Otherwise, the plug-in leaves InDesign's interface unaffected. Other plug-ins might change menus or add their own panels, or both.

 **In some cases, plug-ins may add objects or information to documents that can be recognized only when the plug-in is loaded. If the plug-in is missing, you — or other users — may not be able to open the document, or the document may look different.**

Managing Plug-Ins

After acquiring several plug-ins, you may have trouble managing all the features in InDesign because you'll have new panels, toolbars, and menu options throughout the program. Fortunately, InDesign has a tool to let you manage your plug-ins, so you can turn them on and off as needed, as well as save sets of plug-ins so that you can turn on and off related plug-ins simultaneously.

To manage plug-ins, use the Configure Plug-ins dialog box shown in Figure 36.1. To open this dialog box, choose InDesign ⇨ Configure Plug-Ins on the Mac or choose Help ⇨ Configure Plug-Ins in Windows.

The default list of plug-ins will be very long because so many basic InDesign features are implemented through plug-ins. To help manage the display, you have six options at the bottom of the dialog box that filter what appears: Enabled, Adobe, Required, Disabled, Third Party, and Optional. Deselecting any of these options does not disable the plug-ins themselves; it simply removes them from the dialog box's list.

To manage plug-ins, you want to select Third Party to see non-Adobe plug-ins and Optional to see plug-ins that can be turned off safely. Be sure that Enabled is also selected to see what is turned on or that Disabled is selected to see what plug-ins have been previously turned off. If neither Enabled nor Disabled is selected, you don't see any plug-ins in the list — you have to use these options in combination with each other. For example, selecting Enabled, Adobe, and Required shows only the required Adobe plug-ins that are turned on.

 **Required plug-ins have a lock icon to their left, whereas other plug-ins have a check mark to their left if turned on and nothing if turned off.**

To turn plug-ins on and off, simply click to the left of the plug-in name. If selected, a plug-in is turned on when you relaunch InDesign. If it's not selected, it is turned off when you relaunch. If you're not sure what a plug-in does, you can get more information (the name of the developer, the version, and a brief description) by clicking the plug-in name and then clicking Show Info.

When you first disable plug-ins, InDesign forces you to create a new *set* of plug-ins — sets are essentially a list of which plug-ins should be turned on and which should be turned off. You can copy, edit the name of, and delete sets using the Duplicate, Rename, and Delete buttons. You choose a set of plug-ins to put in use by using the Set pop-up menu at the top of the dialog box. You can also import and export plug-in sets by clicking Import and Export. Click OK when you're done or Cancel to leave the plug-ins as they were when you first opened the Configure Plug-ins dialog box.

FIGURE 36.1

The Configure Plug-ins dialog box

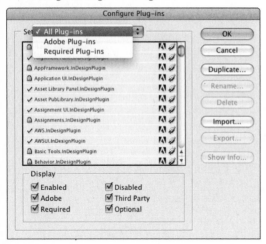

You may want to turn specific plug-ins on and off as needed rather than have them in the way all the time. A good way to do this is to create plug-in sets that you can then switch among. I recommend you create a set of plug-ins called Standard Plugs (at first, it would be the same as the All Plug-ins set, including everything that comes with InDesign out of the box). Then, before you add any new plug-ins, first create a new set named after the new plug-in and activate it in the Set menu. Then quit InDesign and install the new plug-ins. You can decide whether to switch between this plug-in set and Standard plug-ins using the Set pop-up menu or to save this new set as Standard Plug-ins, making the new plug-in part of your standard plug-in set.

 You must quit and relaunch InDesign for any changes to plug-ins to take effect.

Summary

Plug-ins are software modules that serve two purposes in InDesign: incorporating core features into the application and adding special functions. Plug-ins are stored in the Plug-Ins folder within the InDesign application folder. Many established developers of QuarkXPress XTensions and Photoshop plug-ins have developed InDesign plug-ins to provide additional features such as mathematical typesetting and page imposition. When purchasing and using plug-ins, consider whether other users of your workgroup and your service bureau need them as well. Finally, you can manage which plug-ins are in use through the Configure Plug-ins dialog box.

Chapter 37

Using Scripts

Scripting automates many features in InDesign — it's essentially a way to program InDesign to do specific actions. Because InDesign uses standard script languages, you can also run scripts that work with multiple programs in concert, including InDesign. (All the applications must support the same scripting language, of course.) For example, you might use scripts to automate database publishing, such as to run a database search, export data to a text file, import that file into InDesign, and then apply the appropriate formatting.

InDesign supports three scripting languages:

- JavaScript on both Mac and Windows
- AppleScript on the Mac only
- Visual Basic for Applications (VBA), on Windows only

Because only JavaScript is supported by both platforms, I recommend you use it wherever possible so that your scripts can work in cross-platform environments. InDesign doesn't force you to choose just one scripting language, so you could keep using old AppleScript or VBA scripts created for previous versions of InDesign, as well as new scripts written in JavaScript.

As you become comfortable with scriptwriting, you're also likely to discover that virtually everything you do with InDesign is a repetitive task. The more you can free yourself of this kind of work by using scripts, the more time you have to be creative. The possibilities are endless. But before you get too excited, remember that scripting is programming, so most layout artists stay clear of it, using scripts only if they have a programmer available to write them.

Using Scripts

Accessing scripts is easy; they show up in the Scripts panel (choose Window➪Automation➪ Scripts or press Option+⌘+F11 or Ctrl+Alt+F11) if you've placed scripts in the `Scripts` folder inside the folder that contains the InDesign application, as shown in Figure 37.1. Scripts don't have to be in the `Scripts` folder — they can be anywhere on your computer — but to use them outside this folder means you have to double-click them from your desktop rather than have access from within InDesign.

FIGURE 37.1

The Scripts panel in InDesign and its flyout menu

Script tips

When writing scripts, you can associate a script to a specific InDesign menu action so that when a user chooses that menu item, a script runs automatically (technically, by assigning a script to a MenuAction command's Prenotify or Postnotify property when writing the script's code). In InDesign, be sure that Enable Attached Scripts is also enabled in the Scripts panel's flyout menu.

When running scripts, keep the following tips in mind:

■ You can undo all of a script's action by using the InDesign Undo command (choose Edit➪Undo or press ⌘+Z or Ctrl+Z) by ensuring that Undo Affects Entire Script is enabled in the Scripts panel's flyout menu. Otherwise, the undo command reverses just the last action within the script, requiring you to undo several times to "roll back" the complete script action.

■ By enabling the Enable Redraw flyout menu option in the Scripts panel, you can force InDesign to redraw the display while a script is running. This ensures that any changes to the document are immediately visible.

Script locations

Whether you create your own scripts or get them from vendors or other users, you need to save them so that InDesign knows they exist. You have a choice of two locations:

- The `Scripts` folder inside the InDesign application folder (usually `Applications:Adobe InDesign CS4:Scripts` in Mac OS X 10.4 (Tiger) and 10.5 (Leopard), and `Program Files\Adobe\InDesign CS4\Scripts` in Windows XP and Vista). This makes the script available to all users of your computer. If you want the script to start when InDesign launches, place it in the `Startup Scripts` subfolder.

- The `Script Panel` folder. This makes the script available only that specific user (note that it will appear in a folder called `User` in your Scripts panel). The path varies based on your operating system:

  - On the Mac, the path is `Users:user name:Library:Preferences:Adobe InDesign:Version 6.0:Scripts:Script Panel`.

  - In Windows XP, the path is `Documents and Settings\user name\Application Data\Adobe\InDesign\Version 6.0\Scripts\Script Panel`.

  - In Windows Vista, the path is `Users\user name\AppData\Roaming\Adobe\InDesign\Version 6.0\Scripts\Script Panel`.

The script shows up in the Scripts panel. If it doesn't show up immediately, quit and reopen InDesign.

TIP To use scripts developed for InDesign CS3, create a new folder called `Version 5.0 Scripts` inside the Scripts or Script Panel folder and move your old scripts there. They then work in InDesign CS4.

Scripting principles

No matter what scripting language you use, there are several basic principles to observe. These fall into four basic categories:

- **Grammar:** All languages — including programming languages such as Pascal and C++, as well as scripting languages — include grammatical components that are used in standardized sequences. In English, we combine nouns, verbs, adjectives, adverbs, and so on to create sentences. Everybody knows the meaning of "The weather is especially nice today," because it uses common words in a sequence that makes sense. The sentence "Nice is the especially today weather," has the right components but it's arranged in the wrong sequence, so the meaning is lost.

- **Statements and syntax rules:** In JavaScript, AppleScript, and VBA, verbs, nouns, adjectives, and prepositions are combined to create statements; statements are combined to form scripts. Verbs are also called *commands* and *methods*; nouns are called *objects*; and adjectives are called *properties*. Syntax rules specify how statements and scripts must be constructed so that a computer can understand them.

- **Object hierarchy:** All three scripting languages use a structural element called an *object hierarchy*. It's a fancy term for a simple concept. An object hierarchy works like a set of boxes within boxes. A large box contains a smaller box, which contains a smaller box, which contains a smaller box, and so on, until you reach the smallest box, which contains nothing and is the final level in the hierarchy of boxes.

- **InDesign hierarchy:** InDesign contains its own hierarchy, which lends itself nicely to scripting. A document contains pages, pages contain frames, and frames contain text and pictures. You can create scripts that perform actions at any of these levels. In other words, with scripts you can create documents, add pages, add items to pages, and modify the contents of frames, right down to a particular character in a text frame. You can think of this hierarchy in InDesign as a chain of command. You can't talk directly to an item that's at the bottom of the chain. Rather, you must first address the top level, and then the next, and so on, until you've reached the item at the bottom of the chain. This is analogous to the way you use InDesign: You create new documents, add pages, place text and graphics on the pages, and, finally, modify the contents of the frames containing those items.

If you're thinking about dabbling with any of the scripting languages supported by InDesign, the following words of both caution and encouragement are in order. First the encouragement: You don't necessarily need programming experience, scripting experience, or a pocket protector to begin creating scripts. A bit of curiosity and a touch of patience will suffice. Now the caution: Scripting is essentially a euphemism for programming (that is, figuring out the right commands and then typing them for the application to execute). Writing scripts isn't a matter of choosing commands from menus, and clicking and dragging them, or entering values into fields; nor is it like writing a limerick. If you're starting from scratch, know in advance that you have to learn some new skills.

Learning to create scripts is like learning to swim: You can read books, documentation, and articles until your head spins, but eventually you have to get a little wet. The best way to learn about scripting is to write a script. So put on your swimsuit and dive in.

Be forewarned: There's something almost narcotic about creating scripts, and it's not uncommon for novice scriptwriters to get hooked. Don't be surprised if what starts out to be a 15-minute look-see turns into a multihour, late-night programming episode.

> **NOTE**   Because scripting languages differ, you can't always duplicate the functionality of a specific script in one language into a script written in a different language.

> **NOTE**   Adobe has a nearly 2,000-page scripting guide available as a PDF file. It comes with your InDesign or Creative Suite software, residing on the installation CD. You can find additional resources at www.adobe.com.

Exploring JavaScript

JavaScript is a scripting language developed by Netscape Communications, based on Sun Microsystems' Java language that was meant to let Web browsers manage resources on far-flung servers by running scripts to control the servers from a desktop. JavaScript soon became a popular scripting language because, as does Java, it runs on so many types of computers, including Windows, Macintosh, and Unix. But because it is based largely on the object-oriented approach taken by professional computer languages such as C and C++, it can be difficult for nonprogrammers to use.

There are lots of JavaScript editor programs available. Most of these are developed by individuals and small firms, so the list is always changing. I recommend you use the Google search engine (www.google.com) and search for *JavaScript editor* to find the most current programs. A great script-editing program for Mac users is Bare Bones Software's venerable BBEdit; you can get more information at www.barebones.com.

Learning the language

JavaScript is a very complex language based on object-oriented programming, which abstracts items and attributes as objects that are then grouped, changed, or otherwise manipulated. This means that JavaScript is less "Englishlike" than other scripting languages because it requires you to spend a fair amount of time setting up the objects before you can manipulate them.

```
myObject.strokeTint = newValue;
```

This example shows that there is a current object named strokeTint that is being set to a new value; the actual value for newValue is set earlier in the script.

What you need to write and run scripts

You need a program that can display, edit, and test your JavaScript; there is no bundled JavaScript editor in Windows or Mac OS X. Such editors typically format the JavaScript code for you, indenting it automatically, graying out comments, and highlighting certain keywords.

You can use a word processor or text editor to write and edit scripts, but such programs can't check the syntax or automatically format the script text to help show nested loops, conditional branches, and so forth. Also, you can usually use an HTML editor such as Adobe Dreamweaver in which to edit JavaScripts, though they also typically don't provide any debugging tools to help you track and fix coding (syntax) errors. (Figure 37.2 shows a JavaScript script being edited in Dreamweaver.) In this case, you need to open the error window in your browser as you test the code and see if it identifies the error location to help you find it in your HTML editor.

FIGURE 37.2

A JavaScript program viewed in Adobe Dreamweaver

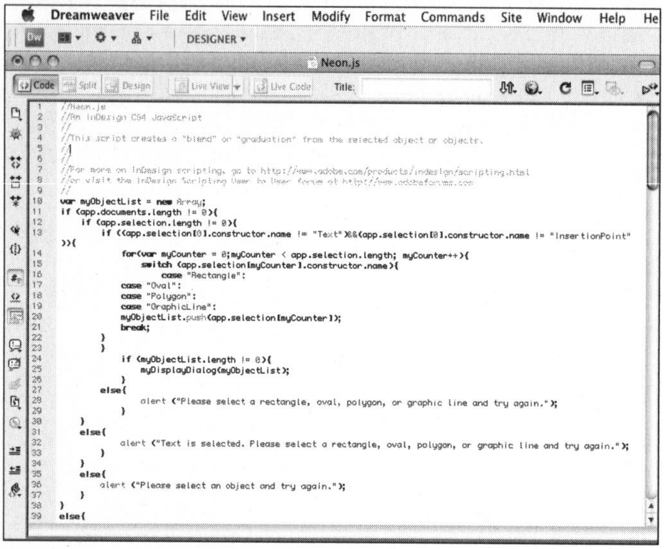

Getting More Information on JavaScript

Before you venture too far into scripting, you should review the JavaScript-related information provided with InDesign:

- **JavaScript documentation and tools:** Sun places the very technical JavaScript documentation on its Web site at http://java.sun.com/javascript/index.jsp

- **InDesign scripting documentation:** The InDesign installation CD contains a 2,000-plus-page PDF file that explains scripting for InDesign. This document, although a bit on the technical side, is a valuable resource. It includes an overview of JavaScript scripting and the object model, as well as a list of InDesign-specific scripting terms and scripting examples.

If you want still more information about JavaScript, several books are available, including *Beginning JavaScript,* 2nd Edition, by Paul Wilton and *JavaScript Bible,* 6th Edition, by Danny Goodman and Michael Morrison (both from Wiley Publishing).

Running your script

The easiest way to run a script is to double-click it in the Scripts panel within InDesign. But you also can simply double-click the script file; note that InDesign may need to be open. Also, while you're developing the script, you can run the script directly from the application in which you created it — again, InDesign may need to be open. If you've done everything correctly, you see InDesign become the active program, and then the actions you put in your script take place. Voilà and congratulations! You can now call yourself a scripter without blushing. That's all there is to creating and running a script.

Saving your script

When you're finished writing and testing a script, choose Save from the script editor's File menu. Name your script and choose its storage location. Move or copy the saved script to one of the two locations I describe earlier in this chapter.

Exploring AppleScript

AppleScript is a scripting language developed by Apple and initially released with System 7.5 that can be used to control Macs, networks, and scriptable applications, including InDesign. The AppleScript language was designed to be as close to normal English as possible so that average Mac users — specifically, those who aren't familiar with programming languages — can understand and use it.

 **InDesign can run text-only AppleScripts in addition to compiled (binary) ones.**

Learning the language

Many of the actions specified in AppleScripts read like sentences you might use in everyday conversation, such as:

```
set color of myFrame to "Black"
```

or

```
set applied font of myCharacterStyle to "Times"
```

Getting More Information on AppleScript

Before you venture too far into scripting, you should review the AppleScript-related information provided with the Mac OS and with InDesign:

- **Mac scripting documentation and tools:** Apple places the AppleScript documentation on its Web site at `www.apple.com/applescript`. In your hard drive's `Applications` folder, you should have a folder called `AppleScript` that contains the Script Editor program, along with a folder of example scripts and the AppleScript Script Menu that adds the Script menu to the Finder. Apple also offers a professional AppleScript editor called AppleScript Studio for download at its developer Web site, `www.apple.com/macosx/features/xcode/`. Apple makes AppleScript Studio part of its Xcode scripting tool, so you need to get Xcode to get AppleScript Studio.

- **InDesign scripting documentation:** The InDesign CD contains a 2,000-plus-page PDF file that explains scripting, including AppleScript programming, for InDesign. This document, although a bit on the technical side, is a valuable resource. It includes an overview of Apple events scripting and the object model, as well as a list of InDesign-specific scripting terms and scripting examples.

If you want still more information about AppleScript, several books are available, including *AppleScript For Dummies,* 2nd Edition, by Tom Trinko, and *Beginning AppleScript,* by Stephen G. Kochan (both from Wiley Publishing).

What you need to write and run scripts

The Script Editor provided with the Mac OS lets you write scripts. You find the Script Editor inside the `AppleScript` folder inside your `Applications` folder (at the root level of your hard drive). An uncompiled script is essentially a text file, so you can actually write scripts with any word processor. The Script Editor, however, was created for writing AppleScripts and includes several handy features for scriptwriters.

> **TIP** To see what AppleScript commands that InDesign supports, you can view the InDesign object model — the supported commands — within the Script Editor; just choose File ⇨ Open Dictionary and then scroll to the InDesign application icon and click Open.

Checking for syntax errors

The next step is to determine whether the statements are correctly constructed. Click the Check Syntax button. If the Script Editor encounters a syntax error, it alerts you and highlights the cause of the error. If the script's syntax is correct, all statements except the first and last are indented and a number of words are displayed in bold, as illustrated in Figure 37.3. Your script has been compiled and is ready to test.

Running your script

To run a script from InDesign, double-click the script in the Scripts panel. Alternatively, double-click the script file itself (InDesign may need to be open). When developing the script, click the Run button in the Script Editor; InDesign becomes the active program, and your script is running.

FIGURE 37.3

This Script Editor window contains sample AppleScript text. When you check the syntax of a script, the Script Editor applies formatting and indents.

If you have trouble getting a script to run, double-check the name that InDesign uses for itself. It might use InDesign® CS4 or simply InDesign® (yes, the name may include the registered trademark symbol). If you run a script from AppleScript (rather than just double-clicking it) and AppleScript can't find InDesign, it gives you a dialog box with which you find the InDesign program. When you've found and selected the InDesign application, AppleScript will find out what InDesign's filename is and use that in your script.

Saving your script

When you're finished writing and testing a script, choose Save from the Script Editor's File menu. Name your script, choose its storage location, and choose Compiled Script from the Format pop-up menu. Move or copy the saved script to one of the two locations I describe earlier in this chapter.

If you save the script in Application format and want to edit your script later, you must open it by dragging and dropping it on the Script Editor application. This is because Application-format scripts are designed to immediately run when double-clicked. You would choose the Application format when creating scripts for use by others because chances are you don't want them to open the script in Script Editor but instead simply want them to use the script by double-clicking it like any other application. (It doesn't matter whether the script is in Application format if you run it from InDesign's Scripts panel.)

Locating more AppleScript tools

A few software utilities are also available for AppleScripters. The most widely used is Script Debugger, from Late Night Software ($199, www.latenightsw.com); it's an interface development tool that quickly creates AppleScript-based applications that have the standard Mac look and feel. Apple also offers its AppleScript Studio as a free download to developers who register at the Apple site (www.apple.com/macosx/features/xcode); this is more capable than the basic Script Editor that comes with Mac OS X. AppleScript Studio is part of Apple's Xcode scripting tool, so you need to get Xcode to get AppleScript Studio.

Exploring VBA

VBA, and its subset version VBScript, is Microsoft's technology for writing your own programs, both those that run in other programs (scripts) and those that run by themselves (custom applications). InDesign works with both VBA and VBScript. The Visual Basic language that underlies both VBA and VBScript is not meant for everyday computer users; knowledge of programming is very useful in taking advantage of this technology. Although based on the Basic language developed in the 1970s to help new users write their own programs, it has evolved a lot since then and is no longer so simple.

Learning the language

Many of the actions specified in VBA have some degree of English, such as:

```
set myTextFrame = InDesign.Documents.Item(1).Spreads.Item(1).
    TextFrames.Add
```

or

```
mySelection.RotationAngle = 30
```

But as you can see, that degree of English is slight. The first code segment, for example, means to add a text frame to the first spread in the first document. The second means to rotate the selected object by 30 degrees.

Getting More Information on VBA

Before you venture too far into scripting, you should review the VBA-related information provided by Microsoft and with InDesign:

- **Microsoft scripting documentation and tools:** Microsoft has a lot of information on VBA, VBScript, and Visual Basic on its Web site. Unfortunately, it's not well organized and thus is hard to find and understand. There's no tutorial that simply explains how a new scripter needs to get started. However, you can search on the Microsoft site for VBA, VBScript, and Visual Basic to get links to documents that may prove useful.

- **InDesign scripting documentation:** The InDesign CD contains a 2,000-plus-page PDF file that explains scripting in InDesign, including VBA programming. This document, although definitely on the technical side, is a valuable resource. It includes an overview of VBA scripting and the object model, as well as a list of InDesign-specific scripting terms and scripting examples.

If you want still more information about VBA and its two "sister" technologies, several books are available, including *VBScript Programmer's Reference,* 2nd Edition, by Adrian Kingsley-Hughes, Kathie Kingsley-Hughes, and Daniel Read; *VBA For Dummies,* 5th Edition, by John Paul Mueller; and *Mastering Microsoft VBA,* 2nd Edition, by Guy Hart-Davis (all from Wiley Publishing).

What you need to write and run scripts

To use InDesign scripting in Windows, you need Microsoft Visual Basic or an application that contains VBA; these include Microsoft Office, Microsoft Visio, and AutoCAD. In Microsoft Office, you can run the Microsoft Script Editor by choosing Tools ➪ Macro ➪ Microsoft Script Editor, which lets you create scripts, edit them, test your code, and fix errors. Figure 37.4 shows the editor with a sample script. (Note that the script editor's dialog box has the self-important name Microsoft Development Environment rather than Microsoft Script Editor.)

You can also write scripts in VBScript, a VBA subset, in a text editor such as WordPad. You need Microsoft's free Windows Scripting Host (`WSCRIPT.EXE`), which is usually installed with Windows, and you can download it from Microsoft's Web site.

There's a third choice for your scriptwriting: You can also use the full Microsoft Visual Basic product from Microsoft.

NOTE To use InDesign scripting in Windows, your user profile must have Administrator privileges.

TIP To see what Visual Basic commands InDesign supports, you can view the InDesign object model — the supported commands — within Microsoft's Visual Basic product; just choose Project ➪ References and then select Adobe InDesign CS4 Type Library in the References dialog box and click OK.

Running your script

There are a few ways to run a VBScript. You can double-click the script in the Scripts panel within InDesign or double-click the script file itself from a folder. When developing scripts, you can run the script directly from the application in which you created a VBA or Visual Basic script, such as the Microsoft Script Editor. (VBScripts can be run from the Scripting Host application.) In all these cases, InDesign becomes the active program, and your script is running.

The Microsoft Development Environment window contains sample VBA text. When you work on a script, the Microsoft Development Environment applies indents automatically.

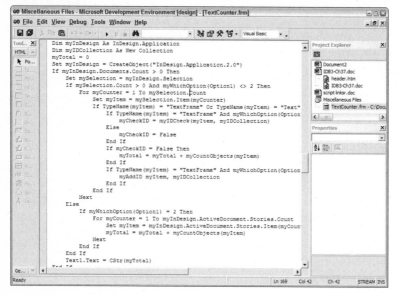

Saving your script

When you're finished writing and testing a script, choose Save from the script editor's File menu. Name your script and choose its storage location. Move or copy the saved script to one of the two locations I describe earlier in this chapter.

Creating and Running Scripts

At this point, I'm assuming that the appropriate scripting software is installed on your computer. If this is the case, you're ready to begin. For your first trick, you're going to make InDesign roll over — sort of. Actually, you're going to rotate an EPS graphic. First, you'll prepare InDesign for its role.

Launch the program and then create a new document (do not select Automatic Text Frame). In the middle of the first page, place an EPS graphic. Make sure that it remains active after you place it.

Writing simple scripts

The following three scripts, taken from Adobe's InDesign script examples, do the same thing in JavaScript, AppleScript, and VBA — they rotate an EPS graphic and its frame.

CROSS-REF All the scripts in this chapter are available for download at www.InDesignCentral. com. Just cut and paste them from the text files into the appropriate scripting editor. Adobe's user forums are also a good place to go for scripting help.

Type the lines that follow this paragraph exactly as they're written for the scripting language you've chosen. Type a return character at the end of each line. Note also the use of straight quotation marks instead of curly typesetter's quotes (the script editor does this for you). Be very careful when you type the text: Typos are script killers.

NOTE In the code samples below, the ¬ symbol indicates where a line of code is broken to fit the page width; in the actual script, there would be no ¬ character, and the line that follows would be combined with the line that now ends in ¬.

JavaScript

```
var myLink, myEPs, myFrame;
if(app.documents.length != 0){
 if(app.activeDocument.links.length != 0){
  for(var myLinkCounter = 0; myLinkCounter < ¬
     app.activeDocument.links.length; myLinkCounter ++){
   myLink = app.activeDocument.links.item(myLinkCounter);
   if(myLink.linkType == "EPS"){
    myEPS = myLink.parent;
    myFrame = myEPS.parent;
    myFrame.rotationAngle = 30;
    }
   }
  }
 }
```

This script first searches through all the items on the page and checks whether any are EPS; if so, it sets the rotation of the item to 30. (Thanks to Adobe's InDesign scripting guru, Olav Martin Kvern, for developing the JavaScript code example.) Note the sequence of actions: First you verify that there is a nonempty document open, and then you check the content type of objects. For those objects that are of the EPS type, you activate the frame and then apply the rotation to that frame. JavaScripts require you to set your own variables (the `var` statements) that define what the object is. (Here, `myLink` is used for each object, `myEPS` is the object that contains the EPS attribute, and `myFrame` is the parent frame containing the EPS graphic.) You work with those variables to see what their attributes are and then change those attributes.

If you're in an adventurous mood, try substituting the statement myFrame.rotationAngle = 30; in the preceding script with each of the following statements:

```
myFrame.shearAngle = 30;
myFrame.verticalScale = 200;
```

If you want to get really fancy, combine all the myFrame. statements into a single script so that you can use the script to make all the changes at one time.

AppleScript

```
tell application "Adobe InDesign CS4"
 activate
 set myPageItems to {EPS, oval, rectangle, polygon}
 set mySelection to selection
 if class of item 1 of mySelection is in myPageItems
    and (count mySelection) > 0 then
  if class of item 1 of mySelection is EPS then
   set myFrame to parent of mySelection
  else
   set myFrame to item 1 of mySelection
  end if
  set rotation angle of myFrame to 30
 end if
end tell
```

> **NOTE**   Be sure that a document is open and that you have selected at least one frame of any type before starting the script. Also in the script itself, make sure to type the name of your InDesign program exactly as it appears in the Finder. Because you're free to rename your program, the name may not match the name in the first line of the script.

If you're feeling daring, try substituting the statement set rotation angle of myFrame to 30 in the preceding script with each of the following statements:

```
set shear angle of myFrame to 30
set vertical scale of myFrame to 200
```

Here again, you can get fancy by combining all the set statements into a single script so that you can use the script to make all the changes at one time.

VBA

```
Dim myInDesign As InDesign.Application
Set myInDesign = CreateObject("InDesign.Application.CS4")
Set mySelection = myInDesign.Selection
If TypeName(mySelection.Item(1)) = "EPS" Then
 mySelection.Parent.RotationAngle = 30
Else
 mySelection.RotationAngle = 30
End If
```

You might satisfy your adventurous streak by substituting the statement `mySelection.RotationAngle = 30` in the preceding script with each of the following statements:

```
set the color of the current box to "Blue"
set the shade of the current box to 50
set the width of the frame of the current box to 10
set the box shape of the current box to ovular
```

Go to town if you want: Combine all the `set` statements into a single script so that you can use the script to make all the changes simultaneously.

> **TIP** Perhaps you noticed the chain of command used in the preceding scripts. First the script addresses InDesign, then the active document (layout), and finally the active frame. If you understand this concept, you'll be scripting like a pro in no time.

Labeling items

As you can see from the examples in the previous section, scripts often refer to items by their type and location in the document. But there's another way to refer to objects that makes sure you can select an item precisely: You can label, or name, an item. You do so in the Script Label panel (choose Window➪Automation➪Script Label). The process is easy: Select the object and then type a name in the panel. That's it!

When writing scripts, you refer to the labeled object as follows. In these examples, the label is *TargetFrame*, and don't worry that the samples seem to do different things — they in fact are unrelated examples, not variations of the same command.

JavaScript

```
with(app.documents.item(0).pages.item(0)){
 myTargetFrame = textFrames.item("myTargetFrame");
}
```

AppleScript

```
select (page item 1 of page 1 of myTargetDocument whose ¬
label is "TargetFrame")
```

VBA

```
Set myAsset = myLibrary.Assets.Item("TargetFrame")
```

Writing conditional scripts

Some scripts simply automate a set of tasks in documents whose content is predictable. But more often than not, documents differ, so you need conditional statements to evaluate certain things to see whether they are true before applying a script's actions. Otherwise, you get an error message when something turns out not to be true. As a simple example, a script that does a search and replace needs to have a document open and a frame selected. If no frame is selected, the script won't know what to search, and the user will get an error message.

The same issue arises for repeated series of actions, where you want the script to do something for all occurrences. The script needs to know what to do when it can't find any more such occurrences. As an example, look at the following script, which counts all open documents. For it to work, at least one document has to be open, so the script checks first to see whether in fact any documents are open and then delivers an error message that the user can understand if none is open. The rotate-EPS-graphic script earlier also used a conditional to make sure there was an EPS graphic in the document. Notice that in all three scripting languages, you use the command if to set up such conditionals.

JavaScript

```
if (app.documents.length==0){
alert("No InDesign documents are open!");
}
```

 **NOTE**   JavaScript uses == for comparing values (as in the example above) and = for assigning values. Visual Basic and AppleScript use = for both purposes.

AppleScript

```
tell application "Adobe InDesign CS4"
 activate
 set myNumberOfDocuments to (count documents)
 if myNumberOfDocuments = 0 then
  display dialog "No InDesign publications are open!"
 end if
end tell
```

VBA

```
Dim myInDesign as InDesign.Application
 Set myInDesign = CreateObject ("InDesign.Application.CS4")
 If myInDesign.Documents.Count
  MsgBox "No InDesign publications are open!"
 End If
End Sub
```

Another form of conditional is what's called a *control loop*, in which an action occurs either for a specified number of iterations or until a condition is met. The following scripts show an example of each for each language. Note the use of comments in the scripts — a handy way to document what you're doing for later reference. In JavaScript, a single-line comment begins with //, whereas a multiline comment begins with /* and ends with */. In AppleScript, a comment begins with -- and continues until you press Enter or Return. In VBA, it begins with Rem followed by a space, and it continues until you press Enter or Return.

JavaScript

```
for (var myCounter = 0; myCounter < 20; myCounter++){
 //do something
}
while (myStop == false){
 /* do something, at some point setting myStop to true
 to leave the loop. */
}
```

AppleScript

```
repeat with counter from 1 to 20
 --do something
end repeat

set myStop to false
repeat while myStop = false
 --do something, at some point setting myStop to true to ¬
 leave the loop.
end repeat
```

VBA

```
For counter = 1 to 20
 Rem do something
Next counter

Do While myStop = false
 Rem do something, at some point setting myStop to true ¬
 to leave the loop.
loop
```

Summary

If your workflow goes beyond original designs for each client and reaches into repetitive production, scripting is for you. Scripts are ideal for automating repetitive tasks — from importing pictures to creating and formatting entire documents. You can even link InDesign to other scriptable applications.

Because InDesign supports JavaScript on the Mac and Windows, as well as AppleScript on the Mac only and VBA on Windows only, you can choose the script language you're most familiar with and/or that is compatible with your other applications. Even better, you can use more than one scripting language with InDesign (though any individual script can use only one language).

Part XI

Appendixes

Appendix A

Installing or Upgrading InDesign

Installing InDesign CS4 is surprisingly easy, but before installing or upgrading, make sure your system meets the InDesign CS4 system requirements. The key requirements are that you are running Mac OS X 10.4 (Tiger), Mac OS X 10.5 (Leopard), Windows XP (with Service Pack 2 or later), or Windows Vista. Then use the steps in this appendix to make quick work of the installation process. If you're upgrading from an earlier version, you'll actually perform a new installation. But read the section on upgrading near the end of this appendix for information about making the transition to InDesign CS4.

IN THIS APPENDIX

Understanding CS4 system requirements

Installing InDesign CS4

Upgrading from prior versions of InDesign

Reinstalling or uninstalling InDesign

Understanding InDesign CS3 System Requirements

InDesign CS4 does not require extraordinary resources. If you have a Mac or PC that runs one of the required operating systems, you can run InDesign CS4. Just be sure to have enough hard-drive space and memory to be able to work with large images, many fonts, and multiple projects, as well, so that you can have additional applications, such as Adobe Photoshop, open at the same time.

Here are the official requirements:

- For Macintosh systems, an Intel processor or a PowerPC G4, or G5 processor, running Mac OS X version 10.4.8 or later (Tiger) or 10.5 (Leopard).

- For Windows systems, an Intel Centrino (including Duo), Core (including Duo), Pentium (4 or later), or Xenon processor — or AMD K6, Athlon (any version), Opteron, Sempron, or Turion processor — running Windows XP (with Service Pack 2 or later) or Windows Vista.

- At least 1.6GB of free hard-drive space on the Mac and 1.8GB of free hard-drive space in Windows for installation (installation also requires free disk space on the startup drive, even if you install InDesign CS4 software on a different drive). (InCopy requires an additional 1GB both on the Mac and in Windows.)

- A DVD-ROM drive.

- At least 256MB of RAM in PowerPC-based Macs and in Windows XP PCs, and 512MB in Intel-based Macs and Windows Vista PCs. Realistically, you want at least 1GB in a production environment so that you can run other programs responsively at the same time.

- Sixteen-bit color depth (thousands of colors) at 1024-x-768 monitor resolution. Realistically, you want to run InDesign at 24-bit color (millions of colors) at a higher monitor resolution — InDesign's user interface barely fits in the 1024-x-768 resolution typical of a 17-inch monitor.

- For PostScript printing, Adobe PostScript Language Level 2 or Adobe PostScript 3.

- For the multimedia features, QuickTime 7.

Installing InDesign CS4

Before beginning the installation process, make sure that you have your serial number provided by Adobe and that you have an Internet connection so that you can activate the software after installation.

Running the installation program

Both the Mac OS and Windows installers for InDesign CS4 provide easy-to-follow on-screen instructions:

1. **Be sure that all other programs are closed.** InDesign typically does not install if other programs are running, even non-Adobe programs. (But it's fine to let your system utilities, such as antivirus software, continue to run.)

2. **Insert the installation DVD in the DVD-ROM drive or access the installation image over the network.** If necessary, double-click the DVD icon to open the DVD.

3. **Double-click the installer program (Setup).** (On the Mac and in Windows Vista, you may be asked for a system password to allow the installation of new software.) The installer runs through an initialization step; be patient while it does so.

4. **Read the License Agreement, and click Accept to continue.** You can select a different language using the pop-up menu at the top of the dialog box.

5. **The InDesign installer asks you what language to install: English or English International.** Choose one and click Continue. *English* means the dialect of English used in the United States. *English International* means British English, the dialect used in the United Kingdom, Canada, Australia, and most former British colonies.

6. **The next dialog box gives you the opportunity to decide where to install InDesign.** If you have multiple disks attached to your computer, you see a list; select the desired disk. By default, the installer places InDesign in the `Applications` folder (Mac) or `Program Files\Adobe` folder (Windows) on your startup hard drive. If you want to change the location (for example, to your Applications folder), click the Browse button. Select or create another folder and click Choose. When that's done, click Next.

7. **In the next dialog box, type your name, company (leave it blank if you're an individual, such as a self-employed designer), and serial number and then click Continue.** A new dialog box appears, in which you can confirm your name, company, and serial number. If the information is correct, click Continue; if it's incorrect, click Back. You're also given the chance to register your copy of InDesign or to skip registration for a later time.

8. **InDesign presents the installation settings for final review.** Click Install to accept them and begin the installation or press Back to change them. Click Finish when the installation is complete, or click the Launch InDesign CS4 Now button to run the program immediately.

InDesign CS4 is now installed!

Activating and registering

You may have additional setup work to do if this is the first time you've installed InDesign CS4 on this computer:

1. **Launch InDesign by double-clicking its icon from the application folder or from the dock (Mac) or Start menu (Windows) if the icon appears there.** You get a dialog box that has you reconfirm the license; click Accept to continue.

2. **In the Software Setup dialog box, enter your serial number, or select the I Want to Try Adobe InDesign Free for 30 Days option to run an unlicensed copy in tryout mode.** Click Next. (You can also click the Product License Agreement hyperlink at the bottom of the dialog box to open the license in a browser window, from which you can print it.)

3. **In the Activate dialog box that appears, choose whether to activate your software.** (You need an Internet connection to do so.) Click Activate Now to activate the software or Activate Later to run InDesign unactivated. If you click Activate Now, InDesign connects to the Adobe server to activate your software and then displays the Activation Complete dialog box. Click Next to continue on from that dialog box.

4. **The installer also asks whether you want to register online.** If you have an Internet connection and are ready to register, click Yes. Doing so launches your default browser and takes you through the registration process. After you register online, an alert may prompt you to restart your computer, depending on whether system-level files were installed. In contrast to activation, registration is optional and lets Adobe know who is entitled to technical support. (You can also register from within InDesign by choosing Help ⇨ Register.)

The activation process downloads a unique ID from Adobe's servers to your computer, so if someone else installs InDesign, the Adobe server sees the additional installation and checks further. (It does not transmit any information about you to Adobe.) You can upgrade major pieces of hardware without requiring reactivation, and you may install and activate the software on two computers (typically a desktop and a laptop) per the Adobe software license. If the Adobe server thinks you are trying to install a third copy, it requires you to call Adobe for reactivation so that a technician can determine whether you are simply trying to reinstall the program on a replacement computer or if you really are installing a third copy.

If you do not activate the software within 30 days of installation, it no longer runs. During those 30 days, InDesign asks you each time you launch it whether you want to activate the software. You can also choose Help ⇨ Activate within InDesign to run the activation program.

> **TIP** To deactivate InDesign so that you can transfer the license to a different computer, choose Help ⇨ Deactivate. Then activate the software on the new computer when you install it. Your license will be transferred. If you don't deactivate the old copy, the new installation counts as an additional installation. Remember: Adobe lets you have just two installations activated at any one time.

Finishing your setup

When you first launch InDesign after installing it, you get the dialog box that appears in Figure A.1. Its options include creating new documents, opening documents, and seeing information on new features. If you don't want one of these options, you can just go to the program by clicking Close. This is similar to quick-start dialog boxes in other programs, such as Microsoft Office, aimed at novice users. If you want to disable it so that you go straight into InDesign, just select the Don't Show Again check box.

> **TIP** To see this dialog box again after disabling it, choose Help ⇨ Welcome Screen. If you deselect the Don't Show Again option, it continues to appear each time you launch InDesign — until you check that option again, of course.

After you install InDesign CS4, there's one more setup step you should take: Tell InDesign CS4 how often to check for program updates via the Web. To do so, choose Help ⇨ Update. InDesign looks for any new updates and then displays a dialog box that has a button labeled Preferences. Click Preferences to open a dialog box in which you enable monthly update checks and tell InDesign whether to automatically install them or ask your permission first. You also select which Adobe software you want to have these settings applied to (not just InDesign).

FIGURE A.1

This Welcome Screen dialog box loads each time you open InDesign, unless you disable it.

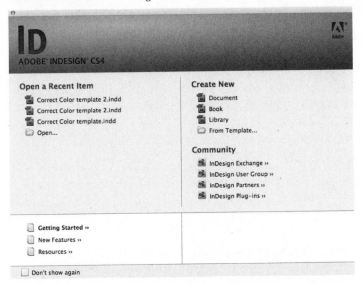

Upgrading from Prior Versions of InDesign

All installations of InDesign CS4 are new installations; there is no option to upgrade a previous version. The installer creates a new folder and places your new copy of InDesign in it, regardless of whether you were using a previous version of InDesign. The only difference between purchasing a new product and upgrading is the price you pay for the software.

Installing new software has its good points and bad points. On the plus side, your existing, earlier-version copy of InDesign is available for future use. You never know when you need it — for example, for that new client who is still using InDesign CS2, for which there is no back-saving capability from InDesign CS4 — so it can be worth keeping on your machine or at least storing on a DVD or other removable disk. The drawback is, of course, that you need space in which to store this old software.

A bigger drawback to the fact that InDesign CS4 requires a new installation is that InDesign CS4 doesn't have any of the custom settings you've selected in your earlier version of InDesign; you often don't realize how many preferences you've set over time until you switch to a new version of the software.

If you did put some effort into customizing your previous version of InDesign, when you start using InDesign CS4, do the following:

- Reset your preferences in the Preferences dialog box (choose InDesign ➪ Preferences ➪ General or press ⌘+K on the Mac, or choose Edit ➪ Preferences ➪ General or press Ctrl+K in Windows).

- Copy any color swatch libraries from the previous version of InDesign (as well as from Adobe Illustrator) to the Swatch Libraries folder in the Presets folder in your InDesign application folder.

- If you want to use InDesign CS3 scripts, create a folder called Version 5.0 Scripts, copy the scripts into it, and then move that folder to InDesign's scripts folder. (See Chapter 37 for information on the two locations — global and local — for storing scripts.)

- With no document open, set any preferences such as styles and color definitions that you want to be used in all future documents. You can also load such settings from other documents using the Load menu option in the various panels' flyout menus.

Although the customizing process can be tedious, it's definitely preferable to performing repetitive tasks such as creating the same style for each document.

Reinstalling and Uninstalling InDesign

If you had previously installed InDesign, you get a dialog box with two options when you run the Setup program:

- **Install or Reinstall:** Use this option to repair a damaged installation or install components you did not install the first time. (Select any unselected items to have them installed.)

- **Uninstall Components:** Use this option to remove all or some of the InDesign application files. Then click Next. The next dialog box lists all the installed components to reinstall or uninstall; click Modify to begin the operation.

When the (re)installation or uninstallation is complete, click Finish.

If you uninstall InDesign, you are given the choice to remove the activation (as I cover earlier in this appendix) or leave it installed. Remove the activation if you are transferring your software to a new computer. If for some reason you don't get the deactivation option, cancel the uninstallation and deactivate the software within InDesign by choosing Help ➪ Deactivate. Then uninstall the software.

Appendix B

What's New in InDesign CS4

In its seventh major version (after 1.0, 1.5, 2.0, 3.0 [CS], 4.0 [CS2], and 5.0 [CS3]), InDesign 6.0 — known formally as InDesign CS4 — has become a very strong page-layout program offering a broad range of flexible, powerful tools.

You can find a host of updated features in this latest release, as well as some key new features. Although the chapters in this book identify new features as they come up in discussing publishing techniques, this appendix brings the whole list to you in one place for easy browsing. The new features are arranged in the same order as this book because that reflects the basic workflow of publishing and the major functional divisions.

InDesign Interface

Adobe continued to fiddle with the new user interface introduced in InDesign CS3, so some of the controls over panels have changed in sometimes subtle ways. A bigger shift is evident in how document windows work.

Document windows, workspaces, and dialog boxes

InDesign has more predefined workspaces than before. The [Essentials] workspace is now the default, and it hides most features from you.

Workspaces now save not only the locations of open and docked panels, but also any custom menus in effect when you created the workspace.

IN THIS APPENDIX

Changes to the InDesign interface

What's enhanced for document and object functions

New and revised text functions

Revamped preflight and output options

Enhancements to Web and multimedia functions

What's changed in InCopy functions

Document windows are now by default accessed through a set of tabs below the Control panel, rather than as a series of cascaded windows as in previous versions of InDesign. InDesign CS4 gets rid of — as a default, anyhow — the title bar for documents. That's because documents are now placed in tabs across the top of the screen under the Control panel and the new application bar. This way, all documents are accessible via their tabs. (You can override this tabbed approach if you prefer the old floating-windows interface.)

The new application bar provides faster access to Adobe Bridge, zoom levels, workspaces, and other display options. If you don't like it, you can turn it off.

InDesign introduces the application frame so that the on-screen container for InDesign on the Mac can now match that on Windows. Conversely, the same control in Windows lets InDesign's container appear in Windows as it does on the Mac.

Gone in InDesign CS4's default view is the Structure view and the Show/Hide Structure button at the lower left of the document window. (The Structure feature is used in XML documents.) You now control the Structure view's display by choosing View ⇨ Structure ⇨ Show/Hide Structure or pressing Option+⌘+1 or Ctrl+Alt+1.

The Open a File, Save, and other file-handling dialog boxes no longer have different appearances for when Version Cue is enabled. Thus, the Use Adobe Dialog and Use OS Dialog buttons are also gone.

Several dialog boxes and panels — including the Corner Options dialog box's Size field and the Effects dialog box's Opacity field — now have nudge buttons to help you easily step through their increments.

Tools

The ability to select pop-out tool menus by Control+clicking or right-clicking is new to InDesign CS4. You can still use the old method: Click and hold the mouse over a tool that has a pop-out menu.

InDesign CS4's Tools panel no longer has the Button tool; that function is now handled through the Buttons panel. The Gradient Feather tool has taken its place and is no longer available as a pop-out tool from the Gradient Swatch tool.

When you create new objects, move them, resize them, or rotate them using the various tools, InDesign now provides an indicator near the mouse to show you the object's current status such as size or rotation angle. The Preferences dialog box lets you turn this Show Transformation Values setting off if you don't like it.

Docks and panels

In InDesign CS4, you can no longer close an individual panel — whether inside the main dock or free-floating; there is no longer a Close box on its tab. Instead, you must drag it out into its own free-floating panel and then close that panel using its Close box. (To bring back a closed panel, select it from the Window menu.) The exception: The free-floating Control panel has no Close box, so it must be closed from the Window menu. Note that you *can* close an entire panel group by clicking its Close box.

The ability to make the main dock free floating is new to InDesign CS4. The method to resize it is also new, although you could resize it in InDesign CS3 using a different approach.

You can now collapse floating panel groups in InDesign CS4. They will display as a set of names, just as collapsed panels do in the main dock. Previously, you could reduce the panel group's size to just its tabs, an option no longer available.

Panels new to InDesign CS4 are the Conditional Text, Connections, Kuler, Page Transitions, and Preflight panels. Gone is the Navigator panel, replaced with the new quick zoom option. Also gone is the Command Bar panel. The Buttons panel replaces the previous versions' States panel.

The Pathfinder panel adds the Join Path iconic button and has rearranged the other buttons for better separation among the path, Pathfinder, and shape-conversion functions.

InDesign CS4 has changed the appearance of its panels slightly. The biggest functional, appearance-related change is that the flyout menus are now clearly separated from the collapse/expand buttons, so you don't accidentally collapse a panel when trying to open the flyout menu, as could happen in InDesign CS3.

InDesign CS4 can also be set so that after you hide all panels by pressing Tab, you can have the Tools panel reappear by moving the mouse to the right edge of the screen, and have the main dock reappear when you move the mouse to the left edge of the screen.

Shortcuts and gestures

The shortcut ⌘+J or Ctrl+J that used to highlight the current number in the Page field now opens the Go to Page dialog box instead, which performs the same action.

Gone in InDesign CS4 is the ability to jump into the View field quickly by pressing press Option+⌘+5 or Ctrl+Alt+5, typing a specific value, and then pressing Return or Enter.

The shortcut for adding entries has changed from ⌘+U or Ctrl+U in previous versions to ⌘+7 or Ctrl+7 in InDesign CS4. (The ⌘+U or Ctrl+U shortcut is now used to toggle the smart guides feature on and off.)

With the Hand tool selected, click and hold the mouse button to zoom and then move the mouse to move through the document's pages. Release the mouse when you're at the desired location. This quick zoom action replaces the Navigator panel of previous versions.

If you use a MacBook with a Multi-Touch trackpad, you can use gestures to zoom in or out. Use the pinch gesture (two fingers moving closer) to zoom in and the expand gesture (two fingers moving apart) to zoom out. (At press time, the MacBook Air and the 2008-or-newer-model MacBook Pros supported gestures, a feature derived from the iPhone and iPod Touch.)

Menus

The File menu now includes the Share My Screen option, which lets Adobe Connection subscribers share their live screens with other users, such as to help each other out or look at layouts together. There's no cost for up to three simultaneous users; Adobe sells a service for larger groups.

The File menu's Cross-Media Export option is now gone, and its Dreamweaver and Digital Editions submenus are now on the File menu itself.

The Edit menu now includes the Edit With option, which lets you choose which program to open a file with, such as an image.

The Type menu adds a new menu option: Hyperlinks and Cross-References, providing menu access to some of the Hyperlinks panel's functions.

The Notes menu is gone from InDesign CS4 and is now a submenu of the Type menu.

The View menu adds the Rotate Spread option to make it easier to work on pages that have rotated elements.

The Window menu lets you show and hide the new application bar and application frame, described earlier in this chapter.

The Object ➪ Transform ➪ Clear Transformations menu sequence is new to InDesign CS4.

Preferences

New to InDesign CS4 is the ability to change how many recently saved files are displayed in the Open Recent submenu that appears under the Open option in the File menu after you have opened a file. You can change this number using the Number of Recent Items to Display option in the Saving InDesign Files area of the File Handling pane.

In the Presets folder, the Button Library and Page Transitions subfolders are new to InDesign CS4, providing a location for the presets for these new features. Other new subfolders are Default, Images, and StartPage, which contain items that are used by the InDesign application (and should not be modified).

Also, the New Doc Sizes.txt file, which contains paper size definitions and used to be in the Presets folder along with the subfolders, has been moved in InDesign CS4 to the Page Sizes subfolder.

In the Preferences dialog box, the Links area has moved from the Type pane to the File Handling pane.

In the Dictionary preferences pane, InDesign CS4 adds the All Languages option to the unnamed pop-up menu, which allows for multilingual hyphenation in the document.

The Version Cue control is now gone from the File Handling pane because Version Cue is now managed through Adobe Bridge for all CS4 applications.

Help

The Adobe Community Search capability is new to InDesign CS4. It lets Adobe, other vendors, and other users post information such as tips and advice to help each other better take advantage of InDesign.

Document and Object Functions

InDesign CS4 has introduced several changes that affect documents and objects universally, with many of the revisions centered around page controls and file handling.

Page sizes, elements, and actions

Previous versions of InDesign often miscalculated object positions when you chose the Spine option. That's now been fixed.

The eight Web-page sizes — 600×300, 640×480, 760×420, 800×600, 984×588, 1024×768, 1240×620, and 1280×800 — are new to InDesign CS4. Pity, no iPhone page size (320×416).

In Design CS4 now carries along any objects in the page's bleed and slug area when you move the page. Previous versions left such objects behind.

The ability to control whether the transparency icon displays in the Pages panel is new to InDesign CS4.

The abilities to rotate page views and apply page transitions (the special effects you often see in slideshows) are also new, as are the controls to display the icons in the Pages panel to indicate their usage.

Object handling

The smart guides, smart dimensions, and smart spacing features are new to InDesign CS4. They help you precisely place and size rotate objects via the mouse by providing visual feedback when items are evenly spaced or sized similar to nearby objects.

When placing a graphics file, you can now draw a frame into which InDesign CS4 will then fit that graphic proportionally.

The ability to place multiple graphics and/or text files simultaneously in a grid of frames is new to InDesign CS4. To do so, hold Shift+⌘ or Ctrl+Shift when placing the files. (Previous versions used the Shift+⌘ or Ctrl+Shift option to place all the images in a series of cascading frames, not in a grid.)

The ability to join two paths to create a combined single path is new to InDesign CS4.

Color creation

The new Kuler control panel lets you create a set of color swatches designed to work well together. You can also import Kuler sets created by others and share your own with others via the Kuler.com online service.

File exchange and management

You can now place — but not drag — snippets into text frames as inline graphics.

The IDML format is new to InDesign CS4. It is designed to make it easier for software developers to work with InDesign files in their own applications.

The filename extension for snippets in InDesign CS4 has changed to `.idms` from `.inds` in previous versions.

Gone in InDesign CS4 is the ability to export SVG graphics files.

New to InDesign CS4 is the ability to export documents as Flash project files or playable Flash files (SWFs).

InDesign CS4 lets you specify what program you want to edit a graphic in — not have InDesign choose for you — by selecting the graphic and then choosing Edit ➪ Edit With. The submenu that appears will list all the programs that InDesign thinks can edit the graphic. Pick one or choose Other to browse your computer for a different application.

InDesign lets you relink all instances of a file in your layout, so you have to do the operation only once. InDesign CS4 changes how this worked previously: Now, be sure to hold Option or Alt when clicking the Relink command or Relink iconic button. Also, InDesign is now smarter about finding missing files when you open a file; if the Find Missing Links Before Opening Document option is selected in the File Handling pane of the Preferences dialog box, InDesign CS4 will search your drives for the files and automatically update them if it finds them.

If you've used previous versions of InDesign, you'll note how different the Links panel is in InDesign CS4; Adobe has given it a major overhaul. Among those changes:

- The Relink to Folder menu option, and the ability to change the file types of linked graphics, is new to InDesign CS4.

- The Edit With menu option is new as well.

- Gone is the Purchase This Image option because the Adobe Stock Photos service has been discontinued.

- You can see extensive information about the file in the Link Info section of the Links panel, containing all the attributes that are also available in Adobe's Bridge, such as file dimensions and color profile. To toggle this information off, just click the Show/Hide Item Information iconic button at the bottom left of the Links panel.

- The Panel Options menu option in the Links panel is new to InDesign CS4, as are nearly all the options in the Panel Options dialog box it opens; the one option that isn't new is Row Size, which has been enhanced in this version.

New options in the File Handling pane of the Preferences dialog box for handling missing links include Check Links Before Opening Document, Find Missing Links Before Opening Document, and Default Relink Folder. (This last option lets you tell InDesign to start looking for missing files in the most recent folder in which it found missing files or in the original folder in which it found them.) The Create Links When Placing Text and Spreadsheet Files option has also moved to this pane from the Type pane.

Multidocument projects

InDesign CS4 adds the ability to synchronize across book chapters the conditional text definitions and cross-reference formats, both of which are new capabilities in InDesign CS4. Also new is the ability to update cross-references throughout a book, which you do using the Update All Cross-References option in the book panel's flyout menu.

New to InDesign CS4 is the ability to compare style groups across documents in a book and figure out which contain the same styles so that the style groups are also kept consistent. To enable this feature, be sure the Smart Match Style Groups check box is selected in the Synchronize Options dialog box.

Text Functions

A third area of major focus for InDesign's revisions involves text handling, covering a wide range of functions.

Text import

The smart text reflow options in the Type pane of the Preferences dialog box let you control how and when new pages are added as you import text files.

InDesign CS4 now honors any Microsoft Word style settings and page break settings that assign text to flow to a right-hand page or left-hand page (which are called odd and even pages in both programs). So if you use those settings in Word, InDesign will retain and apply them as well.

For importing text-only files, InDesign CS4 now has 15 additional options in the Character Set pop-up menu; these options serve to expand the supported language encodings.

Text editing

InDesign CS4 now lets you create cross-references within your document and to other documents, such as to have a cross-reference page number, or the current title of a chapter that is cross-referenced, be automatically filled in.

InDesign CS4 offers a new way to have multiple versions of text in a document that gets around these issues: conditional text. You can think of conditional text as sort of a layer that works within text, so if the text moves, the conditional "layers" do, too.

InDesign CS4 now displays the contents of tables in the Story Editor and lets you edit them. You can also insert tables when in the Story Editor. Previous versions showed just an indicator of where a table existed in the story.

InDesign CS4 also tracks any changes to the table's contents so that you can see exactly what has changed and decide whether to accept those changes if you use the companion InCopy software.

Paragraph and character formatting

InDesign CS4 lets you adjust stroke cap, end join, miter limit (if miter join is enabled), and stroke alignment (center or outside) for text; previous versions of InDesign could not apply these stroke settings to text.

The 01, 02, 03, 04 . . . and 001, 002, 003, 004 . . . numbering styles for numbered lists are new to InDesign CS4.

Spelling and indexing

InDesign CS4 adds the Edit button to the Preferences dialog box's Autocorrect pane, so you can edit both the default autocorrections and any you added yourself. In previous versions, you had to remove an autocorrection and then add back the revised one to make changes.

InDesign CS4 adds an All Languages option for its list of dictionaries in the Languages pop-up menu, in the Dictionary pane of the Preferences dialog box. Words added to this dictionary are used for spell-checking and hyphenation no matter what language you've set InDesign to use. It's a great way to make sure that universal terms — such as proper names or industry-specific jargon — are properly spelled no matter what language is in use.

The shortcut to add a new index entry or cross-reference entry to an index has changed to ⌘+7 or Ctrl+7.

Styles

InDesign adds a new form of nested style: nested line styles. It works just the same as other forms of nested styles (explained next) except that it lets you apply a character style to a certain number of lines in a paragraph. This is a popular design approach, such as having the first line in small caps. You specify the desired character style and how many lines you want it applied to, and InDesign does the rest. (Before, you had to use the End Nested Style Character at the end of the line and then hope the line ending didn't change because of text or other alterations in your file.)

In many dialog boxes and panels, InDesign CS4 now lets you create a style, so you don't have to cancel your operation and go to the appropriate style dialog box. For example, when adding a nested style via the Drop Cap & Nested Styles dialog box, you can choose New Character Style in the Character Style pop-up menu to define the desired character style on the spot. Before, you had to close the Drop Cap & Nested Styles dialog box, open the Character Styles panel and create the drop cap style there, and then close that panel and come back to the Drop Cap & Nested Styles dialog box to apply that new style.

Grep styles are a new option in InDesign CS4's New Paragraph Style and Paragraph Style Options dialog boxes. They let you apply Grep conditional formatting as part of a paragraph style.

Preflight and Output Functions

InDesign CS4 has significantly revamped how preflighting works, which has changed all the dialog boxes and most related settings compared to previous versions of InDesign. Preflighting now occurs as you work, and you have new controls to specify exactly what InDesign should be looking for as you work. The new Preflight panel also lists the errors found and includes hyperlinks to the affected pages.

Support for Acrobat 9's PDF 1.8 format is new to InDesign CS4's PDF export options.

InDesign CS4 can now export documents to the Flash player (SWF) and Flash CS4 project exchange formats.

Web and Multimedia Functions

Although not designed primarily as a tool to create Web and interactive documents, InDesign lets you add Web and interactive caoabilities to documents you then refine in other programs. InDesign CS4 enhances these capabilities.

Hyperlinks

A quick way to add a URL-based hyperlink source is simply to enter that URL in the URL field of the Hyperlinks panel and then press Return or Enter. This new InDesign CS4 feature supplements another easy way from pervious versions of InDesign to add a URL hyperlink source: If your text has a URL in it, just highlight that URL with the Type tool and choose New Hyperlink from URL from the Hyperlinks panel's flyout menu.

In InDesign CS4, the New Hyperlink dialog box adds three new types of hyperlinks — Email, File, and Shared Destination — and lets you apply character styles to the hyperlink sources. Gone is the ability to name the hyperlink source; also gone is the All Types option in the Type pop-up menu (which has been moved and renamed Link To).

In some cases, the Hyperlinks panel shows hyperlink destinations. For example, if you select some text, the URL pop-up menu will display all the saved hyperlink destinations. You can then choose one from the list to turn your selected text into a hyperlink that points to that destination.

A new, quick way to use hyperlink destinations — but only if they are URLs — that you previously created is to select them in the Hyperlinks panel's URL pop-up menu. Also, you can easily change a URL destination — if it is a URL — by selecting its hyperlink source in the Hyperlinks panel and changing the URL in the URL field at the top of the panel.

The Rename Hyperlink menu option is new to InDesign CS4. Before, you had to choose the Hyperlink Options menu option and change the name in the Hyperlink Options dialog box. Note that to rename hyperlink destinations, you still must use the Hyperlink Destination Options dialog box, accessed via the Hyperlink Destination Options menu item in the Hyperlinks panel's flyout menu.

Interactivity

There is no longer a Button tool to create buttons that initiate actions in an exported PDF file such as opening a new page or playing a video. Instead, you can convert any object (no longer just frames) into a button.

Buttons and page actions also work in Flash files, which InDesign CS4 now lets you create.

A new type of page action — the special transition effects common to slideshows, called *page transitions* in InDesign — is available for use in exported Flash and full-screen-mode PDF files.

InDesign CS4 comes with a library of buttons you can use, rather than have to create your own. Just choose Sample Buttons from the Buttons panel's flyout menu to open the Sample Buttons library file. Then just drag the desired buttons from that library to your layout. Close the library when you're done.

InDesign CS4 has no controls in the Buttons panel for placing content into states, controls that the previous versions' States panel used. So the Buttons panel's flyout menu and iconic buttons related to content states are gone in InDesign CS4. Instead, you simply use InDesign's standard methods (such as choosing File ⇨ Place or pressing ⌘+D or Ctrl+D or choosing Edit ⇨ Paste Into or pressing Option+⌘+V or Ctrl+Alt+V) to place content into the buttons..

InDesign CS4's Buttons panel radically changes the user interface for associating actions to mouse-related conditions, making such conditions easily accessible through the Event pop-up menu. In previous versions, you set mouse conditions through an option in the hard-to-find Button Options dialog box. But the capabilities are the same, with the sole addition being that you can specify a page to send the user to (something that works only in exported Flash files).

InCopy Functions

Within InDesign CS4, the ability to choose whether to make InCopy assignments compatible with the current or previous version is new to InDesign CS4.

The various InCopy filename extensions differ based on the file version. In InCopy CS4, documents have the filename extension .icml, whereas in CS3 they have .incd. Assignments' filename extensions are .icma (CS4) and .inca (CS3), and packages' extensions are .icap (CS4) and .incp (CS3). InCopy CS4 can work with both the CS4 and CS3 versions.

InCopy CS4 lets you save workspaces with your preferred panels and menus, just as InDesign CS4 does. That also means that not all menu options may display when you launch InCopy CS4. To see all your options, be sure to choose Window ⇨ Workspace ⇨ Show Full Menus.

InCopy CS4 now can display tracked changes in tables, and its Story Editor can display tables' contents.

Appendix C

Using Version Cue

Working with a team — whether on books, magazines, ads, reports, or manuals — means you must deal with managing documents in your workflow to make sure people aren't working at cross-purposes (such as saving over each other's versions) and have access to the project files they need, wherever the files happen to be stored. In Creative Suite 2, Adobe introduced a mechanism called Version Cue, which was meant to serve those twin needs in a way that didn't care what operating system or network servers or share folders might be in use; it presented a common approach for all users and made those Windows and Mac OS X differences invisible. Adobe has continued to refine this vision in each version of Creative Suite, and CS4 carries on that tradition.

Typically, organizations develop their own version-management procedures, such as having layout artists add version numbers or dates to layout iterations, and perhaps moving files from one network-accessible folder to the next based on workflow (such as by using folders named "To Layout," "To Editor," and "To Production"). Version Cue is meant to replace that kind of do-it-yourself approach.

NEW FEATURE Version Cue no longer sets up different dialog boxes for Open a File, Save, and other file-oriented dialog boxes in InDesign CS4 or other CS4 programs. You simply use the regular dialog boxes now. The Version Cue controls that used to be accessible through those special Version Cue dialog boxes are now handled through Adobe Bridge CS4. Also gone is the control in the Preferences dialog box to turn Version Cue on or off in each CS4 application. It's on for all, or for none.

IN THIS APPENDIX

Understanding Version Cue

Setting up Version Cue servers

Working with Version Cue projects in Bridge

Working with Version Cue documents in InDesign

Setting Up Version Cue Servers

For anyone in a workgroup to use Version Cue, a Version Cue server must be running. This server is a Mac or PC that has the Version Cue CS4 server application running. With this application, the administrator then sets up projects, which are collections of files that assigned users have permission to work with.

Anyone can be an administrator if they have the Version Cue Server software. That means an individual designer can make her Mac or his PC a server that is accessible to anyone else on the network. You are not limited to having your network administrator or IT department setting up Version Cue servers on file-server systems. Of course, that freedom for anyone to create his or her own server can lead to chaos, with multiple projects owned by different people in an uncoordinated way. So you'll want to set some standards as to who can create servers and under what conditions, as well as to how these are catalogued so that people know whom to go to.

NOTE The Version Cue Server software comes as part of the Creative Suite bundles. If you buy a single application such as InDesign CS4, the server software is not included. But all CS4 applications can access projects on Version Cue servers.

NOTE If you're not going to be a Version Cue administrator but instead just someone who accesses files available via Version Cue, skip ahead to the "Working with Version Cue in Adobe Bridge" section.

To set up a Version Cue server, first install the Version Cue CS4 Server application that came with your copy of the Creative Suite 4. After it is installed, you make your computer a server, create and manage projects available from the server, and set user permissions using the Version Cue CS4 system preference (Mac) or control panel (Windows):

- On the Mac, choose ⇨ System Preferences and then click the Version Cue CS4 iconic button.

- In Windows, choose Start ⇨ Control Panel (or, in Windows XP when set to Classic Start Menu, choose Start ⇨ Settings ⇨ Control Panel) and then double-click the Version Cue CS4 iconic button.

After the Version Cue system preference or control panel opens, click Start to turn on the server and select the Turn on Server When the Computer Starts option to have the server started automatically in the future. To make your server visible to other users, choose Visible to Others from the Server Visibility pop-up menu. In the Workgroup Size pop-up menu, choose the option that best fits your expected number of users; this sets the appropriate amount of resources to support the expected number of people. You can also change the default memory allocation for the Version Cue Server from the default 128MB by entering a new value in the Memory Usage field, but unless you have a lot of people accessing your computer as a server, the default value is fine. Note that you can change any of these values at any time as your server needs change.

To set up projects and user permissions, click the Server Administration button. Doing so launches your Web browser and loads a Web-based management console for Version Cue Server. Here are the typical steps:

1. In the first window, supply a password to administer your Version Cue server (your username is system), give your server a name (this is the name that will appear on other users' server lists), and choose Visible to Others from the Server Visibility pop-up menu. Click the Save & Continue button at the top of the window to continue.

2. You will be asked in the next window to log in using the settings you just specified. Do so and click Log In.

3. You will be redirected to the Adobe Version Cue CS4 Server Administration page, which has four tabs: Home, Users/Groups, Projects, and Advanced. The Home page is the default page, and it lists four options in the text below the tabs: Manage Users & Groups, Remove Old Versions, Create a Project, and Perform Advanced Tasks. These tasks are available through the four tabs at top as well (Remove Old Versions is available through the Advanced tab).

4. Set up user permissions to access your server's projects, either by clicking the Users & Groups tab or by clicking Manage Users & Groups in the Home page. You'll see two panes, one for users and one for groups. Start in the Users pane and set up each user, one at a time, by clicking New. In the dialog box that displays, enter the user's network name (this is set up on each user's computer in the Computer Name field in the Mac's Sharing system preference, and in the Computer Description field in the Computer Name pane of the System control panel in Windows). Then assign a login ID and password to that user. You can also grant that user permission to create projects and/or to administer the server. Click Save when done. After you've added all your users, you can add them to groups in the Groups pane by clicking New to create a group (name it in the dialog box that appears and then click Save) and then dragging in the users from the Users pane to the appropriate group in the Groups pane.

5. Set up the projects you want to be accessible by others, either by clicking Projects tab or by clicking Create a Project in the Home page. Click the New button to create a new project. In the page that loads, you have four options on how to create the project: start with a blank project; load all the files from a specific folder; load all the files from an FTP server; or load all the files from a WebDAV server.

   In all four cases, you'll first be given a window in which you must give the project a name and where you have the option of sharing the project with others (so that they can work on it). Also, by default, the project is lock-protected, meaning that whoever opens a file first is the only one who can save it while it is open. (Anyone else who opens it during that time can only read it.)

   If you are importing the project's files, click Next; you'll then be asked to locate the folder or server to import the files from. Click Import when done. If you are creating a blank project, there is no Next button; click Create instead.

Click Assign Permissions to specify who may do what with the project files. You'll see the same two panes as in the Users & Groups step, except that below them is a pane that lists read and write permissions with check boxes next to them. Select the users and groups you want to assign permissions to in the top two panes and then enable the appropriate permissions for them in the pane below. Click Save Permissions when done. Figure C.1 shows the window.

You can work on previously created projects, add projects, or change existing user permissions by going to the appropriate tabs — or you can simply close the browser window if you are finished administering Version Cue.

FIGURE C.1

Assigning project permissions in Version Cue Server

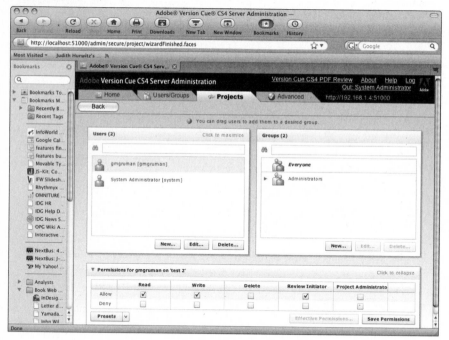

Working with Version Cue in Adobe Bridge

After projects are set up, individual users need to connect to them. So that you can connect to projects, you must make them appear on your computer as if they were network drives, a step you take in Adobe Bridge CS4.

First, make sure Version Cue is enabled in Bridge. Choose Bridge ⇨ Preferences or press ⌘+K on the Mac, or choose Edit ⇨ Preferences or press Ctrl+K in Windows, to open the Preferences dialog box. Go to the Startup Scripts pane and select the Adobe Version Cue CS4 check box. Quit Bridge and relaunch it for Version Cue to become available. Version Cue should now appear in the Favorites list at the left of the Bridge window.

With Version Cue enabled, you can now work with projects. To open a project, choose Tools ⇨ Version Cue ⇨ Connect To, or click the Version Cue icon in the Favorites list and then the Connect To iconic button in the Content pane. Either way, Adobe Drive CS4 will launch.

Adobe Drive is a new program that lets you connect to external resources, including Adobe's Web-based services and Version Cue servers on your network. You'll see an icon for available resources. Double-click the Version Cue icon to get a list of servers you have permission to open. Double-click the desired server to get a login dialog box. Enter your login ID and password and optionally select the Remember Me and Automatically Connect When Computer Starts check boxes to make future access easier. (Never select these boxes if you're working from a public computer, such as at an Internet café, lobby, or computer center. If you do, other people can get to those Version Cue projects from the same computer.)

NOTE If you are a Version Cue Server administrator, you can administer the server using the Administer Server link in Adobe Drive when logging into a server. You can also create new projects from Adobe Bridge by choosing Tools ⇨ Version Cue ⇨ New Project or clicking the New Project iconic button in the Content pane if Version Cue is selected in the Favorites list.

After you've logged in, the Version Cue project will appear as a network drive on your computer. For example, it will appear on the desktop and in the Finder windows' Devices lists on the Mac and in My Computer in Windows. It will also appear as a drive in Creative Suite CS4 applications such as InDesign, letting you access the files the same way you do any files on your computer or on the network. You can double-click files to open them, drag files in and out, create folders, and so on.

CROSS-REF See Chapter 34 for more on using Adobe Bridge.

Working with Version Cue in InDesign

With Version Cue projects now accessible by connecting them with Adobe Bridge (as explained in the previous section), you can now take advantage of Version Cue's version-control features within InDesign — not merely access those files.

Creating file versions

The critical thing to remember about Version Cue is that you must open and save your files to the Version Cue server. Even if that server is a folder on your computer, you must use the server instead of going straight to the folders. For example, say that the file New Notebook.indd is in a folder called Projects in your Documents or My Documents folder, and you made the Projects folder into a Version Cue project called Notebook Project. When you open that file or save it, you would go to the Version Cue server called Notebook Project — *not* to the Projects folder in Documents or My Documents. By using the Version Cue server, you tell InDesign to track the different version of the file. If you bypass the Version Cue server, InDesign won't know to track versions.

The first time you save a file opened via the Version Cue project's server, you'll get a dialog box called Check in of *Filename*. You can type in notes about the changes you made in the Version *x* Comments field (the first time, 1 replaces *x*; on the second save, 2 replaces *x*, and so on). These notes are useful to tell yourself or other designers what you did, such as "Changed the paragraph style definitions to the new standards. Did not yet update table styles or bring in the current logos."

From this point on, choose File ➪ Check In instead of File ➪ Save to update the file in the Version Cue project and to have the opportunity to add your version comments. Each time you check in a file, a new version is created; that way, you can see what happened in each version and even roll back to a previous version if desired.

Note that if you choose File ➪ Save (or press ⌘+S or Ctrl+S), your changes are saved but they aren't stored in a new version. This means you can use Save to periodically save your work and then use File ➪ Check In when you want all the changes (saved or not) since the last check-in to be put into a new version.

Also note that the Links panel (choose Window ➪ Links or press Shift+⌘+D or Ctrl+Shift+D) lets you check out (open from a Version Cue project) and check in the graphics and text imported into your InDesign layout, so you can work with different versions of those source files as well. The

Check Out, Check In, and Versions controls are available as options in the Links panel's flyout menu's Utilities option.

CROSS-REF Chapter 12 covers the Links panel and source linking in more detail.

Working with versions

The benefit to the Version Cue approach is that there is only one document to manage — so your folders don't get cluttered and you can be sure that whoever is working on the document has the latest changes. But this benefit can be realized only if you can see the changes.

To see the various versions of your document, choose Versions from the Version Cue iconic pop-up menu at the bottom of the document window, to the right of the Preflight status/pop-up menu. You will then get the Versions dialog box that lists all the versions of the current document, as Figure C.2 shows. In that dialog box, you can:

- Make a previous version the current version by selecting it and then the clicking Promote to Current Version button. This appears to remove any changes made in all versions created after the one you are promoting. The truth is that those changes are still in the document, but they are stored in the now-superseded versions, and to keep any of those changes, you'll have to duplicate them (through copy and paste or by re-creating them) in the current version. This means you should really use the Promote to Current Version function as a way to undo a series of changes that ended up not working out — sort of as a "reset the document to a previous state" command.

- View any version by selecting it and clicking View Version. Note that if you make changes to any version other than the current version of the document, you can't save those changes as a new version in the document; you instead must save it as a separate file.

- Delete a version by selecting it and clicking Delete. This action does not delete the changes made to the document in those versions but just merges them into the current version.

The Version Cue iconic pop-up menu has two other controls:

- **Reveal in Finder (Mac) or Reveal in Explorer (Windows):** This opens a new window with the folder containing the selected file.
- **Reveal in Bridge:** This opens the Bridge program and shows the selected file's status there.

FIGURE C.2

The Versions dialog box (top) lets you manage and see various versions of your document. You access it by choosing Versions from the Version Cue iconic pop-up menu at the bottom of the document window (bottom).

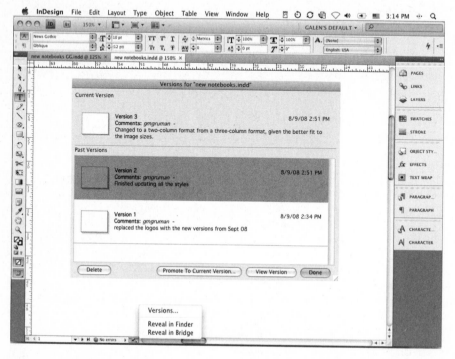

NOTE   You can also promote versions, view versions, and delete versions, as well as check in and check out Version Cue files. Select a project or document in the Content pane for Version Cue (click the Version Cue icon in the Favorites list; double-click a project to open its list of files) and then choose the appropriate submenu option when choosing Tools ⇨ Version Cue menu or from the equivalent iconic buttons at the top of the Content pane.

Appendix D

Shortcuts Cheat Sheet

Shortcuts are essential to making the most of InDesign. Sure, you can access everything from a menu or pane, but shortcuts make the work much faster. This appendix covers InDesign's keyboard shortcuts and working with contextual menus, which lets you use the mouse to find out what options are available for specific objects.

Because there are so many keyboard shortcuts, I've broken them into functional areas to help you find them more easily in the following table. Note that shortcuts marked with an asterisk (*) have changed in InDesign CS4 or are new to InDesign CS4. Features marked with an asterisk are new to InDesign CS4.

Also note that these shortcuts are the default shortcuts for InDesign; you can edit these defaults by choosing Edit ⇨ Keyboard Shortcuts, as covered in Chapter 3.

IN THIS APPENDIX

Using shortcuts in InDesign

Learning shortcuts new to InDesign CS4

TABLE D.1

InDesign Shortcuts

Action or Command	Mac	Windows
Opening/Closing/Saving		
New document	⌘+N	Ctrl+N
New default document	Option+⌘+N	Ctrl+Alt+N
Open document	⌘+O	Ctrl+O
Open library	Option+Shift+⌘+L	Ctrl+Alt+Shift+L
Browse Bridge	Option+⌘+O	Ctrl+Alt+O
Close document	⌘+W	Ctrl+W or Ctrl+F4
Close all documents	Option+Shift+⌘+W	Ctrl+Alt+Shift+W
Quit program	⌘+Q	Ctrl+Q or Alt+F4
Save document	⌘+S	Ctrl+S
Save document as	Shift+⌘+S	Ctrl+Shift+S
Save copy of document	Option+⌘+S	Ctrl+Alt+D
Export document	⌘+E	Ctrl+E
Place text and graphics	⌘+D	Ctrl+D
Viewing		
Hide/show panels	Tab	Tab
Hide/show all panes but Tools panel	Shift+Tab	Shift+Tab
Zoom in	⌘+=	Ctrl+=
Zoom out	⌘+− (hyphen)	Ctrl+− (hyphen)
Fit page/spread in window	⌘+0	Ctrl+0
Fit spread in window	Shift+⌘+0	Ctrl+Alt+0
Fit entire pasteboard in window	Option+Shift+⌘+0	Ctrl+Alt+Shift+0
Display actual size	⌘+1	Ctrl+1
Display at 50%	⌘+5	Ctrl+5
Display at 200%	⌘+2	Ctrl+2
Display at 400%	⌘+4	Ctrl+4
Overprint preview	Option+Shift+⌘+Y	Ctrl+Alt+Shift+Y
Switch between current and previous view	Option⌘+2	Ctrl+Alt+2
Set magnification	Option⌘+5	Ctrl+Alt+5

Action or Command	Mac	Windows
Viewing		
Set all pages to same view	⌘+percent in view percent menu	Ctrl+percent in view percent menu
Switch to previous document window	Shift+⌘+F6	Ctrl+Shift+F6
Switch to next document window	⌘+Y	Ctrl+F6
Show/hide text threads	Option+⌘+Y	Ctrl+Alt+Y
Show/hide frame edges	Control+⌘+H	Ctrl+H
Show/hide rulers	⌘+R	Ctrl+R
Show hidden characters	Option+⌘+I	Ctrl+Alt+I
Fast display mode	Option+Shift+⌘+Z	Ctrl+Alt+Shift+Z
Typical display mode	Option+⌘+Z	Ctrl+Alt+Z
High-quality display mode	Control+Option+⌘+H	Ctrl+Alt+H
Preference/Setup		
Preferences dialog box	⌘+K	Ctrl+K
Document setup	Option+⌘+P	Ctrl+Alt+P
File Info	Option+Shift+⌘+I	Ctrl+Alt+Shift+I
Tools		
Selection tool	V	V
Direct Selection tool	A	A
Position tool	Shift+A	Shift+A
Type tool	T	T
Type on a Path tool	Shift+T	Shift+T
Pen tool	P	P
Add Anchor Point tool	=	=
Delete Anchor Point tool	–	–
Convert Direction Point tool	Shift+C	Shift+C
Pencil tool	N	N
Ellipse tool	L	L
Rectangle tool	M	M
Rectangular Frame tool	F	F
Free Transform tool	E	E
Rotate tool	R	R

continued

TABLE D.1 *(continued)*

Action or Command	Mac	Windows
Tools		
Scale tool	S	S
Shear tool	O	O
Scissors tool	C	C
Button tool	B	B
Measure tool	K	K
Hand tool	H	H
Temporary Hand tool	Shift+spacebar	Shift+spacebar
Zoom tool	Z	Z
Temporary zoom-in tool	⌘+spacebar	Ctrl+spacebar
Temporary zoom-out tool	Option+⌘+spacebar	Ctrl+Alt+spacebar
Gradient Swatch tool	G	G
Gradient Feather tool	Shift+G	Shift+G
Eyedropper tool	I	I
Fill iconic button	X	X
Stroke iconic button	X	X
Swap Fill/Stroke iconic button	Shift+X	Shift+X
Default Fill/Stroke iconic button	D	D
Apply Color iconic button	, (comma)	, (comma)
Apply Gradient iconic button	. (period)	. (period)
Apply None iconic button	/	/
Panels and Panes		
Apply value in field	Option+Enter	Shift+Return
Show Control panel	Option+⌘+6	Ctrl+Alt+6
Show Links panel	Shift+⌘+D	Ctrl+Shift+D
Show Layers panel	F7	F7
Show Pages panel	⌘+F12 or F12	Ctrl+F12 or F12
Show Swatches panel	F5	F5
Show Color panel	F6	F6
Show Glyphs panel	Option+Shift+F11	Alt+Shift+F11
Show Character panel	⌘+T	Ctrl+T
Show Paragraph panel	Option+⌘+T	Ctrl+Alt+T
Show Character Styles panel	Shift+⌘+F11 or Shift+F11	Ctrl+Shift+F11 or Shift+F11

Action or Command	Mac	Windows
Panels and Panes		
Show Paragraph Styles panel	⌘+F11 or F11	Ctrl+F11 or F11
Show Preflight panel*	Option+Shift+⌘+F	Ctrl+Alt+Shift+F
Show Object Styles panel	⌘+F7	Ctrl+F7
Show Quick Apply panel	⌘+Return	Ctrl+Enter
Show Text Wrap panel	Option+⌘+W	Ctrl+Alt+W
Open Text Frame Options dialog box	⌘+B	Ctrl+B
Show Index panel	Shift+F8	Shift+F8
Show Table panel	Shift+F9	Shift+F9
Show Tabs panel	Shift⌘+T	Ctrl+Shift+T
Show Align panel	Shift+F7	Shift+F7
Show Stroke panel	⌘+F10 or F10	Ctrl+F10 or F10
Show Effects panel	Shift+⌘+F10	Ctrl+Shift+F10
Show Separations Preview panel	Shift+F6	Shift+F6
Show Scripts panel	Option+⌘+F11	Ctrl+Alt+F11
Show Info panel	F8	F8
Show Structure panel	Option+⌘+1	Ctrl+Alt+1
Switch to Notes mode	⌘+F8	Ctrl+F8
Guides		
Show/hide guides	⌘+; (semicolon)	Ctrl+; (semicolon)
Lock/unlock guides	Option+⌘+; (semicolon)	Ctrl+Alt+; (semicolon)
Turn on/off smart guides*	⌘+U	Ctrl+U
Snap to guides on/off	Shift+⌘+; (semicolon)	Ctrl+Shift+; (semicolon)
Show/hide baseline grid	Option+⌘+'	Ctrl+Alt+'
Show/hide document grid	⌘+'	Ctrl+'
Snap to document grid on/off	Shift+⌘+'	Ctrl+Shift+'
Select all guides	Option+⌘+G	Ctrl+Alt+G
Create zero-point guidelines	⌘+click zero point when dragging guides	Ctrl+click zero point when dragging guides
Adding and Navigating Pages		
Add new page	Shift+⌘+P	Ctrl+Shift+P
Go to first page	Shift+⌘+PgUp	Ctrl+Shift+Page Up

continued

TABLE D.1   *(continued)*

Action or Command	Mac	Windows
Adding and Navigating Pages		
Go back one page	Shift+PgUp	Shift+Page Up
Go forward one page	Shift+PgDn *or* ⌘+PgDn	Shift+Page Down *or* Ctrl+keypad PgDn
Go to last page	Shift+⌘+PgDn	Ctrl+Shift+Page Down
Go to last page viewed	⌘+PgUp	Ctrl+keypad PgUp
Go forward one spread	Option+PgUp	Alt+Page Up
Go back one spread	Option+PgDn	Alt+Page Down
Object Selection		
Select master page	Shift+⌘+click	Ctrl+Shift+click
Select topmost object	Option+Shift+⌘+]	Ctrl+Alt+Shift+]
Select object above current object	Option+⌘+]	Ctrl+Alt+]
Select bottommost object	Option+Shift+⌘+[	Ctrl+Alt+Shift+[
Select object below current object	Option+⌘+[	Ctrl+Alt+[
Go to last frame in thread	Option+Shift+⌘+PgDn	Ctrl+Alt+Shift+Page Down
Go to next frame in thread	Option+⌘+PgDn	Ctrl+Alt+Page Down
Go to first frame in thread	Option+Shift+⌘+PgUp	Ctrl+Alt+Shift+Page Up
Go to previous frame in thread	Option+⌘+PgUp	Ctrl+Alt+Page Up
Moving Objects		
Move selection 1 point	Left, right, up, and down arrows	Left, right, up, and down arrows
Move selection 10 points	Shift+left, right, up, and down arrows	Shift+left, right, up, and down arrows
Bring object to front	Shift+⌘+]	Ctrl+Shift+]
Bring object forward	⌘+]	Ctrl+]
Send object to back	Shift+⌘+[	Ctrl+Shift+[
Send object backward	⌘+[	Ctrl+[
Object Commands		
Cut	⌘+X	Ctrl+X
Copy	⌘+V	Ctrl+V
Paste	⌘+P	Ctrl+P
Paste into	Option+⌘+V	Ctrl+Alt+V
Paste in place	Option+Shift+⌘+V	Ctrl+Alt+Shift+V
Paste without formatting	Shift+⌘+V	Ctrl+Shift+V
Clear	Backspace	Backspace or Del

Action or Command	Mac	Windows
Object Commands		
Duplicate object	Option+Shift+⌘+D	Ctrl+Alt+Shift+D
Step and repeat	Shift+⌘+U	Ctrl+Shift+U
Resize proportionately	Shift+drag	Shift+drag
Resize frame and content	⌘+drag	Ctrl+drag
Center content	Shift+⌘+E	Ctrl+Shift+E
Fill frame proportionally	Option+Shift+⌘+C	Ctrl+Alt+Shift+C
Fit content proportionally	Option+Shift+⌘+E	Ctrl+Alt+Shift+E
Fit content to frame	Option+⌘+E	Ctrl+Alt+E
Fit frame to content	Option+⌘+C	Ctrl+Alt+C
Decrease size/scale by 1%	⌘+, (comma)	Ctrl+, (comma)
Decrease size/scale by 5%	Option+⌘+, (comma)	Ctrl+Alt+, (comma)
Increase size/scale by 5%	Option+⌘+. (period)	Ctrl+Alt+. (period)
Duplicate	Option+drag, or Option+left, right, up, and down arrows	Alt+drag, or Alt+left, right, up, and down arrows
Group	⌘+G	Ctrl+G
Ungroup	Shift+⌘+G	Ctrl+Shift+G
Lock	⌘+L	Ctrl+L
Unlock	Option+⌘+L	Ctrl+Alt+L
Drop shadow	Option+⌘+M	Ctrl+Alt+M
Transform Again	Option+⌘+3	Ctrl+Alt+3
Transform Sequence Again	Option+⌘+4	Ctrl+Alt+4
Graphics Handling		
Convert text to outlines	Shift+⌘+O	Ctrl+Alt+O
Create outlines without deleting text	Option+Shift+⌘+O	Ctrl+Alt+Shift+O
Make clipping path	Option+Shift+⌘+K	Ctrl+Alt+Shift+K
Make compound path	⌘+8	Ctrl+8
Release compound path	Option+Shift+⌘+8	Ctrl+Alt+Shift+8
Text Selection		
Select all	⌘+A	Ctrl+A
Deselect all	Shift+⌘+A	Ctrl+Shift+A
Select word	double-click	double-click

continued

TABLE D.1	*(continued)*	
Action or Command	**Mac**	**Windows**
Text Selection		
Select one word to left	Shift+⌘+left arrow	Ctrl+Shift+left arrow
Select one word to right	Shift⌘+right arrow	Ctrl+Shift+right arrow
Select range	Shift+left, right, up, and down arrows	Shift+left, right, up, and down arrows
Select paragraph	triple-click	triple-click
Select one paragraph before	Shift+⌘+up arrow	Ctrl+Shift+up arrow
Select one paragraph after	Shift+⌘+down arrow	Ctrl+Shift+down arrow
Select to start of story	Shift+⌘+Home	Ctrl+Shift+Home
Select to end of story	Shift+⌘+End	Ctrl+Shift+End
Moving within Text		
Move left one word	⌘+left arrow	Ctrl+left arrow
Move right one word	⌘+right arrow	Ctrl+right arrow
Move to start of line	Home	Home
Move to end of line	End	End
Move to previous paragraph	⌘+up arrow	Ctrl+up arrow
Move to next paragraph	⌘+down arrow	Ctrl+down arrow
Move to start of story	⌘+Home	Ctrl+Home
Move to end of story	⌘+End	Ctrl+End
Text/Paragraph Formats		
Bold	Shift+⌘+B	Ctrl+Shift+B
Italic	Shift+⌘+I	Ctrl+Shift+I
Normal	Shift+⌘+Y	Ctrl+Shift+Y
Underline	Shift+⌘+U	Ctrl+Shift+U
Strikethrough	Shift+⌘+/	Ctrl+Shift+/
All caps on/off	Shift+⌘+K	Ctrl+Shift+K
Small caps	Shift+⌘+H	Ctrl+Shift+H
Superscript	Shift+⌘+=	Ctrl+Shift+=
Subscript	Option+Shift+⌘+=	Ctrl+Alt+Shift+=
Update character style based on selection	Option+Shift+⌘+C	Ctrl+Alt+Shift+C
Update paragraph style based on selection	Option+Shift+⌘+R	Ctrl+Alt+Shift+R

Action or Command	Mac	Windows
Text/Paragraph Formats		
Drop caps and nested styles	Option+⌘+R	Ctrl+Alt+R
Paragraph rules	Option+⌘+J	Ctrl+Alt+J
Set horizontal scale to 100%	Shift+⌘+X	Ctrl+Shift+X
Set vertical scale to 100%	Option+Shift+⌘+X	Ctrl+Alt+Shift+X
Increase point size by 1 point	Shift+⌘+. (period)	Ctrl+Shift+. (period)
Increase point size by 10 points	Option+Shift+⌘+. (period)	Ctrl+Alt+Shift+. (period)
Decrease point size by 1 point	Shift+⌘+, (comma)	Ctrl+Shift+, (comma)
Decrease point size by 10 points	Option+Shift+⌘+, (comma)	Ctrl+Alt+Shift+, (comma)
Text Alignment and Spacing		
Align left	Shift+⌘+L	Ctrl+Shift+L
Align right	Shift+⌘+R	Ctrl+Shift+R
Align center	Shift+⌘+C	Ctrl+Shift+C
Justify full	Shift+⌘+F	Ctrl+Shift+F
Justify left	Shift+⌘+J	Ctrl+Shift+J
Justify right	Option+Shift+⌘+R	Ctrl+Alt+Shift+R
Justify center	Option+Shift+⌘+C	Ctrl+Alt+Shift+C
Autohyphenation on/off	Option+Shift+⌘+H	Ctrl+Alt+Shift+H
Hyphenation on/off (selected text)	Option+⌘+H	Ctrl+Alt+H
Set spacing and justification	Option+Shift+⌘+J	Ctrl+Alt+Shift+J
Set keep options	Option+⌘+K	Ctrl+Alt+K
Increase leading by 2 points	Option+up arrow	Alt+up arrow
Decrease leading by 2 points	Option+down arrow	Alt+down arrow
Increase leading by 10 points	Option+⌘+up arrow	Ctrl+Alt+up arrow
Decrease leading by 10 points	Option+⌘+down arrow	Ctrl+Alt+down arrow
Use autoleading	Option+Shift+⌘+A	Ctrl+Alt+Shift+A
Increase kerning/tracking by 20 units	Option+right arrow	Alt+right arrow
Increase kerning/tracking by 100 units	Option+⌘+right arrow	Ctrl+Alt+right arrow
Decrease kerning/tracking by 20 units	Option+left arrow	Alt+left arrow

continued

TABLE D.1 *(continued)*

Action or Command	Mac	Windows
Text Alignment and Spacing		
Decrease kerning/tracking by 100 units	Option+⌘+left arrow	Ctrl+Alt+left arrow
Clear all kerning/tracking (set to 0)	Shift+⌘+Q	Ctrl+Shift+Q
Increase baseline shift by 2 points	Option+Shift+up arrow	Alt+Shift+up arrow
Increase baseline shift by 10 points	Option+Shift+⌘+up arrow	Ctrl+Alt+Shift+up arrow
Decrease baseline shift by 2 points	Option+Shift+down arrow	Alt+Shift+down arrow
Decrease baseline shift by 10 points	Option+Shift+⌘+down arrow	Ctrl+Alt+Shift+down arrow
Align to grid on/off	Option+Shift+⌘+G	Ctrl+Alt+Shift+G
Table Editing		
Insert table	Option+Shift+⌘+T	Ctrl+Alt+Shift+T
Insert column	Option+⌘+9	Ctrl+Alt+9
Insert row	⌘+9	Ctrl+9
Select table	Option+⌘+A	Ctrl+Alt+A
Select column	Option+⌘+3	Ctrl+Alt+3
Select row	⌘+3	Ctrl+3
Select cell	⌘+/	Ctrl+/
Delete column	Shift+Delete	Shift+Backspace
Delete row	⌘+Delete	Ctrl+Backspace
Table setup	Option+Shift+⌘+B	Ctrl+Alt+Shift+B
Set cell text options	Option+⌘+B	Ctrl+Alt+B
Find/Change Text, Spelling, and Indexing		
Edit in Story Editor	⌘+Y	Ctrl+Y
Find/change	⌘+F	Ctrl+F
Find next	Option+⌘+F	Ctrl+Alt+F
Search for selected text	Shift+F1	Shift+F1
Add selected text to Find What field	⌘+F1	Ctrl+F1
Add selected text to Change To field	⌘+F2	Ctrl+F2
Change current selection	⌘+F3	Ctrl+F3
Change current selection and search forward	Shift+⌘+F3	Ctrl+Shift+F3

Action or Command	Mac	Windows
Find/Change Text, Spelling, and Indexing		
Check spelling	⌘+I	Ctrl+I
Add new index entry	Option+Shift+⌘+]	Ctrl+Alt+Shift+]
Add new index entry (reversed)	Option+Shift+⌘+[	Ctrl+Alt+Shift+[
New index/open index entry dialog box	⌘+7*	Ctrl+7*
Special Characters		
Bullet (•)	Option+8	Alt+8
Ellipsis (…)	Option+; (semicolon)	Alt+; (semicolon)
Copyright (©)	Option+G	Alt+G
Registered trademark (®)	Option+R	Alt+R
Trademark (™)	Option+2	Alt+2
Paragraph (¶)	Option+7	Alt+7
Section (§)	Option+6	Alt+6
Keyboard double quote (")	Control+Shift+'	Alt+Shift+'
Keyboard single quote/apostrophe (')	Control+'	Alt+'
Switch between keyboard and typographic quotes	Option+Shift+⌘+"	Ctrl+Alt+Shift+"
Em dash (—)	Option+Shift+– (hyphen)	Alt+Shift+– (hyphen)
En dash (–)	Option+– (hyphen)	Alt+– (hyphen)
Nonbreaking hyphen	Option+⌘+– (hyphen)	Ctrl+Alt+– (hyphen)
Discretionary hyphen	Shift+⌘+– (hyphen)	Ctrl+Shift+– (hyphen)
Em space	Shift+⌘+M	Ctrl+Shift+M
En space	Shift+⌘+N	Ctrl+Shift+N
Thin space	Option+Shift+⌘+M	Ctrl+Alt+Shift+M
Nonbreaking space	Option+⌘+X	Ctrl+Alt+X
Soft return	Shift+Enter	Shift+Return
Column break	Keypad Enter	keypad Enter
Frame break	Shift+keypad Enter	Shift+keypad Enter
Page break	⌘+keypad Enter	Ctrl+keypad Enter
Indent to here	⌘+\	Ctrl+\
Right-indent tab	Shift+Tab	Shift+Tab
Insert current page number	Option+Shift+⌘+N	Ctrl+Alt+Shift+N

continued

TABLE D.1   *(continued)*

Action or Command	Mac	Windows
Printing and Output		
Print document	⌘+P	Ctrl+P
Package document	Option+Shift+⌘+P	Ctrl+Alt+Shift+P
Miscellaneous		
Help	Help	F1
Undo	⌘+Z	Ctrl+Z
Redo	Shift+⌘+Z	Ctrl+Shift+Z

Index

Special Characters

A

F

M

N

O

Q

R